ACADEMIC LEGAL DISCOURSE AND ANALYSIS

ASPEN SELECT SERIES

ACADEMIC LEGAL DISCOURSE AND ANALYSIS: ESSENTIAL SKILLS FOR INTERNATIONAL STUDENTS STUDYING LAW IN THE UNITED STATES

Marta Baffy
Georgetown University Law Center

Kirsten Schaetzel
Emory University School of Law

Wolters Kluwer

Published by Wolters Kluwer in New York.

Wolters Kluwer Legal & Regulatory U.S. serves customers worldwide with CCH, Aspen Publishers, and Kluwer Law International products. (www.WKLegaledu.com)

To contact Customer Service, e-mail customer.service@wolterskluwer.com, call 1-800-234-1660, fax 1-800-901-9075, or mail correspondence to:

Wolters Kluwer
Attn: Order Department
PO Box 990
Frederick, MD 21705

Printed in the United States of America.

1 2 3 4 5 6 7 8 9 0

ISBN 978-1-5438-1593-1

Library of Congress Cataloging-in-Publication Data application is in process.

SUSTAINABLE FORESTRY INITIATIVE Certified Sourcing
www.sfiprogram.org
SFI-01051

About Wolters Kluwer Legal & Regulatory U.S.

Wolters Kluwer Legal & Regulatory U.S. delivers expert content and solutions in the areas of law, corporate compliance, health compliance, reimbursement, and legal education. Its practical solutions help customers successfully navigate the demands of a changing environment to drive their daily activities, enhance decision quality and inspire confident outcomes.

Serving customers worldwide, its legal and regulatory portfolio includes products under the Aspen Publishers, CCH Incorporated, Kluwer Law International, ftwilliam.com and MediRegs names. They are regarded as exceptional and trusted resources for general legal and practice-specific knowledge, compliance and risk management, dynamic workflow solutions, and expert commentary.

To our students, who always are our best teachers

Table of Contents

Acknowledgments xix

Introduction 1

Part I. Academic Legal Discourse: Foundations for Writing in a U.S. Law School 5

Introduction to Part I 7

Chapter 1. Introduction to Academic Legal Discourse 9

A. What is Academic Discourse? 9

B. The Role of Culture in Organizing Discourse 10

1. Write with Your Reader in Mind 12

2. Start with Your Main Idea 13

3. Support Your Ideas with Evidence 14

4. Begin with an Introduction and End with a Conclusion 16

a. The Introduction in a Longer Piece of Academic Legal Discourse 16

b. The Conclusion in a Longer Piece of Academic Legal Discourse 18

5. State Every Step of Your Thinking 19

C. Example of Academic Legal Discourse in a Law Review Article 23

D. The Process of Writing 60

Chapter 2. Paragraphs 63

A. Topic Sentences 63

B. Support 69

1. Examples 70

2. Descriptions 70

3. Explanations 71

4. Definitions 73

5. Statistics 73

6. References to Authority 74

7. A Note on Research, Attribution, and Citation 79

8. A Note on Paraphrasing Versus Quoting 79

C. Unity 81

D. Cohesion 86

E. Paragraph Length 92

Chapter 3. Sentences 99

A. Use Word Order That Readers Expect and Find Easy to Understand 99

1. The Problem with Nominalizations 100

2. The Problem with Passive Voice 102

B. Use Correct Word Forms so That Readers Are Not Confused 105

C. Use Correct Sentence Structures to Make Your Meaning Clear 108

1. Simple Sentence 109

2. Compound Sentence 109

3. Complex Sentence 110

4. Compound-Complex Sentence 112

D. Vary Sentence Length and Type to Enhance the Rhythm and Flow of Your Writing 115

Chapter 4. Transitions **119**

A. Transitions within a Paragraph 120

1. Transition Words 121

2. Substantive Transitions 125

a. An Example 126

b. The Structure of Substantive Transitions 127

B. Transitions Between Paragraphs 134

1. Transition Words 134

2. Substantive Transitions 136

a. Using Key Words in Substantive Transitions 140

b. Reminding the Reader of the Topic Under Discussion 140

c. Incorporating Transitions into Topic Sentences 141

C. Transitions between Sections 142

1. Section Headings 142

a. Headings Generally 142

b. Headings and Topic Sentences 144

c. Heading Format 146

d. Heading as Sentences 146

e. A Caveat 146

2. Section Introductions 147

3. Substantive Transitions 149

a. Backward-looking Transitions 149

b. Forward-looking Transitions 150

Chapter 5. Editing and Proofreading **155**

A. Editing 156

1. Editing Checklist 157

2. Using the Editing Checklist 158

B. Proofreading 159

1. Proofreading for Grammar 159

a. Grammar Proofreading Checklist 160

b. Using and Adapting the Grammar Proofreading Checklist 166

2. Proofreading for Punctuation 168

3. Proofreading for Spelling 173

4. Proofreading for Formatting 175

a. Formatting Checklist 175

b. The Importance of Consistency 177

C. Editing and Proofreading During Timed Exams 178

Part II. Academic Legal Analysis: Reading, Discussing, and Writing about Legal Cases 181

Introduction to Part II 183

Chapter 1. Foundations of U.S. Law 187

A. Basic Principles of Common Law 187

1. What is Common Law? 187

2. How is Common Law Created? 188

B. The U.S. Court System 189

1. Hierarchy of Courts 189

2. Federal and State Courts 191

a. Federal Courts 191

b. State Courts 193

C. The Jury System 194

1. General Overview 194

2. The Role of Judge and Jury at Trial 195

3. Who Serves on a Jury? 196

Chapter 2. Reading Cases **199**

A. Elements of a Case 200

1. Sample Case 200

2. Key Elements of an Opinion 204

a. Case Heading 204

b. Name of the Judge 207

c. Facts 207

d. Procedural History 209

e. Issue 210

f. Holding 212

g. Reasoning 214

h. Disposition 216

B. Case Reading Strategies 217

1. Linear Reading Strategies 217

2. Problematizing Reading Strategies 220

3. Evaluative Reading Strategy 222

Chapter 3. Discussing Cases **227**

A. Critiquing the Parties' Claims 228

B. Commenting on the Court's Holding 228

C. Evaluating the Reasons Advanced by the Court 229

D. Applying the Holding or Reasoning of a Case to a Hypothetical 229

E. Comparing the Case to Other Cases You Have Read 230

F. Speculating about the Implications of a Case 231

Chapter 4. Writing about Cases 233

A. Writing Case Briefs 233

1. Suggestions for Effective Case Briefing 235

a. Formulate the "Rule of the Case" 236

b. Be Aware of Obiter Dictum 237

c. The Facts: Include Only the Legally Relevant Facts 237

d. The Issue: Name the Applicable Rule (or Procedure) AND Include Important Facts 238

e. The Holding: Name the Applicable Rule (or Procedure) AND Include Important Facts 239

f. The Reasoning: Be Thorough and Provide All of the Reasons Supplied by the Court 240

2. Benefits of Case Briefing 240

a. Case Briefs Help with Class Participation 241

b. Case Briefs Facilitate Exam Preparation 241

c. Case Briefs Promote Language Development: Paraphrasing 242

B. Writing Course Outlines 248

1. What Does a Course Outline Look Like? 248

a. Student #1's Outline 248

b. Student #2's Outline 249

2. Suggestions for Effective Outlining 251

a. Identify the Major Topics and Subtopics in the Legal Subject 251

b. Organize Your Outline According to Topics, not Case Names 252

c. Organize Information in Visually Appealing Ways 252

d. Start Your Outline about One Month into the Semester, but No Later than One Month Before the Exam 256

e. Create a Long and a Short Outline 256

f. Use Other Outlines to Supplement Your Work, Not to Replace It 256

g. Use Your Outline to Take Past Exams 257

C. Writing Law School Exams 258

1. The "Issue Spotter" Essay Exam 258

a. Torts Essay Question 259

b. Two Sample Answers 261

c. A Framework for Answering Issue Spotter Exam Questions: "IRAC" 263

d. Hedging 269

e. The Direct Answer 269

f. Multiple Issue Spotters 270

g. Red Herrings 270

h. Mistakes to Avoid in Issue Spotter Essay Writing 270

2. Other Exam Questions 278

a. Choice of Law Essay Questions 278

b. Policy Essay Questions 280

c. Short Answer Questions 281

d. Multiple Choice Questions 282

Chapter 5. Torts **285**

A. Torts Case #1 286

B. Torts Case #2 293

C. Torts Case #3 298

D. Torts Vocabulary Exercises (Lists 1-3) 307

E. Torts Essay Question #1 309

F. Torts Case #4 309

G. Torts Essay Question #2 323

H. Torts Case #5 324

I. Torts Vocabulary Exercises (Lists 4-5) 332

J. Torts Case #6 333

K. Torts Essay Question #3 337

L. Torts Case #7 338

M. Torts Case #8 347

N. Torts Case #9 352

O. Torts Case #10 359

P. Torts Essay Question #4 366

Q. Torts Vocabulary Exercises (Lists 6-9) 368

R. Additional Essay Questions 369

Chapter 6. Criminal Procedure **377**

A. Criminal Procedure Case #1 378

B. Criminal Procedure Case #2 395

C. Criminal Procedure Essay Question #1 403

D. Criminal Procedure Case #3 404

E. Criminal Procedure Case #4 412

F. Criminal Procedure Vocabulary Exercises (Lists 1-4) 434

G. Criminal Procedure Essay Question #2 436

H. Criminal Procedure Case #5 437

I. Criminal Procedure Case #6 452

J. Criminal Procedure Essay Question #3 462

K. Criminal Procedure Case #7 463

L. Criminal Procedure Case #8 470

M. Criminal Procedure Essay Question #4 476

N. Criminal Procedure Vocabulary Exercises (Lists 1-8) 477

O. Additional Essay Questions 480

Conclusion. Tips for International Students Studying Law in the United States 487

A. Attending Classes 489

1. Absences 489

2. Latenesses 492

B. Submitting Assignments 493

C. Relationships with Professors 494

D. Relationships with Classmates 496

E. Managing Your Workload 499

Appendix A. List of Torts Vocabulary Terms 501

Appendix B. List of Criminal Procedure Vocabulary Terms 505

Appendix C. Steps in the Civil Litigation Process 507

Appendix D. Steps in the Criminal Justice Process 511

Index 513

Acknowledgments

Marta Baffy

I would like to first thank our editors at Wolters Kluwer, David Herzig and Justin Billing. David took a chance on this project and gave us the creative freedom to develop what is a rather unconventional legal writing text. I would also like to thank my good friend and co-author, Kirsten Schaetzel. Before meeting you, I never imagined collaboration—in teaching, presenting, and writing—could be so effortless and fun.

I would also like to thank all of my students in the course *Academic Legal English* (formerly *Working with Legal Texts*) at Georgetown Law. Without your input over the years as to what readings, activities, and exercises work, this book could not have been written. This project was possible in large part because of you.

Thank you as well to my colleagues at Georgetown: Craig Hoffman, Kia Dennis, Katie Hansen, Andrew Kerr, Almas Khan, Julie Lake, Mari Sakai, Michelle Ueland, and Heather Weger. Your support before and during the writing of this text was crucial. I have learned so much from each of you about teaching Legal English and developing materials that are effective.

I would also like to thank my colleagues who work with foreign-trained lawyers at other institutions: Robert Connor, Pam Dzunu, Cynthia Flamm, Stephen Horowitz, Nell Novara, Shelley Saltzman, Maria Tomeho-Palermino, and Charlotte Wallace. Meeting you and collaborating at the TESOL conference over the past several years has been such a gift. Our conversations have yielded important discoveries about the teaching of Legal English, and many of the lessons I learned from you have been incorporated into this book.

A huge thanks to the following friends and colleagues for their invaluable feedback on various parts of this text. Stephen Horowitz, Andrew Kerr, Julie Lake, Abram Shanedling, Heather Weger, and Maria Zhynovitch—thank you! thank you! This book has benefitted greatly from the keen eye and genius of Stephen in particular, whose innovative approach to legal writing and English as a Second Language instruction is reflected in many of the pages to come.

I would also like to thank my student assistants, Shahin Rafikian for his help editing the manuscript and Anuva Ganapathi for her work on sample case briefs and answers for this book's online supplement.

Finally, I'd like to thank my family: my husband, Stefan, for always being a sounding board for my ideas related to this project and others, and my daughter, Ramona. Though you were in my belly while I wrote much of this book, your imminent arrival was just the motivation I needed to see this project through.

Marta Baffy
Faculty Director, Two-Year LL.M. Program
Georgetown University Law Center

Kirsten Schaetzel

I would like to thank our editors at Wolters Kluwer, David Herzig and Justin Billing, for believing that we could make a valuable contribution to international students studying at law schools in the United States. I want to thank David, too, for his patience as this text went through various manifestations. His encouraging meetings and emails were always welcome.

This book would not have been possible without many people who contributed to and supported it. First, I must thank Marta Baffy, my friend, co-author, and, for several wonderful years, my co-teacher. In addition to teaching me a phenomenal amount about law, she was a wonderful teaching partner.

Second, I must thank Kelly Wilson for her permission to use *Catching the Unique Rabbit: Why Pets Should be Reclassified as Inimitable Property under the Law*. When searching for examples of academic legal writing, Ms. Wilson's article was the one that best fulfilled our criteria for excellent academic legal writing. We are thrilled that she has given us permission to reprint it here.

Third, I also must thank my former colleagues at Georgetown Law: Craig Hoffman, Andrew Kerr, Julie Lake, Michelle Ueland, Megan Vetula, Mary Grilli Jacobs, and Peter Kramer. A huge thank-you to Craig, for taking a chance in hiring me, someone without any legal knowledge, for a new two-year LL.M. program. It was an amazing ride! I would also like to thank my present colleagues at Emory University Law School, especially those who work with our international students: Jessica Dworkin, Nancy Daspit, Hannah Nicole, Rebecca Purdom, and Phoebe Stevenson. I continually learn from all of you.

Fourth, I would like to thank my many international students, in the United States, Bangladesh, Macau, and Singapore. You have taught me so much, especially through your questions. Your hard work and dedication to learning academic and legal English continue to be a source of inspiration for me.

Finally, I must thank my family. The lawyers in my family, Ben Meyer, Jeff Meyer, Roy Schaetzel, and Steve Schaetzel, helped me understand the strange language of the law and offered helpful and insightful suggestions and texts over the years. My husband, Tom, is a constant support and discerning listener. My son, Nate, helps me remember to choose my words carefully.

Above all, I dedicate this text to Karin Nelson Meyer, my beloved sister, who left this world in June 2018 after bravely battling cancer. Karin was a true students' teacher, holding her students to high standards and always striving to make Spanish interesting and accessible. Her dedication to teaching, her love of learning, and her stellar sense of humor are constant inspirations to me.

Many thanks to all of you.

Kirsten Schaetzel
English Language Specialist
Emory University School of Law

This book is designed for international law students either pursuing a law degree or seeking to apply for a law degree in the United States. Accordingly, our aim is to help readers acquire essential skills for succeeding in law classes. These skills include, most fundamentally, writing on the level of texts, paragraphs, and sentences. These skills also encompass reading, discussing, and writing about legal cases that are a mainstay of the U.S. legal educational context.

We have selected many published and non-published (student-written) examples of authentic texts to illustrate various principles of academic legal discourse and analysis. With some exceptions, these examples are reproduced as they appear in their original form.

Sentences in published, long texts such as law review articles and legal cases have been numbered to allow for easy reference to various parts of the text. These numbers do not appear in the original version of these texts but have been added to facilitate class discussion. Legal cases have also been edited, and in most cases abridged, to enhance readability and to help focus readers' attention.

Unless otherwise noted, original footnotes appearing in all of the texts reproduced in this book have been omitted. Because this book focuses on the features of written discourse students should notice when reading texts and emulate when writing documents, it is important that they notice how texts are organized and what they contain. This is easier when the writer's words appear without footnotes.

A handful of published, shorter texts in Part I of this book have also been altered from their original form. Our motivation behind adapting these texts has been to create exercises that call on readers to identify ways to improve the adapted texts. For example, one exercise calls on readers to identify the location of paragraph breaks in texts where these breaks have been intentionally removed. The original form of any adapted text is provided in an online answer key and supplement to this book.

We gratefully acknowledge the following sources, which granted permission to reprint excerpts from the works listed below:

Derek W. Black, *Taking Teacher Quality Seriously*, 57 WM & MARY L. REV. 1597 (2016).

Rebecca Edwalds, *Restructuring Local School Wellness Policies: Amending the Kids Act to Fight Childhood Obesity*, 47 U. MICH. J.L. REFORM 1051 (2014).

Safia Gray Hussain, Note, *Attacking the Dog-Bite Epidemic: Why Breed-Specific Legislation Won't Solve the Dangerous-Dog Dilemma*, 74 FORDHAM L. REV. 2847 (2006).

Huyen Pham, *The Private Enforcement of Immigration Laws*, 96 GEO. L.J. 777 (2008).

Kelly Wilson, *Catching the Unique Rabbit: Why Pets Should be Reclassified as Inimitable Property Under the Law*, 57 CLE. ST. L. REV. 167 (2009).

Introduction

Living in another culture means that many parts of life are different. The first differences you may notice are the weather, the money, and the food. The longer you live in another culture, the more differences you may notice: in punctuality to meetings and classes, in accepted dress for work and leisure, in housewarming gifts for invitations to homes, and in expectations for tipping in restaurants. Just as there are cultural differences in society in general, there are also cultural differences in educational institutions.

You may not realize until you study at a school in a different country that culture also determines what learning means, what professors do and do not do, and what students do and do not do. For example, demonstrating learning in some cultures means that a student memorizes what the professor has presented on PowerPoint slides in class, while doing well on an exam means being able to restate exactly the professor's words. In these types of learning environments, the best student answers will be quite similar. Demonstrating learning in other cultures means reading and understanding the lectures the professor gives, while doing well on an exam means being able to apply the principles the professor has presented to a new situation or problem. In these cultures, the best student answers might be very different, and students may even reach different conclusions. They are the best answers, however, because each student has applied the principles correctly and laid out a clear, logical argument to reach her conclusion. In these two examples, learning in a class and demonstrating learning on an exam are very different.

To do well at an educational institution that is different from one in your native country and culture, it is important to understand what learning means and how learning is measured. This book addresses learning at U.S. law schools: what students are expected to do to learn material presented in classes and readings and how they are expected to demonstrate their learning on exams and in written documents. Before examining what to learn and how to demonstrate your learning, you should understand two characteristics about U.S. law schools. The first is that law school in the United States is graduate-level education and there are particular characteristics of graduate student learners that instruction is tailored to. The second is that law school in the United States is a unique teaching and learning environment and has its own features that make it different from other fields at the graduate level.

What are the characteristics of graduate students that law students are expected to have? First, graduate students are considered adults in American society and, as adults, they are goal-oriented. While undergraduates may struggle to decide on a major, at the graduate level, learners are building on an undergraduate foundation and are specializing in law. Their goal is to learn law, and they approach their classes focused on this goal. Second, graduate students are independent learners. Whereas at lower levels of education, a teacher or professor may tell students what they need to know, at the graduate level, students are expected to figure out what they need to know and how to learn it. This does not mean that professors will not answer questions about the material. However, before going to a professor for help, the professor will expect that students have completed the course reading and worked at understanding it on their own, sometimes consulting other references or their class colleagues for help.

Because graduate students are independent learners, much learning at the graduate level is practical, problem-solving-oriented learning. This is true of law school. As you will learn in the second half of this book, learning to read and understand legal cases is only the first step in demonstrating your learning on exams. Course requirements in a U.S. law school typically require you to describe a problem, analyze it, and suggest a solution by giving and supporting your own opinion.

A final characteristic of graduate students is that they often have work and life experience to consider as they learn. If you have practiced law in your own country or the United States, you will find yourself constantly considering your own experience and comparing it to what you read about in cases and texts and to what you hear your professors and colleagues say in class discussions. You may also write texts bringing together your own experience and the new legal knowledge you are learning. Thus, being goal-oriented, being independent learners, learning through problem-solving, and applying work and life experience to their learning are all characteristics expected of graduate students in the United States.

Even though law students have these characteristics—similar to other graduate students in the United States—law school itself is different from other graduate programs. Law school seeks to transform the way students think from the general intellectual thought of undergraduate study to the specialized and formalized way that lawyers think. In her study of law school language and thought, *The Language of Law School*, Elizabeth Mertz describes law school ideology about language as "one that is part of the larger system to which law students are being socialized,[1] of the written texts they are being trained to read,

---

[1] Socialization refers to the process of learning the communicative norms or "rules" of a particular academic and/or professional community.

and of the way of speaking-and-thinking that their professors urge on them."[2] Law school is not simply a school in which to learn information and law; instead, it is a school in which to learn a new way of reading, thinking, seeing, talking, and writing. All students need to be socialized into these new ways of thinking and communicating—American students as well as international students. For an international student, however, the process may be more complex. This is because if you studied law in a civil law country, there may be a broader gap between your previous education and the education you are now about to receive. This book will help you bridge this gap.

In her 2016 doctoral dissertation, Marta Baffy examined international students' acquisition of academic legal English in a two-year LL.M. program.[3] From her research and our class curricula, we have learned what international students need to know to do well at U.S. law schools. This information and practice exercises form the basis of this book. Our aim is to give you the tools to lessen the gap between your previous educational experiences and what you will encounter in law classes in the U.S. To that end, this book builds on the lawyering skills you have, helps you apply them in a new context, and helps you build skills essential for U.S. law classrooms and practice.

Part I of this book is titled *Academic Legal Discourse: Foundations for Writing in a U.S. Law School*. In these chapters, you will learn the principles of U.S. academic legal discourse: how to organize and present your ideas in writing at the text, paragraph, and sentence levels. You will develop new ways of expressing yourself and encapsulating your ideas in writing. This will make your writing in law school, whether on an essay exam, in a seminar paper, or for a law review article, easy for your reader to understand. Your writing will meet the standards and expectations of the U.S. legal community. Through editing and proofreading your documents, you will also review problematic grammatical and mechanical areas, so that you can express your ideas with accuracy and confidence.

Part II of this book is titled *Academic Legal Analysis: Reading, Discussing, and Writing about Cases*. In these chapters, you will learn how to navigate, understand, and analyze the myriad legal cases assigned in your law classes. You will learn how to extract information from cases and what information to extract. You will learn how to participate in professor-led Socratic discussions about cases, as well as how to begin thinking about the law as professors and attorneys do. Finally, you will develop the language and analytic skills to prepare for, take, and do well on law school exams.

The chapters in Part I and Part II contain language-focused exercises that promote the development of writing skills and legal vocabulary. Many of these

---

[2] ELIZABETH MERTZ, THE LANGUAGE OF LAW SCHOOL: LEARNING TO THINK LIKE A LAWYER 131 (2007).

[3] Marta Baffy, The Academic Discourse Socialization of International Lawyers at a U.S. Law School (April 20, 2016) (unpublished Ph.D. dissertation, Georgetown University) (on file with Georgetown University).

exercises are based on authentic examples of academic legal discourse. Furthermore, the chapters in Part II include tasks that replicate the sorts of assignments students can expect to complete in a doctrinal law class,[4] including case briefs (short case summaries) and essay exams.

It is our hope that by reading this book and doing the exercises contained in it, you will be better prepared to take U.S. law classes. You will feel more at ease in law classes, know better what your professors expect from you, and be able to perform to your utmost potential. We hope this book will lessen the gap between past and present educational experiences, cultures, and countries.

---

[4] A doctrinal law class is one that focuses on a particular subject area. Examples include contracts, criminal law, evidence, and torts. Doctrinal classes can be distinguished from "skills" or "lawyering" courses such as Legal Research and Writing (LRW). LRW courses typically instruct students in how to write two very specific legal documents: the office memorandum and the appellate brief. As numerous books have already been published on the subject, memoranda and appellate briefs are not a focus of this book.

Part I

Academic Legal Discourse: Foundations for Writing in a U.S. Law School

Introduction to Part I

The purpose of Part I of this book is to guide international law students in learning and using U.S. academic legal principles in their writing. Writing for legal audiences in the United States follows certain principles at the whole text, paragraph, and sentence levels. If you can master these and apply them to your writing, your readers will be able to understand more easily the information and ideas you present.

Through the five chapters in Part I, you will learn the characteristics of U.S. academic legal texts and the steps you can make to produce them. Through analyses of authentic texts, you will see how writers follow these principles and their inherent characteristics and learn how to produce them in your own writing.

Chapter 1: *Introduction to Academic Legal Discourse* provides an overview of the principles of U.S. academic legal discourse. It examines the differences in discourse structures from different cultures and highlights the main principles of U.S. academic legal discourse. These principles are: (1) Write with Your Reader in Mind; (2) Start with Your Main Idea; (3) Support Your Ideas with Evidence; (4) Begin with an Introduction and End with a Conclusion; and (5) Show Every Step of your Thinking. Developing these principles in your writing will help it conform to your professors' and others' expectations and meet the criteria for good writing in the U.S. legal community. After explanations and examples of these principles, you will examine a law review article, *Catching the Unique Rabbit: Why Pets Should be Reclassified as Inimitable Property under the Law*, a piece of writing exemplifying these five principles. Following this is a brief description of the writing process used to develop well-written texts.

Chapter 2: *Paragraphs* shows you how to best present your ideas in paragraphs, which form the basis of any piece of writing. The chapter first contains an introduction to the properties of good paragraphs in U.S. academic legal discourse. After demonstrating where and how to state the main idea of a paragraph, the chapter reviews the types of support most common in academic legal discourse. The chapter then defines and illustrates unity and cohesion, two essential characteristics of well-written paragraphs, and gives you techniques to ensure that your paragraphs exhibit these characteristics. The chapter ends with a discussion of the appropriate length of paragraphs in U.S. academic legal discourse.

Chapter 3: *Sentences* introduces you to principles for writing clear, easily understandable sentences. These are: (1) use word order that readers expect and find easy to understand; (2) use the correct forms of words so that readers are not confused; (3) use correct sentence structures to make your meaning clear; and (4) vary sentence length and type to enhance the rhythm and flow of your writing. With clear explanations of these principles and exercises to practice them, you will become skillful at writing sentences.

Now that you have learned about parts of U.S. academic legal discourse at the whole piece, paragraph, and sentence levels, you need to know how to link your sentences and paragraphs together to write a unified and coherent piece. Chapter 4: *Transitions* shows you different devices for linking your ideas to each other. In U.S. academic legal discourse, it is not enough to present your ideas; the reader needs to be led through them. Successful academic legal writers show the reader how one idea relates to the next and how each idea relates to the topic of the whole document.

Finally, you will need to edit and proofread your writing to make sure your ideas are clearly presented and do not suffer from inadvertent grammatical, spelling, punctuation, or formatting mistakes that will mislead your reader. Chapter 5: *Editing and Proofreading* gives you strategies for editing your documents to ensure that they exhibit the characteristics of academic legal discourse outlined in Chapters 2-4. It then provides checklists and other suggestions for examining your documents for the most common grammatical, spelling, punctuation, and formatting mistakes that can lead to misunderstanding.

Through the principles and guidelines presented here and your practice of them, you will be well on your way to exemplifying them in your own writing. This will help you clearly and effectively communicate your ideas to your readers. In turn, you will be able to write more confidently in all of your legal tasks.

Chapter 1
Introduction to Academic Legal Discourse

A. What is Academic Discourse?

Academic discourse is the term given to the patterns and forms of language, spoken or written, that are used to convey meaning in "the academy," or college and university education. When we look at academic writing, such as a paragraph, a paper, or the response to an exam question, the academy has specific and well-defined structures to organize the sentences and the ideas in them. If your writing follows these ways of organization, your professor will easily understand what you are saying. If it does not, then your professor may struggle to understand your ideas because they are not presented in the expected academic way. In addition, academic journal reviewers and editors expect text, and the ideas in it, to be presented and organized according to certain guidelines for academic discourse. Learning and following these guidelines will help a reader easily understand your text and result in a better grade on a paper, a better exam score, or a better chance that an article will be accepted for publication.

Why is academic discourse important to law students? Simply put, it is the foundation for all legal discourse. **Legal discourse** refers to the language used to communicate in legal settings, such as law classes, law firms, and courtrooms. It is not possible to write effective legal discourse without a knowledge of and adherence to the characteristics of academic discourse. The guidelines followed for academic discourse are the same guidelines to follow when writing legal discourse. In fact, legal discourse *is* academic discourse with law as its topic and the use of specialized, legal vocabulary. In this book, we use the term **academic legal discourse** to refer to the written and spoken language used at law school.

Part I of this book teaches the guidelines for written U.S. academic legal discourse: the accepted ways for organizing ideas in writing for class writing assignments, exams, and papers in a U.S. law school context. Learning these accepted ways of writing will help you to make informed decisions about what to write and how to write it if you plan to attend, or are attending, a law school in the United States. The guidelines in Part I will help you, as a writer, learn how to compose a written text that an academic or professional in U.S. society can easily understand.

Although writing is prioritized in this book, we prefer the broader term "discourse" instead of "writing" to refer to what Part I of this book seeks to impart. Discourse, and the plural form "discourses," refers to not only language, but also to "ways of behaving, valuing, thinking, [and] believing . . . that are accepted as instantiations of particular identities . . . by specific groups."[1] By learning the principles of academic legal discourse in Part I of this book, you will become socialized to behaving, valuing, thinking, and believing as law students at a U.S. law school do. Our use of the term "discourse" thus reflects the multifaceted nature of what you are learning and becoming by attending law school and using this book.

Before examining the principles of academic legal discourse in more detail, it is helpful to think about cultural differences in education since you may be coming to U.S. law school from a different country and culture. Writing and education are situated in culture, and noting differences between your educational culture and U.S. educational culture will help you better understand the principles of U.S. academic writing.

B. The Role of Culture in Organizing Discourse

As mentioned in the Introduction, when you live in another culture, you realize that cultural differences are found in more than the food and the holidays. Though these are important cultural differences, differences also exist in institutions and in society in general. Roles for the elderly and the young, for men and women, and for professors and students can also be very different. If you are studying at an educational institution in a culture different from your own, you notice that differences exist in the ways professors and students interact, the type of material students are required to learn, and what learning material means.

How learning is measured, or how professors determine how well students learn the material, can also be different. Many cultures give students exams, but the medium through which an exam is given may vary. In many countries, law students take oral examinations. In these challenging exams, given over many days, a student is orally asked questions over different areas of law by one or several professors. In other countries, law students take principles of law and usually apply them to a hypothetical case they have never seen before. They need to write answers that may be several pages long and follow the guidelines of U.S. academic discourse. The professor will decide whether these exam answers are written in a timed exam period in a classroom or are written in a timed take-home exam.

---

[1] JAMES PAUL GEE, SOCIAL LINGUISTICS AND LITERACIES: IDEOLOGY IN DISCOURSES viii (2008).

In addition to differences in how learning is measured in different countries and cultures, the roles of professor and student are culturally determined. In some cultures, the professor is seen as an expert who knows everything about a topic. She is never questioned publicly in a class; instead, students with questions approach her after class individually or in a small group. If she does not know the answer to their question, she can never say "I don't know," because that would undermine her authority on a subject. In these educational environments, if the students do not understand the professor's answer, they remain silent, because questioning her again shows their lack of understanding.

In other cultures, the professor is also seen as an expert, but as a "learning expert." The professor possesses a large body of knowledge about a subject but is seen as a learning partner within the classroom. The professor advances her own knowledge of the subject with students through the process of learning that happens in the classroom. Students will ask the professor questions in class and may even interrupt the professor to ask a question. If the professor is unsure of the answer, she will usually say, "I'm not sure. Let me look into it and let you know at the next class" or "I have never thought about it that way. That's an interesting question. What do the rest of you think?" and ask the other students for their opinion. In this situation, the professor may or may not give an answer or offer her opinion at the end of the student answers. No one is embarrassed when a professor is unsure, because the professor and students are learning together in the classroom; they are pushing the boundaries of their knowledge.

Just as demonstrations of learning and the roles of professors and students are different in different cultures, so is the way academic discourse is organized and presented. In some cultures, a writer's main idea is presented first in a paper, and in other cultures, it is presented at the end of the paper. In still other cultures, the main idea is somewhere in the middle of the text.[2]

The obligations of reader versus writer also vary according to cultural context. In some cultures, the responsibility for understanding a paper is placed on the reader. If a piece of writing fails to make explicit links between one idea and the next, the reader has to work hard to decipher the writer's text. In other cultures, however, the burden is on the writer to make her paper as clear as possible so that any reader can follow the writer's argument. If a piece of writing contains words, sentences, and paragraphs that are hard to understand, the writer must revise and edit her document.

Understanding the cultural norms of classes and assignments will help you do well when studying in a country or culture that is not your native one. Knowing what your professor expects on a writing assignment or exam answer and knowing how to structure your writing to fulfill those expectations will increase your confidence and make writing an easier endeavor.

---

[2] ROBERT KAPLAN, *Cultural Thought Patterns in Inter-Cultural Education,* 16 LANGUAGE LEARNING 1-2 (1966).

In what follows, we highlight five key principles of academic legal discourse, adhered to by professors and students in U.S. law schools:

1. Write with Your Reader in Mind;
2. Start with Your Main Idea;
3. Support Your Ideas with Evidence;
4. Begin with an Introduction and End with a Conclusion; and
5. Show Every Step of Your Thinking.

1. Write with Your Reader in Mind

One of the main cultural differences in academic writing is the amount of "work" readers and writers have to do to read and write a text. Some cultures are "Reader Responsible" cultures, while others are "Writer Responsible" cultures.[3] In Reader Responsible cultures, the burden of responsibility for understanding a written text is on the reader. The writer will provide a context, make some generalizations, and finish with an explicit argument. However, it is the reader's responsibility to find the logical argument through the context and generalizations, and then to see how this leads to the conclusion that the writer states. The reader is responsible for making these links.

In a Writer Responsible culture, the writer is burdened with making her points clearly and concisely to a reader. The writer begins with her main ideas, clearly supports those ideas, and uses transitional devices to link the ideas and their support together for a reader. The writer defines key concepts for her reader in case she is not familiar with them. The writer also uses language that the reader can easily follow. In a Writer Responsible culture, the writer is always thinking about her reader and how to make her writing easy to understand.

The United States is a Writer Responsible culture. As a writer at a U.S. law school, it is your responsibility to make your points clearly and link them together plainly, so that your reader can easily follow the development of your ideas. If you are from a Reader Responsible culture, you may not be accustomed to stating your main point at the beginning, repeating parts of it throughout your document, and restating your main point again at the end. However, a reader in the U.S. expects that you will follow these principles. You may also feel that the Writer Responsible method forces you to make your points in an overly simple manner and to include unnecessary details. As you work on your writing through the guidelines in this text, you will learn what your reader expects and needs to understand your arguments. If your arguments are clear and organized in the way an American reader expects, then you will do well in writing your legal assignments and law school essay exams.

As you begin to use this book, you will be learning a way of writing characteristic of a Writer Responsible culture. You are learning to write with your

---

[3] MATTHEW MCCOOL, WRITING AROUND THE WORLD (2009).

reader in mind as you compose and revise your writing. Becoming adept at this will help you write well for academic and legal readers, both during law school and for the legal profession in the United States. The next four principles lay out the basics of how to write for a Writer Responsible culture.

2. Start with Your Main Idea

In a U.S. academic setting—be it an undergraduate science course, a graduate history program, or a law classroom—writers are expected to begin with their main idea and then offer evidence to support that idea. This basic pattern characterizes all U.S. academic discourse, and it applies to various levels of discourse. For example, when writing a paper, writers begin with their main idea and then support that idea in the rest of the paper. When writing a section within a paper, writers begin with their main idea and then support that idea in the rest of the section. And even when writing a paragraph within a section within a paper, writers begin with their main idea and then support that idea in the rest of the paragraph.

The main idea → support pattern holds for nearly every type of writing in a legal context. This includes law school papers and essay exams. But it also holds true for professional emails, office memoranda,[4] appellate briefs,[5] and even judicial opinions.[6] Professors, employers, judges, and other legal readers expect writers to get to their point right away. Indeed, they may get impatient if writers "beat around the bush" and keep them waiting and waiting for the main idea.

The following paragraph, pulled from a law review article,[7] illustrates how a writer begins with a main idea and then offers support for that idea in the sentences that follow. (The first sentence has been bolded for emphasis.)

> **Although the right to a jury[8] trial is important, the Supreme Court has determined that the right does not attach in all criminal cases.** The dividing line is whether a crime is classified as

[4] An office memorandum is a professional document usually written for a supervisor at a law firm. This document answers legal questions by explaining how the law will apply to a set of facts.

[5] An appellate brief is a document submitted to an appellate court by lawyers representing opposing parties to a dispute. This document contains the factual context and arguments for why the lawyer's client should win the case.

[6] A judicial opinion is a document written by an appellate judge. You will read many such opinions in Part II of this book.

[7] A law review is a collection of scholarly articles published regularly several times a year. Law reviews are the scholarly journals for the legal field: they contain articles about contemporary legal topics and ideas of interest. Both professors and law students can publish articles in law reviews.

[8] A jury is a body of persons selected to hear and decide a legal case.

> petty. In 1970, the Court decided that any crime with a possibility of imprisonment for at least six months cannot be classified as petty. Therefore, when a defendant's crime carries a penalty of at least six-months imprisonment, a defendant is entitled to a jury trial. Below the six-month threshold, a crime is not automatically classified as petty, but a defendant must prove that it is a serious crime deserving a jury trial before a jury trial will be granted. The Court, in an earlier analysis, described the difficulty in determining what penalty threshold should implicate a jury trial. The Court decided to let legislatures determine the classification of crime above or below the six-month threshold because they are accountable to the electorate and the changing views of society.[9]

The first sentence of this paragraph puts forth the main idea of this paragraph: the Supreme Court has decided that the right to a jury trial does not apply to all criminal cases. This is a general statement. The writer then supports this general statement with more specific details and examples to explain which criminal cases the right to jury attaches to. The reader knows from reading the first sentence of the paragraph what the entire paragraph will be about. U.S. academic legal writers almost always present their main idea at the beginning of a paragraph, as in the example above.

As you will learn in Part I, Chapter 2, the first sentence of a paragraph is called the topic sentence. The topic sentence is important in academic legal discourse because it expresses the topic—that is, the main idea—of the paragraph.

3. Support Your Ideas with Evidence

Since the main idea appears at the beginning of a text, the support, or evidence, for that idea follows. Writing is an active endeavor. A writer puts forth an idea and then uses the following sentences, paragraphs, and sections to give her reader evidence that her idea is reasonable, correct, and believable. So the second part of the main idea → support pattern, giving support after stating the main idea, is another key principle of U.S. academic legal discourse.

In the paragraph above, the main idea of the paragraph is as follows: the Supreme Court has decided that the right to a jury trial does not apply to all criminal cases. What follows this sentence is the specific support—that is, more detailed information about precisely when a defendant does not have the right

---

[9] Taylor E. Whitten, *Under the Guise of Reform: How Marijuana Possession Is Exposing the Flaws in the Criminal Justice System's Guarantee of a Right to a Jury Trial*, 99 IOWA L. REV. 919, 926-27 (2014).

to a jury trial. As a reader you learn the following pieces of information in the rest of the paragraph:

1. The deciding factor for whether the right to a jury applies is if a crime is considered "petty."
2. Petty crimes are those that carry a sentence of less than six months.
3. In some cases, defendants can argue that they committed a serious enough crime to deserve a jury trial, even if the penalty for the crime they have been charged with is less than six months.
4. The Supreme Court has decided to let legislatures classify crimes as petty or not petty.

These pieces of information all support and elaborate upon the writer's main idea for this paragraph, which is that the right to a jury trial does not apply to all criminal cases. This paragraph uses an explanation of what classifies as a case not having a jury trial (Sentence 1 above), a definition (Sentence 2), a possible exception (Sentence 3), and a description of how this plays out (Sentence 4).

As the example above shows, academic legal writers use various types of evidence to support their main ideas. However, the following types of evidence tend to be the most commonly used:

1. Examples;
2. Descriptions;
3. Explanations;
4. Definitions;
5. Statistics; and
6. References to authority.[10]

Texts about different topics use different kinds of evidence to prove the main idea that the writer puts forth. If you are writing about the history of a concept, for example, you might describe to your reader how the concept developed over time. If you want to convince your reader that one case should be decided the same way as another case, you might explain how the decision and logic of the first case is similar to the decision and logic in the second case.

In the paragraph analyzed above, each sentence contains one type of support. However, in some pieces of writing, a piece of support, such as an example or the description of a study, may take several sentences or even paragraphs. The important point is that the support follows the main idea and gives the writer's evidence for her main idea. Part I, Chapter 2 covers in more detail the types of evidence that academic legal writers typically use as support.

---

[10] Reference to authority involves the use of someone else's ideas to support your own arguments. An "authority" is any person or entity that has expertise in the subject matter being discussed.

4. Begin with an Introduction and End with a Conclusion

In addition to starting with the main idea and then giving its support, U.S. academic legal documents usually begin with an introduction and end with a conclusion. The introduction tells the reader the topic the text is about and what the writer will say about this topic. The conclusion restates the topic and summarizes what the writer has said about it. This may seem repetitive. However, in U.S. academic legal discourse, it is standard procedure: a writer announces her topic and opinion about it in the introduction; gives support for it in the middle, or body, of the piece of writing; and then restates the topic and her opinion in the conclusion. It is a clear, straightforward method. By recurrently mentioning the main idea and relating arguments and their support back to the main idea, a convincing piece is written.

Short academic pieces often have only one main idea—for example, a short paragraph answer on an essay exam. In this case, the introduction may be the opening sentence of the paragraph and the conclusion may be the final sentence of the paragraph.[11] (See Part II, Chapter 4 for more information about essay exams.)

a. The Introduction in a Longer Piece of Academic Legal Discourse

Longer written pieces, such as a seminar paper or journal article, may have several main ideas—for example, several reasons the writer is arguing for a particular outcome. In these longer pieces, the introduction briefly states the outcome so that the reader knows the main message of the piece. The introduction may also briefly list the writer's main arguments for her conclusion.

Sometimes, in longer pieces of writing following U.S. academic legal discourse principles, the main idea is accompanied by several other sentences, or a paragraph, that tell the reader how the writer will prove her main idea. This plan for how the writer will prove her main idea is in sentences or paragraphs called a **roadmap**. Roadmap sentences and paragraphs are a "map" for the reader, telling her the direction the paper will follow by clearly stating what ideas will be contained in the piece of writing and how the writer will prove her main idea.

The following example is an introduction from a student-written law review article, *Restructuring Local School Wellness Policies: Amending the Kids Act to Fight Childhood Obesity*. Student-written articles are called "notes." Because this note is a longer piece (28 pages), its introduction is proportionally longer as well (four paragraphs).

---

[11] Note, however, that paragraphs typically do not have a concluding sentence. See Part I, Chapter 2.

INTRODUCTION

Childhood obesity is a growing and omnipresent health issue in the United States. As of 2008, over one-third of all U.S. children and adolescents were overweight, and currently, seventeen percent of overweight children and adolescents are obese. These numbers continue to grow. Children are now at risk for health issues that historically only plagued adults—issues so severe that the average life expectancy in the United States is decreasing.

Most state and federal policies attempting to combat childhood obesity focus on which foods are served in lunchrooms. While the type of food served in schools is important in the battle against childhood obesity, statutes enacted to date have been insufficient and may contribute to the obesity problem. Children need to exercise and learn how to make healthy choices while they are young so that they can make better decisions as adults.

The most recent federal law on point, the Healthy, Hunger-Free Kids Act of 2010 (Kids Act), is a promising step toward fighting childhood obesity. The Kids Act is a significant improvement over the original 1946 school wellness program, codified in the National School Lunch Program. However, the Kids Act has not gone far enough. This Note proposes an amendment to the Kids Act that combines more stringent physical activity requirements with increased physical and nutritional education, all within the existing Local School Wellness Policy framework established by the Kids Act.

Part I of this Note examines the history and current structure of federal legislation surrounding childhood obesity. Part II discusses how the current statutory framework addresses childhood obesity and considers its shortcomings. This Part also explores the guidelines at the center of the Kids Act and argues why such guidelines are inadequate. Finally, Part III proposes an amendment to the Kids Act that will make the Act more effective in teaching children the importance of exercise and healthy eating. Additionally, Part III combats possible criticisms of the proposed amendment by arguing that such criticisms do not override the need for greater action against childhood obesity.[12]

In this introduction, the writer's main idea is in the third paragraph: "However, the Kids Act has not gone far enough. This Note proposes an

[12] Rebecca Edwalds, *Restructuring Local School Wellness Policies: Amending the Kids Act to Fight Childhood Obesity*, 47. U. MICH. J.L. REFORM 1051, 1051-2, (2014).

amendment to the Kids Act that combines more stringent physical activity requirements with increased physical and nutritional education, all within the existing Local School Wellness Policy framework established by the Kids Act." These two sentences tell the reader the writer's main argument, which focuses on critiquing and amending the Kids Act.

In the final paragraph of the introduction, the writer also gives her roadmap. This roadmap describes in detail the direction that the paper will take. Specifically, the roadmap tells readers how the writer plans to prove her main idea. First, the writer provides context to her argument by "examining" the history and structure of legislation on childhood obesity. Next, she "explores" the guidelines in the Kids Act and shows how they are inadequate. Following this, the writer "proposes" a way to amend the Kids Act to make it more effective. Finally, she "combats" criticisms of her proposal. The writer's roadmap helps the reader understand her main arguments from the beginning by allowing the reader to see the scope of and support for these arguments.

b. The Conclusion in a Longer Piece of Academic Legal Discourse

In addition to the introduction stating the writer's main idea and using a roadmap, in longer academic legal pieces, writers often restate the main idea, and sometimes supporting ideas from the roadmap, in their conclusion. The introduction and conclusion mirror each other: the introduction introduces the main idea and the roadmap, and the conclusion restates them to ensure that the reader finishes reading the piece knowing exactly what the writer argued.

Look at the conclusion for the student-written law review article, *Restructuring Local School Wellness Policies: Amending the Kids Act to Fight Childhood Obesity.* Note specifically the underlined words and phrases (added for emphasis), which carry the same ideas that the writer mentions in the Introduction to the paper.

> CONCLUSION
>
> Although the federal government and local educational agencies have been working towards preventing childhood obesity, <u>the efforts to date have not been enough</u>. <u>The government has amended the standards</u> for food served in schools under the National School Lunch Program in an attempt to promote school health. <u>Yet under these same regulations</u>, kids still have access to unhealthy competitive foods. <u>In addition, there is a lack of institutional support</u> for programs geared towards health and exercise throughout the school administration. This makes it more difficult to build an environment emphasizing exercise and healthy living. Finally, even though the Kids Act requires the Secretary of Agriculture to

> provide guidelines to support local wellness policies, as evidenced by the current policies in Texas and Illinois, the guidelines are insufficient to create solid local wellness policies.
>
> Children must receive education about the importance of healthy choices and exercise, just as they are educated about other core academic subjects. The best solution to this problem is amending the Kids Act to require increased activity and physical education classes, more opportunities before and after school for exercise, and health education requirements. In placing importance on health education and physical activity, children may grow up to make independent healthy choices, and prevent themselves from becoming part of the obesity epidemic that plagues the nation.[13]

This conclusion mirrors its introduction (see again pages 17-18) by restating the main idea that current efforts at reducing childhood and adolescent obesity are not doing enough and that the Kids Act needs to be amended to better combat obesity. The underlined words, phrases, and sentences are very similar to those used in the introduction. Use of similar constructions, or synonyms for them, helps the reader see clearly what the writer has argued in the paper.

You may come from a writing tradition in which stating your main ideas in the beginning and restating them again at the end seems very repetitive. However, in U.S. academic legal discourse, this repetition is expected. There is a saying, "In the introduction, we tell the reader what we are going to do, and in the conclusion, we tell the reader what we did." If you have written a carefully argued paper and not veered off course, the main idea, and possible roadmap, in the introduction and conclusion should match.

Similar to the introduction, the conclusion can be of varying length, depending on the length of the text. A longer document will have a longer conclusion and may have an entire section devoted to the conclusion, because there will be more points to review at the end.

5. State Every Step of Your Thinking

Just as you need to state your main idea in your introduction and restate it in your conclusion, you also need to show your reader every step of your thinking. What does this mean?

In academic legal discourse, it is expected that a reader is easily able to understand your arguments, their support, and the logic you use to connect your support to your arguments. Nothing is assumed. Remember that Principle 1 is to Write with Your Reader in Mind. Operationally, this means that your reader needs

---

[13] *Id.* at 1078-79.

to see every step of your thinking. You cannot assume that your reader will understand your conclusion; the reader needs to see how you arrived at your conclusion. Because people in the U.S. come from many different countries and cultures, they do not always share the same cultural references, and they will not always come to the same conclusion when presented with the same arguments and support. Thus, part of your job as a writer in a Writer Responsible culture is to spell out every step of your thinking to be sure your reader understands your arguments and how the support you present proves them.

In the short essay exam answer excerpted below, the writer neatly lays out every step of her thinking. As you will see in Part II of this book, a typical U.S. law school exam consists of a hypothetical scenario—that is, a story—in which people interact in ways that raise legal issues. Students are placed in the role of a legal professional, such as a lawyer or judge, who has to identify these issues and resolve them using the rules of law learned in the course.

In the exam answer below, the student analyzes whether "Cindy," one individual appearing in the hypothetical on the exam, has a claim against "Erica," another individual appearing in the hypothetical. (A claim is a plaintiff's assertion that she is entitled to compensation for her injury. A close synonym is "cause of action.") Notice how the writer walks the reader through every step of her thinking to arrive at the conclusion that Cindy probably does not have a claim against Erica.[14]

> Cindy probably cannot bring a successful claim against Erica. The issue is if Cindy can state a cause of action for the negligent infliction of emotional distress (NIED)[15] after watching her mother's car get struck by another vehicle.
>
> Under the "zone of physical danger" rule, which is the law in Illinois, a plaintiff can make out a claim for NIED if two conditions are met. First, the plaintiff must be in "'such proximity to the accident' that there was 'a high risk of physical impact' so as to cause the plaintiff 'reasonable fear for [her] own safety.'" Second, the plaintiff "'must show a physical injury or illness as a result of the emotional distress.'" *Lewis v. Westinghouse Electric Corp.*
>
> Cindy was in proximity to the accident because she watched it unfold from about 500 feet away. However, Erica could argue that Cindy was not at high risk of physical impact from this distance. Though Cindy could claim that she feared for her own

---

[14] You can read the hypothetical (story) on which this essay question is based in Part II, Chapter 4, along with a detailed analysis of the exam answer excerpted here. Part II, Chapter 4 addresses exam writing and the structure of traditional law school exam answers in greater detail.

[15] The "negligent infliction of emotional distress" is a claim brought by a plaintiff who suffers emotional injury due to the alleged carelessness of a defendant.

> safety, it is unlikely that a court would accept this fear as "reasonable." Cindy was quite a distance from the intersection and safely pulled over on the side of the road. Erica could argue that this situation would not create fear in "the person of ordinary sensibilities." The facts also suggest that Cindy was primarily concerned for her mother's safety, and not her own. Furthermore, a court may be concerned that allowing such a lawsuit to go forward would "encourage neurotic overreactions to trivial hurts" (*Knierim v. Izzo*, cited in *Lewis v. Westinghouse Electric Corp.*), resulting in a greater number of frivolous lawsuits, which may be burdensome on the courts.
>
> Cindy can probably show physical injury as a result of the emotional distress. Though some of Cindy's symptoms appear to be psychological—she has insomnia and nightmares—there are also physical manifestations of her distress. Cindy has back pain, she feels dizzy, and she has panic attacks.
>
> Because Cindy would have a difficult time proving the first part of the NIED zone of danger standard, she likely cannot state a cause of action for NIED against Erica.

The writer's first sentence is her main idea that Cindy does not have a claim against Erica. She then proceeds, step by step, to explain why this is so.

Step 1: The writer first begins by describing the legal issue that is raised by the facts in the hypothetical.

> The issue is if Cindy can state a cause of action for the negligent infliction of emotional distress (NIED) after watching her mother's car get struck by another vehicle.

Step 2: The writer states the legal rule used to determine whether someone has a claim against another individual for negligent infliction of emotional distress, or NIED for short. This rule, as explained by the student, has two components. The writer uses the transition words "first" and "second" to make clear to the reader which component of the rule she is describing.

> Under the "zone of physical danger" rule, which is the law in Illinois, a plaintiff can make out a claim for NIED if two conditions are met. First, the plaintiff must be in "'such proximity to the accident' that there was 'a high risk of physical impact' so as to cause the plaintiff 'reasonable fear for [her] own safety.'" Second,

> the plaintiff "'must show a physical injury or illness as a result of the emotional distress.'" *Lewis v. Westinghouse Electric Corp.*

Step 3: The writer applies the rule to the facts of the hypothetical that she was given on the exam. She begins by applying the first component of the rule. (Note how she uses the key terms "proximity," "physical impact," and "reasonable fear" from the first component of the rule, underlined for emphasis below.)

> Cindy was in proximity to the accident because she watched it unfold from about 500 feet away. However, Erica could argue that Cindy was not at high risk of physical impact from this distance. Though Cindy could claim that she feared for her own safety, it is unlikely that a court would accept this fear as "reasonable." Cindy was quite a distance from the intersection and safely pulled over on the side of the road. Erica could argue that this situation would not create fear in "the person of ordinary sensibilities." The facts also suggest that Cindy was primarily concerned for her mother's safety, and not her own. Furthermore, a court may be concerned that allowing such a lawsuit to go forward would "encourage neurotic overreactions to trivial hurts" (*Knierim v. Izzo*, cited in *Lewis v. Westinghouse Electric Corp.*), resulting in a greater number of frivolous lawsuits, which may be burdensome on the courts.

The writer then applies the second component of the rule. (Note how she uses the key term "physical injury" from the second component of the rule, underlined for emphasis below.)

> Cindy can probably show physical injury as a result of the emotional distress. Though some of Cindy's symptoms appear to be psychological—she has insomnia and nightmares—there are also physical manifestations of her distress. Cindy has back pain, she feels dizzy, and she has panic attacks.

Step 4: The writer concludes that Cindy probably does not have a claim against Erica.

> Because Cindy would have a difficult time proving the first part of the NIED zone of danger standard, she likely cannot state a cause of action for NIED against Erica.

In these few paragraphs, the writer methodically builds her argument that Cindy does not have an NIED claim against Erica. Every step in the writer's thinking is explained completely. If the writer had left out any of these steps, the reader may not follow along or accept her argument. Because the burden for clarity in U.S. academic legal documents is on the writer, a writer must list all of the steps involved in her thinking when making an argument. In U.S. academic legal discourse, readers expect to be led through the text in this way. Writing out every step in your thinking ensures that your reader understands exactly what you are trying to say.

C. Example of Academic Legal Discourse in a Law Review Article

What follows is an example of academic legal discourse. It is a student-written article, referred to as a "note," as mentioned above. The title of the piece is *Catching the Unique Rabbit: Why Pets Should be Reclassified as Inimitable Property under the Law* (hereafter *Catching the Unique Rabbit*). This note demonstrates the five principles discussed in this chapter:

1. Write with Your Reader in Mind;
2. Start with Your Main Idea;
3. Support Your Ideas with Evidence;
4. Begin with an Introduction and End with a Conclusion; and
5. Show Every Step of Your Thinking.

As you begin reading the article below, something will immediately jump out at you: small numbers like this[1] follow nearly every sentence. These numbers represent footnotes, which also appear at the bottom of the page. **Footnotes** perform a variety of functions in U.S. academic discourse. First, they show the reader when the writer has used an authority, another source, for support (something that is not the writer's own thinking). Second, they explain concepts that the writer thinks the reader will find helpful. Finally, footnotes add details that the writer thinks are important, but not important enough to be part of the main writing itself.

In addition to footnotes, you will also find numbers like **(1)**, **(2)**, and **(3)** preceding each sentence. These numbers are not part of the original article; rather, they have been added to make references to sentences in the text, and hence discussion of the article, easier.

The article repeatedly uses certain legal terms. Before the article, you will find definitions of the most commonly used terms. These terms are also highlighted in the text. If you have trouble following the writer's argument because you cannot understand a word or phrase, we encourage you to look up that term in an English-to-English or legal dictionary. As much as possible, however, try to discern the writer's main ideas instead of getting caught up on individual words.

TASK 1.C.1. Questions for Discussion

As you read the article below, answer the following questions. Indicate the sentence(s) in which you found the answer to each question to facilitate a discussion of the questions.

1. Does anything in the article suggest that the writer wrote with her reader in mind? Consider the author's word usage, sentence structure, and paragraph organization.

2. Looking at the paper as a whole, does the writer begin with her main idea? What is this main idea?

3. Looking at the paper as a whole, does the writer end with a conclusion? Does this conclusion mirror the information provided in the introduction?

4. Look at Section II.B., *Favoring the Cat, the Cow, or the Kids: The Importance of Companion Animals to the Modern U.S. Family*. Does the writer begin with her main idea? What is this main idea? Does the writer end the section with a conclusion?

5. Look at Section IV, *Creating a Viable Solution that Can Coexist with Contemporary Jurisprudence and Adequately Compensate Pet Owners: Adopting Inimitable Property.* Find an instance of each of the following types of evidence: (1) example, (2) description, (3) explanation, (4) definition, (5) statistic, and (6) reference to authority.

6. In Section IV, *Creating a Viable Solution that Can Coexist with Contemporary Jurisprudence and Adequately Compensate Pet Owners: Adopting Inimitable Property*, the writer presents her solution. Before giving her arguments, what term does she define? Why?

7. In Section IV.A.4., Anzalone v. Kragness: *The $100,000 Example*, the writer uses an extended example of a case for support. What is the main idea that the writer wishes to support using this case? Where is this main idea located?

8. Look at Section III.A., *Why Allowing Emotional Distress Damages for Pet Loss Fails.* What is the writer's main idea in this section? What steps does the writer go through to prove this idea?

9. Look at Section III.C., *Applying the* Campbell *Exception to Allow a Large Punitive Damage Award in Pet Loss Cases Is Not a Viable Solution.* What

is the writer's main idea in this section? What steps does the writer go through to prove this idea?

Pre-Reading Vocabulary

Damages *(noun)*
A sum of money claimed by the plaintiff, or awarded to the plaintiff, as compensation for injury or loss.

Recover damages *(verb)*
A plaintiff "recovers" damages if she wins the lawsuit and is awarded money. The noun form is "recovery"; the adjective form is "recoverable."

Punitive damages *(noun)*
Punitive damages may also be awarded to the plaintiff. However, punitive damages are awarded not as compensation for injury or loss, but rather to "punish" the defendant or deter future wrongdoing.

Cause of action *(noun)*
A factual situation that provides the grounds for suing another party.

CATCHING THE UNIQUE RABBIT: WHY PETS SHOULD BE RECLASSIFIED AS INIMITABLE PROPERTY UNDER THE LAW

57 CLE. ST. L. REV. 167 (2009).
Kelly Wilson[a1]

INTRODUCTION[1]

(1) When billionaire real estate mogul Leona Helmsley died in August 2007, she left behind contradictory images of both a haughty bourgeoisie

---

[a1] J.D. expected, May 2009, Cleveland State University, Cleveland-Marshall College of Law; B.A. Mount Union College. The Author would like to acknowledge the constant support, love, and guidance of her family, especially her mother, Toni, and grandmother Connie, who have believed in her unfailingly. The Author would also like to thank the members of the Cleveland-Marshall faculty and staff for their helpful comments and advice.

[1] In this Note, the terms *pet* or *pets* (unless noted otherwise) refer specifically to the most widely recognized and typical companion animals: dogs and cats. Although humans keep a number of other species as pets, such as rabbits, birds, fish, or other exotic species of animals, this Note argues in further detail that the unique qualities of the domestic cat and dog set them apart from other types of pets or owned animals, such as typical farm animals or livestock.

businesswoman and a generous philanthropist. [2] **(2)** In her will, Helmsley specifically cut out two of her four grandchildren and made her pampered Maltese, aptly named Trouble, the single largest beneficiary.[3] **(3)** The pooch was the recipient of twelve million dollars worth of caretaking expenses via a trust set up for the pet.[4] **(4)** Trouble's trust exceeded Helmsley's second largest bequest by $2 million; the beneficiary for that bequest was her brother.[5] **(5)** In the very same will, Helmsley also directed that her various residences and belongings were to be sold and the proceeds from the sale were directed to benefit a charitable

---

[2] Alan Feuer, *Helmsley, Through Will, Is Still Calling the Shots*, N.Y. TIMES, Aug. 30, 2007, *available at* http:// www.nytimes.com/2007/08/30/nyregion/30leona.html?em&ex=1188619200&en=49f49958da2265fc&ei=5087%0A. Leona Helmsley was married to Harry Helmsley, one of the most prominent figures in U.S. real estate. RICHARD HAMMER, THE HELMSLEYS: THE RISE AND FALL OF HARRY AND LEONA 37 (1990). Although widely believed to be the owner of the Empire State Building, Harry is actually credited with successfully running and operating the building for many years. *Id.* at 54. Known for driving a hard bargain, Helmsley owned many large residential structures and amassed a fortune; sometimes, the contributions to his opulence came in the form of evicting elderly tenants who had forgotten to pay their rent. *Id.* at 97-98. Leona was a real estate broker when the two met, and after Harry left his wife of thirty-three years and offered Leona a position as senior vice president in one of his companies, the two were eventually married. *Id.* at 137, 149. In addition to residential properties, Helmsley also owned many hotels in New York and other states. *Id.* at 175. Eventually, Leona became president of all the hotels they owned and earned a nasty reputation herself for her extravagant demands and haughty demeanor. *Id.* at 174, 181. One former associate described Leona's character by stating, "She can exude such warmth and love you feel you are being embraced by this rich, glamorous, sexy lady. Then in an instant, she can turn so vicious and verbally violent that you are left flabbergasted." *Id.* at 182.

[3] *See* Feuer, *supra* note 2.

[4] *See id., supra* note 2. It is impossible to leave money to a pet directly through a will as this type of bequest will be declared void and the money intended to go the animal would go to either the residuary or a different beneficiary in the will. *See* MARGARET C. JASPER, PET LAW 47 (2007). Courts will declare these bequests void because animals are still personal property, and one cannot conceivably leave property to another form of property. *Id.* Furthermore, only a little more than half of the states will even allow pet trusts to be established. *Id.* at 87. These states include: Alaska, Arizona, Arkansas, California, Colorado, Florida, Hawaii, Idaho, Illinois, Iowa, Kansas, Maine, Michigan, Missouri, Montana, Nebraska, Nevada, New Hampshire, New Jersey, New Mexico, New York, North Carolina, Oregon, Tennessee, Texas, Utah, Washington, Wisconsin, and Wyoming. *Id.*

[5] *See* Feuer, *supra* note 2.

trust left in both her and her late husband's name.[6] **(6)** Helmsley's belongings are reportedly worth billions of dollars.[7]

(7) While Helmsley's will appears to be a contradiction of greed and generosity, it is significant in the sense that Helmsley prioritized her beloved dog, her pet,[8] higher than certain human members of her family.[9] **(8)** Helmsley's attachment to her dog is one example of the important role a pet can play in a family setting. **(9)** While most pet owners in the United States cannot afford to leave millions to their favorite pets, many pet owners recognize that their pet is part of their family. **(10)** Just as with other family members, pet owners spend significant sums to ensure their pet's safety, health, and happiness.[10] **(11)** Because pet owners go to such great lengths to take care of their pets, it would seem that these unique living creatures would be valued in the law. **(12)** In actuality, most owners would be dismayed to learn that should their pet die by

---

[6] *See id.* It was not until his later years that Harry Helmsley was more philanthropic. *See* HAMMER, *supra* note 2, at 220. Although the Helmsley's had contributed to charities before, the amounts were almost always modest. *Id.* One late-in-life stand-out was a gift of $33 million to a New York hospital that had treated Harry for cardiovascular problems. *Id.* at 221. At the time the gift was made it was one of the "largest gifts ever made by an individual to a single institution." *Id.*

[7] *See* Feuer, *supra* note 2. During her life, Helmsley was known for mistreating her employees, yet she also donated millions of dollars to Hurricane Katrina relief, September 11th funds, hospitals, and made other large and anonymous donations. CNN, *Leona Helmsley, 'Queen of Mean,' Dies at 87*, http://www.cnn.com/2007/US/08/20 /helmsley.obit/index.html (last visited Nov. 30, 2007).

[8] The current trend in animal law articles and texts is to use the term *companion animal* instead of *pet*, and *guardian* instead of *pet owner*. Debra Squires-Lee, *In Defense of Floyd: Appropriately Valuing Companion Animals in Tort*, 70 N.Y.U. L. REV. 1059, 1059 n.2 (1995). This author will use the terms *pet* and *companion animal* interchangeably, but because the thrust of the argument in this Note is that pets should remain classified as property, the term *owner* will still be used. *Id.*

[9] *See* Feuer, *supra* note 2.

[10] *See* Diane Brady & Christopher Palmeri, *The Pet Economy: U.S.s Spend an Astonishing $41 Billion a Year on Their Furry Friends*, BUSINESS WEEK, Aug. 6, 2007, *available at* http://www.businessweek.com/magazine/content/07_ 32/b4045001.htm?chan =search.

being thrown into traffic by an outraged driver,[11] or by suffocation from being left in a sweltering and stifling enclosed area,[12] they could only **recover** nominal **damages** for the market value of their pet.[13] **(13)** They would also be sad to know

---

[11] *See* People v. Burnett, 2 Cal. Rptr. 3d 120, 124 (Ct. App. 2003). Although this is a criminal case, in the state of California an owner is not allowed to recover noneconomic damages for the loss of a pet. *See* Victor E. Schwartz & Emily J. Laird, *Non-Economic Damages in Pet Litigation: The Serious Need to Preserve a Rational Rule*, 33 PEPP. L. REV. 227, 236-37 (2006). Burnett was convicted of animal cruelty for causing the death of a ten-year old Bichon Frise. *Burnett*, 2 Cal. Rptr. 3d at 123. After the owner of the dog committed a small traffic violation which caused her to bump into Burnett's back bumper he got out of his car and as he approached the car the owner rolled down her window. *Id.* When Burnett got to the car he reached in the open window, grabbed the small lap dog out the owner's lap and threw the small dog into the highway. *Id.* It was raining heavily that night and after being thrown across traffic the dog was disoriented. *Id.* In attempting to get back to his owner's car the Bichon was struck and killed by an oncoming motorist who did not see the small dog. *Id.* at 124. These events took place in front of the distraught owner, who was almost hit by a car when attempting to cross traffic to get to the stranded and bewildered dog. *Id.* at 123-24.

[12] Gluckman v. Am. Airlines, Inc., 844 F. Supp. 151, 163 (S.D.N.Y. 1994). On a camping trip in 1988 Andrew Gluckman found an abandoned golden retriever. *Id.* at 153. Gluckman named the dog Floyd, adopted the dog as his pet, and intended to bring the dog back to New York with him. *Id.* at 154. Gluckman paid an additional $110.85 for a special crate and carrying charge for Floyd but was never informed that the airline treated dogs like any other type of baggage. *Id.* On the day of Gluckman's flight, his plane was delayed for over an hour due to a mechanical problem. *Id.* During the delay, the plane sat on the ground in a temperature of 115 degrees Fahrenheit. *Id.* The temperature in the baggage hold of the plane, where Floyd was being kept, reached over 140 degrees Fahrenheit. *Id.* When Floyd was brought to Gluckman to be placed on the next flight the dog was "lying on his side panting; his face and paws were bloody; there was blood all over the crate; and the condition of the cage evidenced a panicked effort to escape." *Id.* Floyd died from being kept in these horrific conditions. Gluckman brought suit seeking emotional distress damages and loss of companionship of his pet (among other claims), but his claims were dismissed and he was denied recovery. *Id.* at 154, 163.

[13] Many courts, including those in Arizona, California, Connecticut, Indiana, Kentucky, Massachusetts, Michigan, Minnesota, Nebraska, New Jersey, North Dakota, Ohio, Oregon, Pennsylvania, Texas, Virginia, Washington, West Virginia, and Wisconsin have neither allowed a pet owner to figure in their emotional distress when calculating damages for a lost pet, nor allowed the owner to recover under a separate cause of action for intentional or negligent infliction of emotional distress. Schwartz & Laird, *supra* note 11, at 236-37.

that should a market even exist, the going rate for an older, previously owned, or impurely bred pet is quite minimal.[14]

(14) This Note introduces a new approach for resolving the issue of inadequate compensation for pet loss by arguing for the adoption of a new classification of personal property called inimitable property. **(15)** The new categorization takes into consideration the live, conscious, and unique qualities of pets that distinguish them from other sorts of inanimate property. **(16)** Part II outlines the historical origins and subsequent shifts in the importance of domestic animals and their status in the law. **(17)** Part III highlights the existing arguments and suggestions for change and addresses why they ultimately fail. **(18)** Part IV introduces the requirements and characteristics of "inimitable property" and explains why it could work if applied to domestic pets by courts or the legislature. **(19)** Finally, Part V concludes that the reclassification of pets as "inimitable property" is a workable solution to compensate owners more adequately when they lose their pets.

II. Origins of the Property Status and Transposed Importance of Domestic Animals

A. Animals as Personal Property: Cats, Cows, and Chairs

(20) People for the Ethical Treatment of Animals' (PETA) rise in popularity, and perhaps infamy,[15] in recent years, may seem to suggest that the concepts of

---

[14] One source estimates that over eighty million dogs are put to sleep every year in pounds and animal shelters because of behavioral problems. Dog Scouts of America, *Responsible Dog Ownership*, http:// www.dogscoutsl.com/Responsible_Ownership.html (last visited Dec. 19, 2008). These problems stem from both poor training and abandonment. *Id.* Such a large number of previously owned dogs being put to sleep before a second owner could be found suggests the lack of a healthy market for a previously owned pet. *Id.*

[15] For an example of animal rights being viewed as infamous, see Jonathan R. Lovvorn, *Animal Law in Action: The Law, Public Perception, and the Limits of Animal Rights Theory as a Basis for Legal Reform*, 12 Animal L. 133, 138 (2006) ("[F]ear of animal rights—and of animal rights activists—is undoubtedly fueled, at least in part, by the violent extremists of the movement and the spectre of direct action, which is also sometimes called animal 'terrorism.'").

animal rights and animal advocacy are modern developments.[16] **(21)** However, the question of what rights, if any, animals (and their owners) have has been debated since ancient times.[17] **(22)** The continuing debate over the legal status of animals is both complex and provocative, as scholars, philosophers, theologians, politicians, and business leaders all weigh in on the subject. **(23)** There are many explanations and allegations for why animals—namely pets—are classified as personal property.[18] **(24)** To better understand the current debate over pets and property law it is necessary to briefly review the origin and evolution of personal property rights in animals.

(25) William Blackstone, a forefather of English and U.S. common law, categorized all animals as either *domitae naturae* (domestic animals) or *ferae naturae* (wild animals).[19] **(26)** Because domestic animals were tame and generally remained close to their owners' homes, their status was defined by their lack of sporadic and frequent movement across property boundaries.[20] **(27)** Wild animals, however, roam freely without regard to property boundaries, making it much harder (perhaps impossible) for humans to possess absolute ownership rights of these animals.[21] **(28)** Since ownership of a domesticated animal is linked

---

[16] *See* U.S. Veterinary Medical Association, *Poll Finds U.S.s Cool Toward Animal Rights*, JAVMA NEWS, July 15, 2003, *available at* http://www.avma.org/onlnews/javma/jul03/030715f.asp (last visited Feb. 7, 2008) ("A Gallup poll testing public reaction to several animal rights goals found that most Americans aren't willing to fundamentally change their views about animals . . . [evidenced by a] majority—71 percent—[of those polled believing] animals are entitled to some protections from harm and exploitation, [while only] 25 percent think that animals deserve the same rights as people."). This poll shows that the concept of animals having the same amount of rights of humans is too new and foreign in comparison to current popular mentality. *Id.*

[17] *Compare* Aristotle, *Politics, in* ANIMAL RIGHTS: A HISTORICAL ANTHOLOGY 6, (Andrew Linzey & Paul Barry Clarke eds., William Ellis trans., 2004) (stating man is the most excellent of all living creatures, and animals, lacking speech or a political or moral sense of good or evil, are inferior), *with* NORM PHELPS, THE LONGEST STRUGGLE: ANIMAL ADVOCACY FROM PYTHAGORAS TO PETA, 26-27 (2007) (recounting that the ancient philosopher, Pythagoras, most known for his work in geometry, was also well known in ancient times as an advocate for a vegetarian lifestyle and diet because he believed, and taught, that all sentient beings have souls of equal worth).

[18] *See generally* ANIMAL RIGHTS: A HISTORICAL ANTHOLOGY (Andrew Linzey & Paul Barry Clarke eds., 2004).

[19] GARY L. FRANCIONE, ANIMALS, PROPERTY, AND THE LAW 41 (2d ed. 2005).

[20] *Id.*

[21] *Id.*

by definition to the ownership of real property, domestic animals could be owned absolutely.[22]

(29) This distinction between domestic and wild animals is important in the evolution of the classification of companion animals. **(30)** Originally, pets were classified as domestic animals. **(31)** Owners could not recover for wrongful injury or death of a pet because the pet had no intrinsic worth to the owner.[23] **(32)** Worth, in this sense, was measured by an animal's contribution to livelihood through farm work, as a source of food through byproducts or their flesh, or as a source of clothing materials and other products made from an animal's body.[24] **(33)** Value was defined solely by monetary worth because these valuable farm animals could be sold or traded for goods.[25] **(34)** According to animal rights advocate and animal law expert Gary L. Francione, "the productive value and the property status of animals are inextricably intertwined" because "[t]he value of animals is dependent on their property status."[26]

(35) Because cattle could be used in a wide variety of ways to help ensure human survival, their status as valuable personal property entitled the owner to

---

[22] *Id.* Additionally, exclusive ownership was also contingent upon the need of tame animals to have a caretaker. Johann Gottlieb Fichte, *The Science of Rights, in* ANIMAL RIGHTS: A HISTORICAL ANTHOLOGY 79-80 (Andrew Linzey & Paul Barry Clarke eds., Columbia University Press 2004). The domestication of animals created an obligation in the owner to not only reap the benefits of the animal, but also to feed, protect, and perform all the actions that wild animals are capable of that domestic animals are not. *Id.*

[23] FRANCIONE, *supra* note 19, at 42. In a case dating back to 1868 the Supreme Judicial Court of Massachusetts opined:

> In regard to the ownership of live animals, the law has long made a distinction between dogs and cats, and other domestic quadrupeds, growing out of the nature of the creatures and the purposes for which they are kept. Beasts which have been thoroughly tamed, and are used for burden or husbandry, or for food, such as horses, cattle and sheep, are as truly property of intrinsic value, and entitled to the same protection, as any kind of goods. But dogs and cats, even in a state of domestication, never wholly lose their wild natures and destructive instincts, and are kept either for uses which depend on retaining and calling into action those very natures and instincts, or else for the mere whim or pleasure of the owner ... [and that] dogs have always been held by the U.S. courts to be entitled to less legal regard and protection than more harmless and useful domestic animals.

Blair v. Forehand, 100 Mass. 136 (Mass. 1868) (cited by the Supreme Court in Sentell v. New Orleans & C. R. Co., 166 U.S. 698, 703 (1897)).

[24] *See* JULIET CLUTTON-BROCK, DOMESTICATED ANIMALS FROM EARLY TIMES 62 (1981).

[25] *See* FRANCIONE, *supra* note 19, at 34. The words chattel, capital, and cattle at one time were all synonymous in European languages. *Id.* The Spanish word for property is also virtually the same as the word for cattle. *Id.* The same holds true in the Latin language where the word for money is a derivative of the word meaning cattle. *Id.*

[26] *Id.* at 28.

recover a large sum of money after a loss.[27] **(36)** In contrast, an owner trying to recover for the loss of a cat or dog would not fare well because those animals offered little or no insurance of survival.[28] **(37)** Despite the status of dogs and cats as personal property, the owner was not entitled to recover for the loss.[29]

B. Favoring the Cat, the Cow, or the Kids: The Importance of Companion Animals to the Modern U.S. Family

(38) When these original distinctions of animals and personal property were being drawn, the U.S. farmer comprised ninety percent of the workforce. **(39)** This made cattle and capital interchangeable.[30] **(40)** In 1990, the percentage of farmers that comprised the workforce had dwindled to less than three percent.[31] **(41)** The drastic decline in U.S. farming shows that the justifications for the original property classifications are horribly outdated. **(42)** No longer is the cow

---

[27] As recently as 2005, a court in California allowed victims of cattle theft to recover four times the worth of the cattle. People v. Baker, 23 Cal. Rptr. 3d 871. 876 (Ct. App. 2005). Ultimately the defendant was held liable in the amount of $22,521 for depriving the owners of the use of cows that might produce valuable offspring. *Id.*

[28] *See supra* note 23.

[29] *See supra* note 23. In contrast with cats and dogs, cows historically have and presently do provide milk, butter, cream, cheese, and beef. CLUTTON-BROCK, *supra* note 24, at 62. If the cow is primarily a draught animal it is used to plow and can provide small amounts of milk. *Id.* When the animal loses utility as a plow animal it can be used as a source of food. *Id.* While alive, the cow also provides a source of free fertilizer for crops through production of manure. *Id.* In addition, the carcass of a cow serves many purposes, including the use of horns, bones, and hide for weapons and clothing; fat can be used to make into candles for lighting, and the hooves can be used to produce glue. *Id.*

[30] Over the course of the past 100 years the number of Americans farming as a profession has declined, although the latest statistics are only available from 1990, it seems reasonable to assume that in the past nineteen years farming as a profession has remained the same or declined even further. ECONOMIC RESEARCH SERVICE, A HISTORY OF U.S. AGRICULTURE, 1607-2000: FARMERS AND THE LAND (2000), *available at* http://www.agclassroom.org/gan/timeline/farmers_land.htm.

[31] *Id.*

the most important animal in Americans' lives.[32] **(43)** With hotels, retailers, insurance companies and other large business sectors pandering to pet owners, it is not far-fetched to assume that in the sixty-three percent of U.S. households who own pets, the role of the most important animal in family life has been taken over by a dog or cat.[33]

(44) However much a pet owner may view his or her pet as a member of the family, there is still an element of ownership and detachment in the relationship. **(45)** This situation is devastatingly apparent for pets caught up in the national mortgage crisis when home owners are being forced to foreclose.[34] **(46)** As families are forced to abandon homes and seek housing by renting, staying with

---

[32] In 2007, the pet industry was worth $41.2 billion, almost double what it was worth ten years ago. *See* U.S. Pet Products Association, *Industry Statistics and Trends: Pet Ownership*, 2007/2008 APPA NATIONAL PET OWNERS SURVEY (2008), *available at* http://www.U.S.petproducts.org/press_ industrytrends.asp (last visited Feb. 1, 2009). On top of an overall increase in the total worth, many companies such as Paul Mitchell (hair care) Harley Davidson (motorcycles) and Old Navy (clothing retail) have product lines available that are specifically designed for family pets. *Id.* Some hotels are beginning to offer plush pet beds and pillows, soft bathrobes for dogs, and treat bags for pets accompanying their owners on vacations. *Id.* There is also a market for high-tech pet gadgets, including electronic toothbrushes, automatic feeders, touch activated toys, and computerized identification tags. *Id.* Pet health is also a burgeoning new market with pet health insurance coverage, pet massages, and pet dance and yoga classes. *Id.* Executing a quick Google search by typing in "pet health insurance" returns six different companies on the first page that offer insurance services for pets. Google, http://www.google.com/search?hl=en&q=pet+health+insurance&btnG=Search (last visited Nov. 19, 2007).

[33] *See* U.S. Pet Products Association, *Industry Statistics and Trends: Pet Ownership*, http://www.U.S.petproducts.org/press_ industrytrends.asp (last visited Feb. 1, 2009).*See also* Elizabeth Paek, *Fido Seeks Full Membership in the Family: Dismantling the Property Classification of Companion Animals by Statute*, 25 U. HAW. L. REV. 481, 482-83 (2003) ("[M]ore than 80% of companion animal guardians consider their companion animals as family members ... [a]nother study revealed that 70% considered their companion animals as children."); Lucy Jen Huang Hickrod & Raymond L. Schmitt, *A Naturalistic Study of Interaction and Frame: The Pet as "Family Member,"* 11 URB. LIFE 55, 59 ("Persons behave toward pets as if they are family members. Pets are named, fed, groomed, photographed, talked to, protected, and mourned. Owners sleep and play with pets. They give them birthday parties [,] . . . . [r]ansom has been paid for pets ... and a dog has participated as the best man in a human wedding.").

[34] Evelyn Nieves, *Foreclosures Lead to Abandoned Animals*, FOX NEWS, Jan. 29, 2008, *available at* http://www.foxnews.com/wires/2008Jan29/0,4670, ForeclosurePets,00.html.

other family members, or worst of all homeless shelters, it is not surprising that pets get left behind.[35]

(47) In Stockton and nearby Modesto, California, for example, where the foreclosure rates are the highest in the United States, animal shelters and rescue services are swamped with pets that families can longer afford or house.[36] **(48)** And although many pet owners consider their pets to be children, human adoption services in Stockton are not reported to be as burdened as are animal shelters. **(49)** From this tragic example one can conclude that pets, although a part of the family, retain subordinate status to human members and therefore retain an element of property and ownership, at least in exigent circumstances.[37]

(50) Although the foreclosure crisis is an extreme example of how pets retain some characteristics and qualities of traditional property, the fact still remains that cattle and companion animals have transposed their positions of importance in most animal owners' households.[38] **(51)** Despite the significant rise in popularity of domestic animals and the trend to include cats, dogs and other pets as family members, law continues to value pets in a manner that suggests they are utterly worthless to an owner. **(52)** The law does this by classifying pets in the same category as a wooden table or used clothing. **(53)** Classifying pets in this manner limits pet owners' recovery in situations of negligent or intentional destruction of their "property" to the fair market value of their pet.[39] **(54)** Rarely is there a remedy for the distraught pet owner, grieving over the death of their "family member," that adequately compensates the owner for his or her loss.

(55) In recent years several states have tried to resolve this problem by either expanding non-economic damage options to pet owners or creating a remedy through statute.[40] **(56)** In addition to the expansion of legal remedies for pet owners, the last two decades have also witnessed a push to make animal law

---

[35] *Id.* ("The problem is exacerbated because most people grappling with foreclosure are returning to rental housing or moving in with relatives—two situations where it can be difficult or impossible to bring pets").

[36] *Id.* ("The abandoned pets are overwhelming animal shelters . . . [in] Stockton and Modesto [which] have some of the nation's highest foreclosure rates.").

[37] *Id.*

[38] *See* Paek, *supra* note 33.

[39] *See* Rebecca J. Huss, *Valuing Man's and Woman's Best Friend: The Moral and Legal Status of Companion Animals*, 86 MARQ. L. REV. 47, 89 (2002). *See also* William C. Root, Note, *Man's Best Friend: Property or Family Member? An Examination of the Legal Classification of Companion Animals and its Impact on Damages Recoverable for Their Wrongful Death or Injury*, 47 VILL. L. REV. 423, 426-28 (2002) (stating that the fair market value of the pet is assessed before injury or death and is based on the amount a stranger at arm's length would be willing to pay for the pet based on pedigree, purchase price, general health and unique traits).

[40] *See* Schwartz & Laird, *supra* note 11, at 243-46.

more scholarly and a worthwhile subject in legal education.[41] **(57)** Since 2000, the number of law schools offering courses in animal law has increased from nine to eighty-nine.[42] **(58)** Some schools even host animal law conferences, moot court competitions, seminars, and fellowships all centering on issues in animal law.[43] **(59)** Some programs were funded in part by former celebrity host of *The Price is Right*, Bob Barker,[44] who was famous for reminding viewers to have their pets spayed or neutered. [45] **(60)** These educational opportunities, including competitions and clinics, are located in some of the most prestigious and influential U.S. law schools, such as Harvard, Stanford University, Columbia University, Duke, Georgetown, and the University of California, Los Angeles.[46] **(61)** These developments demonstrate that significant changes may be forthcoming in the area of animal law.[47]

(62) Despite efforts to change the current system of compensation by expanding legal remedies and educating tomorrow's attorneys and judges in the nuances of animal law, many state courts have refused to adopt new measures or expand damages for injured pets.[48] **(63)** Arguments that have not yet been presented to these courts, however, may eventually prove persuasive. **(64)** The next section is devoted to understanding the current arguments and strategies

---

[41] Paria Kooklan, *Animal Law: Gaining Ground in the United States*, 36 STUDENT LAW at 14, 15 (February 2008).

[42] *Id.*

[43] *Id.* at 16.

[44] *Id.*

[45] Gary Richard Collins II, *Biography for Bob Barker*, http://www.imdb.com/name/nm0054837/bio (last visited Feb. 12, 2008).

[46] *See* Kooklan, *supra* note 41, at 16.

[47] *Id.* at 19 (noting one animal law expert, Stephen Wise, believes that as more people get on the bench who have been exposed to animal law those judges may be more willing to adopt newer ideas about animals without embarrassment).

[48] *See* Schwartz & Laird, *supra* note 11, at 236-37.

for change and explains why these fail to correct the under-valuing of injuries to pet owners.

III. CURRENT SUGGESTED SOLUTIONS AND THEIR INADEQUACIES

A. Why Allowing Emotional Distress Damages for Pet Loss Fails[49]

(65) Allowing a pet owner to recover for his or her emotional distress[50] over the loss of a pet is one primary focus of current reform efforts aimed at fully compensating pet owners.[51] **(66)** But emotional distress,[52] either as a category of recoverable damages or as a separate **cause of action**, in most jurisdictions fails to compensate the pet owner for his or her loss.[53] **(67)** The reason that the emotional distress argument fails to provide a remedy for pet owners is that the

---

[49] Although "emotional distress" can refer to either a measure of damages in personal injury tort cases or a separate tort cause of action, the term, unless otherwise noted, is used here to encompass both definitions.

[50] In Consolidated Rail Corp. v. Gottshall, 512 U.S. 532 (1994), the U.S. Supreme Court reviewed and explained the concept of emotional distress in relation to a Federal Employers' Liability Act (FELA) claim. *Id.* at 544. The Court explained that it must review the claim in light of common law principles and defined emotional distress as an injury that is "mental or emotional harm (such as fright or anxiety) that is caused by the negligence of another and that is not directly brought about by a physical injury." *Id.* Although emotional distress is usually a state issue, for the purposes of this note an exhaustive review on a state by state basis of emotional distress laws is not necessary or prudent. As such, the use of a Supreme Court case which pre-empts state law is meant to be general enough to encompass the scope of the issue.

[51] *See* Steven M. Wise, *Recovery of Common Law Damages for Emotional Distress. Loss of Society, and Loss of Companionship for the Wrongful Death of a Companion Animal*, 4 ANIMAL L. 33, 50-56 (1998) (arguing that emotional distress is calculable and applicable as a measure of loss in wrongful death actions for the loss of a pet); Janice M. Pintar, *Negligent Infliction of Emotional Distress and the Fair Market Value Approach in Wisconsin: The Case for Extending Tort Protection to Companion Animals and Their Owners*, 2002 WIS. L. REV. 735, 761-70 (2002) (arguing that the separate cause of action of negligent infliction of emotional distress should be extended to pet owners who have experienced the loss of a pet due to another's negligence).

[52] The term "emotional distress" as a separate and distinct cause of action (as opposed to a category of damages) as used here encompasses both the tort of negligent infliction of emotional distress and intentional infliction of emotional distress.

[53] With the exception of a few jurisdictions such as Hawaii and Alaska, many state courts have rejected arguments on the issue of expanding non-economic damages, or more specifically, rejected claims of emotional distress damages for pet owners who have experienced a loss. *See* Schwartz & Laird, *supra* note 11; Pintar, *supra* note 51, at 736.

three standard tests used to evaluate emotional distress claims are not well suited to address pet loss or injury claims.

(68) Under the traditional test, or impact test, damages can be recovered for emotional distress only where the defendant's misconduct has resulted in physical contact with the victim (i.e. plaintiff), causing fear and anxiety as well as a physical injury, no matter how slight.[54] **(69)** Under the impact test, a plaintiff could only then recover for his or her own mental distress affiliated with the contact, not the derivative fright or grief because their pet was touched.

(70) Under the second test, the zone of danger test, the plaintiff does not have to prove an actual touch or impact, but instead has to show that he or she was placed in immediate risk of harm due to the defendant's misconduct.[55] **(71)** Here, again, the stress is on the plaintiff's fear of harm to *his or her own body* and not the fear or grief over injury to a pet.[56] **(72)** If, for example, a person was walking a dog and the dog was injured by a car while both the owner and dog were in the cross walk, the owner could recover for his or her own emotional injury. **(73)** But the owner could not pursue a cause of action or claim as an element of damages for the emotional distress resulting from the injuries to the dog per se.

(74) The most viable argument that supports extension of a negligent infliction of emotional distress claim to pet owners involves the use of the bystander test, which allows the plaintiff to recover if the defendant could have foreseen that his or her conduct would cause emotional distress to bystanders.[57] **(75)** In this test, the plaintiff can only recover for emotional distress as the result of witnessing, or by physically experiencing, the injury or death of another person.[58] **(76)** To prevail under the bystander test, plaintiff must prove that he or she was physically in a position to witness the injury, that the resulting shock and mental distress were caused by the contemporaneous observance of the event, and that the plaintiff and the victim were closely related.[59]

(77) At first blush it appears that an owner of an injured pet might be able to recover under the bystander test. **(78)** Most courts, however, limit the last factor so that only very close (human) relatives can recover.[60] **(79)** If, for example, a

---

[54] The physical impact test is only used in a very small minority of U.S. jurisdictions. *Gottshall*, 512 U.S. at 547.

[55] The zone of danger test is followed in a minority, although not a small minority, of jurisdictions, and was the test adopted by the Supreme Court in the case at hand. The court chose this test because of historical considerations and the reduced possibility that claims could be falsified. *Id.* at 547-48, 554-58.

[56] *Id.* at 547-48.

[57] The relative bystander test comes from the California Supreme Court case of *Dillon v. Legg*, 441 P.2d 912 (1968), and the majority of jurisdictions in America have adopted this test. *See also Gottshall*, 512 U.S. at 548.

[58] *See Dillon*, 441 P.2d at 920-21.

[59] *Gottshall*, 512 U.S. at 549.

[60] *Id.*

plaintiff was barred from pursing an emotional distress claim due to the loss of a grandchild or sibling in a particular jurisdiction, allowing a pet owner to recover for the loss of his or her pet family member would never work. **(80)** In short, the conservative pace of common law advancement of personal injury remedies will not allow most courts to adopt measures with such specifically human elements for application to personal property, despite the overwhelming emotional reactions inspired by pets in the modern U.S. family.

B. The Problems with Extending a Wrongful Death Cause of Action or Loss of Companionship Damages for Pet Loss

(81) The arguments for extending either the wrongful death cause of action or loss of companionship action are similar to arguments for a cause of action or category of damages for emotional distress.[61] **(82)** Loss of companionship can be one element in determining the value of a wrongful death of a family member to a living family member who experiences the loss.[62] **(83)** Even though one is a cause of action and the other is a measure of damages, the reasons that both will be unsuccessful are closely related.

(84) Wrongful death actions are created by state legislatures rather than courts.[63] **(85)** The remedial legislation is enacted to provide surviving family members with compensation for the economic and emotional loss they experience when a family member dies due to the wrongful actions of the

---

[61] *See* Margit Livingston, *The Calculus of Animal Valuation: Crafting a Viable Remedy*, 82 NEB. L. REV. 783, 825 (2004); Vasiliki Agorianitis, Comment, *Being Daphne's Mom: An Argument for Valuing Companion Animals as Companions*, 39 J. MARSHALL L. REV. 1453, 1470-71 (2006).

[62] *See* OHIO REV. CODE ANN. § 2125.02(B)(3) (West 2001).

[63] Originally, when the victim of tortious conduct died, all related personal injury causes of action died with them. W. PAGE KEETON ET AL., PROSSER AND KEETON ON THE LAW OF TORTS § 125 (5th ed. 1984). However, this precedent was presumed to give potential plaintiffs incentive to hack up and run over a victim again if the victim was still alive in order to avoid liability. *Id.* Legislatures remedied this situation by enacting wrongful death statutes and survival claims legislation so that family members may recover for both their loss stemming from the wrongful injury, and the loss to which the decedent would have been entitled, had he or she not passed away. *See also* McDavid v. United States, 584 S.E.2d 226, 231-32 (2003).

defendant.[64] **(86)** The statutes contain detailed provisions that dictate who has standing to sue and the type of damages available. **(87)** Like emotional distress claims, wrongful death causes of action are firmly grounded in human relationships and traditional definitions of family, thus preventing courts from extending their reach to people emotionally scarred through the death of a pet.[65] **(88)** Even though loss of companionship is not solely a creature of statute, it is generally used as a measure in wrongful death and loss of consortium claims.[66] **(89)** Such claims were originally only available to husbands who lost the companionship and services of their wives due to the negligent or intentional acts of a third person.[67] **(90)** The right to recover on a loss of consortium claim has only been extended to wives within the last sixty years.[68]

(91) Because these two suggested solutions involve causes of action or terms for the measurement of damages involving close family members, it is unlikely

---

[64] Wrongful death statutes vary from state to state, but in a majority of jurisdictions, are only reserved for relatives related by blood or marriage. *See* David D. Siegel, *Wrongful Death Pleading and Procedural Disputes, in* WRONGFUL DEATH ACTIONS 1967, at 1, 4 (PLI Torts & Personal Injury Law, 1967); *McDavid*, 584 S.E.2d at 231 ("[G]eneralizations are not easy to draw among the fifty-one wrongful death statutes [in the United States], they are capable of being grouped into two major classifications: those representing the majority ... determine damages based on the loss to the survivors of the decedent or statutory beneficiaries ...."). Using Ohio as an example, the right of recovery is extended to "the surviving spouse, children, and parents of the decedent." Clark v. Scarpelli, 744 N.E.2d 719, 731 (Ohio 2001). Also, these named people who are entitled to recover are "rebuttably presumed to have suffered damages by reason of the wrongful death ... [and the right to recover] arises as a result of the suffering incurred by reason of the wrongful death of the decedent." *Id.*

[65] *See* Siegel, *supra* note 64, at 2. Even though most wrongful death statutes are remedial in nature and thus generally entitled to liberal construction, courts often constrain their interpretations of the legislations based on legislative intent. *See McDavid*, 584 S.E.2d at 231-32. Because the purpose of wrongful death statutes is to reverse the harsh common law doctrine that would deny recovery for the decedent's estate or family, it is unlikely that any court would construe a wrongful death statute to extend to pets or pet owners.

[66] Using Ohio as an example, as defined in the wrongful death statute, compensatory damages in a wrongful death action can include "[l]oss of the society of the decedent, including loss of companionship, consortium, care, assistance, attention, protection, advice, guidance, counsel, instruction, training, and education, suffered by the surviving spouse, dependent children, parents, or next of kin of the decedent ...." Action for Wrongful Death: OHIO REV. CODE ANN. § 2125.02(B)(3). For loss of consortium, sec D. Richard Joslyn, Annotation, *Wife's Right of Action for Loss of Consortium*, 36 A.L.R.3d 900 (1971) ("Most courts agree that consortium includes such items as love, companionship, affection, society, comfort, solace, support, sexual relations, and services.").

[67] Joslyn, *supra* note 66, at 900.

[68] *Id.*

that such humanized concepts would be extended for the pet owner who has lost a pet, no matter how much the owner is convinced the pet is his or her child.

C. Applying the Campbell *Exception to Allow a Large Punitive Damage Award in Pet Loss Cases Is Not a Viable Solution*

(92) In the majority of pet loss cases where the court uses the market value approach to assess damages for the loss of a pet, that amount, if any, will be very small.[69] **(93)** Should the pet's death arise in a malicious manner that justifies an award for **punitive damages**, it is also likely that this award, even if relatively modest (for instance under $3,000), will violate U.S. Supreme Court standards that require an appropriate ratio between actual and punitive damage awards.[70] **(94)** However, two exceptions may apply that can suspend the strict application of the ratios.[71] **(95)** The first exception applies in cases where the misconduct is egregious and either causes economic damages in a very small amount, or where the actual injury itself is not easy to detect.[72] **(96)** The second exception is applicable where the non-economic harm is difficult to evaluate in terms of monetary value.[73]

(97) The argument that these exceptions entitle the pet owner to a larger recovery makes a lot of sense. **(98)** However, the first problem that blocks the effectiveness of this solution is that the exception to the limit on punitive

---

[69] *See* Geordie Duckler, *The Economic Value of Companion Animals: A Legal and Anthropological Argument for Special Valuation,* 8 ANIMAL L. 199, 213 (2002) ("[E]ach animal life, apart from the rare instance of a celebrity animal, typically has a low value, with the majority being presumably valueless other than as food or apparel commodities.").

[70] In the defining punitive damage award case the Supreme Court refused to set a precise acceptable ratio for the value of punitive damages compared to compensatory damages. State Farm v. Campbell, 538 U.S. 408, 425-26 (2003). The Court did, however, hold that "[o]ur jurisprudence and the principles it has now established demonstrate . . . few awards exceeding a single-digit ratio between punitive and compensatory damages . . . will satisfy due process." *Id.*

[71] William A. Reppy, Jr., *Punitive Damage Awards in Pet-Death Cases: How Do the Ratio Rules of State Farm v. Campbell Apply?,* 1 J. ANIMAL L. & ETHICS 19, 47, 57 (2006).

[72] *Id.* at 47.

[73] *Id.* at 57.

damages only applies in cases of extreme misconduct by the defendant.[74] **(99)** Punitive damages by nature are meant to punish the type of conduct that is reprehensible not only to the plaintiff, but is also so outlandish that the court wishes to discourage similar conduct in the future.[75]

(100) To determine whether a defendant's conduct warrants punitive damages, courts will consider a number of factors. **(101)** These include whether the harm caused was physical or economic, if the defendant acted with indifference or with reckless disregard for the health and welfare of others, if the target of the conduct was financially vulnerable, if the conduct was repeated or isolated, and if the harm resulted from intentional malice or deceit or if from negligent behavior.[76] **(102)** The application of these factors to pet loss cases will yield disappointing results for most pet owners.

(103) Regarding the first factor, the likeliness that the harm will be physical is very low, as generally the harm to a pet will be categorized as a loss of property, which is considered an economic loss.[77] **(104)** The second factor will also be thwarted because the conduct in question will most likely not reflect a disregard for human health or safety, as the pet—personal property—will be the primary target.[78] **(105)** The third factor focuses on whether the victim is financially vulnerable; however a pet's financial vulnerability seems to be a non-issue.[79] **(106)** The only possible factor that may favor the owner is if defendant has a prior history of targeting or killing pets.[80]

(107) Therefore, punitive damages may only be feasible in a limited number of pet loss cases. **(108)** For instance, in 1964 a court in Florida allowed a pet owner to recover punitive damages when a garbage collector flung an empty garbage can at the owner's small dog who was tied in the front yard.[81] **(109)** Hearing the dog yelp, the owner went outside and saw the garbage collector laughing at his actions as he left.[82] **(110)** The small dog died as a result of the garbage collector's

---

[74] Defendant's misconduct on which punitive damages are based must be heinous because such damages carry criminal punishment connotations. *State Farm,* 538 U.S. at 417. The Court has held that excessive punitive awards constitute an "irrational and arbitrary deprivation of the property of the defendant." *Id.* at 429. The Court has articulated three guideposts for determining the reasonableness of a punitive award, "(1) the degree of reprehensibility of the defendant's misconduct; (2) the disparity between the actual or potential harm suffered by the plaintiff and the punitive damages award; and (3) the difference between the punitive damages awarded by the jury and the civil penalties authorized or imposed in comparable cases." *Id.* at 418.

[75] *Id.* at 416.

[76] *Id.* at 419.

[77] *Id.*

[78] *Id.*

[79] *Id.*

[80] *Id.*

[81] La Porte v. Associated Indeps., Inc., 163 S.2d 267, 269 (Fla. 1964).

[82] *Id.* at 268.

actions.[83] **(111)** Recovery of punitive damages in this case was due to the wanton and malicious actions of the collector. **(112)** More than four decades after this decision, only a handful of cases have succeeded on the punitive damage theory.[84] **(113)** The limited application renders the punitive damages remedy an unlikely solution for pet owners.

D. Why the Declassification of Pets as Property Cannot Work in Contemporary America

(114) Another approach advocated by reformers is derived from focusing more on the rights of the animal rather than the owners. **(115)** Animal rights advocates suggest that domestic animals should no longer be classified as personal property.[85] **(116)** The justifications for declassification are varied, but most stress two common themes. **(117)** The first is that many people today view pets as family members.[86] **(118)** The second stresses that sentient animals have inherent worth outside of our property system and have more than just an interest, indeed a *fundamental right*, in being declassified as chattel.[87] **(119)** At the outset, this seems like a great way to remedy the problem because limits on non-economic damages would no longer apply to the *guardian*—not owner—of

---

[83] *Id.*

[84] Alaskan courts have recognized that punitive damages are recoverable in an action for the death of a pet, however only a handful of other states allow the action at all, and many of the decisions are archaic. *See, e.g.,* Landers v. Municipality of Anchorage, 915 P.2d 614, 620 (Alaska 1996); Parker v. Mise, 27 Ala. 480, 481-82 (1855); Mendenhall v. Struck, 224 N.W. 95, 98 (Iowa 1929); Loeser v. Axtin, 12 Ky. L. Rptr. 636, 636 (1890); Tenhopen v. Walker, 55 N.W. 657, 657-58 (Mich. 1893).

[85] *See* Ariel Simon, *Cows as Chairs: Questioning Categorical Legal Distinctions in a Non-Categorical World, in* PEOPLE, PROPERTY, OR PETS? 7 (Marc D. Hauser et al., eds., 2005) ("An ethical approach to animal rights, in other words, would defy any type of gross generalization, whether it comes in the form of treating animals all as rights-bearing equals or as a morally impoverished form of property. Animals are better understood as dependents . . . "); Paek, *supra* note 33; Root, *supra* note 39.

[86] *See* Paek, *supra* note 33, at 483 ("The relationship between an animal guardian and a companion animal is similar to a parent and child . . . the law recognizes and protects the relationship between family members . . . and . . . courts should recognize that the established legal doctrine of companion animals as property is archaic. . . .").

[87] *See* Gary L. Francione, *Taking Sentience Seriously,* 1 J. ANIMAL L. & ETHICS 1, 17 (2006) ("There is no non-speciesist reason not to recognize that full membership in the moral community requires that we reject the slavery of nonhumans just as we rejected the slavery of humans. This would require that we abolish—and not merely regulate—our exploitation of nonhumans . . . .").

a pet. **(120)** This suggested solution, however, raises too many practical problems to be deemed a viable remedy.[88]

1. Activists are Starving to Get Animals Declassified as Property

(121) The first major obstacle to the recognition of animals as possessing fundamental rights to not be considered chattel is that as guardians of animals, livestock owners could not allow their animals to be killed as a source of food.[89] **(122)** There is also a question about whether guardians of animals such as dairy cows could allow their wards to be milked to produce food, or chickens allowed to produce eggs. **(123)** One theory predicts that such actions would threaten the health and safety of humans because the current state of food production could not support such a large number of vegetarians, or perhaps vegans, and would lead to malnutrition.[90] **(124)** Although there could be a distinction drawn between animals traditionally used as food sources and animals used as companions or for other services, it is unlikely that the proponents of declassification would accept such a distinction. **(125)** The major arguments supporting the declassification of animals as property is that *all* animals have intrinsic rights not to be exploited by humans.[91] **(126)** This presumption is central to this proposed solution, so that if adopted, no distinction could be made between companions and food sources, and would likely have a negative effect on humans.[92]

2. The Disease of Declassification

(127) Another practical problem affecting the health of humans is the end of medical advancements based on animal research.[93] **(128)** Although a very sensitive subject with animal rights activists and others, animal research yields benefits to not only humans, but also animals themselves.[94] **(129)** Great advancements have been made in recent years regarding diseases that affect humans and animals, such as diabetes, that are attributed to biomedical animal research.[95] **(130)** Furthermore, for the same reasons that distinctions could not

---

[88] *See infra* notes 90-99 and accompanying text.

[89] Neha Jadeja, *Why the Status of Animals Should Remain as Property, in* PEOPLE, PROPERTY, OR PETS? 17-18 (Marc D. Hauser et al., eds., 2005).

[90] *Id.* at 18.

[91] *See* Francione, *supra* note 87.

[92] *See* Jadeja, *supra* note 89.

[93] *Id.*

[94] Foundation for Biomedical Research, Survivors: *Animal Research Saves Lives,* http://www.fbresearch.org/ survivors/about/ (last visited Feb. 12, 2008).

[95] Foundation for Biomedical Research, *Survivors: The Truth about Cats and Dogs,* http://www.fbresearch.org/survivors/truth.htm (last visited Feb. 12, 2008).

be made between food source animals and companion animals, a distinction between laboratory mice and other types of animals also would not be feasible.[96] **(131)** This would prove fatal to the benefits of animal research because over ninety-five percent of all animal testing is conducted on laboratory mice and rats.[97] **(132)** Animal testing remains a very controversial issue, however with many horrible terminal diseases, such as HIV/AIDS, still killing humans, the potential advancements to be garnered from biomedical research seem to outweigh the benefit to laboratory mice of shedding their personal property status.[98]

3. Animal Activists Seeking Progressive Judges

(133) The last practical problem with granting animals autonomy is that judges are extremely reluctant to adopt any approach that radically contradicts centuries of well-developed jurisprudence.[99] **(134)** Even if adopted by a legislature, it is easy to foresee problems with enforcement and regulation. **(135)** No longer would the standard be to avoid and punish cruelty. **(136)** The declassification of animals may include a higher standard of well-being and could very possibly place a heavy burden on both courts and executive branch employees.

(137) In sum, the declassification of animals as property might benefit animals, but would arguably do so at the risk of human health, safety, and well-being, and would present practical problems in both enforcement and regulation.

---

[96] *See* Jadeja, *supra* note 89 and accompanying text.

[97] Foundation for Biomedical Research, *Survivors: Quick Facts About Animal Research,* http://www.fbresearch.org/survivors/quickfacts.htm (last visited Feb. 12, 2008).

[98] AVERT, HIV Drugs, Vaccines and Animal Testing, http://www.avert.org/hiv-animal-testing.htm (last visited Feb. 2009) (suggesting that all antiretroviral AIDS drugs were tested at some point on animals). In 2007, HIV/AIDS caused over two million deaths worldwide, and it is estimated that 30.8 million adults are currently living with HIV/AIDS. AVERT, Worldwide HIV & AIDS Statistics, http://www.avert.org/worldstats.htm (last visited Feb. 1, 2008).

[99] *See, e.g.,* Sentell v. New Orleans & C.R. Co., 166 U.S. 698, 701 (1897). ("The very fact that they are without the protection of the criminal laws shows that property in dogs is of an imperfect or qualified nature, and that they stand, as it were, between animals ferae naturae, in which, until killed or subdued, there is no property, and domestic animals, in which the right of property is perfect and complete.").

(138) Therefore, the declassification of animals as property is not a practical solution for today's pet owner.

IV. Creating a Viable Solution that Can Coexist with Contemporary Jurisprudence and Adequately Compensate Pet Owners: Adopting Inimitable Property

(139) To be *inimitable* is to be so rare as to surpass or defy imitation.[100] **(140)** Additionally, to be inimitable means to be without compare and not deserving of imitation.[101] **(141)** The choice of this word to describe a new, hybrid classification of personal property is important because it conveys the unique personal characteristics of pets that the law currently overlooks. **(142)** This section first addresses the shortfalls of leaving pets classified as mere personal property and highlights the need for a new classification system. **(143)** The section then details the features and advantages of inimitable property as a new classification for pets.

A. The Need for Inimitable Property

1. Why Dogs and Cats Are Different from Tables and Chairs

(144) The first obvious distinction that property law fails to take into account is the clear difference between living pets and inanimate objects. **(145)** A pet is a sentient being, capable of feeling pain, fear, aggression, loyalty, and arguably even love. [102] **(146)** Pets are conscious beings and demonstrate their consciousness through their versatility and ability to respond to changing conditions, neurobiological activity which is similar to human brain activity, and their ability to communicate.[103] **(147)** Pets also display preferences and can make choices based on what they want; these choices are not just instinctive responses.[104]

(148) Animals can also adapt their demeanors and personalities depending on the type of environment in which they are raised.[105] **(149)** For instance, if a

---

[100] The Oxford English Dictionary 1122 (2d ed. 1989).

[101] *Id.*

[102] *See* Simon, *supra* note 85, at 6 (stating animals can experience "pain, suffering, fear, preference"). *See also* Herman Daggett, The Rights of Animals: An Oration (1791) *in* Animal Rights: A Historical Anthology 131 (Andrew Linzey & Paul Barry Clarke eds., 2004) (speaking on the rights of animals in 1791, Daggett argued that animals are "sensible beings, and capable of happiness" and that this sentience was deserving of "proportionable tenderness").

[103] Robbie Silverman, *The Thoughts and Feelings of Animals, in* People, Property, or Pets? 119-20 (Marc D. Hauser et al., eds., 2005).

[104] *Id.* at 120-21.

[105] Anmarie Barrie, Cats and the Law 9 (TFH Publications 1990).

kitten is exposed to people and handled frequently by humans when it is two to seven weeks old, it will likely remain an affectionate and friendly cat as it continues to grow through adulthood.[106] **(150)** Conversely, if a kitten at the same age is subjected to a lack of human interaction it may remain unsociable for the duration of its life.[107]

(151) Another feature of pets that is often overlooked, but that sets them apart from other items of property, is that they are named.[108] **(152)** Often, pet names reflect unique characteristics of the pet itself, such as Spot, Fluffy, Red, Princess, or Socks.[109] **(153)** Naming pets sets them apart from wild animals, or even most other types of domestic animals that generally remain nameless.[110] **(154)** Domestic pets also can be trained to respond to their names and make them their own.[111]

(155) The ability of pets to adapt to environments, respond to their names, display affection, and make calculated decisions regarding individual preferences has a significant effect on owners.[112] **(156)** Some owners, faced with losing their

---

[106] *Id.*

[107] *Id.*

[108] LESLIE IRVINE, IF YOU TAME ME: UNDERSTANDING OUR CONNECTION WITH ANIMALS 33 (2004). Boats and ships are also a type of personal property that are named. Leonard O. Townsend, Note, *Love Lies Bleeding: Brownfields in the New Millenium,* 11 FORDHAM ENVTL. L.J. 873, 894 (2000). One maritime author suggests that "[a] ship is the most living of inanimate things . . . every one gives a gender to vessels." *Id.* Even if the ship's name has to do with physical characteristics of the ship, i.e., H.M.S. Titanic, the ship lacks the ability to respond to its name. The distinction between companion animals and ships is obvious.

[109] The name selected by the owner often reflects the uniqueness of each pet. In a recent study of dog and cat owners, a majority of respondents who lived and worked with their pets defined them as "thoughtful, reciprocating, emotional beings with uniquely individual tastes and personalities." IRVINE, *supra* note 108, at 57, 126. As stated in the text, naming often reflects the "individual tastes and personalities" of the animal and reinforces the animal's identity, or self, to their owner. Although naming does not always reflect unique characteristics, it is often the case. This is important because the melding of the animal and owner occurs simultaneously and is dependent upon interaction. *Id.* at 126.

[110] Excluding horses, which generally are named, most species are not routinely named regardless of their intended use by humans. For example, pigs or cows are rarely named unless starring in a Disney movie. *Id.* at 33. Owners do name other types of household pets, such as birds, fish, ferrets, rabbits, turtles, gerbils, etc. However, these pets are not comparable in history of domestication or frequency of ownership. The sentience and emotional reciprocity and sophistication of pets such as birds and fish is also a topic for another paper.

[111] BARRIE, *supra* note 105, at 11. They are also independent enough to often ignore an owner using the pet's name in an effort to convince it to do something or stop doing something.

[112] Companion animals' unique qualities inspire owners to go to great lengths to care for and please their pet. *See* U.S. Pet Products Association, *supra* note 32.

unique pet, wish to not only replace their pet with another, but to also recreate their pet's special personality by cloning.[113] **(157)** While the ground-breaking pet cloning company Genetic Savings and Clone [GSC] was in operation, only a handful of cats were cloned and sold to paying customers.[114] **(158)** Since the company stopped offering pet cloning services, thousands of pet owners have paid over $1,000 to store their pets' DNA in gene banks hoping that one day the process will be more affordable than the original $50,000 price tag.[115] **(159)** Although original efforts in 2001 resulted in a clone that looked substantially different from the DNA donor, the later cats sold by GSC were literal copycats in both appearance and in personality according to the owners of the clones.[116] **(160)** The existence of some owners willing to pay large sums of money to duplicate or bank their pets DNA for potential duplication demonstrates that pets are far removed from other types of property.

(161) Pets are also distinct from other types of property in their ability to reciprocate emotion. **(162)** Marc Bekoff, a noted professor of biology and observer of animal behavior, has written:

> [d]ogs and other companion animals (hereinafter companions) are amazing beings. **(163)** Our companions with whom we share our lives typically have unqualified trust in us—they believe we will always have their best interests in mind, they love us unconditionally when they choose to love us, and they would do almost anything for us. **(164)** And, indeed, often they do, taking care of us and causing themselves harm in selflessly doing so.[117]

(165) Although Professor Bekoff also discusses the emotional capacities of other species in his article, companion animals are unique in the sense that they

---

[113] Maryann Mott, *Cat Cloning Offered to Pet Owners,* NATIONAL GEOGRAPHIC NEWS, Mar. 25, 2004, http://news.nationalgeographic.com/news/pf/57853507.html (last visited Dec. 19, 2008).

[114] Wade Roush, *Genetic Savings and Clone: No Pet Project,* TECHNOLOGY REVIEW, Mar. 2005, *available at* http://www.technologyreview.com/Biotech/14215/.

[115] *Id.*

[116] For testimonials and pictures about the cloned pets provided by GSC, see Genetic Savings and Clone, http://web.archive.org/web/20060615200352/ savingsandclone.com /clients/and_cats.html (last visited Feb. 1, 2009) (on file with author). Genetic Savings and Clone went out of business but the last home site posted for the company can be viewed at Genetic Savings and Clone, http://web.archive.org/web/20060627103935/ savingsandclone.com /clients/index.html (last visited Feb. 1, 2009).

[117] Marc Bekoff, *The Evolution of Animal Play, Emotions, and Social Morality: On Science, Theology, Spirituality, Personhood, and Love,* 36 ZYGON 615, 645 (2001).

express their emotions toward humans, a quality that many other animals do not possess.[118]

(166) All these unique biological and social traits that pets possess enable them to essentially become members of a family.[119] **(167)** The results of one study identify several prominent attitudes held by owners, ranging from pets functioning as family members to occupying "an overlapping but different space from humans in a family."[120] **(168)** Even though owners refer to, or think of, their pets as family members, they realize the pet is not human. **(169)** And yet, many people consider their pets as members of their family based on the way that a pet functions in their households.[121]

(170) While a pet may be able to become a part of the family, it can never attain the same status as a child or human family member.[122] **(171)** This places

---

[118] *Id.* at 634-40.

[119] *See* Susan Phillips Cohen, *Can Pets Function as Family Members?,* 24 WESTERN J. NURSING RESEARCH 621, 624 (2002). In modern America, families extend beyond genetic ties. *Id.* Today, the definition of family extends to the choice of family members, who are considered "functional kin." *Id.* Functional kin become members of a family network and provide services or supplement the services of the biological family members. *Id.* They also can be perceived as "psychological kin," a status that focuses more on the feelings and behaviors of family members toward non-genetic family members. *Id.* These types of functional and psychological kin concepts are far removed from legal concepts that recognized de facto relationships, or from doctrines of equity that recognize a legally protected relationship even though the relationship does not meet all the traditional legal requirements. Such recognition occurs when courts determine that it would be unfair or unjust to not recognize such a relationship. For instance, the doctrine of "equitable adoption" which allows a guardian to stand in as a parent in cases where four elements are met:

> The natural parents of the child have disclaimed or abandoned parental rights to the child;
> The one claiming to be parent has performed the obligations of parenthood for a substantial period of time;
> The child and the one claiming to be parent have held themselves out to be parent and child for a substantial period of time; and
> The relationship between the child and the one claiming to be parent has been publicly recognized.

Lawson v. Atwood, 536 N.E.2d 1167, 1170 (Ohio 1989).

[120] *See* Cohen, *supra* note 119, at 633.

[121] *Id.*

[122] Although one pet, Helmsley's Maltese, Trouble, received the largest bequest in the billionaire real estate mogul's will, the dog is still not considered a family member. *See* Feuer, *supra* note 2. Also, even though eighty percent of pet owners consider their pet a family member, Paek, *supra* note 33, when faced with a choice over whom to abandon, pet owners almost uniformly choose to retain their children and abandon their dogs. *See* Nieves, *supra* note 34.

the pet in quite an uncertain place in the law.[123] **(172)** A pet's half-human, half-property position, however, should not automatically relegate them to the same status as inanimate property owned by humans. **(173)** Companion animals' unique qualities and unique ability to straddle the line between family member and chattel requires a unique classification in property law, as well as a feasible, yet distinct, valuation process. **(174)** Classification of pets as "inimitable property" recognizes this hybrid status, and at the same time creates a measurement process specifically tailored to value the specific relationship between companion animal and owner.

2. Why Previously Owned Dogs and Cats Cannot Be Sold in a Fair Market

(175) The next argument supporting the need for a new classification system challenges the fiction used by the courts in pet loss cases—i.e., that a market exists for previously owned pets. **(176)** With so many previously owned pets being abandoned and put to death, there can hardly be a market in which courts can fairly assess a market value.[124] **(177)** The lack of market for a previously owned pet suggests a serious need to update and reconfigure the valuation process in pet loss cases. **(178)** This update would guarantee that pet owners could be adequately compensated by basing recovery on the true value of the loss to the pet owner rather than a fictitious market.[125]

3. Why Dogs and Cats Are Different from Pigs and Cows

(179) Another reason pets cannot be classified as mere personal property is that placing companion animals in the same legal category as domestic farm animals and livestock fails to recognize crucial differences in the ability of pets to

---

[123] The rules allowing pet owners to recover an adequate amount of compensation vary from state to state. *See* Schwartz & Laird, *supra* note 11, at 236-37.

[124] *Id.* at 240-41.

[125] *See* Duckler, *supra* note 69, at 221 ("Companion animals, to the extent that they have a social 'purpose' created by humans, are most emphatically non-commercial objects valued entirely for the comfort and well-being they impart to their owners as a benefit of ownership.").

bond with humans and their unique and separate histories of domestication.[126] **(180)** The history of the domestication of dogs is especially enlightening and offers reasons why these animals should not be categorized as personal property.[127]

(181) Evidence of the early domestication of dogs dates back to at least 15,000 years ago.[128] **(182)** Alliances between dogs and humans began out of necessity, but have been successful because of the animal's unique characteristics that lend themselves to domestication and the development of social relationships.[129] **(183)** Although the original domestication took place with wolves, Juliet Clutton-Brock, noted author on domestication and archaezoology, explains that within litters each pup would have a different temperament.[130]

(184) It was the occasional pup with just the right "combination of physique and temperament to make the necessary adjustments that would enable it to survive in a human community, live to be an adult, and even to breed. . . . **(185)** [Those offspring] could be protected by people ... and probably [were] given preferential treatment."[131] **(186)** These pups also had unique characteristics like large eyes, attractive coloring, and curled tails which made them more endearing to humans.[132] **(187)** Over time these traits were passed on to new litters, and thus a separate animal, the dog, evolved.[133]

(188) The domestication and history of the cat is also enlightening because it sets the species apart from other types of farm animals. **(189)** Although there are a variety of theories and dates on when cat domestication began, a recent study suggests the process began over 9000 years ago and coincides with the

---

[126] Attorney and doctor of biology, Geordie Duckler, explains the unique nature of companion animals in that:

> [r]oughly 1.5 million species of animal have been identified. Of that number, roughly 1.2 million are insects and arthropods. Of the 300,000 species remaining, the vertebrates comprise about 25,000. Of that number, only 4,000 or so are mammal species. Of that 4,000, it is primarily two, dogs and cats, which historically have formed the most special and intimate relations with us as our social companions. Dogs and cats are a minute component of an immense group, yet only those two species are considered to be potential "companions."

[127] *See supra* note 18 and accompanying text.

[128] JULIET CLUTTON-BROCK, A NATURAL HISTORY OF DOMESTICATED ANIMALS 49 (2d ed. Cambridge Univ. Press 1999).

[129] *Id.* Animal characteristics that facilitate domestication include hardiness, an inclination to like humans, a comfort-loving nature, utility to humans, unimpeded fertility, and relative ease of care. *Id.* at 2. Because even wolves residing in the wild possess these qualities, wolf cubs can be reared by humans and live as domesticated animals. *Id.* at 50.

[130] *Id.* at 51.

[131] *Id.*

[132] *Id.*

[133] *Id.*

early agricultural endeavors of peoples in the fertile crescent.[134] **(190)** As farmers began producing and storing grain, cats were instrumental in controlling the rodent population who fed on grain stores.[135] **(191)** Over time the wild cats dropped their aggressive instinctive behaviors and were incorporated into societies through religious worship, were protected by threat of criminal punishment, and became common in typical ancient households.[136]

(192) As with dogs, what began as a mutually beneficial relationship between humans and cats gave way over time to incorporation into an important place in society, human protection, and cohabitation.[137] **(193)** Even though the domestication of dogs and cats began around the same time that other species were being domesticated,[138] it is only these two animals that have evolved to the point of companionship and cohabitation with humans.[139]

(194) The fact that small cats and dogs could be kept inside the house during ancient times further sets them apart from the much larger ancient ancestor of cattle.[140] **(195)** The first key difference is that rather than assisting humans in hunting like dogs,[141] or protecting grain stores from rodents like cats,[142] cows were domesticated to bear loads and help plow.[143] **(196)** It was the smaller animals, cats and dogs, that were the "easiest to handle and the easiest to house" in ancient societies.[144]

(197) Keeping cows also posed problems for ancient peoples attempting to tame cattle. **(198)** These difficulties included an increased risk of attracting large and dangerous predatory species and the challenge of controlling such large animals that can destroy undergrowth, trample crops, and taint natural sources of water.[145] **(199)** Facing all these disadvantages, the ancient owners of cattle

---

[134] A recent genetic assessment of nearly 1000 cats and their wild ancestors concluded that domestic cats derive from five different wild cats that originated in the Near East and spread to other regions through human movement or migration. Carlos A. Driscoll et al., *The Near Eastern Origin of Cat Domestication,* 317 SCIENCE 519, 521-22 (2007).

[135] *Id.* at 523.

[136] *Id. See also* BARRIE, *supra* note 105, at 11-12.

[137] *See* Driscoll, *supra* note 134, at 523; BARRIE, *supra* note 105, at 11-12.

[138] Driscoll, *supra* note 134, at 523.

[139] *See* Duckler, *supra* note 69.

[140] *See* CLUTTON-BROCK, *supra* note 128, at 59-60, 87, 140.

[141] *Id.* at 56.

[142] *Id.* at 140.

[143] *Id.* at 81. Although cattle may also have been domesticated for the production of milk, this aspect is limited to only certain areas of the world. For instance, a large percentage of African people are lactose intolerant because no tradition existed of milking cows and consuming dairy products. *Id.* at 81-82.

[144] See CLUTTON-BROCK, *supra* note 128, at 88.

[145] *Id.* at 87-88.

began the practice of herding the cattle into corrals, or keeping them in enclosed structures *adjacent to*, not *inside of*, the home when not in use.[146]

(200) The existence of cows, dogs, and cats in ancient societies help explain these animals' demeanors and their ability to connect with humans on differing levels. **(201)** Whereas cattle were kept outside and only interacted with humans while in use, cats and dogs interacted with humans not only while serving human needs, but also when the work day was done.[147] **(202)** It is these interactions—the formation of symbiotic relationships—that truly sets cats and dogs apart from other livestock. **(203)** One expert on archaezoology explains "[t]he domesticated cat extracts from its human partner a home, warmth, affection, and play, whilst humans can assuage their natural inclination to nurture a warm, soft furry animal . . . ."[148]

(204) Another reason pets deserve to be classified separately from inanimate personal property and livestock is because of their unique personalities[149] and genetic structures that cannot be duplicated or replaced through the purchase of another animal of the same breed, age, color, weight, etc.[150] **(205)** Tied in with unique personalities is the unique history of domestication and unique qualities that enable them to respond to and reciprocate human emotions.[151] **(206)** All of these characteristics mean that pets can create social bonds and foster social and emotional developments in families. **(207)** Because pets have such unique characteristics, they deserve to be classified as inimitable property.

(208) The same factors that fostered domestication of cats and dogs but not other animals are the same traits that allow modern humans and their pets to develop unique relationships and bonds distinct from other human-animal interactions. **(209)** Notably, this special relationship is exemplified by the types of activities that humans engage in with their pet that they could not do with livestock, such as sleeping together.[152] **(210)** The fact that dogs and cats have been domesticated for so long for the express purpose of living and interacting

---

[146] *Id.* at 88.

[147] *See infra* note 152 and accompanying text; *infra* note 150 and accompanying text.

[148] *See* CLUTTON-BROCK, *supra* note 128, at 140.

[149] *See* IRVINE, *supra* note 108.

[150] Duckler, *supra* note 69, at 203 ("[A]nimals, by their nature, are inherently unique and irreplaceable objects. Concepts of modern genetics command the recognition that every individual sexually-reproducing animal is a distinct fingerprint of nature, each unlike that of any other.").

[151] *See supra* text accompanying note 118.

[152] *See* Cohen, *supra* note 119, at 622 (citing that as of 2002, 65% of cats and 39% of dogs slept with a family member in their bed).

with humans justifies differential and arguably preferential treatment to farm and wild animals.

4. *Anzalone v. Kragness*: The $100,000 Example

(211) In 2005, Mary Ann Anzalone lost her beloved pet cat, Blackie.[153] **(212)** Anzalone loved her pet so much that hearing of Blackie's death both demolished her emotional stability, and prompted her to bring suit seeking $100,000 in damages from the boarder who was responsible for the cat's demise.[154] **(213)** Anzalone's case epitomizes the inadequate contemporary judicial response to a pet owner's claim and highlights the need to recognize the inimitable property model in such cases.

(214) *Anzalone* begins with the typical story of a doting pet owner, Mary Ann Anzalone, who was enamored with her pet and considered her cat, Blackie, to be her only immediate family and somewhat of a child to her.[155] **(215)** Anzalone boarded Blackie at a local animal hospital, and twelve days later while the cat was let out of her cage for exercise, Blackie was killed by a Rottweiler.[156] **(216)** After hearing of Blackie's horrific death, Anzalone experienced extreme symptoms of distress including weight gain, loss of sleep, and severe feelings of guilt manifested in dreams about the defenseless declawed cat being "ripped apart by a [R]ottweiler."[157]

(217) Despite these and other examples of suffering and guilt, the trial court found that Anzalone failed to state a cause of action for intentional infliction of emotional distress and struck her amended complaint for a failure to adequately plead damages.[158] **(218)** The court's decision seemed to center on the fact that Anzalone was requesting $100,000 in damages in her amended complaint, a seemingly excessive amount for loss of personal property as Illinois law clearly classifies dogs as property.[159] **(219)** The appellate court reversed the lower court's dismissal of Anzalone's claims because complaints should not be dismissed for a valuation or calculation error in damages, and Anzalone met the applicable requirement of proving the existence of damages.[160]

(220) At this point *Anzalone v. Kragness* may seem like any other case, yet beneath the technical requirements, the court's analysis ventures further into the

---

[153] Anzalone v. Kragness, 826 N.E.2d 472, 473 (Ill. App. Ct. 2005).

[154] *Id.* at 473.

[155] *Id.* at 474. Plaintiff was an unmarried woman with no children. *Id.*

[156] An employee of the animal hospital left the door open where Blackie was exercising, which allowed another boarded pet, the Rottweiler, to enter the room and kill Blackie. *Id.*

[157] *Id.*

[158] *Id.* at 474-75.

[159] *Id.* at 476, 478.

[160] *Id.* at 479.

history and future of recovery for pet owners.[161] **(221)** Although Anzalone's claim for intentional infliction of emotional distress was thrown out, she still claimed the loss of her pet, the loss of the pet's *society and companionship* and other financial losses.[162] **(222)** Regarding the loss of companionship claim, the court decisively concluded that "no Illinois statute provides for a 'wrongful death'-type action for the negligent killing of a pet."[163] **(223)** The court observed that because of the peculiar history of wrongful death actions "courts have been reluctant to create a new common law cause of action for the wrongful death of a pet and defer to the legislature the decision to fashion the appropriate cause of action and ... appropriate measure of noneconomic damages."[164]

(224) The Illinois appellate court also recounted the state's history of valuation standards for pets, spanning from fair market value, commercial value, and loss of services.[165] **(225)** The *Anzalone* court then took a progressive stance on the fair market value by noting that in some instances the pet has no market value.[166] **(226)** The court also supported the use of a different standard, the value to the owner, and referenced a comment to the Restatement (Second) of Torts that recommends "where the subject matter cannot be replaced, the measure of the 'value to the owner' is left largely to the discretion of the trier of fact."[167] **(227)** Lastly, the court noted that the actual owner is entitled to demonstrate the value by such proof as the circumstances admit.[168]

(228) One lesson that can be taken from *Anzalone* is that courts are wary of extending existing causes of action that traditionally deal with human injury or death to cases of companion animal death.[169] **(229)** More importantly, this case suggests that some courts are willing to explore new ways to compensate pet

---

[161] *Id.*

[162] *Id.* at 476.

[163] *Id.*

[164] *Id.* This quote further reinforces the arguments laid out in both *supra* Part III section B and *infra* Part IV section B.

[165] *Anzalone,* 826 N.E.2d at 476.

[166] *Id.* at 477.

[167] *Id.*

[168] *Id.* Although there is some question as to whether the use of "value to owner" is a legal fiction purporting to exclude sentiment while allowing for emotional loss in the damage calculation this terminology is often used in small cases where complex monetary calculations "would be unwelcome as too elaborate for the modest occasion. Perhaps the value to owner rule suffices to invite some help from the jury and to the same time to provide a tool for control if the award becomes too generous; if so, maybe no more should be demanded." *Id.* (quoting Dan D. Dobbs, Law of Remedies § 5.16(3) 907 (West 1993)). As with most damage calculations, the "value to the owner" model is not perfect, but it does present the requisite legal form and practical guidance for a jury or judge to make a monetary determination when the item being valued—in this case a pet—is difficult if not impossible to calculate with precision. *Id.*

[169] *Anzalone,* 826 N.E.2d at 476.

owners who are grieving over the loss of their pseudo-family members.[170] **(230)** Lastly, this case demonstrates that many of the current arguments advanced for pet owners seeking adequate compensation are just not viable, and that a new solution is necessary to both fit into the existing framework and update outdated legal notions.

B. Implementing a Solution By Adopting the Inimitable Property Status for Pets: How and Why It Will Work

(231) Functionally, inimitable property will create a hybrid status for pets in the law. **(232)** It will entitle pets to a higher status than ordinary personal property, but will not vest the animals with fundamental rights reserved exclusively to human beings in our civil justice system. **(233)** Such reclassification will work because it is not based on sentience, inherent rights, or anthropomorphic features. **(234)** Rather, it is based on the uniqueness of pets both as independent beings and as creatures that hold irreplaceable positions in our lives and families.[171] **(235)** Although the law already recognizes some forms of special property because of its irreplaceable nature,[172] a classification as merely unique is still insufficient for pets because it fails to account for the living and interactive aspect of pets. **(236)** A rare piece of art may be priceless and irreplaceable, but a piece of art cannot create a special interactive bond with a human. **(237)** The creation of a third category of inimitable property, separate from real property or personal property, would allow courts to use a different measure of valuation which takes in to account a real, factual value that reflects what a pet is worth to an owner.

1. Why Inimitable Property Will Work

(238) Inimitable property will succeed where other proposed solutions fail for several key reasons. **(239)** The first is that it eschews reliance on the fictitious market value for previously owned pets,[173] and instead focuses on the value to

---

[170] By deferring to the legislature, this court recognizes that the issue is both complex and has strong support in contemporary society, and also displays a willingness to help along victims of pet loss by applying the value to owner standard, over the traditional and favored fair market value standard. *Id.* at 476-77.

[171] *See* Bekoff, *supra* note 117, and accompanying text.

[172] In Ohio, the Supreme Court has held value to the owner may be used when fair market value can not be determined. Bishop v. East Ohio Gas Co., 56 N.E.2d 164, 166 (Ohio 1944). Generally, this value to the owner model is used in cases of used personal items such as clothing, but can also be employed in cases of unique or irreplaceable items such as manuscripts, personal photographs, family keepsakes and videotapes.

[173] *See* sources cited *supra* note 14.

the owner, a concept which is already recognized in the law.[174] **(240)** This type of damage calculation can more adequately reflect both compensation for the loss of a pet, and also the loss of what that pet meant—sentimentality aside—to the specific owner.[175] **(241)** Furthermore, adoption of inimitable property would also perform better than other proposed solutions in that it would eliminate the humanized or emotional based framework necessary to evaluate emotional distress claims.[176] **(242)** Based instead on a highly fact-specific, but not easily falsified, factor-balanced analysis, windfalls and fraudulent claims could easily be avoided.

(243) Another reason inimitable property can work is the fact that it will not disrupt or contradict established jurisprudence. **(244)** Inimitable property leaves pets as property, instead of declassifying pets as property altogether. **(245)** Declassification is blatantly at odds with many centuries of precedent that has firmly established pets as a form of property.[177] **(246)** Also, courts would not need to extend any existing causes of action that may already be treated suspiciously, such as negligent or intentional infliction of emotional distress, to make them applicable in pet loss cases. **(247)** Because inimitable property leaves pets classified as a form of personal property, the courts would simply need to apply established torts like trespass to chattel, conversion, or destruction of property.

2. How Inimitable Property Will Work

(248) The need for inimitable property is apparent, but how then will it work? **(249)** If all pets are classified as inimitable property, the process for valuing them after their injury or destruction due to the negligence or the intentional acts of another party will be based on factors and judged on a case-by-case basis. **(250)** Valuing pets based on a multi-factor test also gives courts and legislatures the opportunity to tailor or modify the factors to fit the policy and existing law of a specific jurisdiction. **(251)** The goal of the inimitable property designation is to

---

[174] Value in tort law is defined as "the exchange value or the value to the owner if this is greater than the exchange value." RESTATEMENT (SECOND) OF TORTS § 911 (1979). Value to the owner refers to the "existence of factors apart from those entering into exchange value that cause the article to be more desirable to the owner than to others," even further, a dog trained to obey only one master, will have substantially no value to anyone other than the owner. RESTATEMENT (SECOND) OF TORTS § 911 cmt. e (1979).

[175] Although traditionally the value to owner method is evaluated on an objective basis, the proposed solution can involve both objective and subjective elements to further prevent against windfalls and fraud.

[176] *See* Cohen, *supra* note 119.

[177] Gary L. Francione, *Animals, Property and Personhood, in* PEOPLE, PROPERTY, OR PETS?, 96 n.15 (Marc D. Hauser et al., eds., 2005) ("The status of animals as property has existed for thousands of years.").

value the animal based on its inherent qualities, not the fair market value as with other personal property.[178]

(252) The point of considering various factors is to determine the uniqueness of the animal and the uniqueness and strength of the bond between the pet and the owner. **(253)** Factors to consider include:

- Length of time the pet has been residing with the owner
- Examples of the personal preferences and behavioral traits exhibited by the pet
- Special training or special uses of the pet
- Evidence of the familial-type attachment between the owner and the pet including: photos of the pet paid to be taken or snapshots displayed, extraneous expenditures (treats, massages, birthdays, holidays, etc.), sleep patterns (special bed or with owner).
- Participation in family activities: attending family vacations, shopping trips, or other outings
- Ability of the pet to provide protection, or feelings of safety and wellbeing for the owner
- Ability of the pet to provide comfort, depression reduction or anti-anxiety effects, or other therapeutic effects
- Other aspects of the unique personality of the animal[179]

(254) These elements are able to be easily assessed by juries or factfinders on both a subjective level by focusing on how the particular pet owner and pet interact, and on an objective level by focusing on whether the claims and arguments advanced by the pet owner are reasonable and typical of other similarly situated pet owners in society.

(255) Ideally, this classification scheme would be adopted by legislatures.[180] **(256)** Legislatures are better able to structure laws around the current needs of

---

[178] *See* Huss, *supra* note 39 and accompanying text; Root, *supra* note 39 and accompanying text.

[179] Although not exactly a perfect fit, the factors described by Carolyn B. Matlack in her suggested solution to this problem, which she entitled "Sentient Property," provided guidance for the structuring of these factors. CAROLYN B. MATLACK, WE'VE GOT FEELINGS TOO: PRESENTING THE SENTIENT PROPERTY SOLUTION 88-89 (2006). Matlack bases her solution on the rights due to animals because they are sentient beings. *Id.* She also suggests that the guardian can speak for the animal using the Doctrine of Substituted Judgment. *Id.*

[180] As of 2003, seven states proposed legislation that purported to fix the problem of under compensating owners in pet loss cases. Elaine T. Byszewski, *Valuing Companion Animals in Wrongful Death Cases: A Survey of Current Court and Legislative Action and a Suggestion for Valuing Pecuniary Loss of Companionship,* 9 ANIMAL L. 215, 226-30 (2003). The states with proposed legislation were California, Colorado, Massachusetts, Mississippi, New Jersey, New York, and Rhode Island. *Id.*

society.[181] **(257)** Because inimitable property is a relatively simple idea, law makers would not struggle with complex legal theories or elements, and inimitable property also lends itself to modification and legislatively imposed limitations. **(258)** For instance, Tennessee already has legislation that allows a pet owner to recover noneconomic damages if his or her pet died due to the negligent or intentional acts of a third party.[182] **(259)** Tennessee's statute exemplifies that legislatures need not be [wary] of crafting such legislation because the statute itself limits the maximum award for each pet to $5,000, excludes any other type of pet than a dog or a cat, and exempts veterinarians, and other government agencies or nonprofit agencies that generally act in the public interest.[183] **(260)** Although the Tennessee statute is very forward thinking in creating a statutory remedy for pet owners and increasing the amount that they can recover from basically nothing to $5,000 the statute should most likely be modified and updated. **(261)** Setting the amount of recovery to $5,000 may seriously detract lawyers from accepting cases. **(262)** This problem could be corrected by either upping the maximum recovery or by allowing for punitive damages based on the level of the misconduct.

(263) Finally, although it is recommended that legislatures adopt the inimitable property reclassification scheme, courts will find that it is not such a radical divergence from the current law as to preclude adoption by judicial decision. **(264)** For instance, inimitable property uses established causes of action like destruction of property or trespass to chattel.[184] **(265)** Also, the value to owner standard that is the basis for valuing inimitable property is also derived from a measure already used by courts, although it is updated to reflect the value of the modern pet.[185]

(266) Whether adopted by legislatures or courts, the reclassification of companion animals as inimitable property is necessary to achieve the dual goals

---

[181] *See, e.g., id.* at 225 ("[P]laintiff and others are free to urge the Legislature to visit this issue [extending an existing cause of action to pet owners] in light of public policy considerations, including societal sentiment and treatment of pets, and the prospect of public perception that . . . [the] law does not provide a just and fair remedy to pet owners . . . [who] suffer when their pets are . . . fatally injured . . . .") (quoting Koester v. VCA Animal Hosp., 624 N.W.2d 209, 211 (Mich. Ct. App. 2000)).

[182] TENN. CODE ANN. § 44-17-403 (2000); 2000 Tenn. Pub. Acts, ch. 762 § 1; 2004 Tenn. Pub. Acts. ch. 957 § 7.

[183] Among adding provisions for guide dogs and deleting a size requirement for the county in which this action can be brought, the Tennessee legislature also increased the maximum amount recoverable from $ 4,000 to $ 5,000 in 2004. 2004 Tenn. Pub. Acts. ch. 957 § 3, 7.

[184] Edward H. Ziegler, *Partial Taking Claims, Ownership Rights in Land and Urban Planning Practice: The Emerging Dichotomy Between Uncompensated Regulation and Compsensable Benefit Extraction Under the Fifth Amendment Takings Clause,* 22 J. LAND RESOURCES & ENVTL. L. 1, 3 (2002).

[185] *See* RESTATEMENT (SECOND) OF TORTS § 911 (1979); *supra* note 128.

of preserving existing framework in the law, while updating severely outdated concepts of pets as personal property. **(267)** The benefits realized by this reclassification will not only be reserved for the pet owner, but will also be an advancement for the pets themselves. **(268)** By compromising between the extremely progressive ideals of animal rights activists and the conservative categorization of the common law, the inimitable property valuation model can succeed.

V. Conclusion

(270) Although some people may cringe at the adoption of any reclassification that leaves any animal classified as property,[186] the solution proffered in this Note is not meant to be an elucidation on animal rights, or a discourse on human domination of animals. **(271)** It is proposed as a workable and reasonable solution to a problem that will affect nearly every pet owner who suffers the loss of his or her pet at the hands of another.[187]

(272) The practical problems facing the current suggested solutions require a more modest workable solution that will provide results, yet complement the existing schematic structure of traditional categories in the law.[188] **(273)** Instead of focusing solely on noble, yet ethereal, issues like the sentience of animals, the rights of animals, or emotional bonds between humans and their pets, inimitable property focuses on the unique and scientifically based nature of each individual pet.[189] **(274)** Even though inimitable property focuses on unique traits, the arguments framed here do not deny the possibility that in the future those other solutions might work. **(275)** However, as it stands now, those theories are far too advanced and contradictory to provide results for today's pet owners suffering and grieving over the loss of their companions.

(276) This proposal also works to more justly compensate the owner for his or her very real loss by stressing the irreplaceable value of the pet to the owner, rather than relying on the fair market value. **(277)** The creation of the category of inimitable property for living pets will take into account the unique nature and personality of each pet and from these deductions will allow for a damage award that is an arguably fair compensation for loss. **(278)** Inimitable property will also function to exclude fraudulent cases by incorporating both subjective and

---

[186] *See* Francione, *supra* note 87; Paek, *supra* note 33, at 524 ("Companion animals, like all animals, deserve to be treated with dignity and respect as emotional and sentient beings. The property classification of all animals should be completely abrogated . . . the notion of awarding all animals 'rights' is an issue that must continue to be explored.").

[187] *See* Duckler, *supra* note 69.

[188] *Supra* Part IV.A.

[189] *Supra* Part IV.B.

objective elements into the factored analysis that also serves the benefit of limiting windfalls.[190]

(279) The way that humans interact with pets has changed drastically since animals were classified as personal property.[191] **(280)** Advancements in science, namely emotional and sentience studies and analyses of social networks and familiar relationships, have shown the evolved nature of pets within the family and demand that a reevaluation of our *family members* be completed in our legal framework.[192] **(281)** The time is now, and the only answer acceptable to most judges and workable in our existing system is the inimitable property valuation model.

D. The Process of Writing

When writing any text, a writer goes through multiple steps before ending with a product saying exactly what the writer wants to communicate. The length of this writing process depends on how much time the writer has available to write. The process is quite short and compressed when writing a timed, in-class exam answer. The process is lengthened, and each step is given more time when the writer has several days, weeks, or months to produce the document.

Shown below are steps in the process of writing. These steps are universal and apply to the writing of any document. After each step is listed, a brief description of the activities the writer engages in is given. During exams, writers move through these steps very quickly. While writing other types of documents, writers give amounts of time to each step in proportion to the amount of time they have to deliver the document. It is important, though, that writers go through each step. Progressing through the steps of this writing process result in well-written, clearer, and more accurate final documents.

The Process of Writing

1. **Brainstorming**: List all of the ideas you have on a topic and then organize the best ideas.

2. **Organizing Ideas/Outlining**: Organize your ideas so that they are easily followed and understood by your reader. An **outline** is a writing plan for your document. It lists your main ideas and how you plan to support those ideas. (Outlining exam answers is covered in more detail in Part II, Chapter 4.)

---

[190] *Id.*

[191] *Supra* Part II.

[192] *Supra* Part IV.A.

3. **Drafting**: Follow the list or outline you have created and write your document, from start to finish. If you include information that is not related to your main idea(s), you either need to delete that information or change your main idea(s).

4. **Revising**: Read through your document and put yourself in the shoes of a reader. Are there areas a reader may not understand completely? Or areas that may require more support or evidence to be believable? Or to create a clear picture? If so, make any necessary changes. For papers—but never exams—you may consider asking a colleague to read over your draft.

5. **Rewriting**: Rewrite your document (or portions of your document), addressing any issues that came up during revision. The purpose of revision and rewriting is to make your text more understandable to your reader. Rewriting may mean that you order your points differently; add more examples, definitions, and details; or write a few more sentences explaining something.

6. **Editing**: Edit your document by examining the paragraphs and sentences you have written to ensure that they conform to English academic legal discourse conventions and principles (Editing is covered in more detail in Part I, Chapter 5.)

7. **Proofreading**: Finalize your document by looking at your grammar, punctuation, spelling, and formatting (e.g., font size, spacing, page numbering, etc.). (Proofreading is covered in more detail in Part I, Chapter 5.)

If you follow this process as you write your documents and incorporate the characteristics of academic legal discourse embodied in this textbook, your end product will be carefully conceived and organized. As you write, always keep in mind the five principles of academic legal discourse outlined in this chapter: (1) Write with Your Reader in Mind; (2) Start with Your Main Idea; (3) Support Your Ideas with Evidence; (4) Begin with an Introduction and End with a Conclusion; and (5) Show Every Step of Your Thinking. If you follow these principles, your reader will be able to read your writing and understand your ideas with ease.

Chapter 2
Paragraphs

A paragraph is a collection of sentences organized around one main idea. Paragraphs help writers to organize their ideas and, in turn, help readers to understand those ideas. This chapter addresses four key features of paragraphs in academic legal discourse.

1. Paragraphs begin with a topic sentence (Section A).
2. Paragraphs contain sentences that support and elaborate upon the topic sentence (Section B).
3. Paragraphs are unified around one main idea (Section C).
4. Paragraphs exhibit cohesion, with each sentence building upon the sentence that came before it (Section D).

Before concluding, this chapter also discusses the appropriate length of academic legal paragraphs (Section E).

A. Topic Sentences

Paragraphs have a predictable structure that follows Principles 2 and 3 from Part I, Chapter 1: Start with Your Main Idea and Support Your Ideas with Evidence. The main idea of the paragraph is contained in the first sentence of the paragraph, called the **topic sentence**. The topic sentence introduces the topic that the paragraph will be about and states what the paragraph has to say about the topic (the "main idea"). Support or evidence for the main idea follows in the remaining sentences of the paragraph. These are referred to as **supporting sentences**. Topic sentences are general statements, while supporting sentences contain more specific, detailed information.

Read the following topic sentence from a paragraph in a law review note:

> Clarence Thomas's conduct as a Justice presents a puzzle.[1]

Having read this topic sentence, you know that the rest of the paragraph will be about the conduct of Justice Clarence Thomas, one of the nine justices sitting on the U.S. Supreme Court. Justice Thomas's conduct is therefore the topic of this paragraph. You also learn from this sentence that Justice Thomas's conduct presents a puzzle—in other words, it is confusing. This is the main idea of the paragraph.

To support the idea that Justice Thomas's conduct presents a puzzle, the writer provides details and examples about the Justice's actions on the Court in the remaining, supporting sentences of this paragraph:

> Clarence Thomas's conduct as a Justice presents a puzzle. On one hand, he has more to say than the rest of his colleagues—at least when it comes to written opinions. On this measure, Thomas is far and away the most productive member of the Court. Yet on the other hand, it sometimes seems like he has nothing to say at all. This is especially true when it comes to oral argument; there, he is notorious for not asking questions. In fact, despite the unmatched volume of his written production, some list silence as one of his "signature characteristics."[2]

To illustrate why Justice Thomas's behavior is confusing, the writer draws a contrast between how the Justice acts in a written versus oral medium. Specifically, while Justice Thomas has much to say in his written opinions, he does not ask any questions of lawyers during oral argument.[3] Such contradictory behavior, it is suggested, is confusing. The writer provides these details about Justice Thomas's written and oral behavior to support the idea that Justice Thomas's conduct on the Court presents a puzzle.

On writing tasks in law school—on papers, exams, and other writing assignments—you will organize your writing into similar paragraphs. Your paragraphs will have a topic sentence that names the topic and says something about that topic, followed by specific support for the main idea. Indeed, the only exceptions to the topic sentence + support pattern include introductory, concluding, and transition paragraphs, which can be as short as one or two sentences and thus may not contain a topic sentence.

---

[1] RonNell Andersen & Aaron L. Nielson, *Clarence Thomas the Questioner*, 111 NW U. L. REV. 1185, 1187 (2017).

[2] *Id.*

[3] Oral argument is an event in which lawyers verbally present their arguments to an appellate court (e.g., the Supreme Court of the United States), and the judges ask questions of the lawyers to better understand these arguments.

Topic sentences function a bit like an "introduction" to the paragraph. While paragraphs start with this introduction, however, they need not necessarily have a conclusion. Unlike papers or exams, shorter stretches of text such as paragraphs usually do not require a conclusion at the end.

So when should you add a concluding sentence to your paragraph? A paragraph conclusion is useful if the paragraph is especially long; if it has developed an idea with multiple sub-components; or if the writer wishes to re-emphasize the main idea of the paragraph. Read the following paragraph from a student's seminar paper critiquing a decision handed down by the Supreme Court of South Korea. This paragraph contains a concluding sentence.

> The Court's decision is flawed because the "liability principle" upon which it depends does not take into account the unique nature of a marriage contract. The Court explains that marriage is a "statutory contract that forms the identity of a couple for the purpose of communal life for their lifetime." It is difficult to deny that the marriage has the nature of a contract, since it requires the mutual assent of the two parties. Nevertheless, the substance of marriage is deeply personal because marriage is based on love and trust. When the marriage relationship breaks down, the substance disappears and only the form (that is, a contract) remains. This creates a discrepancy between form and the substance. Under the "liability principle" espoused by the Court, the spouse who wants to divorce would be forced to comply with a contract that is lacking in any substance. It is unreasonable and impracticable to force couples to maintain an outward marital relationship when the love and trust on which the marriage is based no longer exists. Thus, the Court wrongly decided the case.

The last sentence of this paragraph briefly summarizes the main idea developed in the paragraph, which is that the Supreme Court's decision is flawed. This short conclusion helps to remind the reader what has been said in the paragraph and "hammers the point home." Keep in mind, though, that such concluding sentences tend to be the exception, not the rule, when it comes to academic legal paragraphs.

EXERCISE 2.A.1. Topic Sentence Matching

Match the topic sentences on the next page with a paragraph. Write the letter of the topic sentence (a-e) in the space provided before each paragraph (1-5). What clues helped you to make your match?

Topic sentences

a. Over the last twenty years, research about the development of the adolescent brain has changed the way we treat young people who commit crime.

b. During the lengthy journey to adulthood, young people are increasingly relying on their parents for support.

c. Treating young adults differently in the justice system is not a new idea in the U.S. or elsewhere.

d. Parenting is crucial to the lives of children, adolescents, and young adults.

e. Some young adults with disabilities are "gullible."

Paragraphs

1. _____ Attachments to, and involvement from, both mothers and fathers are essential for healthy development throughout the lifespan. From socialization and play in early childhood to monitoring, supervision, and negotiation in adolescence, both mothers and fathers play critical guiding roles in the lives of their children. Children who receive "good enough" parenting are more likely to feel successful and competent, as compared to those who did not and who are more likely to suffer from low self-worth, depression, and other psychological symptomatology.[4]

2. _____ Germany has placed young adults aged 18 to 21 under juvenile jurisdiction since 1953. Switzerland allows young adults to be sentenced as juveniles until age 25. Alabama and Florida have authorized judges to issue more lenient sentences for "youthful offenders" under age 21 since the early 1970s.[5]

3. _____ Put simply, research has confirmed what parents have always known: adolescents have less self-control, are more sensitive to peer pressure and immediate incentives, and have difficulty appreciating the long-term consequences of their behavior. Meanwhile, the adolescent

---

[4] Seth J. Schwartz & Gordon E. Finley, *Mothering, Fathering, and Divorce: The Influence of Divorce on Reports of and Desires for Maternal and Parental Involvement*, 47 FAM. CT. REV. 506, 506 (2009).

[5] Alex A. Stamm, *Young Adults of Different, Too: Why and How We Can Create a Better Justice System for Young People Age 18 to 25*, 95 TEX. L. REV. 72, 79 (2017).

brain is also highly malleable[6] because it is still undergoing massive and profound change.[7]

4. _____ They can be persuaded to sign leases, buy cars or apply for credit cards by others who appear to be their friends. One client was granted guardianship over her 18 year old son who had a low I.Q. Shortly thereafter, he was persuaded by some would-be friends to sign up for a credit card offer that came to the house. When the credit card came, the "friends" took him to a shopping center and they all ran up the credit card to its limit. The client was able to get all of the charges waived and the credit card cancelled because her son had been declared disabled and was not legally able to execute a contract.[8]

5. _____ A key indicator of this trend is the burgeoning number of young adults who live with their parents. As of 2011, 53% of adults between the ages of eighteen and twenty-four, and 39% of those between the ages of eighteen and thirty-four, either lived with their parents or moved back in with their parents temporarily in the past few years. From 1970 to 1990, the proportion of people in their twenties who lived with their parents rose by 50%. The percentage of young adults ages twenty-five to thirty-four living in multigenerational households is now at its highest level in over sixty years.[9]

EXERCISE 2.A.2. Writing Topic Sentences

The following paragraphs are missing topic sentences. Write a topic sentence for each paragraph.

1. ____

____

The probing nature of the Socratic method teaches students the forms of argument that they will engage in as lawyers, as well as the need to justify that argument in a logical manner that can withstand scrutiny.[10]

---

[6] Malleable means adaptable or capable of change.

[7] Stamm, *supra* note 4, at 74.

[8] Mary Denise Cahill & Robert H. Farley, Jr., *Why Does an 18 Year Old with Disabilities Need a Guardian?*, 20 DCBA BRIEF 8, 12 (2008).

[9] Sally F. Goldfarb, *Who Pays for the "Boomerang Generation"?: A Legal Perspective on Financial Support for Young Adults*, 37 HARV. J. L. & GENDER 45, 53 (2014).

[10] Scrutiny refers to an examination or study.

Questioning through the Socratic method also helps highlight basic errors or flaws in reasoning so that students can understand their nature and how to avoid them in the future. The method also encourages students to engage in critical inquiry, not only of their own thoughts, but also of the thoughts of the professor and other students. Further, the Socratic method helps teach precision, not only in the use of language, but also in reasoning itself. Most importantly, the Socratic method encourages students to engage in these concepts independently, by working through the process themselves (albeit with guided direction by the professor) rather than having the arguments simply given to them by the professor.[11]

2. ____

____

Levels of depression increase the most during the third year of law school, as students prepare to transition from student to lawyer. According to one study, by late spring of the first year, 32% of all first-year law students suffer from depression. By the same time in their third year, 40% suffer from depression. This is significant for the legal profession, as 17% of the depressed law students reported they were still depressed, as working lawyers, two years after graduation.[12]

3. ____

____

Professional responsibility courses teach concepts of ethics and responsible participation in the legal profession, and other courses emphasize ethics as well. Moreover, as part of the bar examination process in the United States, law school graduates in nearly all U.S.

---

[11] Jeffrey D. Jackson, *Socrates and Langdell in Legal Writing: Is the Socratic Method a Proper Tool for Legal Writing Courses?*, 43 CAL. W. L. REV. 267, 277-78 (2007).

[12] Jennifer Jolly-Ryan, *Promoting Mental Health in Law School: What Law Schools Can Do for Students to Help Them Become Happy, Mentally Healthy Lawyers*, 48 U. LOUISVILLE L. REV. 95, 99-100 (2009).

If you are struggling with depression or feeling "blue" while in law school, we encourage you to reach out to your Dean of Students or a mental health counselor. Most law schools have a full-time counselor who can provide counseling services free of charge for law students.

jurisdictions are required to pass an examination known as the Multistate Professional Responsibility Examination (MPRE). Other courses also integrate aspects of ethics, morality, and responsible participation into the law school curriculum. In response to pressures to do even more, some law schools have also started requiring students to perform a minimum number of hours of public service, to instill in them the legal profession's obligation to serve the general public. In addition, professional identity is enhanced through opportunities for students to interact with full-time faculty and local practitioners. This is accomplished through one-on-one contact in conjunction with courses, special seminars, networking events, and lecture series.[13]

B. Support

For a reader to understand and accept the main idea that a writer presents in the topic sentence, that idea must be supported with evidence. As you may recall from Part I, Chapter 1, the most common types of evidence in academic legal discourse include:

1. Examples;
2. Descriptions;
3. Explanations;
4. Definitions;
5. Statistics; and
6. References to authority.

Which type of evidence a writer uses depends on the document being written. For example, in a paragraph on a paper, a writer might use statistics to support a claim about the prevalence of a phenomenon. In a paragraph on an essay exam, a writer might define a legal concept and provide an explanation for how courts apply it to factual scenarios. And in a paragraph in an office memorandum,[14] a writer might use an example of a legal case, and details from the case, to show how a court addresses particular legal issues. Most often, writers use a combination of evidence types within a single paragraph.

Below are examples of the six most common types of evidence used in academic legal discourse.

---

[13] Matthew J. Wilson, *U.S. Legal Education Methods and Ideals: Application to the Japanese and Korean Systems*, 18 CARDOZO J. INT'L & COMP. L. 295, 311-12 (2010).

[14] An office memorandum ("memo") is a professional document, usually written for a supervisor at a law firm. It answers a legal question by explaining how the law will apply to a set of facts. Law students write a memo in a Legal Research and Writing class.

1. Examples

An example is an illustration of a prior point that a writer has made. Examples are frequently used in academic legal discourse to support the topic sentence of a paragraph or a sub-point made within the paragraph. This is because examples are useful for making the writer's ideas easier to understand.

The following paragraph from a law review article, titled *Private Enforcement of Immigration Laws*, states as its topic that (1) state and local governments are involved in enforcing immigration laws; and (2) the federal government has encouraged their involvement. To support this topic sentence, the writer first provides an example of how, in 2002, the Department of Justice (a federal executive department) invited local and state police to enforce immigration laws. The writer then provides an example of local law enforcement in three places—Florida, Alabama, and Los Angeles County—that have taken up this invitation.

Topic Example (Beginning with "In 2002 . . . ") (The example continues with "Taking up that invitation . . . ")	State and local governments are getting involved in immigration law enforcement too, with encouragement from the federal government. In 2002, reversing its previous legal position, the Department of Justice invited local and state police to enforce both civil and criminal immigration laws, opining that state governments have "inherent authority" to do so. Taking up that invitation, local law enforcement in Florida, Alabama, and Los Angeles County have entered into training agreements with ICE [Immigration and Customs Enforcement] and currently have immigration law enforcement responsibilities. Other local jurisdictions have pending agreements.[15]

Examples are often introduced with the transition phrase "for example" or "for instance." However, as the paragraph above shows, this need not always be the case.

2. Descriptions

A description is a written representation of a person, place, or event. Descriptions are common in legal writing, especially in the "facts" section of a judicial opinion, office memorandum, or appellate brief (see Part II, Chapter 2 for a discussion of the facts portion of a legal case). When writing about a legal case, it is common practice to begin with a description of who the relevant parties are

---

[15] Huyen Pham, *The Private Enforcement of Immigration Laws*, 96 GEO. L.J. 777, 786 (2008).

(e.g., the plaintiff and defendant); what happened to bring them to court; and what occurred at trial.

The next paragraph is from a legal case, *Posecai v. Wal-Mart Stores*. In this case, the plaintiff sued Wal-Mart Stores after she was robbed at gunpoint in the parking lot at one of its locations (called "Sam's Wholesale Club"). The paragraph appears in the beginning of the case and describes to the reader what happened at trial. More concretely, the paragraph details what two police officers testified[16] to at trial.

Topic Description (Beginning with "Officer Moran testified . . . ") (The description continues with "Officer George Ansardi . . . ")	The plaintiff presented the testimony of two other Kenner police officers. Officer Russel Moran testified that he had patrolled the area around Sam's from 1993 to 1995. He stated that the subdivision behind Sam's, Lincoln Manor, is generally known as a high crime area, but that the Kenner Police were rarely called out to Sam's. Officer George Ansardi, the investigating officer, similarly testified that Lincoln Manor is a high crime area but explained that Sam's is not considered a high crime location. He further stated that to his knowledge none of the other businesses in the area employed security guards at the time of this robbery.[17]

This example is from a professional, not academic, piece of writing: a judicial opinion. Nevertheless, descriptive sentences may also be used to support the ideas in papers, exams, and other writing assignments.

3. Explanations

Explanations consist of reasons or justifications given in support of a particular point or argument. It should come as no surprise that explanations are very common in academic legal paragraphs.

The paragraph below is from a student-written essay about why and how a New York statute governing marital agreements should be amended. After putting forth reasons for why the law ought to be rewritten, the writer outlines her proposed amendment to the law. Following this, in the paragraph excerpted below, she explains to the reader how this amendment would bring about change.

Topic Explanation #1 (Beginning with "First, it would likely alter . . . ")	This proposal would bring change on two levels. First, it would likely alter current practices of matrimonial courts so that property agreements receive more scrutiny than they have in the past. As a result of the amendment,

[16] Testify means to speak in court as a witness. The noun form is "testimony."

[17] Posecai v. Wal-Mart Stores, Inc., 752 So.2d 762, 764 (La. 1999).

Explanation #2
(Beginning with "Second, the proposed amendment would provide . . .")

judges would probably be more willing to look into the external circumstances behind a property distribution contract. Second, the proposed amendment would provide more certainty to both courts and parties signing marital agreements. Specifically, parties signing away their rights to support or property will have no choice but to sign a contract explicitly warning them about the consequences of the agreement.

Explanations are very common in one particular genre of academic legal discourse: essay exams. Indeed, on most exams, law students are expected to provide explanations as to how and why a particular rule applies to a given set of facts. (This is called rule application; you will learn more about essay exam writing in Part II, Chapter 4 of this book.)

See the following paragraph from a student's essay exam answer.

Topic

Explanation
(Beginning with "David did come into physical contact . . .")

David's claim [18] for the negligent infliction of emotional distress (NIED) will fail. This jurisdiction follows the physical impact test for NIED. *Conder v. Wood*. David would have to prove that the defendant's conduct resulted in physical contact with him, which caused him both fear and physical injury. David did come into physical contact with the defendant's vehicle when a piece of the car's tire flew into his hair. However, unlike the plaintiff in the *Conder* case, David did not suffer any physical injury as a result of the emotional trauma he experienced from witnessing the car crash. Therefore, he cannot recover[19] for emotional distress in this jurisdiction.

The topic sentence of this paragraph states that David, the plaintiff in a lawsuit, cannot successfully sue the defendant for the negligent infliction of emotional distress (abbreviated as NIED). You will read about tort law and NIED in Part II of this book; for now, simply note that in the second and third sentences, the writer states the rule and "test" for NIED. This rule is derived from case law—specifically, a case called *Conder v. Wood*. After stating the NIED rule, the writer next explains how the rule would apply to the facts of David's case to argue that David will not win against the defendant in this case.

---

[18] A claim is the plaintiff's assertion that she is entitled to money damages or other remedies.

[19] Recover means to win money in a lawsuit. Usually the verb is used along with the term "damages." For example: "The plaintiff recovered $10,000 in damages."

4. Definitions

Academic legal writers frequently define concepts for their readers. Writers do this because readers come with varying levels of expertise in the topic being written about. If a reader is unfamiliar with a key concept in the writer's text, the reader may fail to understand or fully appreciate the writer's line of argument. Another reason writers define concepts is to prove to readers their familiarity with the subject matter of the text. This may be especially important on an exam.

The following paragraph is from the student-written article, *Catching the Unique Rabbit*, which you read in Part I, Chapter 1. In this paragraph, the writer defines the "bystander test" used by some jurisdictions to determine whether the plaintiff should recover damages for the loss of a pet. In the next paragraph, the writer explains why this test is not a good solution for compensating pet owners who have lost their pets. But first, the writer defines this test so that writers can follow her upcoming argument. Note that this definition is integrated into the writer's topic sentence for the paragraph.

Topic Definition (Beginning with "which allows . . . ")	The most viable argument that supports extension of a negligent infliction of emotional distress claim to pet owners involves the use of the bystander test, which allows the plaintiff to recover if the defendant could have foreseen that his or her conduct would cause emotional distress to bystanders. In this test, the plaintiff can only recover for emotional distress as the result of witnessing, or by physically experiencing, the injury or death of another person. To prevail under the bystander test, plaintiff must prove that he or she was physically in a position to witness the injury, that the resulting shock and mental distress were caused by the contemporaneous observance of the event, and that the plaintiff and the victim were closely related.

Following the definition of the bystander test, the writer continues by providing a detailed description of how this test works ("the plaintiff can only recover for . . ." and "[t]o prevail under the bystander test, the plaintiff must prove . . .").

5. Statistics

The term "statistics" refers to numeric data, such as frequency numbers or percentages. Academic legal writers often use statistics to support claims that a particular phenomenon is either common or uncommon, or simply to show how much there is of something. Statistics tend to be used in papers as opposed to exams because statistics can only be found through extensive research, which students typically do not do for in-class exams.

The paragraph below is from the same article as a previous example in this section, *The Private Enforcement of Immigration Laws*. Here, the writer seeks to support the idea that counterfeit[20] immigration documents are very common. She devotes the entire paragraph to providing examples of enforcement actions in which the Immigration and Naturalization Service (INS) found fraudulent documents. She supports her point that counterfeit documents are widespread by peppering the paragraph with statistics about the prevalence of fraudulent documents. Notice that the writer uses both numbers (e.g., "78,000 fraudulent documents") and percentages ("60% of these cases").

Topic	Just a sampling of enforcement actions shows how widespread counterfeit documents are. In a roughly two-year period, between October 1, 1996 and May 29, 1998,
Statistics (Beginning with "INS conducted 3500 investigations. . . ")	INS conducted 3500 investigations in which it found 78,000 fraudulent documents used to obtain employment for 50,000 unauthorized employees. In about 60% of these cases, INS found that the employer had complied with the verification process and had not knowingly hired unauthorized workers. Of the 78,000 documents, 60% were INS documents like permanent resident cards, 36% were Social Security cards, and the remaining 4% were other documents like drivers' licenses. And in thirty fraud cases investigated during a five-year period (1990-1995), INS confiscated nearly 300,000 counterfeit documents, almost all of which were confiscated in Los Angeles. Finally, in November 1998, INS seized two million counterfeit documents; the seizure took place in Los Angeles but the documents were headed to different distribution points across the country.[21]

6. References to Authority

A reference to authority is when the writer uses the ideas—and occasionally, the exact words—of another person or entity in a position of "authority." Writers draw upon others' ideas and words because this can strengthen their argument. If you make a point that others have similarly made in the past, that point is more likely to be accepted by readers of your text.

---

[20] A counterfeit document is a fake document that imitates something valuable. Often, the term is used with currency (e.g., counterfeit $100 bills).

[21] Pham, *supra* note 15ing, at 807-08.

Who or what counts as an authority depends on the subject matter being written about. In academic legal discourse, there are several authorities upon which writers tend to rely: judges; scholars and professors; and legal, political, or civic organizations. Statutes and regulations, though not a living entity (but certainly written by living lawmakers), also count as authority in academic legal discourse.

In the example below, the author of *The Private Enforcement of Immigration Laws* refers to three different authorities to support her point that employer sanctions (punishments) have not reduced or deterred (prevented) illegal immigration.

Topic Reference to Authority (Beginning with "The Migration. . ") Reference to Authority (Beginning with "And the Government . . . ") Reference to Authority (Beginning with "Finally, Professors . . . ")	After twenty-one years, the almost unanimous conclusion is that federal employer sanctions have not significantly reduced or deterred illegal immigration. The Migration Policy Institute describes employer sanctions as "notoriously ineffective," noting that "employers view the threat of actual punishment under the current system as an acceptable business expense." And the Government Accountability Office, which concluded in 1990 that sanctions had slowed illegal immigration, warned in 2006 that "ongoing weaknesses [in the employment verification process] have undermined its effectiveness" and that employers who circumvent the sanctions face little chance or prosecution. Finally, Professors Aleinikoff, Martin, and Motomura conclude: "Whatever the goals (and hopes) of the Congress that put the employers sanction regime in place in 1986, the statutory provisions have plainly failed of their purpose."[22]

The writer borrows the words of the Migration Policy Institute presumably because, as an organization studying migration, it knows a thing or two about immigration. The writer also borrows the words of the Government Accountability Office because, as a governmental body, its words carry significant weight. Finally, the writer quotes Professors Aleinikoff, Martin, and Motomura, who wrote a textbook on immigration law. Certainly they are authorities on the subject being discussed.

The writer's selection of what to quote is also intentional. She has selected not just any words, but words that serve to underscore her point that employer sanctions do not work well (e.g., the sanctions are "notoriously ineffective"). More will be said below about the decision to quote authorities or to use your

---

[22] *Id.* at 803-04.

own words to describe their ideas. For now, suffice it to say that referencing authorities can be helpful to support the ideas in paragraphs.

EXERCISE 2.B.1. Finding and Identifying Support for the Main Idea

In each paragraph below identify the main idea and name the types of support the writer uses: examples, descriptions, explanations, definitions, statistics, and/or references to authority. Note that a paragraph may use multiple types of support; list all types of support used.

If you have trouble classifying a sentence or group of sentences, try to guess its function.

1. If you plan to litigate,[23] you should learn to draft [a contract] for two reasons. First, you will regularly draft contracts as a litigator. Litigating parties settle more often than they go to trial. The settlement they reach is a business deal, just like any other, and it must be memorialized clearly and accurately. Failure to do so can lead to another dispute and further litigation. Second, knowing how to draft will make you a better litigator. Many of the cases that you litigate will grow out of contract disputes. To represent your client properly, you must be able to analyze a contract and its provisions. If you understand how and why a drafter wrote a provision in a specific way, you will be able to craft more persuasive legal arguments.[24]

   Main idea:

   Type(s) of support used:

2. Piercing the corporate veil is the most litigated issue in corporate law and yet it remains among the least understood. As a general principle, corporations are recognized as legal entities separate from their shareholders, officers, and directors. Corporate obligations remain the liability of the entity and not of the shareholders, directors, or officers who own and/or act for the entity. "Piercing the corporate veil" refers to the judicially imposed exception to this principle by which courts disregard the separateness of the corporation and hold a shareholder responsible for the corporation's action as if it were the shareholder's own. The boundaries of this exception are usually stated in broad terms that offer little guidance to judges or litigants in subsequent cases. In 1926,

[23] Litigate means to bring a lawsuit or to defend against a lawsuit in court.

[24] TINA L. STARK, DRAFTING CONTRACTS 5 (2014).

Benjamin Cardozo described this corner of the law as "enveloped in the mists of metaphor," and courts and commentators have been even less kind in subsequent years. Legal writers have described judicial decisions to pierce the veil as "irreconcilable and not entirely comprehensible," "defying any attempt at rational explanation," and occurring "freakishly."[25]

Main idea:

Type(s) of support used:

3. Recently, there has been an increase in the amount of state and local regulation regarding indoor tanning, especially for minors. Despite the tanning bed industry's strong lobbying efforts greatly diminishing its opponents' ability to pass legislation at both the federal and state level, several organizations that support a complete ban on indoor tanning for minors have been able to push legislation forward. There is a growing trend among states to restrict adolescent access to tanning facilities. In 2003, only Wisconsin, Illinois, and Texas had implemented such restrictions. However, by 2005, there were 21 states, and by 2012, there were 33 states that had implemented age-based restrictions. In the beginning of "2015, [41] states and the District of Columbia [had implemented] some form of" adolescent restrictions, and as of 2016, two more states had implemented these restrictions as well. By the beginning of 2017, 44 states and the District of Columbia had implemented regulations restricting indoor tanning for minors.[26]

Main idea:

Type(s) of support used:

4. By the late nineteenth century, public policy in domestic violence began to move from overt legal approval to toleration, so that men who assaulted their wives were granted immunity from prosecution on grounds of marital privacy and preservation of domestic harmony. This policy of toleration continued up through the 1970s, and wife-beating

---

[25] Robert B. Thompson, *Piercing the Corporate Veil: An Empirical Study*, 76 CORNELL L. REV. 1036, 1036-37 (1991).

[26] Courtney M. Brokloff, *Looks Can Kill: The Dark Side of Indoor Tanning and What States Need to Do to Help Protect Young Adults from This Deadly "Glow"*, 103 IOWA L. REV. 271, 282-83 (2017).

was considered a private matter between husband and wife in which the state should not intrude. Police officers were trained to separate spouses at the scene of a domestic incident and, if necessary, to tell the husband to "cool off" by "'tak[ing] a walk around the block.'" Officers were explicitly instructed not to make an arrest, as domestic violence was not a matter for the criminal justice system. The victims of the abuse were not questioned privately about the incident, nor asked if they needed services or assistance in leaving or if they were in fear of the abuser.[27]

Main idea:

Type(s) of support used:

5. Today, education is perhaps the most important function of state and local governments. Compulsory school attendance laws and the great expenditures for education both demonstrate our recognition of the importance of education to our democratic society. It is required in the performance of our most basic public responsibilities, even service in the armed forces. It is the very foundation of good citizenship. Today it is a principal instrument in awakening the child to cultural values, in preparing him for later professional training, and in helping him to adjust normally to his environment. In these days, it is doubtful that any child may reasonably be expected to succeed in life if he is denied the opportunity of an education. Such an opportunity, where the state has undertaken to provide it, is a right which must be made available to all on equal terms.[28]

Main idea:

Type(s) of support used:

6. Legal academia is awakening to the growing interest in the legal protection of apes and other animals. In 1999, Harvard Law School and Georgetown Law School announced that they would offer their first classes ever in animal law. Less than a year later, Harvard's animal law instructor, Steven Wise, published a book demanding legal rights for chimpanzees and bonobos. In what may be the clearest sign that discussion of great ape legal rights has entered mainstream legal

---

[27] Emily J. Sack, *Battered Women and the State: The Struggle for the Future of Domestic Violence Policy*, 2004 WIS. L. REV. 1657, 1662-63 (2004).

[28] Brown v. Board of Education, 347 U.S. 483 (1954).

discourse, Judge Richard Posner reviewed Wise's book in the *Yale Law Journal.* Although Posner does criticize Wise's approach, he is surprisingly uncritical of Wise's aims and faults Wise principally on methodological grounds.[29]

Main idea:

Type(s) of support used:

7. A Note on Research, Attribution, and Citation

An in-depth discussion of research, attribution, and citation is beyond the scope of this book. It should be mentioned, however, that if you are writing a paper for a seminar course, or a memorandum or appellate brief for a Legal Research and Writing class, you will do research to support your ideas. You will also integrate information gathered from your research into your paragraphs, and in doing so, you will mention the name of the source in a footnote.

The idea of crediting other authors for their ideas is called **attribution**. Information about the sources used, such as the author's name and the title and publication year of the work, is called the **citation**. In U.S. law schools, the form and structure of citations is governed by a guide called *The Bluebook* (included in the list of Further Readings at the end of this chapter).

You may wish to review the titles listed under Further Readings at the end of this chapter if you are interested in conducting legal research or if you know that you will be writing a paper or other assignment for a law class requiring research and citation.

8. A Note on Paraphrasing Versus Quoting

While this book does not address legal research or attribution of sources in detail, it is worth noting that there are two ways to integrate information from sources into paragraphs. The first is **paraphrasing**, or using the writer's own words to describe what someone else has written. Paraphrasing techniques are discussed in Part II, Chapter 4 of this book in the context of case briefing. The second way to integrate information from sources into paragraphs is by **quoting**, or taking another writer's words and inserting those words directly into the paragraph.

See an example of both paraphrasing and quoting in the following paragraph taken from a student's essay exam answer.

---

[29] Adam Kolber, *Standing Upright: The Moral and Legal Standing of Humans and Other Apes* 54 STAN. L. REV. 163, 164 (2001-2002).

> When a suspect is questioned in custody by law enforcement officers, his statements will be admissible[30] against him only if he has received Miranda warnings. The requirement of Miranda warnings applies where the police conduct a "custodial interrogation." The Court has held that the Miranda rule only applies when a suspect is "in custody" (*Oregon v. Mathiason*), which it has defined as "formal arrest or restraint on the freedom of movement of the degree associated with formal arrest." *Stansbury v. California*. Also, the Miranda protections are triggered only by "interrogation" of a subject who is in custody. *Rhode Island v. Innis* expanded the concept of interrogation to include police conduct that, while not formal or express questioning, is its functional equivalent.

To support the idea expressed in the topic sentence, the student has pulled information from three cases: *Oregon v. Mathiason*, *Stansbury v. California*, and *Rhode Island v. Innis*.[31] As the student wrote this paragraph under the time pressure of an in-class exam, she did not have an opportunity to properly cite to these cases using footnotes and *Bluebook* conventions. (Contrast this paragraph with those in *Catching the Unique Rabbit*, which are all properly footnoted.) Instead, the student uses a shorthand citation form: she simply places the case name [in italics] after the clause or sentence containing the information taken from that case.

Notably, the student uses both quotations from the Court's opinions as well as her own words to support the idea expressed in her topic sentence. For example, she quotes the following language from *Stansbury v. California*: "formal arrest or restraint on the freedom of movement of the degree associated with formal arrest." On the other hand, in the last sentence of the paragraph, she uses her own words to state the rule from *Rhode Island v. Innis*.

When writing an academic legal document, writers can quote or paraphrase information to support their topic sentences, though quoting tends to be used rarely. Quoting is reserved for language that is important or powerful—such as the rule from a Supreme Court opinion. Quoting language because it seems too difficult to paraphrase is generally not a good enough reason to quote.

If you plan to write a paper or other document for a law course, peruse the titles under Further Readings at the end of this chapter. Some of the books listed there contain more information about the decision to quote or paraphrase information, as well as how to correctly do so.

---

[30] When evidence is admissible, it means that the evidence can be used in court.

[31] You will read the *Miranda v. Arizona* case and the three other cases referenced in this paragraph in Part II, Chapter 6.

C. Unity

Paragraph unity refers to the idea that all of the sentences in the paragraph are about the same topic. In some cultures, writers may put slightly related topics together in one paragraph. In U.S. academic legal discourse, however, this is generally frowned upon. If you want to include another idea in a paragraph that is interesting and slightly related, then you need to write another paragraph. It is important that your reader is not confronted with topics or sentences that are partially related to the topic, but not directly related.

There are two main ways to create unity in a paragraph, and well-written paragraphs use both of these ways. The first way is to write a topic sentence that introduces the main idea for the paragraph (see again Section A above). The second way to is to recycle key words from the topic sentence of the paragraph, and synonyms for these key words, throughout the paragraph. Key words for a paragraph denote the topic of the paragraph.

Key words are usually nouns because they tend to describe the "thing" or "things" that the paragraph is about. Look again at the following topic sentences, pulled from some of the sample paragraphs you have read in this chapter. Note that key words have been underlined.

> Clarence Thomas's conduct as a Justice presents a puzzle.
>
> > **Topic**: Clarence Thomas's conduct
> > **Main idea**: Clarence Thomas's conduct presents a puzzle
>
> [P]unitive damages may only be feasible in a limited number of pet loss cases.
>
> > **Topic**: Punitive damages in pet loss cases
> > **Main idea**: Punitive damages in pet loss cases are possible in only a small number of cases
>
> David's claim for the negligent infliction of emotional distress (NIED) will fail.
>
> > **Topic**: David's claim for the negligent infliction of emotional distress
> > **Main idea**: David's claim will fail

Now read again the following paragraph from Kelly Wilson's article, *Catching the Unique Rabbit*. What are the key words for this paragraph?

> The domestication and history of the cat is also enlightening because it sets the species apart from other types of farm animals.

> Although there are a variety of theories and dates on when cat domestication began, a recent study suggests the process began over 9000 years ago and coincides with the early agricultural endeavors of peoples in the fertile crescent. As farmers began producing and storing grain, cats were instrumental in controlling the rodent population who fed on grain stores. Over time the wild cats dropped their aggressive instinctive behaviors and were incorporated into societies through religious worship, were protected by threat of criminal punishment, and became common in typical ancient households.

The key words here are "cat" and "domestication."[32] The topic of the paragraph is therefore cat domestication. The main idea of the paragraph is that the domestication of cats is informative in telling us why cats are different from other types of farm animals. If the writer is adept at developing the topic of cat domestication and describing its history to reveal how cats are different from other types of farm animals, the reader should expect to see the words "cat" and "domestication"—and perhaps synonyms for these words—reused throughout the paragraph.

This expectation is borne out. Read again the supporting sentences in the paragraph. The key words "cat" and "domestication" are highlighted, while synonyms are <u>underlined</u>.

> The domestication and history of the cat is also enlightening because it sets the species apart from other types of farm animals. Although there are a variety of theories and dates on when cat domestication began, a recent study suggests <u>the process</u> began over 9000 years ago and coincides with the early agricultural endeavors of peoples in the fertile crescent. As farmers began producing and storing grain, cats were instrumental in controlling the rodent population who fed on grain stores. Over time the wild cats <u>dropped their aggressive instinctive behaviors</u> and were <u>incorporated into societies</u> through religious worship, were protected by threat of criminal punishment, and became common in typical ancient households.

With each supporting sentence, the writer develops the idea of cat domestication throughout history. She mentions the key words "cat," "domestication," or a synonym of these words in every sentence. (Synonyms of domestication include "the process"; "dropped their aggressive instinctive

---

[32] Arguably, "history" is also a key word. However, because domestication refers to the *process* of taming an animal, the idea of history is subsumed under the concept of domestication.

behaviors"; and "incorporated into societies.") These key words and synonyms help the reader to understand how the supporting sentences connect to, and support, the main idea of the paragraph. Because all of the sentences in this paragraph mention the words "cat," "domestication," or a close synonym, the writer has not veered off track. Her entire paragraph is unified around the topic introduced in the topic sentence.

As you write paragraphs on your law school assignments and exams, keep in mind that they should be organized around one main idea. If you feel that your writing contains too many "sub" ideas for one paragraph, you may need to split up your paragraph into multiple paragraphs. Section E below discusses paragraph length, and the idea of splitting up paragraphs, in greater detail.

EXERCISE 2.C.1. Paragraph Unity

Read the topic sentences below and underline the key words in each sentence. You may identify two or three key words or phrases within each sentence. Though key words are often nouns, they could be verbs, adjectives, and adverbs as well.

Topic sentences

a. In recent years, scholars have debated whether healthcare professionals can legally refuse to provide medical services that conflict with their moral or religious beliefs.

b. Conscience clauses are designed to permit healthcare providers to refuse to provide medical services that conflict with their moral, ethical, or religious beliefs.

c. Unfortunate incidents have raised legitimate concerns and indicate that the medical profession must exercise extreme diligence in the proper disposal of medical wastes.

d. Currently, most healthcare professionals are inadequately prepared to deal with disaster events.

e. To prevent dangerous mentally ill persons from obtaining or retaining guns, the SAFE [Secure Ammunitions and Firearms Enforcement] Act imposes reporting obligations on mental healthcare professionals, going far beyond prior New York State and federal laws.

Next, indicate in the blanks below which topic sentence (a-e) belongs to each paragraph.

Finally, underline all key words and synonyms within the paragraphs below. How many times are the key words that you identified used in each paragraph? Are you surprised by this number?

Paragraphs

1. _____ The American Medical Association (AMA) and even the federal government have attempted over the years to encourage, and in some cases even fund, disaster medicine and public health preparedness, education, and training. For example, in 2003, the AMA began working on a "national education and training initiative called the National Disaster Life Support Program (NDLS) to provide physicians, medical students, other health professionals, and other emergency responders with a fundamental understanding and working knowledge of their integrated roles and responsibilities in disaster management and response efforts." Despite these efforts, reports continue to show that the current medical school curriculum related to disaster medicine and public health preparedness is insufficient.[33]

   How many times were key words used in this paragraph?

2. _____ The debate generally focuses on whether healthcare professionals can refuse to provide certain procedures and products such as abortion and contraception. However, this debate also extends to whether healthcare professionals can refuse to provide medical services when they have religious or moral objections to personal characteristics of the patients. Specifically, a major issue is whether healthcare professionals can legally refuse to provide lesbian, gay, or bisexual (LGB) individuals with medical services, such as artificial reproductive technology, where their religious or moral objections pertain to the sexual orientation of the recipient, as opposed to the nature of the services.[34]

   How many times were key words used in this paragraph?

3. _____ The Act requires mental health professionals, using "reasonable professional judgment," to report the names of patients "likely to engage

---

[33] Margaret L. Begalle, *Increasing the Quality of Care During Times of Disaster*, 19 ANNALS HEALTH L. ADVANCE DIRECTIVE 239, 246 (2010).

[34] Rachel Reibman, *The Patient Wanted the Doctor to Treat Her in the Closet, But the Janitor Wouldn't Open the Door: Healthcare Provider Rights of Refusal Versus LGB Rights to Reproductive and Elder Healthcare*, 28 TEMP. J. SCI. TECH. & ENVTL. L. 65, 65-66 (2009).

in conduct that would result in serious harm to self or others." The term "mental health professionals" includes physicians, psychologists, registered nurses and licensed clinical social workers, whether or not they specialize in diagnosing or treating mental illness. There is no requirement that reporting mental healthcare professionals use a risk assessment instrument, or justify their diagnosis and prediction, to a neutral fact finder. There is no opportunity for the person labelled mentally ill and dangerous by a single healthcare professional to dispute the diagnosis and prediction.[35]

How many times were key words used in this paragraph?

4. _____ In light of the Supreme Court's decision in *Roe v. Wade*, which extended the constitutional right to privacy to protect a woman's right to an abortion, initial conscience clause legislation focused on enabling healthcare providers to refuse to perform abortion and sterilization procedures they found morally and religiously objectionable. Today, the federal government and most states have enacted laws enabling doctors and other healthcare providers to refuse to perform abortions and other services on moral, religious, or ethical grounds.[36]

How many times were key words used in this paragraph?

5. _____ In one case, twelve Indianapolis children played with vials of blood that they retrieved from a trash bin outside a medical office; two of these vials were contaminated with HIV (human immunodeficiency virus). At the time, it was legal for the clinic to discard the wastes in an open dumpster. In Ohio, a group of youngsters played doctor by poking each other in the arm with used syringes that they discovered in a dumpster. Five Los Angeles County-USC Medical Center employees filed a $50 million lawsuit against the county after a pipe in the basement of the facility burst, exposing the workers to possibly contaminated blood and fluids.[37]

How many times were key words used in this paragraph?

---

[35] James B. Jacobs & Zoe Fuhr, *Preventing Dangerous Mentally Ill Individuals from Obtaining and Retaining Guns: New York's SAFE Act*, 14 GEO. J. L. & PUB. POL'Y 77, 80 (2016).

[36] Catherine Grealis, *Religion in the Pharmacy: A Balanced Approach to Pharmacists' Right to Refuse to Provide Plan B*, 97 GEO. L.J. 1715, 1718 (2009).

[37] Kamrin T. MacKnight, *The Problems of Medical and Infectious Waste*, 23 ENVTL. L. 785, 789-90 (1993).

D. Cohesion

Cohesion is the idea that the individual parts of something stick together to create a whole (for example, molecules in a glass of water). In the context of academic legal discourse, cohesion means that the sentences in a paragraph fit together like the pieces of a puzzle or like domino tiles, with each individual sentence building upon and adding to the one that came before it.

Paragraph cohesion rests on the idea that readers process information more easily when "old," familiar information is presented to them in the beginning of a sentence, and "new," unfamiliar information is presented at the end. [38] Information is familiar when it has already been mentioned in the text, or if it is something that a reader can be expected to already know.

Look again at the following paragraph from *Catching the Unique Rabbit*. As you read, pay attention to the ideas that the writer places in the beginning and end of her sentences.

> Another approach advocated by reformers is derived from focusing more on the rights of the animal rather than the owners. Animal rights advocates suggest that domestic animals should no longer be classified as personal property. The justifications for declassification are varied, but most stress two common themes. The first is that many people today view pets as family members. The second stresses that sentient animals have inherent worth outside of our property system and have more than just an interest, indeed a *fundamental right*, in being declassified as chattel. At the outset, this seems like a great way to remedy the problem because limits on non-economic damages would no longer apply to the *guardian*—not owner—of a pet. This suggested solution, however, raises too many practical problems to be deemed a viable remedy.

Now let us deconstruct the paragraph sentence by sentence. In each sentence below, "old" information is **bolded**, while "new" information is <u>underlined</u>. The first sentence, the topic sentence, reads as follows:

> **Another approach** advocated by reformers is derived from focusing more on the <u>rights of the animal rather than the owners</u>.

---

[38] This idea is borrowed from DAVID AUSUBEL, EDUCATIONAL PSYCHOLOGY: A COGNITIVE VIEW (1968); see also JOSEPH M. WILIAMS & JOSEPH BIZUP, STYLE: LESSONS IN CLARITY AND GRACE 66-69 (12th ed. 2016).

This paragraph has been taken out of its context, but if you go back and re-read the section from which it is taken, you will remember that in this section the writer presents current suggested solutions to the problem of inadequate compensation for pet loss, as well as the inadequacies of these solutions (review the article in Part I, Chapter 1). In the particular subsection from which this sentence is taken, the writer presents the fourth suggested solution.

The sentence begins with "another approach" ("approach" is a synonym for "solution"). These words—"another approach"— indicate that the writer is now offering another solution whose usefulness will be refuted in the paragraphs to come. This bit of language offers familiar information because the reader has been reading various solutions up to this point in the article. The reader can expect to read more on the topic of solutions.

The end of the sentence, however, offers new information. The "other approach" focuses on the "rights of the animal."

Let us continue reading the paragraph. The next sentence states:

> **Animal rights** advocates suggest that domestic animals should no longer be classified as personal property.

The sentence begins with what is now familiar information that was introduced in the prior sentence: "animal rights." The reader is not surprised by the mention of animal rights here because she has already been told in the previous sentence that the approach to be discussed in this paragraph focuses on the rights of animals.

The writer then provides new information at the end of the sentence, stating that animal rights advocates argue that "animals should no longer be classified as personal property."

Given the pattern exhibited so far, the next sentence begins as you might expect:

> **The justifications for declassification** are varied, but most stress two common themes.

The term "declassification" at the beginning of this sentence is a synonym for "no longer be classified as personal property," mentioned at the end of the previous sentence. This is familiar information with which the writer begins the sentence.

New information again appears again at the end of the sentence. As the reader, you learn that justifications for declassification emphasize "two common themes."

Now examine the next two sentences in the paragraph.

> **The first** is that many people today view pets as family members.

> **The second** stresses that sentient animals have inherent worth outside of our property system and have more than just an interest, indeed a *fundamental right*, in being declassified as chattel.

This pair of sentences begins with "the first" and "the second," words which refer back to the "two common themes" mentioned at the end of the prior sentence. What remains in the two sentences is new information, namely, a brief description of the two themes that underlie declassification of pets as property.

The final two sentences in the paragraph also begin with familiar information:

> At the outset, **this** seems like a great way to remedy the problem because limits on non-economic damages would no longer apply to the *guardian*—not owner—of a pet.
>
> **This suggested solution**, however, raises too many practical problems to be deemed a viable remedy.

In these sentences, the familiar information comes not from the immediately prior sentence, but rather the first sentence of the paragraph. The words "this" and "this suggested solution" refer back to the "approach" that focuses on "animal rights," mentioned in the first sentence. Indeed, these words refer to the topic and focus of the entire paragraph.

With each sentence in this paragraph, the writer develops the idea expressed in her topic sentence by starting each sentence with "old" information and providing "new" information at the end.

When composing your paragraphs, try to think about how to link your sentences so that the ideas within them progressively build upon each other (think: "old" information + "new" information; "old" information + "new" information; etc.). Much of this will come naturally. But if you re-read one of your own paragraphs and it seems disorganized or the ideas seem disjointed, check to make sure that you have followed the principle of cohesion. Usually the problem with such paragraphs is a lack of cohesion.

EXERCISE 2.D.1. Paragraph Cohesion

Look at the four circles, ①, ②, ③, and ④, which indicate where the bold sentence could be added to the passage. Darken the circle where you think the sentence best fits.

1. **The minor complied and dropped a brown vial[39] with a spoon.**

   A police officer encountered a juvenile sitting in a tunnel underneath a bridge. Although the only thing "suspicious" about the youth was that he was wearing a heavy jacket in warm weather, the officer told the minor to come towards him with his hands out of his pockets. ① When the minor did not remove his hands from his pockets as he approached the officer, the officer grabbed the minor's hand and told him to drop whatever he was holding. ② The officer arrested the minor and found drugs during a subsequent search. ③ The Arizona Court of Appeals held that the officer's conduct was not a seizure[40] under the standard set forth in *Terry v. Ohio*. ④ The court further found that even if it were a seizure, it was not an unreasonable one. The court applied a balancing test and held that the public's "strong and legitimate interest in the welfare of *its* children" outweighed the officer's minimal interference with the minor's liberty.[41]

2. **Private organizations also have developed a number of innovative mechanisms designed to aid school officials in decreasing or preventing violence at their schools.**

   All levels of government, as well as private organizations, have responded to the public's call to make schools safer by implementing programs or directives. The federal government has created centers that work to devise solutions to school crime and disciplinary problems, and has introduced legislation supporting local school efforts to reduce violence and promote safety. ① Many states have enacted laws referred to as Safe Schools Acts that generally require safe and peaceful schools and guarantee students' constitutional rights to a "healthful school environment." ② At the local school level, school districts nationwide have implemented practices such as zero tolerance policies, mandatory

[39] A vial is a small cylindrical container usually used for storing medicine.

[40] A seizure in this context refers to the act of taking an object or person (usually by force) by law enforcement officers.

[41] Lourdes M. Rosado, *Minors and the Fourth Amendment: How Juvenile Status Should Invoke Different Standards for Searches and Seizures on the Street*, 73 N.Y.U. L. REV. 762, 762 (1996).

school uniforms, increased security measures, and law enforcement presence at the schools. ③ In addition, the majority of schools also have some sort of formal school violence prevention or reduction program. ④ Efforts of the federal government, state and local governments, and private organizations may be helpful, but these alone cannot tackle the problem of school violence. On a day-to-day basis, school officials must make decisions as to how to respond to the possibility of injury to students.[42]

3. **Parents, in particular, may make use of formidable[43] new tools in monitoring their children.**

As surveillance technology becomes more sophisticated, the power of private citizens to spy on one another increases. ① For example, with a program covertly installed on a smartphone, parents can track the location of a minor child, install equipment on a car to monitor travel and receive detailed data on driving style, and load spyware onto a home computer to capture social media passwords by monitoring keystrokes and browsing history. ② Although parents may profess to use this technology only to protect their children, not all instances of surveillance are so noble. ③ In certain cases, when parents wish to gain bargaining leverage over each other, they may lose sight of their children's best interests. Especially in the context of divorce, children cannot rely on their parents' benevolent discretion in deploying surveillance technology. ④[44]

4. **Both functions coexist within the board, even though the latter has been much less explored.**

A central focus of corporate law scholarship is the function of the board. ① Two basic models have emerged that seek to explain directors' responsibilities and interactions with parties in and around the corporation. ② The dominant model is premised on agency costs, assigning to the board a monitoring function that can improve firm performance by reducing inefficiencies. The second model considers the board to be a provider of management resources, including human capital (such as experience, expertise, and reputation) and relational capital (such as ties to other firms and regulators). ③ Under this "resource dependence" approach, the board spans the divide between

---

[42] Melissa L. Gilbert, *"Time-Out" for Student Threats?: Imposing a Duty to Protect on School Officials*, 49 UCLA L. Rev. 917, 930-31 (2002).

[43] If something is formidable, it is powerful, strong, and/or causes fear or wonder.

[44] Robert D. McCabe, *Children Who Should Not be Heard: Protecting Mature Minors from Parental Wiretaps,* 104 Geo. L.J. 435, 436 (2016).

the company and its external environment, improving firm performance through its ability to assist in managing the company's business. ④[45]

5. **The sanctions'[46] sole success appears to be a symbolic one: establishing the legal principle that employment of unauthorized workers is itself a legal violation (one that penalizes both employers and employees) and underlining the nation's commitment to border control.**

Are private enforcement laws an effective immigration law policy? Though many of these laws are of recent vintage, we can draw upon lessons learned from federal employer sanctions. ① These sanctions provide a good case study because they have been implemented nationally, with substantial federal resources, and their impact over twenty-one years has been widely studied. ② What the studies show is that the sanctions have not deterred illegal immigration, have not resulted in any significant punishment of law-breaking employers, and have caused substantial discrimination against employees. ③ But as employer sanctions continue to be plagued by numerous enforcement problems, the viability of even that symbolism is at risk. ④[47]

EXERCISE 2.D.2. Paragraph Scramble

The following sentences are pulled from a student's essay exam answer. Although these sentences create a unified and cohesive paragraph, they are not in the proper order. Put numbers next to the first (1), second (2), third (3), fourth (4), and fifth (5) sentences in the paragraph.

(If you would like to learn more about how to organize the ideas in a legal analysis, see Part II, Chapter 4.)

_____ As the organizer of the party, Carol is a social host.

_____ As a result of this special relationship, social hosts owe a duty of care to their guests to protect them from unreasonable risks of harm.

_____ If a social host breaches this duty and there is causation between the host's actions and the guest's injury, the social host may be liable in negligence.

---

[45] Lubomir P. Litov, Simone M. Sepe, and Charles K. Whitehead, *Lawyers and Fools: Lawyer-Directors in Public Corporations*, 102 GEO. L.J. 413, 419-20 (2014).

[46] A sanction is a penalty for disobeying a law.

[47] Pham, *supra* note 15, at 803.

_____ The issue in this case is whether Carol is liable in negligence for the head injury that Alice sustained when she attended the party hosted by Carol and fell while rollerblading over a bump on Carol's property.

_____ Social hosts have a "special relationship" with their guests.

E. Paragraph Length

You may have previously learned that paragraphs should be three to five sentences long. While this rule of thumb holds true for most academic legal discourse, some paragraphs are shorter and some are longer. Short paragraphs of two sentences or only one sentence may be seen in introductory, concluding, and transition paragraphs. But such short paragraphs tend to be the exception, not the rule, when it comes to academic legal discourse.

Paragraphs can also be longer than three to five sentences. Trying to squeeze a lot of information into a single paragraph can backfire, however. If you do too much, you run the risk of overwhelming your reader. In many cases it makes sense to break up a long paragraph into two or more paragraphs organized around smaller, sub-ideas.

Read again Section III.A. of *Catching the Unique Rabbit*, reprinted below. As you will see, the writer organizes this section of her article as follows:

- **Paragraph 1**: A short introduction to the idea of emotional distress claims as compensation for pet loss.
- **Paragraph 2**: A discussion of the first test to evaluate emotional distress claims.
- **Paragraph 3**: A discussion of the second test.
- **Paragraphs 4 and 5**: A discussion of the third test.

The writer also includes a brief conclusion for the section at the end of Paragraph 5. As you read, consider why the writer might have decided to use two paragraphs for the third test as opposed to only one.

III. CURRENT SUGGESTED SOLUTIONS AND THEIR INADEQUACIES

A. Why Allowing Emotional Distress Damages for Pet Loss Fails

(1) Allowing a pet owner to recover for his or her emotional distress over the loss of a pet is one primary focus of current reform efforts aimed at fully compensating pet owners. But emotional distress, either as a category of recoverable damages or as a separate cause of action, in most jurisdictions fails to compensate the pet owner for his or her loss. The reason that the emotional distress argument fails to provide a remedy for pet owners is that the three standard tests used to evaluate emotional distress claims are not well suited to address pet loss or injury claims.

(2) Under the traditional test, or impact test, damages can be recovered for emotional distress only where the defendant's misconduct has resulted in physical contact with the victim (i.e. plaintiff), causing fear and anxiety as well as a physical injury, no matter how slight. Under the impact test, a plaintiff could only then recover for his or her own mental distress affiliated with the contact, not the derivative fright or grief because their pet was touched.

(3) Under the second test, the zone of danger test, the plaintiff does not have to prove an actual touch or impact, but instead has to show that he or she was placed in immediate risk of harm due to the defendant's misconduct. Here, again, the stress is on the plaintiff's fear of harm to *his or her own body* and not the fear or grief over injury to a pet. If, for example, a person was walking a dog and the dog was injured by a car while both the owner and dog were in the cross walk, the owner could recover for his or her own emotional injury. But the owner could not pursue a cause of action or claim as an element of damages for the emotional distress resulting from the injuries to the dog per se.

(4) The most viable argument that supports extension of a negligent infliction of emotional distress claim to pet owners involves the use of the bystander test, which allows the plaintiff to recover if the defendant could have foreseen that his or her conduct would cause emotional distress to bystanders. In this test, the plaintiff can only recover for emotional distress as the result of witnessing, or by physically experiencing, the injury or death of another person. To prevail under the bystander test, plaintiff must prove that he or she was physically in a position to witness the injury, that the resulting shock and mental distress were caused by the contemporaneous observance of the event, and that the plaintiff and the victim were closely related.

(5) At first blush it appears that an owner of an injured pet might be able to recover under the bystander test. Most courts, however, limit the last factor so that only very close (human) relatives can recover. If, for example, a plaintiff was barred from pursing an emotional distress claim due to the loss of a grandchild or sibling in a particular jurisdiction, allowing a pet

> owner to recover for the loss of his or her pet family member would never work. In short, the conservative pace of common law advancement of personal injury remedies will not allow most courts to adopt measures with such specifically human elements for application to personal property, despite the overwhelming emotional reactions inspired by pets in the modern American family.

Following the introduction to this section (Paragraph 1), you may have noticed a pattern. For each of the three tests mentioned in the section, the writer first describes the test and then explains why the test fails to adequately compensate pet owners for the injury or loss of their pets. As for the first and second tests, the writer devotes one paragraph to each (Paragraphs 2 and 3).

However, for her discussion of the third test for evaluating emotional distress claims, the writer splits up her ideas into two paragraphs. Paragraph 4 describes the third test, called the "bystander test." Paragraph 5 then explains why the test fails to compensate pet owners.

Why did the writer place these two ideas in two paragraphs instead of merging them together into one paragraph as she did in Paragraphs 2 and 3? Most likely she uses two paragraphs simply because she has more to say about the third test. Instead of trying to fit a great deal of information into one very long paragraph, the writer has recognized that she can more neatly organize her ideas for the reader if she splits up these two ideas into two separate paragraphs.

As you compose paragraphs, always keep in mind Principle 1 from Chapter 1: Write with Your Reader in Mind. To help you remember this principle, you could think of reading as an act of consumption, much like eating. Instead of food, however, readers consume information—and paragraphs help readers to consume this information in manageable chunks. Paragraphs that are too long may be overwhelming, while paragraphs that are too short may seem insignificant and unsatisfying (not unlike taking big versus tiny bites out of food!). When writing, think about how much information you should put in your paragraphs to help your reader "consume" your ideas. Paragraphs reaching one page or more in length are usually too long for the reader to comfortably digest.

EXERCISE 2.E.1. Breaking up Long Paragraphs

The following paragraphs are long and contain several ideas. Try to break up each long paragraph into multiple paragraphs so that every paragraph is organized around one main idea. Put a slash ("/") before each sentence that you believe signals a new paragraph.

1. The research on teacher quality has grown steadily in the last three decades. The research findings consistently conclude

that teacher quality is among the most significant variables in student outcomes. Although a student's socioeconomic status, along with that of his peers, exerts an enormous influence on educational outcomes, teacher quality is generally recognized as the most important school resource affecting student achievement. In addition, although quality teaching is important for all students, it is most important for disadvantaged students. The challenge, however, has been ensuring that all students have "access to competent, caring, qualified teaching in schools organized for success." Students who need qualified teachers the most—poor and minority students—have the least access to them. Students attending predominantly poor and minority schools are assigned to novice teachers at twice the rate as students in low-poverty schools and predominantly white schools. Likewise, students in disadvantaged schools are taught by "out-of-field teachers"[48] at a much higher rate than other students. The long-term effects of this inequality are tremendous. Consistent exposure to low- or high-quality teachers over the course of years has a compounding effect for individual students and the nation as a whole. One prominent study found that "having a top-quartile teacher rather than a bottom-quartile teacher four years in a row would be enough to close the black-white test score gap."[49] This unequal access is sufficiently pervasive that scholars argue that it depresses overall national achievement.[50]

How many new paragraphs did you create? __________

What is the topic and main idea for each of these new, shorter paragraphs?

2. Americans are feeling the bite of a growing dog population. There are approximately sixty-eight million dogs kept as pets in the United States. Every year, these dogs bite an estimated four to five million Americans, representing about two

---

[48] "Out-of-field teaching" refers to a situation where a teacher teaches a subject in which she does not have an academic major or other kind of certification (e.g., a teacher with a degree in history teaching a biology course).

[49] The "black-white test score gap" refers to a difference between how black versus white children score on tests measuring vocabulary, math, and reading skills (among other skills).

[50] Paragraph adapted from Derek W. Black, *Taking Teacher Quality Seriously*, 57 WM. & MARY L. REV. 1597, 1607-09 (2016).

> percent of the population, and that number is on the rise. The Center for Disease Control warns that, each year, Americans have a one in fifty chance of being bitten by a dog. Children are the most frequent bite victims, representing more than fifty percent of the total number of cases. Nearly half of all American children have been bitten before the age of twelve. Serious dog bites may also be on the rise. Notably, while the dog population increased only two percent between 1986 and 1996, the number of dog bites requiring medical attention rose thirty-seven percent. More than 350,000 victims per year, or nearly 960 per day, seek emergency room care for serious dog bites. In fact, dog bites now rank among the top causes of nonfatal injuries, and are responsible second only to baseball and softball injuries for emergency room visits. The increasing number of dog bites has also negatively impacted the insurance industry. Dog bites account for one-third of homeowner insurance claims nationally, and insurance companies pay out approximately $345 million of the more than $1 billion loss associated with dog bites annually. As a result, companies are amending their homeowner insurance policies, with some attempting to limit or exclude coverage for dog bites. Many are now also refusing to write policies for owners of historically dangerous breeds, and most of those refusing coverage for dangerous dogs include pit bulls on the list of uninsurable breeds. [51]

How many new paragraphs did you create? __________

What is the topic and main idea for each of these new, shorter paragraphs?

This chapter has addressed how to write effective paragraphs: where information is located and how it is presented. The following chapter reviews the principles for clear, well-written sentences, the building blocks of paragraphs.

---

[51] Paragraph adapted from Safia Gray Hussain, Note, *Attacking the Dog-Bite Epidemic: Why Breed-Specific Legislation Won't Solve the Dangerous-Dog Dilemma*, 74 FORDHAM L. REV. 2847, 2849-50 (2006).

Further Reading

THE BLUEBOOK: A UNIFORM SYSTEM OF CITATION (20th ed. 2015).

ANNE ENQUIST, LAUREL CURRIE OATES & JEREMY FRANCIS, JUST WRITING: GRAMMAR, PUNCTUATION, AND STYLE FOR THE LEGAL WRITER (5th ed. 2017).

ELIZABETH FAJANS, SCHOLARLY WRITING FOR LAW STUDENTS: SEMINAR PAPERS, LAW REVIEW NOTES & LAW REVIEW COMPETITION PAPERS (5th ed. 2017).

AMY E. SLOAN, BASIC LEGAL RESEARCH: TOOLS AND STRATEGIES (7th ed. 2018).

JOHN M. SWALES & CHRISTINE B. FEAK, ACADEMIC WRITING FOR GRADUATE STUDENTS: ESSENTIAL TASKS AND SKILLS (3d ed. 2012).

EUGENE VOLOKH, ACADEMIC LEGAL WRITING: LAW REVIEW ARTICLES, STUDENT NOTES, SEMINAR PAPERS, AND GETTING ON LAW REVIEW (5th ed. 2016).

Chapter 3
Sentences

Because words and sentences are the building blocks of paragraphs, it is important to use sentences accurately so that readers can easily understand and think about the ideas conveyed in them. Well-written sentences engage readers and invite them to continue reading on. Poorly written sentences do just the opposite. They frustrate readers and may cause them to give up on reading what you have written.

This chapter presents four principles for effectively conveying your ideas in sentences.

1. Use word order that readers expect and find easy to understand (Section A).
2. Use the correct forms of words so that readers are not confused (Section B).
3. Use correct sentence structures to make your meaning clear (Section C).
4. Vary sentence length and type to enhance the rhythm and flow of your writing (Section D).

These four principles apply to all sentences in academic legal discourse, including those in papers, essay exams, and other writing assignments.

A. Use Word Order That Readers Expect and Find Easy to Understand

Read the following two sentences and think about which sentence is easier for you, as the reader, to follow:

1. After six hours of deliberation[1] about the case, a verdict was reached by the jury[2] that the corporations were guilty of pollution of the river.
2. After the jury deliberated for six hours, it found the corporations guilty of polluting the river.

Did you find yourself re-reading Sentence 1 to get the main idea? Was Sentence 2 easier to understand?

If you answered "yes" to these questions, you are like most readers. Most readers understand sentences best when two key pieces of information are placed at the beginning of a sentence:

1. The main character(s) of the sentence; and
2. The actions that they perform.

Indeed, writing is easiest to follow when information about "who is doing what" is made clear at the very start of the sentence.

In the examples above, the jury is the main character in both sentences. And both sentences convey the jury's actions. But it is easiest to understand this meaning if the words "the jury deliberated" are among the first four words in the sentence. In Sentence 1, you do not get to "the jury" until the fifteenth word. You have to wait and wait to find out the person or idea that the sentence is about. Then you have to go back and forth in the sentence to put together exactly which actions were performed by the jury. In Sentence 2, "the jury found" appear in the beginning of the sentence. You know immediately who this sentence is about (the jury) and what this jury did (it deliberated and then found the corporations guilty).

Sentence 1 is more difficult to understand for two additional reasons. To denote the jury's actions, Sentence 1 uses nominalizations and the passive voice. Below is a description of these two grammatical structures, along with an explanation as to why they may present a challenge for clearly conveying your ideas.

1. The Problem with Nominalizations

A **nominalization** is a noun form of an adjective or verb—for example, "deliberation" for the verb "deliberate" and "pollution" for the verb "pollute."

---

[1] Deliberation is the process by which a jury decides a case. The verb "deliberate" means to carefully think about and discuss a matter.

[2] As you will learn in Part II of this book, a jury is a group of ordinary citizens selected to decide a legal case. A jury's decision is called the verdict. Juries reach a verdict by hearing and seeing evidence in the form of testimony (the questioning of witnesses) or exhibits (physical evidence).

Nominalizations often use the noun word endings "-ion," "-ment," and "-ance" or "-ence." See some examples below:

Verb form		Nominalization
deliberate	⇨	deliberation
investigate	⇨	investigation
agree	⇨	agreement
invest	⇨	investment
insure	⇨	insurance
attend	⇨	attendance
refer	⇨	reference
adhere	⇨	adherence

When an action such as "deliberate" is nominalized, it may be difficult for a reader to understand the writer's point. This is because a nominalization hides who performed an action, since it "swallows up" the doer of the action. In Sentence 1 in the example above, the reader has to make an educated guess that the jury is the one that does deliberation. The reader has to do a bit of thinking to arrive at this conclusion.

Using verbs instead of nominalizations to denote actions makes it easier to understand a writer's point. In Sentence 2 in the example above, the reader does not have to expend much effort to connect the jury with the action of deliberating. The sentence makes this connection clear by linking the character with the actions it performed: "the jury deliberated . . . it found."

Although it is a good idea to think twice before using a nominalization, it is not that you should never use a nominalization. Sometimes a nominalization is the subject of your sentence, as in the following example:

> Congressional deliberations on the federal budget lasted several weeks.

In this sentence, the writer must use the nominalization "deliberation" because this is the topic and grammatical subject of the sentence. This sentence is different from the use of "deliberation" in Sentence 1 above:

> After six hours of deliberation about the case, a verdict was reached by the jury that the corporations were guilty of pollution of the river.

Here, again, "deliberation" is used to describe the action of the jury doing its work. Since the nominalization stands in for an action, the verb form is preferable to the nominalization.

When you catch yourself writing a nominalization in a sentence, ask yourself whether you need to use this form of the word. If the nominalization represents an action, always consider using the verb.[3] Most readers understand sentences best when actions are expressed in verbs instead of nominalizations.

2. The Problem with Passive Voice

Nominalizations are not the only structures that obscure the writer's point. The passive voice is another grammatical construction that conceals "who is doing what" in a sentence.

The **passive voice** helps a writer to emphasize not the doer of an action, but rather the person or thing that is acted upon. The passive voice is a counterpart to the **active voice**, which is the default sentence type in English. In an active voice sentence, the grammatical subject of the sentence corresponds to the character who is performing an action. Read the following example:

> The detectives investigated the murder.
> ⇧
> Subject = doer of action

This sentence begins with the subject "the detectives," who perform the action "investigated." In this active voice sentence, it is quite easy to see who is doing what.

In a passive voice sentence, on the other hand, the grammatical subject of the sentence is not the character that is performing the action, but rather the person or thing that is acted upon. Below is the same example, rewritten in the passive voice:

> The murder was investigated by the detectives.
> ⇧
> Subject = person or thing acted upon

The sentence now begins with the object of the verb: "murder." The characters performing the action ("the detectives") are relegated to the very end of the sentence. Indeed, using the passive voice, the detectives can be deleted from the sentence altogether:

> The murder was investigated.

---

[3] That said, maybe your goal is to conceal the actions of an actor. This may be the case if you represent a client whose misdeeds you do not want to emphasize. Instead of saying, for instance, "When my client robbed the bank, she was under duress," you could say, "When the robbery occurred, my client was under duress." Though your client may well have committed the crime of robbery, you may use the nominalization to obscure this fact. When used strategically, nominalizations can be a powerful tool in the advocate's toolbox.

Because "the detectives" are deleted from this sentence, the reader has to make a guess as to who carried out the investigation.

The passive voice is formed with a "be" verb + the past participle (e.g., "the document is written"; "an agreement was reached"; "the manuscript will be published"). It is the preferred grammatical structure in the following situations:

1. When the writer's goal is to hide who performed an action;
2. When the writer does not know who performed an action; or
3. When it is not important who performed an action.

If none of these situations apply to a sentence, it is best to avoid the passive construction.

Let us look at another example. Read the following two sentences and consider which reads better:

1. A suggestion for the elimination of the second paragraph was made by the professor.
2. The professor suggested eliminating the second paragraph.

For most readers, Sentence 2, written in the active voice, is easier to understand. In this sentence, "who is doing what" is made crystal clear: the professor is making a suggestion. The reader does not have to wait until the end of the sentence to learn who this sentence is about. Further, the act of suggesting is housed not in a nominalization, but rather in a verb.

Sentence 1 is written using the passive voice. It contains two nominalizations, "suggestion" and "elimination." (You may have noticed that nominalizations and the passive voice tend to go hand in hand.) In Sentence 1, the reader has to do extra mental work to link the professor, located at one end of the sentence, to the act of suggesting, located at the other end of the sentence. This can significantly impede the reader's understanding of the sentence.

As a writer, you may feel that Sentence 2 in the example above sounds too simplistic. Perhaps you think that longer sentences containing nominalizations and passive constructions sound better. Indeed, you may have previously learned that long words and long sentences are preferable because they lend writing a certain sophistication. However, long words and sentences often cause readers to scratch their heads to figure out the writer's meaning. If you want your reader to understand and engage with your ideas, surely this cannot be your goal.

As you may recall from Chapter 1, in U.S. academic discourse it is the writer's responsibility to make her meaning clear. As a writer in this setting, aim to write in a way that makes your ideas accessible to your reader. Your ideas and arguments should be nuanced and sophisticated, but your sentences should not be overly complex. If you make your sentences too long and complicated, you will likely lose your reader's attention and interest. In law school, this may cause you to lose points on a paper, exam, or other written assignment. And in professional practice, if a judge or supervisor does not understand your writing, you may lose a case—or worse, an important client.

When you catch yourself using the passive voice in a sentence, ask yourself whether the active voice might be more appropriate to make your meaning clear and easy for the reader to understand.

EXERCISE 3.A.1. Sentence Revision

In each of the sentences below, circle the main character(s) of the sentence and underline any nominalizations that express actions. Next, revise the sentences so that actions are expressed in verbs and characters are performing the actions. You may need to create a character for the sentence.

EXAMPLE

> The usage of the property by the plaintiffs was for the storage of their boat and camper.
>
> *The plaintiffs used the property to store their boat and camper.*

1. The defendant made a referral to Scott Thompson, an insurance broker, so that he could provide my client with advice in buying insurance.
2. The arrest of Mr. Jones was the result of a failure to appear in court.
3. There is an allegation by the plaintiff that the intention of the defendant was the commission of a crime.
4. There was a modification of the order by the judge due to the securement of a job by the child's mother.
5. The protection of customers from the foreseeable criminal acts of third parties is the responsibility of commercial landowners.
6. The belief of the police officer was that the investigation by the detective of the two murders was done superficially.
7. The obligation to pay child support must continue until the graduation from high school of the father's child.

B. Use Correct Word Forms so That Readers Are Not Confused

As a legal academic writer, try to make clear to your reader "who is doing what" in every sentence. Words, grammatical constructions, and sentence structures that obscure this information, or make it difficult for your reader to figure out this information, should generally be avoided—unless, of course, hiding this information is precisely your goal.

To figure out "who is doing what" in a sentence, English readers often look at word endings. There are endings that mark nouns, verbs, adjectives, and adverbs. Table 3.1 summarizes these major word forms.[4]

Table 3.1. Word Forms

	Noun	Verb	Adjective	Adverb
DEFINITION	A noun refers to a person, place, or thing	A verb describes an action or a state of being	An adjective modifies a noun and describes what the noun is like	An adverb modifies a verb, an adjective, or another adverb; it describes how something is or is done
EXAMPLES	lawyer, courtroom, statement	sue, realize, be	innocent, guilty, strategic	quickly, lately, contractually
COMMON ENDINGS	-age, -al, -ance/-ence, -dom, -er/-or, -hood, -ism, -ty, -ment, -ness, -ship, -ion	-ate, -ify, -ize	-al, -ble, -en, -ent, -ful, -ic, -ish, -ive, -less, -ly, -ous, -y	-ly

[4] Nouns, verbs, adjectives, and adverbs are content words. Content words carry meaning, and you can look up this meaning in the dictionary. Content words may be contrasted with function words. Function words create grammatical relationships between content words. They include pronouns, prepositions, and articles. You can think of function words as the "glue" that holds sentences together.

If you use a word without using its correct form, you may confuse your reader. See the following sentence:

> Unlike the inquisitorial legal system in other countries, the U.S. legal system is adversary.

This sentence could pose difficulty for a reader. This is because it is unclear what the writer means by the word "adversary" at the end of the sentence. Does the writer mean that the U.S. legal system *is* an adversary—that is, an opponent—to another system? Perhaps. However, this meaning is unlikely for two reasons.

First, legal systems generally do not have adversaries or opponents—people or nations do. Second, the first part of the sentence, "unlike the inquisitorial legal system in other countries," suggests that the writer seeks to compare the legal system of the U.S. with the legal system of other countries. Even if you do not know what "inquisitorial" means, you can deduce that "inquisitorial" is an adjective used to describe a legal system. In the second part of the sentence about the U.S. legal system, the writer is likely trying to present similar information—that is, a word that similarly describes the U.S. system.

Thus, the writer probably wants to use the adjective "adversarial." An adversarial legal system is one in which opposing sides to a dispute present their arguments to a neutral decision-maker. In an adversarial system, a judge usually plays a passive role at trial and makes sure that legal rules and procedures are followed. The adversarial system can be contrasted with the inquisitorial legal system used in many other parts of the world. In an inquisitorial system, judges take a more active role during trial, investigating the facts of the case and examining evidence. In this sentence, and presumably what follows this sentence, the writer wishes to compare these two different systems of law.

What is confusing about this sentence, then, is that the writer uses the noun "adversary" instead of the adjective "adversarial." As a result, a reader may incorrectly believe that the writer wishes to make a point about the legal system having an opponent of some sort. Because this makes little sense, the reader will probably figure out the writer's intended meaning eventually. The reader might think about the sentence a little bit or read the surrounding sentences to figure out what the writer is trying to say. Unfortunately, however, this requires the reader to do extra cognitive "work." In a Writer Responsible culture, readers do not expect to have to do this kind of work. They expect to understand the writer's point quickly and easily (recall Principle 1 in Part I, Chapter 1: Write with Your Reader in Mind). Academic legal writers strive to compose sentences clearly and accurately so that readers easily understand the ideas and arguments contained in their sentences.

Try to always use the correct form of a word so that you do not confuse your reader. If you are in doubt, check an English-to-English dictionary. Dictionaries are an excellent resource because they often list all possible forms of a word.

EXERCISE 3.B.1. Word Form Identification

The following chart gives you practice in thinking about and using different word forms. The chart lists some common legal terms in only one form of the word. Where there is a blank box in the chart, add the correct form of the word or an "X" if the word does not exist in that form. The first line has been completed for you.

If you do not know the meaning of a word, look it up in an English-to-English dictionary or a legal dictionary.[5] A dictionary may also list other word forms to help you fill in the chart.

Noun form	Verb form	Adjective form	Adverb form
admission	*admit*	*admissible*	*admittedly*
	allege		
appeal			
	assume		
		bankrupt	
	comply		
	confirm		
consideration			
			contractually
	convict		
		equitable	
evidence			
	exclude		
	judge		

[5] See, for example, BLACK'S LAW DICTIONARY.

			innocently
litigation			
	object		
	prosecute		
statute			
testimony			

C. Use Correct Sentence Structures to Make Your Meaning Clear

Different languages have different criteria for what constitutes a sentence. In English, a sentence is a group of words that does two things. First, a sentence contains a subject and a verb. Second, a sentence expresses one complete thought. A writer can put more than one thought in a sentence, but a sentence must have at least one complete thought to function as a sentence.

You may remember the following terms from your English grammar classes:

- **Clause**: A clause is a group of words containing a subject (a person or thing) and a verb (an action or state).
- **Independent clause**: An independent clause is a complete sentence that can stand on its own. An independent clause contains a subject and a verb.
- **Dependent clause**: A dependent clause is not a complete sentence and cannot stand on its own. Though a dependent clause also contains a subject and a verb, it must be connected to an independent clause to be complete.

This section reviews the most common ways to write and link together independent and dependent clauses in sentences. Connecting clauses correctly is essential for making your meaning clear to the reader.

There are four main sentence types in English:

1. Simple sentence;
2. Compound sentence;
3. Complex sentence; and
4. Compound-Complex sentence.

Each of these sentence types are described below and illustrated with sample sentences.

1. Simple Sentence

A simple sentence is made up of one independent clause. This independent clause should contain at least a subject and verb.

EXAMPLE: Lawyers are zealous advocates for their clients.

2. Compound Sentence

A compound sentence is made up of two or more independent clauses. There are three patterns for connecting two or more independent clauses.

Pattern 1: Connect the independent clauses with a coordinating conjunction ("and," "but," "for," "or," "nor," "so," "yet").

EXAMPLE: Lawyers are zealous advocates for their clients, **but** there are limits to what they can do while pursuing their clients' claims.

- You may use a comma before the coordinating conjunction if the first clause is particularly long or if the subjects of the two clauses are different.

Pattern 2: Connect the independent clauses with a period (.) or a semicolon (;). Use a semicolon instead of a period when you wish to link two related ideas and you do not want to create a firm break between them.

EXAMPLE: Lawyers are zealous advocates for their clients**. T**hey work hard to protect their clients' interests.

EXAMPLE: Lawyers are zealous advocates for their clients**;** they work hard to protect their clients' interests.

- You cannot use only a comma to connect two independent clauses. See also Part I, Chapter 5 on editing and proofreading for more information.

EXAMPLE: ~~Lawyers are zealous advocates for their clients, they work hard to protect their clients' interests.~~

Pattern 3: Connect the independent clauses with an independent marker (e.g., "in addition," "however," "therefore"). See Table 3.2 below for a list of independent markers.

EXAMPLE: Lawyers are zealous advocates for their clients; **therefore,** they are usually handsomely compensated.

EXAMPLE: Lawyers are zealous advocates for their clients. **Therefore,** they are usually handsomely compensated.

- You must use a semicolon or period + independent marker + comma with this pattern. You cannot use a comma to link two independent clauses.

EXAMPLE: ~~Lawyers are zealous advocates for their clients, **therefore,** they are usually handsomely compensated.~~

3. Complex Sentence

A complex sentence is made up of independent and dependent clauses. There are several patterns for connecting independent and dependent clauses; three of the most common patterns are listed below.

Pattern 1: Connect the independent and dependent clause by starting with the dependent clause first. The independent clause has been underlined.

EXAMPLE: **Because** lawyers are zealous advocates for their clients, they are often handsomely compensated.

- Dependent clauses always begin with a dependent clause marker. These are words like "because," "before," "since," "while," "although," "if," "until," "when," "after," "as if," etc. See Table 3.3 below for a list of dependent markers.
- With this pattern, use a comma between the two clauses.

Pattern 2: Connect the independent and dependent clause by starting with the independent clause first.

EXAMPLE: Lawyers are often handsomely compensated **because** they are zealous advocates for their clients.

- With this pattern, do not use a comma between the two clauses unless the clauses are particularly long and/or you wish to set apart the ideas contained in the clauses.

Pattern 3: Connect the independent clause to an adjective clause. An **adjective clause** is a type of dependent clause. Adjective clauses usually begin with the adjective clause pronouns "that," "which," "who(m)," or "whose."

EXAMPLE: Lawyers advocate for clients **that/who** need their help.
EXAMPLE: Lawyers must take an exam **that/which** qualifies them to practice law.
EXAMPLE: The lawyer represented a client **whose** house burned down.

Adjective clauses can be placed at the end of a sentence or in the middle of a sentence. Either way, they must always directly follow the noun that they are modifying.

EXAMPLE: She wrote a document **that** detailed her arguments.
EXAMPLE: The document **that** detailed her arguments was in the judge's hands.

- Note that in the second example, the independent or main clause is "The document was in the judge's hands." The dependent or adjective clause is "that detailed her arguments." This adjective clause is inserted in the middle of the independent clause.

The use of commas with adjective clauses depends on whether the writer wishes to do one of the following: (1) provide essential, identifying information about the noun being modified (no commas), or (2) provide merely "extra information" about the noun being modified (commas).

EXAMPLE: The students **who** got an A went out to dinner.
EXAMPLE: The students, **who** got an A, went out to dinner.

- In the first example, only a select number of students received an A, not all of them. The writer is identifying precisely which students went out to dinner: the ones who got an A. The students who did not get an A did not go out to dinner.
- In the second example, all of the students received an A. This meaning is signaled by the commas around the adjective clause. These commas indicate that the information contained in the adjective clause is "extra information" that is not necessary for identifying which students went out to dinner.

Adjective clauses can also be reduced into shorter adjective phrases.

EXAMPLE: Lawyers advocate for clients **that need** their help.
⇨ Lawyers advocating for clients **needing** their help.

Pattern 4: Connect the independent clause to a noun clause. A **noun clause** is a clause that replaces a noun or a pronoun in a sentence. Noun clauses may be in the subject or object position of a sentence.

Noun clauses may begin with a question word (e.g., "who," "what," "where").

EXAMPLE: I wonder **why** she didn't attend class.
EXAMPLE: **Where** the next meeting will be is yet to be determined.

Noun clauses may begin with "whether" or "if."

EXAMPLE: The issue is **whether** the trial court erred.
EXAMPLE: I do not know **if** that case is worth appealing.

Noun clauses may begin with "that."

EXAMPLE: Mr. Cohen discovered **that** someone had stolen his tractor.
EXAMPLE: The defendant is worried **that** the judge will deny his motion.

A detailed discussion of adjective and noun clauses is beyond the scope of this book. We suggest consulting a grammar reference book for more information. See a list of recommended texts at the end of this chapter.

4. Compound-Complex Sentence

A compound-complex sentence is made up of at least two independent clauses and one or more dependent clauses. Compound-complex sentences are simply a combination of the two sentence types. As there are numerous possible combinations, they are not all listed here. Below are a few representative examples.

EXAMPLE: Mariah would like to specialize in labor law and she can pursue this dream **if** she is accepted to law school next year.
EXAMPLE: Erika is upset **because** she lost the case; however, she plans to appeal.
EXAMPLE: The students **who** just finished their exam went out to dinner; they decided to celebrate.
EXAMPLE: Ying made it to the deposition, but she missed the meeting with the big client **that** her firm represents.

Table 3.2. List of Independent Clause Markers for Compound Sentences

Addition	Cause and Effect	Summary/Conclusion
also	accordingly	finally
finally	as a consequence	in brief
first, second, third, etc.	as a result	in conclusion
further	consequently	in short
furthermore	hence	in sum
in addition	therefore	in summary
last, lastly	thus	to conclude
moreover		to sum up
next		to summarize
Contrast	**Illustration**	**Intensification**
however	as an illustration	in fact
in contrast	for example	indeed
nevertheless	for instance	of course
nonetheless	specifically	surely
on the other hand	to illustrate	undoubtedly
		without a doubt
Similarity	**Clarification**	
by the same token	in other words	
in a similar fashion	that is to say	
in the same way	to clarify	
likewise		
similarly		

Table 3.3. List of Dependent Clause Markers for Complex Sentences

Cause and Effect	Condition	Time	
because	even if	after	every time
now that	if	as	once
since	in case	as soon as	since
	only if	as/so long as	until
	unless	before	when
		by the time	whenever
			while
Contrast			
although			
even though			
though			
whereas			
while			

EXERCISE 3.C.1. Sentence Structure Error Correction

Below are several sentences written by students. Each sentence contains an error with respect to sentence structure. Try to identify the errors and correct them so that the sentences are grammatical.

1. For example, no knowledge and no skill.
2. In 2009, after Ahmed had completed high school with a very high grade point average.
3. You should ask Yang she worked on that case last year.
4. A federal grand juror in New York is looking at a possible prison sentence he pled guilty to disclosing details of the indictment to the boyfriend of the woman who was charged with manslaughter.
5. The federal judge struck down the voter ID law. Infringes on the right to vote under the Fourteenth Amendment's Equal Protection Clause. Violates the National Voter Registration Act.
6. The defendant filed a motion for judgment as a matter of law, the judge denied the motion.
7. While this text contains no words, but it has a huge impact.
8. Although, Oliver did not speak French or Russian; he was planning to get from Paris to Moscow, without a phone or a map.
9. Although the plaintiff had a famous lawyer. The defendant won.
10. Priya applied to lots of firms however they rejected her applications.
11. If you want to meet Bob, who is the district attorney.
12. Banning the death penalty for inmates with severe mental illness.

D. Vary Sentence Length and Type to Enhance the Rhythm and Flow of Your Writing

Law professor Richard Wydyck, author of the popular legal writing book, *Plain English for Lawyers*, cautions that "Long sentences make legal writing hard to understand."[6] As you read more and more legal academic texts, you will find that successful academic legal writers heed Professor Wydyck's advice and include only one, two, or at most three ideas in a sentence. Too many long sentences clutter up your writing and may confuse the reader of your text.

Recall from earlier in this chapter the following long sentence:

> After six hours of deliberation about the case, a verdict was reached by the jury that the corporations were guilty of pollution of the river.

Now imagine reading sentence after sentence after sentence like that. Not easy, right?

Long sentences place a heavy burden on the reader to try to understand a text. In a Writer Responsible culture such as the United States, this kind of writing is generally discouraged. (See again Part I, Chapter 1 for a discussion of Writer Responsible versus Reader Responsible cultures.) Professor Wydyck's recommendation is to put no more than twenty-five words within a sentence. Because counting words may be time-consuming, we advise instead that you try not to exceed three lines of text per sentence.

Generally speaking, it is best to keep your sentences short. But if you write only short sentences, your writing will sound choppy, as if you chopped your ideas into tiny little pieces. Read the following paragraph:

> **(1)** There are challenges to the ban on lawyer advertising. **(2)** These challenges began in the middle of the 20th century. **(3)** The challenges were often articulated in First Amendment terms. **(4)** The First Amendment was drafted to protect against government restriction of speech. **(5)** However, in *Valentine v. Chrestensen*, the Supreme Court held that the government can restrict purely commercial advertising. **(6)** The promotion of legal services fell under this category. **(7)** This means that lawyer advertising could be prohibited. **(8)** The Court followed this case for several decades. **(9)** It reconsidered this decision in the mid-1970s.

Nearly all of the nine sentences in this paragraph are simple sentences composed of a single independent clause; the only exception is Sentence 5, which

[6] Richard Wydyck, *Plain English for Lawyers*, 66 CALIF. L. REV., 727 741 (1978).

is a complex sentence. If you try reading the paragraph aloud, you may get the sense of starting and stopping and starting and stopping, kind of like a car stuck in heavy traffic.

To give your reader a smoother reading experience, try to vary sentence length and sentence type. You may leave some of your thoughts in short, simple sentences. But also consider combining other thoughts in longer, compound, complex, or compound-complex sentences. Read the same paragraph, edited to include a mix of short and long sentences.

> **(1)** Challenges to the ban on lawyer advertising, which began in the middle of the 20th century, were often articulated in First Amendment terms. **(2)** The First Amendment was drafted to protect against government restriction of speech. **(3)** However, in *Valentine v. Chrestensen*, the Supreme Court held that the government can restrict purely commercial advertising. **(4)** Because the promotion of legal services fell under this category, lawyer advertising could be prohibited. **(5)** The Court followed this case for several decades until it reconsidered its decision in the mid-1970s.

Sentences (1), (2), and (3) of the original paragraph have been combined into one longer complex sentence: "Challenges to the ban on lawyer advertising, which began in the middle of the 20th century, were often articulated in First Amendment terms." Sentences (6) and (7) from the original paragraph have been merged to create another complex sentence: "Because the promotion of legal services fell under this category, lawyer advertising could be prohibited." Sentences (8) and (9) of the original paragraph have been combined into a compound sentence: "The Court followed this case for several decades until it reconsidered its decision in the mid-1970s." The new version of the paragraph does not seem as choppy as the original. It contains a combination of short and long sentences, giving the paragraph a nice rhythm and flow.

In your writing, try to similarly alternate sentence length and type. Too many long sentences clutter up your writing and may make your sentences and paragraphs hard to understand. Too many short sentences make your writing seem unconnected and jerky. A mix of longer and shorter sentences and sentence types will enhance the rhythm and flow of your text.

EXERCISE 3.D.1. Sentence Length and Type Analysis

Read again the first paragraph of *Catching the Unique Rabbit* on the next page. How long is the longest sentence? How short is the shortest sentence? (For this exercise, it may help to count the number of words in each sentence.)

> **(1)** When billionaire real estate mogul Leona Helmsley died in August 2007, she left behind contradictory images of both a haughty bourgeoisie businesswoman and a generous philanthropist. **(2)** In her will, Helmsley specifically cut out two of her four grandchildren and made her pampered Maltese, aptly named Trouble, the single largest beneficiary. **(3)** The pooch was the recipient of twelve million dollars worth of caretaking expenses via a trust set up for the pet. **(4)** Trouble's trust exceeded Helmsley's second largest bequest by $2 million; the beneficiary for that bequest was her brother. **(5)** In the very same will, Helmsley also directed that her various residences and belongings were to be sold and the proceeds from the sale were directed to benefit a charitable trust left in both her and her late husband's name. **(6)** Helmsley's belongings are reportedly worth billions of dollars.

Circle the type of sentence represented by each numbered sentence in the paragraph: simple, compound, complex, or compound-complex. (See again Section B.1 in this chapter for a review of sentences types.)

Sentence (1):	simple	compound	complex	compound-complex
Sentence (2):	simple	compound	complex	compound-complex
Sentence (3):	simple	compound	complex	compound-complex
Sentence (4):	simple	compound	complex	compound-complex
Sentence (5):	simple	compound	complex	compound-complex
Sentence (6):	simple	compound	complex	compound-complex

Do you think this paragraph reads smoothly? You might try reading the paragraph out loud. If you do not think the paragraph reads smoothly, can you suggest any improvements?

This chapter has outlined four key principles for effectively conveying your ideas in sentences: (1) Use word order that readers expect and find easy to understand; (2) Use the correct forms of words so that readers are not confused; (3) Use correct sentence structures to make your meaning clear; and (4) Vary sentence length and type to enhance the rhythm and flow of your writing. The following chapter addresses transitions, devices for helping to link the ideas expressed in your sentences and paragraphs.

Further Reading

BETTY S. AZAR & STACY A. HAGEN, CHARTBOOK: A REFERENCE GRAMMAR FOR UNDERSTANDING AND USING ENGLISH GRAMMAR (2010).

NIGEL CAPLAN, GRAMMAR CHOICES FOR GRADUATE AND PROFESSIONAL WRITERS (2012).

JAN FRODESEN & MARGI WALD, EXPLORING OPTIONS IN ACADEMIC WRITING: EFFECTIVE VOCABULARY AND GRAMMAR USE (2016).

NADIA NEDZEL, LEGAL REASONING, RESEARCH, AND WRITING FOR INTERNATIONAL GRADUATE STUDENTS (2008).

JOHN B. THORNTON, U.S. LEGAL REASONING, WRITING, AND PRACTICE (2014).

JOSEPH M. WILIAMS & JOSEPH BIZUP, STYLE: LESSONS IN CLARITY AND GRACE (12th ed. 2016).

Chapter 4
Transitions

Read the following short text:

> The Socratic Method is the preferred pedagogy of law classes across the U.S. The Socratic Method is a highly interactive form of teaching that involves asking students a series of questions to challenge their assumptions and promote their analytical skills. It has been used to teach law students since the 1800s. While lecturing, professors stand in front of the classroom and talk to students without asking any questions. Lecturing is often used by professors to clarify a point of law or to share an anecdote from professional practice.

Do you have trouble understanding the writer's point? Or seeing the relationship between the first idea that the Socratic Method involves asking questions and the second idea that lecturing involves *not* asking questions? Don't blame yourself if you do. The reason that you are confused is because the writer has failed to use a transition to show the connection between two seemingly contradictory ideas.

Transitions are words, phrases, and sentences that serve as "bridges between what has been read and what is about to be read."[1] They "help readers move from sentence to sentence . . . [and] also alert readers to more global connections of ideas—those between paragraphs or even larger blocks of text."[2] Without transitions, your ideas may seem scattered and your writing incoherent. It is therefore vital to use them in academic legal discourse.[3]

Now re-read the same, but slightly amended, text:

> The Socratic Method is the preferred pedagogy of law classes across the U.S. The Socratic Method is a highly interactive form

---

[1] Diana Hacker, The Bedford Handbook 103 (1998).

[2] *Id.*

[3] Indeed, this is why we have dedicated an entire chapter to the subject.

> of teaching that involves asking students a series of questions to challenge their assumptions and promote their analytical skills. It has been used to teach law students since the 1800s. **Like the Socratic Method, lecturing is also used by professors in U.S. law schools.** While lecturing, professors stand in front of the classroom and talk to students without asking any questions. Lecturing is often used by professors to clarify a point of law or to share an anecdote from professional practice.

Notice that a sentence has been added in the middle of the paragraph. The paragraph now makes more sense because the relationship between the Socratic Method and lecturing has been made clearer. The sentence, "Like the Socratic Method, lecturing is also used by professors in U.S. law schools" is the bridge between the information we learn about the Socratic Method and lecturing. In particular, the phrase "like the Socratic Method" and the word "also" help us to see that the writer is adding a new idea to the discussion about the Socratic Method. (It should be mentioned that this paragraph would also benefit from a unifying topic sentence. This could be along the lines of: "Professors in U.S. law school employ two methods to teach their students.")

You are probably familiar with transition words such as "however" and "therefore." These are not the only transitions in the writer's toolbox. As shown above, and as you will soon see below, phrases and entire sentences can serve as transitions. Transitions can also bridge texts of various lengths. In this chapter you will learn how to use transitions within a paragraph (Section A) and between paragraphs (Section B)—that is, from one paragraph to the next. You will also learn how to use transitions between sections, which are longer blocks of text that are usually multiple pages in length (Section C).

A. Transitions within a Paragraph

Transitions within a paragraph help to connect ideas from one sentence to the next. There are two main ways to create such transitions. First, writers can use **transition words**, which are individual words or short phrases that highlight the connection between two ideas. Examples include "however," "nevertheless," and "in addition."[4]

Second, writers can link two ideas in a paragraph by using substantive transitions.[5] **Substantive transitions** are words, phrases, and entire sentences that repeat content from another sentence in order to help bridge ideas. The

---

[4] Transition words are also called "independent markers" because they join ideas between two independent clauses. See Part I, Chapter 3.

[5] This terminology is borrowed from ANNE ENQUIST, LAUREL OATES & JEREMY FRANCIS, JUST WRITING: GRAMMAR, PUNCTUATION, AND STYLE FOR THE LEGAL WRITER 53-61 (5th ed. 2017).

example in the introduction to this chapter contains a substantive transition: "Like the Socratic Method, lecturing is also used by professors in U.S. law schools." The repetition of the phrase "Socratic Method," coupled with the words "like" and "also," shows the reader how prior information about the Socratic Method relates to coming information about lecturing: the two methods of teaching are alike.

As shown below, substantive transitions often connect ideas more precisely than transition words can. It is therefore good practice to use transition words in conjunction with substantive transitions on papers, exams, and other writing assignments.

1. Transition Words

Transition words help the writer to link sentences within a paragraph by highlighting the relationship between ideas. Table 4.1 below lists transition words commonly used in academic legal discourse and indicates the logical relationships that they signify.

Table 4.1. Transition Words Commonly Used in Academic Legal Discourse[6]

Addition	Cause and Effect	Summary/Conclusion
also	accordingly	finally
finally	as a consequence	in brief
first, second, third, etc.	as a result	in conclusion
further	consequently	in short
furthermore	hence	in sum
in addition	therefore	in summary
last, lastly	thus	to conclude
moreover		to sum up
next		to summarize
Contrast	**Illustration**	**Intensification**
however	as an illustration	in fact
in contrast	for example	indeed
nevertheless	for instance	of course
nonetheless	specifically	surely
on the other hand	to illustrate	undoubtedly
		without a doubt

[6] Table 4.1 should look familiar. In Part I, Chapter 3, the same words were referred to as "independent markers." We use different terminology here because the focus in Chapter 3 was on the syntactic (grammatical) function of the words, while this chapter focuses on the semantic (meaning) function of the words. The different terms emphasize these different functions.

Similarity	Clarification
by the same token	in other words
in a similar fashion	that is to say
in the same way	to clarify
likewise	
similarly	

Transition words are useful in showing the reader the relationship between ideas. But in using them, keep the following in mind. First, double check that you are using these words correctly. In the following sentence, the transition "in other words" is used improperly:

> The New Hampshire government does not collect income tax or sales tax. **In other words**, it imposes high property taxes to generate revenue.

"In other words" is a transition used to clarify or restate an idea stated in a previous sentence by using different words. In this example, however, the idea in the first sentence (in New Hampshire there is *no* income tax or sales tax) is quite different from the idea in the second (in New Hampshire there *is* property tax). A more appropriate transition to connect these two sentences would be one that shows contrast:

> The New Hampshire government does not collect income tax or sales tax. **However**, it imposes high property taxes to generate revenue.

Also appropriate would be a transition that shows cause and effect:

> The New Hampshire government does not collect income tax or sales tax. **As a result**, it imposes high property taxes to generate revenue.

(Perhaps it is precisely because the government does not collect income or sales tax that it must impose high property taxes.)

It can be difficult to appreciate the subtle differences between transition words. Even two transitions signifying a contrast are not necessarily used in the same context. By reading academic legal texts and noticing how these words and phrases are used in context—and recording these uses in your notes or a language journal—you will get a better feel for how to use these transitional elements in your own writing.

A second word of advice regarding transition words: do not overuse them. As a rule of thumb, you should use no more than one or two transition words per paragraph. See, for instance, the following paragraph:

> The New Hampshire government does not collect income tax or sales tax. **As a result**, it imposes high property taxes to generate revenue. **Indeed**, New Hampshire property taxes are among the highest in the U.S. **However**, this does not mean that the overall tax burden of New Hampshire residents is higher than the average. **In fact**, one recent study found that residents of the state give a relatively low portion of their income to the government. **Specifically**, the state ranks 44th in the U.S. in terms of percent of income paid toward taxes. **Therefore**, New Hampshire residents do not carry a heavy tax burden.

In this paragraph, the writer relies on transition words to make nearly all of the logical connections between the sentences. But if the ideas are logically connected and build on each other, there is usually no need to add transition words to make the connection for the reader. See the same paragraph with four of the five transitions deleted and some of the sentences rearranged:

> The New Hampshire government does not collect income tax or sales tax. It does impose high property taxes to generate revenue, making New Hampshire property taxes among the highest in the U.S. However, the overall tax burden of New Hampshire residents is not higher than the average. One recent study found that residents of the state give a relatively low portion of their income to the government: the state ranks 44th in the U.S. in terms of percent of income paid toward taxes. New Hampshire residents do not carry a heavy tax burden.

Try to think of transition words and phrases as a tool for *emphasizing* the relationships between ideas, not for *creating* the relationships. Too many transition words and phrases in one paragraph can be distracting. It also suggests "faked coherence,"[7] or the idea that a genuine logical connection between the sentences is missing.

EXERCISE 4.A.1. Transition Words

Study the list of transition words in Table 4.1. If there is a word or phrase that you are unfamiliar with, look up its definition in an English-to-English dictionary.

---

[7] Joseph M. Williams and Joseph Bizup, Style: Lessons in Clarity and Grace 75 (12th ed. 2016.)

Also look at example sentences containing the transition in the Corpus of Contemporary American English (COCA).[8] You may type the transition word or phrase into the search box and study the sentences in which the word or phrase appears. This will give you a better sense of the contexts in which the transition is typically used.

Once you have reviewed the transition words, fill in the blanks below with an appropriate transition. More than one answer may be possible.

1. Many states have enacted laws allowing citizens to protect their homes from an intruder. In Florida, ____________________, a person has the right to use "deadly force if he or she reasonably believes that using or threatening to use such force is necessary to prevent imminent death or great bodily harm."[9]

2. [T]here are a significant number of children whose disabilities involve serious behavioral problems. These children can often exhibit aggressive and even violent behavior. ____________________, schools are increasingly using physical restraints to manage these students and maintain safety.[10]

3. The non-disciplinary cases fall into two categories. ____________________, there are those cases in which the buyer is suing to enforce a covenant not to compete. ____________________, there are those cases in which the seller is suing to receive his payment or the buyer is suing to have his obligation set aside. These cases are treated separately.[11]

4. Under Pennsylvania law, if a juvenile is convicted of first-degree murder, she may be sentenced to 35 years in prison. ____________________, a juvenile convicted of first-degree murder in Louisiana must serve a minimum of 35 years.[12]

---

[8] CORPUS OF CONTEMPORARY AMERICAN ENGLISH, https://corpus.byu.edu/COCA/ (last visited Mar. 12, 2019). The Corpus of Contemporary American English (COCA) is a collection of texts containing more than 560 million words. The texts are from different sources, including fiction, magazines, and academic journals (including law reviews). Users can search for words or phrases and the corpus will provide a list of texts containing the word or phrase.

[9] FLA. STAT. ANN. § 776.013 (West 2017).

[10] Sarah Marquez, *Protecting Children with Disabilities: Amending the Individuals with Disabilities Education Act to Regulate the Use of Physical Restraints in Public Schools*, 60 SYRACUSE L. REV. 617, 628 (2010).

[11] Stephen E. Kalish, *The Sale of a Law Practice: The Model Rules of Professional Conduct Point in a New Direction*, 39 U. MIAMI L. REV. 471, 480 (1985).

[12] Cara H. Drinan, *The* Miller *Revolution* 101 IOWA L. REV. 1787, 1818 (2016).

5. Landlords are required to allow a prospective tenant to rent the property unless they have a reasonable basis for the refusal. Reasonable objections are "objective" and include the financial responsibility of the tenant and lawfulness of the proposed use of the property. ____________________, "subjective" factors related to race, religion, or ideology are typically unacceptable.[13]

6. The plaintiff had serious concerns about the treatment plan that the doctor had proposed. ____________________, she signed the informed consent form[14] and agreed to the treatment.

7. Community members had mixed reactions to the proposal that teachers integrate social media into their lessons. ____________________, older community members felt that social media would be a distraction in the classroom. ____________________, younger community members, many of whom grew up with Facebook, Instagram, and Snapchat, supported the idea.

2. Substantive Transitions

Transition words are versatile because their meaning does not depend on context. Wherever you plug them in, they retain their meaning. As a result, transition words are a fairly easy, consistent way to show a reader the relationship between your ideas.

But the versatility of transition words comes at a cost: they sometimes lack precision. The benefit of using substantive transitions instead is that they repeat and summarize content from another sentence (or multiple sentences) to make the link between two ideas clear for the reader.

a. An Example

Re-read the following paragraphs from the introduction to *Catching the Unique Rabbit*. Note the substantive transition underlined in the second paragraph.

---

[13] Daphna Lewinsohn-Zamir, *More Is Not Always Better than Less: An Exploration in Property Law*, 92 MINN. L. REV. 634, 649 (2008).

[14] Informed consent refers to a patient's agreement to a certain medical procedure or course of treatment after the physician presents the patient with information about the patient's diagnosis, available medical interventions, and the risks and benefits of all of the patient's options.

> When billionaire real estate mogul Leona Helmsley died in August 2007, she left behind contradictory images of both a haughty bourgeoisie businesswoman and a generous philanthropist. In her will, Helmsley specifically cut out two of her four grandchildren and made her pampered Maltese, aptly named Trouble, the single largest beneficiary. The pooch was the recipient of twelve million dollars worth of caretaking expenses via a trust set up for the pet. Trouble's trust exceeded Helmsley's second largest bequest by $2 million; the beneficiary for that bequest was her brother. In the very same will, Helmsley also directed that her various residences and belongings were to be sold and the proceeds from the sale were directed to benefit a charitable trust left in both her and her late husband's name. Helmsley's belongings are reportedly worth billions of dollars.
>
> While Helmsley's will appears to be a contradiction of greed and generosity, it is significant in the sense that Helmsley prioritized her beloved dog, her pet, higher than certain human members of her family. Helmsley's attachment to her dog is one example of the important role a pet can play in a family setting. While most pet owners in the United States cannot afford to leave millions to their favorite pets, many pet owners recognize that their pet is part of their family. Just as with other family members, pet owners spend significant sums to ensure their pet's safety, health, and happiness. **Because pet owners go to such great lengths to take care of their pets**, it would seem that these unique living creatures would be valued in the law. In actuality, most owners would be dismayed to learn that should their pet die by being thrown into traffic by an outraged driver, or by suffocation from being left in a sweltering and stifling enclosed area, they could only recover nominal damages for the market value of their pet. They would also be sad to know that should a market even exist, the going rate for an older, previously owned, or impurely bred pet is quite minimal.

The substantive transition in the second paragraph reads, "because pet owners go to such great lengths to take care of their pets." This transition repeats—indeed, it sums up—content from the previous sentences in the two paragraphs. These prior sentences focus primarily on how much money pet owners are willing to spend on their pets, thereby illustrating how important pets are to humans. The phrase "such great lengths" alludes to the striking example of Leona Helmsley leaving twelve million dollars to her pet, described in detail in the first paragraph. So, this substantive transition cleverly links an idea developed over several sentences and paragraphs (pet owners do a lot for their pets, showing how important they are to humans) to a coming idea (one would think pets would be valued in the law, but they are not).

Notably, the writer could have used the transition phrase "as a result" to link her ideas:

> . . . Just as with other family members, pet owners spend significant sums to ensure their pet's safety, health, and happiness. **As a result**, it would seem that these unique living creatures would be valued in the law. . . .

But this transition phrase, though appropriate, does not fully capture the main idea developed over several sentences and paragraphs (again, that pet owners do a lot for their pets, which demonstrates how important they are to humans). In fact, like most transition words and phrases, "as a result" seemingly refers back to only the immediately prior sentence: "Just as with other family members, pet owners spend significant sums to ensure their pet's safety, health, and happiness." The substantive transition, in contrast, encapsulates an idea developed over multiple sentences and paragraphs. The transition phrase alone cannot summarize information the same way that the substantive transition can.

b. The Structure of Substantive Transitions

Although substantive transitions can take on a variety of forms, they tend to contain one or more of the following features. These features appear in a variety of different combinations.

1. "This" or "These";
2. Summarizing phrase;
3. Connecting word; and/or
4. Words from other sentences.

Definitions and examples of these features follow.

"This" + summarizing phrase

One of the most common ways to create a substantive transition is to begin a sentence by using words that refer back to an idea expressed in one or more prior sentences. This is usually done by using the demonstrative pronouns "this" or "these" coupled with a summarizing phrase. A **summarizing phrase** is a phrase that sums up an idea expressed in a previous sentence or sentences.[15]

---

[15] ANNE ENQUIST ET AL., JUST WRITING: GRAMMAR, PUNCTUATION, AND STYLE FOR THE LEGAL WRITER 54-57 (5th ed. 2017).

See how the writer of *Catching the Unique Rabbit* uses "this" + a summarizing phrase in the following paragraph.

> In Stockton and nearby Modesto, California, . . . where the foreclosure rates are the highest in the United States, animal shelters and rescue services are swamped with pets that families can longer afford or house. And although many pet owners consider their pets to be children, human adoption services in Stockton are not reported to be as burdened as are animal shelters. **<u>From this tragic example one can conclude</u>** that pets, although a part of the family, retain subordinate status to human members and therefore retain an element of property and ownership, at least in exigent circumstances.

The transition highlighted in this paragraph is "from this tragic example one can conclude." "Tragic example" is a summarizing phrase: it sums up information conveyed in the previous sentences, namely, that pets are dropped off at animal shelters as a result of home foreclosures. The writer labels this information as a "tragic example"; she then refers back to it using the demonstrative pronoun "this." The writer signals that this tragic example allows readers to draw a conclusion by stating, "From this tragic example one can conclude."

Notably, the writer could have used the transition word "therefore" (or "as a result" or "consequently" or any other transition expressing cause and effect). Read the same paragraph with the transition word "therefore" instead.

> In Stockton and nearby Modesto, California, . . . where the foreclosure rates are the highest in the United States, animal shelters and rescue services are swamped with pets that families can longer afford or house. And although many pet owners consider their pets to be children, human adoption services in Stockton are not reported to be as burdened as are animal shelters. **<u>Therefore</u>**, although pets a part of the family, they retain subordinate status to human members and therefore retain an element of property and ownership, at least in exigent circumstances.

Although "therefore," works in this context, it lacks precision. This is because the transition word does not (it cannot) explicitly state precisely which two ideas are being linked. Thus, in the original text, the writer provides a substantive transition to more directly link one idea (that pets, unlike children, are dropped off at shelters as a result of houses being foreclosed upon) to the next idea (that pets do not have the same status as family members). The strength of substantive transitions lies in their ability to more precisely link ideas.

Connecting word + words from other sentences

Another common way to create a substantive transition is to begin a sentence with a connecting word plus specific words from other sentences. **Connecting words** are usually dependent markers (e.g., "although," "because," "even though") or prepositions (e.g., "despite," "like," "unlike"). As the name implies, connecting words help to connect two ideas much like transition words. Connecting words, however, occur in different grammatical environments.

As you may recall from Part I, Chapter 3, transition words (called "independent markers" there)[16] precede independent clauses:

> She is young. **Nevertheless,** she is a skilled litigator.
> ("Nevertheless" is a transition word or independent marker.)

On the other hand, connecting words precede (and create) dependent clauses:

> **Although** she is young, she is a skilled litigator.
> ("Although" is a dependent marker.)
>
> **Because** she wanted to meet some of the partners at the firm, Rui went to a networking event.
> ("Because" is a dependent marker.)

Connecting words, in the form of prepositions, also precede nouns and noun phrases, including gerunds (verb + "-ing"):

> **Despite** her young age, she is a skilled litigator.
> ("Despite" is a preposition.)
>
> **In addition to** passing the Bar Exam, Mohammed secured a job at a top law firm.
> ("In addition to" is a preposition.)[17]

Table 4.2 summarizes commonly used connecting words.

---

[16] *See supra* note 6.

[17] Some transition phrases can be changed into prepositional connecting words. These include "in addition **to**"; "as a result **of**"; "as a consequence **of**"; and "in contrast **to**." With the addition of a preposition at the end of each phrase, the transition words become connecting words that must be followed by a noun or noun phrase.

Table 4.2. Connecting Words Commonly Used in Academic Legal Discourse

Addition	Cause and effect	Contrast
in addition to	as a result of as a consequence of *because*	in contrast to despite in spite of *even though* *although* *though* unlike *while*
Similarity		
like		

NOTE: Non-italicized words are prepositions, while the *italicized* words are dependent markers.

See how the writer of *Catching the Unique Rabbit* uses a connecting word + words from previous sentences to create a transition in the following paragraph.

> Another reason pets deserve to be classified separately from inanimate personal property and livestock is because of their unique personalities and genetic structures that cannot be duplicated or replaced through the purchase of another animal of the same breed, age, color, weight, etc. Tied in with unique personalities is the unique history of domestication and unique qualities that enable them to respond to and reciprocate human emotions. All of these characteristics mean that pets can create social bonds and foster social and emotional developments in families. **Because pets have such unique characteristics**, they deserve to be classified as inimitable property.

This example contains the substantive transition, "Because pets have such unique characteristics." This transition begins with the dependent marker "because," which signals a cause-and-effect relationship between what has already been said and coming information. The transition also contains key words for the paragraph, "pets" and "unique characteristics." The writer's repetition of these words explicitly connects the idea described in the paragraph as a whole (that pets have unique characteristics) and the writer's proposal that pets should be classified as inimitable property ("they deserve to be classified as inimitable property").

Again, the writer may well have used the transition word "therefore" or any of its synonyms here:

> Another reason pets deserve to be classified separately from inanimate personal property and livestock is because of

> their unique personalities and genetic structures that cannot be duplicated or replaced through the purchase of another animal of the same breed, age, color, weight, etc. Tied in with unique personalities is the unique history of domestication and unique qualities that enable them to respond to and reciprocate human emotions. All of these characteristics mean that pets can create social bonds and foster social and emotional developments in families. **Therefore**, they deserve to be classified as inimitable property.

But the transition "because pets have such unique characteristics" more accurately sums up the idea of the entire paragraph (indeed, this sentence is a conclusion for the paragraph). A lone transition word cannot capture this information with such precision.

Other combinations

Substantive transitions can be created using other combinations of the four features mentioned above. Substantive transitions may also be used in combination with transition words. See the following short examples.

Connecting word + "this" + summarizing phrase

> The patent system has traditionally been viewed as having two primary functions: the reward function and the prospect function. **Although these theories** do explain some behavior which results from the practical applications of the patent system, they also overlook some behavior of the patent system which indicates a failure of these functions.[18]

Connecting word + words from other sentences

> Today the Federal Rules of Criminal Procedure grant federal courts broad authority to punish criminal contempt. **Unlike criminal contempt**, civil contempt has no legislation specifically authorizing or restricting it.[19]

---

[18] Seth A. Cohen, *To Innovate or Not to Innovate, That is the Question: The Functions, Failures, and Foibles of the Reward Function Theory of Patent Law in Relation to Computer Software Platforms*, 5 MICH. TELECOMM. & TECH. L. REV. 1, 2 (1999).

[19] Jessica Kornberg, *Rethinking Civil Contempt Incarceration*, 44 NO 1 CRIMLAWBULL ART 4 (2008).

Transition word + "this" + summarizing phrase

> [P]reventive detention was, and still is, subject to continuing criticism. One difficulty with this measure is the inclination to detain for an indeterminate period too many unsuitable offenders. For instance, prior to the 1970s' reform, a vast majority of people detained in Finland were property crime recidivists. **In addition, this method** is challenged on the grounds of human rights violations.[20]

When adding transitions to connect two ideas in a paragraph, try to use substantive transitions in addition to transition words and phrases. This will make your writing more precise and may in turn enhance the readability of your writing assignments.

EXERCISE 4.A.2. Transition Matching

The following sentences begin with a transition. Match each sentence with its paragraph. Write the letter of the sentence (a-e) in the space provided within each paragraph (1-5).

Which feature(s) of the transition helped you to make your match?

Sentences

a. Because children are in danger due to these types of environmental hazards, decision makers must consider young persons when making public policy and determining environmental standards.

b. However, these children's plight is of humanitarian concern.

c. Despite children's right to procreation, their access to birth control and to abortion can be more easily limited than adult's access to birth control and to abortion.

d. As a result, children are exposed to higher doses of toxins from the environment.

e. For these children, how the court procedurally handles their case determines where they will live and what benefits they may receive or lose.

---

[20] Elena Kantorowicz-Reznichenko, *The Secret of a Cheaper Sentencing System: Lessons from Europe*, 53 NO 2 CRIMLAWBULL ART 4 (2017).

Paragraphs

1. The Supreme Court has also carved out a series of constitutional protections for children. The Court has concluded that the protections afforded minors are more limited than those of their adult counterparts. For example, although children have the right to free speech, what they can read and the circumstances under which they can speak are notably limited, at least in the context of the school environment. Children's right to free expression of their religion is also more restricted than their parent's right to exercise religion. __________ Additionally, although children have the right to counsel in delinquency proceedings that may lead to incarceration and in at least some judicial proceedings arising out of abuse or neglect allegations, children's rights to criminal procedural safeguards such as representation by counsel are severely limited in other types of proceedings because of the context in which these claims arise and the superseding rights of the child's parents to care and control.[21]

2. Being a teenager is already hard enough, but when children find themselves in front of a judge for reasons they may not understand, they are scared and, oftentimes, their future will depend on factors beyond their control. This is especially true for children who fall within the dual jurisdiction of the juvenile court. __________ In California, the fate of dual jurisdiction children is largely dependent upon which county the child is fortunate or unfortunate enough to live in.[22]

3. Why are children likely to be more sensitive to toxic chemicals? Children expend more energy than adults and consequently eat more food, breathe more air, and drink more water per pound of body weight than an adult. __________ Since the dose of toxics per pound of body weight in a child is higher, children are more susceptible to injury from environmental toxins than adults. Additionally, children are growing rapidly and certain toxins cause more damage to rapidly dividing cells. The higher percentage of rapidly dividing cells in a child compared to an adult makes the child more vulnerable to toxins than adults.[23]

---

[21] Sarah Katz, *When the Child is a Parent: Effective Advocacy for Teen Parents in the Child Welfare System*, 79 TEMP. L. REV. 535, 541-42 (2006).

[22] Jessica R. Springer, *Orange County's Answer to the Dual Jurisdictional Dilemma*, 56-NOV ORANGE COUNTY LAW. 30 (2014).

[23] A.C. Zahalsky & P.R. McConnachie, *Comments of an Expert: Biomarker Evidence Following Exposure to Pollutants*, 4 VILL. ENVTL. L.J. 41, 47 (1993).

4. Many toxins enter the water supply, which can be a primary source of exposure to pollutants. Every year millions of Americans drink unsafe water, yet water standards for pollutants are based upon the anticipated effects on adults, and do not satisfactorily protect children from the adverse effects of drinking water. Consequently, children are particularly at risk from drinking contaminated water. __________ Thus, concern that children are in danger from environmental hazards, and the recently emerging focus on children's safety, is long overdue.[24]

5. As is true of all immigration proceedings, adult and juvenile alike, the law does not provide a right to counsel. These children do not have the resources to avail themselves of the relief available if there is no one advocating on their behalf, and virtually all UACs [unaccompanied alien children] are unable to afford paying for representation. Some argue that taxpayers should not be responsible for representation of individuals who have knowingly entered the U.S. unlawfully. __________ Our justice system provides a right to counsel in criminal proceedings regardless of immigration status because we as a society believe life and liberty are fundamental rights. Here, a child's only "crime" is often a desperate attempt to escape persecution and the consequences of being returned to the status quo can be a death sentence. Certainly then, the determinations made by immigration adjudicators in these matters affect these children's life and liberty.[25]

B. Transitions Between Paragraphs

Even the most well-written paragraphs are ineffective in getting one's meaning across if the relationship between the ideas expressed in those paragraphs is unclear to the reader. Thus, it is especially important to add transitions between paragraphs.

Transitions between paragraphs, like transitions within paragraphs, generally come in two forms: transition words and substantive transitions.

1. Transition Words

Writers often begin a paragraph with a transition word to signal to the reader that they are building upon an idea developed in the previous paragraph.

---

[24] Blake P. Temple, *Chapter 731: Protecting the Children of California From Environmental Hazards by Taking Them Into Account When Ascertaining and Implementing Environmental Standards*, 31 McGeorge L. Rev. 438, 440 (2000).

[25] Sara V. C. Goldberg & Joy E. Sanders, *A Place to Call Home: Protecting the Rights of Unaccompanied Immigrant Children*, 48-DEC Hous. Law. 22, 25-26 (2010).

This new paragraph can do any number of things: make a comparison (e.g. "similarly"); draw a contrast (e.g., "in contrast"); describe a result or effect (e.g., "as a result"); provide an illustration (e.g., "for example"); or simply add additional information (e.g., "in addition").

The following example is drawn from a law review article titled *Domestic Violence, Domestic Torts and Divorce: Constraints and Possibilities*. In this article, the author examines the obstacles to tort claims against domestic batterers and offers suggestions to overcome these obstacles. The two paragraphs below are from a section of the paper titled "The Dynamics of Abuse." Here, the writer seeks to explain why battered women stay in relationships despite being abused. Note that the writer uses the transition word "first" to begin the second paragraph.

> For those with relatively little experience or understanding of the dynamics of abusive relationships, confronted with a situation involving prolonged and serious abuse, the first question is often "Why doesn't she leave?" Indeed, expert testimony on battered woman syndrome in self-defense cases was in large measure designed to answer this question—to explain how a woman who reasonably feared for her life could still be living in an intimate relationship with her batterer. The explanations preferred today still draw from that earlier testimony, but in the years since, our understanding both of battered woman syndrome, and of the many other aspects of women's situations that keep them in battering relationships has become more sophisticated and more complicated.
>
> **First**, women do not fall in love with batterers, but with individuals who often treat them with an almost exaggerated respect and attention, and can be extraordinarily appealing. Often, by the time the abuse begins, the woman has already made a strong emotional commitment to the relationship, which is not easy to abandon. It is commonplace for women to decide that the first acts of violence are aberrational, and that the batterers' contrition and vows that the violence will not be repeated are sincere. It is also sometimes easier for women to take responsibility for "provoking" the violence, because then they can imagine that they can control it by making changes in their own behavior, rather than demanding change from their partners. This is all the easier because the batterer, although remorseful, may also be telling her that she caused his outburst.[26]

---

[26] Clare Dalton, *Domestic Violence, Domestic Torts and Divorce: Constraints and Possibilities*, 31 New Eng. L. Rev. 319, 336-37 (1997).

The first paragraph starts with the notion that people may not understand why a woman in an abusive relationship would stay. The writer states that the answer to this question used to be the focus of testimony in self-defense cases (presumably, in cases where a battered woman killed her abusive partner). The writer then goes on to say that "the explanations preferred today" stem from some of this testimony combined with a more refined understanding of battered woman syndrome and "women's situations." The second paragraph answers the question posed in the first paragraph ("Why doesn't she leave?"). In doing so, it provides some explanations for why women stay in abusive relationships. The transition word "first" indicates to the reader that a number of explanations are forthcoming in the paragraph.

In this example, the writer uses a transition word in the beginning of one paragraph to build upon the idea developed in the previous paragraph. Starting paragraphs with transition words in this way is commonplace in academic legal discourse.

2. Substantive Transitions

When used to link two paragraphs, substantive transitions can carry meaning in two directions. They can relate the idea in one paragraph to an idea in a previous paragraph; this is called a **backward-looking transition**. Substantive transitions can also relate the idea in one paragraph to an idea in the next paragraph; this is called a **forward-looking transition**. Substantive transitions may contain both backward- and forward-looking elements within a single sentence.

The following example from *Catching the Unique Rabbit* contains a substantive, backward-looking transition:

> William Blackstone, a forefather of English and American common law, categorized all animals as either *domitae naturae* (domestic animals) or *ferae naturae* (wild animals). Because domestic animals were tame and generally remained close to their owners' homes, their status was defined by their lack of sporadic and frequent movement across property boundaries. Wild animals, however, roam freely without regard to property boundaries, making it much harder (perhaps impossible) for humans to possess absolute ownership rights of these animals. Since ownership of a domesticated animal is linked by definition to the ownership of real property, domestic animals could be owned absolutely.

Backward-looking transition

> **This distinction between domestic and wild animals** is important in the evolution of the classification of companion animals. Originally, pets were classified as

> domestic animals. Owners could not recover for wrongful injury or death of a pet because the pet had no intrinsic worth to the owner. Worth, in this sense, was measured by an animal's contribution to livelihood through farm work, as a source of food through byproducts or their flesh, or as a source of clothing materials and other products made from an animal's body. Value was defined solely by monetary worth because these valuable farm animals could be sold or traded for goods. According to animal rights advocate and animal law expert Gary L. Francione, "the productive value and the property status of animals are inextricably intertwined" because "[t]he value of animals is dependent on their property status."

In the first of the two paragraphs, the writer classifies animals as either "domestic" or "wild" and describes the properties of each. In the second paragraph, the writer states that historically pets were classified as domestic animals. She then moves on to defining the worth and value of domestic animals and explains what this means for compensation if an owner's pet is injured.

At the beginning of the second paragraph, the writer begins with, "This distinction between domestic and wild animals." This is a backward-looking substantive transition that relates the new information in this second paragraph (the ideas of worth and value of domestic animals and what this means for compensation) back to the classification of domestic and wild animals mentioned in the first paragraph. The writer's use of "this," coupled with key words from the first paragraph ("domestic" and "wild"), helps the reader follow and understand the writer's line of reasoning. With this transition, the writer has created a bridge between the ideas contained in the two paragraphs.

Forward-looking and backward-looking transitions also work together across multiple paragraphs. Look at the following excerpt from *Catching the Unique Rabbit* to see how substantive transitions work together to facilitate a reader's understanding of the writer's thought process. In this part of the article, the writer makes arguments as to why the declassification of pets as property—a current solution to the problem of inadequate compensation for pet injury or loss—is ineffective.

> *D. Why the Declassification of Pets as Property Cannot Work in Contemporary America*
>
> Another approach advocated by reformers is derived from focusing more on the rights of the animal rather than the owners. Animal rights advocates suggest that domestic animals should no longer be classified as personal property. The justifications for declassification

are varied, but most stress two common themes. The first is that many people today view pets as family members. The second stresses that sentient animals have inherent worth outside of our property system and have more than just an interest, indeed a *fundamental right,* in being declassified as chattel. At the outset, this seems like a great way to remedy the problem because limits on non-economic damages would no longer apply to the *guardian*—not owner—of a pet. **This suggested solution, however, raises too many practical problems to be deemed a viable remedy.**

Backward and forward-looking transition

1. Activists are Starving to Get Animals Declassified as Property

Backward-looking transition

The first major obstacle to the recognition of animals as possessing fundamental rights to not be considered chattel is that as guardians of animals, livestock owners could not allow their animals to be killed as a source of food. There is also a question about whether guardians of animals such as dairy cows could allow their wards to be milked to produce food, or chickens allowed to produce eggs. One theory predicts that such actions would threaten the health and safety of humans because the current state of food production could not support such a large number of vegetarians, or perhaps vegans, and would lead to malnutrition. Although there could be a distinction drawn between animals traditionally used as food sources and animals used as companions or for other services, it is unlikely that the proponents of declassification would accept such a distinction. The major arguments supporting the declassification of animals as property is that *all* animals have intrinsic rights not to be exploited by humans. This presumption is central to this proposed solution, so that if adopted, no distinction could be made between companions and food sources, and would likely have a negative effect on humans.

2. The Disease of Declassification

Backward-looking transition

Another practical problem affecting the health of humans is the end of medical advancements based on animal research. Although a very sensitive subject with animal rights activists and others, animal research yields benefits to not only humans, but also animals themselves. Great advancements have been made in recent years regarding diseases that affect humans and animals, such as diabetes, that are attributed to biomedical animal research. Furthermore, for the same reasons that distinctions could not be made between food source animals and companion animals, a distinction between laboratory mice and other types of animals also would not be feasible. This would prove fatal to the benefits of animal research because over ninety-five percent of all animal testing is conducted on laboratory mice and rats. Animal testing remains a very controversial issue, however, with many horrible terminal diseases, such as HIV/AIDS, still killing humans, the potential advancements to be garnered from biomedical research seem to outweigh the benefit to laboratory mice of shedding their personal property status.

3. Animal Activists Seeking Progressive Judges

Backward-looking transition

The last practical problem with granting animals autonomy is that judges are extremely reluctant to adopt any approach that radically contradicts centuries of well-developed jurisprudence. Even if adopted by a legislature, it is easy to foresee problems with enforcement and regulation. No longer would the standard be to avoid and punish cruelty. The declassification of animals may include a higher standard of well-being and could very possibly place a heavy burden on both courts and executive branch employees.

In sum, the declassification of animals as property might benefit animals, but would arguably do so at the risk of human health, safety, and well-being, and would present practical problems in both enforcement and regulation. Therefore, the declassification of animals as property is not a practical solution for today's pet owner.

At the end of the first paragraph is a backward- and forward-looking substantive transition. First, the transition refers back to the main idea of the paragraph about declassification of pets as a solution: "This suggested solution, however, ..." Second, the transition forecasts for the reader what is to come in the following paragraphs: " . . . raises too many practical problems to be deemed a viable remedy."

The second part of the sentence indicates (and sets up an expectation) that what is coming next is a list of problems with declassification as a remedy. And indeed, the next paragraphs delineate specific problems with declassification. The writer argues that there are three problems and devotes one paragraph to each.

a. Using Key Words in Substantive Transitions

Notably, each of the next paragraphs—in sections D.1., D.2, and D.3—begins with a backward-looking substantive transition that refers back to key words mentioned in the first paragraph of Section D. Recall that the last sentence of the first paragraph states, "This suggested solution, however, raises too many practical problems to be deemed a viable remedy." "Practical problems" are key words in this sentence and the section as a whole. Not surprisingly, the writer begins every paragraph with either these key words or a close synonym:

> **Paragraph in D.1.**: "The first major obstacle . . . " (synonym for problem)
> **Paragraph in D.2.**: "Another practical problem . . . "
> **Paragraph in D.3.**: "The last practical problem . . . "

The writer helps the reader follow her train of thought and makes it clear that in these paragraphs she is detailing the problems that she alluded to in the first paragraph of Section D. Reusing these key words in the topic sentence of each paragraph helps the reader to see the connection between the ideas contained in each paragraph and the section as a whole.

b. Reminding the Reader of the Topic Under Discussion

In addition to reusing the key words "practical problem" or a synonym, in two of the three paragraphs, the writer also repeats the claim that she is refuting. She does not simply list the problems as follows (assume "X," "Y," and "Z" represent the specific problems she is writing about):

> "The first major obstacle is X."
> "Another problem is Y."
> "The last problem is Z."

Rather, she reminds the reader of the idea that she is challenging in this section—namely, that animals should be declassified as personal property. She uses synonyms to express this idea:

> "The first major obstacle to the recognition of animals as possessing fundamental rights to not be considered chattel is that . . . "
>
> "The last problem with granting animals autonomy is that . . . "

When listing things like problems, reasons, or suggestions, it is good practice to remind the reader of the exact topic being discussed. In the following abbreviated examples, "A" stands for the topic, while "X," "Y," and "Z" stand for a problem, reason, and suggestion.

"The first problem is X."	⇨	"The first problem with A is X."
"The second reason is Y."	⇨	"The second reason for A is Y.
"The final suggestion is Z."	⇨	"The final suggestion for A is Z."

The sample sentences on the right represent the preferred way. This is because reminding a reader of the topic ensures that the reader does not have to go back to an earlier paragraph or section in the paper to remind herself of why the writer is making a list in the first place.

c. Incorporating Transitions into Topic Sentences

In academic legal discourse, it is common to incorporate backward-looking substantive transitions into the topic sentence of a paragraph. Usually, the writer begins the sentence with the backward-looking transition *before* providing information about the new topic of the paragraph. This is consistent with the notion of cohesion introduced in Part I, Chapter 3 on paragraphs. Readers process information more easily when familiar information is presented to them in the beginning of a sentence and unfamiliar information is presented at the end. Thus, it makes good sense to begin the topic sentence with the backward-looking transition and then introduce the topic and main idea for the paragraph.

In paragraphs D.1, D.2, and D3., following each transition, the writer introduces the main idea for the paragraph (that is, the various problems with declassification as a remedy):

> "The first major obstacle to the recognition of animals as possessing fundamental rights to not be considered chattel is that as guardians of animals, livestock owners could not allow their animals to be killed as a source of food."
>
> "Another practical problem affecting the health of humans is the end of medical advancements based on animal research."

> "The last practical problem with granting animals autonomy is that judges are extremely reluctant to adopt any approach that radically contradicts centuries of well-developed jurisprudence."

To facilitate the reader's comprehension of a text, writers often combine substantive transitions with topic sentences in this way.

EXERCISE 4.B.1. Transitions Between Paragraphs

Review the article *Catching the Unique Rabbit* in Part I, Chapter 1. Identify at least five transitions between paragraphs and underline them. Try to find both backward-looking and forward-looking transitions. With backward-looking transitions, has the writer effectively incorporated the transition into the topic sentence of the paragraph?

C. Transitions between Sections

A "section" or "part" of a piece of academic legal discourse refers to just that: a section of text that is unified around one main idea. Long texts, such as seminar papers, law review articles, memoranda, and some exam answers may have multiple sections that are several pages in length. These sections are often further subdivided into smaller subsections organized around sub-ideas.

There are three ways to create transitions between sections:

1. Section headings;
2. Section introductions; and
3. Substantive transitions.

1. Section Headings

A commonly used transition in academic legal discourse is a section heading. A **heading** is a title for a section of a text such as a paper or exam answer. Headings are used for the section as whole (e.g., Section II), as well as any smaller subsections contained within the section (e.g., Section II.A, Section II.B, etc.). Titles for subsections are called **subheadings**.

a. Headings Generally

In academic legal discourse, well-written section headings do two things. They introduce the topic of the section, and they state the writer's main idea for the section.

When students write headings, they often include only the topic, usually in the form of a noun or short noun phrase. Below are examples of headings from three different student-written papers:

> THE CURRENT TAX SYSTEM
> MEDICAL MALPRACTICE CLAIMS
> RESIDENT ALIENS AND ADMINISTRATIVE POSITIONS

Unfortunately, these headings are not particularly informative for the reader. Though they say the "thing" that each section is about, the headings do not reveal what the writer has to say about the topic. What point does the writer want to make about the current tax system? What about medical malpractice claims? And what is the connection between resident aliens and administrative positions?

Below are the same headings re-written to include information about what the writer plans to say about each topic:

> PROBLEMS WITH THE CURRENT TAX SYSTEM
> POSSIBLE SOLUTIONS FOR REDUCING MEDICAL MALPRACTICE CLAIMS
> ARGUMENTS FOR WHY RESIDENT ALIENS SHOULD HOLD ADMINISTRATIVE POSITIONS

Headings that state the writer's main idea for a section are more effective in preparing the reader for what is to come in that section. Hence, they are better transitions. (Two exceptions: an introduction and conclusion, which can be called, simply, "Introduction" and "Conclusion.")

Look again at the headings and subheadings from Part III of *Catching the Unique Rabbit*:

> III. CURRENT SUGGESTED SOLUTIONS AND THEIR INADEQUACIES
>
> *A. Why Allowing Emotional Distress Damages for Pet Loss Fails*
>
> *B. The Problems with Extending a Wrongful Death Cause of Action or Loss of Companionship Damages for Pet Loss*
>
> *C. Applying the* Campbell *Exception to Allow a Large Punitive Damage Award in Pet Loss Cases Is Not a Viable Solution*
>
> *D. Why the Declassification of Pets as Property Cannot Work in Contemporary America*

These subheadings encapsulate not only the topic of each subsection, but also what the writer wishes to say about the topics. As stated succinctly in the section heading ("Current Suggested Solutions and their Inadequacies"), each subsection tackles one solution to the problem of inadequate compensation for pet loss and explains why the solution will not work. The four subheadings capture this idea, making it easy for the reader to follow the writer's train of thought:

A. Why Allowing Emotional Distress Damages for Pet Loss Fails

Topic: Emotional distress damages
Main idea: Emotional distress damages will not work (and why)

B. The Problems with Extending a Wrongful Death Cause of Action or Loss of Companionship Damages for Pet Loss

Topic: Wrongful death cause of action or loss of companionship damages
Main idea: Wrongful death cause of action or loss of companionship damages will not work (and why)

C. Applying the Campbell *Exception to Allow a Large Punitive Damage Award in Pet Loss Cases Is Not a Viable Solution*

Topic: The *Campbell* exception
Main idea: The *Campbell* exception will not work (and why)

D. Why the Declassification of Pets as Property Cannot Work in Contemporary America

Topic: Declassification of pets as property
Main idea: Declassification of pets as property will not work (and why)

b. Headings and Topic Sentences

Headings are similar to topic sentences for paragraphs. Headings introduce the topic and main idea of a section; topic sentences introduce the topic and main idea of a paragraph. Headings, however, should be more concise than topic sentences for paragraphs. Headings are designed to grab the reader's attention and provide a quick snapshot of the writer's main idea for an entire section of a document that may be multiple paragraphs in length. As a general rule of thumb, headings should not exceed two lines of text.

Headings also should not take the place of topic sentences in paragraphs. You cannot assume that a reader will read all of your headings. Sometimes, if a reader gets involved in your arguments, she will skip the headings and just focus on the paragraphs. So, perhaps think of headings like the title of a book. A section heading, like the title of a book, is separate from the accompanying text. You do not have to know the title of a book to understand the information contained in the book. It is the same with section headings and paragraphs.[27]

Figure 4.1. Heading Format (Sample)

PAPER TITLE

(all caps, 14 pt., center)

INTRODUCTION

(small caps,[28] capitalize each word,[29] 13 pt., center)

I. SECTION HEADING

(small caps, capitalize each word, 13 pt., center)

A. SUBSECTION HEADING LEVEL ONE

(small caps, italicize, capitalize each word, 12 pt., center)

1. Subsection Heading Level Two

(capitalize each word, 12 pt, align left)

a. Subsection Heading Level Three

(capitalize each word, 12 pt, align left)

i. Subsection Heading Level Four

(capitalize each word, 12 pt, align left)

CONCLUSION

(small caps, capitalize each word, 13 pt., center)

---

[27] A suggestion: when writing a paper, try to write a first draft without any headings. This will ensure that you do not forget to write topic sentences with transitions in them. You can then add in headings at a later time.

[28] Note that there is a difference between "all caps" (WHICH LOOKS LIKE THIS) and "small caps" (WHICH LOOKS LIKE THIS). If you are using Microsoft Word as your word processor, you will find small caps under the "Format" tab if you click on "Font."

[29] Rules of capitalization dictate that every word should be capitalized except for articles (*a*, *an*, *the*) and prepositions shorter than five words. If any these words begin a title or follow a colon, however, they must be capitalized.

c. Heading Format

In academic legal discourse, there is no set format for headings. Unless your professor gives you specific instructions, you have some freedom in how you format your headings. The key is consistency. If your first section heading uses Roman numerals (I, II, etc.) and is **BOLDED AND CAPITALIZED**, make sure the next section heading at the same level looks the same.

Headings are usually formatted using a combination of letters and numbers. Figure 4.1 depicts the heading format typically used by law review journals.

Under this sample format, the Introduction and Conclusion do not use any numerals—though some writers choose to number these as well. The other main section headings use Roman numerals (I, II, III, IV, etc.). The subsection immediately below the main headings use capital letters (A, B, C, D, etc.). Subsections of capital letter sections use Arabic numerals (1, 2, 3, 4, etc.). Subsections of Arabic numeral sections use lowercase letters (a, b, c, d, etc.). Finally, subsections of Arabic numeral sections use lowercase Roman numerals (i, ii, iii, iv, etc.). You should not add a subsection unless there is more than one. So, for example, there should not be a subsection "A" in a paper unless there is a corresponding subsection "B"; there should not be a subsection "1" unless there is also a corresponding subsection "2"; and so forth.

(More will be said about headings for exam answers in Part II, Chapter 4.)

d. Headings as Sentences

You may have noticed that some of the headings in *Catching the Unique Rabbit* are declarative sentences. For example, the heading for Section III.C reads: "Applying the *Campbell* Exception to Allow a Large Punitive Damage Award in Pet Loss Cases is Not a Viable Solution." Such sentence-form headings are perfectly acceptable, so long as they are concise and do not exceed about two lines of text. Headings in papers and on exams—even if in the form of a declarative sentence—should not contain a period at the end.

e. A Caveat

Although section headings are helpful in forecasting the main idea of a section of text, do not rely solely on headings to create transitions for you. By themselves, headings usually are not enough to "carry" your reader from one idea to the next. It is advisable to use section headings in combination with a short introduction to the section and substantive transitions to make clear the links between the ideas in your section. We turn to these two transition types next.

EXERCISE 4.C.1. Section Headings

Visit the website(s) of your school's law review journal(s). If you do not currently attend law school, visit the law review journal websites of a school that you are interested in attending. Select two or three recently published articles and examine the headings. Are the headings informative? What format do they follow? Do you have any suggestions for improvement?

2. Section Introductions

When a section of a text is particularly long and contains multiple subsections (e.g., on a paper), it is useful to explain to the reader what the writer will be doing in that section. This is usually done by adding a short introduction to the section. This introduction typically contains two elements:

1. A brief statement of the main idea of the section.
2. A **"roadmap"** that lays out for the reader step by step what the writer will be writing about in the section (e.g., "In this section, I will first describe . . . . Second, I will argue . . . . Third, I will conclude . . . ."). This roadmap is a partial version of the roadmap for the entire document, which can be stated in the introduction to a longer document (See Principle 4 in Part I, Chapter 1: Begin with an Introduction and End with a Conclusion).

The second component of the introduction, the "roadmap," is a substantive transition. The roadmap of a section introduction serves as a bridge between a previous section and a new section by preparing the reader for what is to come in the new section.

Roadmaps in academic legal English always contain metadiscourse. **Metadiscourse** refers to the language in a written document that refers to the writer or the text itself. The purpose of metadiscourse is to help the reader understand the organization of the writer's text. Writers may use the first-person pronoun "I" when referencing this organization (e.g., "In this section, I argue that . . . ") or the noun "this section" or "this part" instead (e.g., "This section argues that . . . ").

If you skim *Catching the Unique Rabbit* in Part I, Chapter 1, you will find that it has five parts: Part I, Part II, Part III, Part IV, and Part V. Each part has a title and, with the exception of the introduction (Part I) and conclusion (Part V), is divided into smaller subsections. The writer begins Part IV of *Catching the Unique Rabbit* with a short introduction:

IV. CREATING A VIABLE SOLUTION THAT CAN COEXIST WITH CONTEMPORARY JURISPRUDENCE AND ADEQUATELY COMPENSATE PET OWNERS: ADOPTING INIMITABLE PROPERTY

Forward-looking transition

To be *inimitable* is to be so rare as to surpass or defy imitation. Additionally, to be inimitable means to be without compare and not deserving of imitation. The choice of this word to describe a new, hybrid classification of personal property is important because it conveys the unique personal characteristics of pets that the law currently overlooks. **This section first addresses the shortfalls of leaving pets classified as mere personal property and highlights the need for a new classification system. The section then details the features and advantages of inimitable property as a new classification for pets**.

This introductory paragraph to Part IV of the author's paper is made up of a few sentences containing the following information:

1. The main idea for this section of the paper: inimitable property is a new classification system that takes into account the unique characteristics of pets.
2. A roadmap that forecasts what the writer will do in the section: "This section first addresses . . . . The section then details . . . ."

Section introductions tell the reader the major points and arguments the writer will be making in the section. The roadmap in the paragraph is a useful forward-looking transition because it prepares the reader for what is to come. It is quite common in academic legal discourse, especially in texts with multiple subsections.

EXERCISE 4.C.2. Section Introductions

The following paragraphs are from student-written papers. They each provide an example of a section introduction. Although both paragraphs are well-written, do you think one of them is more effective in preparing the reader for what is to come in the section? Why?

Furthermore, in Example 1, what do you think is the function of the first phrase, "despite the objections mentioned above"?

Example 1

IV. SUGGESTIONS FOR ADOPTING PLEA BARGAINING IN THE SOUTH KOREAN CRIMINAL JUSTICE SYSTEM

Despite the objections mentioned above, many legal professionals are considering adopting plea bargaining in the criminal justice system of South Korea. As there is not enough public consensus on plea bargaining, however, it is desirable to gradually introduce it and borrow from the U.S. plea bargaining model. This part of the paper posits some suggestions for adopting plea bargaining and ways to minimize its drawbacks.

Example 2

II. THE AUTHORIZATION OF MULTIPLE VOTING RIGHTS UNDER FRENCH LAW WOULD OFFER TWO LANDMARK ADVANTAGES

The adoption of multiple voting rights under French law would provide various benefits. First, in Section II.A. I will demonstrate that it would furnish to family companies easier access to the securities market and financing of their activities. Second, in Section II.B. I will explain that multiple voting rights will bestow to the management team of a company the opportunity to focus its efforts on long-term investments without the fear of oppression by potential self-interested shareholders focused on rapid and short-term value.

3. Substantive Transitions

Like the roadmap in the section introduction, substantive transitions between sections also contain metadiscourse, or language that explicitly tells the reader what the writer is doing with the text. These substantive transitions can be either backward-looking or forward-looking.

a. Backward-looking Transitions

The following paragraph is from a law review article titled *Valuable Patents*. The authors of this article analyze what makes patents[30] valuable and outline the

[30] A patent is the exclusive privilege of an inventor to use or sell an invention. A patent is a form of intellectual property.

key characteristics of valuable patents. The paragraph below is the first paragraph in Part III of their paper.

III. WHOSE PATENTS ARE LITIGATED

Backward-looking transition

The previous section focused on the characteristics of the patent itself. In this section, we move up one level of generality and examine who is obtaining the patents in our studies. We tested several different characteristics of patent applicants: whether they are foreign or domestic; whether they are corporations, governments or individuals; how many inventors were named on the patent; and whether the applicant claimed "small entity" status as either an individual, a non-profit, or a small company. All of these factors differed significantly between litigated and non-litigated patents.[31]

The substantive transition in this paragraph ties together the information from the previous section of the paper to the information in this section. Such transitions are useful when a writer wishes to emphasize how the new section builds upon the ideas offered in the previous section (for example, the new section might offer additional information, contrasting information, and so forth).

b. Forward-looking Transitions

Forward-looking transitions that prepare the reader for the next section are more common than backward-looking transitions. As an example, read the following paragraphs from *Catching the Unique Rabbit*. The forward-looking transition underlined here appears in the last paragraph of Part II of the article and prepares the reader for what is to come in the following section, Part III.

Forward-looking transition

Despite efforts to change the current system of compensation by expanding legal remedies and educating tomorrow's attorneys and judges in the nuances of animal law, many state courts have refused to adopt new measures or expand damages for injured pets. Arguments that have not yet been presented to these courts, however, may eventually prove persuasive. **The next section is devoted to understanding the current arguments and strategies for change and explains why**

[31] John R. Allison et al., *Valuable Patents*, 92 GEO L.J. 435 (2004).

> **these fail to correct the under-valuing of injuries to pet owners**.
>
> III. Current Suggested Solutions and Their Inadequacies
>
> *A. Why Allowing Emotional Distress Damages for Pet Loss Fails*
>
> Allowing a pet owner to recover for his or her emotional distress over the loss of a pet is one primary focus of current reform efforts aimed at fully compensating pet owners. But emotional distress, either as a category of recoverable damages or as a separate cause of action, in most jurisdictions fails to compensate the pet owner for his or her loss. The reason that the emotional distress argument fails to provide a remedy for pet owners is that the three standard tests used to evaluate emotional distress claims are not well suited to address pet loss or injury claims.

The transition underlined at the end of Part II tells the reader what to expect next, in Part III. This is helpful in focusing the reader's thoughts and preparing the reader for the writer's coming ideas.

EXERCISE 4.C.3. Substantive Transitions

Read the following sentences containing substantive transitions pulled from law review articles. All of these transitions appear at the end of one section and prepare the reader for information provided in the next section.

Underline the verbs that the writers use to describe what they will do in the following section of their paper. The first example has been done for you.

Copy these verbs into your notes or a language journal. They will come in handy when you have to write your own transitions and roadmaps. As you read more and more legal texts, you can add more verbs to your list. If you are not sure how to use these verbs in your own writing, you can read additional sentences using COCA.[32]

---

[32] Corpus of Contemporary American English, *supra* note 8.

1. The next section analyzes how such a national scheme has been applied successfully to increase the efficiency and uniformity of foreign judgment recognition and enforcement procedures in English courts.[33]

2. The next section will present the state's arguments that its compelling interest in an impartial judiciary outweighs the First Amendment protection accorded candidates for judicial office.[34]

3. The following section of this paper outlines the two defenses available to musicians utilizing samples in a copyright infringement case. . . . The following section also highlights how the fair use and *de minimis* use defenses do not provide samplers or copyright holders with clear guidance of what constitutes copyright infringement and what does not.[35]

4. The next Part explores the ideals theorists claim would be abridged if employers obtained meaningful remedies for employee breaches of contract.[36]

5. As the next section explains, this is too high a burden for state law and is asking an irrelevant question when applied to federal law.[37]

6. Finally, the next Part considers the strengths and weaknesses of alternatives to political process theory advanced in recent legal scholarship and judicial opinions concerning sexual orientation and the Equal Protection Clause.[38]

---

[33] Brian Richard Paige, *Foreign Judgments in American and English Courts: A Comparative Analysis*, 26 SEATTLE U. L. REV. 591, 606 (2003).

[34] Ferris K. Nesheiwat, *Judicial Restraint: Resolving the Constitutional Tension Between First Amendment Protection of Political Speech and the Compelling Interest in Preserving Judicial Integrity During Judicial Elections*, 24 QUINNIPIAC L. REV. 757, 762 (2006).

[35] John W. Gregory, *A Necessary Global Discussion for Improvements to U.S. Copyright Law on Music Sampling*, 15 GONZ. J. INT'L L. 4 (2011-2012).

[36] Christopher T. Wonnell, *The Contractual Disempowerment of Employees*, 46 STAN. L. REV. 87, 98 (1993).

[37] Gwendolyn Mckee, *Injury Without Relief: The Increasing Reluctance of Courts to Allow Negligence Per Se Claims Based on Violations of FDA Regulations*, 83 UMKC L. REV. 161, 202 (2014).

[38] Darren Lenard Hutchinson, *"Not Without Political Power": Gays and Lesbians, Equal Protection and the Suspect Class Doctrine*, 65 ALA. L. REV. 975, 994 (2014).

7. The next part will examine federal court jurisdiction and will describe the Congressional grant of the FDIC's federal jurisdiction in title 12 § 1819(b)(2)(A).[39]

8. The next section of this Article will evaluate the statute and its effect on these individuals.[40]

9. In the next part, I describe two examples from criminal law and the unsuccessful efforts, so far, to change those laws using the old ways.[41]

10. In the next Part, I will introduce an alternative to Chief Justice Rehnquist's invocation of truth.[42]

11. U.S. laws that limit employment at-will are discussed in the next section.[43]

12. As the next part demonstrates, however, combining the fact of prior sovereignty with some version of cultural relativism does not resolve the dispute between proponents and opponents of Indian government; it merely shifts the disagreement onto even more contentious terrain.[44]

13. But as I will detail in the next Part, the bulk of family law cases challenge the idea that more procedure is always better for individual litigants.[45]

14. However, the next Part of this article argues that this theory is insufficient to forbid the genuine use of religious principles in public debate.[46]

---

[39] Nicole Sabado, *Adopting a Jurisdictional Approach to the Rights of Asset Purchasers from the FDIC*, 69 FORDHAM L. REV. 287, 296 (2000).

[40] Cecilia M. Espenoza, *The Illusory Provisions of Sanctions: The Immigration Reform and Control Act of 1986*, 8 GEO. IMMIGR. L.J. 343, 357 (1994).

[41] Paul Butler, *By Any Means Necessary: Using Violence and Subversion to Change Unjust Law*, 50 UCLA L. REV. 721, 728 (2003).

[42] John M. Kang, *In Praise of Hostility: Antiauthoritarianism as Free Speech Principle*, 35 HARV. J.L. & PUB. POL'Y 351, 366 (2012).

[43] Lindsay B. Jackson, *A Lesson from Germany on How the United States Could Reform Its Laws on Dismissal*, 4 GEO. J. L. & PUB. POL'Y 521, 526 (2006).

[44] Patrick Macklem, *Distributing Sovereignty: Indian Nations and Equality of Peoples*, 45 STAN. L. REV. 1311, 1335 (1993).

[45] Rebecca Aviel, *Why Civil Gideon Won't Fix Family Law*, 122 YALE L.J. 2106, 2114 (2013).

[46] Jason Carter, *Toward a Genuine Debate about Morals, Religion, Politics, and Law: Why America Needs a Christian Response to the "Christian" Right*, 41 GA. L. REV. 69, 81 (2006).

15. Can we really characterize these repeat players as medical malpractice specialists? The next Part addresses this question.[47]

This chapter has described how transitions may be used to bridge the ideas from one sentence, paragraph, or section of text to the next. The following, final chapter of Part I of this book addresses editing and proofreading, which represent the final steps in the writing process.

Further Reading

MARY BETH BEAZLEY & MONTE SMITH, LEGAL WRITING FOR LEGAL READERS: PREDICTIVE WRITING FOR FIRST-YEAR STUDENTS (2d ed. 2019).

CATHY BIRKENSTEIN, GERALD GRAFF, TONY CRAINE & CYNDEE MAXWELL, THEY SAY, I SAY: THE MOVES THAT MATTER IN ACADEMIC WRITING (3d ed. 2014).

ANNE ENQUIST, LAUREL CURRIE OATES & JEREMY FRANCIS, JUST WRITING: GRAMMAR, PUNCTUATION, AND STYLE FOR THE LEGAL WRITER (5th ed. 2017).

---

[47] Stephen Daniels and Joanne Martin, *Plaintiffs' Lawyers, Specialization, and Medical Malpractice*, 59 VAND. L. REV. 1051, 1060 (2006).

Chapter 5
Editing and Proofreading

When writing and revising, writers focus primarily on organization and content, making sure to follow academic legal discourse conventions and put forth well-reasoned, well-supported arguments. When editing, writers focus instead on whether the language they use adequately conveys their ideas. They pay particular attention to clarity, precision, and cohesion. Finally, when proofreading, writers check "surface" features of the text to remedy any errors with respect to grammar, spelling, punctuation, or the formatting of the text.

Writing, revising, editing, and proofreading are a bit like building a house. Writing and revising represent building the foundation, installing windows and doors, painting the walls, and so forth. This is the most labor-intensive part of the process. Editing, on the other hand, entails closely inspecting an already finished house to check that the foundation is solid, the windows and doors are sealed properly, and the paint is the right color—and making alterations as necessary.

After constructing a home, inspecting it, and making changes, dust and debris may collect. This needs to be cleaned and swept away so that the home looks clean and ready to go on the market. The same goes for writing. The last step of the writing process is proofreading. Proofreading involves checking to make sure that the grammar, punctuation, spelling, and formatting in the text is correct and consistent. You can think of proofreading as the final "clean-up" before submitting your document.

Though they come at the end of the writing process, editing and proofreading are undeniably important. If your professor cannot understand your train of thought because of errors, inaccuracies, or inconsistencies in your language use, surely you cannot score in the top of your class. Similarly, if your supervisor cannot understand the argument laid out in a client's defense, your boss may become frustrated (and perhaps assign the case to someone else). It is therefore essential that you edit and proofread all of your documents. This advice applies not only to papers, but also to exams, even if you have only one or two minutes to spare.

This chapter addresses how to edit and proofread your documents. The chapter first covers editing on the paragraph and sentence level, as well as how to ensure that smooth transitions have been provided for the reader (Section A).

The chapter then outlines ways to proofread documents for grammar, punctuation, spelling, and formatting conventions (Section B). Finally, the chapter closes with suggestions for editing and proofreading timed, in-class final exams (Section C).

A. Editing

Editing involves carefully reading over an already written document to see whether it follows appropriate writing conventions and whether the text reads clearly and easily. Editing happens *after* the writer has written a complete draft of a document and revised it to be sure her ideas are clearly organized and presented.

While editing, writers apply the principles and conventions covered in Chapters 2, 3, and 4 in Part I of this book. Recall that in Chapter 2 on paragraphs, you learned that paragraphs in academic legal discourse have the following four features:

1. Paragraphs begin with a topic sentence;
2. Paragraphs contain sentences that support and elaborate upon the topic sentence;
3. Paragraphs are unified around one main idea; and
4. Paragraphs exhibit cohesion, with each sentence building upon the sentence that came before it.

Recall as well that in Chapter 3 on sentences, you learned four principles for writing effective sentences:

1. Use word order that readers expect and find easy to understand;
2. Use the correct forms of words so that readers are not confused;
3. Use correct sentence structures to make your meaning clear; and
4. Vary sentence length and type to enhance the rhythm and flow of your writing.

Finally, recall that in Chapter 4 on transitions, you learned of three ways to create transitions between your ideas:

1. Transitions within paragraphs;
2. Transitions between paragraphs; and
3. Transitions between sections.

When writing a paper, exam, or any other document, keep in mind all of these principles and features of academic legal English. That said, try not to spend too much time while writing to check that you have followed them. Making sure that each sentence, paragraph, or transition is "perfect" before moving on to the next one is not only time consuming, but also potentially counterproductive. As you re-read and revise your document, you may have to add or delete ideas—and hence entire sentences or paragraphs—if, for example, the ideas in those sentences or paragraphs are no longer relevant to your line of argument. You do not want to get too attached to a sentence or paragraph that you spent hours perfecting only to have to delete it later on.

When writing, first try to get your ideas down. Make sure that the foundation of your paper, exam answer, or other piece of writing is solid. Pay particular attention to the "big picture" and whether you have followed the five key principles of academic legal discourse outlined in Part I, Chapter 1. These principles are:

1. Write with Your Reader in Mind;
2. Start with Your Main Idea;
3. Support your Ideas with Evidence;
4. Begin with an Introduction and End with a Conclusion; and
5. Show Every Step of Your Thinking.

Once you feel confident in the structure and content of what you have written, begin editing your text by applying the more specific principles and features of academic legal discourse covered in Part I, Chapters 2, 3, and 4.

1. Editing Checklist

One of the most effective ways to edit a document is by using a checklist. A checklist is a list that contains action items which you must perform. As you move through the list, you can check off ("✓") any item that you have addressed. People often use checklists to organize their daily schedule. Such a checklist might contain the following items: buy groceries, pick up dry cleaning, and go to a doctor's appointment.

A checklist can also be useful for editing and proofreading documents. This is because the checklist serves as an important reminder of key areas for which you should edit your paper, exam, or other written assignment. As you move read through and edit your document, you can check off any items that you have addressed.

On the next page is an editing checklist that you may use to edit your assignments and, if time permits, your essay exams. The checklist covers the following areas: paragraphs, sentences, and transitions. Note that under each heading in the checklist are the principles and characteristics of academic legal discourse covered in Part I, Chapters 1 through 4. These are the areas to pay attention to while editing your documents.

Editing Checklist

PARAGRAPHS

- ☐ ***Begin with a topic sentence.***[1]
- ☐ ***Support topic sentences with evidence.***[2]
- ☐ ***Unify paragraphs around one main idea.***
- ☐ ***Write cohesive paragraphs.***

SENTENCES

- ☐ ***Use word order that readers expect and find easy to understand.***[3]
- ☐ ***Use the correct forms of words so that readers are not confused.***
- ☐ ***Use correct sentence structures to make your meaning clear.***
- ☐ ***Vary sentence length and type to enhance the rhythm and flow of your writing.***

TRANSITIONS

Try to use the following transitions to help your reader see the connections between your ideas:

- ☐ ***Transitions within paragraphs***
- ☐ ***Transitions between paragraphs***
- ☐ ***Transitions between sections***

2. Using the Editing Checklist

After you have written a draft of your document, you can use the checklist above in two ways. One option is to go through the text and apply each of the points one by one. That is, read your document once to check for topic sentences. Then read your document a second time to check your supporting sentences.

---

[1] Introductory, concluding, and transition paragraphs may not have topic sentences. See again Part I, Chapter 2.

[2] The most common types of evidence in academic legal discourse include examples, descriptions, explanations, definitions, statistics, and reference to authority. Review Part I, Chapter 2 for more detail.

[3] Specifically, begin sentences with characters and actions and watch out for nominalizations and the passive voice. Review Part I, Chapter 3 for more detail.

Then read your document a third time to check that your paragraphs are unified around one main idea. And so on.

A second option is to re-read your document but apply only those points that tend to pose a particular challenge for you. For instance, you may have no problem using correct word forms, but you might struggle with creating smooth transitions between your paragraphs. If so, you could focus primarily on transitions and disregard word forms (unless, of course, you notice a word form error while reading—then you should fix it). This second option is useful for experienced writers who are familiar with their strengths and weaknesses. If you are still new to academic legal discourse, you may wish to stick to the first option until you get a better sense of where your strengths and weaknesses lie.

EXERCISE 5.A.1. Editing

Using the checklist above, edit a document that you have recently written. As you edit, you may change or replace words, modify word order, add punctuation, and shorten or combine sentences. How many edits did you make? Did you find the checklist useful?

B. Proofreading

Editing entails re-reading a document closely to ensure that the paragraphs, sentences, and transitions in the document follow the principles and conventions of academic legal discourse. The primary goal of editing is to create a document that is clear and easy for the reader to understand.

Proofreading is a little different. When writers proofread, they focus on surface features of English: grammar, spelling, punctuation, and the formatting of their document. Proofreading, as mentioned in the introduction to this chapter, is akin to cleaning or polishing; it is the very last step of the writing process. This section provides information and suggestions for proofreading your documents for grammar, spelling, punctuation, and formatting.

1. Proofreading for Grammar

As with editing, it is a good idea to use a checklist as you scan documents for common grammar errors. The checklist below contains suggestions for how to proofread your documents for grammar. The grammar points in the checklist represent errors most commonly found in international students' academic legal discourse. Below each grammar point is an illustration and brief explanation of how to apply the relevant grammar rule.

If you wish to review any of the grammar rules contained in the checklist in greater detail, you are invited to peruse the reference books listed at the end of this chapter.

a. Grammar Proofreading Checklist

1. Verbs

Verbs are one of the most important parts of a sentence, doing the work of describing people, things, actions, and events.

☐ ***Provide a verb in every sentence.***

INCORRECT: The Bar Exam tests students on a variety of subjects. **For example, property and torts.**

- The second sentence is referred to as a sentence fragment. It is incorrect because the sentence is missing a verb.

CORRECT: The Bar Exam tests students on a variety of subjects. **For example, property and torts questions appear on the exam.**

☐ ***Be consistent in your use of verb tenses.***

INCORRECT: The plaintiff filed suit against the defendant doctor last year. She alleged that the doctor was negligent because he **does not warn** her of the drug's side effects.

- "Does not warn" is incorrect because it is the simple present simple tense, while the other sentences describe past actions, using the simple past tense.

CORRECT: The plaintiff filed suit against the defendant doctor last year. She alleged that the doctor was negligent because he **did not warn** her of the drug's side effects.

2. Subject-Verb Agreement

Standard word order in English is subject-verb-object. A subject is a person or thing that a sentence is about. The verb is what the subject does or is. The object is a person or thing that is affected by the verb. In the sentence, "She passed the exam," "she" is the subject, "passed" is the verb, and "the exam" is the object. Note that a sentence must have at least a subject and a verb, but it need not have an object.

☐ ***Make your subjects and verbs agree.***

INCORRECT: The statute **provide** that violators must pay compensation.

- "Provide" is incorrect because it does not agree with its subject "the statute," which is a third person, singular noun. An "s" must be added to the end of the verb.

CORRECT: The statute **provides** that violators must pay compensation.

3. Pronoun Reference

A pronoun is a word used to refer to a noun. There are different kinds of pronouns in English, but the most common are subject pronouns ("I," "you," "he/she/it," "we," "you," "they") and object pronouns ("me," "you," "him/her/it," "us," "you," "them").

☐ ***Make your pronouns agree with the nouns to which they refer.***

INCORRECT: The regulations required foreigners to be domiciled in the country in order to acquire resident status, but **it** did not expressly require them to have a stay permit.

- The word "it" incorrectly refers back to "the regulations" in the beginning of the sentence. The pronoun should be "they" since "the regulations" is plural.

CORRECT: The regulations required foreigners to be domiciled in the country in order to acquire resident status, but **they** did not expressly require them to have a stay permit.

4. Clauses

A clause is a group of words that contains a subject and a verb. An independent clause is one that is a complete sentence on its own. A dependent clause is not a complete sentence on its own; it must be attached to an independent clause. Both types are addressed below. See also Part I, Chapter 3 for examples.

☐ ***Do not use a comma to separate two independent clauses.***

INCORRECT: The court granted the defendant's motion**,** the plaintiff appealed.

- The comma is incorrectly used in this sentence. Two independent clauses must be separated by either a period (.), semicolon (;), or coordinating conjunction ("and," "but," "for," "nor," "or," "so," "yet").

CORRECT: The court granted the defendant's motion**.** **The** plaintiff appealed.

OR: The court granted the defendant's motion**;** the plaintiff appealed.

OR: The court granted the defendant's motion**, and** the plaintiff appealed.

☐ ***Do not let a dependent clause stand on its own.***

INCORRECT: The plaintiff will be compensated for his injury. **Although his compensation will be reduced by his share of fault.**

- The second clause is a dependent clause because it begins with the dependent clause marker "although." A dependent clause—which always begins with a dependent clause marker (e.g., "although," "because," "even if," "while," etc.)—must be attached to an independent clause to form a complete sentence.

CORRECT: The plaintiff will be compensated for his injury **although his compensation will be reduced by his share of fault**.

5. Articles and Nouns

There are two types of articles in English: (1) the indefinite article "a" or "an," and (2) the definite article "the." There are also two types of nouns in English: (1) countable nouns that are countable in the grammatical sense because there is a plural form of the word (e.g., one table, two tables, etc.), and (2) non-countable nouns which are not countable in the grammatical sense because there is no possible plural form of the word (e.g., money).

☐ ***Use an article ("a"/"an" or "the") in front of every countable, singular noun.***

INCORRECT: Mr. Vargas argued that this was not contract.

- If a noun is countable and in singular form, it will always require an article before it. "Contract" is a singular, countable noun. Therefore, it should be preceded by "a," "an," or "the." Which of the three articles is used depends on the word and the context.

CORRECT: Mr. Vargas argued that this was not **a** contract.

☐ ***Use the indefinite article ("a"/"an") in front of the first mention of a countable, singular noun that is not known to the reader.***

INCORRECT: Mr. Vargas retained lawyer.

- Because "lawyer" is a countable, singular noun, it must be preceded by an article. Assuming that this is the first mention of this lawyer to the reader, "a" should be used.

CORRECT: Mr. Vargas retained **a** lawyer.

☐ ***Use the definite article ("the") in front of a noun that is known to the reader because it has already been mentioned.***

INCORRECT: Mr. Vargas retained a lawyer. **A** lawyer had experience with medical malpractice cases.

- The lawyer is introduced in the first sentence and mentioned a second time in the second sentence. Because the lawyer is now known to the reader in the second sentence, the definite article "the" should be used here (and every subsequent mention of the lawyer).

CORRECT: Mr. Vargas retained a lawyer. **The** lawyer had experience with medical malpractice cases.

☐ ***Use the definite article ("the") in front of a noun of which there is only one in a particular context.***

INCORRECT: She argued a case in front of Supreme Court.

- As there is only one Supreme Court, this noun should be preceded by the definite article "the." Similarly, use the definite article with nouns such as "the legislature," "the president," and "the government."
- Note that there are multiple supreme courts (and legislatures, presidents, and governments) in the world. However, your use of "the" assumes a particular context or place—such as the United States. What this context or place is should be made clear to the reader reading your document.
- Further note that it is also possible to use the indefinite article "a" or "an" in front of the nouns "supreme court," "legislature," and so forth. This can be done when writing about these nouns in the abstract (e.g., "**A** supreme court usually hears cases in the area of constitutional law").

CORRECT: She argued a case in front of **the** Supreme Court.

☐ ***Do not use "a"/"an" or a plural form with a non-countable noun.***

INCORRECT: The lawyer presented **evidences** to the jury.

- The word "evidence" is not a countable noun in English. As a result, it is ungrammatical to use a plural form. It is also ungrammatical to say "an evidence." Instead, it would be possible to say "some evidence," "an item or piece of evidence," or simply, "evidence."

CORRECT: The lawyer presented **evidence** to the jury.

☐ ***Use a plural form with a countable noun when making a generalization.***

INCORRECT: Do you think the government should censor **film** and **book**?

- This writer is speaking about censoring not one film and not one book, but rather films and books in general. In such situations, a plural form of a countable noun should be used.

CORRECT: Do you think the government should censor **films** and **books**?

6. Passive Voice

The passive is formed with the verb "be" + the past participle. For example: "The brief <u>was written</u> by Singh." This is in contrast to the active voice. The same sentence stated in the active voice would be: "Singh wrote the brief."

The passive voice is used to emphasize some ideas and de-emphasize others. It allows the writer to minimize or "hide" what someone or something has done. The passive voice tends to be used in three situations: (1) when the writer does not know or care who the doer of an action is (e.g., "thousands of phones are sold every day"); (2) the writer wants to focus attention on the object of an action (e.g., "my client was arrested"); or (3) the writer wants to strategically conceal who performed an action (e.g., "the wallet was stolen").

☐ ***Use the passive voice when beginning a clause with the <u>object</u> of a verb.***

INCORRECT: The treaty provision **violate** by two member states.

- The active form of this sentence would read: "Two member states violated the treaty provision" ("two member states" is the subject, "violated" is the verb, "the treaty provision" is the object).

- The passive voice is used when the writer wishes to start a clause with the object of a verb. If "the treaty provision" is moved into the subject position of the sentence, as it is here, the passive voice must be used.

CORRECT: The treaty provision **was violated** by two member states.

☐ ***Use the passive voice only with transitive verbs.***

INCORRECT: She was taken to the emergency room after the accident **was occurred**.

- Transitive verbs are those that can take grammatical objects. For example, "eat" is a transitive verb because it can take an object: "She ate the food" ("she" is the subject, "ate" is the verb, and "the food" is the object).
- The passive voice can only be formed with transitive verbs. The verb "occur" is an intransitive verb (just like its close synonym "happen"). As an intransitive verb, it cannot take grammatical objects. As result, the passive voice cannot be used with this verb.

CORRECT: She was taken to the emergency room after the accident **occurred**.

7. Parallel Structure

Parallel structure is the repetition of a grammatical form in a sentence. Repeating items or ideas in a sentence using the same grammatical form adds clarity to writing and enhances the readability of your documents.

☐ ***Use parallel structure to connect two or more items in a list.***

INCORRECT: This technique consists of **stopping** a person on the streets because he looks suspicious, **interrogate** the person, and **to search** the person for weapons.

- The verbs "stop," "interrogate," and "search" represent three separate items in a list. To make it easier for the reader to understand this complex sentence, the writer needs to use parallel grammatical form. In this case, that form is the gerund (verb + "ing"), as required by the phrasal verb "consist of."

CORRECT: This technique consists of **stopping** a person on the streets because he looks suspicious, **interrogating** the person, and **searching** the person for weapons.

b. Using and Adapting the Grammar Proofreading Checklist

The checklist above contains grammar points that tend to be problematic for many international students, but it is not one-size-fits-all. You may have different strengths and weaknesses than the checklist above suggests. For instance, you might have no trouble with sentence structure and clauses generally, but you may struggle with nouns and articles. You might also find that the checklist does not contain a particular grammar point that is difficult for you. For example, you may have trouble with the prepositions *at* versus *on*; however, prepositions are not listed above.

When proofreading, you should focus on the areas that tend to be problematic for you. Thus, you can modify the checklist above so that you are proofreading your documents for errors related to the grammar points that *you* find particularly troublesome. Adapting the checklist to suit your needs allows you to proofread your documents more effectively because you will be checking for errors that *you* tend to make.

EXERCISE 5.B.1. Using and Adapting the Grammar Proofreading Checklist

Proofread a written assignment (paper, exam answer, memorandum, etc.) using the grammar proofreading checklist provided in this chapter. Go through each item in the checklist. That is, first read through your entire document, making sure that there is a verb in every sentence. Next, read through your document, making sure that you are consistent in your use of verb tenses. Third, read through your document, making sure that all of your subjects and verbs agree, and so forth, all the way until you have proofread your document for each of the items on the checklist. This may take a couple of hours.

After you have finished, take stock of your proofreading strategy. How helpful were the items in the checklist? Were any items unnecessary? Were you able to combine any items? Are there any grammar points that you would like to add?

Using the simplified version of the checklist below, modify it to suit your own proofreading needs. Cross out any items that you feel you DID NOT need and add any items you feel you DID need. You may add items under the grammar points already provided or add your own grammar point(s). If you cross out an item on the list, your document should contain ample evidence that you do not have trouble with that particular grammar point.

Grammar Proofreading Checklist

VERBS

- ☐ ***Provide a verb in every sentence.***
- ☐ ***Be consistent in your use of verb tenses.***

SUBJECT-VERB AGREEMENT

- ☐ ***Make your subjects and verbs agree.***

PRONOUN REFERENCE

- ☐ ***Make your pronouns agree with the nouns to which they refer.***

CLAUSES

- ☐ ***Do not use a comma to separate two independent clauses.***
- ☐ ***Do not let a dependent clause stand on its own.***

ARTICLES AND NOUNS

- ☐ ***Use an article ("a"/"an" or "the") in front of every countable, singular noun.***
- ☐ ***Use the indefinite article ("a"/"an") in front of the first mention of a countable, singular noun that is not known to the reader.***
- ☐ ***Use the definite article ("the") in front of a noun that is known to the reader because it has already been mentioned.***
- ☐ ***Use the definite article ("the") in front of a noun of which there is only one in a particular context.***
- ☐ ***Do not use "a"/"an" or a plural form with a non-countable noun.***
- ☐ ***Use a plural form with a countable noun when making a generalization.***

PASSIVE VOICE

- ☐ ***Use the passive voice when beginning a clause with the <u>object</u> of a verb.***
- ☐ ***Use the passive voice only with transitive verbs.***

PARALLEL STRUCTURE

- ☐ ***Use parallel structure to connect two or more items in a list.***

OTHER:

- ☐ ____
- ☐ ____

2. Proofreading for Punctuation

Proofreading for punctuation involves scanning your document for errors related to punctuation use. This section addresses appropriate use of the following punctuation marks in academic legal English:

Comma	,
Semicolon	;
Period	.
Quotation marks	" " and ' '
Question mark	?
Hyphen	-
Em dash	—

Take the quiz below to determine what you already know about punctuation use in English. Answers to the quiz and brief explanations follow the quiz.

EXERCISE 5.B.2. Punctuation Quiz

Read the following sentences and mark whether you believe they are grammatically correct (C) or incorrect (I). If you think they are incorrect, try to fix them. Pay attention to punctuation in particular.

1. _____Yang took property, evidence, criminal law, and torts.
2. _____She submitted the memo on May 27 2018.
3. _____The defendant moved for summary judgment, however, the judge denied the motion.
4. _____Participants in today's workshop will learn when to make a complaint; how to file the paperwork; and whom to contact for a follow-up appointment.
5. _____The lawyers submitted the following documents: a memorandum and a report.
6. _____Intentional torts include: assault and battery.
7. _____Since the terms are 'commercially unreasonable', the contract should not be enforced.
8. ____ Maria testified that she "didn't drink alcohol that night."

9. ____ The professor asked, "What are the facts?"

10. _____ Does this qualify as an "excused violation?"

11. _____ Jo began to suffer "migraine symptoms"; as a result, she contacted her physician.

12. _____ The judge stated, "I will apply the 'preexisting duty rule.'"

13. _____ A second year student won the award.

14. _____ Officials refused to prepare a deed of sale—a prerequisite for the legality of such transactions—because they were concerned that the non-citizen spouse would occupy the property.

Answer Key and Explanations

1. _____ Yang took property, evidence, criminal law, and torts.

This sentence is **CORRECT.**

Items in a list should be separated by commas. Before the final item, the word "and" or "or" must be used. The final comma between the words "criminal law" and "and" is referred to as an Oxford comma. This comma is optional.

2. _____ She submitted the memo on May 27 2018.

This sentence is **INCORRECT.**

With dates, a comma should be inserted between the day and year.

Correct version: She submitted the memo on May 27, 2018.

3. _____ The defendant moved for summary judgment, however, the judge denied the motion.

This sentence is **INCORRECT.**

There are two independent clauses here: "The defendant moved for summary judgment" and "however, the judge denied the motion." As discussed in Section A of this chapter, two independent clauses may not be separated by a comma. A period (.) or a semicolon (;) should be used instead. Semicolons are appropriate when the ideas expressed in the independent clauses are closely related.

Correct version: The defendant moved for summary judgment; however, the judge denied the motion. OR: The defendant moved for summary judgment. However, the judge denied the motion.

4. _____ Participants in today's workshop will learn when to make a complaint; how to file the paperwork; and whom to contact for a follow-up appointment.

This sentence is **CORRECT.**

Semicolons may be used in lieu of commas when stating items in a list. Semicolons are preferred instead of commas when the separated items are particularly long; when the items are clauses; or when the items contain commas (e.g., "She went to the grocery store to buy fruit, such as bananas; to pick up some bread, including her favorite, sourdough; and to check the price of fish.").

5. _____ The lawyers submitted the following documents: a memorandum and a report.

This sentence is **CORRECT.**

A colon is properly used after (1) an independent clause or (2) introductory words like "the following," "as follows," or "namely." Colons are used when the material following the colon explains, illustrates, or expands upon the information provided before the colon.

6. _____ Intentional torts include: assault and battery.

This sentence is **INCORRECT.**

A colon should not be used between a subject and its verb, or a verb and its object. Here, "assault and battery" are the object of the verb "include."

Correct version: International torts include assault and battery.

7. _____ Since the terms are 'commercially unreasonable', the contract should not be enforced.

This sentence is **INCORRECT.**

There are two problems here. First, in American English, double quotation marks (“ ”) should be used. Second, commas and periods go INSIDE quotation marks, not outside.

Correct version: Since the terms are “commercially unreasonable,” the contract should not be enforced.

8. ____ Maria testified that she “didn’t drink alcohol that night.”

This sentence is **CORRECT.**
As mentioned above, commas and periods go INSIDE quotation marks.

9. ____ The professor asked, “What are the facts?”

This sentence is **CORRECT.**
Question marks go inside quotation marks if they are part of the quoted material. Here, the writer is quoting a question (What are the facts?). The question mark is part of what is being quoted. Therefore, the question mark should go inside the quotation marks. There is no need for an additional period at the end of the sentence.

NOTE: Use a comma after a reporting verb (e.g., say, state, ask, etc.) and before the quotation. E.g., His client said, “I have nothing to hide.” A colon may also be used after the reporting verb if the quote is longer. E.g., His client said: “I have nothing to hide. I am willing to cooperate with the investigation because I am completely innocent. If this goes to trial, I don’t see how a jury could ever convict me.”

NOTE: Capitalize the first letter of a direct quote if the quoted material is a complete sentence. If the quoted material is only part of a sentence, such as a word or phrase, use a lowercase letter. E.g., His client said that he has “nothing to hide.” Further note that in this example, no comma is used before the quotation because the quotation is grammatically incorporated into the sentence. A reporting verb (e.g., say, state, ask, etc.) is not used.

10. _____Does this qualify as an “excused violation?”

This sentence is **INCORRECT.**
Here, the quotation mark should not be placed inside the quoted material, “excused violation.” The sentence as a whole (beginning with “Does this

qualify. . .") is a question. Therefore, the question mark should go OUTSIDE the quotation marks.

Correct version: Does this qualify as an "excused violation"?

11. _____Jo began to suffer "migraine symptoms"; as a result, she contacted her physician.

This sentence is **CORRECT.**

Although periods and commas always go inside quotation marks, semicolons (;) and colons (:) never do.

12. _____The judge stated, "I will apply the 'pre-existing duty rule.'"

This sentence is **CORRECT.**

When placing a quotation within a quotation, single quotation marks should be used. Here, "pre-existing duty rule" is a quotation within the longer quotation, "I will apply the . . . ." Note that the end punctuation is the period, to end the quoted sentence; the single quotation mark, to end the quotation within a quotation; and finally the double quotation marks, to show where the main quotation ends.

13. _____A second year student won the award.

This sentence is **INCORRECT.**

Use hyphens with two-word, compound adjectives before nouns (e.g., child-friendly hotel, sugar-free drink).

Correct version: A second-year student won the award.

14. _____Officials refused to prepare a deed of sale—a prerequisite for the legality of such transactions—because they were concerned that the non-citizen spouse would occupy the property.

This sentence is **CORRECT.**

The em dash is used in two ways. First, it can set off extra information that is not necessary to understand the rest of the sentence. You can think of the material contained within the em dash as a "by the way" remark. This is the way the em dash is used in sentence 14. The phrase "a prerequisite for the legality of such transactions" is extra information about the noun preceding it, "a deed of sale." In this case, commas and parentheses could also be used instead of the em dash, but to slightly different effect. Parentheses tend to minimize the importance of the information contained within them, while the em dash tends to foreground or emphasize the information. Commas are neutral.

Second, the em dash can show a break in a sentence similar to how a comma, semicolon, or colon might be used. E.g., "Officials were very concerned that the non-citizen spouse would occupy the property—they refused to prepare a deed of sale."

3. Proofreading for Spelling

Proofreading for spelling, like proofreading for punctuation, also entails scanning your document for spelling errors. If you use word processing software like Microsoft Word, it will underline most spelling errors with a red wavy line. On occasion, the software will also autocorrect an error with its best guess as to your intended spelling. The spell check feature is very useful; however, overreliance on it can lead to some unexpected spelling errors in your document. A word of advice: do not rely on spell check to do the proofreading for you. Spell check may autocorrect to a spelling you did not intend.[4] Furthermore, it does not catch every spelling error in your document. Carefully proofread your documents yourself.

Below are some words that are commonly misused in academic legal texts. Notably, none of the words are actually misspelled, and spell check would not flag them as problematic. To the right are the words that students typically wish to use in their texts. To the left are the words that they mistakenly type in their document instead. Can you see why such misspellings might be problematic?

adopt – adapt
disposition – deposition
form – from
law – low
statute – statue
trial – trail
waive – wave

To avoid making this kind of spelling error, proofread your documents very carefully. Spelling errors of any kind may negatively affect your grade on a written assignment.

---

[4] For example, one of the author's students submitted a final paper about the constitution of his country. In one sentence, the word "constitution"—presumably misspelled by the student when he typed it—was autocorrected to "constipation."

EXERCISE 5.B.3. Proofreading for Grammar, Punctuation, and Spelling

Each of the following paragraphs contains a number of grammar, punctuation, and spelling errors. Try to identify and correct all of the errors. The number of errors in each paragraph is indicated in parentheses. You may use an English-to-English or legal dictionary to look up unfamiliar terms.

1. In many proximate cause cases, the defendant argues that, even if she was negligent, a later act supersedes her negligence and 'breaks the causal chain.' An example from the casebooks are *Derdiarian v. Felix Contracting Corp*. In *Derdiarian*, the defendant contractor was working in an excavation on a roadway and failed to erect a barrier (such as truck or concrete blocks) to protect workers from traffic. Dickens, an epileptic who had failed to take his medication, suffered a seizure, lost control of his car, and careening into the excavation. This throws Derdirarian into the air, were his body caught fire from a kettle of hot enamel in use for the repairs.[5] **(6 errors)**

2. There are some good arguments for why a violation of a statue should be treated as "negligence per se," that is, negligence in itself. If legislature has decreed that certain precautions must be taken, or that certain acts should not done, a person who violates the statute has ignored the standard of care established by the legislature.[6] **(3 errors)**

3. An injury to one person is likely to cause a variety of emotional reactions in others. A bystander who witness traumatic injury to family member may suffer acute emotional shock form the unexpected, wrenching experience of witnessing serious physical injury to a loved one. She may also experience feelings of grief, loss, sympathize or sadness due to the fact that the immediate victim has injured or killed.[7] **(5 errors)**

4. While cases sometimes refer to a "misuse defense", misuse of a product may effect a strict products liability claim in several ways. Sometimes misuse defeats the plaintiff's prima facie claim because it indicates that the product was not defective, in other cases, it constitutes a from of plaintiff misconduct that reduce or bars recovery.[8] **(5 errors)**

---

[5] Adapted from JOSEPH W. GLANNON, EXAMPLES AND EXPLANATIONS: THE LAW OF TORTS 252 (5th ed. 2015).

[6] Adapted from *Id.* at 145.

[7] Adapted from *Id.* at 303.

[8] Adapted from *Id.* at 379.

4. Proofreading for Formatting

Before submitting a paper or an exam, students usually receive instructions on how to format their assignments. These instructions are either handed out in an earlier class session or attached as a cover sheet to an exam. Instructions typically provide guidelines regarding:

- Document margins (usually one inch);
- Font (type and size);
- Spacing (single or double);
- Word count (maximum and/or minimum);
- Page numbers (whether to provide them and/or location on page); and
- Whether (and how) course and other identifying information should be included in the document (e.g., your name).

Some professors are very particular when it comes to formatting (you may see many guidelines on their assignments), while others are more lax (you may see few guidelines on their assignments). Either way, if a professor gives you instructions on how to format your document, you should follow those instructions.

The best way to avoid mistakes in formatting is pretty simple: read your professor's instructions closely. Most formatting mistakes are made because students do not read instructions carefully enough. Though formatting may seem trivial to you, your professor might be irked by seemingly minor errors or inconsistencies in your document (e.g., if you use Times New Roman font in one section of your paper, but Cambria font in another section).

Law professors occasionally deduct points from assignments or final grades if students fail to follow formatting instructions. This is probably most common when students do not adhere to guidelines regarding word limits (e.g., writing 8,000 words instead of a prescribed 7,000 word maximum). In fact, some professors simply do not read or give credit to any answers beyond the prescribed limit.

a. Formatting Checklist

Once you have finished writing, revising, and editing your document—and proofreading for grammar, punctuation, and spelling—proofread for formatting. An effective way to do this is to utilize a modified checklist approach. This involves the following steps:

1. Begin your assignment or exam by reading the instructions carefully and highlighting or underlining all relevant information about formatting.

2. When you have finished writing, revising, and editing, proofread your document and check off the formatting instructions one by one.

Imagine, for example, the following cover page on a contracts exam:

CONTRACTS FINAL EXAM

Instructions

You have **3 hours** to answer five questions. You may allocate your time as you wish, but it is recommended that you spend some time organizing your thoughts and planning out your response before you begin writing. You are also advised to spend 15 minutes at the end to proofread your entire exam answer.

Take this time to set up your computer.

1. Open a new Microsoft Word document. Type the response in the document and save the document. Do NOT include your name either in the document or file name.
2. Your response may not exceed 7,000 words.
3. Your document must have one-inch margins throughout.
4. Your document must be double spaced.
5. When you are finished typing up your response, upload the file to the course website under "Contracts Final Exam."

THIS EXAM IS CLOSED BOOK. YOU ARE PERMITTED TO USE ONLY AN OUTLINE.

YOU ARE **NOT PERMITTED** TO USE A DICTIONARY OR THE INTERNET DURING THE EXAM.

You would probably want to highlight or underline the following formatting instructions before beginning work on your answer:

- Do NOT include your name in the document or file name;
- Do not exceed 7,000 words;
- Use one-inch margins; and
- Use double spacing.

Then, once you have finished writing and editing your response, and after you have scanned your document for grammar, punctuation, and spelling errors, go back and check that you have followed all four of these formatting guidelines one by one. After you check your document for each guideline—or after you make changes to your document to ensure conformity with a guideline—write a check mark next to that item.

A marked-up, checked-off cover page might look something like this:

CONTRACTS FINAL EXAM

Instructions

You have **3 hours** to answer five questions. You may allocate your time as you wish, but it is recommended that you spend some time organizing your thoughts and planning out your response before you begin writing. You are also advised to spend 15 minutes at the end to proofread your entire exam answer.

Take this time to set up your computer.

1. Open a new Microsoft Word document. Type the response in the document and save the document. Do NOT include your name either in the document or file name. ✓
2. Your response may not exceed 7,000 words. ✓
3. Your document must have one-inch margins throughout. ✓
4. Your document must be double spaced. ✓
5. When you are finished typing up your response, upload the file to the course website under "Contracts Final Exam."

THIS EXAM IS CLOSED BOOK. YOU ARE PERMITTED TO USE ONLY AN OUTLINE.

YOU ARE **NOT PERMITTED** TO USE A DICTIONARY OR THE INTERNET DURING THE EXAM.

b. The Importance of Consistency

When proofreading, it is important to check documents for consistency. Do you use the same spacing in every part of your document? The same margins? The same font type and size? These should be consistent.

Note as well that unless instructed otherwise, you should use black color font throughout your document. When students copy and paste from the Internet, the copied text often turns up dark gray. This dark gray color is usually an indication that the student has copied from another source, which in turn raises serious issues of plagiarism. Plagiarism is not covered in depth in this book, though see Part II, Chapter 4 for paraphrasing techniques in the context of case briefing. Also peruse the titles under Further Readings in Part II, Chapter 4 for more information on plagiarism in law school.

Try to go through your paper with a fine-tooth comb to make sure that your spacing, margins, and fonts are all consistent.

C. Editing and Proofreading During Timed Exams

While the suggestions in this chapter are useful, it is probably not feasible to follow them on a timed in-class exam. If you have only three or four hours to answer several questions, you will not have the time to go through your document using editing or grammar checklists. But this does not mean that you should not edit and proofread what you have written. You will simply need to adapt your approach given the time pressure of the exam.

When writing a timed exam, focus first and foremost on content. Identify the relevant issues and write well-reasoned analyses. Part II of this book provides detailed information about how to write effective exam answers. Do keep an eye on the clock, however, and be sure to leave at least five minutes, but preferably ten to fifteen, for editing and proofreading at the end. When you have finished writing and are ready to edit and proofread your document, quickly scan your answer to check for errors and inconsistencies. If you do not catch every mistake, that is generally okay. Your professor understands that a timed exam answer is not your most polished work. Just do the best that you can.

Luckily, the more practice exams you take under timed conditions, the more adept you will become at writing effective exam answers in a short amount of time, as well as quick editing and proofreading. The practice essay exam questions in Part II, Chapters 5 and 6 of this book will help you to develop these skills.

In this chapter, you learned skills for editing and proofreading your documents. These skills will serve you well in your academic and professional life to ensure that the documents you write conform to the characteristics of U.S. academic legal discourse.

Likewise, by following the principles outlined in Part I, you will be able to create and finalize academic legal pieces that clearly state your ideas to your reader. Understanding U.S. academic legal discourse; exemplifying its features at the whole text, paragraph, and sentence levels; using the right tools to link your ideas together; and thoroughly editing and proofreading your text will safeguard your text against being misunderstood. Your well-written text will also demonstrate that you can write effectively for the U.S. legal community.

Further Reading

BETTY S. AZAR AND STACY A. HAGAN, UNDERSTANDING AND USING ENGLISH GRAMMAR (5th ed. 2016).

NIGEL CAPLAN, GRAMMAR CHOICES FOR GRADUATE AND PROFESSIONAL WRITERS (2012).

BRYAN GARNER, THE REDBOOK: A MANUAL ON LEGAL STYLE (4th ed. 2018).

MEGAN MCALPIN, BEYOND THE FIRST DRAFT: EDITING STRATEGIES FOR POWERFUL LEGAL WRITING (2014).

RUTH ANN MCKINNEY AND KATIE ROSE GUEST PRYAL, CORE GRAMMAR FOR LAWYERS (2011).

Part II

Academic Legal Analysis: Reading, Discussing, and Writing about Legal Cases

Introduction to Part II

Part II of this book is designed to help you acquire the linguistic and analytic skills required to succeed in U.S. law classes. In particular, this part of the book prepares you for courses that use the written opinions of judges—what are commonly referred to as "cases"—as the main source of learning material. This part of the book also prepares you for courses in which grades are based on a final exam. Examples of such case-heavy, exam-based classes include constitutional law, contracts, corporations, criminal law, evidence, property, and torts, to name just a few examples. Many of these foundational courses are mandatory for students enrolled in both J.D. and LL.M. programs. Not coincidentally, many of these subjects are also tested on the Multistate Bar Exam.

In order to develop the linguistic and analytic skills necessary for successful participation in U.S. law classes, you need both a solid understanding of the U.S. legal system as well as familiarity with the pedagogy of law classes. To this end, in Chapter 1: *Foundations of U.S. Law*, you are first introduced to basic concepts in U.S. law and the structure of the U.S. court system. Following this brief introduction, you will be familiarized with the readings (Chapter 2: *Reading Cases*), discussions (Chapter 3: *Discussing Cases*), and writing tasks (Chapter 4: *Writing About Cases*) that you can expect to encounter in a U.S. law class. Collectively, these chapters lay the groundwork for the next two chapters in Part II of the book.

Chapter 5: *Torts* and Chapter 6: *Criminal Procedure* look like a typical casebook that students use in U.S. law classes. A **casebook** is a textbook containing cases in a particular area of law. Unlike texts in other disciplines, casebooks do not lay out and explain legal rules; instead, they contain judicial opinions with little to no commentary or explanation. Using casebooks, students do most of the "heavy lifting" to figure out the legal rules for themselves. It is commonly believed that teaching law using this **Case Method** helps students to acquire the skills needed to analyze legal problems on exams, and ultimately, in the real world of professional practice.

The focus of Chapters 5 and 6 is tort law and criminal procedure law, respectively. Tort law deals with civil wrongs that cause injury or loss, resulting in liability (legal responsibility). Criminal procedure law prescribes the procedures that the government must follow in the enforcement of criminal law. Chapters 5 and 6 contain a number of cases illustrating legal concepts and rules in these two key areas of U.S. law. These chapters also contain tasks and exercises—in reading, writing, discussion, and legal vocabulary—that are designed to build your linguistic competence for participating in law classes and taking final exams. In short, these two chapters provide an opportunity to apply what you have learned in earlier parts of the book on reading, discussing, and writing about cases.

It is important to mention that the purpose of Chapters 5 and 6 is not to familiarize you with the fine details of either tort or criminal procedure law, though you will certainly increase your knowledge of these two subjects. Rather, by completing the readings and exercises in these two chapters, you will develop the skills that will help you better navigate your law classes and do well on law school exams.

Specifically, the cases in Chapters 5 and 6 provide the content for developing the following important skills:

- Working within a common law system in which the written opinions of judges create rules for courts to follow;
- Reading cases and extracting key information from them;
- Using legal terms of art in class discussions and on essay exams;
- Participating in class discussions grounded in the Socratic Method;[1]
- Synthesizing legal rules into an outline and on essay exams answers; and
- Identifying, analyzing, and resolving legal issues on "issue-spotter" essay exams[2] (i.e., legal analysis).

Because our objective in Part II of this book is to familiarize you with the U.S. legal system and legal cases, the book does not focus on enacted law. **Enacted law** refers to laws written by elected lawmakers, including statutes and administrative regulations. While a great deal of U.S. law has been written in the form of enacted law, and U.S. law students read enacted law during law school (particularly in courses such as Evidence or Federal Income Tax), an overwhelming majority of law professors employ the Case Method and use legal cases as the primary vehicle for legal instruction. Accordingly, we believe it makes good sense to prioritize legal cases in this book.

Part II of the book focuses on legal cases for an additional reason. For most international students, judicial opinions represent a new, unfamiliar form of

---

[1] The Socratic Method is a style of teaching in which a professor asks questions of the students instead of giving answers. The rationale behind the Socratic Method is that students learn best when their knowledge and assumptions are challenged through questions, and not when they are "spoon fed" information through lecture. The Socratic Method is the subject of Part II, Chapter 3.

[2] Issue-spotter essay question are the most common type of exam question in law school; they are also the type of questions students can expect to see on the essay portion of the Bar Exam. Such exam questions include a hypothetical factual scenario containing one or more legal issues that the student must resolve using legal rules learned in class. Issue-spotter exam questions are addressed in Part II, Chapter 4.

writing. As a result, this part of the book focuses on familiarizing you with this new text type to give you the skills to effectively read, discuss, and write about legal cases in the U.S. law classroom.

Chapter 1
Foundations of U.S. Law

There are several features of the U.S. legal system that distinguish it from the legal systems of other countries. One distinctive feature of the U.S. legal system is that legal rules are created not only by legislators—that is, elected lawmakers—but also by judges, through their written opinions. Such judge-made law is referred to as common law. Another distinguishing feature of the U.S. legal system is that it is composed of two parallel legal systems: one for the central, federal government and another one for each of the individual states. Finally, a key feature of the U.S. legal system is that it is adversarial. This means that opposing parties to a dispute gather evidence, question witnesses, and make legal arguments to a jury, a group of individuals that decides which side has made the more convincing arguments and hence who should "win" the case.

This chapter addresses each of these three features of U.S. law. It begins with a description of the basic principles of common law (Section A) before providing a brief sketch of the U.S. court system (Section B). The chapter concludes with a discussion of the jury system and the differing roles of the judge and jury at trial (Section C).

A. Basic Principles of Common Law

1. What is Common Law?

Common law refers to legal rules created by judges through their written decisions, called **judicial opinions** or **cases**. In a common law system, when a judge decides a case between two disputing parties, she creates a rule for courts to follow in similar cases in the future. The case becomes **precedent** (pronounced **PREH**-SIH-DINT)[1] for later cases involving similar facts and legal issues. The court,

---

[1] Pronunciation of challenging legal terms are provided in parentheses.

and other lower courts in the same geographic area or **jurisdiction**,[2] are required or "bound" to follow the legal rule established in the earlier case.

The doctrine of precedent is often referred to as ***stare decisis*** (pronounced **STAR**-EE DIH-**SIGH**-SIS). This is Latin for "to stand by things decided." The principle of *stare decisis* is the backbone of U.S. common law. Several areas of U.S. law such as torts, contracts, and property are governed largely by common law rules. The key benefits of requiring courts to follow legal rules established in prior cases are predictability, consistency, and fairness.

Although the United States is often referred to as a common law country, not every legal rule in the United States is judge-made. On the contrary, many rules are written by elected lawmakers such as those sitting in the U.S. Congress or on state legislatures. **Enacted laws** take the form of constitutions, statutes, and administrative regulations. It is somewhat misleading to call the U.S. a common law country because the federal government and individual states have promulgated thousands of enacted laws. Nevertheless, because legal cases feature so prominently in U.S. law school curricula, this book focuses primarily on judge-made common law.

2. How is Common Law Created?

When deciding a legal dispute between two parties, a judge first determines whether there is an enacted law that governs the dispute. This is because rules created by legislatures are more powerful than common law rules created by judges. If a judge—let us call her Judge Smith—identifies such an enacted law, she applies it to the case at hand. In the process, she will often interpret and explain how the law ought to apply. Judge Smith would also try to find prior cases in which other judges have applied and interpreted the same law. She would use these cases to inform her own interpretation.

Sometimes no enacted law governs a dispute. Instead, the relevant rule is contained in an opinion written by another judge—that is, it might be a common law rule. Judge Smith would then apply this rule to the case at hand. She might interpret and develop the original rule in the process.

In still other situations, there is neither a statute (enacted law) nor judge-made rule (common law) to govern the dispute. Such situations are called **cases of first impression**, because the exact legal issue has never been seen or dealt with before in the jurisdiction. Under these circumstances, Judge Smith would likely resolve the dispute by creating a new common law rule.[3]

---

[2] The term "jurisdiction" has a couple of meanings. One meaning of the term, as it is used here, is "a geographic area within which political or judicial authority may be exercised." *Jurisdiction*, BLACK'S LAW DICTIONARY (3d Pocket Ed. 2006).

[3] "Creating" a common law rule could mean making up an entirely new rule, extending a rule from a previous case to a new factual situation, or synthesizing (combining) rules from previous cases to form a coherent rule.

Because many legal rules in the United States are both created and interpreted by judges, law students cannot avoid reading judicial opinions. In fact, the main method of instruction at U.S. law schools is the Case Method. The **Case Method** is built on the idea that students learn law best by reading real-world cases and analyzing the arguments judges make to resolve disputes. Using this book, you will become intimately familiar with the language and structure of legal cases; in addition, you will learn the skills required for reading, speaking, and writing about these cases in your law classes.

What follows is a brief sketch of the U.S. court system, which provides the context for better understanding the cases that you will be reading in this book and throughout law school.

B. The U.S. Court System

1. Hierarchy of Courts

The U.S. court system is made up of different levels of courts, namely, trial and appellate (pronounced UH-**PELL**-IT) courts. Judges sitting on these courts have the authority to do different sorts of things.

Disputes are first heard in **trial courts**. This is where each party—the plaintiff[4] and defendant—has the opportunity to argue her case by presenting evidence in the form of **testimony** (the questioning of witnesses) or **exhibits** (physical evidence). Each trial is overseen by one **trial judge** who acts much like a referee in a sporting event.

Trial judges have three main duties. First, they pay careful attention during trial to make sure that the parties and their attorneys follow rules of procedure and evidence. Second, they rule on motions. **Motions** are requests made by the parties—for example, to exclude certain kinds of evidence. Finally, trial judges apply pre-existing enacted or common law to resolve the case. In a jury trial, trial judges "instruct" the jury on what rules to apply to help the jury make its decision (more on the role of the jury in Section C below).

Importantly, trial judges do not create law.

If a party is dissatisfied with a trial court's decision, in certain situations she can **appeal** to a higher court. These higher courts are called **appellate courts**. The judges sitting on appellate courts are, appropriately enough, called **appellate judges**. Appellate courts have varying numbers of appellate judges depending on the jurisdiction.

By and large, the role of appellate judges is to review lower court decisions to determine if the lower court judges made any mistakes in applying and

---

[4] In a criminal case there is no plaintiff. Rather, the government (state) initiates legal proceedings.

interpreting legal rules. To help make their determination, appellate judges read written arguments (called appellate briefs) and hear oral arguments by attorneys for opposing sides to the dispute. Appellate judges typically **affirm** (agree with) or **reverse** (disagree with) the lower court's decision. Appellate judges use only the factual evidence that was presented at trial to make their determination. They do not retry a case, and they typically do not hear any new evidence. In the process of reviewing lower court decisions, appellate judges write judicial opinions in which they interpret pre-existing rules and/or create new common law rules to resolve the dispute.

Unlike trial judges, appellate judges _do_ have the power to create law through their written opinions.

Figure 1.1. Hierarchy of Courts

Level of court	Term of address for judge	Number of judges	Role of judge
TRIAL COURT	Judge + last name (e.g., Judge Rodriguez)	1	• Ensure that parties are following rules of procedure and evidence • Rule on motions • Apply pre-existing rules to resolve the case and/or instruct a jury on what rules to apply to resolve the case
INTERMEDIATE APPELLATE COURT	Judge/Justice + last name (e.g., Judge Kim or Justice Kim)	Varies, depending on jurisdiction A panel of 3 judges usually reviews case	• Review lower court decisions • Read appellate briefs and hear oral arguments • Write judicial opinions
HIGHEST APPELLATE ("SUPREME") COURT	Justice + last name (e.g., Justice Marshall)	Varies, depending on jurisdiction (usually 5-9 justices) The full court usually reviews case	• Review lower court decisions • Read appellate briefs and hear oral arguments • Write judicial opinions

In most jurisdictions, there are two levels of appellate courts: intermediate appellate courts and the highest "supreme" court.[5] Appellate judges sitting on intermediate appellate courts usually review cases in panels of three judges. Appellate judges sitting on the highest court review cases **en banc** (pronounced ON-**BONK**), that is, as a full court. Judges on the highest court, and sometimes on an intermediate appellate court, are called **justices**.

2. Federal and State Courts

The United States was founded on the principle of **federalism**, or the idea that two levels of government should manage the affairs of the country. On the one hand, there is a federal government with limited power to govern issues of national importance, such as money making and war. On the other hand, smaller individual state governments address more local issues, such as public health and education.[6] The founders of the United States set up such a federalist system because they were concerned that one central government would be too powerful.

The concept of federalism is reflected in the legislative and judicial branches of government. On the legislative side, there are both federal and state legislatures. Similarly, on the judicial side, two hierarchical court systems run in parallel: a federal system comprised of federal courts, and a state system made up of state courts.

a. Federal Courts

Federal courts have limited jurisdiction. The term "jurisdiction" in this context means the authority to hear a case.[7]

Trial courts in the federal system, called **U.S. District Courts**, have jurisdiction over two main types of cases. First, they have authority to resolve questions arising under the U.S. Constitution or a federal law. This is called **federal question jurisdiction**. In a case brought under federal question jurisdiction, one party usually claims that the other party violated the Constitution or a federal law. Examples of federal law includes the Civil Rights Act, the Fair Housing Act, and the Immigration and Nationality Act.

Second, federal courts have power to hear cases in which the disputing parties are citizens of different states (U.S. or foreign) *and* the amount in controversy—that is, the amount of money at stake—exceeds $75,000. If both of these conditions are met, the federal court can hear the case regardless of the

---

[5] Depending on the jurisdiction, these courts have different names.

[6] For a brief, but thorough discussion of federalism, see Justice Roberts' opinion in National Federation of Independent Business v. Sebelius, 132 S.Ct. 2566, 2576-80 (2012).

[7] This is a different meaning of the term "jurisdiction" than provided in note 2 above.

subject matter involved. The dispute does not have to involve a question of federal law. This is called **diversity of citizenship jurisdiction**.

There are also more specialized trial courts in the federal system, including U.S. Bankruptcy Courts, the U.S. Court of International Trade, and the U.S. Court of Federal Claims (this court hears money claims,[8] usually involving tax refunds).

Cases in the federal system are first heard in 1 of 94 U.S. District Courts or the specialized trial courts named above. Appeals are sent to one of 13 **U.S. Courts of Appeals**, which typically review cases to determine if the District Courts made any mistakes in applying legal rules. The location of both District Courts and Courts of Appeals are, for the most part, geographically determined. There is at least one District Court in every state, though some states have multiple District Courts.

Courts of Appeals are organized into 13 "circuits" (see circuit map below). Twelve of these circuits are regional—that is, based on geography. However, one circuit, the U.S. Court of Appeals for the Federal Circuit, is located in in Washington, D.C. This court has the authority to review cases from all U.S. District Courts and it often handles matters related to patents.

Figure 1.2. U.S. Courts of Appeals

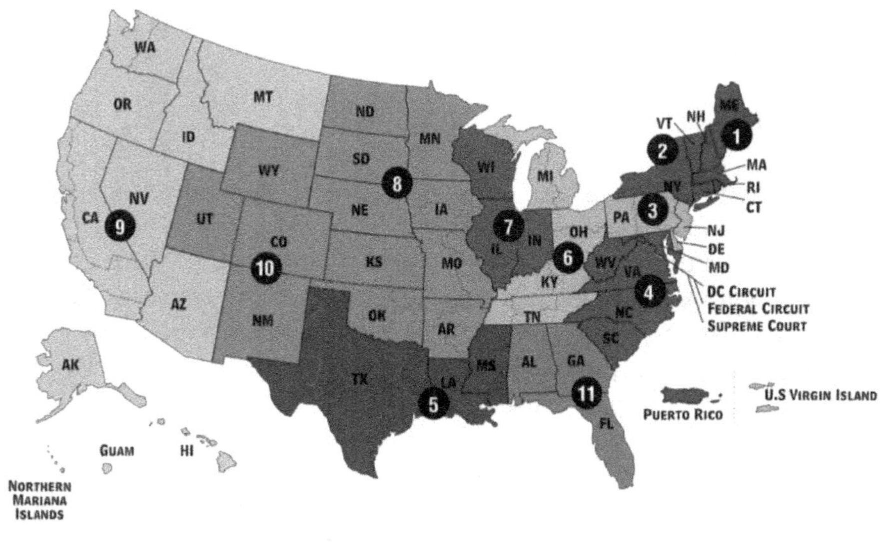

Source: *U.S. Federal Courts Circuit Map*, U.S. COURTS, http://www.uscourts.gov/sites/default/files/u.s._federal_courts_circuit_map_1.pdf (last visited May 3, 2018).

---

[8] A claim is the plaintiff's assertion that she is entitled to money damages or other remedies.

Appeals from U.S. Courts of Appeals are made to the U.S. Supreme Court, the highest court in the United States. Appeals to the Supreme Court are not guaranteed. Dissatisfied parties must request the court to review their case through a **petition for a writ of certiorari** ("certiorari" is pronounced SIR-SHEE-EH-**RAH**-REE). A petition for a writ of certiorari is a document asking the Supreme Court to review a case to determine if lower courts made any mistakes in interpreting or applying legal rules. The Supreme Court has the freedom to **grant** or **deny** certiorari; it is generally under no obligation to review any particular case. This is called **discretionary review**. When the Court does grant certiorari, it is usually because the case involves issues of national importance, such as gun control or marriage equality.

Figure 1.3. The Federal Court System

SUPREME COURT	**U.S. Supreme Court**
INTERMEDIATE APPELLATE COURTS	U.S. Courts of Appeal (13)
TRIAL COURTS	U.S. District Courts (94) U.S. Bankruptcy Courts U.S. Court of International Trade U.S. Court of Federal Claims

b. State Courts

State courts have jurisdiction over claims that arise under state law. State law includes enacted law, such as a provision in the state constitution or a state statute. State law also includes common law. Many areas of the law are governed almost exclusively by state law, including family law, property, and torts. State courts have general jurisdiction, which means they have the authority to hear cases related to a variety of subjects.

States vary in how they name their courts, though in most cases, it is obvious from the name of the court whether a trial, intermediate appellate, or highest appellate court is deciding a case. One notable exception is the court system of the state of New York. In New York, trial courts are called the "Supreme Court," intermediate appellate courts are called the "Supreme Court, Appellate Division," and the highest appellate court is called the "Court of Appeals." During law school you will likely read many cases from New York state courts because they have written landmark (influential) decisions, particularly in the areas of contracts and torts. This book contains a couple of New York Court of Appeals decisions in Part II, Chapter 5.

C. The Jury System

1. General Overview

A unique feature of the U.S. legal system is the **jury**, a group of people assembled to decide a case. The jury plays a role only at trial, and its duties are twofold. First, it hears and reviews evidence presented by the parties—the plaintiff and defendant—to determine what happened in the case. Because this function of the jury is referred to as "finding" or "trying" the facts, juries are often referred to as **fact finders** or **triers of fact**. Second, upon hearing and reviewing all of the evidence presented at trial, the jury makes a determination as to whether it believes the defendant is **liable** (in a civil case) or **guilty** (in a criminal case).

Because juries are usually composed of people who have no training in law, the trial judge must "instruct" the jury on what law to apply to the case to help the jury make its determination. The trial judge also instructs the jury on the level of proof needed to find the defendant liable or guilty. In civil cases, the required standard is a **preponderance of the evidence**. This means that the jury must find that the defendant is "more likely than not" liable. In criminal cases, the required standard is **proof beyond a reasonable doubt**. Reasonable doubt is "[t]he doubt that prevents one from being firmly convinced of a defendant's guilt, or the belief that there is a real possibility that a defendant is not guilty."[9] To find a defendant guilty in a criminal case, juries must believe beyond a reasonable doubt that the evidence presented has established the defendant's guilt.

The following hypothetical case illustrates how parties use evidence at trial. Imagine a civil case involving a customer and a supermarket chain. The customer slipped and fell on a banana peel in one of the chain's stores, resulting in a broken leg. The customer (plaintiff) brings suit against the supermarket chain (defendant), alleging that store employees were careless in not cleaning up the banana peel, thereby causing her injury. At trial, the plaintiff would support her case by offering testimony from various witnesses. One witness may be called by the plaintiff to speak to the defendant's supposed carelessness. This witness, perhaps a fellow customer, might state that she saw the banana peel in the store two hours before the plaintiff's accident, suggesting that the defendant had plenty of time to notice and clean up the peel, but failed to do so. The plaintiff might also present physical evidence. She could use security camera footage from the store to corroborate (support) the witness's testimony that the banana peel was on the supermarket floor hours before the accident.

The defendant then has the opportunity to present her own evidence—though the defendant is under no obligation to present any evidence at all. The defendant could call a witness, maybe one of the store employees, to rebut

---

[9] *Reasonable Doubt*, BLACK'S LAW DICTIONARY (3d Pocket Ed. 2006).

(contradict) the plaintiff's assertion that the defendant was careless in not noticing the banana peel. The employee could explain that she walked through every aisle looking for spills and fallen items just thirty minutes before the accident. However, she could not see the banana peel because it was hidden underneath a shopping cart at the time she walked down the aisle in question. The defendant could even use the same security footage to support the employee's claim that the banana peel was impossible to see.

After both the plaintiff and defendant have presented evidence, the jury must "weigh" this evidence and determine which version of the events it finds more convincing: the plaintiff's or defendant's. The jury receives instructions from the trial judge as to what law to apply to decide whether the defendant is liable. In this example, the judge would likely provide the jury with a legal definition of carelessness (e.g., "A defendant is careless if she does X, Y, and Z"). The judge would probably also provide the jury with the legal rules for determining how the plaintiff should be compensated if the jury decides that the defendant was, indeed, careless. Applying these rules to the facts of the case, the jury would decide if the defendant is liable and, if so, how much money to award the plaintiff for her injuries.

The final phase of the trial is referred to as **jury deliberation**. The term "deliberation" means to carefully think about and discuss a matter. During deliberation, jury members meet privately to decide who should win the case. Once the jury has made up its mind, it returns a **verdict** containing its decision. The verdict is read out loud in court.

2. The Role of Judge and Jury at Trial

As the example above demonstrates, the jury and judge play different roles at trial. The jury hears and reviews evidence presented by the parties and ultimately decides a **question of fact**: what actually happened in this case? The judge plays no part in this factual determination. Although the judge is present throughout the trial, it is not the judge's role to weigh the evidence and determine whether the defendant is liable or guilty. This falls squarely on the shoulders of the jury.

Instead, the trial judge determines **questions of law**. Such questions call on the judge to use her legal expertise to decide questions about whether to admit evidence or grant motions. (Recall that a motion is a request by a party for the judge to do something, such as throwing out the case or excluding evidence.) Questions of law also include decisions about what rules to include in jury instructions before the jury is sent off to deliberate. Such are the *legal* determinations made by trial judges.

Understanding the distinction between questions of fact versus law is important because it helps to appreciate the difference between the role of the jury and judge at trial. This distinction is also significant because parties dissatisfied with the outcome of a case can usually only appeal by arguing that the trial judge made a mistake in deciding a question of law. This is often referred to as a legal error. Very rarely can the jury's factual findings and verdict be challenged.

An exception to the jury/judge and question of fact/question of law distinction is a bench trial. In a **bench trial**, the judge acts as the fact finder instead of the jury. In a bench trial there is no jury.[10] Under the U.S. Constitution, criminal defendants have a right to a jury trial. Similarly, depending on the amount in controversy, parties in civil suits also have this right. For various reasons, however, parties may wish to give up their right to a jury and ask the judge to make both the legal and factual decisions in their case. One reason a criminal defendant might wish to give up her right to a jury trial is because she believes the judge will be a more neutral decision maker than a jury.

3. Who Serves on a Jury?

Juries are composed of ordinary citizens who are called in for "jury duty." Jury duty is a civic responsibility for all U.S. citizens. Once a year or every few years, U.S. citizens receive a letter in the mail asking them to come down to the courthouse for jury selection.

The jury selection process is called **voir dire** (pronounced VWAR-**DEER**). This is a French term that means "to speak the truth." During voir dire, potential jurors who have been called in for jury duty are questioned by lawyers for both sides of a case. The purpose of this questioning is to determine the suitability of each **juror** for the case. Attorneys usually avoid selecting jurors who might be prejudiced against their client. Their aim is to select individuals who may be sympathetic towards their client or have at least a neutral opinion about the subject matter of the case. Attorneys therefore ask potential jurors questions that might reveal any hidden biases. For instance, an attorney representing a defendant charged with drunk driving might ask jurors whether any of them or their close family or friends have been injured in a drunk driving accident. Jurors who answer "yes" are probably eliminated. Though attorneys need not always provide a reason for dismissing a potential juror, the elimination cannot have a discriminatory basis, such as racial bias.

Trial juries range in size from 6 to 12 jurors. Civil juries are typically composed of 6 jurors, while juries in criminal cases usually number 12 individuals.

Knowing the difference between the role of juries and trial courts is critical for understanding the written opinions of appellate judges—in other words, cases. In many of your law classes, cases will make up the bulk of your reading

[10] Trials in which the judge finds the facts are called bench trials because the "bench" refers to the raised area reserved for the judge in a courtroom. See *Bench*, BLACK'S LAW DICTIONARY (3d Pocket Ed. 2006).

assignments. These cases often make reference to questions of fact, questions of law, juries, and trial courts.

The next three chapters address how to read, discuss, and write about cases in the U.S. law school context.

Chapter 2
Reading Cases

The average law student spends anywhere from 4 to 8 hours a day studying for law classes, reading hundreds of cases per semester.[1] With so many cases to get through, learning to read them effectively is integral to a law student's success.[2] In fact, as law professor Ruth Ann McKinney points out, "To be understood, law has to be read, and read well."[3]

So what can you do to "read law well"? Most fundamental is an understanding of the basic structural elements of a judicial opinion. An awareness of the organizational structure of a text facilitates comprehension.[4] Another way to enhance your understanding of cases is by employing effective reading strategies. Finally, familiarity with legal (and non-legal) vocabulary is essential to understanding a court's decision.

To help you become a successful reader of case law, this chapter begins with an overview of the key elements of a legal case (Section A). Following this is a description of three reading strategies designed to help you read effectively (Section B). Definitions of key legal terms are provided before the two cases in this chapter.

---

[1] Sarah Mui, *In Law School, How Many Hours Per Day Did You Study?*, ABA LAW JOURNAL (Oct. 21, 2009, 5:37 PM), http://www.abajournal.com/news/article/in_law_school_how_many_hours_per_day_did_you_study/.

[2] Leah M. Christensen, *Legal Reading and Success in Law School: An Empirical Study*, 30 SEATTLE UNIV. L. REV. 603 (2007).

[3] RUTH ANN MCKINNEY, READING LIKE A LAWYER: TIME-SAVING STRATEGIES FOR READING LAW LIKE AN EXPERT 53 (2d ed. 2012).

[4] Peter Dewitz, *Legal Education: A Problem of Learning from Text*, 23 N.Y.U. REV. L. & SOC. CHANGE 225, 227 (1997).

A. Elements of a Case

Nearly all of the cases that you will read in law school contain the same elements, presented in roughly the same order. The torts case below contains notes in the left-hand margin indicating which element of the case each sentence corresponds to. A detailed explanation of these elements then follows the opinion.

1. Sample Case

Pre-Reading Vocabulary

Damages *(noun)*

A sum of money claimed by the plaintiff, or awarded to the plaintiff, as compensation for injury or loss. The plural form "damages" is always used to denote this meaning of the word.

Seek damages *(verb)*

A plaintiff usually "seeks," that is, requests, damages when she files a civil lawsuit.

Recover damages *(verb)*; **recovery** *(noun)*

A plaintiff "recovers" damages if she wins the lawsuit and is awarded money. The noun form is "recovery."

Motion to dismiss the complaint *(noun)*

A **motion** is a request made by one party (plaintiff or defendant) for a trial court to rule on a particular issue. The court either **grants** (allows) or **denies** (rejects) the motion.

A **complaint** is a legal document containing the plaintiff's reasons for bringing suit against the defendant. In the complaint, the plaintiff alleges specific facts that form the basis of her lawsuit.

To **dismiss** a case means to "throw out" or terminate the lawsuit or part of the lawsuit.

When a defendant files a **motion to dismiss the complaint**, she asserts that the plaintiff does not have a legal claim. A **claim** is a plaintiff's assertion that she is entitled to money damages or other legal remedies. In other words, the defendant's argument is that *even if* everything that the plaintiff states in the complaint is true, the law does not recognize her claim as one for which relief (e.g., money damages) can be granted. For instance, if a colleague is rude to you, it might make you feel bad, but you probably cannot sue her. This is because the pain you feel due to others' rudeness does not constitute a valid legal claim.

Cause of action *(noun)*

A factual situation that provides the grounds for suing another party.

Case heading

LEWIS v. WESTINGHOUSE ELECTRIC CORP.

Appellate Court of Illinois, 1985.

139 Ill.App.3d 634, 487 N.E.2d 1071, 94 Ill.Dec. 194.

Last name of judge writing the opinion

JIGANTI, Presiding Justice:

Facts (1-2)

Procedural history (3-4)

(1) . . . [T]he plaintiff, Lucille Lewis, **sought damages** from the defendants, Westinghouse Elevator Co., a division of Westinghouse Electric Corporation and the Chicago Housing Authority (CHA) for the negligent infliction of emotional distress. **(2)** The defendants **moved to dismiss the plaintiff's complaint** for failure to state a **cause of action**. **(3)** The trial court granted the motion to dismiss. **(4)** The plaintiff now appeals the dismissal of the complaint.

Facts (5-11)

(5) The plaintiff is a resident at one of the apartments owned by the defendant CHA. **(6)** The defendant Westinghouse maintains and services the elevators at the CHA building. **(7)** On August 16, 1983, the plaintiff entered the elevator on the first floor and rode it to the 16th floor. **(8)** As she attempted to exit the elevator, however, the elevator stalled and the doors remained closed. **(9)** The elevator remained in this position for approximately 40 minutes. **(10)** The plaintiff alleges that during that time she was in danger of "suffocation and serious physical harm." **(11)** In addition plaintiff alleges that as a result of the incident she suffered an unstable angina and aggravation of her coronary arteriosclerotic heart disease and hypertension.

Issue (12)

Reasoning (13-16) The court begins its analysis by stating the applicable pre-existing rule

(12) The central issue to be resolved on appeal is whether the plaintiff has stated a cause of action for the negligent infliction of emotional distress under *Rickey v. Chicago Transit Authority* (1983), 98 Ill.2d 546, 75 Ill.Dec. 211, 457 N.E.2d 1. **(13)** In *Rickey,* the plaintiff, age eight, sought damages for the emotional distress he suffered as a result of watching his five year old brother's near strangulation by an article of clothing which became entangled in a CTA escalator. **(14)** In determining whether the plaintiff could **recover**, the court adopted the zone of physical danger standard. **(15)** In order to state a cause of action under that standard the plaintiff must have been in "such proximity to the accident" that there was "a high risk of physical impact" so as to cause the plaintiff "reasonable fear for his own safety." **(16)** Additionally the plaintiff "must show a physical injury or illness as a result of the emotional distress." (*Rickey v. Chicago Transit Authority* (1983), 98 Ill.2d 546, 555, 75 Ill.Dec. 211, 215, 457 N.E.2d 1, 5.) . . .

Holding (17)
Reasoning (18-36)

(17) For at least two reasons we do not believe the plaintiff has stated a cause of action. **(18)** First, we find that the plaintiff did not have a reasonable fear for her own safety. **(19)** Whether a fear is reasonable is determined by the objective standard of whether a particular incident would produce fear in the person of ordinary sensibilities. (*Knierim v. Izzo* (1961), 22 Ill.2d 73, 86, 174 N.E.2d 157, 165.) **(20)** In this case the elevator merely stalled and the doors failed to open. **(21)** This is not a case such as *Bass v. Nooney Co.* (Mo.1983), 646 S.W.2d 765, where water began to rise in the elevator so that the party reasonably feared drowning. **(22)** Apprehensive or uncomfortable it may have been for the plaintiff, but, absent something more, the incident in this case was not one which produces fear of suffocation.

(23) Secondly, we find that for the same reasons stated above, the plaintiff was not in a high risk of physical impact. **(24)** The elevator merely stalled. **(25)** There is no suggestion in this case that any outside force was present that would injure the plaintiff. **(26)** In our estimation the facts here cannot lead to the conclusion that there was a high risk to the plaintiff of physical impact.

(27) In making these judgments concerning high risk of physical impact and reasonable fear we believe that this is a question of law and not a question of fact. **(28)** We recognize nevertheless that the line between those questions is hazy at best. **(29)** The determination is usually made on a common sense or intuitive basis. (*See Consolino v. Thompson* (1984), 127 Ill.App.3d 31, 82 Ill.Dec. 160, 468 N.E.2d 422.) **(30)** Moreover, in making that judgment we are mindful of the admonition of the Illinois Supreme Court in a case involving an intentional infliction of emotional distress, *Knierim v. Izzo* (1961), 22 Ill.2d 73, 174 N.E.2d 157. **(31)** In *Knierim* the court stated that "[i]ndiscriminate allowance of actions for mental anguish would encourage neurotic overreactions to trivial hurts, and the law should aim to toughen the psyche of the citizen rather than pamper it." *Knierim v. Izzo* (1961), 22 Ill.2d 73, 85, 174 N.E.2d 157, 164. . . .

(32) It might be argued that this is not a neurotic overreaction to a trivial hurt since the plaintiff has alleged a resulting physical injury, aggravation of her angina condition. **(33)** However, the *Knierim* court favorably commented on the case of *Slocum v. Food Fair Stores of Florida, Inc.* (Fla.1958), 100 So.2d 396, in which the plaintiff suffered a heart attack as a result of an aggravation of a pre-existing condition. **(34)** The Florida court found that there was no cause of action because the defendant's conduct must cause distress to a person of "ordinary sensibilities." **(35)** The finding of the Florida court, in which the Illinois Supreme Court agreed, was that this was not a person of ordinary sensibilities. **(36)** We judge that to be the situation in this instance. . . .

Holding (37)

(37) For the reasons stated above we believe the plaintiff has not satisfied the elements necessary to state a cause of action for negligent infliction of emotional distress. **(38)** The order of the trial court is affirmed. . . .

Disposition (38)

TASK 2.A.1. Questions for Discussion

Answer the following questions to assist you during a class discussion of the case. Indicate the sentence(s) in which you found the answer to each question.

1. What is the name of the tort that the defendant supposedly committed? (A tort is a civil wrong that causes injury or loss.) Do you know what each of the terms in this multi-word tort mean? If not, look up the definitions in either a law dictionary[5] or an English-to-English dictionary.

2. What was the court's decision in this case? Who won? What reasons did the court provide to support its decision?

---

[5] Black's Law Dictionary is probably the most reputable law dictionary in the U.S. The small "pocket edition" is a good investment. Nearly all of the legal vocabulary terms contained in this book can be found in the pocket edition of Black's Law Dictionary.

2. Key Elements of an Opinion

a. Case Heading

Each opinion begins with a heading containing the following information:

- The names of the parties (this is the "name" or "title" of the case);
- The name of the court that decided the case and the year it decided the case; and
- The citation for the case.

Recall the heading for the *Lewis* case above:

LEWIS v. WESTINGHOUSE ELECTRIC CORP.
Appellate Court of Illinois, 1985.
139 Ill.App.3d 634, 487 N.E.2d 1071, 94 Ill.Dec. 194.

(1) Name of the Case

At trial court, the name of the plaintiff is listed first, followed by the name of the defendant. The name that appears in trial court documents is therefore always *Plaintiff v. Defendant*. Once parties appeal a decision, however, the order of the names may change. In some appellate courts, the appealing party (the **appellant** or **petitioner**) is listed first, followed by the responding party (the **appellee** or **respondent**) even if the appealing party is the original defendant at the trial level. In other jurisdictions, the original order of *Plaintiff v. Defendant* is maintained throughout the entire appeals process. Different courts follow different conventions and often you will not know who is the original plaintiff or defendant until you read the case closely.

Use only the last (family) names of the parties when referring to a case.

(a) Typeface

When referring to cases in writing, you should italicize or underline the name of the case. Italicization is the term for slanted text that looks like *this*. When writing about the case Lewis v. Westinghouse Electric Corp., for example, you would type *Lewis v. Westinghouse Electric Corp.* or Lewis v. Westinghouse Electric Corp. (Italicization of case names is more common than underlining. Underlining of case names is used mostly in court documents.)

(b) Naming Conventions

When referring to a case, you may often abbreviate the name of the case by using only one of the parties' last names instead of both the plaintiff's and defendant's names. *Lewis v. Westinghouse Electric Corp.* could be referred to as, simply, *Lewis*.[6]

When using this abbreviated form, it is convention to use the first party's name (for example, *Lewis*). However, the first party's name is sometimes quite long; in that case, use the second party's shorter name. Furthermore, individual states and the U.S. government are occasionally parties to a lawsuit, especially in criminal cases. This makes for case names such as *Oregon v. Mathiason* or *North Carolina v. Butler* (cases you will read in Part II, Chapter 6). As far as case abbreviations go, *Oregon* and *North Carolina* are not particularly informative, considering there are thousands of cases involving the states of Oregon and North Carolina. So when abbreviating case names involving individual states or the United States, you could use the other party's name instead. Thus, *Oregon v. Mathiason* would shorten to *Mathiason*, while *North Carolina v. Butler* would become *Butler*.

LANGUAGE TIP

You may use two grammatical constructions when talking about cases:

1. In *Lewis*, the issue was whether . . . .
2. In **the** *Lewis* **case**, the court held that . . . .

Notice that in the second version, if you use the word "case" after the case name, you must also use the definite article "the" before the case name. This rule applies to both full and abbreviated case names. That is, you could also say or write:

1. In *Lewis v. Westinghouse Electric Corp.*, the issue was whether . . . .
2. In **the** *Lewis v. Westinghouse Electric Corp.* **case**, the court held that . . . .

(2) Name of the Court

Most of the cases you will read in law school, and certainly all of the cases you will read in this book, have been decided by appellate courts. Therefore, in

[6] In writing, first cite the case name in full and then use the abbreviated form. See THE BLUEBOOK: A UNIFORM SYSTEM OF CITATION R. 10.2, at 96-101 (Columbia Law Review Ass'n et al. eds., 20th ed. 2015).

case headings you will often see a reference to "appellate court," "court of appeals," or "supreme court."

(3) Citation

The **citation** of a case contains information about where to find the case. Appellate cases are published in multi-volume books called **reporters** or **reports**. The citation refers to the particular book, volume, and page number on which a case appears. Cases are organized in each reporter chronologically by date. Some cases are published in multiple reporters and will have several citations.

Law libraries contain physical copies of reporters, but nowadays you can use a citation to find most cases on the internet through a legal database such as Westlaw or LexisNexis. The formatting of citations are governed by rules that may differ from jurisdiction to jurisdiction, though the most widely used system of citation is contained in a guide called *The Bluebook* (if you take a legal writing or a scholarly writing class, you will become familiar with *The Bluebook*).

The citations for *Lewis v. Westinghouse Electric Corp.* are:

139 Ill.App.3d 634, 487 N.E.2d 1071, 94 Ill.Dec. 194.

Three citations are provided for the case, with each citation separated by a comma. This means that *Lewis* appears in three reporters. The first number in each of the citations refers to the volume number in which the case is printed. Each reporter is made up of many volumes because new cases are argued every year and they cannot all fit into one book. The abbreviation in the middle refers to the name of the reporter in which the case is published. The second number in the citation is the first page on which the case begins in the reporter.

Looking at the first citation, 139 Ill.App.3d 634: *Lewis* is in volume 139, that is, the 139th book of this particular reporter. "Ill.App.3d" is the abbreviation for the reporter, that is, the *Illinois Appellate Court Reports, Third Series*. As the name implies, this reporter contains appellate court opinions for the Illinois Appellate Court. The second number in this first citation is 634. This means that *Lewis* begins on page 634 in the 139th volume of the Illinois Appellate Court Reports, Third Series.

Figure 2.1. Citation of a Case

Volume number ⇩ First page of case ⇩

139 Ill.App.3d 634

⇧ Name of reporter

The *Lewis* case is printed in two other reporters as well: "N.E.2d" and "Ill.Dec." N.E.2d refers to the *North Eastern Reporter Second*, a regional case reporter that publishes appellate decisions for Illinois, Indiana, Massachusetts, New York, and Ohio. Ill.Dec. refers to *West's Illinois Decisions* (West is the name a publishing company), a reporter that contains Illinois Appellate Court and Illinois Supreme Court decisions. As you may not always be familiar with a reporter abbreviation, you can look these up either online or in a copy of *The Bluebook*. That said, knowing the name of the particular reporter in which a case is published is usually not of critical importance.

b. Name of the Judge

After the heading, you will find the name of the judge who authored the opinion. While there are multiple appellate judges sitting on each appellate court, one judge is usually responsible for writing the opinion for the court. Most courts will provide only the judge's last name, followed by a comma and the word "judge," "justice," or the abbreviation "J" (which stands for judge or justice).

c. Facts

Courts will often begin their opinions by describing the facts. The facts include the events that sparked the lawsuit and some of the events that occurred during trial.

A variety of actions may trigger formal court proceedings. A violation of a contract provision, a domestic dispute, or the commission of a serious crime are all grounds for initiating a lawsuit. The facts surrounding these actions are the very reason that one party has decided to bring suit in civil court or the government has decided to prosecute a criminal defendant. Judicial opinions usually begin with a detailed description of these facts. You may refer to these as **conflict facts**[7] because they describe the problem or dispute that landed the parties in court—in other words, the facts that came before a lawsuit was filed.

The conflict facts only give part of the picture, however. As you may remember from Part II, Chapter 1, parties can appeal an adverse decision only by alleging that the trial court made a legal error. The party appealing a lower court decision must therefore argue that the lower court made a mistake in applying or interpreting the law. These mistakes tend to center on one of the following legal determinations made by trial judges:

---

[7] McKinney, *supra* note 3, at 134, 138-41 (explaining that conflict facts are "facts about the real-life events that happened between the parties that gave rise to the present disagreement."). Another term that is used is "operative facts." Michael Hunter Schwartz, Expert Learning for Law Students 105 (2d ed. 2008) ("Operative facts are all the events that transpired before someone involved the courts.").

1. The trial judge's grant or denial of a motion (either before trial or during trial);
2. The trial judge's ruling on the admissibility of evidence; or
3. The trial judge's instruction to the jury regarding the applicable law.

When telling the facts of a case, courts will almost always describe these legal decisions by lower courts. In addition, courts often give details about the legal arguments the parties made in preparation for trial, at trial, and/or on appeal. You may refer to these facts as the **legal facts**[8] because these facts refer to events that occurred during the legal proceedings.

Table 2.1. Conflict Facts and Legal Facts

Conflict facts	Legal facts
Description of the actions and events that led to a dispute between the parties (in a civil case); or description of the actions and events that led to prosecution of the defendant (in a criminal case) Examples • A husband (allegedly) failed to pay child support for six months • A man (allegedly) stole $20,000 worth of jewelry	1. Description of the legal decisions of the trial judge before and during trial Examples • The trial judge denied a motion to dismiss • The trial judge excluded certain evidence 2. Description of the actions and arguments of the parties and their lawyers in preparation for trial, during trial, and on appeal Examples • The plaintiff claimed that her doctor was negligent in her care • The defendant argued that the police obtained evidence against him illegally

Conflict facts are easier to understand because they describe the everyday actions of ordinary people that led to a conflict and hence a lawsuit. On the other hand, legal facts focus on what the parties to the lawsuit, the parties' lawyers,

---

[8] McKinney, *supra* note 3, at 133, 135-38 (defining legal facts as "facts about how this case came up through the courts, facts about how pre-trial papers were filed or a trial was conducted, facts about the legal arguments the parties may have made to the lower courts before the case came up on appeal[.]").

and judges said or did during the legal proceedings. These descriptions contain specialized legal vocabulary pertaining to legal theories, concepts, and arguments.

When you read the facts section of a case, try to categorize the facts into conflict facts and legal facts. This may help to better understand why the losing party appealed.

TASK 2.A.2. Facts of *Lewis*

Look back to the *Lewis* case. The facts are contained in sentences (1)-(2) and (5)-(11). Which of the facts can be classified as conflict facts? Which of the facts are legal facts? How can you tell?

d. Procedural History

In addition to describing the facts of the case, a court will almost always include a story about how the case moved through the court system. This is called the procedural history or procedural posture of the case. When describing this story of the case, courts focus on which lower courts heard or reviewed the case and what they decided to do with the case.

To determine what counts as the procedural history of a case, consider the following questions:

- **Who won in the trial court and how**: The plaintiff? The defendant? On a jury verdict? On a motion to dismiss? On another kind of motion?
- **Who appealed the lower court's decision**: The plaintiff? The defendant?
- **Which court is this case in**: Intermediate appellate court or highest court? State court or federal court?
- **How did the appellate court(s) "dispose" of the case**: Did the court(s) affirm (agree with) the lower court's judgment? Did the court(s) reverse (disagree with) the lower court's judgment?

Generally, the procedural history of the case appears right before or right after a description of the facts. This is because before getting to the substance of an opinion, courts like to provide the reader with information about how the case got to the appellate court in the first place.

TASK 2.A.3. Procedural History of *Lewis*

Who won in the trial court in *Lewis*? How did this party win? Who appealed the trial court's decision?

e. Issue

The issue or "issue on appeal" is the legal question that a court must resolve. It dictates what the entire case will be about. A case might have one or more issues depending on the subject matter and the complexity of the case. The issue is often located at the very beginning of an opinion—for example, in the first paragraph—and again before a detailed discussion of the court's decision.

(1) Signposting

In locating the issue, look for the words "issue," "question," "decide," and "whether." Sometimes it will be easy to identify the issue because courts may preface it with an introductory phrase such as "the issue is whether"; "the question presented is"; or "today we must decide." These phrases are called signposts. Circle or highlight signposts when you see them in the text.

(2) Word of Caution

While the words "issue," "question," "decide," and "whether" are useful signposts for the issue, you should be aware that these words can be misleading. Courts may use these words to describe minor questions in the case that need to be answered before getting to the "real" issue on appeal. Occasionally, courts also provide overly broad formulations of the issue. Further, courts do not always state the issue explicitly. Sometimes they do not write an express issue at all, leaving you to infer it from the case as a whole. Although *Lewis* is a fairly straightforward case, you will read other cases in this book and in law school that will not provide an explicit issue. In order to determine the issue in such cases, you will need to read the case very closely.

(3) Procedural and Substantive Issues

Recall from Part II, Chapter 1 that the role of appellate courts is to review the decisions of lower courts to determine whether the lower court has made a legal error. Appellate courts do not usually disturb the factual findings made by the factfinder, be that a jury or a judge. At the heart of any case, then, lie "procedural" questions such as:

> "Was evidence appropriately admitted?"
> "Did the trial court err in dismissing the case?"
> "Were instructions to the jury (regarding the applicable law) correct?"

Issues focusing explicitly on the appropriateness of the trial court's legal determinations are procedural in nature because they address the legal procedures followed by the court.

But while the job of appellate courts is to review the legal decisions made by lower courts, they do not always frame issues in such procedural terms. This is because procedural issues ultimately reflect and give way to broader questions of "substantive" law. Substantive law refers to the specific rules that govern the rights and obligations of individuals within a particular area of law. For example, a question about the appropriateness of jury instructions often entails a more fundamental decision about what is really the appropriate rule in the first place.

Courts often frame issues in substantive rather than procedural terms because they would like to draw attention to the substantive legal questions raised by lower court decisions rather than mere procedural concerns. Some examples of issues framed in terms of substantive law:

> [The issue is] whether the defendants owed plaintiffs a duty to exercise reasonable care in the marketing and distribution of the handguns they manufacture[.][9]

> The question . . . is whether the plaintiff may recover for bodily injury or sickness resulting from fear for her safety caused by a negligent defendant, where the plaintiff was placed in danger by such negligence, although there was no physical impact.[10]

> In this case we are asked to determine whether an order prohibiting a father from taking his children to religious services . . . during periods of lawful custody or visitation violated the father's constitutional rights . . . .[11]

> We have held that the Fourth Amendment permits police officers to approach individuals at random in airport lobbies and other public places to ask them questions and to request consent to search their luggage, so long as a reasonable person would understand that he or she could refuse to cooperate. This case requires us to determine whether the same rule applies to police encounters that take place on a bus.[12]

These issues do not focus on the correctness of the trial court's actions, but rather seek an answer in the form of a substantive rule of law. The terms "duty," "negligence," "constitutional rights," and "Fourth Amendment" suggest that these issues address substantive rules of tort, family, and criminal procedure law.

---

[9] Hamilton v. Beretta U.S.A. Corp., 96 N.Y.2d 222 (2001).

[10] Falzone v. Busch, 45 N.J. 559 (1965).

[11] Zummo v. Zummo, 394. Pa.Super. 30 (1990).

[12] Florida v. Bostick, 501 U.S. 429 (1991).

Keep in mind that both versions of the issue, procedural and substantive, are correct. A substantive formulation is forward-looking and more directly frames the court's decision as a rule of law with precedential effect for future cases. In contrast, the procedural version is backward-looking and shines a light on the actions of the lower court instead—that is, whether the court's decisions were correct or incorrect. Courts will occasionally offer both procedural and substantive formulations of the issue, though they frequently opt for one or the other.

When reading a case, try to articulate both a procedural and substantive issue.

TASK 2.A.4. Issue of *Lewis*

The issue in *Lewis* is contained in sentence (12). Is this a procedural or substantive issue? Why?

f. Holding

The holding is the court's answer to the specific issue or issues raised on appeal. Imagine that a court stated the following issue in a case involving a landowner and an injured trespasser:

> "Does a landowner owe a duty to warn trespassers on the property of hazardous conditions?"

In a perfect world, the court's holding would read something like this:

> "No. We hold that a landowner does not owe a duty to warn trespassers on the property of hazardous conditions."

Unfortunately, however, you will rarely see such beautiful symmetry between the issue and holding, or such precision and explicitness in the language of a judicial opinion. In fact, locating the holding in a case can be a challenging task.[13]

---

[13] You may be relieved to learn that identifying holdings can be challenging not only for law students, but even seasoned legal professionals. In fact, the concept of a holding is a debated topic in contemporary legal theory. If you are interested in learning more, see Maxwell L. Stearns and Michael Abramowicz, *Defining Dicta*, 56 STANFORD L. REV. 953 (2005).

(1) Signposting

Sometimes courts make your job easier by employing the following phrases to introduce the holding: "we hold that"; "we decide that"; and "we conclude that." Look out for such signposts and circle or underline them in the opinion when you see them.

(2) Another Word of Caution

As with the issue, however, exercise caution when you see the phrases "we hold that"; "we decide that"; and "we conclude that." Though often helpful, such wording may be misleading. Courts occasionally use language suggestive of a holding but make a statement that does not accurately answer the issue on appeal. Sometimes the statement is too broad. Sometimes the statement is incomplete. And still other times the statement does something entirely different. To further complicate matters, courts may fail to provide an express holding at all, leaving you once again to infer it from the opinion as a whole.

(3) Procedural and Substantive Holdings

You already know that issues can be framed in procedural or substantive terms. So too can holdings. A procedural holding is the answer to a procedural issue before the court. Procedural issues include questions like:

"Did the trial court err in dismissing the case?"
"Were the trial court's instructions to the jury correct?"

Holdings that answer these questions are procedural because they rule on the appropriateness of the legal procedure used by the trial judge. Holdings for these hypothetical issues may be along the lines of:

"The trial court was correct in dismissing the case."
"The trial court's instructions to the jury were incorrect."

As mentioned, however, procedural issues sometimes reflect broader questions of substantive law (see again examples of substantive issues above). Thus, a court might answer an issue with a holding that focuses on substantive law.

TASK 2.A.5. Holding of *Lewis*

The holding of the *Lewis* case is contained in sentence (17) and again in sentence (37). Is this holding a direct answer to the issue in the case? Do you think this holding is procedural or substantive in nature?

g. Reasoning

To support a decision, courts must supply reasons, which collectively make up the reasoning or rationale of the opinion. Depending on the case, courts provide different kinds of support, though they tend to fall into three broad categories:

- Courts apply pre-existing rules, derived from enacted or case law, to the situation at hand. This is called **rule application**.
- Courts compare the instant case (the case before the court) to prior cases involving similar issues and facts. This is called **reasoning by analogy**.
- Courts provide policy reasons to support their decisions (**policy** refers to the values and interests promoted by a rule). These reasons are called **policy rationales**.

Courts may offer reasons in any order they believe makes the most sense, but they typically begin by applying pre-existing rules first. Depending on the case, the source of these rules may be enacted law (e.g., statutes), common law, or a combination of these two sources of law.

Next, courts will frequently reason by analogy to other cases that raise similar issues and facts, explaining how the present case is either similar to or different from those other cases decided in the past. Such reasoning by analogy is the bedrock of common law analysis and it is how common law rules develop and evolve over time. If there is no controlling case or enacted law (that is, no opportunity to apply a pre-existing rule), the case is one of first impression. In cases of first impression, courts almost always analogize to prior cases because there simply is no pre-existing rule to apply.

Finally, courts often provide policy rationales for their decisions. For example, a court may reason that its decision is necessary in order to preserve justice or fairness in the legal system.

Depending on the complexity or significance of the case, courts may furnish anywhere from one to a dozen or more reasons to support their decisions. These reasons tend to fall into the three categories outlined above, though courts may provide other kinds of reasons as well. What follows is a detailed description of the three types of reasons typically supplied by courts.

(1) Rule Application

When a court cites to rules from prior cases or enacted law such as a statute, it is a good indication that the court is about to begin providing reasons for its decision. Perhaps not surprisingly, this usually—though not always—follows a statement containing the holding. When reading a judicial opinion, make note of the pre-existing rule(s) that the court applies to decide the case. This is probably the most common way for a court to support its decision. Note that rules from case law only apply if the present case raises the same or similar issues and has substantially similar facts. Further, courts are "bound" by only the rules from their own jurisdiction. Rules from other jurisdictions, whether enacted or common law rules, may guide courts, but courts are not under any obligation to follow them.

TASK 2.A.6. Applying Pre-existing Rules in *Lewis*

What is the pre-existing rule referred to in the *Lewis* case? What is the source of this rule: enacted law or case law? In which sentence(s) is this rule applied to the facts of the case?

(2) Reasoning by Analogy

In addition to applying pre-existing rules, courts also reason by analogy. Reasoning by analogy, also referred to as analogical reasoning, involves making comparisons. In the context of judicial decision making, as well as common law analysis more generally, reasoning by analogy means comparing the present case to prior cases to determine how the case should be decided.

Courts reason by analogy in two ways. First, they analogize the instant case to a previous case, pointing out how the two cases are factually similar. Because the cases are so similar, the argument goes, they should yield similar results. Second, courts distinguish the instant case from a previous case, explaining how the two cases are factually dissimilar. Because the cases are so different, the argument goes, the present case should be decided differently.

You will see lots of reasoning by analogy in the cases you read. This is because our common law system is built on comparison. If two cases raise the same issue and present similar facts, the principles of precedent and *stare decisis* dictate that the outcome of the two cases should be similar as well.

(3) Policy Rationales

To support a decision, courts sometimes offer other reasons that go beyond the application of a rule or a comparison of cases. They will often justify their opinions by explaining what policies the decision will advance. A policy is a value or interest that promotes a healthy, well-functioning society and government. There are some policy arguments that you will see recycled throughout judicial opinions. They include:

- **Social policy arguments**: The court's decision promotes a social goal and will thus create a better society. Social goals include things like freedom, safety, and privacy.
- **Fairness and justice policy arguments**: The court's decision advances fairness and justice. Fairness and justice are usually based on the notion that like cases, people, and situations ought to be treated alike.
- **Economic policy arguments**: The court's decision promotes economic efficiency and/or a free-market economy. For instance, courts occasionally undertake a cost-benefit analysis to argue that the rule's benefits exceed its costs.
- **Separation of powers policy arguments**: The court's decision respects the separation of powers between the three branches of government, that is, the judiciary, legislature, and executive. For example, courts often defer to the legislature when they believe that the branch of government that has been elected through popular vote (i.e., the legislature) is in a better position to make a change in the law.
- **Judicial administration policy arguments**: The court's decision creates a rule that is practical and easy (or easier) for courts to apply. For example, courts often assert that the rules they announce will reduce judges' workload. In addition, courts often talk of rigid, "bright line" rules that may lack flexibility, but can be easily applied in future cases.[14]

TASK 2.A.7. Reasoning of *Lewis*

Apart from applying a pre-existing rule to the facts of the case, does the *Lewis* court supply any other reasons to support its decision? Does the court analogize to or distinguish between this case and a previous case? Does the court argue that a particular policy, or social goal, is advanced by its decision?

h. Disposition

The disposition refers to the specific action that the court takes to "dispose" of the case. Typically, you will see appellate courts do one or a combination of the following:

---

[14] For a more detailed discussion of these and other policy arguments, see HELEN S. SHAPO ET AL., WRITING AND ANALYSIS IN THE LAW 264-68 (5th ed. 2008).

- **Affirm** the judgment (agree with the lower court and uphold its decision);
- **Reverse** the judgment (disagree with the lower court and overrule its decision); and
- **Remand** the case (send the case back to the trial court for further proceedings consistent with the appellate court's opinion).

The disposition often appears in the beginning of a case and almost always at the very end. It is often in all capital letters (e.g., AFFIRMED). This part of the opinion is also called the result or judgment.

TASK 2.A.8. Disposition of *Lewis*

What is the court's disposition in *Lewis*? What do you predict the losing party will do next?

B. Case Reading Strategies

This section presents three strategies for more effective case reading: (1) linear, (2) problematizing, and (3) evaluative reading strategies.[15]

1. Linear Reading Strategies

Consider the strategies you currently use to read. Perhaps you underline or highlight words or sentences in the text; make notes in margins; or summarize information in a notebook or Word document. These are called linear or "default"[16] reading strategies because they require you to move through the text in a linear, step-by-step fashion. (The term "linear" means to progress in a series of steps or in a straight line.) These strategies are probably the most commonly used by students of all ages, as they tend to be the first strategies novice readers are taught in school.

When reading cases, try to employ the following linear strategies to help you better understand the text.

---

[15] These strategies have been adapted from Dorothy Deegan, *Exploring Individual Differences Among Novices Reading in a Specific Domain: the Case of Law*, 30 READING RES. Q. 154, 161 (1995). See also Christensen, *supra* note 2, at 608-10; Peter Dewitz, *supra* note 4, at 228.

[16] Deegan, *supra* note 15, at 161.

- **Skim the case to get a sense of the main idea of the case and how the text is organized**

Before you begin reading the case closely, try reading the first paragraph and last paragraph of the opinion. It is a convention of U.S. academic and legal writing that writers place their main idea in the very beginning and again at the end of a text (see again Part I, Chapter 1 of this book). Knowing the writer's main idea and keeping this in mind while reading the text more carefully may help you stay focused on the big picture instead of getting lost in the weeds (that is, confused by all the minute details of the opinion).

Next, try skimming the case to get an idea of how it is structured. **Skimming** means to read a text quickly to get a general sense of the text. How many pages is the case? Is the text divided into sections? What are these sections about? Judges often split up their opinions into sections and provide informative section headings (**headings** are titles for a section of text). When used in judicial opinions, headings are useful because they help to guide the reader through the various parts of the text. Pay attention to these headings, if they are provided.

After skimming the case, read it more carefully a second time, focusing on the details of the case.[17] It will probably take you a long time to read a case closely. Students report that reading a page of a judicial opinion can take up to 30-45 minutes in the beginning. Rest assured that you will become a faster reader with time and practice. Keep in mind, however, that cases are dense and will always require a time commitment. Do not expect to breeze through a case in 10 minutes; at least, not if you expect to understand it.

- **Underline, highlight, and/or circle important sentences or words**

During your second, closer reading of the case, underline, highlight, and/or circle important sentences or words. Sentences worth highlighting include those that contain the key elements of the case: the facts, issue, holding, and so on. In addition, you may wish to circle key words in the opinion. These key words might include the plaintiff's legal claim (e.g., in *Lewis*, this is the negligent infliction of emotional distress), or words such as "issue" or "hold," which might serve as signposts for important parts of the opinion.

Something to avoid is highlighting or underlining *everything* in the text. The purpose of highlighting or underlining is to make certain parts of the text stand out. If you mark up the entire case, you will not be able to discern what is most important in the case.

---

[17] For a multi-step approach to reading legal cases, see Mary A. Lundberg, *Metacognitive Aspects of Reading Comprehension: Studying Understanding in Legal Case Analysis*, 22 READING RES. Q. 407, 430-32.

- **Write brief notes in the margins to signal important sections and ideas in the case**

In addition to highlighting or underlining parts of the case, you can also write brief notes in the margins of the page. This is called **annotating**. You can annotate the opinion by indicating which sentences or paragraphs refer to key elements of the case. You may also wish to write notes about more specific information. Some information worth annotating includes the plaintiff's legal arguments, the defendant's legal arguments, the source of pre-existing rules, and the kind of reasoning undertaken by the court (e.g., analogical reasoning or policy justification).

The purpose of annotating is to help you find information that a professor might ask you about during class discussions. In addition, annotating might be useful when you review a case while preparing for an end-of-semester final exam. Shorter annotations tend to be more useful than essay-length comments, which you will likely not have the time or patience to read through during class or exam preparation.

Figure 2.2 below provides a highlighted and annotated page from the *Lewis* case. Notice that the reader has highlighted only the most important portions of the text—not everything. The reader has also circled two important words, "issue" and "zone of physical danger standard" (the rule applied in *Lewis*), presumably to make this information better stand out when she reviews the case. Finally, the reader has annotated the text with abbreviations, words, numbers, and short phrases. Some of these words and phrases indicate elements of the opinion (e.g., "facts") or information about the parties (e.g., "P resident; D elevator co."), while other phrases provide definitions of key terms and reminders (e.g., damages, which the reader defines as "$$, compensation for injury. Always use 's'!)").

It helps to come up with your own abbreviations to save time and space when making annotations. "P" for plaintiff, "D" for defendant, "CofA" for cause of action, and "PH" for procedural history are only some examples of abbreviations you can use when marking up a case. Try to create an abbreviation system of your own.

Figure 2.2. Highlights and Annotations

LEWIS v. WESTINGHOUSE ELECTRIC CORP.

Appellate Court of Illinois, 1985.

139 Ill.App.3d 634, 487 N.E.2d 1071, 94 Ill.Dec. 194.

JIGANTI, Presiding Justice:

$$, Compensation for injury. Always use "s"!

(1) . . . [T]he plaintiff, Lucille Lewis, sought damages from the defendants, Westinghouse Elevator Co., a division of Westinghouse Electric Corporation and the Chicago Housing
CofA Authority (CHA) for the negligent infliction of emotional distress. **(2)** The defendants moved to dismiss the plaintiff's complaint for

PH failure to state a cause of action. **(3)** The trial court granted the motion to dismiss. **(4)** The plaintiff now appeals the dismissal of the complaint.

Facts

P resident, D elevator Co.

(5) The plaintiff is a resident at one of the apartments owned by the defendant CHA. **(6)** The defendant Westinghouse maintains and services the elevators at the CHA building. **(7)** On August 16, 1983, the plaintiff entered the elevator on the first floor and rode it to the 16th floor. **(8)** As she attempted to exit the elevator, however, the elevator stalled and the doors remained closed. **(9)** The elevator remained in this position for approximately 40 minutes. **(10)** The plaintiff alleges that during that time she was in danger of "suffocation and serious physical harm." **(11)** In addition plaintiff alleges that as a result of the incident she suffered an unstable angina and aggravation of her coronary arteriosclerotic heart disease and hypertension.

Issue

(12) The central issue to be resolved on appeal is whether the plaintiff has stated a cause of action for the negligent infliction of emotional distress under *Rickey v. Chicago Transit Authority* (1983), 98 Ill.2d 546, 75 Ill.Dec. 211, 457 N.E.2d 1. **(13)** In *Rickey,* the plaintiff, age eight, sought damages for the emotional distress he suffered as a result of watching his five year old brother's near strangulation by an article of clothing which became entangled in a CTA escalator. **(14)** In determining whether the plaintiff could recover, the court adopted the zone of physical danger standard. **(15)** In order to state a cause of action under that standard the plaintiff must have been in "such proximity to the accident" that there was "a high risk of physical impact" so as to cause the plaintiff "reasonable fear for his own safety." **(16)** Additionally the plaintiff "must show a physical injury or illness as a result of the emotional distress." (*Rickey v. Chicago Transit Authority* (1983), 98 Ill.2d 546, 555, 75 Ill.Dec. 211, 215, 457 N.E.2d 1, 5.) . . .

Zone of danger standard: Two components

1

2

2. Problematizing Reading Strategies

Problematizing[18] reading strategies require the reader to engage or interact with the text on a more meaningful level than linear strategies. Unlike linear reading strategies, which place you in a somewhat passive role as a recipient of information, problematizing strategies require you to be an active participant in the construction of your own knowledge. Four strategies fall under the umbrella of problematizing.

[18] Deegan, *supra* note 15, at 161.

- **Contextualize the case**

Before you begin reading the case, situate the case within your course syllabus. Think about how the case fits into what you are working on in the class and why the professor might have assigned this case for you to read at this time. To help place the case into context, you can look at (1) section headings in your casebook (e.g., to determine the subject matter discussed in the case); (2) comments or explanations preceding the case (e.g., to learn about the rules and principles discussed in the case); and (3) the case heading (e.g., to ascertain who the parties are, when the case was decided, and what court decided the case). This information is valuable because it may help you to understand why you are reading this case and how it might connect to other cases and topics you have already covered in class.

- **Ask yourself questions while reading the case**

As you read the case, stop yourself periodically to ask questions about it. You might consider writing these questions either in the margins of the text or in your notes as you read. You could look up the answers to these questions after you have finished reading the case. Alternatively, you can ask your professor these questions when you go over the case in class.

Some examples of questions you can ask yourself include (this list is not exhaustive):

"Why did the plaintiff sue this defendant and not another defendant?"
"Why didn't the defendant argue. . . ?"
"What does a motion for summary judgment mean?"
"Why didn't the judge make the point that. . . ?"

Research has shown that when readers ask questions about a text, their comprehension of the text improves.[19] The more you inquire about the cases you read, the more likely you are to understand them. Read with an inquisitive mind.

- **Make predictions about the case**

In addition to contextualizing the case and asking yourself questions, you could also make predictions as you read. For example, after you have read the conflict facts, try to predict what the plaintiff's legal argument might be. Similarly, once you have read the plaintiff's legal argument, try to predict the defendant's counterargument. You can also make predictions about the reasons that the court will put forth to support its decision. After you have read the court's holding

---

[19] Nell K. Duke and P. David Pearson, *Effective Practices for Developing Reading Comprehension,* 189 J. OF EDUCATION 107, 113-14 (2008/2009).

for the case, try to make predictions about why the court decided as it did. Making these predictions does not have to take longer than 10-20 seconds or so.

Briefly stopping as you read to predict what will happen in the case will help to sharpen your legal argumentation skills. Predictions require you to come up with hypotheses about the case that you can then confirm or reject by reading the opinion. As you read more cases and become more familiar with common law argumentation, your predictions will likely become more accurate.

- **Connect your reading of the case to a real world purpose**

Research shows that connecting your reading of a case to a real world purpose helps to better understand the case,[20] perhaps because you become more invested in the case. A real world purpose generally includes putting yourself in the shoes of an attorney, not simply a law student who has to prepare for class. When you read a case, consider casting yourself in the role of an attorney who has to explain the case to a client or supervisor.

3. Evaluative Reading Strategy

A third reading strategy involves reading a case with a critical eye. While reading, "talk back to the text"[21] instead of unquestioningly accepting the court's decision and rationale.

You could ask questions along the lines of:

"How did the court interpret pre-existing law? Do I agree with this interpretation? Why or why not?"
"Is there anything missing from the court's opinion?"
"Are there any logical inconsistencies in the opinion?
"Was this case correctly decided? Why or why not?"
"What are the implications of the court's decision?"

Evaluating every case you read might be time-consuming, but it is worthwhile. When called on in class, you will often be asked to go beyond merely retelling the key elements of a case. Instead, you may be called on to critique the court's decision, speculate about why the court decided as it did, and/or make arguments about alternative ways the court could have resolved the issue in the case. Employing an evaluative reading strategy is an excellent way to anticipate some of the tougher questions professors will ask you in class.

---

[20] Christensen, *supra* note 2, at 634-36.

[21] Elizabeth Fajans and Mary Falk, *Against the Tyranny of the Paraphrase: Talking Back to Texts*, 78 CORNELL L. REV. 163, 163 (1993) (arguing that "[t]o be effective counselors and advocates, lawyers cannot take legal documents at their word" and that law students should "talk back to the text.").

Further, like the problematizing strategies discussed above, using the evaluative strategy requires you to become more engaged in reading the text. This increases the likelihood that you will understand the case, its implications, and its connections to other cases.

Successful law students use all of the reading strategies discussed in this chapter. However, the strongest law students tend to employ problematizing and evaluative reading strategies to a greater extent than linear strategies.[22] Less successful students, in contrast, rely primarily on linear strategies.[23] In fact, the more time students spend on problematizing and evaluating a case, the higher their grade point average (GPA).[24] It is thus important to engage with a case beyond merely highlighting and annotating. As Professor Christensen explains:

> Successful law students (and lawyers) question court decisions, evaluate the results of cases, and consider the implications of rules. Reading the law is far more than making notes or highlighting text. . . . The best students (and lawyers) are open to the possibility that any given text may be interpreted in several different ways.[25]

TASK 2.B.1. Reading Strategies

Read the following case, *Ross v. Cheema*, also about the tort of negligent infliction of emotional distress. This case is from a different jurisdiction than *Lewis* (see again pages 201-03). *Lewis* is an Illinois case, while *Ross* was decided by the Supreme Court of Indiana.[26] Keep this in mind as you read.

Use at least one linear, problematizing, and evaluative reading strategy while reading the case. Then answer the questions below.

1. **Linear strategies**: Which strategy/strategies did you use? Did the strategy/strategies help you to better understand the case?
2. **Problematizing strategies**: Which strategy/strategies did you select? Did the strategy/strategies deepen your understanding of the case?
3. **Evaluative strategy**: Ask yourself one of the sample questions posed above, or come up with your own evaluative question. (And be sure to

---

[22] Christensen, *supra* note 2, at 625-46; Laurel C. Oates, *Beating the Odds: Reading Strategies of Law Students Admitted Through Alternative Admissions Programs*, 83 IOWA L. REV. 139 (1997).

[23] Christensen, *supra* note 2, at 625-46.

[24] *Id.*

[25] *Id.* at 646.

[26] Illinois and Indiana are adjacent states in the "Midwest" of the U.S. They are located roughly in the middle of the country.

answer the question.) Did using the evaluative strategy deepen your understanding of the case?

Pre-Reading Vocabulary

Motion for summary judgment *(noun)*

A motion for summary judgment is a request for the court to dismiss a case or part of a case. A party filing a motion for summary judgment maintains that there are no material facts in dispute and therefore nothing for the fact finder to decide. As a result, the party making the motion is entitled to judgment "as a matter of law."

Imagine a plaintiff's case against a defendant doctor in which the plaintiff alleges that the doctor performed her hand surgery on the wrong hand (e.g., the left instead of the right hand). If there is no dispute between the parties as to whether this fact occurred, the only question that remains is whether the defendant was negligent as a matter of law in performing the surgery on the plaintiff's left hand. Under these circumstances, if the plaintiff moved for summary judgment, she would probably be granted the motion. This is because there is no question as to whether the doctor performed the surgery on the left hand; the only issue that remains to be resolved is whether this act was negligent.[27]

Trial judges either **grant** or **deny** a motion.

ROSS v. CHEEMA

Supreme Court of Indiana, 1999.
716 N.E.2d 435.

SULLIVAN, Justice.

(1) While sitting in her living room, Plaintiff Joyce Ross was frightened by loud knocking at her door. **(2)** We find that Ross did not sustain the requisite direct impact necessary to maintain an action in Indiana for negligent infliction of emotional distress.

Background

(3) On December 6, 1995, Ross was sitting in a chair in her living room when someone rang the doorbell. **(4)** Before Ross could answer the door, the person pounded loudly on the door. **(5)** Ross then heard the screen door pop open, followed by the twisting of the door knob, and then more pounding on the door. **(6)** Ross rose from her chair, ran to the kitchen, looked out the window and saw an unfamiliar car. **(7)** Frightened, she placed a steak knife in her pants before

[27] In a situation so clear-cut as this hypothetical, the parties would probably come to an agreement before a lawsuit is even filed. The example nevertheless illustrates that a motion for summary judgment will be granted to the moving party if she can demonstrate that there are no material facts in dispute.

going to answer the door. **(8)** Upon opening the door, Defendant Raminder Cheema, making a delivery for his employer, Defendant Pillow Express Delivery Services, Inc., handed Ross a clipboard and stated "I have a letter for you. **(9)** Sign here." **(10)** Ross signed for the letter, but as she closed the door, she noticed that the screen door lock was broken and that the door knob was very loose.

(11) On August 3, 1996, Ross filed a complaint for damages against Cheema and Pillow Express, alleging negligent infliction of emotional distress. **(12)** At trial, Defendants successfully moved for summary judgment, arguing that the Indiana impact rule barred Ross's recovery. **(13)** The Court of Appeals reversed, finding that because Ross sustained a direct impact from Defendant's negligence, she was not precluded by the modified impact rule from maintaining her action for negligent infliction of emotional distress. *Ross v. Cheema,* 696 N.E.2d 437, 439 (Ind.Ct.App.1998).

Discussion

(14) Defendants contend that the Court of Appeals erred in reversing the trial court's grant of summary judgment. **(15)** Specifically, they argue that the Court of Appeals improperly concluded that Ross sustained the "direct impact" necessary to maintain an action for negligent infliction of emotional distress under Indiana's modified impact rule. **(16)** We agree.

(17) In *Shuamber v. Henderson,* 579 N.E.2d 452 (Ind.1991), this Court set forth the rule governing negligent infliction of emotional distress claims. **(18)** *Shuamber* modified prior Indiana law, which held that damages for emotional distress were recoverable only where the emotional distress is accompanied by, and results from, a contemporaneous physical injury. *See,e.g., New York, Chicago, & St. Louis R.R. Co. v. Henderson,* 237 Ind. 456, 477, 146 N.E.2d 531, 543 (1957). **(19)** In doing so, this Court did away with the physical injury requirement, concluding instead that:

> When . . . a plaintiff sustains a direct impact by the negligence of another and, by virtue of that direct involvement sustains an emotional trauma which is serious in nature and of a kind and extent normally expected to occur in a reasonable person, we hold that such a plaintiff is entitled to maintain an action to recover for that emotional trauma without regard to whether the emotional trauma arises out of or accompanies any physical injury to the plaintiff.

Shuamber, 579 N.E.2d at 456. **(20)** Hence, the modified rule maintains the requirement of a direct impact, but that impact need not result in a physical injury, nor need the emotional trauma result from a physical injury.

(21) In the present case, Ross was sitting in her living room when Cheema began the pounding on her door that is alleged to have caused her emotional distress. **(22)** This pounding, Ross asserts, constitutes a "direct impact" within the meaning of Indiana's modified impact rule, and thereby entitles her to maintain her action for negligent infliction of emotional distress. **(23)** It does not. **(24)** Prior to *Shaumber,* Indiana's impact rule required a direct impact, which resulted in physical injury, which in turn resulted in the actionable emotional distress. *Boston v. Chesapeake & O. Ry.,* 223 Ind. 425, 428–29, 61 N.E.2d 326, 327 (1945). **(25)** In causing the requisite physical injuries, the direct impact is properly understood as being "physical" in nature. **(26)** Though removing the physical injury element, *Shaumber* in no way altered the "impact" element of the rule. **(27)** For purposes of the modified rule, the direct impact sustained by the plaintiff must necessarily be a "physical" one. **(28)** It is clear from the facts of this case that Ross, in merely hearing a loud pounding at her door, did not sustain the direct "physical" impact necessary to maintain an action for negligent infliction of emotional distress under the modified impact rule.

Conclusion

(29) For these reasons, we . . . vacate the opinion of the Court of Appeals . . . and affirm the judgment of the trial court.

TASK 2.B.2. Questions for Discussion

Answer the following questions to assist you during a class discussion of the case. Indicate the sentence(s) in which you found the answer to each question.

1. What are the facts of this case?

2. What is the procedural history?

3. What is the issue? What is the court's holding?

4. What reason(s) does the court offer to support its decision? Do you find these reasons convincing? Why or why not?

5. What is the court's disposition?

6. How is this case similar to *Lewis v. Westinghouse Electric Corp.*? How is it different?

Chapter 3
Discussing Cases

Law professors often start class discussions by asking about the key elements of a case. These questions are along the lines of:

"What are the facts of this case?"
"What is the issue on appeal?"
"What did the court hold?"

But if these were the only kinds of questions that professors asked about the numerous cases you read for homework, class discussions would quickly become rather dry and, frankly, quite boring.

Most professors challenge their students with questions that require them to look beyond the surface of a case. This is because law professors view their job not so much as imparting information—what you might think of as "the law"—but rather teaching a set of analytic skills that will help you to "think like a lawyer." Thinking like a lawyer means being able to identify, analyze, and resolve legal issues using rules of law. One benefit of the Case Method is that the hundreds of judicial opinions you will read in law school serve as great models for helping you to develop this skill.

Law professors devote a great deal of class time to dissecting judicial opinions and asking you to think about *how* and *why* courts reached a particular decision. Their goal is to help you make similar arguments on law school exams and, later, in professional practice. The tool that professors use to help foster your legal analytic skills is the Socratic Method. The **Socratic Method** is a style of teaching that involves questioning instead of lecturing or spoon feeding students information. Using the Socratic Method, professors ask questions that challenge students to think more deeply about a case. They will often start out asking those "easy" questions about the main elements of a judicial opinion: the facts, the issue, the holding, and so on. This line of inquiry will then give way to more thought-stimulating questions that will ask students to do one or more of the following: critique the parties' claims; comment on the court's holding; evaluate the reasons advanced by the court; apply the holding of the case to a hypothetical;

compare the case to other cases you have read; and speculate about the implications of a decision.

A. Critiquing the Parties' Claims

Sample questions:

> "What do you think of the plaintiff's argument that . . . ?"
> "Do you agree with the defendant that . . . ?"
> "Are you convinced by the defendant's claim that . . . ?"

One reason why professors ask students to critique parties' arguments is to socialize students into our adversarial legal system.[1] There are always two opposing sides in a lawsuit and who prevails is often a matter of who makes the better, more persuasive arguments. When professors ask you to critique the parties' claims and defenses, they facilitate your socialization because they push you to think critically about the arguments and consider possible counterarguments. As a lawyer, you will win your client's case only if you convince the jury or the court. You will therefore spend a lot of time crafting your own arguments and rebuttals to your opponent's counterarguments. These questions are designed to help you develop this skill.

B. Commenting on the Court's Holding

Sample questions:

> "What does the court mean when it says . . . ?"
> "Did the court state a broad or narrow holding?"
> "Was this the right decision?"

Professors might ask questions about the holding of a case to test your understanding of what the court has decided. Sometimes it is unclear what the court means exactly, perhaps because the court does not provide an explicit holding, or because it uses very broad language. Your professors' questions can help you to figure this out. Your professors also ask questions about the holding to cast light on (and correct) any misunderstandings or unwarranted assumptions you might have about the case.

---

[1] Socialization refers to the process of learning the communicative norms or "rules" of a particular academic and/or professional community.

By asking you to comment on and potentially criticize the court's holding, professors also push you to think about the case more deeply. They may ask whether you believe a court "got it right" and whether the decision is sound. You may feel that you are not in a position to critique a court's decision, being just a law student. But remember that your professors' goal is to foster your ability to think critically and make arguments. This will be useful in professional practice and, more immediately, on your exams.

C. Evaluating the Reasons Advanced by the Court

Sample questions:

> "Why do you think the court applied this rule . . . ?"
> "Do you agree with the court's analysis that this case is similar to . . . ?"
> "What was the underlying policy rationale for the decision? Are you convinced by this rationale?"

Generally speaking, professors do not want students to unquestioningly accept what the court says without giving it some thought. This is why they ask questions that go beyond those structural elements of the case in the first place (such as the facts, issue, and holding). Since the rationale behind a decision is one of the most important parts of the opinion, professors will often ask you not only to state what those reasons are, but also to evaluate those reasons. They may ask whether you are convinced by the court's reasoning because this will promote your critical thinking and legal analytic skills—in other words, your ability to "think like a lawyer."

D. Applying the Holding or Reasoning of a Case to a Hypothetical

Sample questions:

> "Imagine that Lewis was actually injured by the elevator. What result would follow?"
> "Suppose that instead of 'merely stalling,' the elevator jumped erratically between floors. Would this change the court's analysis?"

If you have ever tried a new sport, you know that you cannot truly learn how to play the sport well until you *apply* the rules you have learned while playing an actual game. It is the same with legal rules. Though you might have a sense of how a rule operates, you cannot fully understand its scope until you apply it to another case.

To help you get a better sense of how legal rules work, professors will ask you many hypotheticals (often called hypos) in class. A **hypothetical** is a factual scenario that is a slight variation on the facts of the case you read for homework. By applying the holding, and perhaps the reasoning, of a case to a new situation, you gain a much deeper understanding of the court's decision and when or how the rule of the case applies. As you can see from the examples provided above, hypotheticals frequently begin with the phrase "imagine that" or "suppose that."

Hypothetical questions are also designed to challenge assumptions that you might have about the case and governing law. By working through hypotheticals, these hidden assumptions usually come to light. For example, your answer to a hypothetical about emotional distress damages may reveal the erroneous assumption that such damages are recoverable for purely emotional trauma suffered as a result of the defendant's negligence. (They are not; see again *Lewis v. Westinghouse Electric Corp.* and *Ross v. Cheema* in Part II, Chapter 2). Hypotheticals are a great tool for probing such assumptions, and professors use them frequently in class.

E. Comparing the Case to Other Cases You Have Read

Sample questions:

"How is this case similar to . . . ?"
"Is this case distinguishable from . . . ?"
"How do you reconcile this case with . . . ?"

Common law analysis often involves reasoning by analogy. Under the principle of *stare decisis*, like cases must be treated alike. Professors try to sharpen your ability to reason by analogy, and hence assist your socialization into the U.S. legal system, by asking questions that directly call on you to compare two or more cases that you have read for class. Such questions also reveal the kinds of factors courts may use to draw parallels or make distinctions between cases.

Words and expressions you will often hear in class include: <u>analogize</u> X case <u>to</u> Y case (show how two cases are similar); <u>distinguish</u> X case <u>from</u> Y case (show how two cases are different); and <u>reconcile</u> X case <u>with</u> Y case (show how two cases that are seemingly different are nevertheless compatible).

F. Speculating about the Implications of a Case

Sample questions:

> "What are the consequences of this case for . . . ?"
> "Does this case create a slippery slope . . . ?"
> "Will this case open the floodgates for more litigation on . . . ?"

Cases do not happen in a vacuum but rather in a broader legal and social context. Professors may therefore ask questions that invite you to think about the potential effects of a decision.

Two phrases you might hear in this context include "slippery slope" and "opening the floodgates." The metaphor of slippery slope refers to a course of action that leads to a series of events with a final, usually negative, consequence (not unlike a very slippery slide). As an example, parents of teenagers often make slippery slope arguments about the use of alcohol that might go something like this. If you drink alcohol, you will become drunk; if you become drunk, you will lose your inhibitions; if you lose your inhibitions, you will get in a car even when it is not safe; if you get in a car when it is not safe (because you are drunk), you will get into an accident. Professors will similarly ask you to identify slippery slope arguments in a legal opinion or to make them yourself.

The metaphor of opening the floodgates refers to an action that makes it possible for something else to happen in very large numbers. (A floodgate is a gate that is designed to keep out or allow in a large amount of water.) In the context of law, this "something" is almost always increased litigation in a particular area of law. Professors may ask whether you believe a decision will result in more lawsuits and potentially overburden the legal system—or, whether the court was concerned about opening the floodgates in reaching its decision.

You can almost certainly expect to be asked the questions in this chapter in a U.S. law class. That said, law professors also ask other kinds of questions depending on their perspective or approach to law. A torts professor with a degree in economics, for example, might ask questions about how court decisions do (or do not) promote economic efficiency. Or a civil procedure professor with twenty years of litigation experience may focus on the more practical aspects of trial procedure.

Pay special attention to the questions your professor asks you—and in particular, the kinds of hypotheticals put to you in class. These are often a window into the kinds of questions you can expect to see on the professor's final exam.

Chapter 4
Writing about Cases

By and large, U.S. law students write three types of documents in a lecture-based exam class: case briefs, course outlines, and exams.

Case briefs and course outlines are "writer based"[1] documents. As the name implies, the intended audience for a writer-based document is the writer herself. The purpose of a writer-based document is to help the writer study, organize, and reflect on information. Other examples of writer-based documents include class notes, flash cards, and journal entries.

Unlike case briefs and course outlines, exams are "reader-based" [2] documents that are produced specifically to communicate with a reader: a professor, supervisor, or editor. Reader-based documents are usually formal and tend to be more polished than their writer-based counterparts. Examples of reader-based documents include letters written for a client, legal memoranda written for a supervisor, and appellate briefs written for an appellate judge.

As a law student, you will produce both writer- and reader-based documents for class. Writer-based documents often precede and lay the groundwork for subsequent reader-based documents. For instance, case briefs and course outlines are both key ingredients for a successful exam answer.

This chapter begins by describing how to write effective case briefs (Section A) and create useful course outlines (Section B). The chapter then continues with a discussion of law school exams (Section C).

A. Writing Case Briefs

A **case brief** is a summary of a case that contains all of the key elements of a case outlined in Part II, Chapter 2. It is a study tool that helps with class participation and exam preparation.

---

[1] Linda Flower, *Writer-Based Prose: A Cognitive Basis for Problems in Writing* 41 College Eng. 19 (1979).

[2] *Id.*

Below is a sample brief of the *Lewis* case. (To refresh your memory of the case, look back to pages 201 to 203.)

Lewis v. Westinghouse Electric Corp.

Appellate Court of Illinois, 1985.

RULE OF THE CASE: A plaintiff cannot state a cause of action for negligent infliction of emotional distress (NIED) unless she can demonstrate (1) "such proximity to the accident" that it created a "high risk of physical impact" that would cause "reasonable fear for [her] own safety"; and (2) physical injury or illness as a result of the emotional distress.

Facts: Plaintiff (Lewis) lived in an apartment building owned by one of the defendants, Chicago Housing Authority (CHA). The other defendant, Westinghouse Electric Corp. (WEC), maintained and serviced elevators in the building. Upon trying to exit the elevator in the building one day, she got stuck for 40 minutes when the doors failed to open. As a result of the accident, the plaintiff alleged that she feared suffocation and bodily harm, and that her previous medical conditions worsened. The plaintiff sued both CHA and WEC for NIED. The defendants filed a motion to dismiss the plaintiff's complaint for failure to state a cause of action, and the trial court granted the motion.

Procedural History: Defendant prevailed at trial (on a motion to dismiss). The plaintiff appealed.

Issue: Did the plaintiff state a cause of action for NIED against an elevator company and housing authority after being stuck in a stalled elevator for 40 minutes?

Holding: No. The plaintiff did not state a cause of action for NIED against an elevator company and housing authority after being stuck in a stalled elevator for 40 minutes.

Reasoning:

Rule application: According to *Rickey v. Chicago Transit Authority*, a plaintiff can recover for NIED if she is in the "zone of physical danger." This means that (1) the plaintiff must be in "such proximity to the accident" that there is a "high risk of physical impact" so as to cause the plaintiff "reasonable fear for [her] own safety"; and (2) the plaintiff "must show a physical injury or illness as a result of the emotional distress." Both conditions must be met. The plaintiff has failed to meet the first of these conditions. Her fear was not reasonable per the objective standard of "whether a particular incident would produce fear in the person of ordinary sensibilities" (*Knierim v. Izzo*). The court suggests that she was not a person of ordinary sensibilities. Second, the plaintiff was not at high risk of physical impact. The elevator simply stopped, and there is no indication that any outside force could have caused a danger of physical impact.

Reasoning by analogy: This case is not like *Bass v. Nooney Co*, in which water rose in an elevator such that the plaintiff feared drowning. Rising water elicited a reasonable fear on the part of the plaintiff. In this case, however, the elevator merely stalled. A stalled elevator does not produce reasonable fear in a person of ordinary sensibilities.

Policy rationale: The law should not "encourage neurotic overreactions to trivial hurts" but rather "aim to toughen the psyche of the citizen rather than pamper it."

Disposition: Trial court's decision is affirmed.

Comments: [This part is optional. You may include notes for yourself about the case: look up and define terms or legal principles you do not know; jot down questions you want to ask your professor in class; connect this case to other cases you have read in class; etc.]

1. Suggestions for Effective Case Briefing

As illustrated by the sample brief above, a thorough case brief usually contains the following sections:

1. Case name, court, and date;
2. Rule of the case;
3. Facts;
4. Procedural history;
5. Issue;
6. Holding;
7. Reasoning; and
8. Disposition.

These sections more or less correspond to the key elements of a case previously outlined in Part II, Chapter 2.

Students wishing to further reflect on the case after their reading can also include an optional comments section at the end of the case brief. This optional section is one way to engage or "interact" with the case on a deeper level and experiment with the reading strategies discussed in Part II, Chapter 2. It is strongly recommended that you take the time to think about and provide comments on each of your cases in this optional section.

More detailed suggestions for writing an effective case brief follow.

a. Formulate the "Rule of the Case"

The holding of a case is the court's answer to the issue raised on appeal. It is a statement of law as applied to the facts of a *particular* case. The **rule of the case**, on the other hand, is a more *general* legal principle that the case you are reading "stands for." It is the rule that courts are bound to follow and apply to future cases.

Courts often will not state an explicit rule, but will leave it for readers to figure out from reading the opinion. In fact, sometimes readers simply cannot be sure about what the rule of a case is until later courts in later cases interpret and clarify the rule. This uncertainty may be frustrating for new law students, but it illustrates the malleability and flexibility of common law.

The difference between a holding and a rule is often a matter of wording. Holdings are more closely tied to the facts of the particular case, while rules are more general statements of law. For example:

1. "We hold that Amy did not owe a duty to aid Ben, a stranger who had been injured in a car accident not caused by the defendant."
2. "We decide that individuals do not owe a duty to aid strangers who have been injured in an accident not caused by the individual."

The first statement is specific: it refers to the particular individuals in the case (Amy and Ben) and the kind of accident in which Ben was involved (a car accident). The second statement is more general: it refers to "individuals," "strangers," and "accidents." The first statement therefore sounds more like a holding, while the second statement sounds more like a rule. Additionally, holdings may be formulated in the present or past tense, but rules are always stated in the present tense.

As mentioned, courts do not always state an explicit rule (or holding) in their opinion. You might need to derive this rule for yourself following a close reading of the case. The rule of a case will often be a matter of interpretation, and two people can construe or "read" a case quite differently (often depending on their goals and the clients they are representing). Again, this demonstrates the flexibility of common law.

In *Lewis*, the court does not articulate an explicit rule of law. It is your task as the reader to figure out what the "*Lewis* rule" is. Of course, the court does apply a pre-existing rule from the *Rickey* case, cited in the opinion in sentences (13)-(16). However, this pre-existing rule might not be the same as the "*Lewis* rule."

As it turns out, *Lewis* does not do anything revolutionary. It more or less stands for the same rule as the one articulated in *Rickey*. Frequently, however, the pre-existing rule(s) <u>applied in</u> the case and the rule <u>of</u> a case are different.

This is because in a common law system, cases usually further develop and define the scope of rules established in previous cases.

Try to capture both the holding and rule of a case in your case brief.

TASK 4.A.1. The *Ross* Rule?

Look again at the *Ross* decision. Does the court create a completely new rule in this case? Or does it further develop a pre-existing common law rule?

b. Be Aware of Obiter Dictum

Courts are only bound by the rule for which a case stands. They are not bound to follow other statements made in an opinion that do not address the issue or issues raised in the particular case. Yet, sometimes courts make pronouncements that look awfully similar to rules or reasons for rules, and it can be difficult to discern what constitutes a rule or reasoning that future courts must follow and what is other "stuff."

Imagine that the *Lewis* court stated: "If the elevator had jerked and dropped several floors, the plaintiff could have had a cause of action for the negligent infliction of emotional distress." This hypothetical "if . . . then" construction does not convey what actually happened in the *Lewis* case. Rather, it is a slight manipulation of the facts to suggest the scope of the court's rule. Courts occasionally provide such hypotheticals in their opinions. However, these hypotheticals do *not* constitute the rule of the case and they do *not* bind later courts. Courts do not announce rules of law through hypotheticals. They announce rules through definitive statements.

The hypothetical in the paragraph above is an example of dictum (plural form dicta). **Dictum** is an abbreviated form of the Latin term obiter dictum (plural form obiter dicta), which literally means "something said in passing" or "a remark by the way." **Dicta** are statements made in judicial opinions—like hypotheticals—that are helpful for understanding the court's decision, but are not necessary to the resolution of the issue or issues in the particular case. When reading a case, try to tease out or separate the rule from the dicta. And remember that the rule is the general legal principle that the decision represents.

c. The Facts: Include Only the Legally Relevant Facts

Facts that are essential to the outcome of a case are called the **legally relevant facts**. These are the only facts that you should include in your short case brief. Though most facts that courts include in their opinions tend to be relevant, they also provide information about names, dates, and other identifying information that usually does not affect the outcome of a case and therefore are not legally relevant. The ability to determine or "boil down" a case to its legally relevant facts is a key skill developed in law school. Law professors, bar examiners, and judges will test you on this skill throughout law school and beyond.

A good way to determine whether a fact is legally relevant is by asking yourself: "If this fact had NOT occurred, would it have changed the court's conclusion?" If your answer is "yes," then the fact is legally relevant (because the fact affected the court's decision). If the answer is "no," then the fact is not legally relevant (because it did not affect the court's decision).

TASK 4.A.2. Legally Relevant Facts in *Lewis*

In the facts section of the *Lewis* case brief, the writer does NOT include the date on which the incident in question occurred. However, the writer DOES include the amount of time that the elevator stalled. Why do you think one of these facts is legally relevant but the other is not?

d. The Issue: Name the Applicable Rule (or Procedure) AND Include Important Facts

Issues can be formulated in a number of ways. But to be as precise as possible, your formulation of the issue should make reference to two pieces of information: (1) the applicable rule (or procedure) and (2) important facts. All of this should be done in one sentence: either a yes/no question or a statement beginning with "the issue is whether. . . ."

Here is the issue from the *Lewis* case brief:

> "Did the plaintiff state a cause of action for NIED against an elevator company and housing authority after being stuck in a stalled elevator for 40 minutes?"

What is the applicable rule here? If you guessed NIED (negligent infliction of emotional distress), you guessed right. This is the legal rule at the heart of the *Lewis* case. So the issue should certainly mention this rule by name. The rest of the issue provides only the most important facts: *Lewis* involved an individual who was stuck in an elevator that stalled for 40 minutes.[3]

---

[3] Many legal rules are made up of multiple elements or components that must be satisfied. In certain cases, only one element of a rule is disputed by the parties (e.g., the plaintiff claims she has proved the particular element, while the defendant argues that she has not successfully proved the element). In these situations, you would focus in on the element or component in dispute. You will see examples of issues revolving around a single element in the cases contained in Part II, Chapters 5 and 6.

As you may recall, issues can be phrased in procedural terms, that is, with a focus on the appropriateness of the lower court's legal decision. The issue in *Lewis* can also be formulated in this way:

> "Did the trial court err in dismissing the plaintiff's complaint for failure to state a cause of action for NIED against an elevator company and housing authority after she was stuck in a stalled elevator for 40 minutes?"

The relevant procedure here is dismissing the plaintiff's complaint. And the issue is whether the court erred in doing so. The important facts otherwise remain the same. Procedural issues will often begin with the phrase, "Did the trial court err . . .?"

LANGUAGE TIP

The verb "err" is followed by the preposition "in" and the gerund (verb + "-ing"). For example:

1. Did the court err <u>in granting</u> the motion for summary judgment?
2. Did the court err <u>in allowing</u> the jury to hear the evidence?

As you first start writing case briefs, it is good practice to try to formulate the issue in terms that are both substantive (with a focus on the applicable legal rule) and procedural (with mention of the applicable legal procedure).

e. The Holding: Name the Applicable Rule (or Procedure) AND Include Important Facts

The holding in your case brief should directly answer the issue in your brief. You can start with a simple "yes" or "no," and then provide a longer explanation. Just as you included the applicable rule (or procedure) and important facts in your statement of the issue, you should do the same with the holding. Notice that in the sample *Lewis* brief above, the holding mirrors the issue word-for-word:

> "The plaintiff did not state a cause of action for NIED against an elevator company and housing authority after being stuck in a stalled elevator for 40 minutes."

Try to create the same kind of symmetry between your issue and holding, so that the holding is a mirror image of the issue.

f. The Reasoning: Be Thorough and Provide All of the Reasons Supplied by the Court

The court's reasoning is one of the most important parts of the opinion for two reasons. First, this section provides necessary support for the court's conclusion. Second, the reasoning is a great example of legal analysis. By reading the court's reasoning carefully—and for *every* case that you are assigned[4]—you will gradually start to see patterns of legal analysis that you can then apply to your law school exam answers.

In your case briefs, try to be as thorough as possible and note all of the separate reasons provided by the court. Also useful is to jot down the type of reasoning applied by the court: rule application? reasoning by analogy? policy rationale? The more you scrutinize the way courts reason, the more likely it is that you will be able to apply the same kind of legal reasoning to your final exams.

While the suggestions above make it likely that you will write an effective case brief, it should be noted that there is no single "right" way to write a brief. It is difficult to predict what your professor (or employer or judge) will consider important about a case. You may well include material in your brief that your professor does not cover in class at all. Or vice versa, you may fail to include information that your professor asks about in detail. Over time, you will develop a feel for what information should be included in your brief and what information can be left out.

2. Benefits of Case Briefing

You may be wondering why you should take the time and effort to write a summary of each case instead of simply reading closely and following the reading strategies outlined in Part II, Chapter 2. Writing a separate summary of each case is a time-consuming exercise and, as you will soon learn, time is a precious commodity in law school. Nevertheless, for the reasons outlined below, it is a good habit to write your own briefs for every case you read.

You may have also heard of "canned" case briefs available either online or in book format. Such pre-written case briefs can be helpful in a pinch (for example, if you did not have time to read a case because of an emergency the night before). However, canned briefs should not replace preparing your own brief. The value of writing a case brief lies in the process of reading the court's decision and

---

[4] Consider the following story about the authors' friend a cautionary tale. One day in torts, the professor called on the friend (now a legal writing professor). The friend had read three out of four cases. When the class began discussing the fourth case, the professor called on the friend and he admitted that he had not read the case. The professor replied, "Read it now. We'll wait." The friend then had to read the case while the professor and other students in the class waited!

extracting the important elements. Furthermore, reading and briefing cases exposes you to patterns of legal reasoning and important legal vocabulary which you can use in your own legal analyses.

a. Case Briefs Help with Class Participation

Imagine that you have read a ten-page case that the class is in the middle of discussing. Unexpectedly, the professor calls on you to explain the policy justifications for denying recovery to the plaintiff. You do not remember the answer to her question off the top of your head. You should not feel bad about this; you will read numerous cases for homework every day, and it will be hard to recall every little detail about every single case. But if all you have in front of you is your casebook, it might take a bit of time for you to locate the information that the professor is asking for. You may remember that the answer is contained in the court's analysis, so you skip to that part of the opinion and quickly scan the text to find the answer. But the clock is ticking and your professor and colleagues are waiting. Even ten seconds of silence can seem like an eternity in the classroom.

If you walk into class having briefed your cases, you will likely avoid this situation. Instead of frantically leafing through the case and scanning the text to find the answer to your professor's question, you have it right in front of you in your notebook or on your computer screen.

Case briefs help you in class because they allow you to answer questions when the professor calls on you unexpectedly. They may also give you the confidence to volunteer answers on your own.

b. Case Briefs Facilitate Exam Preparation

Law school essay exams usually require you to apply the rules you have learned in class to new factual scenarios. If you have written out case briefs for each of the cases that you read throughout the term, you have saved yourself time in the long run. You do not need to re-read hundreds of pages in your casebook to find the rule of each case.[5] Armed with organized case briefs, you have to look through only your (much shorter) briefs to find the rules.

The process of writing case briefs helps with exam preparation in another important way: case briefs help to develop your legal analytic and writing skills. Legal opinions reflect the kind of writing and thinking expected of you on law school essay exams and thus serve as models of legal analysis. By writing down each element of the court's decision, and by teasing out the various reasons and kinds of reasons provided by the court to support its decision, you build a solid foundation for your own exam writing.

---

[5] Keep in mind as well that courts do not always state holdings and rules explicitly, so figuring out this information weeks or months after your initial reading of a case can be challenging.

c. Case Briefs Promote Language Development: Paraphrasing

The more you read and write in a language, the more your language develops. By virtue of reading and writing, you become exposed to new words, expressions, and grammatical structures that you can use in your own writing.

As you read new cases, pay attention to the words and structures used by the court. Consider keeping a vocabulary or grammar journal in which you can jot down new terms or grammatical constructions that you can follow up on later. Paying attention to the court's language use may help you to better retain some of this linguistic information. Again, especially helpful is keeping a journal and committing to practicing the lists of words and structures that you have collected.

Writing case briefs helps you to fine-tune one particular writing skill: paraphrasing. **Paraphrasing** is the act of putting someone else's writing into your own words. Paraphrasing is an essential skill that helps to avoid a charge of plagiarism on exams and seminar papers.[6] Paraphrasing in a case brief means using your own words instead of directly copying language from the opinion. The ability to paraphrase a case demonstrates an understanding of the case. Furthermore, paraphrasing allows you to develop the skill of making complex ideas easier to understand, which is an important skill when working with clients.

A variety of techniques may be used to paraphrase texts. The most common techniques are listed below. These techniques should always be used in combination, with the writer employing three, four, or five techniques within a single paraphrase. Using just one technique from the list below is not enough to create a paraphrase. Each of the examples below illustrates a single paraphrasing technique; none of the techniques, by themselves, are sufficient for creating an effective paraphrase (more on this in Section (6) below).

(1) Using Synonyms

Synonyms are words and expressions that have a similar meaning as the original word or expression. Though using synonyms is a great way to paraphrase, keep in mind that most words in English have a slightly different shade of meaning. Check an English-to-English dictionary when you are in doubt as to the subtle difference between two terms. In addition, read several example sentences with the synonyms you would like to use in your paraphrase. This will give you a better idea of the context in which the words can be used appropriately. A great place to look for example sentences is the Corpus of Contemporary American English

---

[6] Plagiarism is regarded as a very serious offense at academic institutions throughout the United States. This book does not address plagiarism in detail. However, every law school has an academic code of conduct that details the kinds of activities that would constitute plagiarism. Read your school's code of conduct carefully.

(COCA), an online collection of searchable texts (called a "corpus") of over 560 million words.[7]

You should also refrain from using synonyms for legal concepts and specialized vocabulary, often referred to as "terms of art." Creating a synonym for a term of art might create confusion for the reader who may be familiar only with the particular term, but not the phrase you created. For example, you would not want to use a synonym for the term "negligent infliction of emotional distress." This is a fixed legal term that does not have synonyms.

Examples of this paraphrasing technique from *Lewis v. Westinghouse Electric Corp.*:

ORIGINAL:	"she **attempted** to **exit** the elevator"
PARAPHRASE:	she **tried** to **leave** the elevator
ORIGINAL:	"the elevator **stalled**"
PARAPHRASE:	the elevator **stopped**

(2) Changing the Word Form

Another paraphrasing technique involves changing the form of a word. For instance, if a sentence contains the noun "presentation," you could use the verb "present" instead. If a sentence contains the adjective "vulnerable," you could use the noun "vulnerability."

But changing word form comes with one big caveat. When you start playing with word forms, you can end up with a sentence that is too long, clumsy, and potentially unclear. Make sure that your paraphrase is concise and easy for the reader to understand, even if that reader is you.

Examples of this paraphrasing technique from *Lewis v. Westinghouse Electric Corp.*:

ORIGINAL:	"the plaintiff is a **resident** at one of the apartments"
PARAPHRASE:	the plaintiff **resides** at one of the apartments
ORIGINAL:	"his five year old brother's near **strangulation**"
PARAPHRASE:	his five year old brother was nearly **strangled**

---

[7] CORPUS OF CONTEMPORARY AMERICAN ENGLISH, https://corpus.byu.edu/COCA/ (last visited Mar. 12, 2019).

(3) Changing Transitions

Transitions are words that indicate relationships between ideas within a sentence or across sentences (see again Part I, Chapter 4). To show contrast, for example, writers can use the words "however," "nevertheless," or "in contrast." To show cause and effect, writers may use the words "as a result," "consequently," or "as a consequence." When paraphrasing an original sentence with one of these words, you can try to use a different transition.

Examples of this paraphrasing technique from *Lewis v. Westinghouse Electric Corp.*:

ORIGINAL:	"We recognize **nevertheless** that the line between those questions is hazy at best."
PARAPHRASE:	**However**, we recognize that the line between those questions is hazy at best.

ORIGINAL:	"**Additionally**, the plaintiff 'must show a physical injury or illness as a result of the emotional distress.'"
PARAPHRASE:	**Furthermore**, the plaintiff "must show a physical injury or illness as a result of the emotional distress."

(4) Changing the Order of Ideas

You can also swap the order in which you present ideas. Assume, for example, that the original sentence expresses a cause-and-effect relationship, beginning with the cause first and ending with the effect. In a paraphrase, you could begin with the effect first and then the cause.

Another caveat: in using this paraphrasing technique, make sure that you do not end up with a sentence that is awkward or illogical, or one that would disrupt the flow of ideas in a paragraph.

Examples of this paraphrasing technique from *Lewis v. Westinghouse Electric Corp.*:

ORIGINAL:	"**The trial court granted** the motion to dismiss."
PARAPHRASE:	The motion to dismiss **was granted by the trial court**.

ORIGINAL:	"**As she attempted to exit the elevator**, however, the elevator stalled and the doors remained closed."
PARAPHRASE:	However, the elevator stalled and the doors remained closed **as she attempted to exit the elevator**.

(5) Changing Text Structure

Finally, you can change the structure of the original text by breaking a sentence up into multiple sentences, or merging together shorter sentences into one longer sentence.

Examples of this paraphrasing technique from *Lewis v. Westinghouse Electric Corp.*:

ORIGINAL:	"However, the *Knierim* court favorably commented on the case of *Slocum v. Food Fair Stores of Florida, Inc.*, in which the plaintiff suffered a heart attack as a result of an aggravation of a pre-existing condition."
PARAPHRASE:	However, the *Knierim* court favorably commented on the case of *Slocum v. Food Fair Stores of Florida, Inc.* **<u>In this case,</u>** the plaintiff suffered a heart attack as a result of an aggravation of a pre-existing condition.
ORIGINAL:	"The elevator merely stalled. There is no suggestion in this case that any outside force was present that would injure the plaintiff."
PARAPHRASE:	The elevator merely stalled **<u>and</u>** there is no suggestion in this case that any outside force was present that would injure the plaintiff.

(6) Use Paraphrasing Techniques in Combination

When you paraphrase texts, use a combination of the five techniques instead of relying on only one. Using only one technique to paraphrase will result in a sentence that is still plagiarized from the original. In fact, each of the examples provided above do not go far enough. They provide an example of a single paraphrasing technique. By itself, one technique is not sufficient to create a paraphrase.

See, for example, the following original sentence from *Lewis*:

> "In *Rickey,* the plaintiff, age eight, sought damages for the emotional distress he suffered as a result of watching his five year old brother's near strangulation by an article of clothing which became entangled in a CTA escalator."

Now read the following sentence:

> In *Rickey,* the plaintiff, age eight, sought damages for the emotional distress he suffered as a result of watching his five year old brother's near strangulation by an article of clothing which **got trapped** in a CTA escalator.

Though this writer uses the synonym "was trapped" for "entangled," the sentence is nevertheless a plagiarized version of the original. This is because the vast majority of the sentence has not been changed from the original.

The next sentence, on the other hand, is a much more effective paraphrase of the original sentence from *Lewis*.

> The plaintiff in *Rickey* was an eight year old who brought suit against the CTA for negligent infliction of emotional distress. He watched as his five year old brother was almost strangled by clothing that got trapped in a CTA escalator.

This sentence exhibits all of the five paraphrasing techniques. Can you find where, and how, the writer uses the techniques?

A couple of final notes about paraphrasing case briefs. First, you do not necessarily need to paraphrase the holding or key language from the court's reasoning. If the court offers an explicit holding, you can write the holding, word-for-word, in your case brief. Similarly, if the court provides important language in the opinion—for example, to define a key concept—you may also copy that language into your case brief instead of paraphrasing it. Be sure, however, to put quotation marks (" . . . ") around any text that you lift word-for-word from the opinion.

Second, remember that a case brief is a writer-based document. The intended audience for the document is nobody but the writer—that is, you. Less than perfect paraphrasing is usually not a problem if you are the only person who sees your brief. However, plagiarizing on a case brief may easily translate to plagiarizing on an exam if you end up copying sentences from your brief to your exam answer. The best way to avoid this is by paraphrasing your case briefs or by placing quotation marks around anything that is not in your own words.

TASK 4.A.3. Paraphrasing

Paraphrase each of the following sentences pulled from torts cases. Try to use as many of the five techniques from above. You may use a law dictionary or an English-to-English dictionary if you need help understanding any of the words or phrases.

1. Perry testified that he performed a pretrip inspection of the trailer on the day of the accident.[8]

2. Mr. Kinney had shoveled snow from his driveway the previous evening but was not aware that ice had formed overnight.[9]

3. Plaintiff was standing on a platform of defendant's railroad after buying a ticket to go to Rockaway Beach. A train stopped at the station, bound for another place. Two men ran forward to catch it.[10]

4. Carafano is a popular actress. Under the stage name of Chase Masterson, Carafano has appeared in numerous films and television shows, such as "Star Trek: Deep Space Nine," and "General Hospital."[11]

5. This appeal presents the question whether the doctrine of informed consent requires a physician to obtain the patient's consent before implementing a nonsurgical course of treatment.[12]

6. The jury must determine, after considering all the evidence, whether the defendant attempted to aid the victim.[13]

7. At the heart of the First Amendment is the recognition of the fundamental importance of the free flow of ideas and opinions on matters of public interest and concern.[14]

---

[8] McDougald v. Perry, 716 So.2d 783, 784 (Fla. 1998).
[9] Carter v. Kinney, 896 S.W.2d 926, 927 (Missouri 1995).
[10] Palsgraf v. Long Island Railroad Co., 248 N.Y. 339, 340 (1928).
[11] Carafano v. Metrosplash, Inc, 339 F.3d 1119, 1121 (9th Cir. 2003).
[12] Matthies v. Mastromonaco, 160 N.J. 26, 28 (1999).
[13] Farwell v. Keaton, 396 Mich. 281, 287 (1976).
[14] Hustler Magazine, Inc. v. Falwell, 485 U.S. 46, 50 (1988).

B. Writing Course Outlines

A course outline is a summary of the legal concepts and rules of law in a particular legal subject. It contains information collected from case briefs, class notes, and course readings in one clear, organized document. You can think of a course outline as a "cheat sheet" for law school exams. This is because most exams are "open book" and "open notes," which means that students can take study materials, including course outlines, with them into the examination room. In short, a course outline is a summary of your course for the purpose of helping you on an exam.

Though the ostensible purpose of a course outline is to refresh your memory while taking an exam, most students will not have much time to peruse their outlines during the test. Thus, the value of course outlines lies mostly in the process of creating them. Preparing your own outline allows you to review material and organize it in a way that makes sense to you. It also allows you to identify areas of the law that still confuse you, and which you should spend more time reviewing before the exam. Finally, the outline is a great tool to use when answering practice exam questions in preparation for the exam.

This section contains samples of course outlines and suggestions for creating your own.

1. What Does a Course Outline Look Like?

Below are excerpts of two outlines for a family law class, written by two different students. Which one do you think is more helpful for exam preparation and for use on an in-class exam?

a. Student #1's Outline

a. Child Custody

Case #1: *In re Marriage of Carney*
Facts: Husband and wife married when teenagers and had two sons. They separated after the second child was born. Mother gave up custody of the sons to father and they moved to a different state. Four years later, father was injured and he became a quadriplegic. Mother requested custody of both boys. Before father's accident, mother didn't visit her sons or contribute to their support. She called them occasionally and sent some letters. Trial court awarded custody to mother, while father argues that trial court abused its discretion.
Issue: Is a physical disability that affects the parent's ability to participate in physical activities by itself sufficient to take the children from his custody?
Holding: A physical disability that affects the parent's ability to participate in physical activities is not by itself sufficient to take the children from his custody.

Case #2: *Kendall v. Kendall*
Facts: Husband and wife members of different religious beliefs (husband Catholic, wife Jewish). Before marrying, they discussed raising children in Jewish faith. After getting married, husband

became member of a fundamentalist Christian faith; later, the wife adopted Orthodox Judaism. They had two children. The mother tried to limit the children's exposure to father's religion. Mother filed a petition to divorce father. The trial judge granted the divorce, awarded custody to both parents, and stated that "neither [parent] may indoctrinate the children in a manner which substantially promotes their alienation from either parent or their rejection of either parent." Father appealed and argued that the trial judge's order violated his freedom to exercise his religion.
Issue: Was the trial judge's order a limitation on the defendant's religious freedom?
Holding: No, when there is evidence of harm to children, a limitation placed on a party's religious freedom does not violate constitutional rights.

Case #3: *McMillen v. McMillen*
Facts: Husband and wife had one son and divorced four years later. Wyoming court awarded primary custody of son to mother. Next year father instituted an action in Pennsylvania asking for partial custody of son. The custody order was modified a few times in the next few years. The son expressed his preference to live with father, and a Pennsylvania court granted custody to father, arguing that it would be in the best interest of the child. On appeal, the appellate court vacated the custody order and awarded custody to mother.
Issue: Should a child's preference to live with one parent determine who is awarded custody?
Holding: A child's preference is not dispositive in custody determinations, but it is one factor to consider.

b. Student #2's Outline

2. Child Custody

Custody determinations are made in the **best interest of the child (BIOC)**, but the court takes multiple factors into account (**no one factor is controlling**).

Factors considered by the court:	• Child's relationship to parent • Health and welfare of child (emotional, social, educational needs) • Home environments • Parents' care-taking ability • Past evidence of abuse • Stability and continuity • Sex + age of children • Child's preference—if based on mature, intelligent, rational reasons

Applying the BIOC standard:

Factor:	Case name	Rule
Disability	*In re Marriage of Carney*	• Physical handicap is NOT presumptive evidence of unfitness or even of detriment to children. Physical well-being not

		determinative of custody decisions.
Religion	*Kendall v. Kendall*	• When demonstrable evidence of substantial harm to the children has been found, a divorce judgment limiting the children's exposure to religious indoctrination does not burden the parent's right to practice religion under the Free Exercise clauses of the state and federal constitution.
Child's preference	*McMillen v. McMillen*	• Though the express wishes of a child are not controlling in custody decisions, such wishes do constitute an important factor that must be carefully considered in determining the child's best interests.

NOTE: Custody is modifiable with a material change in circumstances!

Outline #2 is probably more helpful both during the exam preparation process and on an exam. This is because the student who created Outline #2 did not merely "dump" her case briefs into the outline, but carefully considered how to organize information in a way that would be helpful if she needs to refresh her memory of child custody rules while taking her family law exam.

Law school exams generally do not call on students to recite information about the cases they have learned in class. Rarely will you see a question on an exam asking you, for example, the facts of *Kendall v. Kendall* or the holding of *McMillen v. McMillen*. Instead, your task on most exams will be to read a hypothetical story and determine what legal issues the story raises and how to resolve those issues using the rules you have learned in class. Student #2 designed a better outline for such an exam.

Let us assume that the family law exam involves a story about child custody. Student #2 can turn to the relevant section of her outline and look at the table she has created for what factors courts consider in awarding custody. Let us further assume that this child custody exam question involves a disabled parent. Student #2 would not have to search long to find that she read a case on disability, *In re Marriage of Carney*. This is clearly shown in the table of cases she has created. Student #2 has the rule from this case right on hand, which she can then apply to the facts of the hypothetical scenario on the exam. Student #1, on the other hand, would need to do some digging around in her outline to try to find the relevant rule to answer the question. Needless to say, this might waste valuable time during the exam.

When creating your course outlines, think about how to organize information in a way that would be helpful for the exam. Below are some further suggestions.

2. Suggestions for Effective Outlining

a. Identify the Major Topics and Subtopics in the Legal Subject

The first step in creating a course outline is to identify the major topics and subtopics covered in class. This will give your outline a structure that you can fill in with more detailed information as the semester progresses. To identify topic areas, you can consult two sources: your casebook and your course syllabus. Look at the table of contents of your casebook and the schedule on your syllabus for topics. Because professors often do not end up covering all of the topics contained in a casebook, your syllabus will probably be more helpful.

Here is an example of the major topics and subtopics covered in a family law class. This is a good starting point for the outline.

FAMILY LAW OUTLINE

I. Defining "Family"

II. Marriage

A. Family Privacy
B. The Fundamental Right to Marry
C. Traditional Model of Marriage and Challenges/Revisions to It
D. Who Can Get Married?
E. Common Law Marriage, Alternatives to Marriage, and Abolishing Marriage

III. Getting out of Marriage

A. Divorce
1. Economic Consequences of Divorce
a. Distribution of Property
b. Alimony
c. Child Support
2. Child's Consequences of Divorce
a. Child Custody
b. Child Visitation
B. Annulment

IV. Jurisdictional Issues in Family Law

b. Organize Your Outline According to Topics, not Case Names

As the example of Student #1's and Student #2's outlines demonstrates, it is usually better to organize an outline by issues and topics covered in the class, and not by case names. As mentioned, law school exams will rarely call on students to directly recite information from the cases they have read (e.g., "What are the facts of X case?"; "What is the holding of Y case?"; "What were the court's reasons in Z case?"). Therefore, an outline that simply contains case briefs is not going be particularly helpful.

Rather, law school exams usually consist of a story—called a "fact pattern"—in which people interact in ways that raise legal issues. Your job on the exam is to identify these issues and figure out how to resolve them using the rules you learned in the course.

It makes more sense to organize your outline based on potential issues or topics that might appear on exam fact patterns. This is what Student #2 did above. On the second table in her outline, she began with "factors" courts might consider in the left column. These are potential topics that might come up in child custody cases. She then provided the case names which stand for these topics (middle column), and then the rules derived from these cases (right column). This is a more user-friendly outline for an exam that calls on students to identify and resolve legal issues.

c. Organize Information in Visually Appealing Ways

Because you will have very little time to consult your outline during an exam, organize your outline so that it is easy to find the information that you are looking for. Below are visuals that you could incorporate into your outline.

(1) Bullet Points

A bullet point is a small symbol, usually a dot or a line (• or -). Bullet points make items in a list stand out. They are useful on outlines as well as in class notes. Here is part of a student's outline for a constitutional law class. Notice how she uses bullet points to organize information.

DORMANT COMMERCE CLAUSE

If Congress has NOT enacted legislation in a particular area of interstate commerce, the states are free to **REGULATE**, so long as the state statutes:

- Do not **discriminate** against out of state commerce
- Do not unduly **burden** interstate commerce
- Do not regulate **extraterritorial** (wholly out of state) activity

(2) Bolding, Underlining, Highlighting

The student who created the constitutional law outline above also uses **bolding**, <u>underlining</u>, and highlighting—sometimes in combination—to make particular text better stand out. Again, because you will have very little time to consult your outline during a timed exam, it makes sense to arrange your outline in a way that makes it easier for you to access important information (such as case names, statutes, specialized terms, and so forth) in a hurry. Bolded, underlined, and highlighted text certainly grabs the reader's attention.

(3) Tables

A table is a visual that consists of columns and rows. Tables may be used to organize certain kinds of information. For example, you could list arguments for and against particular rules, policies, or procedures. As you are creating your outline, think about what information could be best visualized in a table. Lists and comparisons are usually good candidates.

Tables are also especially helpful for organizing information from the cases you have read. As mentioned, you probably should not organize tables by the names of the cases, but rather, by the issues or topics that the cases raise. You saw an example of such a table in Student #2's outline above.

Below is another example, pulled from a student's criminal procedure outline. In the criminal procedure class, this student read many cases involving different types of searches under the Fourth Amendment to the U.S. Constitution. All of these searches have slightly different requirements, which can be difficult to remember. The student compiled all of the information from the cases that she read for class into a table that helped her to better understand the requirements for the different kinds of searches.

The table she created contains the following information:

1. Types of searches, as indicated in the left column;
2. Whether probable cause is required for that type of search, as indicated in the middle column; and
3. Whether a search warrant is required for that type of search, as indicated in the right column.

The student also specified in parentheses which case established or illustrates each of these requirements.

This table took the student many hours to create. After its completion, however, she had a much better understanding of searches under the Fourth Amendment. This is because the process of creating a table helps to understand a topic better. The student also had a visual that made it easy for her to find information while taking the criminal procedure exam.

(4) Checklists

A checklist contains a list of questions that one must (or can) ask in conducting a legal analysis. As you move through the list of questions, you can check off ("✓") any item that you have addressed in your analysis.

The checklist below was created by a student in a contracts class. It contains the questions she wanted to ask herself to make sure she would not miss any potential issues on a contracts fact pattern. A checklist like this is useful because it reminds you of the questions you should address but may forget with the time pressure and anxiety of taking an exam.

Contracts Checklist

1. IS THERE A CONTRACT?

- Offer
    - Must show (1) contractual intent; (2) certain and definite terms; (3) communication to offeree
    - Unilateral or bilateral?
    - Option contract?
    - Is it revocable at any time?
- Acceptance
- Consideration
- Mutual assent

YES. Continue with checklist below.
NO. Do analysis above.

2. IS CONTRACT ENFORCEABLE?

(Statute of frauds: for goods over $500; land not in writing)

- Mistake: mutual vs. unilateral (unless clerical, should enforce)
- Warranty: rescission possible
- Misrepresentation or nondisclosure

YES. Have duties of one party been discharged?

- If something happens that was unexpected (impossibility, impracticability, F or P, accord and satisfaction—meaning parties discharged b/c satisfied in other way)
- Can introduce PER?
    - Partial vs. total integration
    - Restatement § 214 (can bring in evidence)
    - Interpretation (on face or extrinsic)
- Has it been modified by a subsequent agreement? Is this enforceable?
    - To be enforceable, need consideration (change duties on both sides)
    - Or make separate stand alone agreement

NO. Maybe for lack of consideration.
Going off Contract:

- Is there an implied contract?
    - Implied in fact: it's just not in writing, but there is a deal
    - Implied in law: no need for bargain, so unjust enrichment (NOTE: this matters for remedies)
- Is there promissory estoppel?

3. IS THERE A BREACH?

NOTE: (1) when it occurred; (2) material or minor
YES. What damages?

- Expectation, reliance, restitution

- Limitations: duty to mitigate; consequential damages only if foreseeable; no mental distress
- Liquidated damages clause?
- Enforcement in equity? (injunction or specific performance)

NO. Any damages off contract? Under QM? (Look at reasonable value)

(5) Flowcharts

A flowchart is a visual that depicts a process. Flowcharts are useful when there are several available alternatives or procedures to choose from within a process. The flowchart below was created by a student studying criminal procedure to better understand when a statement can be used against a criminal suspect under the rule articulated by the Supreme Court in *Miranda v. Arizona*.

Can a suspect's self-incriminating statements be used against him at trial? (*Miranda* Test)

Custody?
↓ ↘
Yes No → Can be used
↓
Interrogation?
↓ ↘
Yes No → Can be used
↓
Miranda warnings?
↓ ↘
No Yes
↓
Waiver?
↓ ↘
No Yes
↓ ↘
Cannot be used Can be used

The benefit of thinking about how to best organize information you have learned in class cannot be underestimated. Creating tables, checklists, flowcharts, and other visuals requires you to think about how information fits together and how to best conceptualize a particular area of the law. Though all of this thinking is time-consuming, you will find that it is usually well worth it. A well-organized outline will provide you with a better understanding of the material and, in turn, better prepare you for the final exam.

d. Start Your Outline about One Month into the Semester, but No Later than One Month Before the Exam

Even if you are so energized by your first class that you want to run home and get started on your outline right away, you should take a moment. Starting on your outline too soon may turn out to be counterproductive.

It is advisable to begin creating your outline a few weeks into the semester. In the beginning of any class, you cannot yet "see the forest for the trees." This idiom means that you cannot see a situation as a whole because you are lost in all of the tiny details. When you first begin learning a new subject, it can be difficult to understand the "big picture" and see how different cases, statutes, and legal principles fit together. As you learn more about the subject, you gain a better sense of these connections. It is a good idea to wait until you have some of this understanding before you begin to create your outline.

That said, you also should not wait too long to begin assembling your outline. At the latest, you should get started one month before the exam. If you wait until finals period to make your outline and you finish right before the exam, you probably will not gain as much from the process.

e. Create a Long and a Short Outline

Although there is no perfect length for an outline, shorter outlines are generally more useful on exams. Of course, "short" is somewhat subjective: it could mean one, five, or even 30 pages.

One strategy worth trying is making both a longer and shorter outline. The long outline can contain all of your notes and case briefs in a somewhat unpolished form; this outline could be up to 200 pages or more. The long outline can serve as a "master document" from which you create a shorter, more concise outline that contains only the most important information you need for your exam. As the semester progresses and you practice using your outline with hypotheticals and sample exam questions, you will get a good sense of what information is absolutely necessary, as well as how to organize this information in a succinct, visually appealing way that will help you on the exam.

f. Use Other Outlines to Supplement Your Work, Not to Replace It

You do not have to be in law school very long to learn that for many courses, commercial outlines are available for purchase. Commercial outlines are books containing the rules and principles of a particular area of law in a neat, outline format.

Commercial outlines are an excellent resource. However, they should not replace creating your own outline. As already mentioned, much of the value of an outline lies in the process of its creation. You can use a commercial outline to supplement your work—for example, to confirm your understanding of a particular legal principle—but do not let the outline take the place of preparing your own.

The same advice goes for course outlines created by students who took the same course in a previous semester. You might have a friend who took the same class last year and made an outline that she claims earned her an A in the course. Though your friend may well have created an excellent outline, it would still be a good idea to make your own. People organize and conceptualize information in very different ways. What was helpful for your friend may not be helpful for you. Nonetheless, if your friend is willing to share her outline with you, it cannot hurt to take a look. You can certainly use it to guide your own outline. But again, another person's outline should not replace preparing your own.

Some law schools also have "outline banks" available to their law students. This is usually an online portal where students can upload their outlines and share it with others who attend the law school. This is also a great resource, though two caveats are in order. First, if you download an outline from an outline bank, make sure that the student took the same class with the same professor. Professors may cover different material or take a different theoretical approach to the subject matter, even if they teach the same subject. Second, keep in mind that just because an outline has been uploaded to an outline bank does not mean that the outline contains accurate information. This is another reason why you should always create your own outline and use other outlines merely to supplement or double-check your work.

g. Use Your Outline to Take Past Exams

One of the best things you can do with your outline is to put it to the test. As the semester wears on and you feel that you are getting a good handle on the materials covered in a class, try to take past exams to see whether your outline proves to be a useful resource. At most law schools, professors will post their past exams, and occasionally, the best student answer to the exam, online or at the library. You should take a look at these past exams and take them under timed conditions. If a best answer exists, you should also check to see how your answer compares.

In taking past exams, you might find that you do not need to use your outline at all. Maybe you remember all of the information you need to answer a question because you spent so much time outlining that you know all of the rules by heart. Or—and this is much more likely—you might find that to answer a question, you need to use your outline to refresh your memory about a rule, procedure, or other information. If this is the case, consider how helpful your outline was. Did your outline contain the information you needed? Was it easy to find the information? What could you change to make it more accessible?

Taking past exams is not only very useful preparation for the exam, but it also allows you to test out your course outline and make any adjustments before exam day.

C. Writing Law School Exams

Law classes can generally be classified into three categories. The vast majority are **exam classes** in which the student's entire grade is based on a timed final exam administered at the end of the semester. Exam classes tend to be larger lecture courses with over 30 students, where much of the interaction is driven by the question-answer sequence of the Socratic Method. Introductory courses in contracts, constitutional law, corporations, torts, and other major areas of law are exam classes.

Another popular type of class is the **seminar class**. These courses focus on a subfield of law, and they can be rather specialized. Seminar classes tend to be much smaller than exam classes, with courses capped at around 15 or 20 students. If you take a seminar class, your grade is usually based on a long (e.g., 25+ page) scholarly paper on an original topic related to the subject area of the course. You conduct your own research and develop this paper throughout the term and submit it for a final grade at the end.

There is also an increasing push to provide law students with more practical, hands-on training that they can take with them into the workforce. Accordingly, many law schools now offer **experiential classes** and clinics that help students develop the professional skills they need to succeed as lawyers. For instance, classes in arbitration and mediation may have a component that requires students to participate in simulated arbitration hearings or mediation sessions, which may then be factored into students' final grade. Courses in contract drafting teach students how to write contracts. And courses in some specialized subfields may require students to work collaboratively on group projects centered on solving hypothetical client problems.

In spite of the diversity in the law school curriculum, however, it is virtually impossible to go through law school without taking exams. Because a student's grade in an exam class boils down to her exam performance during the "finals period," it is important to become familiar with the ins and outs of exam-taking before taking that first exam. This section serves as an introduction to different kinds of law school exams, with particular emphasis on law professors' favorite: the "issue spotter" essay exam.

1. The "Issue Spotter" Essay Exam

Law school exams come in various forms, though the most common by far is the essay exam. Essay exams are usually administered under timed conditions, ranging anywhere from two to five hours. Essay exams are also typically **in-class exams** because they take place in a classroom. Most in-class exams are "open book" and/or "open notes," and you may take your course materials in with you to the examination room.

In lieu of an in-class exam, some professors give **take-home exams**, which must be completed within a window of time, usually 12 to 48 hours. In-class and take-home essay exams are often quite similar, though the latter are longer and involve more complex legal questions. In addition, professors expect more detailed, sophisticated responses on take-home exams.

Essay exams usually contain made-up scenarios called **fact patterns**, which are stories about people having law-related problems. Your task as test-taker is to identify or "spot" the legal issues raised in the story and determine how to resolve them. As you will soon see, this kind of essay exam, aptly called an "issue spotter," is designed to simulate the work of legal professionals such as attorneys, judges, or legislators. This connection to real-life legal practice is probably why professors like to evaluate students using this type of assessment.

For example, one popular type of issue spotter question on torts exams involves a hypothetical client who has been injured and turns to her lawyer for help. The student, placed in the position of the lawyer, must determine whether the client has a claim against any of the parties that may have harmed her.

There is good reason to include such questions on an exam. Lawyers regularly interview clients who tell detailed stories about the injuries that befell them. It is a lawyer's job to identify what issues are raised by the client's case, determine what rules would apply, and predict the client's chances of success (and hence determine whether the law firm should accept the case).

Below is an example of such a question.

a. Torts Essay Question

QUESTION

Last July, Cindy and her mother Donna went on a mother-daughter shopping trip around town. Because Cindy had another social engagement following the trip, the two of them took separate cars. Donna followed Cindy's car.

The mother-daughter duo was headed to Cindy's favorite store when Cindy stopped at a busy intersection in the center of town, looked around, and then proceeded to pass through the intersection safely. Cindy then stopped on the side of the road, about 500 feet (approximately 150 meters) from the intersection, to wait for Donna's car. When Donna attempted to drive through the intersection, Donna's car was struck on the driver's side by a car driven and owned by Erica.

An initial medical examination right after the accident revealed that Donna sustained injuries to her left rib cage and she strained her abdominal muscles. A second medical examination was conducted approximately four weeks after the

> accident. The report from this second examination stated that there was "no evidence of any remaining physical injuries from the accident."
>
> Because Cindy was waiting on the side of the road for Donna's car to pass through the intersection, she watched the entire accident from her rearview mirror. Seeing that Donna's car was struck, Cindy feared that her mother was seriously injured and became very anxious. To make matters worse, Cindy has not been quite the same in the months since the accident. She has extreme pain in her back, dizzy spells, panic attacks, and episodes of insomnia. She also has recurring nightmares of her mother dying in a car crash.[15]
>
> Cindy came to your law firm last week asking for legal advice. You are a junior associate at the firm and the managing partner, Ms. Ferris, has asked you to write her an email discussing whether Cindy might have a claim against Erica.
>
> For this question, assume that you are working in Illinois.

This question can be separated out into three parts.

First is the **fact pattern**. This fact pattern relates the story of Cindy, Donna, and Erica. Fact patterns are narratives that contain legal issues which you need to identify and resolve in your exam answer. Fact patterns can be shorter than this example or they can be quite a bit longer. Some professors write elaborate fact patterns that can reach up to six or seven (or more) pages.

Second is the **question**. On this exam, the question is as follows:

> Cindy came to your law firm last week asking for legal advice. You are a junior associate at the firm and the managing partner, Ms. Ferris, has asked you to write her an email discussing whether Cindy might have a claim against Erica.

Read the question at least two times to make sure you understand what it is asking you to do. In addition, consider reading the question before reading the fact pattern so that you read with a clearer purpose. Also pay attention to the **role** that question has cast you in and the **task** that you have been assigned. Here, you are a junior associate (your role) who has to write an email about whether a potential client might be able to sue another person (your task). Other roles you might be asked to inhabit include a trial judge (e.g., ruling on a motion), an appellate judge (e.g., writing an opinion), or a lawmaker (e.g., evaluating the merits of a particular law).

[15] Fact pattern adapted from Barnhill v. Davis, 300 N.W.2d 104 (Iowa 1981).

Third is an additional **instruction**:

For this question, assume that you are working in Illinois.

Not all professors provide additional instructions for individual questions. But if they do, pay special attention to them. Failure to follow these additional instructions could negatively affect your grade. Professors might instruct you to use the law of a particular jurisdiction, as this question does here. Professors might also instruct you to stay within a word or page limit or request that you format your response in a particular way.

b. Two Sample Answers

Read the following sample responses to the exam question above. Which response answers the question more effectively?

(1) Student #1's Answer

> The issue here is if Cindy can successfully state a cause of action for the negligent infliction of emotional distress. A plaintiff in a negligent infliction of emotional distress case brought under Illinois law must be in "'such proximity to the accident' that there was 'a high risk of physical impact' so as to cause the plaintiff 'reasonable fear for [her] own safety.'" Cindy was not in proximity to the accident. In addition, it is obvious that Cindy didn't fear for her own safety but was so worried about her mom that she had a panic attack in the car. Therefore, Cindy would not be able to state a cause of action for negligent infliction of emotional distress.

(2) Student #2's Answer

> Dear Ms. Ferris:
>
> I hope this message finds you well. Below you will find my analysis of Cindy's case.
>
> Cindy probably cannot bring a successful claim against Erica. The issue is if Cindy can state a cause of action for the negligent infliction of emotional distress (NIED) after watching her mother's car get struck by another vehicle. Under the "zone of physical danger" rule, which is the law in Illinois, a plaintiff can make out a claim for NIED if two conditions are met. First, the plaintiff must be in "'such proximity to the accident' that there was 'a high risk of physical impact' so as to cause the plaintiff

'reasonable fear for [her] own safety.'" Second, the plaintiff "'must show a physical injury or illness as a result of the emotional distress.'" *Lewis v. Westinghouse Electric Corp.*

Cindy was in proximity to the accident because she watched it unfold from about 500 feet away. However, Erica could argue that Cindy was not at high risk of physical impact from this distance. Though Cindy could claim that she feared for her own safety, it is unlikely that a court would accept this fear as "reasonable." Cindy was quite a distance from the intersection and safely pulled over on the side of the road. Erica could argue that this situation would not create fear in "the person of ordinary sensibilities." The facts also suggest that Cindy was primarily concerned for her mother's safety, and not her own. Furthermore, a court may be concerned that allowing such a lawsuit to go forward would "encourage neurotic overreactions to trivial hurts" (*Knierim v. Izzo*, cited in *Lewis v. Westinghouse Electric Corp.*), resulting in a greater number of frivolous lawsuits, which may be burdensome on the courts.

Cindy can probably show physical injury as a result of the emotional distress. Though some of Cindy's symptoms appear to be psychological—she has insomnia and nightmares—there are also physical manifestations of her distress. Cindy has back pain, she feels dizzy, and she has panic attacks.

Because Cindy would have a difficult time proving the first part of the NIED zone of danger standard, she likely cannot state a cause of action for NIED against Erica. As a result, I would not suggest taking her case.

Please do not hesitate to contact me if you have any further questions.

Kind regards,
Junior Associate

If you felt that Answer #2 responded to the question more effectively, you are correct. (You may also have guessed this was the more effective answer because you first read an excerpt of Answer #2 in Part I, Chapter 1 of this book as well.)

One rather obvious difference between Answer #1 and Answer #2 is length: Answer #2 is much longer than Answer #1. Though the length of a response is never the sole metric for a successful exam answer, it does tend to suggest a more thorough analysis. On the other hand, a long answer could also signal that the writer has veered off track and included too much unnecessary or irrelevant information in the response.

Listed below are the ingredients necessary for an effective exam answer, which are exhibited by Answer #2. Also listed are mistakes to avoid, some of which are evident in Answer #1.

c. A Framework for Answering Issue Spotter Exam Questions: "IRAC"

Issue spotter exam questions call on students to do four things:

1. Identify the legal **issues** raised by the fact pattern;
2. Determine the **rules** that govern the issues identified;
3. **Analyze** how the rules apply to the particular facts of the case; and
4. **Conclude** by predicting what is likely to happen.

The acronym used to refer to these four elements of an exam answer is IRAC, which stands for **I**ssue, **R**ule, **A**nalysis, and **C**onclusion. IRAC is a useful framework for organizing your exam answer and ensuring that you include all relevant information in your response.

(1) Issue

In Answer #2, the writer states the issue in the following sentence:

> The issue is if Cindy can state a cause of action for the negligent infliction of emotional distress (NIED) after watching her mother's car get struck by another vehicle.

As with the issue in a case brief, the writer names the applicable legal rule (NIED) and the important facts ("after watching her mother's car get struck by another vehicle").

(2) Rule

In Answer #2, the writer states the applicable rule in the following sentences:

> Under the "zone of physical danger" rule, which is the law in Illinois, a plaintiff can make out a claim for NIED if two conditions are met. First, the plaintiff must be in "'such proximity to the accident' that there was 'a high risk of physical impact' so as to cause the plaintiff 'reasonable fear for [her] own safety.'" Second, the plaintiff "'must show a physical injury or illness as a result of the emotional distress.'" *Lewis v. Westinghouse Electric Corp.*

The writer explains the rule in some detail, but not too much. Since there are multiple components or elements of the NIED rule, the writer breaks down the rule into these components and briefly describes each component. In the analysis, the writer then applies these components to the facts of the case. (Note that both common law and statutory rules often have multiple components or elements that must be satisfied.)

Keep in mind as well that sometimes you will have to synthesize a rule from multiple sources—for example, three different cases. In other words, the rule you should include in the "R" of IRAC will not always come from one case. Common law rules develop over time, across multiple cases, and you may need to account for this in your rule statement. You will see examples of how rules evolve over time in Part II, Chapters 5 and 6. In these chapters, you will also have an opportunity to practice synthesizing rules from multiple sources.

(3) Analysis

In Answer #2, the writer's analysis is contained in the following paragraphs:

> Cindy was in proximity to the accident because she watched it unfold from about 500 feet away. However, Erica could argue that Cindy was not at high risk of physical impact from this distance. Though Cindy could claim that she feared for her own safety, it is unlikely that a court would accept this fear as "reasonable." Cindy was quite a distance from the intersection and safely pulled over on the side of the road. Erica could argue that this situation would not create fear in "the person of ordinary sensibilities." The facts also suggest that Cindy was primarily concerned for her mother's safety, and not her own. Furthermore, a court may be concerned that allowing such a lawsuit to go forward would "encourage neurotic overreactions to trivial hurts" (*Knierim v. Izzo*, cited in *Lewis v. Westinghouse Electric Corp.*), resulting in a greater number of frivolous lawsuits, which may be burdensome on the courts.
>
> Cindy can probably show physical injury as a result of the emotional distress. Though some of Cindy's symptoms appear to be psychological—she has insomnia and nightmares—there are also physical manifestations of her distress. Cindy has back pain, she feels dizzy, and she has panic attacks.

The analysis is probably the most important part of your entire essay exam answer. It will also likely be the lengthiest section of the IRAC response.

In this analysis, the writer has done four things:

a. Applied the relevant rule to the facts of the hypothetical;
b. Framed points as arguments;
c. Provided counterarguments and rebuttals; and

d. Offered policy justifications.

(a) Applying the Relevant Rule to the Facts of the Hypothetical

In applying the rule to the facts, the writer uses key language from the rule and connects it to the facts of the case. Look again at the writer's statement of the rule:

> Under the "zone of physical danger" rule, which is the law in Illinois, a plaintiff can make out a claim for NIED if two conditions are met. First, the plaintiff must be in "'such proximity to the accident' that there was 'a high risk of physical impact' so as to cause the plaintiff 'reasonable fear for [her] own safety.'" Second, the plaintiff "'must show a physical injury or illness as a result of the emotional distress.'" *Lewis v. Westinghouse Electric Corp.*

This rule contains the following key words and phrases:

"proximity to the accident";
"high risk of physical impact";
"reasonable fear for . . . own safety"; and
"physical injury or illness"

Notably, each of these phrases are pulled directly from the *Lewis* opinion (which, by the way, cites another opinion in the same jurisdiction).

Now look again at the writer's analysis. To better stand out, key words have been **bolded** and the facts are <u>underlined</u>.

> Cindy was in **proximity to the accident** because she <u>watched it unfold from about 500 feet away</u>. However, Erica could argue that Cindy was not at **high risk of physical impact** from this distance. Though Cindy could claim that she **feared for her own safety**, it is unlikely that a court would accept this fear as "**reasonable**." Cindy <u>was quite a distance from the intersection and safely pulled over on the side of the road</u>. Erica could argue that this situation would not create fear in "the person of ordinary sensibilities." The facts also suggest that <u>Cindy was primarily concerned for her mother's safety, and not her own</u>. Furthermore, a court may be concerned that allowing such a lawsuit to go forward would "encourage neurotic overreactions to trivial hurts" (*Knierim v. Izzo*, cited in *Lewis v. Westinghouse Electric Corp.*), resulting in a greater number of frivolous lawsuits, which may be burdensome on the courts.

> Cindy can probably show **physical injury** as a result of the emotional distress. Though some of Cindy's symptoms appear to be psychological—she has insomnia and nightmares—there are also physical manifestations of her distress. Cindy has back pain, she feels dizzy, and she has panic attacks.

The writer applies each of the components of the NIED rule to the facts of the hypothetical case by directly connecting key language from the rule to relevant facts pulled from the fact pattern.

LANGUAGE TIP

A straightforward way to connect key language to the facts is by employing the following structure:

Key language + "because" or "when" + facts

For example:

1. Cindy was **in proximity to the accident** when she watched it unfold from about 500 feet away.
2. Cindy's **fear for her own safety was not reasonable** because she was 500 feet from the intersection and safely pulled over on the side of the road.

(b) Framing Points as Arguments

Student #2 acknowledges that the question on this exam entails a dispute between two parties: Cindy (the putative plaintiff) and Erica (the putative defendant). Therefore, she frames her points as arguments that the two parties would be likely to make:

> "However, Erica **could argue** that Cindy was probably not at high risk of physical impact from this distance."
>
> "Though Cindy **could claim** that she feared for her own safety, it is unlikely that a court would accept this fear as 'reasonable.' Cindy was quite a distance from the intersection and safely pulled over on the side of the road."
>
> "Erica **could argue** that this situation would not create fear in 'the person of ordinary sensibilities.'"

Importantly, these arguments are supported with specific facts pulled from the fact pattern.

(c) Providing Counterarguments and Rebuttals

As shown above, the writer has framed her points as arguments. However, these are presented not as one-sided arguments—that is, all from the perspective of the plaintiff or defendant. Rather, the writer provides two-sided arguments[16] that consist of an argument (made by Erica), a counterargument (made by Cindy), and a rebuttal to the counterargument (made by Erica). See again the three points above: "Erica could argue . . . " + "Though Cindy could claim . . . " + "Erica could argue . . . ."

Two-sided arguments demonstrate to your professor that you have identified arguments for both sides to a dispute. This is a valuable skill for practicing attorneys, who must be able to formulate not only their own arguments, but also anticipate and respond to opposing counsel's arguments. Furthermore, making two-sided arguments suggests to your professor that you picked a side only after careful evaluation of competing arguments.[17]

(d) Offering Policy Justifications

In addition to rule application, Student #2 provides policy reasons for why a court probably would not allow Cindy's lawsuit to go forward. Recall from Part II, Chapter 2 that rule application and policy rationales are two kinds of legal reasoning in judicial opinions. Your exam answer will draw on the same kinds of legal reasoning. Again, this is one of the main reasons to read and brief your cases carefully: the opinions serve as excellent models of legal analysis.

Citing the *Knierim* case (cited in *Lewis*) Student #2 states:

> Furthermore, a court may be concerned that allowing such a lawsuit to go forward would "encourage neurotic overreactions to trivial hurts" (*Knierim v. Izzo*, cited in *Lewis v. Westinghouse Electric Corp.*), resulting in a greater number of frivolous lawsuits, which may be burdensome on the courts.

Here, the writer has made what appears to be both a social policy and judicial administration argument. First, allowing Cindy's NIED claim to go forward may encourage individuals to overreact to problems that are insignificant, which

---

[16] PAUL BERGMAN, PATRICK GOODMAN, AND THOMAS HOLM, CRACKING THE CASE METHOD: LEGAL ANALYSIS FOR LAW SCHOOL SUCCESS 2-3 (2012).

[17] Professors occasionally write exam questions with only one right answer. If you feel that this is the case for a question on an exam you are taking, it is of little use to make such two-sided arguments. Provide the answer that you feel your professor is looking for.

likely is not good for society because it could create "neurotic" and overly sensitive individuals (this sounds like a social policy argument). In a similar vein, allowing Cindy's claim to go forward might "open the floodgates" for increased NIED litigation, which the courts might have trouble handling (this sounds like a judicial administration argument).

Providing policy justifications, when possible and relevant, may support and strengthen your analysis. Review common policy arguments in Part II, Chapter 2.

(e) What about Analogical Reasoning?

You have learned in this book that judges often employ three types of argumentation in their opinions: rule application, reasoning by analogy, and policy rationales. Answer #2 applied rules and offered policy justifications but did not reason by analogy. This is because issue spotter exam answers usually call on students to employ the former two types of argumentation.

Analogical reasoning is not as common on exam answers, perhaps because such reasoning requires a more nuanced, in-depth analysis to which timed exams do not easily lend themselves. That said, there is nothing stopping you from analogizing between a hypothetical on your exam and a case or cases you have read in class. Indeed, this might be exactly what your professor is looking for. Particularly in a course in which you have read very few cases, but you analyzed each case in great detail, your professor might expect you to make such comparisons between the fact pattern and a case or cases you have read for class.

In any event, read each exam question carefully. The question should provide clues as to what kind of analysis your professor is looking for. Additionally, take a look at the professor's past exams (if available) and best answer (if available). Analyze the kinds of arguments in the best answer, and identify instances of counterargument and rebuttal. Notice when the writer uses policy arguments and analogical reasoning with hypotheticals. "Unpacking" a best answer in this way will not only give clues as to the kind of analysis you should provide, but it will make you a more confident exam taker as well.

(4) Conclusion

Student #2 concludes her response in the following sentences:

> Because Cindy would have a difficult time proving the first part of the NIED zone of danger standard, she likely cannot state a cause of action for NIED against Erica. As a result, I would not suggest taking her case.

As a final step in the analysis, the writer concludes by summarizing the points she made in the analysis: Cindy probably cannot prove the first component of the

NIED rule, and therefore she probably does not have a claim against Erica. She makes a prediction about what is probably going to happen in the case.

d. Hedging

Student #2 uses hedging throughout her response. Hedging refers to language that decreases the certainty with which a writer states a claim. Common hedging devices include the modal verbs "might," "may," and "could," and the adverbs "probably" and "likely."

The exam question called on the writer to make a prediction about whether Cindy has a claim against Erica. The writer cannot be one hundred percent sure as to what will happen. So, she uses hedges to temper the certainty with which she delivers her predictions: "Erica **could** argue"; "a court **may** be concerned"; "Cindy can **probably** show"; and "she **likely** cannot state."

Professors usually do not pose questions with one clear-cut, "right" answer. Often, either party could make convincing arguments to resolve the issue at hand.[18] Hedging is one way to demonstrate to your professor your recognition that you are operating within a legal gray area and your predictions cannot be completely accurate. When answering questions that ask you to predict what will or should happen, consider using hedging devices in your response.

e. The Direct Answer

You may have noticed that Answer #2 does not begin with the IRAC analysis. Before delving into IRAC, the writer provides a quick greeting and the following short sentence:

> Cindy probably cannot bring a successful claim against Erica.

The purpose of this short sentence is to directly answer the question that was posed in the exam. As you may recall, the question on this exam was:

> Cindy came to your law firm last week asking for legal advice. You are a junior associate at the firm and the managing partner, Ms. Ferris, has asked you to write her an email **discussing whether Cindy might have a claim against Erica**.

The task in this question is to write an email "discussing whether Cindy might have a claim against Erica." Notice that the writer's response directly answers and mirrors the wording of this question right in the beginning of her response. On

[18] However, some professors do write exam questions with only one right answer in mind. In this case, you should avoid hedging as you will show less confidence in your answer and will probably receive a lower score.

law school exams it is a good idea to get to your point straight away. Law professors read potentially hundreds of student responses. Make your professor's life easier (and increase the chances of her actually enjoying reading your exam answer) by starting out with a direct answer to the question. You can think of this as the "thesis" for your response.

f. Multiple Issue Spotters

The sample exam question in this chapter raises only one legal issue: whether Cindy has a claim of NIED against Erica. However, fact patterns are often significantly longer than this sample question. Longer fact patterns usually contain more issues for students to identify and resolve in their exam answer. Indeed, sometimes professors have a checklist of issues they would like students to spot, and they keep that by their side as they read student answers.

With longer fact patterns containing multiple issues, professors also test students' ability to determine which issues are important (and should be discussed in detail) and which are less important (and should be discussed in less detail). Not all issues are weighted the same. Think of your exam as a test of legal judgment.

On a multiple issue spotter, for each issue identified, write out a separate IRAC analysis containing a statement of the issue, a statement and description of the rule, an analysis, and a conclusion (e.g., Issue #1: IRAC; Issue #2: IRAC; Issue #3: IRAC). Some of the essay practice exercises in Part II, Chapters 5 and 6 contain fact patterns with multiple issues.

g. Red Herrings

Professors occasionally include "red herrings" in fact patterns. A **red herring** is a detail that is intended to distract or mislead the reader. For instance, the torts question above might include a detail about Donna (Cindy's mother) being slightly drunk at the time of the accident. This fact might be relevant if *Donna* brought suit against Erica—perhaps as evidence that Donna was partially at fault for the accident. However, this fact probably has little to do with *Cindy's* NIED claim against Erica. Professors test students on their ability to ignore such red herrings and address only those facts that raise legal issues. Again, they are testing your legal judgment.

h. Mistakes to Avoid in Issue Spotter Essay Writing

(1) Not Managing Your Time

Law school essay exams are usually administered under timed conditions. Students have anywhere from two to five hours for timed in-class exams, and six to 48 hours for take-home exams. As a result, time management is an important skill to develop, particularly for in-class exams. Students who do not manage their time effectively often end up running out of time and may fail to answer one or more questions on the exam.

When you receive your exam and you have been instructed to begin, leaf through all of the pages. Look at each question and check whether your professor has indicated how much the questions are weighted. For example, on a two-hour exam containing three questions, the first question may be worth 50 percent of your score, the second question may be worth 30 percent of your score, while the third question may account for 20 percent of your score. In apportioning your time, plan to spend about an hour on the first question, 35 minutes on the second question, and 25 minutes on the third question. If your professor has not indicated how much each question is weighted, look at how long the fact patterns are and the complexity of the questions (e.g., one question may have multiple sub-questions). This may give you a general sense of how much time you should allot for each question. It may also help to quickly scan each fact pattern and try to determine the general topic or issue(s) that they raise. If you know a lot about the topic in the second question, but less about the topic in the first question, you may wish to begin with the second question to get that quickly out of the way.

As a rule of thumb, you should expect to spend about one-third of your time reading and planning out your response for each question (see the discussion on outlining immediately below). In addition, you may wish to leave 5-10 minutes at the end of the exam to edit and proofread your entire response. Professors understand that you are writing under time pressure and your exam may contain some spelling, punctuation, and minor grammatical errors. However, you do not want to submit an exam that is riddled with mistakes and looks sloppy. This may cause you to lose points.

Above all, always keep an eye on the clock.

(2) Not Outlining Your Exam Answer

As mentioned in Part I, Chapter 1, the process of writing an academic legal text usually involves creating a writing outline, that is, a plan for your piece. Essay exams are no exception.

Because law school exams are timed, students often feel pressured to begin writing as soon as they have finished reading the question(s). With dozens of other test takers typing away on their computers, this pressure only intensifies. However, our suggestion is to try and tune out this distraction. Pay attention only to *your* exam and *your* response. Before you begin writing out your answer, do not hesitate to spend some time outlining (planning) your response.

As mentioned, you should spend about one-third of your time reading and outlining an exam answer. If you have allotted 45 minutes to answering a question, you should spend about 15 minutes reading the question and planning out your response. If you have two hours to answer another question, you should expect to allocate about 40 minutes to reading the question and outlining your answer. If permitted, take ear plugs into the examination room with you so that you are not tempted to follow your neighbors' example and start typing your response right away.

What should an outline for your exam answer look like? There is no set template for a writing outline, and you should develop your own strategy for creating one that works for you. That said, it may be useful to include the following pieces of information in your outline:

1. Your conclusion;
2. The issue(s) that you have identified in the fact pattern;
3. The rule(s) that govern the issue(s);
4. Arguments for and against your conclusion, supported with facts from the fact pattern; and
5. Your conclusion.

Because a well-developed exam answer touches on these points, it makes sense to think about these points before you begin writing.

As an illustration, see Student #2's outline for the answer to the torts exam question posed above. This outline could be written out by hand on a piece of paper. Alternatively, it could be typed into your document and deleted when you have finished typing your response.

Issue: *NIED?*

Rule: *Zone of danger (Illinois)*
Two elements: (1) proximity w/ high risk of physical impact to cause reasonable fear for own safety + (2) physical injury or illness

Arguments FOR NIED	***Arguments AGAINST NIED***
• *Cindy 500 feet away* • *Cindy feared for safety b/c close to accident* • *Cindy had physical injury (back pain, dizziness, panic attacks)*	• *Cindy pulled over on side of road so not very close* • *fear probably not "reasonable"* • *situation not one that would create fear in "person of ordinary sensibilities"* • *Cindy worried about Mom's safety, not own* • *Policy argument: allowing this lawsuit to go forward may open floodgates for frivolous litigation*

Conclusion: *No NIED*

An answer outline like this is useful because it gives the writer a sense of direction. Have you ever started writing something only to realize that as you were writing you changed your mind? On a timed essay exam, this change of heart may cause you to lose precious time.

One of the most useful features of an outline is a FOR/AGAINST table. This table, as shown above, allows the writer to organize all possible arguments for both sides to a dispute. Such a table is helpful when it comes to making the arguments, counterarguments, and rebuttal in the analysis section of the response. In creating such a table, you get a good visual as to which side has more arguments in its favor, which may help you to pick a side. (Though note that not all arguments are weighted the same. Some arguments are stronger than others. Keep this in mind as you decide which side to pick and hence what your conclusion will be.)

Come up with a plan before you write and you will likely end up with a more organized, well-developed response.

(3) Not Using Headings to Organize your Answer

As mentioned in Part I, Chapter 4 of this book, headings are titles for sections of text. Headings help the reader to understand the organization of your text. Good headings also preview for the reader the main idea of an upcoming section in your document. This is important on exams because your professor will be reading potentially hundreds of answers—and rather quickly at that—so it behooves you to organize and highlight your main points as clearly as you possibly can.

You do not need to (and probably shouldn't) create separate headings for each of the IRAC elements. But if you analyze three issues in your answer, it probably makes sense to create a separate section for each issue with informative headings preceding them. For example, on a products liability question in which you identified two different claims that the plaintiff might bring against a defendant, you could include the following section headings:

1. **Claim for Failure to Warn**
2. **Claim for Design Defect**

Or, if you want your heading to be more informative, you can add more detail:

1. **The Plaintiff's Claim for Failure to Warn Will Likely Fail**
2. **The Plaintiff's Claim for Design Defect Will Likely Be Successful**

What you should certainly try to avoid is too many headings (e.g., for each element of IRAC) or no headings at all for long answers with multiple components.

(4) Not Following Instructions

One reason Student #2 has written an effective exam answer is because she has followed the instructions in the exam prompt very closely. Again, the question was:

> Cindy came to your law firm last week asking for legal advice. You are a junior associate at the firm and the managing partner, Ms. Ferris, has asked you to **write her an email** discussing whether Cindy might have a claim against Erica.
> (emphasis added)

In Answer #1, the writer does not format her response as an email. In Answer #2, the writer does format her response as an email. Though it may seem silly to compose an email to an imaginary supervisor, this is exactly what the question calls on students to do. On exams, professors will often cast students in the "real-world" role of an attorney and expect students to really play the part. If a question puts you in the role of a junior associate tasked with writing an email to a supervisor, do precisely that. Take your role and the task that you have been assigned seriously.

Professors will occasionally include such instructions on their exam specifically to help them "weed out" lower scoring answers from higher scoring ones. For example, if a student does not format her response to the exam question as an email, a professor could automatically throw the student's exam answer in a pile reserved for lower scoring answers—even if the response is otherwise well-reasoned and well-structured (of course, this is not true for every professor).

Other instructions you should pay very close attention to include any mention of word and page limits. In large survey courses, professors may have over a hundred students, which means they read over a hundred exam answers. For their own sake, professors in these courses attempt to reduce their workload by placing a length limit on exam responses. If you exceed a word or page limit, the professor might not read the extra words or pages. This could cause you to lose points.

Most exams will have a cover page containing formatting and other instructions for the exam. Some professors send this out before the exam. It is a good use of your time to read this cover page either before or during the exam.

(5) Failing to State and Apply Each Component of a Rule with Multiple Components or Elements

One weakness of Answer #1 is that it does not state each element of the NIED rule from the *Lewis* case. The following sentences, pulled from *Lewis*, provide the relevant rule:

> "[T]he court adopted the zone of physical danger standard. In order to state a cause of action under that standard the plaintiff must have been in 'such proximity to the accident' that there was 'a high risk of physical impact' so as to cause the plaintiff 'reasonable fear for his own safety.' Additionally the plaintiff 'must show a physical injury or illness as a result of the emotional distress.'" (*Rickey v. Chicago Transit Authority* (1983), 98 Ill.2d 546, 555, 75 Ill.Dec. 211, 215, 457 N.E.2d 1, 5.)

In order to state a cause of action for NIED, then, the court uses a "zone of danger" standard. Under this standard, two conditions must be met: (1) the plaintiff must be in such proximity to the accident that there is a high risk of physical impact causing the plaintiff reasonable fear for his own safety; and (2) the plaintiff must show physical injury or illness as a result of the emotional distress. This pre-existing rule, applied in *Lewis*, was established in *Rickey v. Chicago Transit Authority*.

The student who wrote Answer #1 did not state each element of this NIED rule. Instead, she stopped at the first component of the rule (see the underlined portion):

> The issue here is if Cindy can successfully state a cause of action for the negligent infliction of emotional distress. **A plaintiff in a negligent infliction of emotional distress case brought under Illinois law must be in "'such proximity to the accident' that there was 'a high risk of physical impact' so as to cause the plaintiff 'reasonable fear for [her] own safety.'"** Cindy was not in proximity to the accident. In addition, it is obvious that Cindy didn't fear for her own safety but was so worried about her mom that she had a panic attack in the car. Therefore, Cindy would not be able to state a cause of action for negligent infliction of emotional distress.
>
> (emphasis added)

Because Student #1 did not state the second component of the NIED rule, she also did not apply this component to the facts of the hypothetical case. As her analysis is incomplete, she likely lost points on this exam answer.

(6) Making Conclusory Statements

Another weakness of Answer #1 is that it contains a conclusory statement in the analysis. A conclusory statement is a conclusion with an insufficient underlying explanation or analysis. After stating the first component of the NIED rule, Student #1 seemingly applies this rule to the facts of the case. See again her statement of the rule plus application here:

> A plaintiff in a negligent infliction of emotional distress case brought under Illinois law must be in "'such proximity to the accident' that there was 'a high risk of physical impact' so as to cause the plaintiff 'reasonable fear for [her] own safety.'" Cindy was not in proximity to the accident.

Look again at the following sentence: "Cindy was not in proximity to the accident." Does this analysis appear short to you? Are you convinced that Cindy was not in proximity to the accident?

The weakness here is that the student's statement is not backed up with any factual evidence from the fact pattern. Looking at this, a reader would probably think: *Why* was Cindy not in proximity to the accident? *How far away* was Cindy? Can you say more?

In your analysis, pull relevant facts from the fact pattern to support your arguments. If you say that Cindy was not in proximity to the accident, tell the reader *why* that is the case. A more thorough analysis would sound something like: "Cindy was not in proximity to the accident because she was 500 feet away from the crash and pulled over on the side of the road." You can avoid making conclusory statements if you connect key language from the rule ("Cindy was not in proximity to the accident") with relevant facts from the fact pattern ("because she was 500 feet away from the crash and pulled over on the side of the road").

(7) Inventing Facts

Continuing her application of the NIED rule to the hypothetical case, Student #1 states:

> In addition, it is obvious that Cindy didn't fear for her own safety but was so worried about her mom that she had a panic attack in the car.

There are two problems here. Most immediately, there is a factual error: Cindy did not have a panic attack in the car at the time of the accident. Cindy did have panic attacks, but the fact pattern suggests that these occurred *after* the accident. Student #1 "invented" this fact about Cindy's panic attacks.

Inventing facts is a more common mistake than you might think. If you read the fact pattern carefully, you can usually avoid making this mistake.

One suggestion for reading fact patterns on exams is to read them two times. Read over the fact pattern once to try to get the main idea of the narrative. Read over it a second time more closely, paying special attention to—and underlining or highlighting—facts that might raise legal issues. In the margins, write the legal issues that the facts raise.

A second, less serious problem with the sentence from Answer #1 above is that it uses the word "obvious." Some law professors dislike this word. They write fact patterns specifically so that there is no one "obvious" or "right" answer. If you think an issue could be argued either way—that is, either the plaintiff or defendant could prevail—try to avoid using this term.

(8) Requiring the Reader to Infer the Significance of Facts

Another common mistake on exams is making the reader figure out the importance of the facts. Imagine Student #1 wrote the following response to the exam question:

> The issue here is if Cindy can successfully state a cause of action for the negligent infliction of emotional distress. A plaintiff in a negligent infliction of emotional distress case brought under Illinois law must be in "'such proximity to the accident' that there was 'a high risk of physical impact' so as to cause the plaintiff 'reasonable fear for [her] own safety.'"
>
> Cindy stopped on the side of the road, about 500 feet (approximately 150 meters) from the intersection, to wait for Donna's car. When Donna attempted to drive through the intersection, her car was struck on the driver's side by a car driven and owned by Erica. Because Cindy was waiting on the side of the road for Donna's car to pass through the intersection, she watched the entire accident from her rearview mirror. Seeing that Donna's car was struck, Cindy feared that her mother was seriously injured and became very anxious.
>
> Therefore, Cindy would not be able to state a cause of action for negligent infliction of emotional distress.

Look carefully at the middle paragraph. Does it look familiar? It should, because it is copied word-for-word from the fact pattern (see again the torts fact pattern on pages 262-63).

The paragraph lists a number of facts, which is good. However, this description of the facts does not tell the reader *why* or *how* these facts are important. As a result, the paragraph is the opposite of a conclusory statement. Instead of drawing a legal conclusion without providing any factual support, the writer offers a great deal of factual support, but fails to make any connection to key language from the rule. It is unclear what is the legal significance of these facts.

Connect key language from the rule with facts pulled from the fact pattern. This will prevent you from making conclusory statements or making the reader infer the significance of facts. It will also result in a more thorough, well-reasoned analysis.

TASK 4.C.1. Answer #1 Analysis

The writer of Answer #1 above made several avoidable mistakes. Look through Answer #1 again and, using the information you have learned about issue spotter exam writing, find at least two additional weaknesses of the response. How would you suggest correcting these weaknesses?

Weakness:

How to correct weakness:

Weakness:

How to correct weakness:

2. Other Exam Questions

While the issue spotter is the most common type of exam, professors write other kinds of exam questions. These include choice of law essay questions, policy essay exam questions, short answer questions, and multiple choice questions. These question types are not the focus of this book, but as you may come across them on some of your exams, a brief description and example of each question type follows.

a. Choice of Law Essay Questions

Occasionally you will be asked to focus not on how settled law would apply to the facts of a hypothetical, but rather what the applicable law ought to be in the first place. Legal rules are not always settled or uniform across jurisdictions, and your professor may want to test you on your ability to recognize this. Accordingly, essay questions may require you to analyze the more fundamental question of what rule should apply to a particular situation and why.

These questions tend to arise in the following situations:

1. There are two competing rules for resolving a dispute;
2. The case you are presented with is a case of first impression and there is no specific rule on point; or
3. The rule as articulated by a prior court or courts is ambiguous or unclear.

The following hypothetical—a slightly altered version of the torts question on pages 262-63—illustrates what a choice of law question might look like.

QUESTION

Last July, Cindy and her mother Donna went on a mother-daughter shopping trip around town. Because Cindy had another social engagement following the trip, the two of them took separate cars. Donna followed Cindy's car.

The mother-daughter duo was headed to Cindy's favorite store when Cindy stopped at a busy intersection in the center of town, looked around, and then proceeded to pass through the intersection safely. Cindy then stopped on the side of the road, about 500 feet (approximately 150 meters) from the intersection, to wait for Donna's car. When Donna attempted to drive through the intersection, Donna's car was struck on the driver's side by a car driven and owned by Erica.

An initial medical examination right after the accident revealed that Donna sustained injuries to her left rib cage and strained her abdominal muscles. A second medical examination was conducted approximately four weeks after the accident. The report from this second examination stated that there was "no evidence of any remaining physical injuries from the accident."

Because Cindy was waiting on the side of the road for Donna's car to pass through the intersection, she watched the entire accident from her rearview mirror. Seeing that Donna's car was struck, Cindy feared that her mother was seriously injured and became very anxious. To make matters worse, Cindy has not been quite the same in the months since the accident. She has extreme pain in her back, dizzy spells, panic attacks, and episodes of insomnia. She also has recurring nightmares of her mother dying in a car crash.

Cindy sued Erica seeking damages for the negligent infliction of emotional distress (NIED). At trial, the judge instructed the jury that the plaintiff in an NIED claim can recover damages if she can prove that she was physically impacted by the defendant's actions. The jury found no physical impact to Cindy and returned a verdict for the defendant.[19]

---

[19] Fact pattern adapted from Barnhill v. Davis, 300 N.W.2d 104 (Iowa 1981).

> Cindy has appealed the case, arguing that the judge's instructions to the jury were incorrect. You are an appellate judge tasked with reviewing the case and writing an opinion.
>
> Assume that in this jurisdiction, there is no settled NIED rule.

In this altered fact pattern, the role and task of the student has changed significantly. Instead of a junior associate writing an email about a possible NIED claim, the student has been cast in the role of an appellate judge reviewing a lower court decision.

States have created different NIED rules. A student who has taken a torts course probably learned that some states follow the "zone of danger rule" (as illustrated by the *Lewis* case on pages 201-03), while other states follow the so-called "impact rule" (as illustrated by the *Ross* case on pages 225-26). In a semester-long torts class, students usually read cases applying both rules.

The altered exam question states that in this imaginary jurisdiction, the courts have not yet settled on an NIED rule. This is the additional instruction at the very end of the question. Therefore, the question indirectly calls on the exam taker, acting as an appellate judge with the authority to create law, to decide which of the two rules, the zone danger or the impact rule, to apply to the case at hand.

An effective answer to this question would (1) explain that multiple rules can apply to this situation; (2) select a rule to apply to this situation and explain why; and (3) apply the rule to the facts and render judgment. The opinion should also begin with a direct answer. Given the student's role and task, this would likely be a statement as to whether the lower court's decision should be affirmed or reversed.

b. Policy Essay Questions

Another kind of essay question calls on students to evaluate legal rules from a policy perspective. In these policy questions, the student's task is not to identify legal issues and apply existing rules, but rather to explain whether she agrees or disagrees with a rule by using policy arguments to support her opinion.[20]

The following question illustrates what a policy question on an exam might look like.

---

[20] For an excellent, detailed discussion of policy questions (and exam taking generally), see RICHARD MICHAEL FISCHL AND JEREMY PAUL, GETTING TO MAYBE: HOW TO EXCEL ON LAW SCHOOL EXAMS 151-93 (1999).

> **QUESTION**
>
> You are a law clerk to Justice Adams, an appellate judge in your jurisdiction's intermediate appellate court. A new case has landed on Justice Adams' desk involving a claim of negligent infliction of emotional distress (NIED).
>
> The trial judge in the case instructed the jury that the plaintiff in an NIED claim can recover damages if she can prove that she was physically impacted by the defendant's actions. The jury found no physical impact to Cindy and returned a verdict for the defendant. The plaintiff has appealed the case, arguing that the judge's instructions to the jury were incorrect. There is no settled NIED rule in your jurisdiction.
>
> Justice Adams has asked you to write her a short memo explaining why the court should or should not adopt the NIED impact rule going forward.

In this exam question, students have been assigned an entirely different role and task: a law clerk to an appellate judge who must write a memo evaluating a legal rule.

An effective response to such a policy question would (1) provide a direct answer to the judge's question (e.g., "Yes, the court should adopt the impact rule"); (2) support the student's position with at least two or three policy rationales (e.g., the impact rule will reduce fraudulent lawsuits based on purely psychological injury); and (3) state competing policy rationales for the "other side" and minimize the importance of these arguments.

For a list of common policy justifications that courts often use to support their decisions, see again Part II, Chapter 2.

c. Short Answer Questions

As the name implies, short answer questions usually call on a student to respond to a question in a couple of sentences or a short paragraph. Short answer questions can be based on a paragraph-length fact pattern. Or they can be a short, one-sentence question. Below is an example.

> **QUESTION**
>
> What is the zone of danger rule and what are its benefits and drawbacks? Answer in one paragraph not to exceed a page.

An effective answer to this question would do just as the question instructs: (1) explain the zone of danger rule; and (2) outline its pros and cons. The answer would also be limited to one paragraph that is no longer than a page.

d. Multiple Choice Questions

Finally, some professors ask multiple choice questions that ask students to select one or multiple correct answers from a list of answer choices. Multiple choice exams might seem easier than essay or short answer questions because the test taker does not have to produce any written text. However, multiple choice questions can be quite tricky. And, if a student gets a question wrong, she does not get any points for trying. This is unlike an essay or short answer question, where the professor might give partial credit even for incomplete or inaccurate responses.

The following is an example of a multiple choice question.

QUESTION

After witnessing a particularly gruesome accident involving a malfunctioning elevator, Brenda would like to bring suit against the elevator company for the negligent infliction of emotional distress. Under the zone of danger rule, what would Brenda need to prove?

There may be more than one correct answer. Circle the letter of all correct choices.

a. She was near the accident when it occurred.
b. She was in danger of being physically impacted by the accident.
c. She feared for her own safety.
d. She suffered psychological injury.

Based on your reading of the *Lewis* case, you probably know that answer choices a, b, and c, are correct. Answer choice d is incorrect; according to *Rickey* (cited in *Lewis*) the plaintiff "must show a *physical* injury or illness as a result of the emotional distress" (emphasis added). A psychological injury by itself will not suffice.

No matter what kind of final exam you take, it is vital that you adequately prepare for the exam. The final exam is one of the most important and high-stakes reader-based documents you will write during your time in law school. Regularly attend class sessions and pay close attention to what the professor says and asks in class. In addition, write case briefs, prepare course outlines, and practice with hypotheticals and past exams. These are the most effective ways to get ready for the test.

Further Reading

The following texts provide more information about case briefing, outlining, and exam taking.

PAUL BERGMAN, PATRICK GOODMAN, AND THOMAS HOLM, CRACKING THE CASE METHOD: LEGAL ANALYSIS FOR LAW SCHOOL SUCCESS (2012). **(Case briefing, exam taking)**

JOHN C. DERNBACH, WRITING ESSAY EXAMS TO SUCCEED IN LAW SCHOOL (NOT JUST TO SURVIVE) (4th ed. 2014). **(Exam taking)**

RICHARD MICHAEL FISCHL AND JEREMY PAUL, GETTING TO MAYBE: HOW TO EXCEL ON LAW SCHOOL EXAMS (1999). **(Exam taking)**

MICHAEL HUNTER SCHWARTZ, EXPERT LEARNING FOR LAW STUDENTS (2d ed. 2008). **(Case briefing, exam taking)**

ANDREW J. MCCLURG, 1L OF A RIDE: A WELL-TRAVELED PROFESSOR'S ROADMAP TO SUCCESS IN THE FIRST YEAR OF LAW SCHOOL (2013). **(Case briefing, outlining, exam taking)**

NADIA E. NEDZEL, LEGAL REASONING, RESEARCH, AND WRITING FOR INTERNATIONAL GRADUATE STUDENTS (2004). **(Case briefing, outlining, exam taking)**

HERBERT N. RAMY, SUCCEEDING IN LAW SCHOOL (2d ed. 2010). **(Case briefing, outlining, exam taking)**

ALEX SCHIMEL, LAW SCHOOL EXAMS: A GUIDE TO BETTER GRADES (2012). **(Exam taking)**

JOHN DELANEY, HOW TO DO YOUR BEST ON LAW SCHOOL EXAMS (2012). **(Outlining, exam taking)**

KIMM ALAYNE WALTON AND LAZAR EMANUEL, STRATEGIES & TACTICS FOR THE FIRST-YEAR LAW STUDENT: MAXIMIZE YOUR GRADES (2004). **(Case briefing, outlining, exam taking)**

Chapter 5
Torts

The cases in this chapter all concern torts, an area of civil law. A **tort** is a wrongful act (or failure to act) that causes someone to suffer an injury or loss. The injured party may seek compensation for the harm by suing the alleged **tortfeasor**, that is, the individual or other entity who supposedly committed the tort. The party suing is referred to as the **plaintiff**, while the party being sued is the **defendant**. If found liable, the defendant (tortfeasor) must pay money damages to the plaintiff (injured party). Because torts is an area of civil law, we speak of the defendant's potential **liability**, not guilt. There is no jail time attached to committing a tort.

Tort law is mostly common law. Judges create tort law through their written opinions, which announce rules of law that future courts must follow. A small portion of tort rules are enacted by legislatures in the form of statutes, but this is by far the minority. Tort law is also state law, meaning that it is created by state as opposed to federal courts. Since there are 50 states in the United States, there are also 50 separate bodies of tort law. Nonetheless, these different bodies of law are quite similar with only minor variations between them, allowing students to study torts as one major area of law.

Broadly speaking, there exist three kinds of torts: intentional torts, strict liability, and negligence. Intentional torts refer to injuries resulting from deliberate, intentional acts, such as assault and battery. Strict liability is absolute legal responsibility for an injury regardless of fault. It is typically associated with products liability law, which often involves harms from defectively manufactured products. Finally, **negligence** refers to a failure to use the level of care that a reasonable person would use in similar circumstances. This chapter focuses almost exclusively on negligence law.

The tort of negligence is comprised of four elements. This means that a plaintiff who brings a claim of negligence against a defendant must prove that *all* four elements are present in her case. These four elements will be revealed to you through ten negligence cases contained in this chapter.

A. Torts Case #1

The following case addresses the first element of negligence: a **duty** to exercise care.

As a general rule, courts in the United States do not impose a duty on people to act for the sake of others with whom they do not have a relationship. For example, if you walk by a lake and see a stranger drowning in the water, you need not jump in the water or even grab a lifesaver or rope to help rescue the person. If you see a stranger in a restaurant choking on her steak, you need not run over to pat her on the back or perform the Heimlich maneuver. You may sit idly by the water and you may continue to savor your dinner, doing nothing to help these people. This might be in direct contrast to the law in your country, where individuals may be obligated to help others who are in harm's way.

While the "no duty" rule permeates U.S. tort law, courts have carved out some important exceptions to it. Courts have also recognized that when individuals engage in conduct that creates a risk of harm to others, they have a duty to exercise care toward the people who may foreseeably be injured by their conduct. A prime example of such risk-creating conduct is driving. Everyone who drives has a duty to avoid injuring others sharing the road with them, even if they are complete strangers.

In the first case you will read below, the Supreme Court of Minnesota is wrestling with whether to apply the "no duty" rule or whether the plaintiff's case fits into an exception to this rule. As you read the case, try to discern what that exception might be.

EXERCISE 5.A.1. Sentence Identification

Every number in the left-hand column corresponds to a sentence next to it in the opinion. Indicate the information provided by each sentence:

- Facts;
- Procedural history;
- Issue;
- Holding;
- Reasoning; or
- Disposition.

If you feel that a sentence does not fit into any of the categories, try to guess its function in the case.

HARPER v. HERMAN

Supreme Court of Minnesota, 1993.
499 N.W.2d 472.

PAGE, Justice.

(1) **(1)** This case arises upon a reversal by the court of
appeals of summary judgment in favor of the defendant. **(2)**
(2) The court of appeals held that defendant, the owner and
operator of a private boat on Lake Minnetonka, had a duty
to warn plaintiff, a guest on the boat, that water
(3) surrounding the boat was too shallow for diving. **(3)** We
reverse and reinstate judgment in favor of defendant.

(4) **(4)** The facts are undisputed for the purpose of this
(5) appeal. **(5)** On Sunday, August 9, 1986, Jeffrey Harper
("Harper") was one of four guests on Theodor Herman's
(6) ("Herman") 26-foot boat, sailing on Lake Minnetonka. **(6)**
Harper was invited on the boat outing by Cindy Alberg
Palmer, another guest on Herman's boat. Herman and
Harper did not know each other prior to this boat outing.
(7) **(7)** At the time Herman was 64 years old, and Harper was
(8) 20 years old. **(8)** Herman was an experienced boat owner
having spent hundreds of hours operating boats on Lake
(9) Minnetonka similar to the one involved in this action. **(9)** As
owner of the boat, Herman considered himself to be in
(10) charge of the boat and his passengers. **(10)** Harper had
some experience swimming in lakes and rivers, but had no
formal training in diving.

(11) **(11)** After a few hours of boating, the group decided
to go swimming and, at Herman's suggestion, went to Big
(12) Island, a popular recreation spot. **(12)** Herman was familiar
with Big Island, and he was aware that the water remains
shallow for a good distance away from its shore. Harper had
(13) been to Big Island on one previous occasion. **(13)** Herman
positioned the boat somewhere between 100 to 200 yards
from the island with the bow facing away from the island in
an area shallow enough for his guests to use the boat
ladder to enter the water, but still deep enough so they
(14) could swim.[1] **(14)** The bottom of the lake was not visible
(15) from the boat. **(15)** After positioning the boat Herman
proceeded to set the anchor and lower the boat's ladder

[1] Herman disputes that the boat was this far from shore, but for purposes of this appeal stipulates to Harper's allegation. [Footnote appears in original case.—Eds.]

which was at its stern.
(16) **(16)** While Herman was lowering the ladder, Harper
(17) asked him if he was "going in." **(17)** When Herman
responded yes, Harper, without warning, stepped onto the
side of the middle of the boat and dove into approximately
(18) two or three feet of water. **(18)** As a result of the dive,
Harper struck the bottom of the lake, severed his spinal
cord, and was rendered a C6 quadriplegic.
(19) **(19)** Harper then **brought suit**, **alleging** that Herman
owed him a duty of care to warn him that the water was
(20) too shallow for diving. **(20)** On October 23, 1991, the trial
court granted Herman's motion for summary judgment,
(21) ruling that the law does not impose such a duty. **(21)** In
reversing the trial court, the court of appeals concluded
that Herman voluntarily assumed a duty to exercise
reasonable care when he allowed Harper onto his boat, and
that the duty of care included warning Harper not to dive
because he knew that the water was "dangerously
shallow." Harper v. Herman, 487 N.W.2d 908, 910
(Minn.App.1992).
(22) **(22)** The sole issue on appeal is whether a boat owner
who is a **social host** owes a duty of care to warn a guest on
the boat that the water is too shallow for diving.
(23) **(23)** Harper alleges that Herman owed him a duty to
warn of the shallowness of the water because he was an
inexperienced swimmer and diver, whereas Herman was a
(24) veteran boater. **(24)** Under those circumstances, Harper
argues, Herman should have realized that Harper needed
his protection.
(25) **(25)** We have previously stated that an affirmative
duty to act only arises when a special relationship exists
(26) between the parties. **(26)** "The fact that an actor realizes or
should realize that action on his part is necessary for
another's aid or protection does not of itself impose upon
him a duty to take such action . . . unless a special
relationship exists . . . between the actor and the other
which gives the other the right to protection." Delgado v.
Lohmar, 289 N.W.2d 479, 483 (Minn.1979), *reh'g denied,*
(27) Jan. 11, 1980 (citations omitted). **(27)** Accepting, ***arguendo,***
that Herman should have realized that Harper needed
protection, Harper must still prove that a special
relationship existed between them that placed an
affirmative duty to act on the part of Herman.
(28) **(28)** Harper argues that a special relationship requiring

Herman to act for his protection was created when
Herman, as a social host, allowed an inexperienced diver on
(29) his boat. **(29)** Generally, a special relationship giving rise to
a duty to warn is only found on the part of **common
carriers**, **innkeepers**, possessors of land who hold it open
to the public, and persons who have custody of another
person under circumstances in which that other person is
deprived of normal opportunities of self-protection.
(30) **Restatement** (Second) of Torts § 314A (1965). **(30)** Under
this rule, a special relationship could be found to exist
between the parties only if Herman had custody of Harper
under circumstances in which Harper was deprived of
(31) normal opportunities to protect himself.[2] **(31)** These
elements are not present here.

(32) **(32)** The **record** before this court does not establish
that Harper was either particularly vulnerable or that he
(33) lacked the ability to protect himself. **(33)** Further, the
record does not establish that Herman held considerable
power over Harper's welfare, or that Herman was receiving
a financial gain by hosting Harper on his boat. **(34)** Finally,
(34) there is nothing in the record which would suggest that
Harper expected any protection from Herman; indeed, no
such allegation has been made.

(35) **(35)** The court of appeals found that Herman owed
Harper a duty to warn him of the shallowness of the water
because Herman knew that it was "dangerously shallow."
(36) **(36)** We have previously stated that "[a]ctual knowledge of
a dangerous condition tends to impose a special duty to do
something about that condition." *Andrade v. Ellefson,* 391
N.W.2d 836, 841 (Minn.1986) (holding that county was not
immune to charge of improper supervision of day care

---

[2] Prosser describes a circumstance in which one party would be liable in negligence because another party was deprived of normal opportunities for self-protection as occurring when

> the plaintiff is typically in some respect particularly vulnerable and dependent upon the defendant who, correspondingly, holds considerable power over the plaintiff's welfare. In addition, such relations have often involved some existing or potential economic advantage to the defendant. Fairness in such cases thus may require the defendant to use his power to help the plaintiff, based upon the plaintiff's expectation of protection, which itself may be based upon the defendant's expectation of financial gain.

W. Page Keeton et al., *Prosser and Keeton on the Laws of Torts* § 56, at 374 (5th ed. 1984). [Footnote appears in original case.—Eds.]

center where children were abused when county knew
(37) about overcrowding at the center). **(37)** However, superior
knowledge of a dangerous condition by itself, in the
absence of a duty to provide protection, is insufficient to
(38) establish liability in negligence. **(38)** Thus, Herman's
knowledge that the water was "dangerously shallow"
(39) without more does not create liability. **(39)** *Andrade*
involved a group of plaintiffs who had little opportunity to
protect themselves, children in day care, and a defendant
(40) to whom the plaintiffs looked for protection. **(40)** In this
case, Harper was not deprived of opportunities to protect
himself, and Herman was not expected to provide
protection.

(41) **(41)** "There are many dangers, such as those of fire
and water, . . . which under ordinary conditions may
reasonably be expected to be fully understood and
appreciated by any child . . . ." Restatement (Second) of
(42) Torts § 339 cmt. j (1965). **(42)** If a child is expected to
understand the inherent dangers of water, so should a 20-
(43) year-old adult. **(43)** Harper had no reasonable expectation
to look to Herman for protection, and we hold that Herman
had no duty to warn Harper that the water was shallow.

(44) **(44)** Reversed and judgment in favor of defendant
reinstated.

TASK 5.A.2. Case Brief

Write a case brief of *Harper v. Herman* using the following template.

Case name
Court & Year

Rule of the case:
Facts:
Procedural history:
Issue:
Holding:
Reasoning:
Disposition:
Comments:

TASK 5.A.3. Torts Vocabulary Definitions (List 1)

Fill in each definition with the appropriate term from the list below. Consult a law dictionary or an English-to-English dictionary to confirm that you have matched each term with the correct definition.

allege *(verb)*
arguendo (adverb) (pronounced AR-GYOO-**EN**-DOH)
bring suit *(verb)*
common carrier *(noun)*
innkeeper *(noun)*
owe [someone] a duty of care *(verb)*
record *(noun)*
Restatement *(noun)*
social host *(noun)*
superior knowledge *(noun)*

Terms related to torts

1. When an individual ____________________ someone ____________________, it means that she has a responsibility to exercise care to protect the person from harm. Who owes duties to whom is often prescribed by law.

2. A/an ____________________ is a person who hosts a social gathering, not for financial gain. In tort law, the term is often used to refer to individuals who host gatherings where alcohol is served.

3. The ____________________ is a compilation of rules derived from case law. It is not a "primary source," but rather a "secondary source" that courts refer to extensively in contracts and torts cases in particular. A Restatement provision is not binding on a court, unless the highest court in the jurisdiction has accepted that provision as law.

4. ____________________ refers to one person's knowledge of a (usually dangerous) condition that is not obvious to another person exercising reasonable care.

5. A/an ____________________ is an individual or company that provides accommodation for paying guests (e.g., a hotel, hostel, or guest house), and owes them a duty of care.

6. ____________________ is a legal term and it means "for the sake of argument." Writers typically use this when making assumptions. For example: Assuming, arguendo, that the defendant failed to use reasonable care, the plaintiff was nonetheless negligent in bringing about her own injury.

7. A/an ____________________ is a person or entity that transports people and goods for a fee (e.g., bus company or airline).

Terms related to procedure

8. The ____________________ refers to the written account of all of the acts and proceedings at trial as transcribed by a court reporter, as well as any documents filed in the case. When a case is appealed, an appellate court can look only at this record.

9. To ____________________ means to initiate legal proceedings against another party.

10. To ____________________ means to claim or assert wrongdoing. In the legal context, a plaintiff makes allegations in the **complaint**, the document that details the reasons she is suing the defendant and the remedies she is seeking. The defendant then files an **answer**, the document that denies or admits each allegation in the complaint. (See also Appendix C: Steps in the Civil Litigation Process.)

TASK 5.A.4. Questions for Discussion

Answer the following questions to assist you during a class discussion of the case. Indicate the sentence(s) in which you found the answer to each question.

1. Briefly describe the events that led up to the lawsuit (the "conflict facts").

2. Which of the following facts from *Harper* are legally relevant? Which ones are not? Underline only the legally relevant facts.

   a. On Sunday, August 9, 1986, Herman took his 26-foot boat out on Lake Minnetonka.
   b. Harper was a guest on Herman's boat.
   c. Once Herman positioned the boat about 100 to 200 feet from an island, Harper asked Herman if he was "going in." Herman

responded "yes." Then, without warning, Harper dove into two or three feet of water.

d. As a result of the dive, Harper became paralyzed.

3. Why did Harper (plaintiff) sue Herman (defendant)? What did Harper allege?

4. What qualifies as a "special relationship" under Minnesota tort law? Why is it important for the defendant to have a special relationship with the plaintiff?

5. According to the court, is there a special relationship between Harper and Herman? Why or why not?

6. The court states that "Harper was not deprived of opportunities to protect himself." Why does this matter?

7. Who prevailed (won) in this case? The plaintiff or defendant?

B. Torts Case #2

As suggested in *Harper*, individuals generally do not have an affirmative duty to act towards others unless there is a "special relationship" between them. In the next case, a special relationship exists between the parties. The defendant is an innkeeper and the plaintiff's relative was a guest at the inn. The question in this case centers on the scope of an innkeeper's duty.

As you read, consider the following question: Does the court impose a duty on the innkeeper in the particular circumstances of this case? Why or why not?

ESTATE OF RUPPEL v. HYEON JIN, INC.

Appellate Court of Illinois, 1995.

272 Ill.App.3d 527, 650 N.E.2d 645, 208 Ill.Dec. 951.

Justice McCORMICK delivered the opinion of the court:

(1) Plaintiff appeals the trial court's denial of its motion to file a second **amended complaint** and dismissal of its negligence action. **(2)** Plaintiff alleged negligence by defendant in the death of Michael Ruppel (the **deceased**), who, while **intoxicated**, fell down some stairs at the Carriage House Motor Inn (Carriage House) located in Northlake, Illinois. **(3)** Plaintiff contends that the trial court **erred** in finding that defendant owed no duty to the deceased.

. . . **(4)** Plaintiff's amended complaint alleges that at 7:30 p.m. on August 28, 1989, the deceased was drinking alcohol beverages at the Pine Yard Restaurant, which is a part of the Carriage House. **(5)** The deceased became highly intoxicated and left the Pine Yard to return to his room on the second floor of the Carriage House. **(6)** The deceased passed the front desk of the motel, at which the manager, Albert Bernstein, was stationed. **(7)** Bernstein saw the deceased in his intoxicated state and knew that the deceased had to ascend a flight of stairs to return to his room. **(8)** Bernstein neither warned the deceased that the stairs were dangerous, nor attempted to help him up the stairs. **(9)** The deceased began to ascend the stairs and fell. **(10)** He was hospitalized as a result of the fall and died a week later.

(11) The trial court dismissed plaintiff's original complaint and its amended complaint . . . for failure to allege a duty owed to the deceased by defendant. **(12)** Upon dismissal of plaintiff's amended complaint, the trial court **granted** plaintiff leave "to tender a 2nd amended complaint to the court . . . ." **(13)** At a hearing on plaintiff's motion to file its second amended complaint, the trial court found that plaintiff failed to allege either a defect in the stairs or that the deceased had been exhibiting impaired motor skills at the time of his fall. . . . [As a result, the court dismissed the case.]

(14) This appeal followed.

(15) Plaintiff asks that we take a quantum leap and expand the duty owed to an intoxicated person. **(16)** Relying on *Ward v. K–mart Corp.* (1990), 136 Ill.2d 132, 143 Ill.Dec. 288, 554 N.E.2d 223, plaintiff contends that because Bernstein knew the deceased was intoxicated, he could **reasonably** have anticipated that the deceased would get hurt climbing stairs, and therefore, defendant owed a duty to the deceased to warn him or otherwise protect him from the danger presented by the stairs at the Carriage House. **(17)** Plaintiff misapprehends the scope of *Ward.*

(18) In *Ward,* a shopper carrying a large mirror out of a store walked into a post in a parking lot. **(19)** The shopper admitted having seen the post when he entered the store, but he forgot it was there while he was shopping and his view was obstructed by the mirror. **(20)** In finding that K–Mart owed the plaintiff a duty to warn him of or protect him from the post, our supreme court reassessed the standards applicable to determining a defendant's duty to protect plaintiffs in an encounter with an open and obvious dangerous condition. **(21)** Prior to *Ward,* the courts held that defendants owed no duty to plaintiffs injured in such encounters. (*Bialek v. Moraine Valley Community College School Dist. 524* (1994), 267 Ill.App.3d 857, 204 Ill.Dec. 924, 642 N.E.2d 825.) **(22)** The *Ward* court adopted section 343A of the Restatement (Second) of Torts (Restatement (Second) of Torts, § 343A (1965)) in holding that defendants owe a duty to remedy or warn of an open and obvious condition when "the defendant should reasonably anticipate injury to those entrants on his premises who are generally **exercising reasonable care** for their own safety, but who may reasonably be expected to be distracted . . . or forgetful of the condition after having momentarily encountered it." *Ward,* 136 Ill.2d at 152, 143 Ill.Dec. 288, 554 N.E.2d 223.

(23) We observe that although *Ward* warned generally against applying the open and obvious doctrine mechanically "by merely viewing [a] condition in the abstract, wholly apart from the circumstances in which it existed" (*Ward,* 136 Ill.2d at 152, 143 Ill.Dec. 288, 554 N.E.2d 223), it acknowledged, citing other cases, that the focus in such situations remains primarily on the character of the condition on the land, rather than on the physical condition of the plaintiff. **(24)** In *Ward,* the plaintiff, by transporting his purchases from the store to his car, engaged in conduct which was encouraged and expected of him. (*Bialek,* 267 Ill.App.3d at 863, 204 Ill.Dec. 924, 642 N.E.2d 825.) **(25)** Likewise, in **the case at bar**, we may assume that the deceased was expected to ascend the stairs in order to gain access to his room. **(26)** It is doubtful that the deceased, who voluntarily became intoxicated, falls within the class of plaintiffs who are generally exercising reasonable care for their own safety or may be said to have been reasonably distracted or reasonably forgetful, as required by *Ward.*

(27) In light of *Ward,* our courts have held that a stairway is not generally considered "unreasonably dangerous solely because of the normal risks a person undergoes when using stairs." (*Glass v. Morgan Guarantee Trust Co.* (1992), 238 Ill.App.3d 355, 360, 179 Ill.Dec. 552, 606 N.E.2d 384.) **(28)** Thus, "the law does not require a person to foolproof stairs against normal risks." (*Glass,* 238 Ill.App.3d at 361, 179 Ill.Dec. 552, 606 N.E.2d 384.) **(29)** Indeed, "stairs, by their very nature, create the risk that persons using them might be injured by a fall." (*Glass,* 238 Ill.App.3d at 358, 179 Ill.Dec. 552, 606 N.E.2d 384.) **(30)** In *Glass,* the court refused to impose a duty upon owners of stairways to warn or otherwise make "safe" their stairs for shoppers carrying objects. **(31)** The court specifically noted that posting a warning that stairs are dangerous would be "pointless." (*Glass,* 238 Ill.App.3d at 361, 179 Ill.Dec. 552, 606 N.E.2d 384.) **(32)** Here, to the extent that plaintiff's case relies on the physical incapacity that being intoxicated creates, a verbal warning would have been of little or no assistance to the deceased. . . .

(33) In this case, plaintiff failed to allege that the deceased had displayed any outward signs of being physically incapacitated, such as difficulty in walking or balancing. **(34)** Instead, plaintiff relied on the conclusory allegation that Bernstein "saw Michael S. Ruppel [deceased] in a highly intoxicated condition." **(35)** Absent any signs of impaired physical mobility that reasonably informed defendant that the deceased could not safely ascend the stairs, a duty to warn or assist does not exist. **(36)** The conclusory allegation that the deceased was highly intoxicated does not allow us to speculate that he had an observable incapacity to successfully ascend the stairs. **(37)** Hence, the deceased's injury was not reasonably **foreseeable**. **(38)** Moreover, the public policy consideration of imposing on a hotel the burden of escorting intoxicated persons to their destinations would be quite onerous. **(39)** Ultimately, the hotel would be required to provide for the total care and safety of intoxicated persons on its premises. . . .

(40) The trial court correctly **denied** plaintiff's motion for leave to file its second amended complaint and correctly dismissed plaintiff's action.

(41) Affirmed. . . .

TASK 5.B.1. Case Brief

Write a case brief of *Estate of Ruppel v. Hyeon Jin, Inc.* using the template on page 290.

TASK 5.B.2. Torts Vocabulary Definitions (List 2)

Fill in each definition with the appropriate term from the list below. Consult a law dictionary or an English-to-English dictionary to confirm that you have matched each term with the correct definition. If multiple forms of a term are provided, you may not need to use all of the forms in the blanks.

amended *(adjective)*; amend *(verb)*
complaint *(noun)*
deceased *(adjective*; *noun)*
err *(verb)*
"exercise reasonable care" *(verb)*
foreseeable *(adjective)*
grant vs. deny *(verb)*
intoxicated *(adjective)*
reasonably *(adverb)*; reasonable *(adjective)*
"the case at bar" *(noun)*

Terms related to torts

1. When an individual ______________________, she uses the degree of care that a sensible and competent person would exercise in similar circumstances.

2. To act ______________________ means to act in a fair or proper way under the circumstances. The term "reasonable person" is often used in negligence law. It refers to a person of average skill and judgment. It is a fictional person that functions as the standard by which fact finders evaluate a defendant's conduct.

3. If an event or situation is ______________________, it is possible to anticipate and predict its occurrence.

4. A/an ____________________ individual is one who is dead.

5. Someone who is ____________________ is under the influence of alcohol or drugs and has a diminished ability to act with her physical and mental capabilities intact.

Terms related to procedure

6. Courts can either ____________________ (allow) or ____________________ (disallow) a party's request. These two terms are most often used with the word "motion" (e.g., a court grants a motion or denies a motion).

7. To ____________________ means to change the phrasing of a document.

8. A/an ____________________ is the document that details the reasons the plaintiff is suing the defendant and the remedies sought. (See also Appendix C: Steps in the Civil Litigation Process.)

9. If a court ____________________, it made a mistake in applying or interpreting the law. Higher courts often review lower court's decisions to determine if the lower courts made any legal errors.

10. The term ____________________ refers to the case that the court is currently considering. A synonym is "the instant case."

TASK 5.B.3. Questions for Discussion

Answer the following questions to assist you during a class discussion of the case. Indicate the sentence(s) in which you found the answer to each question.

1. What are the facts of this case?

2. What is the issue in this case?

3. What is the plaintiff's argument as to why the defendant owed the deceased a duty of care?

4. What case does the plaintiff rely on to support its argument? How does the court distinguish this case from the plaintiff's case?

5. What is the "open and obvious doctrine"? According to the court, does this doctrine apply to the plaintiff's case? Why or why not?

6. In sentence (37), the court states, "the deceased's injury was not reasonably foreseeable." Why does this matter?

7. What is the court's holding?

8. Which of the following types of reasons does the court supply to support its decision: (a) rule application; (b) analogical reasoning; and/or (c) policy justification?

9. Would the outcome of this case be any different if the plaintiff could prove that the manager (Bernstein) had witnessed the deceased (Ruppel) lose his balance and fall 10 seconds before he began ascending the stairs? Why or why not?

C. Torts Case #3

In the next case, a special relationship exists between the plaintiff and defendant because the defendant is a common carrier and the plaintiff is a customer. This case addresses whether the common carrier breached its duty of care to the customer. **Breach** is the second element of negligence, and it refers to a defendant's failure to meet or satisfy its duty of care.

Whether a duty exists in a particular case is often a question of law: courts and legislatures typically determine who owes duties to whom and under what circumstances. Breach, on the other hand, is usually a question of fact for a fact finder to resolve. As you may recall from Part II, Chapter 1, the term "fact finder" or "trier of fact" refers to an individual or individuals who determine whether and how an event occurred (e.g., Did the defendant run the red light and strike and kill the pedestrian? Was the defendant drunk at the time of the accident?). In U.S. courts, fact finders are usually juries composed of 6 to 12 private citizens called jurors. Juries "find" or "determine" facts at trial by hearing and reviewing evidence presented by both sides to a dispute—that is, the plaintiff and defendant—and ultimately deciding which side is more believable.

In a negligence suit, parties often disagree about whether the defendant's actions rose to the level of a breach, with one side arguing that there *was* a breach (plaintiff) and the other side asserting that there was *no* breach (defendant). Based on all of the evidence the jury has been shown by the two sides, it must decide who is more credible and, ultimately, who should win the case. As you read *Mastriano*, keep in mind the jury's important role at trial.

Pre-Reading Vocabulary

Dissent *(noun; verb)*; "**dissenting opinion**"

To dissent means to disagree. A dissenting opinion is one that disagrees with the majority court's decision, as expressed in the "majority opinion" (you have been reading only majority opinions thus far in this book). Dissenting opinions are optional and need not be included in a decision.

Dissenting opinions are written by one or more judges. They are common at the Supreme Court level, particularly in cases addressing topics on which the Court is divided. Though dissenting opinions can be informative, they are not binding on future courts because they do not count as "the law." Only the rule in the majority opinion is binding on future courts. Dissenting opinions, when they are written, always follow the majority opinion.

In the next case, two of the judges on the Supreme Judicial Court of Maine have joined in writing a dissenting opinion.

MASTRIANO v. BLYER

Supreme Judicial Court of Maine, 2001.
779 A.2d 951, 2001 ME 134.

ALEXANDER, J.

(1) Rachel Mastriano [representing the estate of Douglas K. Dionne] appeals from the summary judgment entered in the Superior Court . . . on her negligence **claims** against Samuel Blyer, [doing business as] Blyer Taxi Service, and Clifford Groder, Jr. (collectively "BTS"), brought pursuant to Maine's Wrongful Death Act, 18–A M.R.S.A. § 2–804 (1998), for the death of Douglas K. Dionne. **(2)** Mastriano argues that the summary judgment was inappropriate because BTS owed Dionne a duty beyond providing him a safe exit from its cab, and because there remain genuine issues of material fact regarding a breach of duty. **(3)** We decline Mastriano's request to expand the special duty common carriers owe to their customers to provide a safe exit in a safe place. **(4)** Accordingly, we affirm.

I. CASE HISTORY

(5) The uncontested facts presented in the parties' statements of material facts may be summarized as follows:

Douglas Dionne spent the early evening hours of August 4, 1997, drinking beer at the Elks Lodge in Skowhegan. **(6)** A long-time friend, Flint Batchelder, observed Dionne drinking between 5:30 and 8:00 that evening. **(7)** At approximately 8:00 P.M., Batchelder observed that Dionne's speech began to be slurred and that he swayed on his feet. **(8)** The bartender refused to serve Dionne any more liquor, and another patron called Blyer Taxi Service to give Dionne a ride home.

(9) When the taxi arrived, Batchelder walked with Dionne to the taxi. **(10)** Dionne walked without physical assistance, but Batchelder observed him sway as he walked. **(11)** Batchelder asked the cab driver, Clifford Groder, Jr., to take Dionne home because he had had too much to drink. **(12)** Batchelder explained that Dionne lived on East Madison Road and that Dionne would show him the way to the house. **(13)** Batchelder offered to pay the fare, but Dionne insisted on paying his own fare. **(14)** When Batchelder last saw Dionne, he was speaking in a clear voice and was able to give instructions to Groder.

(15) Once in the cab, Dionne refused to give Groder directions to his house. **(16)** Instead, he directed Groder to take him to the Kennebec Valley Inn. **(17)** When that establishment proved to be closed, he asked Groder to take him to Bloomfield's Tavern. **(18)** Once there, Dionne paid the fare and exited the cab. **(19)** Groder watched him walk safely into the tavern and left the area to attend to other business.

(20) Groder had considerable experience as a taxi operator. **(21)** With regard to intoxicated passengers, Groder's practice was as follows: (1) for passengers who were so intoxicated that they could not function, as where they had to be picked up and placed in the cab, Groder would take them to the nearest hospital; and (2) for passengers who had consumed alcohol, but could walk and give clear directions, Groder would take them to the location they dictated. **(22)** Once the passengers were safely deposited at the location, Groder would leave.

(23) Around 8:30 or 9:00 P.M., Groder responded to a call from Bloomfield's Tavern to pick up Dionne. **(24)** When Groder arrived at Bloomfield's, Dionne walked straight to the cab and gave Groder clear directions to drive him to a convenience store to purchase cigarettes. **(25)** At the convenience store, Dionne walked straight into the store and Groder observed him speak with the clerk, obtain the cigarettes, pay for them, and walk from the store. **(26)** Once back in the cab, Dionne directed Groder to return him to the Elks Lodge.

(27) At the Elks Lodge, Dionne paid the fare plus a large tip, exited the taxi, and walked past his automobile. **(28)** Groder related that he knew that the automobile was Dionne's because he observed Dionne approach it, kick it, and call it a "piece of junk." **(29)** Dionne walked over to a fence near a horseshoe pit, and Groder stated that he assumed Dionne was going to relieve himself. **(30)** Groder heard other voices in the area and assumed Dionne would be safe. **(31)** Groder then left the Elks Lodge to resume his work. **(32)** Later that evening, Dionne died in a single-car accident while driving his automobile on the East Madison Road. **(33)** At the time of the accident, Dionne's blood-alcohol content was .25. **(34)** The record is silent as to what, if anything, Dionne may have had to drink after he left Groder's cab.

(35) Mastriano sued BTS for negligence. **(36)** BTS moved for a summary judgment arguing that Mastriano had not established that BTS breached any duty of care to Dionne. **(37)** The Superior Court granted BTS's motion, finding that

Mastriano had "failed to raise a genuine issue of material fact to dispute Defendants' statement that the place of discharge was reasonably safe and that the passenger/carrier relationship had ended." **(38)** The court also declined to "extend the carrier's duty to include preventing Dionne from drinking and/or driving after safe discharge in a reasonably safe place." **(39)** Mastriano then timely appealed.

II. LEGAL ANALYSIS

(40) We review a summary judgment by examining the evidence "in the light most favorable to the nonprevailing party to determine whether the record supports the conclusion that there is no genuine issue of material fact and that the prevailing party is entitled to a judgment as a matter of law." *Champagne v. Mid–Maine Med. Ctr.*, 1998 ME 87, ¶ 5, 711 A.2d 842, 844. **(41)** If it is clear that BTS would prevail as a matter of law if Mastriano presented nothing more than what was before the court at the hearing on the motion for summary judgment, then the court was correct to enter the summary judgment. *See id.* ¶ 9, 711 A.2d at 845.

(42) To survive BTS's motion for summary judgment, Mastriano must establish a **prima facie case** for each element of the cause of action that BTS challenges. *See Corey v. Norman, Hanson & DeTroy,* 1999 ME 196, ¶ 9, 742 A.2d 933, 938.

(44) A prima facie case of negligence requires a plaintiff to establish four elements: duty, breach, causation, and damages. **(45)** We recently characterized these elements: "a duty owed, breach of that duty, and an injury to the plaintiff that is proximately caused by a breach of that duty." *Stanton v. Univ. of Maine Sys.*, 2001 ME 96, ¶ 7, 773 A.2d 1045, 1049. *See also McPherson v. McPherson,* 1998 ME 141, ¶ 8, 712 A.2d 1043, 1045; *Searles v. Trustees of St. Joseph's Coll.*, 1997 ME 128, ¶¶ 5, 6, 8, 695 A.2d 1206, 1209. **(46)** "The existence of a duty is a question of law, which we review *de novo. McPherson,* 1998 ME 141, ¶ 8, 712 A.2d at 1045. *See also Stanton,* 2001 ME 96, ¶ 8, 773 A.2d at 1049.

(47) A duty is "an obligation, to which the law will give recognition and effect, to conform to a particular manner of conduct toward another." *Budzko v. One City Ctr. Assocs. Ltd. P'ship,* 2001 ME 37, ¶ 10, 767 A.2d 310, 313 (quoting *Quadrino v. Bar Harbor Banking & Trust Co.*, 588 A.2d 303, 304 (Me.1991)). **(48)** Generally, the duty at issue and its means of fulfillment can be readily identified, leaving only the question of breach for the factfinder. *See Stanton,* 2001 ME 96, ¶ 11, 773 A.2d at 1050. **(49)** Thus, when we talk of duty, we often discuss one's obligation to: (1) operate a motor vehicle safely; (2) provide medical or legal services competently; (3) assure that floors are not slippery; (4) warn of foreseeable risks to persons present on one's property; or (5) otherwise conduct ourselves or our business in ways that do not cause injury to others. **(50)** By contrast, the "duty" urged upon us here has no obvious means of fulfillment.

(51) A common carrier owes its passengers a duty that requires "'the exercise of the highest degree of care compatible with the practical operation of the machine in which the conveyance was undertaken.'" *Roberts v. Yellow Cab Co.*, 240 A.2d 733, 735 (Me.1968) (quoting *Chaput v. Lussier*, 132 Me. 48, 52, 165 A. 573, 575 (1933)). **(52)** This heightened standard of care continues until the carrier has given its passenger a reasonably safe discharge at a reasonably safe location. *See Lipsky v. Padgett*, 730 So.2d 818, 819 (Fla.Dist.Ct.App.1999); *Knoud v. Galante*, 696 A.2d 854, 856 (Pa.Super.Ct.1997).

(53) Mastriano urges that we expand the common carrier's duty to provide a safe exit at a safe place to include an *in loco parentis* type of responsibility to intervene in an arguably intoxicated passenger's life, perhaps against the passenger's wishes, to ensure that the passenger does not harm himself or herself after the common carrier has given the safe exit that the law requires.

(54) The existing rule establishes a bright line dividing the primary obligation of common carriers to provide a safe discharge, and the primary obligation of passengers to accept personal responsibility for their own safety. *See Roberts*, 240 A.2d at 735–36. **(55)** We decline to expand the duty of common carriers by imposing *in loco parentis* oversight responsibilities for those passengers who are possibly **inebriated** or otherwise impaired.

(56) Mastriano focuses on Dionne's .25 blood-alcohol content when Dionne died and Dionne's inferentially obvious drunken state to support her position. **(57)** However, the new rule of law urged upon us makes no distinction between close cases and obvious ones. **(58)** Instead, it would expose common carriers to potential liability anytime someone claims, with the clarity of hindsight and the emotion of subsequent tragedy, that the carrier should have noticed a passenger's possible impairment and, accordingly, taken steps, perhaps against the passenger's wishes, to protect the passenger from each and every potential harm of the passenger's own design. **(59)** Our decisions do not support such an expansive view of duty.

(60) When a plaintiff claims that a defendant had an affirmative duty to act to protect the plaintiff from himself or herself, we have generally held that "absent a special relationship, the law imposes no duty to act affirmatively to protect someone from danger unless the dangerous situation was created by the defendant." *Jackson v. Tedd–Lait Post No. 75, Am. Legion*, 1999 ME 26, ¶ 8, 723 A.2d 1220, 1221. *See also Hughes v. Beta Upsilon Bldg. Ass'n*, 619 A.2d 525, 526–27 (Me.1993). **(61)** As these cases suggest, we are cautious in assigning a duty which imposes an affirmative obligation to act, and we should be even more cautious when the duty urged upon us is a duty to intervene in a plaintiff's life to prevent the plaintiff from injuring himself or herself. . . . **(62)** In this case, any special responsibility ended with Dionne's safe exit at a safe place. **(63)** The cab driver had no further duty . . . to act affirmatively to protect the passenger from himself after his exit.

(64) This is not a case where the forces that would harm the passenger were already unleashed and apparent, and the cab driver released the passenger into those forces—for example allowing a drunk to exit onto a busy highway at night. **(65)** That would be an unsafe exit. **(66)** Nor is this a situation where a danger at the drop-off site was reasonably foreseeable—for example, an ice covered parking lot or a place where vagabonds were known to lurk in the bushes ready to pounce on lonely drunks. **(67)** That could be considered an exit to an unsafe place. **(68)** Here, the cab driver is being asked to anticipate a harm that may or may not occur at some other location and with that anticipation, act affirmatively to limit the passenger's freedom of choice or freedom of movement so that the passenger might not injure himself after he exits the cab safely.

(69) Were we to adopt Mastriano's expansive view of duty, what should a common carrier—the airline, the bus driver, the cab driver—do if they perceive, or arguably should perceive, a passenger to be inebriated or otherwise impaired? **(70)** Should they refuse to let the passenger leave the vehicle and possibly subject themselves to assault or civil liability for illegal restraint? **(71)** Should they refuse to pick up the passenger and leave the person to fend for themselves by the side of the road? **(72)** There is no obvious course of conduct by which any new duty to become an instrument for good could be fulfilled in a manner that is foreseeable or definable to a jury.

(73) The Government acting through the courts or the Legislature can only go so far in requiring common carriers or others to protect people from themselves. **(74)** Common carriers have no duty, to be fulfilled in an unspecified manner, to protect possibly inebriated or impaired passengers from themselves after the carrier provides them with a safe exit in a safe place. **(75)** We decline to extend the law to reach that result.

(76) Mr. Dionne's death was a tragedy, but it was a tragedy caused by his own hand in becoming intoxicated, entering his car, and driving himself to his death. **(77)** The common carrier, who gave Mr. Dionne his contracted ride from Bloomfield's to the Elks Lodge and provided him a safe exit at a safe place, had no further duty to Mr. Dionne to intervene in his life and prevent the subsequent tragedy which Mr. Dionne brought on himself.

. . . **(78)** Judgment affirmed.

. . . **(79)** WATHEN, C.J., with whom DANA, J., joins, **dissenting**.

(80) I respectfully dissent. **(81)** The Court has correctly stated the general rule that the heightened duty a carrier owes its passenger continues until the carrier has discharged the passenger at a reasonably safe location. **(82)** It has failed to recognize, however, that discharging an intoxicated passenger at his or her car may not be discharging the passenger at a reasonably safe location. **(83)** The present case is particularly compelling because, taking the facts in the light most favorable to plaintiff, the carrier was specifically informed at the time of engagement that the passenger had had too much to drink, and he could easily have inferred that the passenger was too drunk to drive.

(84) A place that is reasonably safe for most passengers to disembark may not, under the circumstances, be reasonably safe for a passenger who is intoxicated or otherwise disabled. **(85)** Thus, when a carrier is aware that its passenger has a disability due to intoxication, age, or mental or physical condition, it must exercise reasonable care not to discharge the passenger at a place where, due to the disability, he or she is exposed to an unreasonable risk of harm. *Portier v. Thrifty Way Pharmacy,* 476 So.2d 1132, 1140 (La.Ct.App.1985) *rev'd in part on other grounds,* 479 So.2d 916 (La.1985). **(86)** The carrier's determination of whether a particular location is unreasonably risky involves not only an evaluation of the risks posed by the physical characteristics of the place of discharge, but also the foreseeable risks that may arise through the conduct of the passenger or a third party. *See* RESTATEMENT (SECOND) OF TORTS § 302A (1965) ("An act or omission may be negligent if the actor realizes or should realize that it involves an unreasonable risk of harm to another through the negligent or reckless conduct of the other or a third person."). **(87)** If the carrier fails to exercise the reasonable care required by the circumstances, it may be liable for its passenger's injuries even though the passenger has stepped securely onto the street. *Torres v. Salty Sea Days, Inc.,* 36 Wash.App. 668, 676 P.2d 512, 517 (1984).

(88) This rule does not in any way expand the carrier's duty to discharge its passengers at a reasonably safe location, nor does it impose a paternalistic obligation on the carrier to affirmatively protect a passenger after he or she has disembarked. **(89)** Rather, it arises necessarily from the carrier's general duty in cases, such as the present one, involving passengers who are disabled due to intoxication.

(90) I am not unmindful of the policy implications of this position, but, unlike the majority, I do not find them overwhelming. **(91)** A carrier, pursuant to a reasonably implemented rule of operation, could simply refuse service to an apparently intoxicated individual who requested to be transported to an unsafe location such as his or her car. **(92)** Carriers would continue to provide a socially beneficial service by transporting intoxicated individuals to safe locations such as the individual's home, a hospital, a bus or airline terminal, or even a bar without the threat of liability. **(93)** In this way, the **deterrent** effect of the rule on a carrier's willingness to transport intoxicated individuals would be minimal and would only arise when the individual requested to be transported to an unsafe location.

(94) I am satisfied that a jury could, if it heard nothing more than the evidence presented in the parties' statements of material fact, find that Groder knew that Dionne was disabled due to his intoxication and that discharging Dionne at his car exposed him to an unreasonable risk of harm that resulted in his death. **(95)** I would **vacate** the summary judgment and allow the case to proceed to trial.

TASK 5.C.1. Case Brief

Write a case brief of *Mastriano v. Blyer* using the template on page 290. Include a summary of the dissenting opinion in your brief.

TASK 5.C.2. Torts Vocabulary Definitions (List 3)

Fill in each definition with the appropriate term from the list below. Consult a law dictionary or an English-to-English dictionary to confirm that you have matched each term with the correct definition. If multiple forms of a term are provided, you may not need to use all of the forms in the blanks.

claim *(noun; verb)*
deterrent *(adjective; noun)*
inebriated *(adjective)*
prima facie case *(adjective)* ("prima facie" is pronounced **PREE**-MUH **FAY**-SHUH)
vacate *(verb)*

Terms related to torts

1. To be ____________________ means to be intoxicated.

2. A/an ____________________ is something that discourages, prevents, or impedes. Tort law and criminal law are designed to deter certain behavior by fear of liability or punishment.

Terms related to procedure

3. A/an ____________________ is the plaintiff's assertion that she is entitled to money damages or other remedies. It is a demand for relief.

> Note: The word "claim" is often used with the prepositions "against," "of," and "for."
>
> "Claim against" is used with <u>the name of an opposing party</u> to denote who an individual is suing.
>
> > The plaintiff has a claim **against** <u>the defendant</u>.
> > Ms. Jones brought a claim **against** <u>her employer</u>.
>
> "Claim of" and "claim for" are both used with the <u>name of the particular wrong</u> for which an individual is suing.

The plaintiff brought a claim **of** negligence.
Mr. Wright has a claim **for** wrongful termination.

"Claim of" is also used with the remedy sought by an individual.

The plaintiff has a claim **of** $50,000 in damages.
The court rejected the claim **of** injunctive relief.

4. A/an ____________________ is a case in which a party has produced sufficient evidence to allow a factfinder to rule in the party's favor.

5. When a court ____________________ a prior judgment, it nullifies or cancels it.

TASK 5.C.3. Questions for Discussion

Answer the following questions to assist you during a class discussion of the case. Indicate the sentence(s) in which you found the answer to each question.

1. What are the facts of this case?

2. What is the issue? What is the court's holding?

3. What is the duty of common carriers? According to the court, when does this duty end?

4. How does Mastriano seek to "expand the common carrier's duty"? Why does the court refuse to do so?

5. In sentence (62), the majority states: "any special responsibility ended with Dionne's safe exit at a safe place." Do you agree with the majority that Dionne exited at a safe place? What does the dissent say?

6. In sentence (94), the dissent states: "I am satisfied that a jury could . . . find that Groder knew that Dionne was disabled due to his intoxication and that discharging Dionne at his car exposed him to an unreasonable risk of harm that resulted in his death." Why does it matter what the jury *could* find?

7. Hypotheticals:

    a. Suppose that instead of dropping off Dionne at Elks Lodge, the taxi driver took him to a local lake (per Dionne's request). Would this help the plaintiff's argument that the driver breached his duty of care? Why or why not?

    b. What if the taxi driver dropped off Dionne in a densely wooded park with deep ravines and steep cliffs? Would this strengthen the plaintiff's case? Why or why not?

    c. Finally, what if the taxi driver dropped off Dionne in a high-crime neighborhood with frequent violent muggings? Would this help the plaintiff's case? Why or why not?

D. Torts Vocabulary Exercises (Lists 1-3)

EXERCISE 5.D.1. Fill in the Blanks

Fill in the blanks with the most appropriate form of the words and phrases in the list below. You may have to change word form to create a grammatically correct sentence. Some questions may have more than one correct answer.

allege	err
arguendo	exercise reasonable care
bring suit	foreseeable
claim	grant
common carrier	owe
complaint	record
deceased	Restatement
deny	superior knowledge

1. In *Miller*, the court held that landowners do not ____________________ a duty of care to trespassers. Thus, if someone trespasses on another's property and is injured, the owner of that land will not be held liable.

2. The plaintiff ____________________ that the defendant doctor failed to ____________________ when performing the surgical procedure that left the plaintiff paralyzed.

3. Assuming, ____________________, that the defendant owed and breached the duty of care, the plaintiff still needs to prove the remaining two elements of negligence.

4. The plaintiff ____________________ against the defendant. In other words, she took the defendant to court.

5. The state supreme court held that the trial court ____________________ in ____________________ the defendant's motion to dismiss. The court provided several reasons for why the motion should not have been allowed.

6. Mary has a/an ____________________ against Nathan for the negligent infliction of emotional distress.

7. The plaintiff's ____________________ alleged that it was ____________________ that a customer could slip and fall on the banana peel that was left on defendant's property. The plaintiff argued that the defendant should have anticipated that such an injury might occur. And, since it did not do anything to remove the banana peel, the defendant breached its duty of care.

EXERCISE 5.D.2. Matching

Match the five subjects below with the phrases (1-7) to create a complete sentence. Each subject should be matched with at least one phrase. Some questions may have more than one correct answer.

The court   The defendant   The judge   The jury   The plaintiff

1. ____________________ vacated the judgment.

2. ____________________ granted the motion.

3. ____________________ owes a duty of care to the plaintiff.

4. ____________________ wrote a dissenting opinion.

5. ____________________ filed a complaint.

6. ____________________ denied the motion for summary judgment.

7. ____________________ did not exercise reasonable care, as determined by the jury.

E. Torts Essay Question #1

Answer the following hypothetical using the previous cases in this chapter to inform your answer. Use a piece of paper or a blank document on your computer to outline your response before you begin writing.

Suggested response time: **40 minutes**.

QUESTION

Ally works in downtown Barkton and takes the metro to work every day. The day after a major snowstorm this February, it was a beautiful, sunny day. Though many schools and businesses were still closed for snow cleanup, Ally's office was open. She had no choice but to go in to work. Ally arrived at her usual metro stop and began descending the stairs to catch her train. She noticed a small paper sign taped to the wall in the stairwell reading, "CAUTION: Wet snow. Slippery steps." Ally saw that there was quite an accumulation of snow and slush on the steps—approximately three to four inches. She proceeded carefully because she knew that the steps are slippery even in good weather conditions (the steps are made of a smooth, polished stone). Despite her caution, however, Ally slipped on the fifteenth step, tumbling down the remaining twenty steps. She sustained serious injuries in the fall: a dislocated shoulder, a broken hip, and three broken ribs.

Last Friday, Ally came to your law firm asking whether she should bring suit against the Barkton Transportation Authority (BTA). You are a junior associate at the firm and the managing partner, Ms. Liu, has asked you to write her an email explaining whether Ally has a claim against the BTA.

Ms. Liu already had Dave, the firm's investigator, do some preliminary research on the case. Dave found 23 complaints on the BTA's website, posted by passengers who have previously slipped on the steps. About one-third of them complained that they fell when the steps were dry.

Assume that you are working in a jurisdiction in which the laws of **ALL** states apply.

F. Torts Case #4

Thus far, you have read three cases in the area of negligence law. You know that negligence may be defined as the failure to use the level of care that a reasonable person would use in similar circumstances, resulting in another person's injury or loss. You also know that the tort of negligence is composed of four elements. In order to recover on a claim for negligence, a plaintiff has to prove all four of these elements.

The previous three cases involved the first two elements of negligence: (1) the **duty** to exercise care; and (2) **breach**, that is, the failure to exercise care. The next case addresses the third element of negligence: causation.

DOE v. MANHEIMER

Supreme Court of Connecticut, 1989.
212 Conn. 748, 563 A.2d 699.

GLASS, Associate Justice.

(1) The difficult issue in this case is whether a landowner may be liable in tort for damages arising from the rape of a pedestrian committed on the landowner's property behind brush and trees that shielded the area from view from the nearby public sidewalk and street.

I

(2) The plaintiff, Jane Doe, worked as a meter reader for the Connecticut Light and Power Company in New London. **(3)** On July 30, 1984, her employers assigned her to work in the Green Street area. **(4)** At approximately 8 a.m., as she walked along Green Street, she observed a man on the opposite sidewalk who appeared to be looking for directions. **(5)** She crossed the street to offer assistance. **(6)** As she came near, the man, a stranger, reached into a satchel, removed a gun, and held it against her. **(7)** He forced her from the sidewalk through a paved vacant lot that abutted the street. **(8)** The man then forced her onto adjacent property owned by the named defendant (hereinafter defendant) some fifty to seventy feet from the sidewalk. **(9)** The defendant's property extended approximately six and three-quarter feet from the side of his building to the lot boundary parallel to the building. **(10)** The area into which the plaintiff was forced was bounded by the defendant's building on one side and a retaining wall in the rear. **(11)** On the other side, overgrown sumac bushes and tall grass shielded the area from view from the sidewalk and street.

(12) Behind the sumac bushes, the abductor viciously **assaulted** and raped the plaintiff for thirty minutes. **(13)** In the commission of the assault, the abductor used various items, including a rope and rubber gloves, which he had carried with him in his satchel. **(14)** His possession of these items suggested that the sexual assault had been planned. **(15)** The assailant fled after committing the crime and has never been identified or caught. **(16)** The effect of the sexual assault upon the plaintiff has been severe. **(17)** She has attempted suicide on several occasions.

(18) Her emotional and psychiatric problems have required and continue to require hospital confinement.

(19) The plaintiff brought an action against the defendant for personal injuries sustained in the assault. **(20)** The complaint alleged causes of action based on common law negligence, statutory negligence and public nuisance. **(21)** In essence, she claimed that the defendant had failed to remove the overgrown vegetation although he knew or should have known that, because the neighborhood was a high crime area, third persons might use the overgrowth to conceal the perpetration of crimes against pedestrians. **(22)** She asserted that, had the overgrowth not been present, the area in which the assault occurred would have been visible to passing motorists and pedestrians. **(23)** Consequently, she alleged, the overgrowth caused and contributed to the assault and the duration of the assault.

(24) The action was tried to a jury before the court, *Walsh, J.* Several witnesses described the neighborhood where the sexual assault had been committed as a high crime area. **(25)** Another rape had occurred in a neighborhood building about three months prior to the sexual assault against the plaintiff.

(26) Approximately fourteen months prior to the assault, Clara Manheimer, the defendant's ninety year old mother, had been bound, gagged and robbed in the package store at the front of the building on the defendant's property. **(27)** Prostitution and drug dealing were more prevalent in that section of New London than in other sections. **(28)** Further, derelicts and homeless people frequented the site where the assault occurred and the adjacent vacant lot through which the plaintiff had been forced from the sidewalk. **(29)** Various debris littered the area, including liquor and wine bottles and cans. **(30)** Street people had scattered cardboard boxes, mattresses and blankets that they used when they slept there at night. **(31)** There was also evidence that on occasion, some of those people had been compensated with free liquor for cleaning the vacant lot. **(32)** The police frequently had removed from the area people too drunk to care for themselves.

(33) In addition to testimony concerning the assault and the condition of the site, the plaintiff presented George Rand, an environmental psychologist. **(34)** Rand testified that he personally examined the location of the assault, the surrounding neighborhood, and, for lack of a better term, the cultural activities and history of the area. **(35)** He testified that, in his opinion, the physical configuration of the specific site increased the risk of violent crimes between strangers by creating a "protective" zone that reduced or eliminated visibility and, hence, served as an inducement for crime. **(36)** He summarized the results of his study by testifying that "I've analyzed the local site, the sub area, the presence of adult entertainment, activities, sexually oriented businesses. **(37)** I've looked at prior crimes. . . . The fact that it is an area of the city with a relatively high incidence of crime. **(38)** And I . . . assumed as a result of those observations that there was a persistent and inappropriate use of that site based on the evidence that it was periodically and frequently used by drunks. . . . **(39)** There was fighting.

(40) Police came. **(41)** A history of complaints. **(42)** All those things indicate a condition of environmental disorder that I would contend is potentially related to increasing the risk of crime."

(43) Melvin Jetmore, a building official for the city of New London and one of the authors of the housing code, testified for the plaintiff that the site of the defendant's property where the rape had occurred violated the housing code due to the presence of an "obnoxious" overgrowth of sumac trees and brush, and various debris including papers, shingles and broken glass. **(44)** Jetmore testified that prior to the assault, New London had notified the defendant in March, 1983, and again in February, 1984, of the housing code violations, and that Jetmore had specifically told the defendant to remove all the debris and broken glass and "cut all the bushes and trees down." **(45)** The defendant, however, did not correct the violations.

(46) The plaintiff also presented conflicting testimony concerning the "purpose" of the pertinent housing code provisions. **(47)** Jetmore testified that the relevant provisions of the city housing code were designed to prevent deterioration and "blight" and to keep property clear of "nuisances and hazards to the safety of occupants, pedestrians and so forth." **(48)** Further, Robert Finn, a housing code officer for the town of Plainville, testified initially that in his opinion, it was a function of the housing code to eliminate such hazards as "possible places for concealment of criminal activity." **(49)** On re-**cross-examination**, however, Finn contradicted himself, and testified that it was not a purpose of the housing code to prevent the concealment of persons who intend to commit criminal activity. **(50)** He concluded, "I can't say that those trees should be removed because of an anticipated crime. **(51)** But, they should be removed because they violate the code."

(52) At the close of the plaintiff's case, the defendant rested without presenting evidence and moved for a **directed verdict**. **(53)** The trial court reserved a decision on the defendant's motion. **(54)** Thereafter, the jury returned a general **verdict** in favor of the plaintiff, and awarded her $540,000 in damages. . . . **(55)** Subsequently, however, the trial court **set aside the verdict** on the defendant's motion. **(56)** In setting aside the verdict, the trial court first observed that "[w]ithout the shielding [of the overgrowth], the rape most probably would not have occurred [on the defendant's property]." **(57)** The court implicitly found that the defendant owed the plaintiff a duty of reasonable care, stating that, "[i]n the neighborhood described in the present case, a trier of fact may . . . find the occurrence of violence reasonably foreseeable in such a sheltered location to be perpetrated by someone lying in ambush or by someone also using the public right of way who harbors an intent to drag into concealment and out of public view some other party also using the public right of way to inflict harm." **(58)** It also found that the "breach of duty whether common law or statutory or the creating or permitting of a public nuisance was the position of the sumac bush."

(59) Despite finding a legally cognizable duty and a breach of that duty, the trial court nevertheless ruled that "the shielded bushing did not cause the injury. The rape and assault caused the injury and damages." **(60)** "That shielding [which was described as the building, a retaining wall and sumac trees and/or bushes] could have been provided in that same place and time by some other validly positioned or placed apurtenance." **(61)** The court concluded, therefore, that as a matter of law, the jury could not find that the defendant's maintenance of overgrowth on his property was a "substantial factor" in producing the plaintiff's injuries and, hence, the plaintiff had failed to establish **proximate cause**.

II

(62) The plaintiff appealed to the Appellate Court from the judgment of the trial court granting the defendant's motion to set aside the verdict. **(63)** We transferred the case to ourselves pursuant to Practice Book § 4023. **(64)** On appeal, the plaintiff claims that the trial court erred in setting aside the verdict on the ground that the plaintiff had not established proximate cause as a matter of law. **(65)** She asserts that evidence pertaining to the condition of the defendant's property, in connection with evidence that the neighborhood was a high crime area and that the specific site was frequented by trespassing street people and derelicts, created a question of fact for the jury whether the harm the plaintiff had suffered was reasonably foreseeable to the defendant. **(66)** She avers, therefore, that the trial court erred in concluding that the criminal act of the unknown assailant was the supervening cause of the plaintiff's injuries as a matter of law. **(67)** Further, she argues that the trial court's conclusion that the condition of the defendant's property was not a "substantial factor" in causing the plaintiff's injuries was inconsistent with its prior finding that "the occurrence of violence [was] reasonably foreseeable in such a sheltered location" and that "[w]ithout the shielding, the rape most probably would not have occurred there." **(68)** Consequently, she claims, the court erred in setting aside the jury's verdict in her favor on the ground that she had failed to prove proximate cause. **(69)** We are not persuaded.

A

(70) "Proximate cause" is an element of proof of all three causes of action asserted by the plaintiff. See, e.g., *Catz v. Rubenstein,* 201 Conn. 39, 44 (1986) (elements of negligence are duty, breach, causation and damages); *Madenford v. Interstate Lumber & Mill Corporation,* 153 Conn. 62, 64 (1965) (to be actionable, violation of statute must proximately cause injury); *State v. Tippetts–Abbett–McCarthy–Stratton,* 204 Conn. 177, 183 (1987) (actionable nuisance must proximately cause injuries). **(71)** The plaintiff has not argued that a different proximate cause analysis may or should apply to the different causes of action alleged. . . .

(72) Ordinarily, "the decision to set aside a verdict involves the exercise of a broad legal **discretion** by the trial court which, in the absence of a clear abuse, will not be disturbed; *Lee v. Lee,* [171 Conn. 1, 3, 368 A.2d 11 (1976)]; and further, that in reviewing the exercise of that discretion every reasonable presumption should be indulged in favor of its correctness. *Angelica v. Fernandes,* 174 Conn. 534, 535 (1978); *Ardoline v. Keegan,* 140 Conn. 552, 555 (1954)." *Jacobs v. Goodspeed,* 180 Conn. 415, 416 (1980). **(73)** The trial court's discretion, however, is circumscribed by our recognition that the "issue of proximate cause is ordinarily a question of fact for the trier. *Tetro v. Stratford* 189 Conn. 601, 605, [458] A.2d 5 (1983). **(74)** 'Conclusions of proximate cause are to be drawn by the jury and not by the court.' *Fox v. Mason,* 189 Conn. 484, 489 (1983). **(75)** "It becomes a conclusion of law only when the mind of a fair and reasonable man could reach only one conclusion; if there is room for a reasonable disagreement the question is one to be determined by the trier of fact." . . . '" *Trzcinski v. Richey,* 190 Conn. 285, 295 (1983). **(76)** Thus, the trial court's judgment setting aside the jury's verdict may stand only if there was no "room for a reasonable disagreement" on the question of proximate cause.

B

(77) To prevail on a negligence claim, a plaintiff must establish that the defendant's conduct "legally caused" the injuries. *Wu v. Fairfield,* 204 Conn. 435, 438 (1987); *Hearl v. Waterbury YMCA,* 187 Conn. 1, 4 (1982); W. Prosser & W. Keeton, Torts (5th Ed.) § 41, p. 263. **(78)** As we observed in *Kowal v. Hofher,* 181 Conn. 355, 359 (1980), "[l]egal cause is a hybrid construct, the result of balancing philosophic, pragmatic and moral approaches to causation." **(79)** The first component of "legal cause" is "**causation in fact**." **(80)** "'Causation in fact' is the purest legal application of . . . legal cause. **(81)** The test for cause in fact is, simply, would the injury have occurred were it not for the actor's conduct." Id.

(82) The second component of "legal cause" is proximate cause, which we have defined as "'[a]n actual cause that is a substantial factor in the resulting harm . . . .' *Coburn v. Lenox Homes, Inc.,* 186 Conn. 370, 383 (1982)." *Boehm v. Kish,* 201 Conn. 385, 391 (1986). **(83)** The "proximate cause" requirement tempers the "expansive view of causation [in fact] . . . by the pragmatic . . . shaping [of] rules which are feasible to administer, and yield a workable degree of certainty. 2 Harper & James, Torts § 20.4, p. 1133. **(84)** Remote or trivial [actual] causes are generally rejected because the determination of the responsibility for another's injury is much too important to be distracted by explorations for obscure consequences or inconsequential causes." *Kowal v. Hofher,* supra, 181 Conn. at 359–60. **(85)** "In determining proximate cause, the point beyond which the law declines to trace a series of events that exist along a chain signifying actual causation is a matter of fair judgment and a rough sense of justice. . . .

(86) This court has often stated that the "test" of proximate cause is whether the defendant's conduct is a "substantial factor" in producing the plaintiff's injury. *Wu v. Fairfield,* supra, 204 Conn. at 438; *Boehm v. Kish,* supra; *Tetro v. Stratford,* supra; see also *Ferndale Dairy, Inc. v. Geiger,* 167 Conn. 533, 538 (1975) (defining "substantial factor" as one which "must have continued down to the moment of the damage or, at least, down to the setting in motion of the final active injurious force which immediately produced or preceded the damage") .... **(87)** That negligent conduct is a "cause in fact," however, obviously does not mean that it is also a "substantial factor" for the purposes of a proximate cause inquiry. **(88)** The "substantial factor" test, in truth, reflects the inquiry fundamental to all proximate cause questions; that is, "'whether the harm which occurred was of the same general nature as the foreseeable risk created by the defendant's negligence.' *Merhi v. Becker,* [164 Conn. 516, 521, 325 A.2d 270 (1973)] .... **(89)** In applying this test, we look "'from the injury to the negligent act complained of for the necessary causal connection. *Collins v. City National Bank & Trust Co.,* 131 Conn. 167, 171 [1944].'" *Peterson v. Oxford,* 189 Conn. 740, 749 (1983).

(90) The "scope of the risk" analysis of "proximate cause" similarly applies where, as here, the **risk of harm** created by the defendant's negligence allegedly extends to an intervening criminal act by a third party. See *Tetro v. Stratford,* supra, 189 Conn. 605; *Coburn v. Lenox Homes, Inc.,* supra. **(91)** "We have consistently adhered to the standard of 2 Restatement (Second), Torts § 442B (1965) that a negligent defendant, whose conduct creates or increases the risk of a particular harm and is a substantial factor in causing that harm, is not relieved from liability by the intervention of another person, *except* where the harm is intentionally caused by the third person *and* is not within the scope of the risk created by the defendant's conduct. *Kiniry v. Danbury Hospital,* 183 Conn. 448, 455 (1981); *Merhi v. Becker,* [supra, 164 Conn. at 522]; *Miranti v. Brookside Shopping Center, Inc.,* 159 Conn. 24, 28 (1969)." (Emphasis added.) *Tetro v. Stratford,* supra. **(92)** "The reason [for the general rule precluding liability where the intervening act is intentional or criminal] is that in such a case the third person has deliberately assumed control of the situation, and all responsibility for the consequences of his act is shifted to him." 2 Restatement (Second), Torts § 442B, comment c. **(93)** "Such tortious or criminal acts may in themselves be foreseeable, [however,] and so within the scope of the created risk . . . ." Id.; see also 2 Restatement (Second), Torts §§ 448 and 449.

C

(94) Applying these principles, we first note that the defendant has not argued that his conduct was not a "cause in fact" of the plaintiff's injuries. **(95)** The trial court found that the sexual assault most probably would not have occurred *where it actually occurred* had the overgrown vegetation not been present. **(96)** The court also found that the jury could have found from the evidence that the rapist "by design and plan premeditated that the sexual assault would occur in that exact location." **(97)** Further, there was evidence from which the jury could reasonably have found that the assault would not have lasted thirty minutes absent the shielding provided by the overgrowth. **(98)** "The conception of causation in fact extends not only to positive acts and active physical forces, but also to pre-existing passive conditions which have played a ... part in bringing about the event." W. Prosser & W. Keeton, supra, p. 265. **(99)** Under the circumstances, we have no reason to question the trial court's finding that the injury would not have occurred, where it actually occurred, were it not for the shielding created by the overgrowth. *Boehm v. Kish,* supra; *Kowal v. Hofher,* supra.

(100) We disagree with the plaintiff, however, that there was room for reasonable disagreement over the question whether the condition on the defendant's property proximately caused her injuries. *Trzcinski v. Richey,* supra. **(101)** The plaintiff argues that there was sufficient evidence for the jury to find that the impaired visibility created by the overgrowth, in conjunction with the manner in which the defendant's property was used and the unseemly character of the neighborhood, increased the risk of violent crime between strangers. **(102)** She claims, therefore, that under § 442B of the Restatement, the assailant's act was within the "scope of the risk" created by the condition of the defendant's property. **(103)** We are persuaded, however, that the plaintiff's application of § 442B of the Restatement is unduly broad. **(104)** Contrary to her assertion, the harm she suffered cannot reasonably be understood as within the scope of the risk created by the defendant's conduct. **(105)** We reach this conclusion on the basis of the applicable standards established in our cases as well as by reference to factually analogous precedents.

(106) First, we decline to accept the plaintiff's argument suggesting that it was within the "scope of the risk" that the condition of the defendant's land might catalyze a criminal assault. **(107)** The plaintiff presented expert testimony that conditions of "environmental disorder," such as those present on the defendant's property and within the surrounding neighborhood, stood in a direct and positive relationship with an increased risk of violent crimes between strangers. **(108)** She also **presented evidence** tending to indicate that the assailant had planned the crime around the site. **(109)** Thus, the plaintiff's theory of liability turns in part on the argument that because the overgrowth was instrumental, in a psychological and sociological sense, in fostering the criminal act, the defendant should be held liable.

(110) This argument envisages the rapist's conduct as a "dependent intervening force"; that is, a predictable response or "reaction to the stimulus of a situation for which the actor has made himself responsible by his negligent conduct." 2 Restatement (Second), Torts § 441, comment c. **(111)** This position is untenable. **(112)** First, it is clear that § 442B contemplates *reasonably foreseeable* intervening misconduct, rather than *all* conduct that actually proceeds from a situation created by the defendant. *Coburn v. Lenox Homes, Inc.,* supra, 186 Conn. at 375, 384. **(113)** We are not persuaded that a landowner should reasonably foresee that a condition on his property such as overgrown vegetation might provide a substantial incentive or inducement for the commission of a violent criminal assault between strangers. **(114)** This is true although once such an incident does occur, it necessarily "could" have occurred. **(115)** Violent crimes are actuated by a host of social and psychological factors.

(116) Although, as a matter of fact, it may be true that one of those actuating factors is mere opportunity for concealment, common experience informs us that such a factor is at most incidental. **(117)** A prudent person who owns land abutting a public way would not, in our opinion, infer from his ordinary experience the possibility that overgrown vegetation will prompt or catalyze a violent criminal act. **(118)** This theory ascribes far too much speculative imagination to a "reasonable" or "prudent" person. **(119)** A person of ordinary caution is not required to be accomplished at making such recondite associations.

(120) Moreover, in the present case, there was no evidence tending to demonstrate that the defendant had had any past experience that might reasonably have led him to perceive and act on the atypical association between "natural shields" such as overgrown vegetation and violent criminal activity. **(121)** Indeed, the evidence showed that the prior "criminal activity" occurring in the vacant lot abutting his property and the scene of the crime generally was nonviolent, involving vagrancy and the public consumption of alcohol. **(122)** The plaintiff has not directed our attention to evidence that any of the individuals who frequented the vacant lot threatened or assaulted any passersby or local residents, except to the extent that their mere presence and appearance was "threatening." **(123)** Moreover, evidence that the defendant's mother had been robbed in the liquor store on the defendant's premises, and that a rape had occurred in a nearby building more than two months prior to the assault on the plaintiff, does not require a different conclusion. **(124)** Both incidents occurred indoors. **(125)** The fact that criminals will rob liquor stores is an unfortunate, but not extraordinary, fact of contemporary life, and cannot reasonably be seen as exciting the imagination of a prudent person to suppose that a violent sexual crime will occur behind nearby overgrown vegetation in the area of a vacant lot. **(126)** Further, even if it is assumed that the defendant knew or should have known of the rape in the nearby building, the plaintiff has not presented evidence demonstrating anything distinctive about that inherently atrocious incident that might be reasonably understood as eliciting the type of sensitivity for which she would now hold the defendant accountable. **(127)** In addition, that experts in environmental psychology such as George Rand are attuned to the association between conditions of "environmental disorder," such as overgrown vegetation in a poor neighborhood, and crime is surely a product of special training, knowledge, interest and, especially, perspective. . . .

(128) [The plaintiff erroneously argues] that the condition on the defendant's property, in connection with the "socio-chemistry" of the area, created a foreseeable "opportunity" for the commission of a violent crime and, hence, the harm inflicted on the plaintiff was within the "scope of the risk." **(129)** Our cases make it clear that, to be within the "scope of the risk," the harm actually suffered must be of the same "general type" as that which makes the defendant's conduct negligent in the first instance. *Coburn v. Lenox Homes, Inc.,* supra. **(130)** It is unexceptional to impose upon a landowner liability resulting from injuries caused directly and without intervening criminal conduct by "dangerous conditions" on the land. **(131)** Thus, where the plaintiff stumbles on accumulated debris on the defendant's land, and injures himself, the defendant may be liable. *Miranti v. Brookside Shopping Center, Inc.,* supra. **(132)** We are not prepared, however, to extend the scope of the foreseeable risk presented by "obnoxious overgrowth" or accumulated debris beyond injury produced by physical contact with such conditions. **(133)** Thus, the harm suffered by the plaintiff in this case was not of the same general type that allegedly made the defendant negligent. . . .

(134) *Miranti v. Brookside Shopping Center, Inc.,* supra, on which the plaintiff places much reliance, is factually dissimilar to the present case. **(135)** In *Miranti,* the plaintiff, a fifteen year old boy, was chased and knocked down by a dog, and fell over an accumulation of trash and debris on property alleged to be under the control of the defendants. **(136)** The trial court, concluding that the proximate cause of the fall and resulting injury was solely the action of the dog in knocking the plaintiff down rather than the accumulation of trash and debris, rendered judgment for the defendants on their motion for summary judgment. **(137)** We reversed, holding that the pleadings raised contested issues as to whether an accumulation of trash and debris did, in fact, exist, and, if it did, as to whether it created a condition productive of a foreseeable harm of the general nature of that suffered by the plaintiff, and as to which the defendants could be held legally responsible for the condition in any one or more of the ways claimed by the plaintiff. **(138)** Unlike *Miranti,* where the plaintiff was injured when he fell over the trash and debris on the defendants' property, in this case the plaintiff was injured by the criminal act of her abductor. **(139)** The sumac trees, the bushes, debris or litter on the defendant's property did not injure the plaintiff. **(140)** Nor, unlike *Miranti,* does the "scope of the risk" presented by the "dangerous" condition on the defendant's property extend to the harm of the general nature suffered by the plaintiff. . . .

(141) Finally, we disagree with the plaintiff's assertion that the trial court's conclusion that the occurrence of violence in such a sheltered location was reasonably foreseeable, and that the rape would not have occurred where it did absent the overgrowth, undermined its conclusion that the condition of the defendant's property was not a "substantial factor" of the plaintiff's harm. **(142)** A review of the trial court's memorandum indicates that the court's prior remarks addressed the issues of duty and factual cause rather than proximate cause. **(143)** We conclude, therefore, that there was no "room for a reasonable disagreement" that the plaintiff did not establish that the condition on the defendant's land was a proximate cause of the sexual assault. *Trzcinski v. Richey,* supra. **(144)** Accordingly, the trial court did not err in setting aside the jury's verdict in favor of the plaintiff. See *Magarian v. Bessoni,* 160 Conn. 442 (1971); *Robinson v. Southern New England Telephone Co.,* supra.

(145) There is no error. . . .

TASK 5.F.1. Case Brief

Write a case brief of *Doe v. Manheimer* using the template on page 290.

TASK 5.F.2. Torts Vocabulary Definitions (List 4)

Fill in each definition with the appropriate term from the list below. Consult a law dictionary or an English-to-English dictionary to confirm that you have matched each term with the correct definition. If multiple forms of a term are provided, you may not need to use all of the forms in the blanks.

assault *(verb; noun)*
bring an action *(verb)*
causation in fact *(noun)*; also referred to as "but-for cause"
cross-examination *(noun)*
directed verdict *(noun)*
discretion *(noun)*
present evidence *(verb)*
proximate cause *(noun)*
risk of harm *(noun)*
set aside the verdict *(verb)*
sustain an injury or injuries *(verb)*
testimony *(noun)*; testify *(verb)*
witness *(noun)*
verdict *(noun)*

Terms related to torts

1. ____________________ is a tort that involves intentionally placing another person in apprehension of imminent harmful or offensive contact.

2. There are two components of legal cause:

   a. ____________________
   b. ____________________

   Note: A plaintiff must prove both of these components of legal cause.

3. The term ____________________ refers to the danger that someone will be injured due to the defendant's conduct.

4. When an individual ____________________ an injury, she becomes injured. Courts also use the terms "suffer" or "incur" an injury.

Terms related to procedure

5. During trial, both the plaintiff and defendant have the opportunity to ____________________ in their favor. Because the plaintiff initiates the legal action, she is the first person to present her side of the story. Once the plaintiff finishes, the defendant has the opportunity to tell her side of the story.

   Note: The plaintiff, defendant, and other witnesses cannot talk freely in court. Rather, they answer questions put to them by their own lawyers and lawyers for the other side ("opposing counsel"). In other words, they testify. The stories that they tell are therefore significantly constrained by the question-answer format of courtroom talk.

6. A motion for a/an ____________________ is a motion usually filed by a defendant. After the plaintiff has presented her case, the defendant may ask the court to find in the defendant's favor. The defendant would make this request if she believes that the plaintiff has not produced enough evidence to support the factual allegations made in her claim. If the trial judge grants the motion, the defendant wins. If the trial judge denies the motion, the defendant is allowed to present evidence in her favor. The trial judge may also reserve a decision on the motion and wait to see what the jury decides.

7. A/an ____________________ is a jury's decision as to who should win a case (plaintiff or defendant) as well as its determination as to the amount of damages, if any, that the plaintiff should recover. Juries "return" a verdict.

8. ____________________ refers to the freedom to exercise one's own judgment and freedom to make one's own choices. For example, trial judges have a great deal of this when deciding whether to grant or deny motions.

9. A/an ____________________ is a person who testifies in court.

10. ____________________ refers to a sworn, formal statement given by a witness in a court of law. Witnesses ____________________ in court by answering questions asked by their own attorneys (direct examination)

and attorneys for the other side (cross examination). (See also Appendix C: Steps in the Civil Litigation Process.)

11. A motion to ____________________ is a request by a party for the trial judge to "overturn" a jury verdict. Judges grant this motion if they believe that the evidence to support the verdict is not legally sufficient and no reasonable person could decide for the non-moving party.

12. ____________________ is the phase of a trial where a lawyer questions a witness on the opposing side (e.g., the defense attorney asks questions from one of the plaintiff's witnesses). It is the opposite of direct examination, which is the phase of a trial where an attorney questions her own witness (e.g., the defense attorney asks questions from the defendant). (See also Appendix C: Steps in the Civil Litigation Process.)

13. To ____________________ is a synonym for "bring suit." It means to initiate legal proceedings against another party.

TASK 5.F.3. Questions for Discussion

Answer the following questions to assist you during a class discussion of the case. Indicate the sentence(s) in which you found the answer to each question.

1. What are the facts of this case?

2. Who prevailed at trial court?

3. The court begins the case in sentence (1) by stating the issue as follows: "The difficult issue in this case is whether a landowner may be liable in tort for damages arising from the rape of a pedestrian committed on the landowner's property behind brush and trees that shielded the area from view from the nearby public sidewalk and street." Is this a narrow or broad formulation of the issue?

4. What are the two elements of causation? Must a plaintiff prove both of these elements?

5. The question of proximate cause is usually a question for the fact finder (jury). However, the trial court stated that "as a matter of law," the plaintiff failed to establish proximate cause (see again sentence (61)).

Why did the trial judge decide the question of proximate cause instead of leaving this to the jury?

6. What is the holding of the case? What is the rule of the case?

7. What is the "test" of proximate cause used by the court?

8. When is a "scope of the risk" analysis used? According to the court, was the harm Doe suffered within the scope of the risk created by the defendant's conduct? Why/why not?

9. Hypotheticals:

    a. Imagine the same facts as *Doe*, but instead of raping the plaintiff, the assailant took her wallet and pushed her in the bushes on defendant's property. The plaintiff subsequently broke her leg on a sharp branch sticking out of the ground. Would the result be any different in this case?

    b. What if another woman had been mugged in the same bushes as Doe, two months before the incident with Doe? Would the result be any different in this case?

10. Hypotheticals:

    a. Abe (defendant) fails to stop at a red light and collides into Cathy (plaintiff) as she is crossing the street. Cathy suffers serious injuries as a result.

       Can Cathy prove causation in fact? Can Cathy prove proximate cause?

    b. Abe (defendant) is driving drunk and hits a warehouse full of explosives. There is an explosion as a result. Bob sees the explosion from the street that he is driving on. As he turns around to look at the explosion, he doesn't see Cathy (plaintiff) crossing the street in front of him, and he hits her. Cathy suffers serious injuries as a result.[1]

---

[1] Hypothetical adapted from *Actual and Proximate Causation*, JUSTIA.COM, https://www.justia.com/injury/negligence-theory/actual-and-proximate-cause/ (last visited May 17, 1018).

Can Cathy prove causation in fact? Can Cathy prove proximate cause?

G. Torts Essay Question #2

Answer the following hypothetical using the previous cases in this chapter to inform your answer. Use a piece of paper or a blank document on your computer to outline your response before you begin writing.

Suggested response time: **35 minutes**.

QUESTION

On March 10th of last year, the Emergency Alert System issued an alert stating that there was an incoming ballistic missile to the city island of Cranston. The alert read as follows: "BALLISTIC MISSILE INCOMING. SEEK SHELTER IMMEDIATELY. THIS IS NOT A DRILL." The message went out to all cellphones at 8 am.

After receiving the message, Mark, a longtime resident of Cranston, thought that he was shortly going to die. He and his wife, Nancy, decided that they should die together on the beach. As they made their way to the beach (a three-minute walk from the couple's home), they called family members to say goodbye and tell them that they loved them.

While sitting on the beach and anxiously waiting for the missile to strike, Mark started to feel a severe pain in his chest. The pain became so severe that Nancy thought it best to take her husband to the local hospital. While on their way, Mark and Nancy missed a message sent at 8:45 a.m. stating that the warning was a false alert.

It turns out that Mark suffered a massive heart attack and had to undergo emergency surgery. He alleges that the heart attack has caused permanent damage to his heart and he can no longer participate in activities he once enjoyed due to his fear that he will experience another cardiac arrest.

Mark has sued the city of Cranston for negligence in sending out the false alert. The city has filed a motion to dismiss, arguing that Mark has failed to allege causation. You are the trial judge. How would you rule on the motion?[2]

For this question, assume that you are working in a jurisdiction in which the laws of **ALL** states apply.

---

[2] Hypothetical adapted from Eli Rosenberg, *A Hawaii Man Had a Medical Emergency During the False Missile Alert. Now He's Suing*, The Wash. Post (Nov. 28, 2018, 6:19 PM), https://www.washingtonpost.com/nation/2018/11/28/hawaii-man-had-heart-attack-during-false-missile-alert-now-hes-suing/?utm_term=.0e9ec595034a.

H. Torts Case #5

The next two cases, *Harding v. Deiss* and *Murphy v. Steeplechase Amusement Co.*, address not an element of negligence, but rather defenses to a claim of negligence. In both cases, whose conduct is the defense based upon?

HARDING v. DEISS

Supreme Court of Montana, 2000.
300 Mont. 312, 3 P.3d 1286, 2000 MT 169.

HUNT, Justice.

(1) Marsha Harding (Appellant) appeals from the denial by the Third Judicial District Court, Deer Lodge County, of . . . its issuance of a jury instruction on comparative negligence. **(2)** We reverse.

(3) We restate Appellant's issue[] on appeal as follows: Did the District Court err in allowing Respondents to present argument and jury instructions on comparative negligence? . . .

STATEMENT OF FACTS

(4) On August 3, 1994, Appellant's daughter, Candice Shuck (Candice), went horseback riding at the Fairmont Stables near Anaconda, Montana. **(5)** Candice had asthma, was allergic to horses, and had a long medical history of breathing difficulties. **(6)** During the ride she began to have trouble breathing and eventually collapsed. **(7)** Two of the stables' employees administered CPR at the scene and Candice was transported by ambulance to the Anaconda Hospital emergency room where she was placed under the care of Dr. Zachory Deiss (Dr. Deiss). **(8)** The next day she was transported to St. James Hospital in Butte, Montana, and placed under the care of Dr. Glenn Sublette (Dr. Sublette). **(9)** Candice's family then brought in neurosurgeon Dr. Pius Baggenstos who cared for Candice until her death on August 11, 1994.

(10) Following Candice's death, Appellant brought a wrongful death and survivor action alleging medical negligence by Dr. Deiss and Dr. Sublette (Respondents). **(11)** A jury returned a verdict in Respondents' favor. . . .

(12) The issue before the jury in this medical malpractice case was whether Candice's irreversible brain injury occurred before or after she arrived at the Anaconda hospital. **(13)** Appellant argued Respondents were negligent in their treatment of Candice by failing to intubate her immediately upon her arrival at the hospital, and that their negligence caused Candice's injury and death. **(14)** Respondents claimed that Candice had already suffered a severe brain injury due to oxygen deprivation brought on by her asthma attack and it was her own negligence, not the negligence of Respondents, which caused her death.

(15) Appellant asserts that the conduct of a patient can never be an issue in a claim of medical malpractice, and the issue of whether Candice was negligent should not have been submitted to the jury; whether Candice did something wrong before she was rendered unconscious is irrelevant to whether the Respondents were later negligent in her medical care. **(16)** Appellant specifically argues that Court Instructions Nos. 11 and 12 should not have been given to the jury. **(17)** Court Instruction No. 11 stated:

> [n]egligence on the part of Candice Shuck does not bar **recovery** of the estate of Candice Shuck unless Candice Shuck's negligence was greater than the combined negligence of the defendants. **(18)** However, the total amount of damages that the estate of Candice Shuck would otherwise be entitled to **recover** will be reduced by the court in proportion to the amount of negligence you attribute to Candice Shuck.

(19) Court Instruction No. 12 read:

> [t]he defendants have the **burden of proving** that the Plaintiff Candice Shuck was negligent. **(20)** As to this defense, the defendants have the burden of proving the following:
> (1) That the plaintiff (Candice Shuck) was negligent.
> **(21)** (2) That plaintiff's (Candice Shuck) negligence was the cause of Plaintiff's injury.

(22) Appellant claims that these two instructions "in essence put before the jury the notion that they could determine whether Candice Shuck was legally negligent and then compare her negligence to the negligence of the [Respondents]." **(23)** Appellant asserts that giving comparative negligence instructions in a medical malpractice case presents an opportunity to nullify every possible case against a physician for malpractice.

(24) Respondents assert that a jury instruction on comparative negligence is appropriate in this action because it was Candice's negligence which caused her injury. **(25)** They further claim that the jury never reached the issue of Candice's negligence because they concluded that Respondents were not negligent, and therefore, the issue of the jury instruction is moot.

(26) We review jury instructions in a civil case for **abuse of discretion**. *Federal Mutual Insurance Co. v. Anderson,* 1999 MT 288, ¶ 44, 297 Mont. 33, ¶ 44, 991 P.2d 915, ¶ 44. **(27)** Furthermore,

> [a] district court has broad discretion in deciding whether to give or refuse a party's proposed jury instruction. **(28)** In reviewing whether a particular jury instruction was properly given or refused, we must consider the instruction in its entirety, as well

> as in connection with the other instructions given and with the evidence introduced at trial.

In re Estate of Lande, 1999 MT 162, ¶ 44, 295 Mont. 160, ¶ 44, 983 P.2d 308, ¶ 44 (citing *Moore v. Imperial Hotels Corp.,* 1998 MT 248, ¶ 21, 291 Mont. 164, ¶ 21, 967 P.2d 382, ¶ 21).

(29) . . . Appellant correctly asserts that [the issue of comparative negligence in a case like this] has not been directly addressed in Montana, [but] other jurisdictions have given the matter significant consideration, often in the context of the related defense of **contributory negligence**. **(30)** We find other jurisdictions' analyses of the defenses of contributory and comparative negligence in medical malpractice actions helpful in resolving this issue.

(31) According to one author, "[c]ase law is replete with instances where the physician charged the plaintiff with contributory negligence for behavior that occurred before the patient sought treatment, but courts generally agree that the prior conduct should not be considered in assessing damages." Madelynn R. Orr, Comment, *Defense of a Patient's Contribution to Fault in Medical Malpractice Actions,* 25 Creighton L.Rev. 665, 667, (1992). **(32)** Courts have, however, acknowledged the propriety of the defense of contributory or comparative negligence in certain circumstances. **(33)** In an action for **medical malpractice**, the improper diagnosis of a patient's medical condition coupled with improper treatment resulted in the amputation of the patient's foot. *Durphy v. Kaiser,* 698 A.2d 459, 466 (D.C.1997). **(34)** Defendants raised the defense of contributory negligence claiming that the patient had failed to cooperate in his treatment. **(35)** In discussing the standard for contributory negligence the court stated, "[i]n medical malpractice cases, contributory negligence is a valid defense if the patient's negligent act occurs with that of the physician and creates an unreasonable risk of improper medical treatment." *Durphy,* 698 A.2d at 467. *See also Champs v. Stone* 74 Ohio App. 344, 58 N.E.2d 803 (1944) (patient was contributorily negligent when he allowed a "grossly intoxicated" physician to give him an injection which resulted in the patient's injury).

(36) Courts have noted that in assisting a jury to decide a case involving the patient's fault as a defense in medical malpractice cases, it is necessary to first clarify the sequence of events in relation to the interwoven doctrines of contributory or comparative negligence, proximate cause, and avoidable consequences. *Bryant v. Calantone,* 286 N.J.Super. 362, 669 A.2d 286, 288 (1996). **(37)** In *Bryant,* a patient with a heart condition was advised by his cardiologist that he must be given antibiotics upon having any type of dental work performed. **(38)** According to the patient, when he arrived to have his teeth cleaned, the Dentist handed him a dose of medication and said "this is all you need." *Bryant,* 669 A.2d at 287–88. **(39)** Within two weeks of treatment, the patient became very ill and required several serious heart surgeries. **(40)** In addressing the defendant's claim that the district court erred in not issuing a jury instruction on comparative negligence, the court stated "the patient's conduct must be divided into three categories in determining whether the patient shares any fault and if so, what principles of law to apply to that fault." *Bryant,* 669 A.2d at 288.

(41) "The three temporal headings under which the patient's conduct is to be examined are 1) the pre-treatment period[,] 2) the treatment period during which the alleged malpractice occurred, and 3) the post-malpractice period." *Bryant,* 669 A.2d at 288. **(42)** The *Bryant* court noted [t]he pre-treatment health habits of a patient are not to be considered as evidence of fault . . . . *Bryant,* 669 A.2d at 289.

(43) The *Durphy* court held similarly, stating

> where the patient's negligent act merely precedes that of the physician and provides the occasion for medical treatment, contributory negligence is not a permissible defense. **(44)** Where that occurs, the doctor's negligent act is considered an intervening cause which does not bar the patient from recovering.

Durphy, 698 A.2d at 467.

(45) In *Whitehead v. Linkous, M.D.,* 404 So.2d 377 (Fla.Dist.Ct.App.1981) patient Whitehead consumed the drugs Valium and Darvocet in conjunction with a large amount of beer in an apparent suicide attempt. *Whitehead,* 404 So.2d at 378. **(46)** A nurse administered Whitehead a medicine to induce vomiting. **(47)** The nurse later noted that his color "didn't look right." *Whitehead,* 404 So.2d at 378. **(48)** Whitehead lost consciousness and later died. **(49)** The hospital asserted that his acts in attempting to commit suicide were a contributing cause of his death and thus, were subject to a jury instruction on comparative negligence. *Whitehead,* 404 So.2d at 378–79. **(50)** The court held that any conduct by Whitehead before he entered the hospital which contributed to his death was not a proximate, legal cause of the damages sought, and the trial court erred in submitting the instruction on comparative negligence. *Whitehead,* 404 So.2d at 379. *See also Spence v. Aspen Skiing Co.,* 820 F.Supp. 542 (D.Colo.1993) (noting that it would be inconsistent with the reasonable and normal expectations of both parties for the court to excuse or reduce the provider's liability simply because it was the patient's own fault that she required care in the first place).

(51) We agree with the foregoing decisions and conclude that comparative negligence as a defense does not apply where a patient's pre-treatment behavior merely furnishes the need for care or treatment which later becomes the subject of a malpractice claim. **(52)** The patient's conduct before seeking medical treatment is merely a factor the physician should consider in treating the patient. **(53)** Candice's actions are clearly pre-treatment conduct and as such are not to be considered as evidence of fault which may offset any negligent conduct by the Respondents. **(54)** Acceptance of Respondents' argument (that Candice's act of riding a horse while having asthma is a negligent act which should be offset against any negligent act by Respondents in her treatment) would lead to an absurd result. **(55)** Under such a theory, in any case where the patient was responsible for events that led to her hospitalization, the treating physician would not be liable for negligent treatment. **(56)** We hold that in medical malpractice actions, jury instructions on a patient's comparative negligence are appropriate only where the patient's negligent conduct occurs contemporaneous with or subsequent to treatment. **(57)** We conclude that because Candice's allegedly negligent acts were pre-treatment conduct, the District Court's issuance of jury instructions on comparative negligence was an abuse of discretion. . . .

(58) Reversed. . . .

TASK 5.H.1. Case Brief

Write a case brief of *Harding v. Deiss* using the template on page 290.

TASK 5.H.2. Torts Vocabulary Definitions (List 5)

Fill in each definition with the appropriate term from the list below. Consult a law dictionary or an English-to-English dictionary to confirm that you have matched each term with the correct definition. If multiple forms of a term are provided, you may not need to use all of the forms in the blanks.

abuse of discretion *(noun)*
burden of proof *(noun)*; have the burden of proving [something] *(verb)*
comparative negligence *(noun)*
contributory negligence *(noun)*
jury instructions *(noun)*; instruct the jury *(verb)*
medical malpractice *(noun)*
recovery *(noun)*; recover [damages] *(verb)*
return a verdict in favor of [someone] *(verb)*

Terms related to torts

1. ____________________ is a defense to a claim of negligence based on the plaintiff's conduct. If a defendant succeeds in arguing this defense, the plaintiff cannot recover any damages if she has contributed to her injury (even if she is merely 1 percent at fault). Only a handful of states permit defendants to use this "all-or-nothing" defense.

2. ____________________ is also a defense to a claim of negligence based on the plaintiff's conduct. Under this more "forgiving" view, the plaintiff's damages are reduced based on her share of fault.

3. ____________________ refers to the failure of a medical professional to render services that meet the requisite standard of care.

4. If the plaintiff is successful in her case against the defendant, she is awarded money damages. In other words, the plaintiff ____________________ damages. The noun form ____________________ refers to the amount of money that a plaintiff is awarded in a lawsuit.

Terms related to procedure

5. ____________________ refers to a party's responsibility to prove or disprove a disputed fact by producing relevant evidence to persuade the factfinder.

> Recall from Part II, Chapter 1 that in civil cases, this responsibility rests with the plaintiff, who bears a burden of proving her claim by a "preponderance of the evidence" (this means that more than 50 percent of the evidence should point in the plaintiff's favor). In criminal cases, the responsibility is on the prosecution, who has a burden of proving the defendant's guilt "beyond a reasonable doubt."

6. ____________________ refers to a judge's failure to make reasonable legal decisions. Appellate courts review certain trial court decisions to determine whether the judge abused her discretion.

7. When judges ____________________, they tell the jury what law to apply in making its decision. Another term for this is "charging the jury."

8. Juries ____________________ a verdict in favor of either the plaintiff or the defendant.

TASK 5.H.3. Questions for Discussion

Answer the following questions to assist you during a class discussion of the case. Indicate the sentence(s) in which you found the answer to each question.

1. Why did the plaintiff sue the defendant doctors? In other words, what was the plaintiff's claim?

2. Who prevailed at trial? How?

3. What were the plaintiff's and defendant's arguments on appeal?

4. Why does the Supreme Court of Montana look to other jurisdictions to help resolve the issue in this case?

5. What is the rule established in this case? What reasons does the Court supply to support its decision?

6. Do you agree with the Court that a patient's pre-treatment behavior should not be considered by the jury as evidence of comparative negligence? Why or why not?

7. Hypotheticals:

    a. Amanda stepped on a nail that pierced her shoe and the sole of her foot. She removed the shoe and found blood where the nail had entered her skin. Amanda immediately washed her foot and disinfected the area with antibacterial lotion. Two days later, she felt a sharp pain in her foot and noticed a red bump over the area where the nail had pierced her skin. She again applied antibacterial lotion on her skin. When the pain and redness did not go away four days later, she called Dr. Benson, who examined her foot. By this point, her entire foot was red and badly swollen. Dr. Benson prescribed Amanda a wash solution, painkillers, and told her to place her foot in a high position. Amanda followed these instructions. However, one day later, her leg was discolored up to her knee. Amanda went to the Emergency Room, where she was told that her lower leg would have to be amputated. Amanda brought suit against Dr. Benson alleging medical malpractice.

Based on the rule articulated in *Harding v. Deiss*, is this a situation where the court could instruct the jury on comparative negligence?[3]

b. Francine was injured in an automobile accident. While her injuries were not life-threatening, she had to get surgery to repair a broken shoulder. To calm her nerves, Francine had three glasses of her favorite wine two hours prior to her surgery, though she was instructed by a nurse not to consume any food or water 12 hours before the operation. The doctor thought she smelled alcohol on Francine's breath, but when she asked Francine about it, Francine denied having had anything to drink. The doctor decided to go ahead with the surgery. Due to the alcohol in Francine's body, her blood did not clot properly during surgery and she lost a massive amount of blood. She is now brain dead. Francine's relatives have brought suit against her surgeon alleging medical malpractice.

   Based on the rule articulated in *Harding v. Deiss*, is this a situation where the court could instruct the jury on comparative negligence?

A final note on contributory versus comparative negligence

Though courts sometimes use the terms "contributory negligence" and "comparative negligence" interchangeably, these two terms refer to different concepts. Contributory negligence is the idea that a plaintiff cannot recover damages if she has contributed at all to her injury—even if her share of fault is only 1 percent. Very few jurisdictions adhere to this doctrine.

Comparative negligence is perhaps the fairer approach, as this reduces the plaintiff's recovery based on her share of fault. Two types of comparative negligence have emerged over the years: "pure" comparative negligence and "modified" comparative negligence. In a **pure comparative negligence** regime, a plaintiff's recovery is reduced by her share of fault, whether it is 10 percent, 50 percent, or 99 percent. In a **modified comparative negligence** system, a plaintiff's recovery is again reduced by her share of fault, but only up to a point. If the plaintiff's fault exceeds a certain level—usually 50 percent or more—she is entirely barred from recovery. This is a popular approach that has been adopted by statute in many states.

---

[3] Hypothetical adapted from Sales v. Bacigalupi, 47 Cal.App.2d 82 (1941).

I. Torts Vocabulary Exercises (Lists 4-5)

EXERCISE 5.I.1. Fill in the Blanks

Fill in the blanks with the most appropriate form of the words and phrases in the list below. You may have to change word form to create a grammatically correct sentence. Some questions may have more than one correct answer.

causation in fact
comparative negligence
contributory negligence
cross-examination
decedent
discretion
instruct the jury
proximate cause
recovery

1. During ____________________, the plaintiff testified that she did not remember everything that happened on the night of the accident. She admitted this after the defendant's lawyer questioned her on this point for almost 20 minutes.

2. The defendant argued that the plaintiff was ____________________ negligent and was responsible for some of her own injuries.

3. Public school districts have a great deal of ____________________ in creating dress codes for their students. In other words, they have the freedom to decide what students are allowed to wear with little interference from the government.

4. After the plaintiff has proved causation ____________________, she must also prove that the defendant ____________________ caused her injuries.

5. The plaintiff's ____________________ was reduced by her share of fault, which the jury found to be 25 percent.

EXERCISE 5.I.2. Matching

Match the five subjects on the next page with the phrases (1-7) to create a complete sentence. Each subject should be matched with at least one phrase. Some questions may have more than one correct answer.

The attorney   The defendant   The judge   The jury   The plaintiff

1. ____________________ set aside the verdict.

2. ____________________ returned a verdict in favor of the defendant.

3. ____________________ recovered $500,000 in damages.

4. ____________________ presented evidence regarding the plaintiff's work history.

5. ____________________ sustained serious injuries when the defendant collided into her car.

6. ____________________ has the burden of proving the plaintiff's negligence.

7. ____________________ instructed the jury that common carriers owe a duty of reasonable care to their customers.

J. Torts Case #6

MURPHY v. STEEPLECHASE AMUSEMENT CO.

Court of Appeals of New York, 1929.
250 N.Y. 479, 166 N.E. 173.

CARDOZO, C. J.

(1) The defendant, Steeplechase Amusement Company, maintains an amusement park at Coney Island, N. Y. **(2)** One of the supposed attractions is known as "the Flopper." **(3)** It is a moving belt, running upward on an inclined plane, on which passengers sit or stand. **(4)** Many of them are unable to keep their feet because of the movement of the belt, and are thrown backward or aside. **(5)** The belt runs in a groove, with padded walls on either side to a height of four feet, and with padded flooring beyond the walls at the same angle as the belt. **(6)** An electric motor, driven by current furnished by the Brooklyn Edison Company, supplies the needed power.

(7) Plaintiff, a vigorous young man, visited the park with friends. **(8)** One of them, a young woman, now his wife, stepped upon the moving belt. **(9)** Plaintiff followed and stepped behind her. **(10)** As he did so, he felt what he describes as a sudden jerk, and was thrown to the floor. **(11)** His wife in front and also friends behind him were thrown at the same time. **(12)** Something more was here, as every one understood, than the slowly moving escalator that is common is shops and public places. **(13)** A fall was foreseen as one of the risks of the adventure. **(14)** There would have been no point to the whole thing, no adventure about it, if the risk had not been there. **(15)** The very name, above the gate, "the Flopper," was warning to the timid. **(16)** If the name was not enough, there was warning more distinct in the experience of others. **(17)** We are told by the plaintiff's wife that the members of her party stood looking at the sport before joining in it themselves. **(18)** Some aboard the belt were able, as she viewed them, to sit down with decorum or even to stand and keep their footing; others jumped or fell. **(19)** The tumbling bodies and the screams and laughter supplied the merriment and fun. **(20)** "I took a chance," she said when asked whether she thought that a fall might be expected.

(21) Plaintiff took the chance with her, but, less lucky than his companions, suffered a fracture of a knee cap. **(22)** He states in his complaint that the belt was dangerous to life and limb, in that it stopped and started violently and suddenly and was not properly equipped to prevent injuries to persons who were using it without knowledge of its dangers, and in a bill of particulars he adds that it was operated at a fast and dangerous rate of speed and was not supplied with a proper railing, guard, or other device to prevent a fall therefrom. **(23)** No other negligence is charged.

(24) We see no adequate basis for a finding that the belt was out of order. **(25)** It was already in motion when the plaintiff put his foot on it. **(26)** He cannot help himself to a verdict in such circumstances by the addition of the facile comment that it threw him with a jerk. **(27)** One who steps upon a moving belt and finds his heels above his head is in no position to discriminate with nicety between the successive stages of the shock, between the jerk which is a cause and the jerk, accompanying the fall, as an instantaneous effect. **(28)** There is evidence for the defendant that power was transmitted smoothly, and could not be transmitted otherwise. **(29)** If the movement was spasmodic, it was an unexplained and, it seems, an inexplicable departure from the normal workings of the mechanism. **(30)** An aberration so extraordinary, if it is to lay the basis for a verdict, should rest on something firmer than a mere descriptive epithet, a summary of the sensations of a tense and crowded moment. Matter of Case, 214 N. Y. 199; Dochtermann v. Brooklyn Heights R. R. Co., 32 App. Div. 13, 15; Id., 164 N. Y. 586; Foley v. Boston & M. R. R. Co., 193 Mass. 332, 335; Work v. Boston Elevated R. Co., 207 Mass. 447, 448; N. & W. Ry. Co. v. Birchett (C. C. A.) 252 F. 512, 515. **(31)** But the jerk, if it were established, would add little to the case. **(32)** Whether the movement of the belt was uniform or irregular, the risk at greatest was a fall. **(33)** This was the very hazard that was invited and foreseen. Lumsden v. L. A. Thompson Scenic Ry. Co., 130 App. Div. 209, 212, 213.

(34) Volenti non fit injuria. **(35)** One who takes part in such a sport accepts the dangers that inhere in it so far as they are obvious and necessary, just as a fencer accepts the risk of a thrust by his antagonist or a spectator at a ball game the chance of contact with the ball. Pollock, Torts (11th Ed.) p. 171; Lumsden v. L.

A. Thompson Scenic Ry. Co., supra; Godfrey v. Connecticut Co., 98 Conn. 63; Johnson v. City of New York, 186 N. Y. 139, 148; McFarlane v. City of Niagara Falls, 247 N. Y. 340, 349; cf. 1 Beven, Negligence, 787; Bohlen, Studies in the Law of Torts, p. 443. **(36)** The antics of the clown are not the paces of the cloistered cleric. **(37)** The rough and boisterous joke, the horseplay of the crowd, evokes its own guffaws, but they are not the pleasures of tranquility. **(38)** The plaintiff was not seeking a retreat for meditation. **(39)** Visitors were tumbling about the belt to the merriment of onlookers when he made his choice to join them. **(40)** He took the chance of a like fate, with whatever damage to his body might ensue from such a fall. **(41)** The timorous may stay at home.

(42) A different case would be here if the dangers inherent in the sport were obscure or unobserved (Godfrey v. Connecticut Co., supra; Tantillo v. Goldstein Bros. Amusement Co., 248 N. Y. 286), or so serious as to justify the belief that precautions of some kind must have been taken to avert them (cf. O'Callaghan v. Delwool Park Co., 242 Ill. 336). **(43)** Nothing happened to the plaintiff except what common experience tells us may happen at any time as the consequence of a sudden fall. **(44)** Many a skater or a horseman can rehearse a tale of equal woe. **(45)** A different case there would also be if the accidents had been so many as to show that the game in its inherent nature was too dangerous to be continued without change. **(46)** The president of the amusement company says that there had never been such an accident before. **(47)** A nurse employed at an emergency hospital maintained in connection with the park contradicts him to some extent. **(48)** She says that on other occasions she had attended patrons of the park who had been injured at the Flopper, how many she could not say. **(49)** None, however, had been badly injured or had suffered broken bones. **(50)** Such testimony is not enough to show that the game was a trap for the unwary, too perilous to be endured. **(51)** According to the defendant's estimate, 250,000 visitors were at the Flopper in a year. **(52)** Some quota of accidents was to be looked for in so great a mass. **(53)** One might as well say that a skating rink should be abandoned because skaters sometimes fall.

(54) There is testimony by the plaintiff that he fell upon wood, and not upon a canvas padding. **(55)** He is strongly contradicted by the photographs and by the witnesses for the defendant, and is without corroboration in the testimony of his companions who were witnesses in his behalf. **(56)** If his observation was correct, there was a defect in the equipment, and one not obvious or known. **(57)** The padding should have been kept in repair to break the force of any fall. **(58)** The case did not go to the jury, however, upon any such theory of the defendant's liability, nor is the defect fairly suggested by the plaintiff's bill of particulars, which limits his complaint. **(59)** The case went to the jury upon the theory that negligence was dependent upon a sharp and sudden jerk.

(60) The judgment of the Appellate Division and that of the Trial Term should be reversed, and a new trial granted, with costs to abide the event.

(61) POUND, CRANE, LEHMAN, KELLOGG, and HUBBS, JJ., concur.

(62) O'BRIEN, J., dissents on the authority of Tantillo v. Goldstein Bros. Amusement Co., 248 N. Y. 286.

(63) Judgments reversed, etc.

TASK 5.J.1. Case Brief

Write a case brief of *Murphy v. Steeplechase Amusement Co.* using the template on page 290.

TASK 5.J.2. Questions for Discussion

Answer the following questions to assist you during a class discussion of the case. Indicate the sentence(s) in which you found the answer to each question.

1. What are the facts of this case?

2. What is the rule of the case?

3. What is the court's reasoning for the rule it announces? In your own words, explain what you think *volenti non fit injuria* means.

4. Hypotheticals:

   a. Billy and Cyrus went white water rafting[4] in the Shenandoah River. When their raft collided with a rock, it capsized[5] and they both fell into the water. Billy, who was wearing a life jacket at the time, hit his head on a rock underwater, lost consciousness, and drowned. Billy's wife brought suit against the outfitter that organized the trip and provided the raft, alleging negligence. Would Billy's wife be likely to prevail? Why or why not?

   b. Imagine that instead of being injured by a rock in the water, Billy was bitten by a black widow spider[6] that was on the raft. As a

---

[4] White water rafting is a recreational outdoor activity in which an inflatable raft (boat) is used to navigate rough water.

[5] When a boat capsizes, it flips over in the water.

[6] Black widow spiders are one of the most dangerous, venomous spiders in the United States.

result of the bite, Billy has had extensive medical problems and was hospitalized twice. He brought suit against the outfitter, alleging negligence. Would he be likely to prevail? Why or why not?

c. What if Billy could prove that this was the third time that a customer had been bitten by a spider on one of the outfitter's rafts? Would this make a difference?

K. Torts Essay Question #3

Answer the following hypothetical using the previous cases in this chapter to inform your answer. Use a piece of paper or a blank document on your computer to outline your response before you begin writing.

Suggested response time: **40 minutes**.

QUESTION

Andy was a guest at the Golden Spur Hotel and Casino when he became involved in an unfortunate incident. After eating dinner at the hotel restaurant, he decided to try his luck at one of the poker tables in the adjoining casino. He was seated at the table with Barry and Clark. Barry was a regular at the casino—he played poker and blackjack at least once or twice a week—and had a history of getting into shouting matches and physical altercations[7] with other patrons when he lost. Indeed, he was banned from the casino for about six months two years ago after he had threatened to kill another patron. Clark had never visited the casino before, but he was an expert poker player, having competed in poker competitions for most of his adult life.

After a few rounds of losing to Clark, Barry had had enough. He started screaming obscenities[8] at Clark and accused him of cheating. While Clark sat there unresponsive, Barry punched him in the face and Clark collapsed onto the ground. As Clark struggled to get back on his feet, he reached into his pocket and pulled out a gun, aiming it directly at Barry. At this point, Andy decided to intervene, telling Clark calmly, "Come on, this guy isn't worth your energy." Andy then reached out to grab Clark's gun out of his hands, at which point Clark accidentally fired the gun in Andy and Barry's direction. The bullet hit Andy in the right shoulder.

---

[7] An altercation is a public argument or disagreement; it can be verbal and/or physical.

[8] Obscenities are offensive words and expressions; they are also referred to as "swear words."

As a result of this accident, Andy, who is right-handed, can no longer use his right hand. He also has chronic pain in his shoulder which radiates down into his arm. This pain will likely stay with him for the rest of his life.

Andy would like to sue the Golden Spur Hotel and Casino. He has come to your law firm asking whether you think he has a case against the hotel. Your supervisor, Mr. Cruz, has asked you to write him (that is, Mr. Cruz) an informal memo evaluating Andy's chances of success.

For this question, assume that you are working in a jurisdiction in which the laws of **ALL** states apply.

L. Torts Case #7

The next two cases address liability for injury caused by defective products, an area of tort law known as **products liability**. Plaintiffs who bring suit against product manufacturers may sue under a theory of negligence, though strict liability often applies. Recall from the introduction to this chapter that strict liability is absolute legal responsibility for an injury regardless of fault.

Plaintiffs sue product manufacturers for defects (problems or imperfections) with respect to the manufacture of a product, the design of a product, or the warnings attached (or not attached) to a product. As you read the following two cases, think about what the plaintiff in each case alleges: a manufacturing, design, or warning defect?

BROWN FORMAN CORP. v. BRUNE

Court of Appeals of Texas, 1994.

893 S.W.2d 640.

Justice YAÑEZ, Justice.

(1) This is a products liability and negligence case involving a tequila distiller and a college freshman, an underage drinker, who died from ethanol poisoning after she consumed a large quantity of tequila within a relatively short period of time. **(2)** At issue is whether the distiller, Brown–Forman, may be liable for **damages** because it failed to warn of the possibility of death following overconsumption of alcohol within a short amount of time and failed to provide instructions about the safe use of its tequila. **(3)** The question of whether a distiller had either duty has not been addressed by Texas courts.

(4) We conclude that under the facts of this case, Brown–Forman had no duty to provide a warning of the possibility of death following overconsumption of a large quantity of tequila within a short amount of time and had no duty to provide instructions for the safe use of its tequila. **(5)** We reverse the trial court's judgment, **render** judgment in favor of Brown–Forman, and render that Brune take nothing.

(6) On the afternoon of November 14, 1983, eighteen-year-old, college freshman, Marie Brinkmeyer and a friend went to a bar to drink alcoholic beverages. **(7)** In Texas, in 1983, the legal age for purchasing alcoholic beverages was nineteen. **(8)** Apparently, the bar personnel did not ask to see her identification and served her alcoholic beverages despite the fact that she was an underage drinker. **(9)** Testimony from friends accompanying her that afternoon was that she drank a 32–ounce pitcher of hurricanes and an unknown number of white russians. **(10)** It was at the bar that Marie and a friend planned a tequila party for that evening. **(11)** Marie and a friend left the bar late in the afternoon. **(12)** On the way back to the college campus, Marie and a friend stopped at a liquor store where she illegally purchased a bottle of Pepe Lopez tequila. **(13)** Brown–Forman manufactures Pepe Lopez tequila. **(14)** That evening, at the party, she continued the drinking she had begun that afternoon and began drinking tequila without mixing it with any nonalcoholic beverage. **(15)** Marie drank a glass half filled with only tequila and then straight from the tequila bottle. **(16)** While at the party, and after drinking heavily and rapidly, Marie became unconscious. **(17)** Friends took Marie to her room about 10:00 p.m. and laid her on her bed. **(18)** The next morning, Marie's roommate found her in bed, dead. **(19)** An autopsy revealed that the cause of her death was related to her ingesting large amounts of ethanol.

(20) Joyce Brune, Marie's mother, sued Brown–Forman claiming that the company was responsible for the **wrongful death** of her daughter. **(21)** Brune asserted that the tequila contained a marketing defect in that it was an unreasonably dangerous product in the absence of a warning and/or instructions for appropriate use. **(22)** Brune asserted this claim as a strict liability action and a negligence action. . . .

(23) . . . [T]he case proceeded to a jury trial. The jury determined that a marketing defect existed when the tequila left Brown–Forman's possession which caused Marie's death. **(24)** Additionally, the jury determined that Brown–Forman's negligence caused Marie's death. **(25)** The jury **awarded damages** to Brune which the court reduced by the percentage the jury found to be Marie's comparative responsibility. **(26)** Brown–Forman now appeals from the judgment.

(27) Among several points of error, Brown–Forman contends . . . that it owed Marie no duty to warn of the risk of death from overconsumption of alcohol within a short amount of time and that no duty exists by which it must provide instructions about the "proper" use of tequila.

(28) In 1983, when this case arose, there existed no state or federal warning requirements for alcoholic beverages. . . . [The court notes that in 1988 a federal law was passed requiring a "Government Warning" on all containers of alcoholic beverages. This warning provides that (1) "women should not drink alcoholic beverages during pregnancy because of the risk of birth defects"; and (2) "[c]onsumption of alcoholic beverages impairs [the] ability to drive a car or operate machinery, and may cause health problems." Because the case occurred in 1983, however, the court reviews the case as if no federal warnings existed.—Eds.]

(29) A "marketing defect" occurs when the defendant knows or should know of a potential risk of harm presented by the product, but sells it without adequately warning consumers of the danger or providing instructions for safe use. *Bristol–Meyers v. Gonzales,* 561 S.W.2d 801, 804 (Tex.1978). **(30)** Thus, even a product safely designed and manufactured may be unreasonably dangerous as marketed because of a lack of adequate warnings or instructions for safe use. *Joseph E. Seagram & Sons, Inc. v. McGuire,* 814 S.W.2d 385, 387 (Tex.1991). **(31)** In a marketing defect case, the focus is on whether the product's risks were reasonably foreseeable by the manufacturer or seller at the time of manufacture, whether the lack of warnings or instructions created an unreasonable danger, and whether the warnings given, if any, were adequate. **(32)** The adequacy of the warning is defined in terms of the likelihood of its being noticed and its ability to be understood and to convey a sufficient indication of the risks involved. **(33)** It is the absence of a warning that makes use of the product unreasonably dangerous. *Blackwell Burner Co. v. Cerda,* 644 S.W.2d 512, 516 (Tex.App.—San Antonio 1982, writ ref'd n.r.e.).

(34) It is fundamental that the existence of a **legally cognizable** duty is a prerequisite to all tort liability. *Graff v. Beard,* 858 S.W.2d 918, 919 (Tex.1993) (citing *Greater Houston Transp. Co. v. Phillips,* 801 S.W.2d 523, 525 (Tex.1991)). **(35)** Whether a legal duty exists under a set of facts is a question of law. *Greater Houston Transp.,* 801 S.W.2d at 525. **(36)** Therefore, . . . the threshold question is whether Brown–Forman had a duty to warn of the risk of death from overconsumption of alcohol in a short period of time. **(37)** We note that because there existed no federal or state legislation in 1983 regarding warnings on alcoholic beverage containers, does not mean that distillers may not be found liable for a failure to warn should courts find such a duty exists. **(38)** As the *Poole* court noted, considering "the creation of new concepts of duty in tort is historically the province of the judiciary." *El Chico v. Poole,* 732 S.W.2d 306, 314 (Tex.1987). **(39)** Therefore, we consider whether a common law duty existed in 1983 for distillers to warn that overconsumption of tequila within a short amount of time may cause death and whether there existed a duty to provide instructions about the safe use of tequila. **(40)** We proceed with our analysis keeping in mind that the absence of the warning is what must render the tequila unreasonably dangerous.

(41) Determining whether a legal duty exists necessarily entails the interpretation and application of legal precedent as well as policy considerations. **(42)** We consider social, economic, and political questions and their applicability to the facts at hand. *Graff,* 858 S.W.2d at 920 (citing *Mitchell v. Missouri–Kansas–Texas R.R. Co.,* 786 S.W.2d 659, 662 (Tex.1990)). **(43)** Other factors to be considered include the extent of the risk involved, "the foreseeability and likelihood of injury weighed against the social utility of the actor's conduct, the magnitude of the burden of guarding against the injury, and the consequences of placing the burden on the defendant." *Graff,* 858 S.W.2d at 920 (quoting *Greater Houston Transp.,* 801 S.W.2d at 525). **(44)** We note that foreseeability alone is not a sufficient basis for creating a new duty. *Bird v. W.C.W.,* 868 S.W.2d 767, 769 (Tex.1994). **(45)** In a failure to warn case, we consider the extent to which the tort system is capable of devising an adequate warning.

(46) In assessing whether a legal duty exists under the facts before us, we find Justice Kilgarlin's words distinguishing moral and legal duties particularly instructive:

> In spite of a societal dynamic to expand duty, Texas still follows a general rule that Texans do not owe others general amorphous legal duties. **(47)** The rule in Texas still distinguishes between moral and legal duty. **(48)** Although one may have a moral duty to prevent a blind person from crossing a busy street against a light, a person has no legal duty to do so unless additional factors exist. **(49)** These other factors include the existence of familial or voluntary relationships which impose a duty, statutes or ordinances which may legally require action, or special circumstances, such as having placed the blind man in his precarious position in the first place. **(50)** These relationships and circumstances may be born of contract as well as other voluntary or legal origins. **(51)** These are the duties that must expand and mutate in response to changes in society.

Malek v. Miller Brewing Co., 749 S.W.2d 521, 523 (Tex.App.—Houston [1st Dist.] 1988, writ denied) (quoting Kilgarlin & Sterba–Boatwright, *The Recent Evolution of Duty in Texas,* 28 S.Tex.L.Rev. 241, 245 (1986)).

(52) The common law has long recognized that the alcoholic beverage drinker maintains the ultimate power and thus the obligation to control his own drinking behavior. *Graff,* 858 S.W.2d at 921. **(53)** We believe that the common law should remain focused on the drinker as the person primarily responsible for his behavior.

(54) Though no Texas court has had to decide whether a distiller has a duty to warn of the risk of death from overconsuming alcohol in a short period of time, Texas courts have addressed whether alcoholic beverage manufacturers must warn of other risks and dangers associated with alcoholic beverages. **(55)** All concluded that the alcoholic beverage manufacturer had no duty to warn of whatever risk or danger was asserted.

(56) Before the federal labelling act became effective, a Houston court of appeals addressed whether a brewer owed a duty to place a warning on its beer stating that it may cause intoxication and render drinkers unable to operate a car. *Malek v. Miller Brewing Co.,*749 S.W.2d 521, 523 (Tex.App.—Houston [1st

Dist.] 1988, writ denied). **(57)** The *Malek* court held that the manufacturer had no legal duty to warn even though the federal government later enacted the 1988 legislation requiring manufacturers to place a specific warning on their products about driving after drinking. **(58)** The *Malek* court reviewed several cases from other jurisdictions and noted that courts have had difficulty devising an adequate warning of the particular tolerance of each consumer. *Malek,* 749 S.W.2d at 523. **(59)** The *Malek* court noted that the Tennessee Supreme Court's holding that the risk to a minor of death from ingestion of Everclear grain alcohol was not a hidden or unknown danger requiring a warning. *Malek,* 749 S.W.2d at 523 (citing *Pemberton v. American Distilled Spirits Co.,* 664 S.W.2d 690 (Tenn.1984)).

(60) In *Pemberton,* an individual died after overconsuming Everclear in a short amount of time. **(61)** The Tennessee Supreme Court found that the manufacturer had no duty to warn of the possibility of death in such an incident because the danger was generally known and recognized. *Pemberton,* 664 S.W.2d at 692.

(62) We note that in 1988, when Congress enacted the federal labeling law it decided to place labels on bottles of alcoholic beverages despite existing case law concluding that manufacturers had no duty to warn consumers about the product's dangers. **(63)** Before the enactment of the required federal warning, Texas courts, among others across the country, determined that manufacturers of alcoholic beverages did not owe a duty to warn that drinking alcoholic beverages may cause alcoholism or intoxication, or to warn of the dangers of driving after drinking alcoholic beverages. *Seagram & Sons, Inc. v. McGuire,* 814 S.W.2d 385 (Tex.1991) (manufacturer has no duty to warn of danger of developing alcoholism from prolonged and excessive consumption of product); *Malek v. Miller Brewing Co.,* 749 S.W.2d 521 (Tex.App.—Houston [1st Dist.] 1988, writ denied) (no duty to warn that beer may cause intoxication); *Morris v. Adolph Coors Co.,* 735 S.W.2d 578 (Tex.App.—Fort Worth 1987, writ ref'd n.r.e.) (manufacturer has no duty to warn that overconsumption of alcoholic beverage may impair the motor skills and judgment necessary to drive automobile). **(64)** Despite this case law, the only warnings the federal government required to be placed on alcoholic beverage bottles were regarding drinking during pregnancy and driving after drinking. **(65)** The federal government when considering the federally mandated warning label, did not require a warning about consuming large quantities of beverage alcohol within a short period of time.

(66) When choosing to enter the business of manufacturing alcoholic beverages a manufacturer should make an effort to inform its users about risks and dangers associated with its product. **(67)** That effort may include a larger public education campaign rather than simply labelling a bottle. **(68)** In fact, education may be the only remedy we have in preventing binge drinking. **(69)** Despite education, however, there will always be individuals who, though informed about the dangers associated with the use of alcoholic beverages, choose to misuse the product. **(70)** The circumstances behind an individual's choice to misuse beverage alcohol are profoundly complex and will not be addressed by placing a few warning words on the outside of a bottle. **(71)** The warning and education must come long before an individual reaches for a bottle of alcohol. **(72)** Holding an alcoholic beverage manufacturer financially responsible for the death of an individual who consumed a large quantity of alcohol in a short amount of time does not answer the more direct question about why the individual would consume a known dangerous product in such a quantity.

(73) As with smoking, perhaps with an increase in education to the public about the dangers of consuming large amounts of alcoholic beverages within a short period of time, acceptance of such activity will diminish.

(74) Alcoholic beverages are dangerous products. **(75)** Many human tragedies can be traced to an individual's use of alcohol. **(76)** Nevertheless, this country has made a political decision to allow alcoholic beverages to be sold in the marketplace. **(77)** The use of alcoholic beverages has been regulated greatly both at the federal and state levels of government. **(78)** While alcohol is accepted as a dangerous product, it has been found not "unreasonably dangerous." **(79)** The Restatement provides that manufacturers of alcoholic beverages are not required to warn about the dangers of its product when "consumed in excessive quantity."

(80) The standard for common knowledge is the overall knowledge common to the community that is a basis for determining a duty to warn, not what individual users may or may not know. **(81)** Many products cannot possibly be made entirely safe for all consumption. Restatement § 402A, comment i. **(82)** The product sold must be dangerous to an extent beyond that which would be contemplated by the ordinary consumer who purchases it, with the ordinary knowledge common to the community as to its characteristics. *Id.* **(83)** While courts have determined that it is within common knowledge that harm may come to those drinking alcohol, we cannot accept that one would think that drinking a large quantity of alcohol quickly would somehow be less harmful. **(84)** While morally it might appear prudent to require manufacturers of alcoholic beverages to place a warning on alcoholic beverages about the danger of death after ingesting large amounts of alcohol over a short period of time, we find no legal duty to do so.

(85) Considering the extensive involvement of the federal and state government in regulating alcoholic beverages, we conclude that the subject of warnings on alcoholic beverages and placing instructions for use on an alcoholic beverage container should be left to the legislative process. **(86)** The issues relevant to this case have for so long been political issues we conclude that courts are ill-equipped to develop effective and feasible warnings and instructions. . . .

(87) We understand that binge drinking and underage drinking is a problem. **(88)** However, merely because it is foreseeable that an underage drinker may gain access to alcoholic beverages and misuse them is not a reason to impose a duty to warn about death from overconsumption and impose liability for the drinker's death upon the distiller. **(89)** When considering the social, economic, and political questions and their applicability to the facts at hand, we conclude that no legal duty existed on the part of Brown–Forman to place a warning on its containers of tequila that overconsumption of tequila within a short period of time may cause death.

(90) Additionally, because of the inability to fashion effective instructions about the proper use of tequila, we conclude that no legal duty exists on the part of Brown–Forman to place instructions for proper use on its containers of tequila. **(91)** Brune suggested placing a chart on bottles of alcoholic beverages that would provide general information for the "average" person about levels of alcohol consumption. **(92)** However, Joe Darnell, former TABC [Texas Alcoholic Beverage Commission] general counsel, testified that a chart like the one proposed by Brune would not have been approved by the TABC because it would have implied a safe "dosage" of alcohol consumption—a deceptive implication. **(93)** There are too many variables, such as weight, age, and health among other things that affect blood alcohol levels and their effect on a person that such a warning would be ineffective. *See Malek,* 749 S.W.2d at 523; *Graff,* 858 S.W.2d at 921.

(94) Even if a warning could be fashioned, there existed no evidence that Marie would have heeded the warning. **(95)** The evidence was that Marie had received and disregarded warnings about the abuse of alcoholic beverages generally. **(96)** We note that a textbook used by Marie in her high school health class explains that after drinking 10–20 cocktails, death can result. **(97)** She was intoxicated when she illegally purchased the tequila and continued to drink it after her friends took the bottle away from her and told her to stop drinking. **(98)** If we assume that a warning had been on the bottle advising about the dangers of drinking large quantities of alcohol within a short period of time, the evidence shows that she would have disregarded it. . . .

(99) Finding that Brown–Forman had no legal duty to warn Marie about the dangers of consuming a large amount of tequila over a short time period and no duty to provide instructions about the proper use of tequila, we reverse the trial court's judgment, render judgment for Brown–Forman, and render that Brune take nothing.

TASK 5.L.1. Case Brief

Write a case brief of *Brown Forman Corp. v. Brune* using the template on page 290.

TASK 5.L.2. Torts Vocabulary Definitions (List 6)

Fill in each definition with the appropriate term from the list below. Consult a law dictionary or an English-to-English dictionary to confirm that you have matched each term with the correct definition. If multiple forms of a term are provided, you may not need to use all of the forms in the blanks.

damages *(noun)*; award damages *(verb)*
legally cognizable *(adjective)*
render *(verb)*
wrongful death *(noun)*

Terms related to torts

1. If a jury finds that a defendant in a negligence case is liable for the plaintiff's injuries, it will ____________________ to the plaintiff. In other words, the jury will order the defendant to compensate the plaintiff.

2. The verb ____________________ has two meanings: (1) to provide or give, and (2) to cause to become or make.

   Indicate which meaning, (1) or (2), each sentence below illustrates.

   a. The judge rendered a decision.
   b. Because the evidence was obtained illegally, it was rendered inadmissible.
   c. The accident rendered him a quadriplegic.
   d. The jury rendered a verdict.

   Do the two meanings require the use of different grammatical structures? What do you notice?

3. A/an ____________________ lawsuit is one in which the plaintiff alleges that the defendant's negligence caused the death of another person (usually a relative).

Term related to procedure

4. If a duty is ____________________, it means that the duty is recognized by law. This expression is often used with the term "claim." A legally cognizable claim is one that the law recognizes and which courts have the power to adjudicate.

TASK 5.L.3. Questions for Discussion

Answer the following questions to assist you during a class discussion of the case. Indicate the sentence(s) in which you found the answer to each question.

1. What happened in this case?

2. What were the issues, and what did the Court hold?

3. Do you agree with the Court's conclusion that placing a label on an alcoholic beverage about the danger of death is a moral obligation and not a legal one?

4. Who do you think is in the best position to control drinking behavior? The consumer or alcohol manufacturer?

5. The Court states in sentence (88) that "merely because it is foreseeable that an underage drinker may gain access to alcoholic beverages and misuse them is not a reason to impose a duty to warn about death from overconsumption and impose liability for the drinker's death upon the distiller." Do you agree with the Court?

6. What are the arguments for *not* providing detailed warnings on a bottle of alcohol, including the warning that overconsumption may lead to death?

7. The Court suggests that it is "common knowledge" and obvious that consuming too much alcohol can lead to death. What about the following scenarios? Are these more or less clear-cut than *Brune*?

   a. Lack of a warning on a gun that it may cause fatal injury.
   b. Lack of a warning on a microwave that placing metal objects inside it can cause a fire.
   c. Lack of a warning on a box of hard candy that it could pose a choking hazard for young children.

M. Torts Case #8

LEDAY. v. CLAIROL, INC.
Court of Appeal of Louisiana, Third Circuit, 1990.
571 So.2d 866.

STOKER, Judge.

(1) This is a products liability suit by Lisa Leday to recover damages and costs for a moderate scalp irritation and loss of hair allegedly caused by application of Clairol's "Nice 'N Easy" hair color kit. **(2)** Plaintiff alleges that the hair color kit contains **inadequate** warnings as to the danger and nature of an allergic reaction to the hair dye. **(3)** Clairol, Inc. defended on the basis that plaintiff **misused** the product in failing to conduct a patch test for the prescribed twenty-four hours. **(4)** The trial judge found that the warning provided in the kit was inadequate to engage the attention of "those who will foreseeably use the product" and did not adequately convey the nature of the danger of a reaction to the hair dye. **(5)** The trial judge awarded plaintiff $1000 in general damages and $430.56 for medical expenses.

(6) Clairol, Inc. appeals the judgment, contending that the trial judge erred in finding that the warning was inadequate. **(7)** Clairol, Inc. also argues that plaintiff Leday's failure to perform a patch test for twenty-four hours was misuse of the product by her; therefore, Leday was at fault in causing her injuries. . . .

FACTS

(8) On May 1, 1986, Leday purchased and used a Clairol "Nice 'N Easy" hair dye kit. **(9)** Prior to full application, plaintiff conducted a patch test on the inside of her arm at her elbow for eight hours. **(10)** Despite the fact that the instructions prescribed a twenty-four-hour test period, Leday decided to fully apply the hair dye to her hair after only an eight-hour test period since she had suffered no reaction in that time. **(11)** Within twenty-four hours of application of the dye plaintiff suffered an allergic reaction to the dye, the symptoms of which were swelling, irritation, redness and hair loss. **(12)** Leday testified that she had used the hair dye kit about five months previously, employing an eight-hour patch test at that time as she did in this case. **(13)** On that occasion she did not suffer a reaction to the dye.

(14) The box containing the "Nice 'N Easy" bottle of color material included an instruction sheet. **(15)** In clearly readable print, under a bold heading reading STEP ONE PREPARATION, the user was advised: "Twenty-four hours before you color your hair be sure to: read this instruction sheet all the way through [and] do the Allergy Test and Strand Test. . . ." **(16)** Two other instructions not pertinent here follow the language just quoted. **(17)** Next, in bold type approximately 5/16 of an inch high, appear the words "ALLERGY TEST." **(18)** The following paragraph appears under the words allergy test:

> Certain people may be allergic to foods, drugs, cosmetics or other substances usually considered harmless. **(19)** Allergies can sometimes develop suddenly. **(20)** You might have been non-allergic to a certain substance last week but be allergic to the same thing today. **(21)** That's why you must do this test for sensitivity 24 hours before each and every hair color application. **(22)** And don't forget to preview your new hair color at the same time (see Strand Test instructions).

(23) After this language three separate numbered paragraphs are distributed laterally across the page of instructions. **(24)** Each of these three paragraphs are spaced so that they stand apart from one another. **(25)** Each number appears in bold type approximately 5/16 of an inch high and appears to the side of the printed paragraph to which it applies. **(26)** The numbers are prominent on the printed page, catch the eye and function to visually separate the three points presented. **(27)** The first paragraph sets forth instructions for mixing the color for the allergy test and the strand test. **(28)** Paragraphs two and three appear as follows:

> **2** **Apply**
> With mild soap and water, wash an area about the size of a quarter inside your arm at your elbow. Pat dry. With a cotton swab, apply a few drops of the color mixture to the test area.

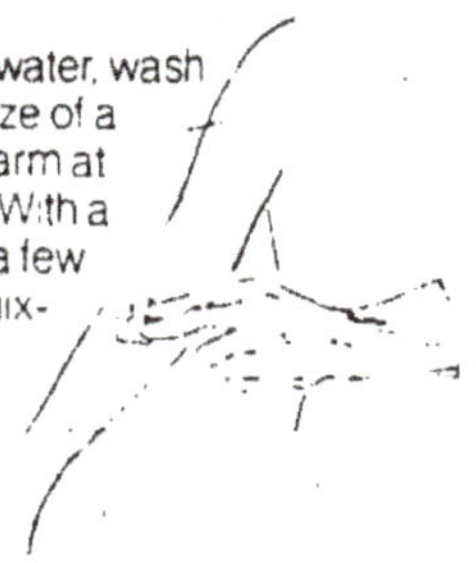

> **3** **Let Mixture Dry on Skin**
> Leave test area uncovered and undisturbed for 24 hours. If there is no adverse reaction, go ahead and color your hair. If you notice any reddening of the skin, burning, itching, or other irritation in or around the test area, you are allergic to the product and must not use it. If any allergic reaction occurs, return the UNMIXED portions of this product to Clairol Consumer Satisfaction, 345 Park Avenue, New York, N.Y. 10154 for a full refund. Please state the price you paid. Be sure to include your name and address.

(29) Dr. John Tassin, an expert in general medicine, testified that he treated Leday's scalp irritation and discharged her after two and one-half months. **(30)** Tassin testified that Leday suffered a moderate chemical irritation, presumably from the hair dye, which caused an acute dermatitis. **(31)** He prescribed cortisone lotion, antibiotics, benedryl and a shampoo to treat the dermatitis. **(32)** Upon discharge on July 22, 1986, Leday's dermatitis was improved and her scalp looked good.

(33) Dr. James Smith, an expert in dermatology, saw Leday in September 1987 and in September 1988 for a complaint of persistent hair loss. **(34)** Dr. Smith testified that he had never seen permanent hair loss caused by an allergic reaction to hair dye. **(35)** Dr. Tassin believed that the hair loss plaintiff suffered in

1987 and 1988 was caused by tension on her hair due to use of tight hair rollers rather than her prior allergic reaction to the hair dye. **(36)** He also testified that it is very important to perform a patch test for twenty-four hours every time hair dye is used because a person may become sensitive to it at any time.

OPINION

(37) Clairol, Inc. contends on appeal that the trial judge erred in finding that the warnings provided in the hair dye kit were inadequate to convey the nature of the danger of an allergic reaction to the hair dye product, especially to users with little education such as Leday (Leday has a seventh grade education). **(38)** Clairol, Inc. also contends that Leday was at fault in failing to conduct a patch test for twenty-four hours prior to full application of the hair dye and that this failure to follow instructions constituted misuse of the product.

(39) In Louisiana, a manufacturer of a product may be held liable for injuries caused by its product, without any particular act of negligence being proven, if a plaintiff shows by a preponderance of the evidence: (1) that the product was in normal use; (2) there was a defect in the product, i.e., the product was unreasonably dangerous in that use; and (3) the plaintiff's injuries were caused by the defect. **(40)** A manufacturer must also give warnings of any danger inherent in its product's normal use which is not within the knowledge of an ordinary user. *Ardoin v. Wal Mart,* 525 So.2d 150 (La.App. 3d Cir.1988); *Spurlock v. Cosmair, Inc.,* 509 So.2d 826 (La.App, 1st Cir.1987); *Booker v. Revlon Realistic Professional Products, Inc.,* 433 So.2d 407 (La.App. 4th Cir.1983).

(41) In order for a product to be considered **defective**, it must be shown that it is unreasonably dangerous in normal use. **(42)** For a product to be considered in normal use, the user must comply with the directions and warnings provided by the manufacturer of the product. **(43)** A plaintiff bears the burden of proving the product was in normal use at the time of his injury. *Duncan v. Louisiana Power & Light Co.,* 532 So.2d 968 (La.App. 5th Cir.1988); *Ardoin v. Wal Mart,* supra; *Spurlock v. Cosmair, Inc.,* supra; *Booker v. Revlon Realistic Professional Products, Inc.,* supra; *Rhodes v. Max Factor, Inc.,* 264 So.2d 263 (La.App. 4th Cir.1972); *Thomas v. Gillette Company,* 230 So.2d 870 (La.App. 3d Cir.), writ denied, 233 So.2d 249 (La.1970).

(44) The determination of whether a warning is **adequate** depends upon a balancing of considerations including, among other factors, the severity of the danger, the likelihood that the warning will catch the attention of those who will foreseeably use the product and convey the nature of the danger to them, the intensity and the form of the warning, and the cost of improving the strength or the mode of the warning. *Bloxom v. Bloxom,* 512 So.2d 839 (La.1987); also, *Walker v. Maybelline,* 477 So.2d 1136 (La.App. 1st Cir.), writ denied, 481 So.2d 1333 (La.1986).

(45) An essential element of a cause of action for failure to adequately warn of a product's danger is that there be some reasonable connection between the omission of the manufacturer and the damage which the plaintiff has suffered.

(46) Once a plaintiff proves that the lack of an adequate warning or instruction rendered the product unreasonably dangerous, his cause in fact burden is eased by a presumption: when a manufacturer fails to give adequate warnings or instructions, a presumption arises that the user would have read and heeded such admonitions. **(47)** The presumption may, however, be rebutted if the manufacturer produces contrary evidence which persuades the trier of fact that an adequate warning or instruction would have been futile under the circumstances. *Bloxom v. Bloxom,* supra, at 850; also, *Ingram v. Caterpillar Machinery Corp.,* 535 So.2d 723 (La.1988).

(48) In this case, Leday failed to properly follow the instructions in the Allergy Test section which specifically warns the user against using the product if redness, burning, itching or irritation of the skin occurs in or around the elbow test area within twenty-four hours. **(49)** It was established at trial that plaintiff read and understood the Allergy Test section, but that she chose to shorten the test time to eight hours. **(50)** We find the warning is specific as to the symptoms of an allergic reaction. **(51)** The fact that it does not specifically warn against hair loss is of little significance since proper conduct of the patch test will disclose whether or not a person is allergic to the product.

(52) We note that the Allergy Test section stands out well in the instruction sheet and was not obscured by numerous other warnings and instructions. **(53)** We fail to see how further highlighting of the Allergy Test section could have been accomplished. **(54)** We fail to see how the warning could have been made more clear or emphatic. **(55)** Leday *did* read the section and purposely chose to ignore the manufacturer's explicit instructions. **(56)** Such misuse of the product was the cause of plaintiff's injuries. **(57)** Had plaintiff conducted the patch test for twenty-four hours, she would have discovered that she was then allergic to the product and would have known that she should not apply the product to her hair. **(58)** Therefore, the trial court manifestly erred in holding Clairol, Inc. liable for Leday's injuries. **(59)** We find that Leday was 100% at fault for her injuries.

CONCLUSION

(60) For the reasons given, the judgment of the trial court is reversed and the plaintiff's action is dismissed. . . .

(61) REVERSED.

TASK 5.M.1. Case Brief

Write a case brief of *Leday v. Clairol, Inc.* using the template on page 290.

TASK 5.M.2. Torts Vocabulary Definitions (List 7)

Fill in each definition with the appropriate term from the list below. Consult a law dictionary or an English-to-English dictionary to confirm that you have matched each term with the correct definition.

adequate vs. inadequate *(adjective)*
defective *(adjective)*
misuse *(noun)*

Terms related to torts

1. The term ____________________ means sufficient or enough. In warning defect cases, the plaintiff often alleges that the manufacturer's warning provided on or with the product was ____________________, while the defendant manufacturer argues that the warning was sufficient.

2. If a product is ____________________, it means that it is not working properly and may cause harm or injury.

3. The defense of ____________________ refers to the defendant's argument that the plaintiff did not use the product correctly and was injured as a result.

TASK 5.M.3. Questions for Discussion

Answer the following questions to assist you during a class discussion of the case. Indicate the sentence(s) in which you found the answer to each question.

1. What happened in this case? What is the plaintiff's claim?

2. What do you make of the following sentences (12-13) in the court's opinion: "Leday testified that she had used the hair dye kit about five months previously, employing an eight-hour patch test at that time as she did in this case. On that occasion she did not suffer a reaction to the dye." Does this fact help the plaintiff's case? Why or why not?

3. The court mentions that Leday has a seventh grade education. Is this relevant to the resolution of the case? Why or why not?

4. What factors does the court take into account to determine whether a warning is adequate? Which of these factors do you think it should weigh the heaviest? Why?

5. The court states in sentence (51): "The fact that it does not specifically warn against hair loss is of little significance since proper conduct of the patch test will disclose whether or not a person is allergic to the product." Would a patch test necessarily reveal "consistent hair loss" on the user's head?

6. Hypothetical: Sue bought a "seafood boiling kit" that contained a pot, a burner, and a propane tank.[9] The tank was manufactured by ProTank Corporation. Sue's sixteen-year-old son, Tom, had a history of gas inhalation and had been treated at a substance abuse clinic. One day, Tom filled a plastic bag with propane from the tank and sniffed it to get "high." Unfortunately, Tom inhaled so much of propane that he lost consciousness and eventually died two days later. Sue brought suit against ProTank Corporation, arguing that the warning on the tank was not adequate to warn against the dangers of inhalation. The warning on the propane tank stated: "DANGER: Flammable liquid and gas under pressure can explode if mixed with air. Keep away from heat and flame. Store and use with adequate ventilation." The trial judge determined that the warning on the propane tank was inadequate. ProTank Corporation has appealed, arguing that (1) the warning was adequate; and (2) a more detailed warning including the risks of inhalation would have been useless under the circumstances.[10]

   You are the appellate judge reviewing the case. What is your decision?

N. Torts Case #9

The next two cases address the final element of negligence: damages. As you read through the cases, try to determine the two types of damage awards and specific damage items that may be awarded to compensate injured plaintiffs.

---

[9] Propane is a flammable gas that is used in stoves and grills. A propane tank is a tank that stores propane.

[10] Hypothetical adapted from Kelly v. Hanover Insurance Co., 722 So.2d 1133 (La. 1999).

CLARK v. CANTRELL

Supreme Court of South Carolina, 2000.
339 S.C. 369, 529 S.E.2d 528.

WALLER, Justice.

(1) John Kevin Clark and Maggie Lee Anderson sued Annette Rochelle Cantrell for injuries and damages they **incurred** as a result of an automobile accident. **(2)** A jury awarded actual and punitive damages to Clark and Anderson. **(3)** The Court of Appeals affirmed the verdicts and awards. *Clark v. Cantrell,* 332 S.C. 433 (Ct.App.1998). **(4)** We granted Cantrell's **petition for a writ of certiorari** to review that decision. **(5)** We affirm as modified.

FACTS

(6) Shortly after dark on November 1, 1993, Cantrell, driving a late-model Mustang GT with hazard lights flashing, sped down Highway 24 toward Anderson. **(7)** The driver of a pickup truck that Cantrell passed on a two-lane stretch of road estimated Cantrell was traveling 75 to 80 mph, and she nearly collided with the pickup truck while swerving back into the right lane. **(8)** The pickup driver believed the Mustang, which continued to pass other vehicles in a similarly hazardous manner, had to be headed for the hospital.

(9) Some distance down the highway, Anderson and a friend were headed to Georgia to buy tickets in the new lottery. **(10)** Anderson, a nursing assistant at the local hospital, intended to gas up her 1980 Oldsmobile Cutlass and was waiting to turn left into a Hess service station.

(11) Cantrell sped through an intersection a short distance from the Hess station, entering a busy stretch of four-lane highway flanked by restaurants and other retail businesses. **(12)** The speeding Mustang scared a man whose wife, accompanied by their three boys, was taking him to his night-shift textile job. **(13)** The man estimated the Mustang was traveling 75 to 100 mph.

(14) Anderson waited for a car or two to go by, then began turning left across two lanes of traffic. **(15)** The front of her car was at the entrance of the service station lot when Anderson glimpsed a small "turbo car" speeding toward her. **(16)** The textile worker, still watching Cantrell's speeding car from the nearby intersection, saw it strike the right rear side of Anderson's Oldsmobile. **(17)** The impact flung Anderson's friend, David James, from the car, killing him.

(18) A state Highway Patrol trooper who reconstructed the accident scene pegged the Mustang's speed at 67 to 71 mph when Cantrell first applied her brakes. **(19)** An accident reconstruction expert hired by Cantrell estimated her car was traveling 57 mph. **(20)** The posted speed limit was 35 mph. **(21)** The trooper and Cantrell's expert testified that, if she had been traveling 35 mph, the accident probably would not have occurred. **(22)** Cantrell's expert also testified that he believed the primary cause of the accident was Anderson's decision to turn left in front of Cantrell's oncoming car.

(23) When Cantrell emerged from her car, she was upset and screaming about the condition of her car, demanding that bystanders look at what had happened to it. **(24)** She laughed as a trooper talked to her a short while later, although her laughter ended when she was informed someone had died in the accident. **(25)** Cantrell told a trooper the next day that she was speeding because her car was low on gas and she was in a hurry to reach a station.

(26) Anderson and Clark alleged that Cantrell had caused their injuries and damages by speeding on the busy highway. **(27)** Cantrell's primary defense was that Anderson caused the accident by turning left in front of her. **(28)** The jury found Anderson sixteen percent at fault and Cantrell eighty-four percent at fault in the accident. **(29)** The jury awarded Anderson $75,000 in **actual damages** and $25,000 in **punitive damages**; and Clark, the vehicle's owner, $3,000 in actual damages and $750 in punitive damages. **(30)** The trial judge reduced the actual damages, but not the punitive damages, by the proportion of Anderson's fault.

ISSUE[]

(31) Did the Court of Appeals err in holding that punitive damages are not reduced by the proportion of the plaintiff's negligence under comparative negligence?

DISCUSSION . . .

(32) Cantrell contends the Court of Appeals erred in holding that punitive damages, unlike actual damages, are not reduced by the proportion of the plaintiff's negligence under comparative negligence. **(33)** Cantrell argues punitive damages should be reduced proportionately because such damages serve, in part, a compensatory role. **(34)** She relies on several cases decided before the adoption of comparative negligence in 1991. **(35)** Further, Cantrell asserts that reducing punitive damages is consistent with the adoption of comparative negligence because it focuses on both parties' degree of fault in causing an accident. **(36)** We disagree.

(37) We are free to decide this novel question of law with no particular deference to the lower court. *See* S.C. Const. art. V, §§ 5 and 9; S.C.Code Ann. §§ 14-3-320 and -330 (1976 & Supp.1999); S.C.Code Ann. § 14-8-200 (Supp.1999) (granting Supreme Court and Court of Appeals the jurisdiction to correct errors of law in both law and equity actions); *I'On v. Town of Mt. Pleasant,* 338 S.C. 406 (2000).

(38) Comparative negligence is the law in South Carolina. *Nelson v. Concrete Supply Co.,* 303 S.C. 243 (1991). **(39)** The jury must apportion fault between the plaintiff and defendant in a negligence action. **(40)** The plaintiff may recover damages when his or her negligence is not greater than that of the defendant. **(41)** The plaintiff's damages, however, are reduced in proportion to the amount of his or her negligence. *Id.* **(42)** The parties agree that *Nelson* requires the reduction of plaintiff's actual damages. **(43)** The novel issue presented in this case is whether the court must reduce *punitive* damages won by the plaintiff in proportion to the amount of his or her negligence.

(44) The purpose of actual or compensatory damages is to compensate a party for injuries suffered or losses sustained. **(45)** The goal is to restore the injured party, as nearly as possible through the payment of money, to the same position he or she was in before the wrongful injury occurred. *Barnwell v. Barber-Colman Co.,* 301 S.C. 534, 537 (1989); *Laird v. Nationwide Ins. Co.,*243 S.C. 388, 396 (1964); *Carrigg v. Blue,* 283 S.C. 494, 499 (Ct.App.1984); F.P. Hubbard & R.L. Felix, *The South Carolina Law of Torts* 535-36 (1997).

(46) The purposes of punitive damages are to punish the wrongdoer and deter the wrongdoer and others from engaging in similar **reckless**, **willful**, **wanton**, or **malicious** conduct in the future. *Barnwell, supra.* **(47)** Punitive damages also serve to vindicate a private right of the injured party by requiring the wrongdoer to pay money to the injured party. *Harris v. Burnside,* 261 S.C. 190, 196, 199 S.E.2d 65, 68 (1973); Hubbard & Felix, *supra,* at 581-93. **(48)** This Court has explained the important role that punitive damages play in the American system of justice generally, and in South Carolina in particular since at least 1784.

> **(49)** Exemplary or punitive damages go to the plaintiff, not as a fine or penalty for a public wrong, but in vindication of a private right which has been willfully invaded; and indeed, it may be said that such damages in a measure compensate or satisfy for the willfulness with which the private right was invaded, but, in addition thereto, operating as a deterring punishment to the wrongdoer, and as a warning to others. . . . **(50)** Punitive damages have now come, however, to be generally, though not universally, regarded, not only as punishment for wrong, but as vindication of private right. **(51)** This is the basis upon which they are now placed in this state. *Rogers v. Florence Printing Co.,* 233 S.C. 567, 573 (1958) (citations omitted) . . . .

(52) Cases mentioning the compensatory aspect of punitive damages provide little support for Cantrell's position. **(53)** All merely illustrate the obvious truth that punitive damages serve at least three important purposes: punishment of the defendant's reckless, willful, wanton, or malicious conduct; deterrence of similar future conduct by the defendant or others; and compensation for the reckless or willful invasion of the plaintiff's private rights. **(54)** While there is a compensatory aspect to punitive damages, we find unpersuasive Cantrell's attempt to blur all distinctions between actual and punitive damages by unduly emphasizing that compensatory aspect.

(55) We affirm the Court of Appeals' holding on this issue for four related reasons. **(56)** First, allowing the defendant to shift a portion of the cost of a punitive award back to the plaintiff through comparative negligence would reduce the punishment and deterrent effect of the award. **(57)** The defendant's punishment would be lessened simply because the plaintiff was somewhat negligent. **(58)** That is illogical and violates the underlying rationale of punitive damages.

(59) As the Court of Appeals explained in this case, the overwhelming majority of other jurisdictions considering this issue have concluded that an award of punitive damages is not reduced under comparative negligence. **(60)** Courts uniformly have held that allowing such a reduction would nullify the punishment and deterrence goals underlying punitive damages. *Clark,* 332 S.C. at 442 n. 5 (listing cases). **(61)** In *Anderson v. Trent,* 685 S.W.2d 712 (Tex.Ct.App.1984), the court reasoned that

> if exemplary damages were *only* for compensating the plaintiff, then an argument could be made that they should be reduced by the percentage of the plaintiff's comparative negligence. **(62)** However, the paramount purpose for awarding exemplary damages is *not* to compensate the plaintiff, but to punish and set an example for others. **(63)** Consequently, it is incorrect to view the award of exemplary damages from the eyes of the recovering plaintiff; rather, the award should be viewed from the eyes of public policy. *Id.* at 714 (emphasis in original) (citations omitted). . . .

(64) Second, any reduction in the defendant's punishment inflicts a corresponding amount of punishment on the plaintiff. **(65)** Shifting a portion of the cost of the punitive award back to the plaintiff essentially would punish him or her along with the defendant. **(66)** In this case, Anderson would be punished by the loss of $4,000 (sixteen percent of $25,000 in punitive damages), money which the jury believed she rightly deserved. **(67)** Yet Anderson in no way contributed to the willful or reckless nature of the defendant's conduct, and did nothing for which she should be punished.

(68) Third, it would be inappropriate to reduce the punitive damages by comparing the plaintiff's *negligence* with the defendant's *reckless* or *willful* conduct. **(69)** It is proper to reduce Anderson's actual damages in this case because the jury decided her negligent decision to turn left in front of Cantrell's speeding car contributed to causing the accident. **(70)** But Anderson's negligent conduct was not willful or reckless. **(71)** Conduct that is merely negligent should not be used to reduce damages the jury decided Cantrell should pay as a means of punishing her willful and reckless conduct, and deterring similar conduct by her and others in the future.

(72) Fourth, when considering the negligence attributable to each party, the focus is on the actions of both plaintiff and defendant. **(73)** What did each do, or not do, that contributed to the cause of an injury? **(74)** With punitive damages, however, the focus is on only the defendant. **(75)** The central inquiry is whether the defendant's conduct was so reckless, willful, wanton, or malicious that the defendant should be punished and deterred by requiring him or her to pay money to the plaintiff. *See Gamble v. Stevenson,* 305 S.C. 104, 110 (1991) (listing factors focusing on defendant that court must consider in post-trial review of punitive award).

(76) Cantrell also argues that the Court of Appeals erred because Anderson did not present clear and convincing evidence of Cantrell's reckless, willful, wanton, or malicious conduct. **(77)** We conclude the Court of Appeals correctly reasoned that Cantrell's excessive speed, her disregard for the commercial nature of the highway, her lack of remorse, and her frivolous reason for speeding amply support the award of punitive damages.

(78) In sum, we hold that punitive damages are not reduced by the proportion of the plaintiff's negligence under comparative negligence. **(79)** We also affirm the award of punitive damages to Anderson and Clark. . . .

TASK 5.N.1. Case Brief

Write a case brief of *Clark v. Cantrell* using the template on page 290.

TASK 5.N.2. Torts Vocabulary Definitions (List 8)

Fill in each definition with the appropriate term from the list below. Consult a law dictionary or an English-to-English dictionary to confirm that you have matched each term with the correct definition.

actual damages *(noun)*
incur [injuries or damages] *(verb)*
malicious *(adjective)*
petition for a writ of certiorari *(noun; verb)*
punitive damages *(noun)*
reckless *(adjective)*
wanton *(adjective)*
willful *(adjective)*

Terms related to torts

1. Another way to say that someone has suffered an injury or damages is to say that she has ____________________ an injury or damages.

2. ____________________ refer to the money awarded to an injured party to compensate her for loss and injury. Another term for this is compensatory damages.

3. ____________________ refer to damages awarded to punish the defendant for engaging in outrageous conduct and to discourage the defendant from engaging in similar conduct in the future. This money is not intended to compensate the injured party. Courts sometimes refer to this as exemplary damages.

4. When an individual is ____________________, she is disregarding the consequences of her actions. If she is acting in a/an ____________________ and ____________________ manner, she is engaging in illegal behavior intentionally. Finally, if she is ____________________, she is acting with a deliberate intention to cause others harm. These four adjectives are often used together to describe the kinds of actions that may subject a defendant to punitive damages.

Term related to procedure

5. A/an ____________________ is a request by a losing party to a state's highest court (or the Supreme Court of the United States) to review a lower court's decision. Another term that is used in some jurisdictions is "grant leave to appeal." (See also Appendix C: Steps in the Civil Litigation Process.)

TASK 5.N.3. Questions for Discussion

Answer the following questions to assist you during a class discussion of the case. Indicate the sentence(s) in which you found the answer to each question.

1. Briefly describe the facts leading up to the lawsuit. What is the relationship between Clark, Anderson, and Cantrell?

2. What was Anderson and Clark's claim against Cantrell at trial? What was Cantrell's defense at trial?

3. Did the jury award damages to Anderson and Clark? What kind of damages? How much?

4. What is the issue, and what did the Court hold?

5. In sentence (70), the court states that "Anderson's negligent conduct was not willful or reckless." Why does this matter?

6. Are there any problems with awarding punitive damage awards to plaintiffs?

7. Create your own question. For inspiration, review the list of common question types in Part II, Chapter 3.

O. Torts Case #10

MCDOUGALD v. GARBER

Court of Appeals of New York, 1989.

73 N.Y.2d 246, 536 N.E.2d 372, 538 N.Y.S.2d 937, 57 USLW 2519.

WACHTLER, Chief Judge.

(1) This appeal raises fundamental questions about the nature and role of **nonpecuniary damages** in personal injury litigation. **(2)** By nonpecuniary damages, we mean those damages awarded to compensate an injured person for the physical and emotional consequences of the injury, such as **pain and suffering** and the loss of the ability to engage in certain activities. **(3)** **Pecuniary damages**, on the other hand, compensate the victim for the economic consequences of the injury, such as **medical expenses**, **lost earnings** and the **cost of custodial care**.

(4) The specific questions raised here deal with assessment of nonpecuniary damages and are (1) whether some degree of cognitive awareness is a prerequisite to recovery for **loss of enjoyment of life** and (2) whether a jury should be instructed to consider and award damages for loss of enjoyment of life separately from damages for pain and suffering. **(5)** We answer the first question in the affirmative and the second question in the negative.

I.

(6) On September 7, 1978, plaintiff Emma McDougald, then 31 years old, underwent a Caesarean section and tubal ligation at New York Infirmary.

(7) Defendant Garber performed the surgery; defendants Armengol and Kulkarni provided anesthesia. **(8)** During the surgery, Mrs. McDougald suffered oxygen deprivation which resulted in severe brain damage and left her in a permanent comatose condition. **(9)** This action was brought by Mrs. McDougald and her husband, suing derivatively, alleging that the injuries were caused by the defendants' acts of malpractice.

(10) A jury found all defendants liable and awarded Emma McDougald a total of $9,650,102 in damages, including $1,000,000 for conscious pain and suffering and a separate award of $3,500,000 for loss of the pleasures and pursuits of life. **(11)** The balance of the damages awarded to her were for pecuniary damages—lost earnings and the cost of custodial and nursing care. **(12)** Her husband was awarded $1,500,000 on his **derivative claim** for the loss of his wife's services. **(13)** On defendants' posttrial motions, the Trial Judge reduced the total award to Emma McDougald to $4,796,728 by striking the entire award for future nursing care ($2,353,374) and by reducing the separate awards for conscious pain and suffering and loss of the pleasures and pursuits of life to a single award of $2,000,000 (*McDougald v. Garber,* 132 Misc.2d 457). **(14)** Her husband's award was left intact. **(15)** On cross appeals, the Appellate Division affirmed (135 A.D.2d 80) and later granted defendants leave to appeal to this court.

II.

(16) We note at the outset that the defendants' liability for Emma McDougald's injuries is unchallenged here . . . .

(17) Also unchallenged are the awards in the amount of $770,978 for loss of earnings and $2,025,750 for future custodial care—that is, the pecuniary damage awards that survived defendants' posttrial motions.

(18) What remains in dispute, primarily, is the award to Emma McDougald for nonpecuniary damages. **(19)** At trial, defendants sought to show that Mrs. McDougald's injuries were so severe that she was incapable of either experiencing pain or appreciating her condition. **(20)** Plaintiffs, on the other hand, introduced proof that Mrs. McDougald responded to certain stimuli to a sufficient extent to indicate that she was aware of her circumstances. **(21)** Thus, the extent of Mrs. McDougald's cognitive abilities, if any, was sharply disputed.

(22) The parties and the trial court agreed that Mrs. McDougald could not recover for pain and suffering unless she were conscious of the pain. **(23)** Defendants maintained that such consciousness was also required to support an award for loss of enjoyment of life. **(24)** The court, however, accepted plaintiffs' view that loss of enjoyment of life was compensable without regard to whether the plaintiff was aware of the loss. **(25)** Accordingly, because the level of Mrs. McDougald's cognitive abilities was in dispute, the court instructed the jury to consider loss of enjoyment of life as an element of nonpecuniary damages separate from pain and suffering. **(26)** The court's charge to the jury on these points was as follows:

> **(27)** If you conclude that Emma McDougald is so neurologically impaired that she is totally incapable of experiencing any unpleasant or painful sensation, then, obviously, she cannot be awarded damages for conscious pain. . . .
>
> **(28)** It is for you to determine the level of Emma McDougald's perception and awareness. **(29)** Suffering relates primarily to the emotional reaction of the injured person to the injury. **(30)** Thus, for an injured person to experience suffering, there, again, must be some level of awareness. **(31)** If

> Emma McDougald is totally unaware of her condition or totally incapable of any emotional reaction, then you cannot award her damages for suffering. **(32)** If, however, you conclude that there is some level of perception or that she is capable of an emotional response at some level, then damages for pain and suffering should be awarded. . .
>
> **(33)** Damages for the loss of the pleasures and pursuits of life, however, require no awareness of the loss on the part of the injured person. **(34)** Quite obviously, Emma McDougald is unable to engage in any of the activities which constitute a normal life, the activities she engaged in prior to her injury. . . . **(35)** Loss of the enjoyment of life may, of course, accompany the physical sensation and emotional responses that we refer to as pain and suffering, and in most cases it does. **(36)** It is possible, however, for an injured person to lose the enjoyment of life without experiencing any conscious pain and suffering. **(37)** Damages for this item of injury relate not to what Emma McDougald is aware of, but rather to what she has lost. **(38)** What her life was prior to her injury and what it has been since September 7, 1978 and what it will be for as long as she lives.

(39) We conclude that the court erred, both in instructing the jury that Mrs. McDougald's awareness was irrelevant to their consideration of damages for loss of enjoyment of life and in directing the jury to consider that aspect of damages separately from pain and suffering.

III.

(40) We begin with the familiar proposition that an award of damages to a person injured by the negligence of another is to compensate the victim, not to punish the wrongdoer (*see, Sharapata v. Town of Islip,*56 N.Y.2d 332, 335; Prosser and Keeton, Torts, at 7 [5th ed.]). **(41)** The goal is to restore the injured party, to the extent possible, to the position that would have been occupied had the wrong not occurred (1 Minzer, Nates, Kimball, Axelrod & Goldstein, Damages in Tort Actions §§ 1.00, 1.02). **(42)** To be sure, placing the burden of compensation on the negligent party also serves as a deterrent, but purely punitive damages—that is, those which have no compensatory purpose—are prohibited unless the harmful conduct is intentional, malicious, outrageous, or otherwise aggravated beyond mere negligence . . . .

(43) Damages for nonpecuniary losses are, of course, among those that can be awarded as compensation to the victim. **(44)** This aspect of damages, however, stands on less certain ground than does an award for pecuniary damages. **(45)** An economic loss can be compensated in kind by an economic gain; but recovery for noneconomic losses such as pain and suffering and loss of enjoyment of life rests on "the legal fiction that money damages can compensate for a victim's injury" (*Howard v. Lecher,* 42 N.Y.2d 109, 111). **(46)** We accept this fiction, knowing that although money will neither ease the pain nor restore the victim's abilities, this device is as close as the law can come in its effort to right the wrong. **(47)** We have no hope of evaluating what has been lost, but a monetary award may provide a measure of solace for the condition created (*see, Skelton v. Collins,* 115 CLR 94, 130 [Austl H C]).

(48) Our willingness to indulge this fiction comes to an end, however, when it ceases to serve the compensatory goals of tort recovery. **(49)** When that limit is met, further indulgence can only result in assessing damages that are punitive. **(50)** The question posed by this case, then, is whether an award of damages for loss of enjoyment of life to a person whose injuries preclude any awareness of the loss serves a compensatory purpose. **(51)** We conclude that it does not.

(52) Simply put, an award of money damages in such circumstances has no meaning or utility to the injured person. **(53)** An award for the loss of enjoyment of life "cannot provide [such a victim] with any consolation or ease any burden resting on him. . . . **(54)** He cannot spend it upon necessities or pleasures. **(55)** He cannot experience the pleasure of giving it away" (*Flannery v. United States,* 4th Cir., 718 F.2d 108, 111, *cert. denied* 467 U.S. 1226).

(56) We recognize that, as the trial court noted, requiring some cognitive awareness as a prerequisite to recovery for loss of enjoyment of life will result in some cases "in the paradoxical situation that the greater the degree of brain injury inflicted by a negligent defendant, the smaller the award the plaintiff can recover in general damages" (*McDougald v. Garber,* 132 Misc.2d 457, 460, *supra*). **(57)** The force of this argument, however—the temptation to achieve a balance between injury and damages—has nothing to do with meaningful compensation for the victim. **(58)** Instead, the temptation is rooted in a desire to punish the defendant in proportion to the harm inflicted. **(59)** However relevant such retributive symmetry may be in the criminal law, it has no place in the law of civil damages, at least in the absence of **culpability** beyond mere negligence.

(60) Accordingly, we conclude that cognitive awareness is a prerequisite to recovery for loss of enjoyment of life. **(61)** We do not go so far, however, as to require the fact finder to sort out varying degrees of cognition and determine at what level a particular deprivation can be fully appreciated. **(62)** With respect to pain and suffering, the trial court charged simply that there must be "some level of awareness" in order for plaintiff to recover. **(63)** We think that this is an appropriate standard for all aspects of nonpecuniary loss. **(64)** No doubt the standard ignores analytically relevant levels of cognition, but we resist the desire for analytical purity in favor of simplicity. **(65)** A more complex instruction might give the appearance of greater precision but, given the limits of our understanding of the human mind, it would in reality lead only to greater speculation.

(66) We turn next to the question whether loss of enjoyment of life should be considered a category of damages separate from pain and suffering.

IV.

(67) There is no dispute here that the fact finder may, in assessing nonpecuniary damages, consider the effect of the injuries on the plaintiff's capacity to lead a normal life. **(68)** Traditionally, in this State and elsewhere, this aspect of suffering has not been treated as a separate category of damages; instead, the plaintiff's inability to enjoy life to its fullest has been considered one type of suffering to be factored into a general award for nonpecuniary damages, commonly known as pain and suffering.

(69) Recently, however, there has been an attempt to segregate the suffering associated with physical pain from the mental anguish that stems from the inability to engage in certain activities, and to have juries provide a separate award for each . . . .

(70) Some courts have resisted the effort, primarily on the ground that duplicative and therefore excessive awards would result (*see, e.g., Huff v. Tracy,* 57 Cal.App.3d 939, 944; *Poyzer v. McGraw,* 360 N.W.2d 748, 752–753 [Iowa]). **(71)** Other courts have allowed separate awards, noting that the types of suffering involved are analytically distinguishable (*see, e.g., Rufino v. United States,* 2nd Cir., 829 F.2d 354 [applying its prediction of New York law]; *Thompson v. National R.R. Passenger Corp.,* 6th Cir., 621 F.2d 814, *cert. denied* 449 U.S. 1035; *Mariner v. Marsden,*610 P.2d 6 [Wyo]; *Lebesco v. Southeastern Pa. Transp. Auth.,* 251 Pa.Super. 415). **(72)** Still other courts have questioned the propriety of the practice but held that, in the particular case, separate awards did not constitute reversible error (*see, e.g., Swiler v. Baker's Super Mkt.,* 203 Neb. 183; *Pierce v. New York Cent. R.R. Co.,* 6th Cir., 409 F.2d 1392, 1398–1399).

(73) In this State, the only appellate decisions to address the question are the decision of the Appellate Division, First Department, now under review (135 A.D.2d 80, *supra*), and the decision of the Second Department in *Nussbaum v. Gibstein,* 138 A.D.2d 193, *revd.* 73 N.Y.2d 912 [decided today]). **(74)** Those courts were persuaded that the distinctions between the two types of mental anguish justified separate awards and that the potential for duplicative awards could be mitigated by carefully drafted jury instructions. **(75)** In addition, the courts opined that separate awards would facilitate appellate review concerning the excessiveness of the total damage award.

(76) We do not dispute that distinctions can be found or created between the concepts of pain and suffering and loss of enjoyment of life. **(77)** If the term "suffering" is limited to the emotional response to the sensation of pain, then the emotional response caused by the limitation of life's activities may be considered qualitatively different (*see,* Comment, *Loss of Enjoyment of Life as a Separate Element of Damages,* 12 Pac.L.J. 965, 969–973). **(78)** But suffering need not be so limited—it can easily encompass the frustration and anguish caused by the inability to participate in activities that once brought pleasure. **(79)** Traditionally, by treating loss of enjoyment of life as a permissible factor in assessing pain and suffering, courts have given the term this broad meaning.

(80) If we are to depart from this traditional approach and approve a separate award for loss of enjoyment of life, it must be on the basis that such an approach will yield a more accurate evaluation of the compensation due to the plaintiff. **(81)** We have no doubt that, in general, the total award for nonpecuniary damages would increase if we adopted the rule. **(82)** That separate awards are advocated by plaintiffs and resisted by defendants is sufficient evidence that larger awards are at stake here. **(83)** But a larger award does not by itself indicate that the goal of compensation has been better served.

(84) The advocates of separate awards contend that because pain and suffering and loss of enjoyment of life can be distinguished, they must be treated separately if the plaintiff is to be compensated fully for each distinct injury suffered. **(85)** We disagree. **(86)** Such an analytical approach may have its place when the subject is pecuniary damages, which can be calculated with some precision. **(87)** But the estimation of nonpecuniary damages is not amenable to such analytical precision and may, in fact, suffer from its application. **(88)** Translating human suffering into dollars and cents involves no mathematical formula; it rests, as we have said, on a legal fiction. **(89)** The figure that emerges is unavoidably distorted by the translation. **(90)** Application of this murky process to the component parts of nonpecuniary injuries (however analytically distinguishable they may be) cannot make it more accurate. **(91)** If anything, the distortion will be amplified by repetition.

(92) Thus, we are not persuaded that any salutary purpose would be served by having the jury make separate awards for pain and suffering and loss of enjoyment of life. **(93)** We are confident, furthermore, that the trial advocate's art is a sufficient guarantee that none of the plaintiff's losses will be ignored by the jury.

(94) The errors in the instructions given to the jury require a new trial on the issue of nonpecuniary damages to be awarded to plaintiff Emma McDougald. **(95)** Defendants' remaining contentions are either without merit, beyond the scope of our review or are rendered academic by our disposition of the case.

(96) Accordingly, the order of the Appellate Division, insofar as appealed from, should be modified, with costs to defendants, by granting a new trial on the issue of nonpecuniary damages of plaintiff Emma McDougald, and as so modified, affirmed. . . .

(97) Order, insofar as appealed from, modified, with costs to defendants, by granting a new trial on the issue of nonpecuniary damages of plaintiff Emma McDougald and, as so modified, affirmed.

TASK 5.O.1. Case Brief

Write a case brief of *McDougald v. Garber* using the template on page 290.

TASK 5.O.2. Torts Vocabulary Definitions (List 9)

Fill in each definition with the appropriate term from the list below. Consult a law dictionary or an English-to-English dictionary to confirm that you have matched each term with the correct definition. If multiple forms of a term are provided, you may not need to use all of the forms in the blanks.

cost of custodial care *(noun)*
culpability *(noun)*; culpable *(adjective)*
derivative claim *(noun)*
loss of enjoyment of life *(noun)*
lost earnings *(noun)*
medical expenses *(noun)*
nonpecuniary damages *(noun)*
pain and suffering *(noun)*
pecuniary damages *(noun)*

Terms related to torts

1. There are two types of compensatory or actual damages: ____________________ and ____________________. The former refers to damages awarded to compensate an injured person for the economic consequences of her injury, while the latter compensates the person for the physical and emotional consequences of her injury.

2. The following are pecuniary damages: (a) ____________________: the costs incurred for the treatment or prevention of injury or disease; (b) ____________________: the costs incurred for non-medical care that assists people with activities of daily living such as bathing, eating, and dressing; and (c) ____________________: the potential earnings an individual was unable to receive due to injury or illness.

3. The following are nonpecuniary damages: (a) ____________________: the mental and physical pain associated with injury (past, present, and future) and (b) ____________________: negative changes to a person's life or the inability to participate in activities or pleasures of life as a result of injury.

4. ____________________ means responsibility for a wrong.

Term related to procedure

5. A/an ____________________ is brought by someone closely associated with the injured party (e.g., a spouse). The claim derives from the plaintiff's primary injury claim.

TASK 5.O.3. Questions for Discussion

Answer the following questions to assist you during a class discussion of the case. Indicate the sentence(s) in which you found the answer to each question.

1. What are the facts of this case?

2. What is the issue, and what does the Court hold?

3. In sentence (44), the Court states that damages for nonpecuniary losses "stands on less certain ground than does an award for pecuniary damages." Why is this so?

4. Which approach do you believe is more appropriate: one general award for pain and suffering or separate awards for pain and suffering and loss of enjoyment of life? What are potential problems associated with each approach?

5. What is the "paradoxical situation" to which the Court refers in sentence (56)? Do you find the Court's reasoning convincing on this point?

6. Hypothetical: Suppose that instead of going into a permanent coma, Mrs. McDougald died on the operating table after suffering five minutes of oxygen deprivation. What damage items would/would not be recoverable?

7. Create your own question. For inspiration, review the list of common question types in Part II, Chapter 3.

P. Torts Essay Question #4

Answer the following hypothetical using the previous cases in this chapter to inform your answer. Use a piece of paper or a blank document on your computer to outline your response before you begin writing.

Suggested response time: **35 minutes**.

QUESTION

Henry, a professional pianist and piano instructor, purchased an electric saw to perform repairs to his home. The saw was designed and manufactured by the Kutter Company. The saw had two blade guards that shielded almost the entire saw blade. The top guard was made of metal, while the bottom guard was made of transparent plastic.

Instructions in the operator's manual, located inside the packaging, suggested that the saw should be used with the blade guards in place. Specifically, the owner's manual stated: "The saw works best with blade guards attached." The manual further added: "Do not use the saw to cut material more than five inches in height." The saw itself did not contain any other instructions or warnings.

Two days after purchasing the saw, Henry used it to cut a piece of wood about five inches deep. As he attempted to cut the piece of wood, he found that the plastic lower blade guard prevented the blade from passing completely through the piece of wood. As a result, Henry removed both blade guards from the saw to cut the wood. He then continued to work with the saw blade fully exposed.

Approximately ten minutes after removing the blade guards, while Henry was working on cutting another piece of wood, the spinning blade unexpectedly flew off the saw and back toward Henry. The flying blade amputated his left thumb and index finger.

Without the use of his two fingers, Henry can no longer play the piano. He has had to quit his job with the local orchestra and has lost all of his private students.

Henry has brought suit against the Kutter Company, alleging that it is liable for his injury. You are a lawyer representing the Kutter Company. Your supervisor, Mr. Tanaka, has asked you to write an informal memo to him evaluating the merits of Henry's case against the company.[11]

This lawsuit has been filed in a Louisiana trial court, and Louisiana tort law applies. Accordingly, Mr. Tanaka has advised you to use Louisiana case law to inform your analysis. Note that Louisiana is a pure comparative negligence jurisdiction.

[11] Hypothetical adapted from Hood v. Ryobi America Corp., 181 F.3d 608 (4th Cir. 1999).

Q. Torts Vocabulary Exercises (Lists 6-9)

EXERCISE 5.P.1. Fill in the Blanks

Fill in the blanks with the most appropriate form of the words and phrases in the list below. You may have to change word form to create a grammatically correct sentence. Some questions may have more than one correct answer.

actual damages	malicious
award	punitive damages
culpable	reckless
derivative claim	recover
deter	wanton
incur	willful

1. The plaintiff ____________________ $500,000 in damages.
2. The jury deliberated for nearly five hours before reaching a verdict. It found the defendant liable for negligence and ____________________ the plaintiff $50,000 in ____________________ damages for pain and suffering.
3. Many believe that the death penalty has a/an ____________________ effect on serious crime. However, statistics show that capital punishment doesn't seem to have any effect on homicide rates.
4. The jury found that the defendant was ____________________ and awarded money damages to the plaintiff.
5. The attorney argued that her client ____________________ a serious injury as a result of the defendant's negligence.

EXERCISE 5.P.2. Matching

Match each hypothetical below with the type of damages that the situation calls for. Note that the hypotheticals might be matched with more than one term from the list below. Try select only the most relevant terms.

lost earnings
punitive damages
pain and suffering

cost of custodial care
loss of enjoyment of life
nonpecuniary damages

1. Eve, 70 years old, was a professional dancer for much of her life. As she grew older, she gave up dancing professionally but continued to dance for fun because, in her words, it "gave my life meaning." Last year, she was injured in an automobile accident that left her paralyzed from the waist down. She claims that she can no longer dance, which has significantly diminished her quality of life. What type of damages might she seek to recover in a claim against the driver?

   ____

2. Patricia brought suit against the defendant doctor who provided anesthesia during her husband's operation on his wrist. She claims that the doctor was negligent, which is why her husband, Dave, lost so much oxygen during the procedure and ultimately became "brain dead." As a result of his current condition, Dave needs round-the-clock care from a nurse. What type of damages might Patricia seek to recover in a claim against the defendant doctor?

   ____

3. Bill was killed when a car crashed into him while he was riding his bike on the street. He died immediately on impact. Bill's father sued Corey, the driver of the car that hit him. During trial, the plaintiff presented evidence that Corey was both under the influence of alcohol and texting at the time of the car accident. What type of damages might the jury award in such a case?

   ____

R. Additional Essay Questions

Answer the following hypotheticals using the twelve cases in this chapter and Part II, Chapter 2 to inform your answers. Use a piece of paper or a blank document on your computer to outline your response before you begin writing.

Suggested response time for Question 1: **45 minutes.**

QUESTION 1

Aaron and Betsy got married in June of last year and spent their honeymoon at the Blue Beach Resort Hotel. They were very excited about their trip to this all-inclusive resort with 8 pools, an 18-hole golf course, as well as kayaking, paddle boarding, and rock climbing opportunities on site.

Early on the second day of the honeymoon, Aaron decided to take a dip in one of the hotel pools. The pool was 3 ½ feet[12] at the shallow end and 8 feet at the deep end, though this was not marked anywhere on or by the pool. A 7-foot water slide was positioned at the shallow end of the pool, leading directly into the pool. Large signs located at both ends of the pool stated, "DANGER! No running on pool grounds."

After swimming a couple of laps in the deep end, Aaron got out and sat on a lounge chair next to the pool. While drying off, he observed a group of young children taking turns sliding into the pool head first, doing "belly slides." The lifeguard on duty clapped every time one of the kids made a particularly splashy entrance into the pool. Though Aaron didn't see any adults using the slide, feeling young and adventurous, he decided to also give the slide a try. He climbed up to the top of the slide and proceeded to slide down head first with his arms positioned straight ahead of him. Right after he hit the water, however, Aaron's head struck the bottom of the pool. He immediately felt pain in his head and neck, and a large bruise began to develop on the right side of his head.

Aaron was determined not to let a little pain detract from his romantic honeymoon with Betsy. Later that day, he and Betsy went to play a round of golf, their favorite activity, on the hotel's golf course. But no sooner had they arrived at the first hole than Aaron was hit in the shoulder by a flying golf ball. This is because Daren, another guest at the hotel whom Aaron did not know prior to this incident, accidentally hit his golf ball in the wrong direction. (It turns out that Daren was just learning how to play golf and did not have very good control of his golf swing.) A nasty bruise started forming on Aaron's shoulder.

Because of the injuries he sustained that day, Aaron has developed some serious health issues. When he slid into the pool and hit his head, he fractured one of his vertebrae.[13] As a result, he is not able to control his bladder and bowel function. When he was hit by the golf ball in his shoulder, a tendon[14] tore, requiring surgery. Now he can't raise his arms above shoulder level.[15]

Aaron has come to your law firm inquiring whether he should bring suit against any the parties involved in his case. Your direct supervisor, Mr. Jennings,

[12] Three feet equals approximately one meter.

[13] A vertebra is a small bone that forms that backbone.

[14] A tendon is a piece of human tissue that attaches a muscle to a bone.

[15] Hypothetical adapted from Louis v. Louis, 636 N.W.2d 314 (Minn. 2001).

has handed this case off to you. Mr. Jennings has asked you to write him an email in which you evaluate all of the potential claims that Aaron might have.

Assume that you are working in a jurisdiction in which the laws of **ALL** states apply. For assessing damages, further assume that this is a modified comparative negligence jurisdiction, where plaintiffs cannot recover if they are more than 50 percent at fault.

Suggested response time for Question 2: **35 minutes**.

QUESTION 2

Lacy Miller was the owner of a two-year-old German Shepherd dog, Bodie. The dog was known in the neighborhood as friendly and got along well with Lacy's friends, neighbors, and children.

One April night at 8:30 pm, Bodie broke loose from Lacy's backyard without her knowledge. Within the next two hours, the police received three calls from different residents stating that there was a dangerous wolf roaming the neighborhood.

At 2:30 am that same night, police officers Chris North and Dianne Olson spotted a stray animal standing on the southwest corner of Main Street and 11th Avenue. Both officers believed the animal to be the wolf that residents had called about. The officers began to quietly approach the animal, and when they were roughly a half block away on 11th Avenue, Dianne took aim at the animal with her gun. She shot at it three times, missing each time. As the animal tried to run away, Chris ran after it and shot at it an additional twenty-two times before it fell to the ground.

Earlier in the night, at approximately 2:00 am, Lacy discovered that Bodie had escaped from her backyard. She began calling his name and looking for him around the neighborhood. She spotted Bodie sniffing a mailbox on the southwest corner of Main Street and 11th Avenue, which was one block away from where Lacy was standing on Main Street. Neither Lacy nor the officers could see each other because they were approaching the dog from different streets. Dense vegetation in the neighborhood, as well as the dark of night, decreased visibility. As Lacy walked toward Bodie, she heard three gunshots. She saw Bodie retreat, running away from the gunshots on 11th Avenue. Lacy began screaming Bodie's name and ran toward him to try and shield him from the shots. Chris stopped shooting at Bodie as soon as Lacy came into his view. However, it was too late, and he accidentally shot Lacy twice in the leg.

Bodie was shot multiple times in the head and torso. He died at the scene. Lacy was rushed to the emergency room to be treated for her bullet wounds. Lacy had to undergo two surgeries and two months of physical therapy. While Lacy has made a full physical recovery, she claims to be "traumatized" after the loss of her "best friend."

Lacy, a lawyer, plans to sue the police department for negligent infliction of emotional distress and common law negligence. You have been retained by Lacy to represent her in the case against the police department. Lacy has asked you to write her an honest letter in which you analyze her chances of success.[16]

Assume that you are working in a jurisdiction in which the laws of **ALL** states apply. For assessing damages, further assume that this is a pure comparative negligence jurisdiction.

Suggested response time for Question 3: **45 minutes.**

QUESTION 3

Amber (age 24) is a famous singer known for three *Billboard* Hot 100 chart-topping singles. Last April she set out on a world tour that was scheduled to last four months, but the tour had to be cut short.

Following Amber's third show on the tour in Miami, Florida, she went out with her backup singers, manager, and some fans to get a taste of that famous Miami nightlife. She stayed out until 4 a.m., and was somewhat inebriated when she arrived at her hotel, The Alton. Amber decided to take a bath as soon as she arrived in her room. The bathtub was a freestanding white tub with a smooth interior, without no-slip mats or treads[17] on the tub floor. Amber put an entire container of bubbling bath soap in the water, sat back, relaxed, and drank some champagne.

About fifteen minutes (and two glasses of champagne) into her bath, Amber decided to clean her ears, as she does once or twice a week. She stood up in the tub and reached over to the sink, roughly four feet from the tub, to grab a cotton swab.[18] The swabs, manufactured by Clean Ears, were placed on the sink inside a small plastic container that contained only the following information: "Clean Ears® Cotton Swabs, 100% Cotton, Paper Sticks, Double Tipped." After reaching for one swab, Amber sat back down in the tub and started to clean her left ear by placing the swab inside her ear canal and moving it around. While working on her left ear, Amber decided to stand up and reach toward the sink for another swab to clean her right ear. However, at this point Amber slipped and fell in the tub since the tub floor was very slippery. Unfortunately, because the swab was still inside her left ear, and Amber fell on her left side, the cotton swab was pushed inside her ear as she hit the floor of the tub. This partially ruptured Amber's left ear drum.

---

[16] Hypothetical adapted from Soucek v. Banham, 503 N.W.2d 153 (Minn. 1993).

[17] Treads are rubberized stickers that can be stuck to the floor of a bathtub to improve traction and safety.

[18] A cotton swab is a small ball of cotton that is wrapped around both ends of a short stick. They are often called "Q-tips."

Amber stepped out of the shower and immediately called an ambulance. She then got dressed and headed to the ground floor to wait for the ambulance to arrive. While waiting, her left ear began to bleed.

At the hospital, Amber was treated by Dr. Franklin, a resident[19] in emergency medicine. Dr. Franklin, who had never removed an object from a patient's ear before, chose to irrigate[20] Amber's ear using an electric ear syringe,[21] assuming that the water would push out the swab. However, the cotton at the end of the swab swelled with water instead, and the water pressure from the syringe ruptured Amber's ear drum completely. In the end, Dr. Franklin had to use pliers[22] to pull out the swab. As a result of the rupture, Amber has lost all sense of hearing in her left ear and she will never regain her hearing in that ear.

This incident has caused Amber a great deal of physical and psychological pain. The accident has also interfered with her ability to sing. Since she cannot hear in one of her ears, Amber's pitch has been off, and she cannot quite sing the way that she used to. As a result, she has not performed or recorded any new songs since the incident. In addition, because of her injuries and recovery time, Amber also had to cancel the rest of her tour. She lost out on about $40 million as a result.

Amber has come to your law firm asking whether she might have a claim against any of the parties involved in her case. You are a junior associate at the firm and the managing partner, Ms. Abboud, has asked you to write her (that is, Ms. Abboud) an informal memo about what claims Amber might have, and against whom. Ms. Abboud has asked you to consider all potential defendants, even if you believe that the claims against them will not be successful.

Assume that you are working in a jurisdiction in which the laws of **ALL** states apply. For assessing damages, further assume that this is a pure comparative negligence jurisdiction.

---

[19] A resident is a doctor who is still completing her training, usually in a hospital setting.

[20] To "irrigate" means to supply a continuous flow of water. This word is used when referring to watering land or crops, or in medicine, when applying water to a wound or an organ (such as an ear).

[21] An electric ear syringe is a device that is used to propel water into the ear canal. It is similar to a hose used for watering plants, but the "hose" is small enough to fit into an ear.

[22] Pliers are small hand tools that are used for holding, picking up, and pulling out small objects. Pliers are similar to pincers or tweezers.

Suggested response time for Question 4: **45 minutes**.

QUESTION 4

This past June, Alice (aged 13) was invited to a "90s Rollerblade[23] Party" to celebrate her friend Brooke's 12th birthday. Alice had never tried rollerblading before going to this party, but thought it sounded fun. The party was organized and hosted by Brooke's mother, Cindy Daleford. The kids were encouraged to wear 90s clothing and makeup[24] while rollerblading around the Dalefords' sprawling property, which has over 10 miles of paved trails where Cindy trains for marathons.

Alice received the following invitation to the party:

YOU ARE INVITED TO BROOKE'S

90's Rollerblading Birthday Party

Saturday, June 10 from 11 a.m. – 1 p.m.
1324 Shady Grove St

Whether you are a seasoned rollerblader or a complete newbie, you are welcome! Everyone will be taught rollerblading basics by Brooke's mom, a rollerblading expert.

Rollerblades will be provided. Please send us your shoe size. Helmets and knee/elbow pads will not be provided. Please bring these with you.

On the day of the party, Alice arrived at Brooke's house at 11:05 a.m. and was immediately fitted for rollerblades. She did not bring a helmet or knee and elbow pads, and none were provided for her. At around 11:25 a.m., Cindy held a short rollerblading "lesson," in which she taught Alice and Brooke's other friends how to balance and move their legs using the rollerblades, as well as how to avoid potentially dangerous bumps on the trails. She instructed the girls to stay away from any bumps that were marked with bright yellow cones.

Soon after the lesson, the girls began rollerblading on the paved trail. Cindy also put on her rollerblades and supervised the girls, guiding some of the less confident ones and helping up anyone who fell. After half an hour or so, Alice got

[23] A rollerblade is a type of skate that has a single line of wheels at the bottom. This was a popular form of skating in the 1990s.

[24] The 1990s were characterized by bright, neon colors; lots of blue eye shadow; and big, voluminous hair.

the hang of[25] rollerblading. She began gliding faster and faster. Initially, she steered clear of marked bumps on the trail, but soon decided it could be a fun challenge to skate over on top of them. The third time Alice did this, she lost her balance, fell, and hit her head on a thick tree branch. She was not wearing a helmet.

Cindy saw Alice fall and was soon by her side. Alice seemed to be okay—she did not have any cuts or scratches, just minor redness on her head. To be on the safe side, however, Cindy took Alice to the local emergency room. She asked her husband, Ed, to look after the other kids at the party.

While waiting for a doctor to see Alice, Cindy called Alice's mother, Felicity, to fill her in on what had happened. Felicity drove to the hospital at once and arrived just as Alice was called into the examination room to be seen by the emergency room physician, Dr. Garrett. Felicity was relieved to find that Alice seemed to be completely fine.

Dr. Garrett conducted both a physical and neurologic exam on Alice. He checked her head for evidence of scalp trauma and skull fractures and found a small area of redness and bruise. He checked her vision, reflexes, and range of arm and leg motion. All of these were normal. He also asked Alice a series of questions (e.g., What day is it? Do you know where you are? How old are you?) to ascertain whether she was cognitively impaired. Alice answered all of these questions correctly. She also informed the doctor that she was not in any pain. Dr. Garrett let Alice go without any further testing. However, he advised Alice to return immediately if she experienced a headache, dizziness, or vomiting. Felicity took her daughter home while Cindy returned to Brooke's birthday party.

Alice took a short nap as soon as she arrived home. When she woke up, she felt a mild headache coming on and took some ibuprofen.[26] She watched some TV and then went back to sleep for about two hours. When Alice woke up the second time, the headache had gotten much worse and she was feeling quite dizzy. She told Felicity about her symptoms, who then rushed Alice to the emergency room. On the way to hospital, Alice lost consciousness.

At the hospital, Dr. Garrett ordered a CT scan[27] to check for any bleeding on Alice's brain. The scan revealed that Alice had an epidural hematoma, a collection of blood outside the brain, which was compressing the surrounding brain tissue. Alice was taken into emergency surgery immediately to relieve the pressure on her brain, but it was too late to be of any help. Alice is now in a permanent coma and requires machine-supported breathing and other forms of life support. There is little chance that she will ever regain consciousness.

Last Friday, Felicity came to your law firm inquiring whether she has a claim of negligence against any of the parties involved in her daughter's case (she would

---

[25] Getting the hang of something means to learn how to do something.

[26] Ibuprofen is an over-the-counter medication used to relieve pain.

[27] A computerized tomography (CT) scan is a type of x-ray that creates cross-sectional images of the bones, blood vessels, and tissues inside the body.

be suing on behalf of Alice). You are a lawyer at the firm and Ms. Singh, your supervisor, has asked you to write her (that is, Ms. Singh) an email in which you analyze what claims Felicity might have and against whom. Ms. Singh has asked you to consider all potential defendants, even if you believe that the claims against them will not be successful.

Assume that you are working in a jurisdiction in which the laws of **ALL** states apply. For assessing damages, further assume that this is a contributory negligence jurisdiction.

Further Reading

The following hornbooks provide more in-depth coverage of tort law. A **hornbook** is a textbook that covers a particular area of law. Unlike a casebook, a hornbook contains detailed explanations and summaries of legal rules and principles. It is a study aid frequently used by law students to supplement what they learn through cases and class discussions.

Titles marked with an asterisk (*) contain practice exercises in the form of hypotheticals.

*ANITA BERNSTEIN, QUESTIONS & ANSWERS: TORTS (4th ed. 2018).

KENNETH ABRAHAM, THE FORMS AND FUNCTIONS OF TORT LAW (5th ed. 2017).

*JOSEPH W. GLANNON, EXAMPLES & EXPLANATIONS: THE LAW OF TORTS (5th ed. 2015).

EDWARD J. KIONKA, TORTS IN A NUTSHELL (6th ed. 2015).

MARSHALL SHAPO, PRINCIPLES OF TORT LAW (4th ed. 2016).

Chapter 6
Criminal Procedure

The cases in this chapter all concern criminal procedure, the area of law that sets forth the procedures that the government must follow when enforcing substantive criminal law. The laws regulating this process come from a variety of sources, including criminal procedure codes, constitutions, and court decisions. In certain areas of criminal procedure law, U.S. Constitutional provisions, as they are interpreted by the Supreme Court of the United States, comprise the primary form of regulation. The focus of this chapter is on one of these areas of criminal procedure law.

In the pages to follow, you will read U.S. Supreme Court decisions that prescribe the procedures that law enforcement authorities must follow in their investigation of crimes. More specifically, you will read several cases that address **police interrogation** and the rules that police officers must comply with when interviewing witnesses and suspects.

This area of criminal procedure law concerns the **Fifth Amendment** to the U.S. Constitution. This amendment provides that "No person . . . shall be compelled in any criminal case to be a witness against himself." The Supreme Court has interpreted this language to mean that neither the federal nor state governments can force individuals to confess to wrongdoing at a criminal trial or while the individual is in police custody. We call this right the **privilege against self-incrimination** (see definitions on the next page).

So what are the specific rules that police officers must follow to ensure that individuals' Fifth Amendment rights are protected? The Supreme Court established these procedures in the landmark case, *Miranda v. Arizona*—the first case that you will read in this chapter. *Miranda* is one of the most influential cases in U.S. Supreme Court jurisprudence. But because it leaves some questions unanswered, the remaining cases in this chapter clarify its scope.

A. Criminal Procedure Case #1

The famous *Miranda* case is actually four cases consolidated and decided at once: *Miranda v. Arizona*; *Vignera v. New York*; *Westover v. United States*; and *California v. Stewart*. Our concern here is not so much the particular facts of any of the cases, but rather the rule the Court announces for law enforcement officers to follow. Therefore, read this case primarily for *what* this new rule is and *why* the Court has created it.

Pre-Reading Vocabulary

self-incrimination *(noun)*
The act of exposing oneself to an accusation of a crime, usually by making a statement. An example of self-incrimination would involve a suspect in a robbery investigation saying, "My friend and I broke into the house." Other forms: incriminate *(verb)*; incriminating *(adjective)*.

privilege *(noun)*
A right given to particular groups of people. Courts refer to the "privilege against self-incrimination," which is the right of individuals to refrain from making any statements that would incriminate them.

custody *(noun)*
In the context of criminal law, custody refers to a situation where a person who is suspected, charged, or convicted of a crime is physically held in the care of law enforcement. Note that "custody" has a different meaning in the context of civil law (e.g., torts, family law).

interrogation *(noun)*
The act of questioning a suspect or witness by law enforcement officers.

MIRANDA v. ARIZONA
Supreme Court of the United States, 1966.
384 U.S. 436, 86 S.Ct. 1602, 16 L.Ed.2d 694.

Mr. Chief Justice WARREN delivered the opinion of the Court.

(1) The cases before us raise questions which go to the roots of our concepts of American criminal jurisprudence: the restraints society must observe consistent with the Federal Constitution in **prosecuting** individuals for crime. **(2)** More specifically, we deal with the **admissibility** of statements obtained from an individual who is subjected to custodial police interrogation and the necessity for procedures which assure that the individual is accorded his privilege under the Fifth Amendment to the Constitution not to be compelled to incriminate himself.

(3) We dealt with certain phases of this problem recently in Escobedo v. State of Illinois, 378 U.S. 478 (1964). **(4)** There, as in the four cases before us, law enforcement officials took the defendant into custody and interrogated him in a police station for the purpose of obtaining a confession. **(5)** The police did not effectively advise him of his right to remain silent or of his right to consult with his attorney. **(6)** Rather, they confronted him with an alleged accomplice who accused him of having perpetrated a murder. **(7)** When the defendant denied the accusation and said "I didn't shoot Manuel, you did it," they handcuffed him and took him to an interrogation room. **(8)** There, while handcuffed and standing, he was questioned for four hours until he confessed. **(9)** During this interrogation, the police denied his request to speak to his attorney, and they prevented his retained attorney, who had come to the police station, from consulting with him. **(10)** At his trial, the State, over his objection, introduced the confession against him. **(11)** We held that the statements thus made were constitutionally **inadmissible**.

(12) This case has been the subject of judicial interpretation and spirited legal debate since it was decided two years ago. **(13)** Both state and federal courts, in assessing its implications, have arrived at varying conclusions. **(14)** A wealth of scholarly material has been written tracing its ramifications and underpinnings. **(15)** Police and **prosecutor** have speculated on its range and desirability. **(16)** We granted certiorari in these cases . . . in order further to explore some facets of the problems, thus exposed, of applying the privilege against self-incrimination to in-custody interrogation, and to give concrete constitutional guidelines for law enforcement agencies and courts to follow.

(17) We start here, as we did in *Escobedo*, with the premise that our holding is not an innovation in our jurisprudence, but is an application of principles long recognized and applied in other settings. **(18)** We have undertaken a thorough re-examination of the *Escobedo* decision and the principles it announced, and we reaffirm it. **(19)** That case was but an explication of basic rights that are enshrined in our Constitution—that "No person . . . shall be compelled in any criminal case to be a witness against himself," and that "the accused shall . . . have the Assistance of Counsel"—rights which were put in jeopardy in that case through official overbearing. . . .

(20) Our holding will be spelled out with some specificity in the pages which follow but briefly stated it is this: the **prosecution** may not use statements, whether **exculpatory** or **inculpatory**, stemming from custodial interrogation of the defendant unless it demonstrates the use of procedural safeguards effective to secure the privilege against self-incrimination. **(21)** By custodial interrogation, we mean questioning initiated by law enforcement officers after a person has been taken into custody or otherwise deprived of his freedom of action in any significant way. **(22)** As for the procedural safeguards to be employed, unless other fully effective means are devised to inform accused persons of their right of silence and to assure a continuous opportunity to exercise it, the following measures are required. **(23)** Prior to any questioning, the person must be warned that he has a right to remain silent, that any statement he does make may be used as evidence against him, and that he has a right to the presence of an attorney, either retained or appointed. **(24)** The defendant may **waive** effectuation of these rights, provided the **waiver** is made voluntarily, knowingly and intelligently. **(25)** If, however, he indicates in any manner and at any stage of the process that he wishes to consult with an attorney before speaking there can be no questioning. **(26)** Likewise, if the individual is alone and indicates in any manner that he does not wish to be interrogated, the police may not question him. **(27)** The mere fact that he may have answered some questions or volunteered some statements on his own does not deprive him of the right to refrain from answering any further inquiries until he has consulted with an attorney and thereafter consents to be questioned.

I.

(28) The constitutional issue we decide in each of these cases is the admissibility of statements obtained from a defendant questioned while in custody or otherwise deprived of his freedom of action in any significant way. **(29)** In each, the defendant was questioned by police officers, detectives, or a prosecuting attorney in a room in which he was cut off from the outside world. **(30)** In none of these cases was the defendant given a full and effective warning of his rights at the outset of the interrogation process. **(31)** In all the cases, the questioning elicited oral admissions, and in three of them, signed statements as well which were admitted at their trials. **(32)** They all thus share salient features—**incommunicado** interrogation of individuals in a police-dominated atmosphere, resulting in self-incriminating statements without full warnings of constitutional rights.

(33) An understanding of the nature and setting of this in-custody interrogation is essential to our decisions today. **(34)** The difficulty in depicting what transpires at such interrogations stems from the fact that in this country they have largely taken place incommunicado. **(35)** From extensive factual studies undertaken in the early 1930's, including the famous Wickersham Report to Congress by a Presidential Commission, it is clear that police violence and the "third degree" flourished at that time. **(36)** In a series of cases decided by this Court long after these studies, the police resorted to physical brutality—beatings, hanging, whipping—and to sustained and protracted questioning incommunicado in order to **extort confessions**. **(37)** The Commission on Civil Rights in 1961 found much evidence to indicate that "some policemen still resort to physical force to **obtain confessions**," 1961 Comm'n on Civil Rights Rep., Justice, pt. 5, 17. **(38)** The use of physical brutality and violence is not, unfortunately, relegated to the past or to any part of the country. **(39)** Only recently in Kings County, New York, the police brutally beat, kicked and placed lighted cigarette butts on the back of a potential witness under interrogation for the purpose of securing a statement incriminating a third party. People v. Portelli, 15 N.Y.2d 235 (1965).

(40) The examples given above are undoubtedly the exception now, but they are sufficiently widespread to be the object of concern. **(41)** Unless a proper limitation upon custodial interrogation is achieved—such as these decisions will advance—there can be no assurance that practices of this nature will be eradicated in the foreseeable future. . . .

(42) . . . [T]he modern practice of in-custody interrogation is psychologically rather than physically oriented. **(43)** As we have stated before, "Since Chambers v. State of Florida, 309 U.S. 227, this Court has recognized that **coercion** can be mental as well as physical, and that the blood of the accused is not the only hallmark of an unconstitutional inquisition." Blackburn v. State of Alabama, 361 U.S. 199, 206 (1960). **(44)** Interrogation still takes place in privacy. **(45)** Privacy results in secrecy and this in turn results in a gap in our knowledge as to what in fact goes on in the interrogation rooms. **(46)** A valuable source of information about present police practices, however, may be found in various police manuals and texts which document procedures employed with success in the past, and which recommend various other effective tactics. **(47)** These texts are used by law enforcement agencies themselves as guides. **(48)** It should be noted that these texts professedly present the most enlightened and effective means presently used to obtain statements through custodial interrogation. **(49)** By considering these texts and other data, it is possible to describe procedures observed and noted around the country.

[The Court details police interrogation procedures by quoting extensively from police manuals and other documents.]

(50) From these representative samples of interrogation techniques, the setting prescribed by the manuals and observed in practice becomes clear. **(51)** In essence, it is this: To be alone with the subject is essential to prevent distraction and to deprive him of any outside support. **(52)** The aura of confidence in his guilt undermines his will to resist. **(53)** He merely confirms the preconceived story the police seek to have him describe. **(54)** Patience and persistence, at times relentless questioning, are employed. **(55)** To obtain a confession, the interrogator must "patiently maneuver himself or his quarry into a position from which the desired objective may be attained." **(56)** When normal procedures fail to produce the needed result, the police may resort to deceptive stratagems such as giving false legal advice. **(57)** It is important to keep the subject off balance, for example, by trading on his insecurity about himself or his surroundings. **(58)** The police then persuade, trick, or cajole him out of exercising his constitutional rights.

(59) Even without employing brutality, the "third degree" or the specific stratagems described above, the very fact of custodial interrogation exacts a heavy toll on individual liberty and trades on the weakness of individuals. . . .

(60) In the cases before us today, given this background, we concern ourselves primarily with this interrogation atmosphere and the evils it can bring. **(61)** In . . . *Miranda v. Arizona*, the police arrested the defendant and took him to a special interrogation room where they secured a confession. . . . [The Court describes the other three cases decided along with *Miranda*.]

(62) In these cases we might not find the defendants' statements to have been involuntary in traditional terms. **(63)** Our concern for adequate safeguards to protect precious Fifth Amendment rights is, of course, not lessened in the slightest. . . . **(64)** [T]he defendant was thrust into an unfamiliar atmosphere and run through menacing police interrogation procedures. . . . **(65)** To be sure, the records do not evince overt physical coercion or patent psychological ploys. **(66)** The fact remains that in none of these cases did the officers undertake to afford appropriate safeguards at the outset of the interrogation to insure that the statements were truly the product of free choice.

(67) It is obvious that such an interrogation environment is created for no purpose other than to subjugate the individual to the will of his examiner. **(68)** This atmosphere carries its own badge of intimidation. **(69)** To be sure, this is not physical intimidation, but it is equally destructive of human dignity. **(70)** The current practice of incommunicado interrogation is at odds with one of our Nation's most cherished principles—that the individual may not be compelled to incriminate himself. **(71)** Unless adequate protective devices are employed to dispel the **compulsion** inherent in custodial surroundings, no statement obtained from the defendant can truly be the product of his free choice.

(72) From the foregoing, we can readily perceive an intimate connection between the privilege against self-incrimination and police custodial questioning. **(73)** It is fitting to turn to history and precedent underlying the Self-Incrimination Clause to determine its applicability in this situation.

II.

(74) We sometimes forget how long it has taken to establish the privilege against self-incrimination, the sources from which it came and the fervor with which it was defended. **(75)** Its roots go back into ancient times. . . . [The Court traces the history of the privilege against self-incrimination clause.]

(76) . . . [W]e may view the historical development of the privilege as one which groped for the proper scope of governmental power over the citizen. **(77)** As a "noble principle often transcends its origins," the privilege has come rightfully to be recognized in part as an individual's substantive right, a "right to a private enclave where he may lead a private life. **(78)** That right is the hallmark of our democracy." United States v. Grunewald, 233 F.2d 556, 579, 581—582 (Frank, J., dissenting), rev'd, 353 U.S. 391 (1957). **(79)** We have recently noted that the privilege against self-incrimination—the essential mainstay of our adversary system—is founded on a complex of values, Murphy v. Waterfront Comm. of New

York Harbor, 378 U.S. 52, 55—57, n. 5; Tehan v. United States ex rel. Shott, 382 U.S. 406, 414—415, n. 12 (1966). **(80)** All these policies point to one overriding thought: the constitutional foundation underlying the privilege is the respect a government—state or federal—must accord to the dignity and integrity of its citizens. **(81)** To maintain a "fair state-individual balance," to require the government "to shoulder the entire load," 8 Wigmore, Evidence 317 (McNaughton rev. 1961), to respect the inviolability of the human personality, our accusatory system of criminal justice demands that the government seeking to punish an individual produce the evidence against him by its own independent labors, rather than by the cruel, simple expedient of **compelling** it from his own mouth. Chambers v. State of Florida, 309 U.S. 227, 235—238 (1940). **(82)** In sum, the privilege is fulfilled only when the person is guaranteed the right "to remain silent unless he chooses to speak in the unfettered exercise of his own will." Malloy v. Hogan, 378 U.S. 1, 8 (1964).

(83) The question in these cases is whether the privilege is fully applicable during a period of custodial interrogation. **(84)** In this Court, the privilege has consistently been accorded a liberal construction. . . . **(85)** We are satisfied that all the principles embodied in the privilege apply to informal compulsion exerted by law-enforcement officers during in-custody questioning. **(86)** An individual swept from familiar surroundings into police custody, surrounded by antagonistic forces, and subjected to the techniques of persuasion described above cannot be otherwise than under compulsion to speak. **(87)** As a practical matter, the compulsion to speak in the isolated setting of the police station may well be greater than in courts or other official investigations, where there are often impartial observers to guard against intimidation or trickery. . . .

(88) Our decision in Malloy v. Hogan, 378 U.S. 1 (1964), necessitates an examination of the scope of the privilege in state cases as well. **(89)** In *Malloy*, we squarely held the privilege applicable to the States, and held that the substantive standards underlying the privilege applied with full force to state court proceedings. . . . **(90)** The implications of this proposition were elaborated in our decision in Escobedo v. State of Illinois, 378 U.S. 478, decided one week after *Malloy* applied the privilege to the States.

(91) Our holding there stressed the fact that the police had not advised the defendant of his constitutional privilege to remain silent at the outset of the interrogation, and we drew attention to that fact at several points in the decision, 378 U.S., at 483, 485, 491. **(92)** This was no isolated factor, but an essential ingredient in our decision. **(93)** The entire thrust of police interrogation there, as in all the cases today, was to put the defendant in such an emotional state as to impair his capacity for rational judgment. **(94)** The abdication of the constitutional privilege—the choice on his part to speak to the police—was not made knowingly or competently because of the failure to **apprise him of his rights**; the compelling atmosphere of the in-custody interrogation, and not an independent decision on his part, caused the defendant to speak.

(95) A different phase of the *Escobedo* decision was significant in its attention to the absence of counsel during the questioning. **(96)** There, as in the cases today, we sought a protective device to dispel the compelling atmosphere of the interrogation. **(97)** In *Escobedo*, however, the police did not relieve the defendant of the anxieties which they had created in the interrogation rooms. **(98)** Rather, they denied his request for the assistance of counsel, 378 U.S., at 481, 488, 491. **(99)** This heightened his dilemma, and made his later statements the product of this compulsion. Cf. Haynes v. State of Washington, 373 U.S. 503, 514 (1963). **(100)** The denial of the defendant's request for his attorney thus undermined his ability to exercise the privilege—to remain silent if he chose or to speak without any intimidation, blatant or subtle. **(101)** The presence of counsel, in all the cases before us today, would be the adequate protective device necessary to make the process of police interrogation conform to the dictates of the privilege. **(102)** His presence would insure that statements made in the government-established atmosphere are not the product of compulsion.

(103) It was in this manner that *Escobedo* explicated another facet of the pre-trial privilege, noted in many of the Court's prior decisions: the protection of rights at trial. **(104)** That counsel is present when statements are taken from an individual during interrogation obviously enhances the integrity of the fact-finding processes in court. **(105)** The presence of an attorney, and the warnings delivered to the individual, enable the defendant under otherwise compelling circumstances to tell his story without fear, effectively, and in a way that eliminates the evils in the interrogation process. **(106)** Without the protections flowing from adequate warning and the rights of counsel, "all the careful safeguards erected around the giving of testimony, whether by an accused or any other witness, would become empty formalities in a procedure where the most compelling possible evidence of guilt, a confession, would have already been obtained at the unsupervised pleasure of the police." Mapp v. Ohio, 367 U.S. 643, 685 (1961) (Harlan, J., dissenting). Cf. Pointer v. State of Texas, 380 U.S. 400 (1965).

III.

(107) Today, then, there can be no doubt that the Fifth Amendment privilege is available outside of criminal court proceedings and serves to protect persons in all settings in which their freedom of action is curtailed in any significant way from being compelled to incriminate themselves. **(108)** We have concluded that without proper safeguards the process of in-custody interrogation of persons suspected or accused of crime contains inherently compelling pressures which work to undermine the individual's will to resist and to compel him to speak where he would not otherwise do so freely. **(109)** In order to combat these pressures and to permit a full opportunity to **exercise the privilege against self-incrimination**, the accused must be adequately and effectively apprised of his rights and the exercise of those rights must be fully honored.

(110) It is impossible for us to foresee the potential alternatives for protecting the privilege which might be devised by Congress or the States in the exercise of their creative rule-making capacities. **(111)** Therefore we cannot say that the Constitution necessarily requires adherence to any particular solution for the inherent compulsions of the interrogation process as it is presently conducted. **(112)** Our decision in no way creates a constitutional straitjacket which will handicap sound efforts at reform, nor is it intended to have this effect. **(113)** We encourage Congress and the States to continue their laudable search for increasingly effective ways of protecting the rights of the individual while promoting efficient enforcement of our criminal laws. **(114)** However, unless we are shown other procedures which are at least as effective in apprising accused persons of their right of silence and in assuring a continuous opportunity to exercise it, the following safeguards must be observed.

(115) At the outset, if a person in custody is to be subjected to interrogation, he must first be informed in clear and unequivocal terms that he has the right to remain silent. **(116)** For those unaware of the privilege, the warning is needed simply to make them aware of it—the threshold requirement for an intelligent decision as to its exercise. **(117)** More important, such a warning is an absolute prerequisite in overcoming the inherent pressures of the interrogation atmosphere. **(118)** It is not just the subnormal or woefully ignorant who succumb to an interrogator's imprecations, whether implied or expressly stated, that the interrogation will continue until a confession is obtained or that silence in the face of accusation is itself damning and will bode ill when presented to a jury. **(119)** Further, the warning will show the individual that his interrogators are prepared to recognize his privilege should he choose to exercise it.

(120) The Fifth Amendment privilege is so fundamental to our system of constitutional rule and the expedient of giving an adequate warning as to the availability of the privilege so simple, we will not pause to inquire in individual cases whether the defendant was aware of his rights without a warning being given. **(121)** Assessments of the knowledge the defendant possessed, based on information as to his age, education, intelligence, or prior contact with authorities, can never be more than speculation; a warning is a clearcut fact. **(122)** More important, whatever the background of the person interrogated, a warning at the time of the interrogation is indispensable to overcome its pressures and to insure that the individual knows he is free to exercise the privilege at that point in time.

(123) The warning of the right to remain silent must be accompanied by the explanation that anything said can and will be used against the individual in court. **(124)** It is only through an awareness of these consequences that there can be any assurance of real understanding and intelligent exercise of the privilege. **(125)** Moreover, this warning may serve to make the individual more acutely aware that he is faced with a phase of the adversary system—that he is not in the presence of persons acting solely in his interest.

(126) The circumstances surrounding in-custody interrogation can operate very quickly to overbear the will of one merely made aware of his privilege by his interrogators. **(127)** Therefore, the right to have counsel present at the interrogation is indispensable to the protection of the Fifth Amendment privilege under the system we delineate today. **(128)** Our aim is to assure that the individual's right to choose between silence and speech remains unfettered throughout the interrogation process. **(129)** A once-stated warning, delivered by those who will conduct the interrogation, cannot itself suffice to that end among those who most require knowledge of their rights. **(130)** A mere warning given by the interrogators is not alone sufficient to accomplish that end. **(131)** Prosecutors themselves claim that the admonishment of the right to remain silent without more "will benefit only the recidivist and the professional." Brief for the National District Attorneys Association as amicus curiae, p. 14. **(132)** Even preliminary advice given to the accused by his own attorney can be swiftly overcome by the secret interrogation process. Cf. Escobedo v. State of Illinois, 378 U.S. 478, 485, n. 5. **(133)** Thus, the need for counsel to protect the Fifth Amendment privilege comprehends not merely a right to consult with counsel prior to questioning, but also to have counsel present during any questioning if the defendant so desires.

(134) The presence of counsel at the interrogation may serve several significant subsidiary functions as well. **(135)** If the accused decides to talk to his interrogators, the assistance of counsel can mitigate the dangers of untrustworthiness. **(136)** With a lawyer present the likelihood that the police will practice coercion is reduced, and if coercion is nevertheless exercised the lawyer can testify to it in court. **(137)** The presence of a lawyer can also help to guarantee that the accused gives a fully accurate statement to the police and that the statement is rightly reported by the prosecution at trial. See Crooker v. State of California, 357 U.S. 433, 443—448 (1958) (Douglas, J., dissenting).

(138) An individual need not make a pre-interrogation request for a lawyer. **(139)** While such request affirmatively secures his right to have one, his failure to ask for a lawyer does not constitute a waiver. **(140)** No effective waiver of the right to counsel during interrogation can be recognized unless specifically made after the warnings we here delineate have been given. **(141)** The accused who does not know his rights and therefore does not make a request may be the person who most needs counsel. **(142)** As the California Supreme Court has aptly put it:

> Finally, we must recognize that the imposition of the requirement for the request would discriminate against the defendant who does not know his rights. **(143)** The defendant who does not ask for counsel is the very defendant who most needs counsel. **(144)** We cannot penalize a defendant who, not understanding his constitutional rights, does not make the formal request and by such failure demonstrates his helplessness. **(145)** To require the request would be to favor the defendant whose

> sophistication or status had fortuitously prompted him to make it. People v. Dorado, 62 Cal.2d 338, 351 (1965) (Tobriner, J.). . . .

(146) Accordingly we hold that an individual held for interrogation must be clearly informed that he has the right to consult with a lawyer and to have the lawyer with him during interrogation under the system for protecting the privilege we delineate today. **(147)** As with the warnings of the right to remain silent and that anything stated can be used in evidence against him, this warning is an absolute prerequisite to interrogation. **(148)** No amount of **circumstantial evidence** that the person may have been aware of this right will suffice to stand in its stead. **(149)** Only through such a warning is there ascertainable assurance that the accused was aware of this right.

(150) If an individual indicates that he wishes the assistance of counsel before any interrogation occurs, the authorities cannot rationally ignore or deny his request on the basis that the individual does not have or cannot afford a retained attorney. **(151)** The financial ability of the individual has no relationship to the scope of the rights involved here. **(152)** The privilege against self-incrimination secured by the Constitution applies to all individuals. **(153)** The need for counsel in order to protect the privilege exists for the **indigent** as well as the affluent. **(154)** In fact, were we to limit these constitutional rights to those who can retain an attorney, our decisions today would be of little significance. **(155)** The cases before us as well as the vast majority of confession cases with which we have dealt in the past involve those unable to retain counsel. **(156)** While authorities are not required to relieve the accused of his poverty, they have the obligation not to take advantage of indigence in the administration of justice. **(157)** Denial of counsel to the indigent at the time of interrogation while allowing an attorney to those who can afford one would be no more supportable by reason or logic than the similar situation at trial and on appeal struck down in Gideon v. Wainwright, 372 U.S. 335 (1963), and Douglas v. People of State of California, 372 U.S. 353 (1963).

(158) In order fully to apprise a person interrogated of the extent of his rights under this system then, it is necessary to warn him not only that he has the right to consult with an attorney, but also that if he is indigent a lawyer will be appointed to represent him. **(159)** Without this additional warning, the admonition of the right to consult with counsel would often be understood as meaning only that he can consult with a lawyer if he has one or has the funds to obtain one. **(160)** The warning of a right to counsel would be hollow if not couched in terms that would convey to the indigent—the person most often subjected to interrogation—the knowledge that he too has a right to have counsel present. **(161)** As with the warnings of the right to remain silent and of the general right to counsel, only by effective and express explanation to the indigent of this right can there be assurance that he was truly in a position to exercise it.

(162) Once warnings have been given, the subsequent procedure is clear. **(163)** If the individual indicates in any manner, at any time prior to or during questioning, that he wishes to remain silent, the interrogation must **cease**. **(164)** At this point he has shown that he intends to exercise his Fifth Amendment privilege; any statement taken after the person **invokes his privilege** cannot be other than the product of compulsion, subtle or otherwise. **(165)** Without the right to cut off questioning, the setting of in-custody interrogation operates on the individual to overcome free choice in producing a statement after the privilege has been once invoked. **(166)** If the individual states that he wants an attorney, the interrogation must cease until an attorney is present. **(167)** At that time, the individual must have an opportunity to confer with the attorney and to have him present during any subsequent questioning. **(168)** If the individual cannot obtain an attorney and he indicates that he wants one before speaking to police, they must respect his decision to remain silent.

(169) This does not mean, as some have suggested, that each police station must have a "station house lawyer" present at all times to advise prisoners. **(170)** It does mean, however, that if police propose to interrogate a person they must make known to him that he is entitled to a lawyer and that if he cannot afford one, a lawyer will be provided for him prior to any interrogation. **(171)** If authorities conclude that they will not provide counsel during a reasonable period of time in which investigation in the field is carried out, they may refrain from doing so without violating the person's Fifth Amendment privilege so long as they do not question him during that time.

(172) If the interrogation continues without the presence of an attorney and a statement is taken, a heavy burden rests on the government to demonstrate that the defendant knowingly and intelligently waived his privilege against self-incrimination and his right to retained or appointed counsel. Escobedo v. State of Illinois, 378 U.S. 478, 490, n. 14. **(173)** This Court has always set high standards of proof for the waiver of constitutional rights, Johnson v. Zerbst, 304 U.S. 458 (1938), and we reassert these standards as applied to in custody interrogation. **(174)** Since the State is responsible for establishing the isolated circumstances under which the interrogation takes place and has the only means of making available corroborated evidence of warnings given during incommunicado interrogation, the burden is rightly on its shoulders.

(175) An express statement that the individual is willing to make a statement and does not want an attorney followed closely by a statement could constitute a waiver. **(176)** But a valid waiver will not be presumed simply from the silence of the accused after warnings are given or simply from the fact that a confession was in fact eventually obtained. **(177)** A statement we made in Carnley v. Cochran, 369 U.S. 506, 516 (1962), is applicable here:

> Presuming waiver from a silent record is impermissible. **(178)** The record must show, or there must be an allegation and evidence

> which show, that an accused was offered counsel but intelligently and understandingly rejected the offer. **(179)** Anything less is not waiver.

See also Glasser v. United States, 315 U.S. 60 (1942). **(180)** Moreover, where in-custody interrogation is involved, there is no room for the contention that the privilege is waived if the individual answers some questions or gives some information on his own prior to invoking his right to remain silent when interrogated.

(181) Whatever the testimony of the authorities as to waiver of rights by an accused, the fact of lengthy interrogation or incommunicado incarceration before a statement is made is strong evidence that the accused did not validly waive his rights. **(182)** In these circumstances the fact that the individual eventually made a statement is consistent with the conclusion that the compelling influence of the interrogation finally forced him to do so. **(183)** It is inconsistent with any notion of a voluntary relinquishment of the privilege. **(184)** Moreover, any evidence that the accused was threatened, tricked, or cajoled into a waiver will, of course, show that the defendant did not voluntarily waive his privilege. **(185)** The requirement of warnings and waiver of rights is a fundamental with respect to the Fifth Amendment privilege and not simply a preliminary ritual to existing methods of interrogation.

(186) The warnings required and the waiver necessary in accordance with our opinion today are, in the absence of a fully effective equivalent, prerequisites to the admissibility of any statement made by a defendant. **(187)** No distinction can be drawn between statements which are direct confessions and statements which amount to "admissions" of part or all of an offense. **(188)** The privilege against self-incrimination protects the individual from being compelled to incriminate himself in any manner; it does not distinguish degrees of incrimination. **(189)** Similarly, for precisely the same reason, no distinction may be drawn between inculpatory statements and statements alleged to be merely "exculpatory." **(190)** If a statement made were in fact truly exculpatory it would, of course, never be used by the prosecution. **(191)** In fact, statements merely intended to be exculpatory by the defendant are often used to impeach his testimony at trial or to demonstrate untruths in the statement given under interrogation and thus to prove guilt by implication. **(192)** These statements are incriminating in any meaningful sense of the word and may not be used without the full warnings and effective waiver required for any other statement. **(193)** In *Escobedo* itself, the defendant fully intended his accusation of another as the slayer to be exculpatory as to himself.

(194) The principles announced today deal with the protection which must be given to the privilege against self-incrimination when the individual is first subjected to police interrogation while in custody at the station or otherwise deprived of his freedom of action in any significant way. **(195)** It is at this point that our adversary system of criminal proceedings commences, distinguishing itself at the outset from the inquisitorial system recognized in some countries. **(196)** Under the system of warnings we delineate today or under any other system which may be devised and found effective, the safeguards to be erected about the privilege must come into play at this point.

(197) Our decision is not intended to hamper the traditional function of police officers in investigating crime. See Escobedo v. State of Illinois, 378 U.S. 478, 492. **(198)** When an individual is in custody on **probable cause**, the police may, of course, seek out evidence in the field to be used at trial against him. **(199)** Such investigation may include inquiry of persons not under restraint. **(200)** General on-the-scene questioning as to facts surrounding a crime or other general questioning of citizens in the fact-finding process is not affected by our holding. **(201)** It is an act of responsible citizenship for individuals to give whatever information they may have to aid in law enforcement. **(202)** In such situations the compelling atmosphere inherent in the process of in-custody interrogation is not necessarily present.

(203) In dealing with statements obtained through interrogation, we do not purport to find all confessions inadmissible. **(204)** Confessions remain a proper element in law enforcement. **(205)** Any statement given freely and voluntarily without any compelling influences is, of course, **admissible in evidence**. **(206)** The fundamental import of the privilege while an individual is in custody is not whether he is allowed to talk to the police without the benefit of warnings and counsel, but whether he can be interrogated. **(207)** There is no requirement that police stop a person who enters a police station and states that he wishes to confess to a crime, or a person who calls the police to offer a confession or any other statement he desires to make. **(208)** Volunteered statements of any kind are not barred by the Fifth Amendment and their admissibility is not affected by our holding today.

(209) To summarize, we hold that when an individual is taken into custody or otherwise deprived of his freedom by the authorities in any significant way and is subjected to questioning, the privilege against self-incrimination is jeopardized. **(210)** Procedural safeguards must be employed to protect the privilege and unless other fully effective means are adopted to notify the person of his right of silence and to assure that the exercise of the right will be scrupulously honored, the following measures are required. **(211)** He must be warned prior to any questioning that he has the right to remain silent, that anything he says can be used against him in a court of law, that he has the right to the presence of an attorney, and that if he cannot afford an attorney one will be appointed for him prior to any questioning if he so desires. **(212)** Opportunity to exercise these rights must be afforded to him throughout the interrogation. **(213)** After such warnings have been given, and such opportunity afforded him, the individual may knowingly and intelligently waive these rights and agree to answer questions or make a statement. **(214)** But unless and until such warnings and waiver are demonstrated by the prosecution at trial, no evidence obtained as a result of interrogation can be used against him.

IV.

(215) A recurrent argument made in these cases is that society's need for interrogation outweighs the privilege. **(216)** This argument is not unfamiliar to this Court. See, e.g., Chambers v. State of Florida, 309 U.S. 227, 240—241 (1940). **(217)** The whole thrust of our foregoing discussion demonstrates that the Constitution has prescribed the rights of the individual when confronted with the power of government when it provided in the Fifth Amendment that an individual cannot be compelled to be a witness against himself. **(218)** That right cannot be abridged. . . .

(219) If the individual desires to exercise his privilege, he has the right to do so. **(220)** This is not for the authorities to decide. **(221)** An attorney may advise his client not to talk to police until he has had an opportunity to investigate the case, or he may wish to be present with his client during any police questioning. **(222)** In doing so an attorney is merely exercising the good professional judgment he has been taught. **(223)** This is not cause for considering the attorney a menace to law enforcement. **(224)** He is merely carrying out what he is sworn to do under his oath—to protect to the extent of his ability the rights of his client. **(225)** In fulfilling this responsibility the attorney plays a vital role in the administration of criminal justice under our Constitution.

(226) In announcing these principles, we are not unmindful of the burdens which law enforcement officials must bear, often under trying circumstances. **(227)** We also fully recognize the obligation of all citizens to aid in enforcing the criminal laws. **(228)** This Court, while protecting individual rights, has always given ample latitude to law enforcement agencies in the legitimate exercise of their duties. **(229)** The limits we have placed on the interrogation process should not constitute an undue interference with a proper system of law enforcement. **(230)** As we have noted, our decision does not in any way preclude police from carrying out their traditional investigatory functions. **(231)** Although confessions may play an important role in some convictions, the cases before us present graphic examples of the overstatement of the "need" for confessions. **(232)** In each case authorities conducted interrogations ranging up to five days in duration despite the presence, through standard investigating practices, of considerable evidence against each defendant. . . .

(233) It is also urged upon us that we withhold decision on this issue until state legislative bodies and advisory groups have had an opportunity to deal with these problems by rule making. **(234)** We have already pointed out that the Constitution does not require any specific code of procedures for protecting the privilege against self-incrimination during custodial interrogation. **(235)** Congress and the States are free to develop their own safeguards for the privilege, so long as they are fully as effective as those described above in informing accused persons of their right of silence and in affording a continuous opportunity to exercise it. **(236)** In any event, however, the issues presented are of constitutional dimensions and must be determined by the courts. **(237)** The admissibility of a statement in the face of a claim that it was obtained in violation of the defendant's constitutional rights is an issue the resolution of which has long since been undertaken by this Court. See Hopt v. People of Territory of Utah, 110 U.S. 574 (1884). **(238)** Judicial solutions to problems of constitutional dimension have evolved decade by decade. **(239)** As courts have been presented with the need to enforce constitutional rights, they have found means of doing so. **(240)** That was our responsibility when *Escobedo* was before us and it is our responsibility today. **(241)** Where rights secured by the Constitution are involved, there can be no rule making or legislation which would abrogate them.

V.

(242) Because of the nature of the problem and because of its recurrent significance in numerous cases, we have to this point discussed the relationship of the Fifth Amendment privilege to police interrogation without specific concentration on the facts of the cases before us. **(243)** We turn now to these facts to consider the application to these cases of the constitutional principles discussed above. **(244)** In each instance, we have concluded that statements were obtained from the defendant under circumstances that did not meet constitutional standards for protection of the privilege. . . . [The Court applies the principles to the cases considered and renders judgment in each case.]

(245) *It is so ordered*. . . . [Justices Clark, Harlan, and White wrote concurring and/or dissenting opinions, which are omitted here.]

TASK 6.A.1. Case Brief

Write a case brief of *Miranda v. Arizona* using the template below.

Case name
Court & Year

Rule of the case:
Facts:
Procedural history:
Issue:
Holding:
Reasoning:
Disposition:
Comments:

TASK 6.A.2. Criminal Procedure Vocabulary Definitions (List 1)

Fill in each definition with the appropriate term from the list below. Consult a law dictionary or an English-to-English dictionary to confirm that you have matched each term with the correct definition. If multiple forms of a term are provided, you may not need to use all of the forms in the blanks.

admissibility *(noun)*; admissible *(adjective)*; "admissible in evidence"
apprise [someone] of her/his rights *(verb)*
cease *(verb)*
circumstantial evidence *(noun)*
coercion *(noun)*; coerce *(verb)*
compulsion *(noun)*; compel *(verb)*
exercise/invoke a privilege *(verb)*
exculpatory vs. inculpatory *(adjective)*
extort vs. obtain a confession *(verb)*
inadmissible *(adjective)*
incommunicado *(adjective)*
indigent *(adjective)*
probable cause *(noun)*
prosecute *(verb)*; prosecutor *(noun)*; prosecution *(noun)*
waive *(verb)*; waiver *(noun)*

1. In ____________________ interrogations, the interrogated party cannot communicate with anyone apart from her interrogators.

2. If a police officer ____________________ a confession from a suspect, she uses physical force, threats of physical force, and/or other aggressive tactics to obtain the confession.

3. To ____________________ someone to do something means to influence that person to undertake some action by using force or threats. A very close synonym is the verb ____________________.

4. The verb ____________________ refers to the act of instituting criminal proceedings against an individual.

5. A/an ____________________ is the act of giving up a right to something. In the interrogation setting, individuals can give up their privilege against self-incrimination by letting the police officers know that they wish to speak and/or do not want to consult an attorney.

6. If a person is ____________________, she is very poor and cannot afford legal representation.

7. When an individual communicates to police officers that she wants to remain silent and/or wishes to consult with an attorney, she ____________________ or ____________________ her privilege against self-incrimination.

8. ____________________ evidence is evidence that tends to show that an individual is *not* guilty. ____________________ evidence, in contrast, is evidence that tends to show that an individual *is* guilty.

9. ____________________ is the amount of suspicion required to arrest a suspect, conduct a search, or obtain a warrant. It requires a reasonable basis for believing that a suspect has committed or is going to commit a crime (for arrest), or that evidence of a crime will be found in the place to be searched (for a search).

10. ____________________ is a synonym for discontinuing or putting an end to something.

11. If a piece of evidence (e.g., a statement, an object) is ____________________, the trial court allows the factfinder to hear or see that evidence. The noun form is ____________________. The antonym is ____________________.

12. ____________________ refers to "indirect" evidence that requires one extra step—an inference—to connect it to a factual conclusion. Fingerprints at a crime scene (e.g., murder) are a good example. They do not directly prove a person's guilt, but suggest that the individual was at the crime scene and may have committed the murder.

13. When police officers ____________________ someone of her rights, they inform or advise her of her rights (e.g., the right to remain silent).

TASK 6.A.3. Questions for Discussion

Answer the following questions to assist you during a class discussion of the case. Indicate the sentence(s) in which you found the answer to each question.

1. What "procedural safeguards" does the Court establish to protect the privilege against self-incrimination?

2. What are the Court's reasons for creating these procedural safeguards? In other words, why does the privilege against self-incrimination (as enshrined in the Fifth Amendment) need protection?

3. In what situation(s) must these procedural safeguards be employed? To what situation(s) do these rules *not* apply?

4. According to the Court, what is the relationship between the Fifth and Sixth Amendments to the U.S. Constitution? (Note: the Sixth Amendment provides a right to counsel.)

5. Can a suspect give up her privilege against self-incrimination? How so?

6. What are the consequences of law enforcement authorities *not* informing suspects of their rights? Do you think this is just? Why or why not?

B. Criminal Procedure Case #2

In *Miranda*, the Court held that law enforcement officers have to provide a warning if they subject an individual to "custodial interrogation." This warning must contain the following information:

1. You have the right to remain silent;
2. Anything you say can and will be used against you in a court of law;
3. You have a right to an attorney; and
4. If you cannot afford an attorney, one will be appointed for you.

The *Miranda* Court also held that individuals may choose to waive their privilege against self-incrimination, but they must do so knowingly and intelligently.

Though *Miranda* provides detailed, specific instructions for police officers to follow, it is quite vague in other ways. For example, what qualifies as being "in custody or otherwise deprived of [one's] freedom of action in any significant way"? Is a suspect in custody, for the purposes of *Miranda*, if she is questioned by police officers on the side of a road? In an office building? At home? Furthermore, what exactly constitutes "interrogation"? Is a suspect interrogated if she overhears a conversation between police officers and feels compelled to speak? What does it mean to "knowingly and intelligently" waive one's rights? Does nodding one's head qualify as a knowing and intelligent waiver? Or is this insufficient? The cases in this chapter provide some answers to these questions.

The next three cases address the "in custody" element of *Miranda*.

STANSBURY v. CALIFORNIA

Supreme Court of the United States, 1994.
511 U.S. 318, 114 S.Ct. 1526, 128 L.Ed.2d 293, 62 USLW 4279.

PER CURIAM.

(1) This case concerns the rules for determining whether a person being questioned by law enforcement officers is held in custody, and thus entitled to the warnings required by *Miranda v. Arizona,* 384 U.S. 436 (1966). **(2)** We hold, not for the first time, that an officer's subjective and undisclosed view concerning whether the person being interrogated is a suspect is irrelevant to the assessment whether the person is in custody.

I

(3) Ten-year-old Robyn Jackson disappeared from a playground in Baldwin Park, California, at around 6:30 p.m. on September 28, 1982. **(4)** Early the next morning, about 10 miles away in Pasadena, Andrew Zimmerman observed a large man emerge from a turquoise American sedan and throw something into a nearby flood control channel. **(5)** Zimmerman called the police, who arrived at the scene and discovered the girl's body in the channel. **(6)** There was evidence that she had been raped, and the cause of death was determined to be asphyxia complicated by blunt force trauma to the head.

(7) Lieutenant Thomas Johnston, a detective with the Los Angeles County Sheriff's Department, investigated the **homicide**. **(8)** From witnesses interviewed on the day the body was discovered, he learned that Robyn had talked to two ice cream truck drivers, one being **petitioner** Robert Edward Stansbury, in the hours before her disappearance. **(9)** Given these contacts, Johnston thought Stansbury and the other driver might have some connection with the homicide or knowledge thereof, but for reasons unimportant here Johnston considered only the other driver to be a leading suspect. **(10)** After the suspect driver was brought in for interrogation, Johnston asked Officer Lee of the Baldwin Park Police Department to contact Stansbury to see if he would come in for questioning as a potential witness.

(11) Lee and three other plainclothes officers arrived at Stansbury's trailer home at about 11:00 that evening. **(12)** The officers surrounded the door and Lee knocked. **(13)** When Stansbury answered, Lee told him the officers were investigating a homicide to which Stansbury was a possible witness and asked if he would accompany them to the police station to answer some questions. **(14)** Stansbury agreed to the interview and accepted a ride to the station in the front seat of Lee's police car.

(15) At the station, Lieutenant Johnston, in the presence of another officer, questioned Stansbury about his whereabouts and activities during the afternoon and evening of September 28. **(16)** Neither Johnston nor the other officer **issued *Miranda* warnings**. **(17)** Stansbury told the officers (among other things) that on the evening of the 28th he spoke with the victim at about 6:00, returned to his trailer home after work at 9:00, and left the trailer at about midnight in his housemate's turquoise, American-made car. **(18)** This last detail aroused Johnston's suspicions, as the turquoise car matched the description of the one Andrew Zimmerman had observed in Pasadena. **(19)** When Stansbury, in response to a further question, admitted to prior convictions for rape, kidnaping, and child molestation, Johnston terminated the interview and another officer **advised Stansbury of his *Miranda* rights**. **(20)** Stansbury declined to make further statements, requested an attorney, and was arrested. **(21)** **Respondent** State of California **charged** Stansbury with first-degree murder and other crimes.

(22) Stansbury filed a pretrial **motion to suppress** all statements made at the station, and the evidence discovered as a result of those statements. **(23)** The trial court denied the motion in relevant part, ruling that Stansbury was not "in custody"—and thus not entitled to *Miranda* warnings—until he mentioned that he had taken his housemate's turquoise car for a midnight drive. **(24)** Before that stage of the interview, the trial court reasoned, "the focus in [Lieutenant Johnston's] mind certainly was on the other ice cream [truck] driver," Tr. 2368; only "after Mr. Stansbury made the comment . . . describing the . . . turquoise-colored automobile" did Johnston's suspicions "shif[t] to Mr. Stansbury," *ibid.* **(25)** Based upon its conclusion that Stansbury was not in custody until Johnston's suspicions had focused on him, the trial court permitted the prosecution to introduce in its case in chief the statements Stansbury made before that time. **(26)** At trial, the jury **convicted** Stansbury of first-degree murder, rape, kidnaping, and lewd act on a child under the age of 14, and fixed the penalty for the first-degree murder at death.

(27) The California Supreme Court affirmed. **(28)** Before determining whether Stansbury was in custody during the interview at the station, the court set out what it viewed as the applicable legal standard:

> In deciding the custody issue, the totality of the circumstances is relevant, and no one factor is **dispositive**. **(29)** However, the most important considerations include (1) the site of the interrogation, (2) whether the investigation has focused on the subject, (3) whether the objective indicia of arrest are present, and (4) the length and form of questioning. 4 Cal.4th 1017, 1050 (1993) (internal quotation marks omitted).

(30) The court proceeded to analyze the second factor in detail, in the end accepting the trial court's factual determination "that suspicion focused on [Stansbury] only when he mentioned that he had driven a turquoise car on the night of the crime." *Id.,* at 1052. **(31)** The court "conclude[d] that [Stansbury] was not subject to custodial interrogation before he mentioned the turquoise car," and thus approved the trial court's ruling that *Miranda v. Arizona,* did not bar the admission of statements Stansbury made before that point. 4 Cal.4th, at 1054.

(32) We granted certiorari. 510 U.S. 943 (1993).

II

(33) We held in *Miranda* that a person questioned by law enforcement officers after being "taken into custody or otherwise deprived of his freedom of action in any significant way" must first "be warned that he has a right to remain silent, that any statement he does make may be used as evidence against him, and that he has a right to the presence of an attorney, either retained or appointed." 384 U.S., at 444. **(34)** Statements elicited in noncompliance with this rule may not be admitted for certain purposes in a criminal trial. **(35)** Compare *id.,* at 492, 494, with *Harris v. New York,* 401 U.S. 222 (1971). **(36)** An officer's obligation to administer *Miranda* warnings attaches, however, "only where there has been such a restriction on a person's freedom as to render him 'in custody.'" *Oregon v. Mathiason,* 429 U.S. 492, 495 (1977) *(per curiam);* see also *Illinois v. Perkins,* 496 U.S. 292, 296 (1990). **(37)** In determining whether an individual was in custody, a court must examine all of the circumstances surrounding the interrogation, but "the ultimate inquiry is simply whether there [was] a 'formal arrest or restraint on freedom of movement' of the degree associated with a formal arrest." *California v. Beheler,* 463 U.S. 1121, 1125 (1983) *(per curiam)* (quoting *Mathiason, supra,* 429 U.S., at 495).

(38) Our decisions make clear that the initial determination of custody depends on the objective circumstances of the interrogation, not on the subjective views harbored by either the interrogating officers or the person being questioned. **(39)** In *Beckwith v. United States,* 425 U.S. 341 (1976), for example, the defendant, without being advised of his *Miranda* rights, made incriminating statements to Government agents during an interview in a private home. **(40)** He later asked that *Miranda* "be extended to cover interrogation in non-custodial circumstances after a police investigation has focused on the suspect." 425 U.S., at 345 (internal quotation marks omitted). **(41)** We found his argument unpersuasive, explaining that it "was the compulsive aspect of custodial interrogation, and not the strength or content of the government's suspicions at the time the questioning was conducted, which led the Court to impose the *Miranda* requirements with regard to custodial questioning." *Id.,* at 346–347 (internal quotation marks omitted). **(42)** As a result, we concluded that the defendant was not entitled to *Miranda* warnings: "Although the 'focus' of an investigation may indeed have been on Beckwith at the time of the interview . . . , he hardly found himself in the custodial situation described by the *Miranda* Court as the basis for its holding." 425 U.S., at 347.

(43) *Berkemer v. McCarty,* 468 U.S. 420 (1984), reaffirmed the conclusions reached in *Beckwith.* **(44)** *Berkemer* concerned the roadside questioning of a motorist detained in a traffic stop. **(45)** We decided that the motorist was not in custody for purposes of *Miranda* even though the traffic officer "apparently decided as soon as [the motorist] stepped out of his car that [the motorist] would be taken into custody and charged with a traffic offense." 468 U.S., at 442. **(46)** The reason, we explained, was that the officer "never communicated his intention to" the motorist during the relevant questioning. *Ibid.* **(47)** The lack of communication was crucial, for under *Miranda* "[a] policeman's unarticulated plan has no bearing on the question whether a suspect was 'in custody' at a particular time"; rather, "the only relevant inquiry is how a reasonable man in the suspect's position would have understood his situation." 468 U.S., at 442. **(48)** Other cases of ours have been consistent in adhering to this understanding of the custody element of *Miranda.* See, *e.g., Mathiason, supra,* 429 U.S., at 495 ("Nor is the requirement of warnings to be imposed simply because . . . the questioned person is one whom the police suspect. *Miranda* warnings are required only where there has been such a restriction on a person's freedom as to render him 'in custody'"); *Beheler, supra,* 463 U.S., at 1124, n. 2 ("Our holding in *Mathiason* reflected our earlier decision in *[Beckwith],* in which we rejected the notion that the 'in custody' requirement was satisfied merely because the police interviewed a person who was the 'focus' of a criminal investigation"); *Minnesota v. Murphy,* 465 U.S. 420, 431 (1984) ("The mere fact that an investigation has focused on a suspect does not trigger the need for *Miranda* warnings in noncustodial settings, and the probation officer's knowledge and intent have no bearing on the outcome of this case") (citation omitted); cf. *Pennsylvania v. Bruder,* 488 U.S. 9, 11, n. 2 (1988).

(49) It is well settled, then, that a police officer's subjective view that the individual under questioning is a suspect, if undisclosed, does not bear upon the question whether the individual is in custody for purposes of *Miranda.* See F. Inbau, J. Reid, & J. Buckley, Criminal Interrogation and Confessions 232, 236, 297–298 (3d ed. 1986). **(50)** The same principle obtains if an officer's undisclosed assessment is that the person being questioned is not a suspect. **(51)** In either instance, one cannot expect the person under interrogation to probe the officer's innermost thoughts. **(52)** Save as they are communicated or otherwise manifested to the person being questioned, an officer's evolving but unarticulated suspicions do not affect the objective circumstances of an interrogation or interview, and thus cannot affect the *Miranda* custody inquiry. **(53)** "The threat to a citizen's Fifth Amendment rights that *Miranda* was designed to neutralize has little to do with the strength of an interrogating officer's suspicions." *Berkemer, supra,* 468 U.S., at 435, n. 22.

(54) An officer's knowledge or beliefs may bear upon the custody issue if they are conveyed, by word or deed, to the individual being questioned. Cf. *Michigan v. Chesternut,* 486 U.S. 567, 575, n. 7 (1988) (citing *United States v. Mendenhall,* 446 U.S. 544, 554, n. 6 (1980) (opinion of Stewart, J.)). **(55)** Those beliefs are relevant only to the extent they would affect how a reasonable person in the position of the individual being questioned would gauge the breadth of his or her "'freedom of action.'" *Berkemer, supra,* 468 U.S., at 440. **(56)** Even a clear statement from an officer that the person under interrogation is a prime suspect is not, in itself, dispositive of the custody issue, for some suspects are free to come and go until the police decide to make an arrest. **(57)** The weight and pertinence of any communications regarding the officer's degree of suspicion will depend upon the facts and circumstances of the particular case. **(58)** In sum, an officer's views concerning the nature of an interrogation, or beliefs concerning the potential culpability of the individual being questioned, may be one among many factors that bear upon the assessment whether that individual was in custody, but only if the officer's views or beliefs were somehow manifested to the individual under interrogation and would have affected how a reasonable person in that position would perceive his or her freedom to leave. **(59)** (Of course, instances may arise in which the officer's undisclosed views are relevant in testing the credibility of his or her account of what happened during an interrogation; but it is the objective surroundings, and not any undisclosed views, that control the *Miranda* custody inquiry.)

(60) We decide on this state of the record that the California Supreme Court's analysis of whether Stansbury was in custody is not consistent in all respects with the foregoing principles. **(61)** Numerous statements in the court's opinion are open to the interpretation that the court regarded the officers' subjective beliefs regarding Stansbury's status as a suspect (or nonsuspect) as significant in and of themselves, rather than as relevant only to the extent they influenced the objective conditions surrounding his interrogation. . . . **(62)** So understood, the court's analysis conflicts with our precedents. **(63)** The court's apparent conclusion that Stansbury's *Miranda* rights were triggered by virtue of the fact that he had become the focus of the officers' suspicions . . . is incorrect as well. **(64)** Our cases make clear, in no uncertain terms, that any inquiry into whether the interrogating officers have focused their suspicions upon the individual being questioned (assuming those suspicions remain undisclosed) is not relevant for purposes of *Miranda.* See generally 1 W. LaFave & J. Israel, Criminal Procedure §6.6(a), pp. 489–490 (1984).

(65) The State acknowledges that Lieutenant Johnston's and the other officers' subjective and undisclosed suspicions (or lack thereof) do not bear upon the question whether Stansbury was in custody, for purposes of *Miranda,* during the station house interview. **(66)** It maintains, however, that the objective facts in the record support a finding that Stansbury was not in custody until his arrest. **(67)** Stansbury, by contrast, asserts that the objective circumstances show that he was in custody during the entire interrogation. **(68)** We think it appropriate for the California Supreme Court to consider this question in the first instance. **(69)** We therefore reverse its judgment and remand the case for further proceedings not inconsistent with this opinion.

(70) *It is so ordered. . . .*

TASK 6.B.1. Case Brief

Write a case brief of *Stansbury v. California* using the template on page 392.

TASK 6.B.2. Criminal Procedure Vocabulary Definitions (List 2)

Fill in each definition with the appropriate term from the list below. Consult a law dictionary or an English-to-English dictionary to confirm that you have matched each term with the correct definition.

advise [someone] of her rights *(verb)*
charge [someone] with a crime *(verb)*
convict [someone] of a crime *(verb)*
dispositive *(adjective)*
homicide *(noun)*
issue *Miranda* warnings *(verb)*
motion to suppress *(noun)*
per curiam (adjective)
petitioner *(noun)*
respondent *(noun)*

1. ____________________ refers to the unlawful killing of a human being. Murder and manslaughter are two types.

2. A/an ____________________ opinion is issued in the name of the entire Court as opposed to an individual Justice. These opinions tend to be written when a case can or must be disposed of quickly.

3. Police officers must ____________________ individuals of their right to remain silent when they take them into custody and interrogate them. In other words, they have to inform them of their rights by ____________________ *Miranda* warnings.

4. When the defendant files a/an ____________________, she requests the court to exclude evidence because she claims that it was obtained illegally.

5. The ____________________ is the person who was not satisfied with a lower court's decision and requests the Court to review her case (by filing what's called a "petition for a writ of certiorari"). The person against whom the petition is filed is called the ____________________. In courts other than the Supreme Court of the United States, the terms "appellant" and "appellee" may be used instead. Note that either party could be the original plaintiff or defendant.

6. When law enforcement authorities ____________________ an individual with a crime, they allege that the person has committed a criminal offense. It is a formal accusation of wrongdoing. (See Appendix D: Steps in the Criminal Justice Process.)

7. An individual is ____________________ of a crime when, following a trial, the factfinder returns a guilty verdict. (See Appendix D: Steps in the Criminal Justice Process.)

8. If a question, situation, or evidence is ____________________, it brings a case to an end. In essence, it provides the "solution" for the case.

TASK 6.B.3. Questions for Discussion

Answer the following questions to assist you during a class discussion of the case. Indicate the sentence(s) in which you found the answer to each question.

1. What crime is being investigated in this case?

2. Why was Stansbury questioned by the police? Where was he questioned?

3. Was Stansbury advised of his *Miranda* rights? At what point? Why?

4. Briefly state the facts and procedural history of the case.

5. What test did the California Supreme Court use to determine custody? According to the Supreme Court, why does this "conflict[] with our precedents"? (See sentence (62).) What are the disadvantages of this test?

6. What test does the United States Supreme Court use to determine custody? What are the advantages of this test?

7. The Court states in sentence (52), "Save as they are communicated or otherwise manifested to the person being questioned, an officer's evolving but unarticulated suspicions do not affect the objective circumstances of an interrogation or interview, and thus cannot affect the *Miranda* custody inquiry." Can you explain in your own words what this means?

8. Hypothetical: Alan's wife, Beth, was killed while she was working after hours in her office. Beth's death is being investigated as a homicide, and the police have three suspects: Beth's boss, a jealous coworker, and Alan. The police strongly believe that Alan might have had a motive to kill Beth, as several friends and neighbors indicated that the two had "explosive" fights in the weeks leading up to Beth's murder. Detectives stop by Alan's house to ask him some questions, telling him that he is a "witness" who might be able to provide valuable information about his wife's work relationships. Alan invites the officers into his house and within two minutes breaks down, confessing: "I killed my wife. She was cheating on me." The detectives promptly arrest Alan and advise him of his *Miranda* rights.

   Could the statement that Alan killed his wife be used against him at trial?

   What if the officers inform Alan that he is one of the suspects in the murder investigation? Would this change your answer?

C. Criminal Procedure Essay Question #1

Answer the hypothetical on the next page using the previous cases in this chapter to inform your answer. Use a piece of paper or a blank document on your computer to outline your response before you begin writing.

Suggested response time: **30 minutes**.

QUESTION

Late one evening, police officer Mike saw a car suspiciously weaving in and out of a lane on a local road. He followed the car for one mile before pulling it over. Mike parked his police vehicle right behind the car, which belonged to Nick. He walked over to Nick's car and asked him to step out of the vehicle. Mike asked Nick if he had had anything to drink. Nick answered, "No, I don't drink alcohol." Mike then performed a roadside sobriety test consisting of a walk-and-turn and a one-leg stand.[1] Nick could not keep his balance. This led Mike to believe that Nick was drunk. Mike pushed Nick up against the side of the police car and yelled at him to keep his hands on the car where Mike could see them. Mike then walked over to Nick's car and peered inside the window using a flashlight. He asked again, "Are you sure you didn't have anything to drink?" Still pressed up against the police car, Nick exclaimed, "Okay, I had three beers and smoked a little weed,[2] but I am fine to drive. You won't find anything in the car." Upon hearing this, Mike walked back over to Nick, placed him under arrest, and handcuffed him. He also read Nick his *Miranda* rights.

Nick has been charged with driving under the influence and other criminal offenses based on evidence seized during a search of his vehicle. Would Nick's statements be admissible against him at trial?

D. Criminal Procedure Case #3

OREGON v. MATHIASON

Supreme Court of the United States, 1977.
429 U.S. 492, 97 S.Ct. 711, 50 L.Ed.2d 714.

PER CURIAM.

(1) Respondent Carl Mathiason was convicted of **first-degree burglary** after a **bench trial** in which his confession was critical to the State's case. **(2)** At trial he moved to suppress the confession as the fruit of questioning by the police not preceded by the warnings required in Miranda v. Arizona, 384 U.S. 436 (1966). **(3)**

---

[1] Roadside sobriety tests are used by police officers to determine whether a driver is under the influence of alcohol. The walk-and-turn test entails walking in a straight line with the heel of one foot touching the toes of another, and then turning around and doing the same until returning to the point where the driver began the test. The one-leg stand entails standing with one foot about six inches off the ground while counting to 30 seconds. If a driver is not able to stay balanced during the tests, uses her arms to maintain balance, starts hopping, steps out of the line, and/or can't follow instructions, it suggests that she is under the influence of alcohol.

[2] "Weed" is a colloquial term for marijuana.

The trial court refused to exclude the confession because it found that Mathiason was not in custody at the time of the confession.

(4) The Oregon Court of Appeals affirmed respondent's conviction, but on his petition for review in the Supreme Court of Oregon that court by a divided vote reversed the conviction. **(5)** It found that although Mathiason had not been arrested or otherwise formally detained, "the interrogation took place in a 'coercive environment'" of the sort to which *Miranda* was intended to apply. **(6)** The court **conceded** that its holding was contrary to decisions in other jurisdictions, and referred in particular to *People v. Yukl*, 25 N.Y.2d 585 (1969). **(7)** The State of Oregon has petitioned for certiorari to review the judgment of the Supreme Court of Oregon. **(8)** We think that court has **read *Miranda* too broadly**, and we therefore reverse its judgment.

(9) The Supreme Court of Oregon described the factual situation surrounding the confession as follows:

> An officer of the State Police investigated a theft at a residence near Pendleton. **(10)** He asked the lady of the house which had been **burglarized** if she suspected anyone. **(11)** She replied that the defendant was the only one she could think of. **(12)** The defendant was a parolee and a 'close associate' of her son. **(13)** The officer tried to contact defendant on three or four occasions with no success. **(14)** Finally, about 25 days after the burglary, the officer left his card at defendant's apartment with a note asking him to call because 'I'd like to discuss something with you.' **(15)** The next afternoon the defendant did call. **(16)** The officer asked where it would be convenient to meet. **(17)** The defendant had no preference; so the officer asked if the defendant could meet him at the state patrol office in about an hour and a half, about 5:00 p.m. **(18)** The patrol office was about two blocks from defendant's apartment. **(19)** The building housed several state agencies.
>
> **(20)** The officer met defendant in the hallway, shook hands and took him into an office. **(21)** The defendant was told he was not under arrest. **(22)** The door was closed. **(23)** The two sat across a desk. **(24)** The police radio in another room could be heard. **(25)** The officer told defendant he wanted to talk to him about a burglary and that his truthfulness would possibly be considered by the **district attorney** or judge. **(26)** The officer further advised that the police believed defendant was involved in the burglary and (falsely stated that) defendant's fingerprints were found at the scene. **(27)** The defendant sat for a few minutes and then said he had taken the property. **(28)** This

> occurred within five minutes after defendant had come to the office. **(29)** The officer then advised defendant of his *Miranda* rights and took a taped confession.
>
> **(30)** At the end of the taped conversation the officer told defendant he was not arresting him at this time; he was released to go about his job and return to his family. **(31)** The officer said he was referring the case to the district attorney for him to determine whether criminal charges would be brought. **(32)** It was 5:30 p.m. when the defendant left the office.
>
> **(33)** The officer gave all the testimony relevant to this issue. **(34)** The defendant did not **take the stand** either at the hearing on the motion to suppress or at the trial. 275 Or. 1, 3-4 (1976).

(35) The Supreme Court of Oregon reasoned from these facts that:

> We hold the interrogation took place in a 'coercive environment.' **(36)** The parties were in the offices of the State Police; they were alone behind closed doors; the officer informed the defendant he was a suspect in a theft and the authorities had evidence incriminating him in the crime; and the defendant was a **parolee** under supervision. **(37)** We are of the opinion that this evidence is not overcome by the evidence that the defendant came to the office in response to a request and was told he was not under arrest. Id., at 5.

(38) Our decision in *Miranda* set forth rules of police procedure applicable to "custodial interrogation." **(39)** "By custodial interrogation, we mean questioning initiated by law enforcement officers after a person has been taken into custody or otherwise deprived of his freedom of action in any significant way." 384 U.S., at 444. **(40)** Subsequently we have found the *Miranda* principle applicable to questioning which takes place in a prison setting during a suspect's term of imprisonment on a separate offense, *Mathis v. United States*, 391 U.S. 1 (1968), and to questioning taking place in a suspect's home, after he has been arrested and is no longer free to go where he pleases, *Orozco v. Texas*, 394 U.S. 324 (1969).

(41) In the present case, however, there is no indication that the questioning took place in a context where respondent's freedom to depart was restricted in any way. **(42)** He came voluntarily to the police station, where he was immediately informed that he was not under arrest. **(43)** At the close of a ½-hour interview respondent did in fact leave the police station without hindrance. **(44)** It is clear from these facts that Mathiason was not in custody "or otherwise deprived of his freedom of action in any significant way."

(45) Such a noncustodial situation is not converted to one in which *Miranda* applies simply because a reviewing court concludes that, even in the absence of any formal arrest or restraint on freedom of movement, the questioning took place in a "coercive environment." **(46)** Any interview of one suspected of a crime by a police officer will have coercive aspects to it, simply by virtue of the fact that the police officer is part of a law enforcement system which may ultimately cause the suspect to be charged with a crime. **(47)** But police officers are not required to **administer** *Miranda* warnings to everyone whom they question. **(48)** Nor is the requirement of warnings to be imposed simply because the questioning takes place in the station house, or because the questioned person is one whom the police suspect. **(49)** *Miranda* warnings are required only where there has been such a restriction on a person's freedom as to render him "in custody." **(50)** It was that sort of coercive environment to which *Miranda* by its terms was made applicable, and to which it is limited.

(51) The officer's false statement about having discovered Mathiason's fingerprints at the scene was found by the Supreme Court of Oregon to be another circumstance contributing to the coercive environment which makes the *Miranda* rationale applicable. **(52)** Whatever relevance this fact may have to other issues in the case, it has nothing to do with whether respondent was in custody for purposes of the *Miranda* rule.

(53) The petition for certiorari is granted, the judgment of the Oregon Supreme Court is reversed, and the case is remanded for proceedings not inconsistent with this opinion.

(54) So ordered. . . .

Mr. Justice MARSHALL, dissenting.

(55) The respondent in this case was interrogated behind closed doors at police headquarters in connection with a burglary investigation. **(56)** He had been named by the victim of the burglary as a suspect, and was told by the police that they believed he was involved. **(57)** He was falsely informed that his fingerprints had been found at the scene, and in effect was advised that by cooperating with the police he could help himself. **(58)** Not until after he had confessed was he given the warnings set forth in *Miranda v. Arizona*, 384 U.S. 436 (1966).

(59) The Court today holds that for constitutional purposes all this is irrelevant because respondent had not "'been taken into custody or otherwise deprived of his freedom of action in any significant way.'" Ante, at [sentence 40], quoting *Miranda v. Arizona*, supra, at 444. **(60)** I do not believe that such a determination is possible on the record before us. **(61)** It is true that respondent was not formally placed under arrest, but surely formalities alone cannot control. **(62)** At the very least, if respondent entertained an objectively reasonable belief that he was not free to leave during the questioning, then he was "deprived of his freedom of action in a significant way." **(63)** Plainly the respondent could have so believed, after being told by the police that they thought he was involved in a burglary and that his fingerprints had been found at the scene. **(64)** Yet the majority is content to note that "there is no indication that . . . respondent's freedom to depart was restricted in any way," ante, at [sentence 42], as if a silent record (and no state-court findings) means that the State has sustained its burden, see Lego v. Twomey, 404 U.S. 477, 489 (1972), of demonstrating that respondent received his constitutional due.

(65) More fundamentally, however, I cannot agree with the Court's conclusion that if respondent were not in custody no warnings were required. **(66)** I recognize that *Miranda* is limited to custodial interrogations, but that is because, as we noted last Term, the facts in the *Miranda* cases raised only this "narrow issue." Beckwith v. United States, 425 U.S. 341, 345 (1976). **(67)** The rationale of *Miranda*, however, is not so easily cabined.

(68) *Miranda* requires warnings to "combat" a situation in which there are "inherently compelling pressures which work to undermine the individual's will to resist and to compel him to speak where he would not otherwise do so freely." 384 U.S., at 467. **(69)** It is of course true, as the Court notes, that "[a]ny interview of one suspected of a crime by a police officer will have coercive aspects to it." Ante, at [sentence 47]. **(70)** But it does not follow that because police "are not required to administer *Miranda* warnings to everyone whom they question," ibid., that they need not administer warnings to anyone, unless the factual setting of the *Miranda* cases is replicated. **(71)** Rather, faithfulness to *Miranda* requires us to distinguish situations that resemble the "coercive aspects" of custodial interrogation from those that more nearly resemble "(g)eneral on-the-scene questioning . . . or other general questioning of citizens in the fact-finding process" which *Miranda* states usually can take place without warnings. 384 U.S., at 477.

(72) In my view, even if respondent were not in custody, the coercive elements in the instant case were so pervasive as to require *Miranda*-type warnings. **(73)** Respondent was interrogated in "privacy" and in "unfamiliar surroundings," factors on which *Miranda* places great stress. Id., at 449-450; see also Beckwith v. United States, supra, at 346 n. 7. **(74)** The investigation had focused on respondent. **(75)** And respondent was subjected to some of the "deceptive stratagems," *Miranda v. Arizona*, supra, at 455, which called forth the *Miranda* decision. **(76)** I therefore agree with the Oregon Supreme Court that to excuse the absence of warnings given these facts is "contrary to the rationale expressed in *Miranda*." 275 Or. 1, 5 (1976).

(77) The privilege against self-incrimination "has always been 'as broad as the mischief against which it seeks to guard.'" Miranda v. Arizona, supra, at 459-460, quoting Counselman v. Hitchcock, 142 U.S. 547, 562 (1892). **(78)** Today's decision means, however, that the Fifth Amendment privilege does not provide full protection against mischiefs equivalent to, but different from, custodial interrogation. See also Beckwith v. United States, supra. **(79)** It is therefore important to note that the state courts remain free, in interpreting state constitutions, to guard against the evil clearly identified by this case.

(80) I respectfully dissent.

Mr. Justice STEVENS, dissenting.

(81) In my opinion the issues presented by this case are too important to be decided summarily. **(82)** Of particular importance is the fact that the respondent **was on parole** at the time of his interrogation in the police station. **(83)** This fact lends support to inconsistent conclusions.

(84) On the one hand, the State surely has greater power to question a parolee about his activities than to question someone else. **(85)** Moreover, as a practical matter, it seems unlikely that a *Miranda* warning would have much effect on a parolee's choice between silence and responding to police interrogation. **(86)** Arguably, therefore, *Miranda* warnings are entirely inappropriate in the parole context.

(87) On the other hand, a parolee is technically in legal custody continuously until his sentence has been served. **(88)** Therefore, if a formalistic analysis of the custody question is to determine when the *Miranda* warning is necessary, a parolee should always be warned. **(89)** Moreover, *Miranda* teaches that even if a suspect is not in custody, warnings are necessary if he is "otherwise deprived of his freedom of action in any significant way." **(90)** If a parolee being questioned in a police station is not described by that language, today's decision qualifies that part of *Miranda* to some extent. **(91)** I believe we would have a better understanding of the extent of that qualification, and therefore of the situations in which warnings must be given to a suspect who is not technically in custody, if we had the benefit of full argument and plenary consideration.

(92) I therefore respectfully dissent from the Court's summary disposition.

TASK 6.D.1. Case Brief

Write a case brief of *Oregon v. Mathiason* using the template on page 392. Also include a summary of the dissenting opinions in your brief.

TASK 6.D.2. Criminal Procedure Vocabulary Definitions (List 3)

Fill in each definition with the appropriate term from the list on the next page. Consult a law dictionary or an English-to-English dictionary to confirm that you have matched each term with the correct definition. If multiple forms of a term are provided, you may not need to use all of the forms in the blanks.

administer [*Miranda* warnings] *(verb)*
bench trial *(noun)*
concede *(verb)*
district attorney *(noun)*
first-degree burglary *(noun)*; burglarize *(verb)*
parolee *(noun)*; be on parole *(verb)*
read [a case] broadly *(verb)*
take the stand *(verb)*

1. When a witness ____________________, she testifies in court.

2. To ____________________ something means to admit that something is true.

3. A/an ____________________ refers to a trial in which there is no jury. The judge acts as the factfinder in the case.

4. A/an ____________________ is someone who has been released early from prison. Once the individual is released, she is said to be ____________________, meaning that she is supervised by a parole officer.

5. When courts read a case ____________________, they interpret the case to have wide-ranging effects, with application to a large class of cases. The opposite is reading a case narrowly.

6. A/an ____________________ is a lawyer who represents the government in the prosecution of a crime.

7. ____________________ is a criminal offense involving the unlawful breaking and entering of a building with the purpose to commit a crime. When a crime is characterized as "first-degree," it is usually the most serious form of the offense (crimes may also be classified as "second-degree," "third-degree," and so on).

8. When a police officer ____________________ *Miranda* warnings, she reads the suspect her *Miranda* rights.

TASK 6.D.3. Questions for Discussion

Answer the questions on the next page to assist you during a class discussion of the case. Indicate the sentence(s) in which you found the answer to each question.

1. How and where was the defendant in this case questioned by the police? What was the questioning about?

2. Was the defendant advised of his *Miranda* rights? When? Was the defendant arrested?

3. What did the Supreme Court of Oregon hold? How does this conflict with the *Miranda* decision? What does the Supreme Court of the United States hold?

4. Would Justice Marshall like to expand or narrow the scope of *Miranda*? Why? And how?

5. In sentence (73), Justice Marshall states: "In my view, even if respondent were not in custody, the coercive elements in the instant case were so pervasive as to require *Miranda*-type warnings." Why and how does this statement conflict with the *Miranda* rule as it has been interpreted by the Supreme Court?

6. Justice Stevens writes a separate dissenting opinion, taking issue with the Court's custody determination. What is the focus of Justice Stevens' dissent?

7. Which facts in this case work <u>FOR</u> custody? Which facts work <u>AGAINST</u> custody? Which fact do you think weighs (or should weigh) most heavily in favor of custody?

<u>FOR custody</u>	<u>AGAINST custody</u>

8. Whose reading of *Miranda* do you find more convincing: the majority's or Justice Marshall's? Why?

E. Criminal Procedure Case #4

J.D.B. v. NORTH CAROLINA

Supreme Court of the United States, 2011.
564 U.S. 261, 131 S.Ct. 2394, 180 L.Ed.2d 310, 79 USLW 4504, 11 Cal. Daily Op. Serv. 7346, 2011 Daily Journal D.A.R. 8827, 22 Fla. L. Weekly Fed. S 1135.

Justice SOTOMAYOR delivered the opinion of the Court.

(1) This case presents the question whether the age of a child subjected to police questioning is relevant to the custody analysis of *Miranda v. Arizona,* 384 U.S. 436 (1966). **(2)** It is beyond dispute that children will often feel bound to submit to police questioning when an adult in the same circumstances would feel free to leave. **(3)** Seeing no reason for police officers or courts to blind themselves to that commonsense reality, we hold that a child's age properly informs the *Miranda* custody analysis.

I

A

(4) Petitioner J.D.B. was a 13-year-old, seventh-grade student attending class at Smith Middle School in Chapel Hill, North Carolina when he was removed from his classroom by a uniformed police officer, escorted to a closed-door conference room, and questioned by police for at least half an hour.

(5) This was the second time that police questioned J.D.B. in the span of a week. **(6)** Five days earlier, two home break-ins occurred, and various items were stolen. **(7)** Police stopped and questioned J.D.B. after he was seen behind a residence in the neighborhood where the crimes occurred. **(8)** That same day, police also spoke to J.D.B.'s grandmother—his legal guardian—as well as his aunt.

(9) Police later learned that a digital camera matching the description of one of the stolen items had been found at J.D.B.'s middle school and seen in J.D.B.'s possession. **(10)** Investigator DiCostanzo, the **juvenile** investigator with the local police force who had been assigned to the case, went to the school to question J.D.B. **(11)** Upon arrival, DiCostanzo informed the uniformed police officer on detail to the school (a so-called school resource officer), the assistant principal, and an administrative intern that he was there to question J.D.B. about the break-ins. **(12)** Although DiCostanzo asked the school administrators to verify J.D.B.'s date of birth, address, and parent contact information from school records, neither the police officers nor the school administrators contacted J.D.B.'s grandmother.

(13) The uniformed officer interrupted J.D.B.'s afternoon social studies class, removed J.D.B. from the classroom, and escorted him to a school conference room. **(14)** There, J.D.B. was met by DiCostanzo, the assistant principal, and the administrative intern. **(15)** The door to the conference room was closed. **(16)** With the two police officers and the two administrators present, J.D.B. was questioned for the next 30 to 45 minutes. **(17)** Prior to the commencement of questioning, J.D.B. was given neither *Miranda* warnings nor the opportunity to speak to his grandmother. **(18)** Nor was he informed that he was free to leave the room.

(19) Questioning began with small talk—discussion of sports and J.D.B.'s family life. **(20)** DiCostanzo asked, and J.D.B. agreed, to discuss the events of the prior weekend. **(21)** Denying any wrongdoing, J.D.B. explained that he had been in the neighborhood where the crimes occurred because he was seeking work mowing lawns. **(22)** DiCostanzo pressed J.D.B. for additional detail about his efforts to obtain work; asked J.D.B. to explain a prior incident, when one of the victims returned home to find J.D.B. behind her house; and confronted J.D.B. with the stolen camera. **(23)** The assistant principal urged J.D.B. to "do the right thing," warning J.D.B. that "the truth always comes out in the end." App. 99a, 112a.

(24) Eventually, J.D.B. asked whether he would "still be in trouble" if he returned the "stuff." *Ibid.* **(25)** In response, DiCostanzo explained that return of the stolen items would be helpful, but "this thing is going to court" regardless *Id.,* at 112a; *ibid.* ("[W]hat's done is done[;] now you need to help yourself by making it right"); see also *id.,* at 99a. **(26)** DiCostanzo then warned that he may need to seek a secure custody order if he believed that J.D.B. would continue to break into other homes. **(27)** When J.D.B. asked what a secure custody order was, DiCostanzo explained that "it's where you get sent to **juvenile detention** before court." *Id.,* at 112a.

(28) After learning of the prospect of juvenile detention, J.D.B. confessed that he and a friend were responsible for the break-ins. **(29)** DiCostanzo only then informed J.D.B. that he could refuse to answer the investigator's questions and that he was free to leave. **(30)** Asked whether he understood, J.D.B. nodded and provided further detail, including information about the location of the stolen items. **(31)** Eventually J.D.B. wrote a statement, at DiCostanzo's request. **(32)** When the bell rang indicating the end of the schoolday, J.D.B. was allowed to leave to catch the bus home.

B

(33) Two juvenile petitions were filed against J.D.B., each alleging one **count** of breaking and entering and one count of **larceny**. **(34)** J.D.B.'s **public defender** moved to suppress his statements and the evidence derived therefrom, arguing that suppression was necessary because J.D.B. had been "interrogated by police in a custodial setting without being afforded *Miranda* warning[s]," App. 89a, and because his statements were involuntary under the totality of the circumstances test, *id.,* at 142a; see *Schneckloth v. Bustamonte* 412 U.S. 218 (1973) (due process precludes admission of a confession where "a defendant's will was overborne" by the circumstances of the interrogation). **(35)** After a suppression hearing at which DiCostanzo and J.D.B. testified, the trial court denied the motion, deciding that J.D.B. was not in custody at the time of the schoolhouse interrogation and that his statements were voluntary. **(36)** As a result, J.D.B. entered a transcript of admission to all four counts, renewing his objection to the denial of his motion to suppress, and the court adjudicated J.D.B. **delinquent**.

(37) A divided panel of the North Carolina Court of Appeals affirmed. *In re J.D.B.,* 196 N.C.App. 234 (2009). **(38)** The North Carolina Supreme Court held, over two dissents, that J.D.B. was not in custody when he confessed, "declin[ing] to extend the test for custody to include consideration of the age . . . of an individual subjected to questioning by police." *In re J.D.B.,* 363 N.C. 664 (2009).

(39) We granted certiorari to determine whether the *Miranda* custody analysis includes consideration of a juvenile suspect's age.

II

A

(40) Any police interview of an individual suspected of a crime has "coercive aspects to it." *Oregon v. Mathiason,* 429 U.S. 492, 495, 97 S.Ct. 711, 50 L.Ed.2d 714 (1977) *(per curiam)*. **(41)** Only those interrogations that occur while a suspect is in police custody, however, "heighte[n] the risk" that statements obtained are not the product of the suspect's free choice. *Dickerson v. United States,* 530 U.S. 428, 435 (2000).

(42) By its very nature, custodial police interrogation entails "inherently compelling pressures." *Miranda,* 384 U.S., at 467. **(43)** Even for an adult, the physical and psychological isolation of custodial interrogation can "undermine the individual's will to resist and . . . compel him to speak where he would not otherwise do so freely." *Ibid.* **(44)** Indeed, the pressure of custodial interrogation is so immense that it "can induce a frighteningly high percentage of people to confess to crimes they never committed." *Corley v. United States,* 556 U.S. 303, –—— (2009) (citing Drizin & Leo, The Problem of False Confessions in the Post–DNA World, 82 N.C.L.Rev. 891, 906–907 (2004)); see also *Miranda,* 384 U.S., at 455, n. 23. **(45)** That risk is all the more troubling—and recent studies suggest, all the more acute—when the subject of custodial interrogation is a juvenile. See Brief for Center on Wrongful Convictions of Youth et al. as ***Amici Curiae*** 21–22 (collecting empirical studies that "illustrate the heightened risk of false confessions from youth").

(46) Recognizing that the inherently coercive nature of custodial interrogation "blurs the line between voluntary and involuntary statements," *Dickerson,* 530 U.S., at 435, this Court in *Miranda* adopted a set of **prophylactic** measures designed to safeguard the constitutional guarantee against self-incrimination. **(47)** Prior to questioning, a suspect "must be warned that he has a right to remain silent, that any statement he does make may be used as evidence against him, and that he has a right to the presence of an attorney, either retained or appointed." 384 U.S., at 444; see also *Florida v. Powell,* 559 U.S. ——, —— (2010) ("The four warnings *Miranda* requires are invariable, but this Court has not dictated the words in which the essential information must be conveyed"). **(48)** And, if a suspect makes a statement during custodial interrogation, the burden is on the Government to show, as a "prerequisit[e]" to the statement's admissibility as evidence in the Government's case in chief, that the defendant "voluntarily, knowingly and intelligently" waived his rights. *Miranda,* 384 U.S., at 444, 475–476; *Dickerson,* 530 U.S., at 443–444.

(49) Because these measures protect the individual against the coercive nature of custodial interrogation, they are required "'only where there has been such a restriction on a person's freedom as to render him "in custody."'" *Stansbury v. California,* 511 U.S. 318, 322 (1994) *(per curiam)* (quoting *Oregon v. Mathiason,* 429 U.S. 492, 495 (1977) *(per curiam)*). **(50)** As we have repeatedly emphasized, whether a suspect is "in custody" is an objective inquiry.

> **(51)** Two discrete inquiries are essential to the determination: first, what were the circumstances surrounding the interrogation; and second, given those circumstances, would a reasonable person have felt he or she was at liberty to terminate the interrogation and leave. **(52)** Once the scene is set and the players' lines and actions are reconstructed, the court must apply an objective test to resolve the ultimate inquiry: was there a formal arrest or restraint on freedom of movement of the degree associated with formal arrest. *Thompson v. Keohane,* 516 U.S. 99, 112 (1995) (internal quotation marks, alteration, and footnote omitted).

See also *Yarborough v. Alvarado,* 541 U.S. 652, 662–663 (2004); *Stansbury,* 511 U.S., at 323; *Berkemer v. McCarty,* 468 U.S. 420, 442, and n. 35 (1984). **(53)** Rather than demarcate a limited set of relevant circumstances, we have required police officers and courts to "examine all of the circumstances surrounding the interrogation," *Stansbury,* 511 U.S., at 322, including any circumstance that "would have affected how a reasonable person" in the suspect's position "would perceive his or her freedom to leave," *id.,* at 325. **(54)** On the other hand, the "subjective views harbored by either the interrogating officers or the person being questioned" are irrelevant. *Id.,* at 323, 114 S.Ct. 1526. **(55)** The test, in other words, involves no consideration of the "actual mindset" of the particular suspect subjected to police questioning. *Alvarado,* 541 U.S., at 667, 124 S.Ct. 2140; see also *California v. Beheler,* 463 U.S. 1121, 1125, n. 3, 103 S.Ct. 3517, 77 L.Ed.2d 1275 (1983) *(per curiam).*

(56) The benefit of the objective custody analysis is that it is "designed to give clear guidance to the police." *Alvarado,* 541 U.S., at 668, 124 S.Ct. 2140. But see *Berkemer,* 468 U.S., at 441, 104 S.Ct. 3138 (recognizing the "occasiona[l] . . .

difficulty" that police and courts nonetheless have in "deciding exactly when a suspect has been taken into custody"). **(57)** Police must make in-the-moment judgments as to when to administer *Miranda* warnings. **(58)** By limiting analysis to the objective circumstances of the interrogation, and asking how a reasonable person in the suspect's position would understand his freedom to terminate questioning and leave, the objective test avoids burdening police with the task of anticipating the idiosyncrasies of every individual suspect and divining how those particular traits affect each person's subjective state of mind. See *id.,* at 430–431, 104 S.Ct. 3138 (officers are not required to "make guesses" as to circumstances "unknowable" to them at the time); *Alvarado,* 541 U.S., at 668, 124 S.Ct. 2140 (officers are under no duty "to consider . . . contingent psychological factors when deciding when suspects should be advised of their *Miranda* rights").

B

(59) The State and its *amici* contend that a child's age has no place in the custody analysis, no matter how young the child subjected to police questioning. **(60)** We cannot agree. **(61)** In some circumstances, a child's age "would have affected how a reasonable person" in the suspect's position "would perceive his or her freedom to leave." *Stansbury,* 511 U.S., at 325. **(62)** That is, a reasonable child subjected to police questioning will sometimes feel pressured to submit when a reasonable adult would feel free to go. **(63)** We think it clear that courts can account for that reality without doing any damage to the objective nature of the custody analysis.

(64) A child's age is far "more than a chronological fact." *Eddings v. Oklahoma,* 455 U.S. 104, 115 (1982); accord, *Gall v. United States,* 552 U.S. 38, 58 (2007); *Roper v. Simmons,* 543 U.S. 551, 569 (2005); *Johnson v. Texas,* 509 U.S. 350, 367 (1993). **(65)** It is a fact that "generates commonsense conclusions about behavior and perception." *Alvarado,* 541 U.S., at 674 (BREYER, J., dissenting). **(66)** Such conclusions apply broadly to children as a class. **(67)** And, they are self-evident to anyone who was a child once himself, including any police officer or judge.

(68) Time and again, this Court has drawn these commonsense conclusions for itself. **(69)** We have observed that children "generally are less mature and responsible than adults," *Eddings,* 455 U.S., at 115–116, 102 S.Ct. 869; that they "often lack the experience, perspective, and judgment to recognize and avoid choices that could be detrimental to them," *Bellotti v. Baird,* 443 U.S. 622, 635, 99 S.Ct. 3035, 61 L.Ed.2d 797 (1979) (plurality opinion); that they "are more vulnerable or susceptible to . . . outside pressures" than adults, *Roper,* 543 U.S., at 569, 125 S.Ct. 1183; and so on. . . . **(70)** Addressing the specific context of police interrogation, we have observed that events that "would leave a man cold and unimpressed can overawe and overwhelm a lad in his early teens." *Haley v. Ohio,* 332 U.S. 596, 599, 68 S.Ct. 302, 92 L.Ed. 224 (1948) (plurality opinion); see also *Gallegos v. Colorado,* 370 U.S. 49, 54, 82 S.Ct. 1209, 8 L.Ed.2d 325 (1962) ("[N]o matter how sophisticated," a juvenile subject of police interrogation "cannot be compared" to an adult subject). **(71)** Describing no one child in particular, these observations restate what "any parent knows"—indeed, what any person knows—about children generally. *Roper,* 543 U.S., at 569, 125 S.Ct. 1183.

(72) Our various statements to this effect are far from unique. **(73)** The law has historically reflected the same assumption that children characteristically lack the capacity to exercise mature judgment and possess only an incomplete ability to understand the world around them. See, *e.g.,* 1 W. Blackstone, Commentaries on the Laws of England 464–465 (hereinafter Blackstone) (explaining that limits on children's legal capacity under the common law "secure them from hurting themselves by their own improvident acts"). **(74)** Like this Court's own generalizations, the legal disqualifications placed on children as a class—*e.g.,* limitations on their ability to alienate property, enter a binding contract enforceable against them, and marry without parental consent—exhibit the settled understanding that the differentiating characteristics of youth are universal.

(75) Indeed, even where a "reasonable person" standard otherwise applies, the common law has reflected the reality that children are not adults. **(76)** In negligence suits, for instance, where liability turns on what an objectively reasonable person would do in the circumstances, "[a]ll American jurisdictions accept the idea that a person's childhood is a relevant circumstance" to be considered. Restatement (Third) of Torts §10, Comment *b,* p. 117 (2005); see also *id.,* Reporters' Note, pp. 121–122 (collecting cases); Restatement (Second) of Torts §283A, Comment *b,* p. 15 (1963–1964) ("[T]here is a wide basis of community experience upon which it is possible, as a practical matter, to determine what is to be expected of [children]").

(77) As this discussion establishes, "[o]ur history is replete with laws and judicial recognition" that children cannot be viewed simply as miniature adults. *Eddings,* 455 U.S., at 115–116, 102 S.Ct. 869. **(78)** We see no justification for taking a different course here. **(79)** So long as the child's age was known to the officer at the time of the interview, or would have been objectively apparent to any reasonable officer, including age as part of the custody analysis requires officers neither to consider circumstances "unknowable" to them, *Berkemer,* 468 U.S., at 430, 104 S.Ct. 3138, nor to "anticipat[e] the frailties or idiosyncrasies" of the particular suspect whom they question, *Alvarado,*541 U.S., at 662, 124 S.Ct. 2140 (internal quotation marks omitted). **(80)** The same "wide basis of community experience" that makes it possible, as an objective matter, "to determine what is to be expected" of children in other contexts, Restatement (Second) of Torts §283A, at 15; see *supra,* at 2403, and n. 6, likewise makes it possible to know what to expect of children subjected to police questioning.

(81) In other words, a child's age differs from other personal characteristics that, even when known to police, have no objectively discernible relationship to a reasonable person's understanding of his freedom of action. **(82)** *Alvarado* holds, for instance, that a suspect's prior interrogation history with law enforcement has no role to play in the custody analysis because such experience could just as easily lead a reasonable person to feel free to walk away as to feel compelled to stay in place. 541 U.S., at 668, 124 S.Ct. 2140. **(83)** Because the effect in any given case would be "contingent [on the] psycholog[y]" of the individual suspect, the Court explained, such experience cannot be considered without compromising the objective nature of the custody analysis. *Ibid.* **(84)** A child's age, however, is different. **(85)** Precisely because childhood yields objective conclusions like those we have drawn ourselves—among others, that children are "most susceptible to influence," *Eddings,* 455 U.S., at 115, 102 S.Ct. 869, and "outside pressures," *Roper,* 543 U.S., at 569, 125 S.Ct. 1183—considering age in the custody analysis in no way involves a determination of how youth "subjectively affect[s] the mindset" of any particular child, Brief for Respondent 14.

(86) In fact, in many cases involving juvenile suspects, the custody analysis would be nonsensical absent some consideration of the suspect's age. **(87)** This case is a prime example. **(88)** Were the court precluded from taking J.D.B.'s youth into account, it would be forced to evaluate the circumstances present here through the eyes of a reasonable person of average years. **(89)** In other words, how would a reasonable adult understand his situation, after being removed from a seventh-grade social studies class by a uniformed school resource officer; being encouraged by his assistant principal to "do the right thing"; and being warned by a police investigator of the prospect of juvenile detention and separation from his guardian and primary caretaker? **(90)** To describe such an inquiry is to demonstrate its absurdity. **(91)** Neither officers nor courts can reasonably evaluate the effect of objective circumstances that, by their nature, are specific to children without accounting for the age of the child subjected to those circumstances.

(92) Indeed, although the dissent suggests that concerns "regarding the application of the *Miranda* custody rule to minors can be accommodated by considering the unique circumstances present when minors are questioned in school," *post,* at [sentence 279] (opinion of ALITO, J.), the effect of the schoolhouse setting cannot be disentangled from the identity of the person questioned. **(93)** A student—whose presence at school is compulsory and whose disobedience at school is cause for disciplinary action—is in a far different position than, say, a parent volunteer on school grounds to chaperone an event, or an adult from the community on school grounds to attend a basketball game. **(94)** Without asking whether the person "questioned in school" is a "minor," *ibid.,* the coercive effect of the schoolhouse setting is unknowable.

(95) Our prior decision in *Alvarado* in no way undermines these conclusions. **(96)** In that case, we held that a state-court decision that failed to mention a 17-year-old's age as part of the *Miranda* custody analysis was not objectively unreasonable under the deferential standard of review set forth by the

Antiterrorism and Effective Death Penalty Act of 1996 (AEDPA), 110 Stat. 1214. **(97)** Like the North Carolina Supreme Court here, . . . we observed that accounting for a juvenile's age in the *Miranda* custody analysis "could be viewed as creating a subjective inquiry," 541 U.S., at 668. **(98)** We said nothing, however, of whether such a view would be correct under the law. . . . **(99)** To the contrary, Justice O'Connor's concurring opinion explained that a suspect's age may indeed "be relevant to the 'custody' inquiry." *Alvarado,* 541 U.S., at 669.

(100) Reviewing the question *de novo* today, we hold that so long as the child's age was known to the officer at the time of police questioning, or would have been objectively apparent to a reasonable officer, its inclusion in the custody analysis is consistent with the objective nature of that test. **(101)** This is not to say that a child's age will be a determinative, or even a significant, factor in every case. . . . **(102)** It is, however, a reality that courts cannot simply ignore.

III

(103) The State and its *amici* offer numerous reasons that courts must blind themselves to a juvenile defendant's age. **(104)** None is persuasive.

(105) To start, the State contends that a child's age must be excluded from the custody inquiry because age is a personal characteristic specific to the suspect himself rather than an "external" circumstance of the interrogation. Brief for Respondent 21; see also *id.,* at 18–19 (distinguishing "personal characteristics" from "objective facts related to the interrogation itself" such as the location and duration of the interrogation). **(106)** Despite the supposed significance of this distinction, however, at oral argument counsel for the State suggested without hesitation that at least some undeniably personal characteristics—for instance, whether the individual being questioned is blind—are circumstances relevant to the custody analysis. See Tr. of Oral Arg. 41. **(107)** Thus, the State's quarrel cannot be that age is a personal characteristic, without more.

(108) The State further argues that age is irrelevant to the custody analysis because it "go[es] to how a suspect may internalize and perceive the circumstances of an interrogation." Brief for Respondent 12; see also Brief for United States as ***Amicus Curiae*** 21 (hereinafter U.S. Brief) (arguing that a child's age has no place in the custody analysis because it goes to whether a suspect is "particularly susceptible" to the external circumstances of the interrogation (some internal quotation marks omitted)). **(109)** But the same can be said of every objective circumstance that the State agrees is relevant to the custody analysis: Each circumstance goes to how a reasonable person would "internalize and perceive" every other. See, *e.g., Stansbury,* 511 U.S., at 325. **(110)** Indeed, this is the very reason that we ask whether the objective circumstances "add up to custody," *Keohane,* 516 U.S., at 113,instead of evaluating the circumstances one by one.

(111) In the same vein, the State and its *amici* protest that the "effect of . . . age on [the] perception of custody is internal," Brief for Respondent 20, or "psychological," U.S. Brief 21. **(112)** But the whole point of the custody analysis is to determine whether, given the circumstances, "a reasonable person [would] have felt he or she was . . . at liberty to terminate the interrogation and leave." *Keohane,* 516 U.S., at 112. **(113)** Because the *Miranda* custody inquiry turns on the mindset of a reasonable person in the suspect's position, it cannot be the case that a circumstance is subjective simply because it has an "internal" or "psychological" impact on perception. **(114)** Were that so, there would be no objective circumstances to consider at all.

(115) Relying on our statements that the objective custody test is "designed to give clear guidance to the police," *Alvarado,* 541 U.S., at 668, the State next argues that a child's age must be excluded from the analysis in order to preserve clarity. **(116)** Similarly, the dissent insists that the clarity of the custody analysis will be destroyed unless a "one-size-fits-all reasonable-person test" applies. *Post,* at 2415. **(117)** In reality, however, ignoring a juvenile defendant's age will often make the inquiry more artificial, see *supra,* at 2404 – 2405, and thus only add confusion. **(118)** And in any event, a child's age, when known or apparent, is hardly an obscure factor to assess. **(119)** Though the State and the dissent worry about gradations among children of different ages, that concern cannot justify ignoring a child's age altogether. **(120)** Just as police officers are competent to account for other objective circumstances that are a matter of degree such as the length of questioning or the number of officers present, so too are they competent to evaluate the effect of relative age. **(121)** Indeed, they are competent to do so even though an interrogation room lacks the "reflective atmosphere of a [jury] deliberation room," *post,* at [sentence 263]. **(122)** The same is true of judges, including those whose childhoods have long since passed, see *post,* at 2416. **(123)** In short, officers and judges need no imaginative powers, knowledge of developmental psychology, training in cognitive science, or expertise in social and cultural anthropology to account for a child's age. **(124)** They simply need the common sense to know that a 7-year-old is not a 13-year-old and neither is an adult.

(125) There is, however, an even more fundamental flaw with the State's plea for clarity and the dissent's singular focus on simplifying the analysis: Not once have we excluded from the custody analysis a circumstance that we determined was relevant and objective, simply to make the fault line between custodial and noncustodial "brighter." **(126)** Indeed, were the guiding concern clarity and nothing else, the custody test would presumably ask only whether the suspect had been placed under formal arrest. *Berkemer,* 468 U.S., at 441; see *ibid.* (acknowledging the "occasiona[l] . . . difficulty" police officers confront in determining when a suspect has been taken into custody). **(127)** But we have rejected that "more easily administered line," recognizing that it would simply "enable the police to circumvent the constraints on custodial interrogations established by *Miranda*." *Ibid.*; see also *ibid.,* n. 33.

(128) Finally, the State and the dissent suggest that excluding age from the custody analysis comes at no cost to juveniles' constitutional rights because the due process voluntariness test independently accounts for a child's youth. **(129)** To be sure, that test permits consideration of a child's age, and it erects its own barrier to admission of a defendant's inculpatory statements at trial. . . . **(130)** But *Miranda*'s procedural safeguards exist precisely because the voluntariness test is an inadequate barrier when custodial interrogation is at stake. . . . **(131)** To hold, as the State requests, that a child's age is never relevant to whether a suspect has been taken into custody—and thus to ignore the very real differences between children and adults—would be to deny children the full scope of the procedural safeguards that *Miranda* guarantees to adults.

(132) The question remains whether J.D.B. was in custody when police interrogated him. **(133)** We remand for the state courts to address that question, this time taking account of all of the relevant circumstances of the interrogation, including J.D.B.'s age at the time. **(134)** The judgment of the North Carolina Supreme Court is reversed, and the case is remanded for proceedings not inconsistent with this opinion.

(135) *It is so ordered.*

Justice ALITO, with whom THE CHIEF JUSTICE, Justice SCALIA, and Justice THOMAS join, dissenting.

(136) The Court's decision in this case may seem on first consideration to be modest and sensible, but in truth it is neither. **(137)** It is fundamentally inconsistent with one of the main justifications for the *Miranda* rule: the perceived need for a clear rule that can be easily applied in all cases. **(138)** And today's holding is not needed to protect the constitutional rights of minors who are questioned by the police.

(139) *Miranda*'s prophylactic regime places a high value on clarity and certainty. **(140)** Dissatisfied with the highly fact-specific constitutional rule against the admission of involuntary confessions, the *Miranda* Court set down rigid standards that often require courts to ignore personal characteristics that may be highly relevant to a particular suspect's actual susceptibility to police pressure. **(141)** This rigidity, however, has brought with it one of *Miranda*'s principal strengths—"the ease and clarity of its application" by law enforcement officials and courts. See *Moran v. Burbine,* 475 U.S. 412, 425–426 (1986). **(142)** A key contributor to this clarity, at least up until now, has been *Miranda*'s objective reasonable-person test for determining custody.

(143) *Miranda*'s custody requirement is based on the proposition that the risk of unconstitutional coercion is heightened when a suspect is placed under formal arrest or is subjected to some functionally equivalent limitation on freedom of movement. **(144)** When this custodial threshold is reached, *Miranda* warnings must precede police questioning. **(145)** But in the interest of simplicity the custody analysis considers only whether, under the circumstances, a hypothetical reasonable person would consider himself to be confined.

(146) Many suspects, of course, will differ from this hypothetical reasonable person. **(147)** Some, including those who have been hardened by past interrogations, may have no need for *Miranda* warnings at all. **(148)** And for other suspects—those who are unusually sensitive to the pressures of police questioning—*Miranda* warnings may come too late to be of any use. **(149)** That is a necessary consequence of *Miranda*'s rigid standards, but it does not mean that the constitutional rights of these especially sensitive suspects are left unprotected. **(150)** A vulnerable defendant can still turn to the constitutional rule against *actual* coercion and contend that that his confession was extracted against his will.

(151) Today's decision shifts the *Miranda* custody determination from a one-size-fits-all reasonable-person test into an inquiry that must account for at least one individualized characteristic—age—that is thought to correlate with susceptibility to coercive pressures. **(152)** Age, however, is in no way the only personal characteristic that may correlate with pliability, and in future cases the Court will be forced to choose between two unpalatable alternatives. **(153)** It may choose to limit today's decision by arbitrarily distinguishing a suspect's age from other personal characteristics—such as intelligence, education, occupation, or prior experience with law enforcement—that may also correlate with susceptibility to coercive pressures. **(154)** Or, if the Court is unwilling to draw these arbitrary lines, it will be forced to effect a fundamental transformation of the *Miranda* custody test—from a clear, easily applied prophylactic rule into a highly **fact-intensive** standard resembling the voluntariness test that the *Miranda* Court found to be unsatisfactory.

(155) For at least three reasons, there is no need to go down this road. **(156)** First, many minors subjected to police interrogation are near the **age of majority**, and for these suspects the one-size-fits-all *Miranda* custody rule may not be a bad fit. **(157)** Second, many of the difficulties in applying the *Miranda* custody rule to minors arise because of the unique circumstances present when the police conduct interrogations at school. **(158)** The *Miranda* custody rule has always taken into account the setting in which questioning occurs, and accounting for the school setting in such cases will address many of these problems. **(159)** Third, in cases like the one now before us, where the suspect is especially young, courts applying the constitutional voluntariness standard can take special care to ensure that incriminating statements were not obtained through coercion.

(160) Safeguarding the constitutional rights of minors does not require the extreme makeover of *Miranda* that today's decision may portend.

I

(161) In the days before *Miranda,* this Court's sole metric for evaluating the admissibility of confessions was a voluntariness standard rooted in both the Fifth

Amendment's Self–Incrimination Clause and the Due Process Clause of the Fourteenth Amendment. See *Bram v. United States,* 168 U.S. 532, 542 (1897) (Self–Incrimination Clause); *Brown v. Mississippi,* 297 U.S. 278 (1936) (due process). **(162)** The question in these voluntariness cases was whether the particular "defendant's will" had been "overborne." *Lynumn v. Illinois,* 372 U.S. 528, 534 (1963). **(163)** Courts took into account both "the details of the interrogation" *and* "the characteristics of the accused," *Schneckloth v. Bustamonte,* 412 U.S. 218, 226 (1973), and then "weigh[ed] . . . the circumstances of pressure against the power of resistance of the person confessing." *Stein v. New York,* 346 U.S. 156, 185 (1953).

(164) All manner of individualized, personal characteristics were relevant in this voluntariness inquiry. **(165)** Among the most frequently mentioned factors were the defendant's education, physical condition, intelligence, and mental health. . . . **(166)** The suspect's age also received prominent attention in several cases, *e.g., Gallegos v. Colorado,* 370 U.S. 49, 54 (1962), especially when the suspect was a "mere child." *Haley v. Ohio,* 332 U.S. 596, 599 (1948) (plurality opinion). **(167)** The weight assigned to any one consideration varied from case to case. **(168)** But all of these factors, along with anything else that might have affected the "individual's . . . capacity for effective choice," were relevant in determining whether the confession was coerced or compelled. See *Miranda v. Arizona,* 384 U.S. 436, 506–507 (1966) (Harlan, J., dissenting).

(169) The all-encompassing nature of the voluntariness inquiry had its benefits. **(170)** It allowed courts to accommodate a "complex of values," *Schneckloth, supra,* at 223, 224, and to make a careful, highly individualized determination as to whether the police had wrung "a confession out of [the] accused against his will." *Blackburn v. Alabama,* 361 U.S. 199, 206–207 (1960). **(171)** But with this flexibility came a decrease in both certainty and predictability, and the voluntariness standard proved difficult "for law enforcement officers to conform to, and for courts to apply in a consistent manner." *Dickerson v. United States,* 530 U.S. 428, 444 (2000).

(172) In *Miranda,* the Court supplemented the voluntariness inquiry with a "set of prophylactic measures" designed to ward off the "'inherently compelling pressures' of custodial interrogation." See *Maryland v. Shatzer,* 559 U.S. ——, –—— (2010) (quoting *Miranda,* 384 U.S., at 467). **(173)** *Miranda* greatly simplified matters by requiring police to give suspects standard warnings before commencing any custodial interrogation. See *id.,* at 479. **(174)** Its requirements are no doubt "rigid," see *Fare v. Michael C.,* 439 U.S. 1310, 1314 (1978) (Rehnquist, J., in chambers), and they often require courts to suppress "trustworthy and highly probative" statements that may be perfectly "voluntary under [a] traditional Fifth Amendment analysis." *Fare v. Michael C.,* 442 U.S. 707, 718 (1979). **(175)** But with this rigidity comes increased clarity. **(176)** *Miranda* provides "a workable rule to guide police officers," *New York v.*

Quarles, 467 U.S. 649, 658 (1984) (internal quotation marks omitted), and an administrable standard for the courts. **(177)** As has often been recognized, this gain in clarity and administrability is one of *Miranda*'s "principal advantages." *Berkemer v. McCarty,* 468 U.S. 420, 430 (1984); see also *Missouri v. Seibert,* 542 U.S. 600, 622 (2004) (KENNEDY, J., concurring in judgment).

(178) No less than other facets of *Miranda,* the threshold requirement that the suspect be in "custody" is "designed to give clear guidance to the police." *Yarborough v. Alvarado,* 541 U.S. 652, 668, 669 (2004). **(179)** Custody under *Miranda* attaches where there is a "formal arrest" or a "restraint on freedom of movement" akin to formal arrest. *California v. Beheler,* 463 U.S. 1121, 1125 (1983) *(per curiam)* (internal quotation marks omitted). **(180)** This standard is "objective" and turns on how a hypothetical "reasonable person in the position of the individual being questioned would gauge the breadth of his or her freedom of action." *Stansbury v. California,* 511 U.S. 318, 322–323, 325 (1994) *(per curiam)* (internal quotation marks omitted).

(181) Until today, the Court's cases applying this test have focused solely on the "objective circumstances of the interrogation," *id.,* at 323, not the personal characteristics of the interrogated. *E.g., Berkemer, supra,* at 442, and n. 35; but cf. *Schneckloth,* 412 U.S., at 226 (voluntariness inquiry requires consideration of "the details of the interrogation" *and* "the characteristics of the accused"). **(182)** Relevant factors have included such things as where the questioning occurred, how long it lasted, what was said, any physical restraints placed on the suspect's movement, and whether the suspect was allowed to leave when the questioning was through. **(183)** The totality of *these* circumstances—the external circumstances, that is, of the interrogation itself—is what has mattered in this Court's cases. **(184)** Personal characteristics of suspects have consistently been rejected or ignored as irrelevant under a one-size-fits-all reasonable-person standard. *Stansbury, supra,* at 323 ("[C]ustody depends on the objective circumstances of the interrogation, not on the subjective views harbored by either the interrogating officers or the person being questioned").

(185) For example, in *Berkemer v. McCarty, supra,* police officers conducting a traffic stop questioned a man who had been drinking and smoking marijuana before he was pulled over. *Id.,* at 423. **(186)** Although the suspect's inebriation was readily apparent to the officers at the scene, *ibid.,* the Court's analysis did not advert to this or any other individualized consideration. **(187)** Instead, the Court focused only on the external circumstances of the interrogation itself. **(188)** The opinion concluded that a typical "traffic stop" is akin to a "*Terry* stop" and does not qualify as the equivalent of "formal arrest." *Id.,* at 439.

(189) *California v. Beheler, supra,* is another useful example. **(190)** There, the circumstances of the interrogation were "remarkably similar" to the facts of the Court's earlier decision in *Oregon v. Mathiason,* 429 U.S. 492 (1977) *(per curiam)*—the suspect was "not placed under arrest," he "voluntarily [came] to the police station," and he was "allowed to leave unhindered by police after a brief interview." 463 U.S., at 1123, 1121. **(191)** A California court in *Beheler* had nonetheless distinguished *Mathiason* because the police knew that Beheler "had been drinking earlier in the day" and was "emotionally distraught." 463 U.S., at 1124–1125. **(192)** In a summary reversal, this Court explained that the fact "[t]hat the police knew more" personal information about Beheler than they did about Mathiason was "irrelevant." *Id.,* at 1125. **(193)** Neither one of them was in custody under the objective reasonable-person standard. *Ibid.;* see also *Alvarado, supra,* at 668, 669 (experience with law enforcement irrelevant to *Miranda* custody analysis "as a *de novo* matter").

(194) The glaring absence of reliance on personal characteristics in these and other custody cases should come as no surprise. **(195)** To account for such individualized considerations would be to contradict *Miranda*'s central premise. **(196)** The *Miranda* Court's decision to adopt its inflexible prophylactic requirements was expressly based on the notion that "[a]ssessments of the knowledge the defendant possessed, based on information as to his age, education, intelligence, or prior contact with authorities, can never be more than speculation." 384 U.S., at 468–469.

II

(197) In light of this established practice, there is no denying that, by incorporating age into its analysis, the Court is embarking on a new expansion of the established custody standard. **(198)** And since *Miranda* is this Court's rule, "not a constitutional command," it is up to the Court "to justify its expansion." Cf. *Arizona v. Roberson,* 486 U.S. 675, 688 (1988) (KENNEDY, J., dissenting). **(199)** This the Court fails to do.

(200) In its present form, *Miranda*'s prophylactic regime already imposes "high cost[s]" by requiring suppression of confessions that are often "highly probative" and "voluntary" by any traditional standard. *Oregon v. Elstad,* 470 U.S. 298, 312 (1985); see *Dickerson,* 530 U.S., at 444 (under *Miranda* "statements which may be by no means involuntary, made by a defendant who is aware of his 'rights,' may nonetheless be excluded and a guilty defendant go free as a result"). **(201)** Nonetheless, a "core virtue" of *Miranda* has been the clarity and precision of its guidance to "police and courts." *Withrow v. Williams,* 507 U.S. 680, 694 (1993) (internal quotation marks omitted); see *Moran,* 475 U.S., at 425 ("[O]ne of the principal advantages of *Miranda* is the ease and clarity of its application" (internal quotation marks omitted)). **(202)** This increased clarity "has been thought to outweigh the burdens" that *Miranda* imposes. *Fare,* 442 U.S., at 718. **(203)** The Court has, however, repeatedly cautioned against upsetting the careful "balance" that *Miranda* struck, *Moran, supra,* at 424, and it has "refused to sanction attempts to expand [the] *Miranda* holding" in ways that would reduce its " clarity." See *Quarles,* 467 U.S., at 658 (citing cases). **(204)** Given this practice, there should be a "strong presumption" against the Court's new departure from the established custody test. See *United States v. Patane,* 542 U.S. 630, 640

(2004) (plurality opinion). **(205)** In my judgment, that presumption cannot be overcome here.

A

(206) The Court's rationale for importing age into the custody standard is that minors tend to lack adults' "capacity to exercise mature judgment" and that failing to account for that "reality" will leave some minors unprotected under *Miranda* in situations where they perceive themselves to be confined. See *ante,* at [sentences 72 and 74]. **(207)** I do not dispute that many suspects who are under 18 will be more susceptible to police pressure than the average adult. **(208)** As the Court notes, our pre-*Miranda* cases were particularly attuned to this "reality" in applying the constitutional requirement of voluntariness in fact. *Ante,* at [sentence 74] (relying on *Haley,* 332 U.S., at 599 (plurality opinion), and *Gallegos,* 370 U.S., at 54). **(209)** It is no less a "reality," however, that many persons *over* the age of 18 are also more susceptible to police pressure than the hypothetical reasonable person. See *Payne,* 356 U.S., at 567 (fact that defendant was a "mentally dull 19–year–old youth" relevant in voluntariness inquiry). **(210)** Yet the *Miranda* custody standard has never accounted for the personal characteristics of these or any other individual defendants.

(211) Indeed, it has always been the case under *Miranda* that the unusually meek or compliant are subject to the same fixed rules, including the same custody requirement, as those who are unusually resistant to police pressure. *Berkemer,* 468 U.S., at 442, and n. 35 ("[O]nly relevant inquiry is how a reasonable man in the suspect's position would have understood his situation"). **(212)** *Miranda*'s rigid standards are both overinclusive and underinclusive. **(213)** They are overinclusive to the extent that they provide a windfall to the most hardened and savvy of suspects, who often have no need for *Miranda*'s protections. . . . **(214)** And *Miranda*'s requirements are underinclusive to the extent that they fail to account for "frailties," "idiosyncrasies," and other individualized considerations that might cause a person to bend more easily during a confrontation with the police. See *Alvarado,* 541 U.S., at 662 (internal quotation marks omitted). **(215)** Members of this Court have seen this rigidity as a major weakness in *Miranda*'s "code of rules for confessions." See 384 U.S., at 504 (Harlan, J., dissenting); *Fare,* 439 U.S., at 1314 (Rehnquist, J., in chambers) ("[T]he rigidity of [*Miranda*'s] prophylactic rules was a principal weakness in the view of dissenters and critics outside the Court"). **(216)** But if it is, then the weakness is an inescapable consequence of the *Miranda* Court's decision to supplement the more holistic voluntariness requirement with a one-size-fits-all prophylactic rule.

(217) That is undoubtedly why this Court's *Miranda* cases have never before mentioned "the suspect's age" or any other individualized consideration in applying the custody standard. See *Alvarado, supra,* at 666. **(218)** And unless the *Miranda* custody rule is now to be radically transformed into one that takes into account the wide range of individual characteristics that are relevant in determining whether a confession is voluntary, the Court must shoulder the burden of explaining why age is different from these other personal characteristics.

(219) Why, for example, is age different from intelligence? **(220)** Suppose that an officer, upon going to a school to question a student, is told by the principal that the student has an I.Q. of 75 and is in a special-education class. Cf. *In re J.D.B.,* 363 N.C. 664, 666 (2009). **(221)** Are those facts more or less important than the student's age in determining whether he or she "felt . . . at liberty to terminate the interrogation and leave"? See *Thompson v. Keohane,* 516 U.S. 99, 112 (1995). **(222)** An I.Q. score, like age, is more than just a number. . . . **(223)** And an individual's intelligence can also yield "conclusions" similar to those "we have drawn ourselves" in cases far afield of *Miranda. Ante,* at [sentence 84]. . . .

(224) How about the suspect's cultural background? **(225)** Suppose the police learn (or should have learned . . .) that a suspect they wish to question is a recent immigrant from a country in which dire consequences often befall any person who dares to attempt to cut short any meeting with the police. **(226)** Is this really less relevant than the fact that a suspect is a month or so away from his 18th birthday?

(227) The defendant's education is another personal characteristic that may generate "conclusions about behavior and perception." *Ante,* at [sentence 64] (internal quotation marks omitted). **(228)** Under today's decision, why should police officers and courts "blind themselves," *ante,* at [sentence 3], to the fact that a suspect has "only a fifth-grade education"? See *Clewis,* 386 U.S., at 712 (voluntariness case). **(229)** Alternatively, what if the police know or should know that the suspect is "a college-educated man with law school training"? See *Crooker v. California,* 357 U.S. 433, 440 (1958), overruled by *Miranda, supra,* at 479, and n. 48. **(230)** How are these individual considerations meaningfully different from age in their "relationship to a reasonable person's understanding of his freedom of action"? *Ante,* at [sentence 80]. **(231)** The Court proclaims that "[a] child's age . . . is different," *ante,* at [sentence 83], but the basis for this *ipse dixit* is dubious.

(232) I have little doubt that today's decision will soon be cited by defendants—and perhaps by prosecutors as well—for the proposition that all manner of other individual characteristics should be treated like age and taken into account in the *Miranda* custody calculus. **(233)** Indeed, there are already lower court decisions that take this approach. . . .

(234) In time, the Court will have to confront these issues, and it will be faced with a difficult choice. **(235)** It may choose to distinguish today's decision and adhere to the arbitrary proclamation that "age . . . is different." *Ante,* at [sentence 83]. **(236)** Or it may choose to extend today's holding and, in doing so, further undermine the very rationale for the *Miranda* regime.

B

(237) If the Court chooses the latter course, then a core virtue of *Miranda*—the "ease and clarity of its application"—will be lost. *Moran,* 475 U.S., at 425; see *Fare,* 442 U.S., at 718 (noting that the clarity of *Miranda*'s requirements "has been thought to outweigh the burdens that the decision . . . imposes"). **(238)** However, even today's more limited departure from *Miranda*'s one-size-fits-all reasonable-person test will produce the very consequences that prompted the *Miranda* Court to abandon exclusive reliance on the voluntariness test in the first place: The Court's test will be hard for the police to follow, and it will be hard for judges to apply. See *Dickerson v. United States,* 530 U.S. 428, 444 (2000).

(239) The Court holds that age must be taken into account when it "was known to the officer at the time of the interview," or when it "would have been objectively apparent" to a reasonable officer. *Ante,* at [sentence 78]. **(240)** The first half of this test overturns the rule that the "initial determination of custody" does not depend on the "subjective views harbored by . . . interrogating officers." *Stansbury,* 511 U.S., at 323. **(241)** The second half will generate time-consuming satellite litigation over a reasonable officer's perceptions. **(242)** When, as here, the interrogation takes place in school, the inquiry may be relatively simple. **(243)** But not all police questioning of minors takes place in schools. **(244)** In many cases, courts will presumably have to make findings as to whether a particular suspect had a sufficiently youthful look to alert a reasonable officer to the possibility that the suspect was under 18, or whether a reasonable officer would have recognized that a suspect's I.D. was a fake. **(245)** The inquiry will be both "time-consuming and disruptive" for the police and the courts. See *Berkemer,* 468 U.S., at 432 (refusing to modify the custody test based on similar considerations). **(246)** It will also be made all the more complicated by the fact that a suspect's dress and manner will often be different when the issue is litigated in court than it was at the time of the interrogation.

(247) Even after courts clear this initial hurdle, further problems will likely emerge as judges attempt to put themselves in the shoes of the average 16–year–old, or 15–year–old, or 13–year–old, as the case may be. **(248)** Consider, for example, a 60–year–old judge attempting to make a custody determination through the eyes of a hypothetical, average 15–year–old. **(249)** Forty-five years of personal experience and societal change separate this judge from the days when he or she was 15 years old. **(250)** And this judge may or may not have been an average 15–year–old. **(251)** The Court's answer to these difficulties is to state that "no imaginative powers, knowledge of developmental psychology, [or] training in cognitive science" will be necessary. *Ante,* at [sentence 122]. **(252)** Judges "simply need the common sense," the Court assures, "to know that a 7–year–old is not a 13–year–old and neither is an adult." *Ante,* at [sentence 123]. **(253)** It is obvious, however, that application of the Court's new rule demands much more than this.

(254) Take a fairly typical case in which today's holding may make a difference. **(255)** A 16 ½-year-old moves to suppress incriminating statements made prior to the administration of *Miranda* warnings. **(256)** The circumstances are such that, if the defendant were at least 18, the court would not find that he or she was in custody, but the defendant argues that a reasonable 16 ½-year-old would view the situation differently. **(257)** The judge will not have the luxury of merely saying: "It is common sense that a 16 ½-year-old is not an 18–year–old. **(258)** Motion granted." **(259)** Rather, the judge will be required to determine whether the differences between a typical 16 ½-year-old and a typical 18–year–old with respect to susceptibility to the pressures of interrogation are sufficient to change the outcome of the custody determination. **(260)** Today's opinion contains not a word of actual guidance as to how judges are supposed to go about making that determination.

C

(261) Petitioner and the Court attempt to show that this task is not unmanageable by pointing out that age is taken into account in other legal contexts. **(262)** In particular, the Court relies on the fact that the age of a defendant is a relevant factor under the reasonable-person standard applicable in negligence suits. *Ante,* at [sentence 75] . . . **(263)** But negligence is generally a question for the jury, the members of which can draw on their varied experiences with persons of different ages. **(264)** It also involves a *post hoc* determination, in the reflective atmosphere of a deliberation room, about whether the defendant conformed to a standard of care. **(265)** The *Miranda* custody determination, by contrast, must be made in the first instance by police officers in the course of an investigation that may require quick decisionmaking. . . .

(266) Equally inapposite are the Eighth Amendment cases the Court cites in support of its new rule. . . . **(267)** Those decisions involve the "judicial exercise of independent judgment" about the constitutionality of certain punishments. . . . **(268)** Like the negligence standard, they do not require on-the-spot judgments by the police.

(269) Nor do state laws affording extra protection for juveniles during custodial interrogation provide any support for petitioner's arguments. See Brief for Petitioner 16–17. **(270)** States are free to enact additional restrictions on the police over and above those demanded by the Constitution or *Miranda*. **(271)** In addition, these state statutes generally create clear, workable rules to guide police conduct. . . . **(272)** Today's decision, by contrast, injects a new, complicating factor into what had been a clear, easily applied prophylactic rule. See *Alvarado, supra,* at 668–669, 124 S.Ct. 2140.

III

(273) The Court's decision greatly diminishes the clarity and administrability that have long been recognized as "principal advantages" of *Miranda*'s prophylactic requirements. See, *e.g., Moran,* 475 U.S., at 425. **(274)**

But what is worse, the Court takes this step unnecessarily, as there are other, less disruptive tools available to ensure that minors are not coerced into confessing.

(275) As an initial matter, the difficulties that the Court's standard introduces will likely yield little added protection for most juvenile defendants. **(276)** Most juveniles who are subjected to police interrogation are teenagers nearing the age of majority. **(277)** These defendants' reactions to police pressure are unlikely to be much different from the reaction of a typical 18–year–old in similar circumstances. **(278)** A one-size-fits-all *Miranda* custody rule thus provides a roughly reasonable fit for these defendants.

(279) In addition, many of the concerns that petitioner raises regarding the application of the *Miranda* custody rule to minors can be accommodated by considering the unique circumstances present when minors are questioned in school. . . . **(280)** The *Miranda* custody rule has always taken into account the setting in which questioning occurs, restrictions on a suspect's freedom of movement, and the presence of police officers or other authority figures. See *Alvarado, supra,* at 665; *Maryland v. Shatzer,* 559 U.S. ——, —— (2010). **(281)** It can do so here as well. . . .

(282) The Court rests its decision to inject personal characteristics into the *Miranda* custody inquiry on the principle that judges applying *Miranda* cannot "blind themselves to . . . commonsense reality." *Ante,* at [sentence 3]. **(283)** But the Court's shift is fundamentally at odds with the clear prophylactic rules that *Miranda* has long enforced. **(284)** *Miranda* frequently requires judges to blind themselves to the reality that many un-Mirandized custodial confessions are "by no means involuntary" or coerced. *Dickerson,* 530 U.S., at 444. **(285)** It also requires police to provide a rote recitation of *Miranda* warnings that many suspects already know and could likely recite from memory. **(286)** Under today's new, "reality"-based approach to the doctrine, perhaps these and other principles of our *Miranda* jurisprudence will, like the custody standard, now be ripe for modification. **(287)** Then, bit by bit, *Miranda* will lose the clarity and ease of application that has long been viewed as one of its chief justifications.

(288) I respectfully dissent.

TASK 6.E.1. Case Brief

Write a case brief of *J.D.B. v. North Carolina* using the template on page 392. Also include a summary of the dissenting opinion in your brief.

TASK 6.E.2. Criminal Procedure Vocabulary Definitions (List 4)

Fill in each definition with the appropriate term from the list below. Consult a law dictionary or an English-to-English dictionary to confirm that you have matched each term with the correct definition. If multiple forms of a term are provided, you may not need to use all of the forms in the blanks.

age of majority *(noun)*
Amicus Curiae; *Amici Curiae (noun)* (pronounced UH-**MEE**-KUS **KYOO**-REE-EYE; UH-**MEE**-KEE **KYOO**-REE-EYE)
count of [name of offense] *(noun)*
delinquent *(adjective; noun)*
fact-intensive *(adjective)*
juvenile *(adjective; noun)*; juvenile detention *(noun)*
larceny *(noun)*
public defender *(noun)*

1. The ____________________ is the threshold age at which a person is considered an adult. In most jurisdictions this is 18.

2. The term ____________________ refers to a/an ____________________ who has violated the law. Children below a certain age are tried not for "crimes" but rather "delinquent acts." Juveniles who commit such delinquent acts are sent to a/an ____________________ center.

3. ____________________ refers to the unlawful taking and carrying away of someone else's personal property without the owner's consent and with the intent to permanently deprive the owner of the property. It is a criminal offense.

4. ____________________ is Latin for "friend of the court." It is a person or group that is not a party to a legal action but has an interest in the matter being litigated. ____________________ (plural form) petition an appellate court to submit "amicus briefs," which may help to influence the court's decision.

5. A/an ____________________ refers to a single criminal charge. Individuals may be charged with one more ____________________ (plural form) of a criminal offense or multiple criminal offenses.

6. ____________________ are attorneys who represent indigent criminal defendants. They are paid by the government.

7. If an analysis is ____________________, it involves an in-depth examination of all of the factual circumstances.

TASK 6.E.3. Questions for Discussion

Answer the following questions to assist you during a class discussion of the case. Indicate the sentence(s) in which you found the answer to each question.

1. Describe the facts of this case.

2. What is the issue and the holding?

3. The majority and dissent disagree on whether age should factor into the *Miranda* custody analysis. What are their main arguments?

   Majority   Dissent

4. The majority states that a child's age is "different" from other personal characteristics. How so? Do you agree with this argument?

5. Do you agree with the dissent that the majority's decision is an "extreme makeover" of *Miranda*? Why or why not?

6. The dissent writes at length about the "voluntariness test" that was used to evaluate the admissibility of confessions before the *Miranda* decision was handed down. What is this voluntariness test and how does it differ from *Miranda*?

7. Do you think it is relevant to a *Miranda* custody analysis whether someone is blind? has a very low IQ? does not understand English very well? Or are these the kinds of "personal characteristics" that shouldn't be factored into the custody analysis? What's the difference between these characteristics and age?

8. State the rule for determining whether a suspect is "in custody" for the purposes of *Miranda*.

9. Hypothetical: Detectives Allman and Bates were investigating the murder of Carlson, a 15-year-old boy. They had reason to believe that the murder was motivated by drug activity in the neighborhood. Allman and Bates received an anonymous tip that Davis, a 16-year-old boy in the same neighborhood, was involved in drug trafficking and had personal "beef" with Carlson after he failed to pay for over three ounces of marijuana. Davis is a well-known troublemaker in the neighborhood who has had numerous run-ins with the police and, after being convicted of grand larceny, did a six-month stint at a juvenile detention facility when he was 15 years old.

   Allman and Bates received the tip at 3 a.m. With Edwards, another colleague, they immediately went to Davis's house to investigate. Davis, who lives with his mother and two siblings, was asleep so Davis's mother let the officers into the house and woke up her son. The officers entered Davis's bedroom and, while Davis was still in bed, said they wanted to ask him "a few questions" about Carlson's murder. They informed Davis that he was not under arrest but that it was important to answer the questions.

   The police officers spoke with Davis for two hours, asking him about his relationship with Carlson and whether anyone would have had a reason to kill him. Davis was cooperative and answered all of the officers' questions. When they asked him about where he was on the night of the murder, however, Davis started to look nervous. As the police officers asked more questions in this vein, eventually admitted to being at the murder scene and owning a firearm. He also told the officers the whereabouts of the gun. At this point the officers read Davis his *Miranda* rights and arrested him. Later tests revealed that Davis's gun fired the shot that killed Carlson. Davis was charged with second-degree murder.

   The trial is about to begin, and Davis is seeking to suppress the statements made in his bedroom. He claims that the statements were obtained in violation of his Fifth Amendment rights because he did not receive *Miranda* warnings. You are the trial judge presiding over the case. How would you rule on the motion to suppress?

F. Criminal Procedure Vocabulary Exercises (Lists 1-4)

EXERCISE 6.F.1. Fill in the Blanks

Fill in the blanks with the most appropriate form of the words and phrases in the list below. You may have to change word form to create a grammatically correct sentence. Some questions may have more than one correct answer.

administer	indigent
admissible	issue
cease	juvenile
charge	motion to suppress
concede	on parole
convict	parolee
count	petitioner
dispositive	prosecute
district attorney	public defender
exercise	respondent
homicide	take the stand
inadmissible	waive

1. The trial judge denied the defendant's ____________________. The defendant's statements made during his questioning at the police station were therefore ____________________.

2. Jill ____________________ her privilege against self-incrimination when she told the police officer that she wished to remain silent.

3. Kyle has been ____________________ with two ____________________ of larceny. His trial is scheduled for next month.

4. The ____________________ wished to appeal the state Supreme Court's opinion, so she petitioned for a writ of certiorari in the Supreme Court of the United States.

5. Joey is a/an ____________________ who has represented hundreds of ____________________ clients who could not afford legal representation. Most of the defendants he has worked with come from the city.

6. Opposing counsel ____________________ that my client's relationship history has nothing to do with the case.

7. Miles was released from prison for good behavior. He is now ____________________ and has to visit with an officer once a month.

8. Five witnesses ____________________ for the prosecution. They each testified that they had seen the defendant remove property from the victim's home.

9. The jury ____________________ the defendant of first-degree murder.

EXERCISE 6.F.2. Matching

Match the three subjects below with the phrases (1-9) to create a complete sentence. Each subject should be matched with at least one phrase. Some questions may have more than one correct answer.

The defendant   Law enforcement officers   The jury

1. ____________________ charged Mr. Smith with first-degree burglary.
2. ____________________ invoked the privilege against self-incrimination.
3. ____________________ extorted a confession from Mr. Smith.
4. ____________________ was apprised of her rights.
5. ____________________ advised Mr. Smith of his rights.
6. ____________________ issued *Miranda* warnings.
7. ____________________ convicted Mrs. Smith of first-degree burglary.
8. ____________________ was convicted of first-degree burglary.
9. ____________________ took the stand.

G. Criminal Procedure Essay Question #2

Answer the following hypothetical using the previous cases in this chapter to inform your answer. Use a piece of paper or a blank document on your computer to outline your response before you begin writing.

Suggested response time: **35 minutes**.

QUESTION

Lorna and her husband Mike are co-owners of the Magic Deli, a delicatessen selling sandwiches, snacks, and drinks. Police officers learned from an informant that the deli is a "front" for selling the drug methamphetamine (also known as "crystal meth"). After obtaining a valid search warrant, the police searched the deli on a morning that Lorna's and Mike's 17-year-old daughter, Naomi, was running the store by herself. The police read Naomi the search warrant and began asking her questions about the deli.

About half an hour into the search of the store and questioning of Naomi, Lorna and Mike drove to the deli—concerned because Naomi was not answering their calls. When Lorna and Mike arrived, they noticed six police cars in the parking lot and the door to the deli was locked. Lorna banged on the door. When an officer opened the door partway, Lorna explained that she was an owner of the store. The police officer permitted Lorna to enter the deli, but when Mike tried to follow behind her, the officer shut the door and locked it from the inside. Mike knocked on the door but to no avail; he waited for about 30 minutes in the parking lot before Lorna, Naomi, and the police officers finally exited the store.

Once inside the deli, Lorna saw and called out to Naomi to ask if she was okay. There were nine police officers inside the deli. Oliver, one of the police officers, warned Lorna not to communicate with Naomi, while Paul, another officer told Lorna to "shut up." Oliver directed Lorna to a small office inside the deli, where he and another officer, Detective Quinn, asked her questions for 20 minutes while seated around a table. The door to the office remained open.

Ten minutes into the questioning, Detective Quinn asked Lorna to identify a small pouch filled with a white substance. Oliver falsely told Lorna that an informant had traced the pouch back to the Magic Deli. Lorna admitted to selling crystal meth from the store, but stated that she'd never seen a pouch like the one Detective Quinn was holding. Without any further questioning, Detective Quinn placed Lorna under arrest and issued *Miranda* warnings.

Lorna was later charged with possession and distribution of a Class B substance. She filed a pre-trial motion to suppress the incriminating statement she made while questioned during the search, arguing that it was obtained in violation of her Fifth Amendment rights. You are the trial judge. How would you rule on the motion to suppress?[3]

H. Criminal Procedure Case #5

The focus of the previous cases has been on the "in custody" element of *Miranda*. But an incriminating statement obtained without the provision of *Miranda* warnings is inadmissible in court only if it was made during "custodial interrogation." Thus, in order to suppress a statement obtained without *Miranda* warnings, it is not enough to prove that the statement was made while an individual was in custody. The individual must also have been subjected to interrogation. In the following case, the Court attempts to clarify what constitutes "interrogation."

RHODE ISLAND v. INNIS

Supreme Court of the United States, 1980.
446 U.S. 291, 100 S.Ct. 1682, 64 L.Ed.2d 297.

Mr. Justice STEWART delivered the opinion of the Court.

(1) In *Miranda v. Arizona*, 384 U.S. 436, 474, the Court held that, once a defendant in custody asks to speak with a lawyer, all interrogation must cease until a lawyer is present. **(2)** The issue in this case is whether the respondent was "interrogated" in violation of the standards promulgated in the *Miranda* opinion.

I

(3) On the night of January 12, 1975, John Mulvaney, a Providence, R.I., taxicab driver, disappeared after being dispatched to pick up a customer. **(4)** His body was discovered four days later buried in a shallow grave in Coventry, R.I. **(5)** He had died from a shotgun blast aimed at the back of his head.

(6) On January 17, 1975, shortly after midnight, the Providence police received a telephone call from Gerald Aubin, also a taxicab driver, who reported that he had just been robbed by a man wielding a sawed-off shotgun. **(7)** Aubin further reported that he had dropped off his assailant near Rhode Island College in a section of Providence known as Mount Pleasant. **(8)** While at the Providence police station waiting to give a statement, Aubin noticed a picture of his assailant on a bulletin board. **(9)** Aubin so informed one of the police officers present. **(10)**

[3] Hypothetical adapted from U.S. v. Kim, 292 F.3d 969 (9th Cir. 2002).

The officer prepared a **photo array**, and again Aubin identified a picture of the same person. **(11)** That person was the respondent. **(12)** Shortly thereafter, the Providence police began a search of the Mount Pleasant area.

(13) At approximately 4:30 a.m. on the same date, Patrolman Lovell, while cruising the streets of Mount Pleasant in a patrol car, spotted the respondent standing in the street facing him. **(14)** When Patrolman Lovell stopped his car, the respondent walked towards it. **(15)** Patrolman Lovell then arrested the respondent, who was unarmed, and advised him of his so-called *Miranda* rights. **(16)** While the two men waited in the patrol car for other police officers to arrive, Patrolman Lovell did not converse with the respondent other than to respond to the latter's request for a cigarette.

(17) Within minutes, Sergeant Sears arrived at the scene of the arrest, and he also gave the respondent the *Miranda* warnings. **(18)** Immediately thereafter, Captain Leyden and other police officers arrived. **(19)** Captain Leyden advised the respondent of his *Miranda* rights. **(20)** The respondent stated that he understood those rights and wanted to speak with a lawyer. **(21)** Captain Leyden then directed that the respondent be placed in a "caged wagon," a four-door police car with a wire screen mesh between the front and rear seats, and be driven to the central police station. **(22)** Three officers, Patrolmen Gleckman, Williams, and McKenna, were assigned to accompany the respondent to the central station. **(23)** They placed the respondent in the vehicle and shut the doors. **(24)** Captain Leyden then instructed the officers not to question the respondent or intimidate or coerce him in any way. **(25)** The three officers then entered the vehicle, and it departed.

(26) While en route to the central station, Patrolman Gleckman initiated a conversation with Patrolman McKenna concerning the missing shotgun. **(27)** As Patrolman Gleckman later testified:

> . . . At this point, I was talking back and forth with Patrolman McKenna stating that I frequent this area while on patrol and [that because a school for handicapped children is located nearby,] there's a lot of handicapped children running around in this area, and God forbid one of them might find a weapon with shells and they might hurt themselves." App. 43–44.

(28) Patrolman McKenna apparently shared his fellow officer's concern: ". . . I more or less concurred with him [Gleckman] that it was a safety factor and that we should, you know, continue to search for the weapon and try to find it." *Id.*, at 53.

(29) While Patrolman Williams said nothing, he overheard the conversation between the two officers: ". . . He [Gleckman] said it would be too bad if the little—I believe he said a girl—would pick up the gun, maybe kill herself." *Id.*, at 59.

(30) The respondent then interrupted the conversation, stating that the officers should turn the car around so he could show them where the gun was located. **(31)** At this point, Patrolman McKenna radioed back to Captain Leyden that they were returning to the scene of the arrest and that the respondent would inform them of the location of the gun. **(32)** At the time the respondent indicated that the officers should turn back, they had traveled no more than a mile, a trip encompassing only a few minutes.

(33) The police vehicle then returned to the scene of the arrest where a search for the shotgun was in progress. **(34)** There, Captain Leyden again advised the respondent of his *Miranda* rights. **(35)** The respondent replied that he understood those rights but that he "wanted to get the gun out of the way because of the kids in the area in the school." **(36)** The respondent then led the police to a nearby field, where he pointed out the shotgun under some rocks by the side of the road.

(37) On March 20, 1975, a **grand jury** returned an **indictment** charging the respondent with the **kidnaping**, **robbery**, and **murder** of John Mulvaney. **(38)** Before trial, the respondent moved to suppress the shotgun and the statements he had made to the police regarding it. **(39)** After an **evidentiary hearing** at which the respondent elected not to testify, the trial judge found that the respondent had been "repeatedly and completely advised of his *Miranda* rights." **(40)** He further found that it was "entirely understandable that [the officers in the police vehicle] would voice their concern [for the safety of the handicapped children] to each other." **(41)** The judge then concluded that the respondent's decision to inform the police of the location of the shotgun was "a waiver, clearly, and on the basis of the evidence that I have heard, and [*sic*] intelligent waiver, of his [*Miranda*] right to remain silent." **(42)** Thus, without passing on whether the police officers had in fact "interrogated" the respondent, the trial court **sustained** the admissibility of the shotgun and testimony related to its discovery. **(43)** That evidence was later introduced at the respondent's trial, and the jury returned a verdict of guilty on all counts.

(44) On appeal, the Rhode Island Supreme Court, in a 3–2 decision, set aside the respondent's conviction. R.I., 391 A.2d 1158. **(45)** Relying at least in part on this Court's decision in *Brewer v. Williams*, 430 U.S. 387, the court concluded that the respondent had invoked his *Miranda* right to counsel and that, contrary to *Miranda's* mandate that, in the absence of counsel, all custodial interrogation then cease, the police officers in the vehicle had "interrogated" the respondent without a valid waiver of his right to counsel. **(46)** It was the view of the state appellate court that, even though the police officers may have been genuinely concerned about the public safety and even though the respondent had not been addressed personally by the police officers, the respondent nonetheless had been subjected to "subtle coercion" that was the equivalent of "interrogation" within the meaning of the *Miranda* opinion. **(47)** Moreover, contrary to the holding of the trial court, the appellate court concluded that the evidence was insufficient to support a finding of waiver. **(48)** Having concluded that both the shotgun and testimony relating to its discovery were obtained in violation of the *Miranda* standards and therefore should not have been admitted into evidence, the Rhode Island Supreme Court held that the respondent was entitled to a new trial.

(49) We granted certiorari to address for the first time the meaning of "interrogation" under *Miranda v. Arizona*. 440 U.S. 934.

II

(50) In its *Miranda* opinion, the Court concluded that in the context of "custodial interrogation" certain procedural safeguards are necessary to protect a defendant's Fifth and Fourteenth Amendment privilege against compulsory self-incrimination. **(51)** More specifically, the Court held that "the prosecution may not use statements, whether exculpatory or inculpatory, stemming from custodial interrogation of the defendant unless it demonstrates the use of procedural safeguards effective to secure the privilege against self-incrimination." *Id.*, 384 U.S., at 444. **(52)** Those safeguards included the now familiar *Miranda* warnings—namely, that the defendant be informed "that he has the right to remain silent, that anything he says can be used against him in a court of law, that he has the right to the presence of an attorney, and that if he cannot afford an attorney one will be appointed for him prior to any questioning if he so desires"—or their equivalent. *Id.*, at 479.

(53) The Court in the *Miranda* opinion also outlined in some detail the consequences that would result if a defendant sought to invoke those procedural safeguards. **(54)** With regard to the right to the presence of counsel, the Court noted:

> Once warnings have been given, the subsequent procedure is clear. . . . **(55)** If the individual states that he wants an attorney, the interrogation must cease until an attorney is present. **(56)** At that time, the individual must have an opportunity to confer with the attorney and to have him present during any subsequent questioning. **(57)** If the individual cannot obtain an attorney and he indicates that he wants one before speaking to police, they must respect his decision to remain silent." *Id.*, at 473–474.

(58) In the present case, the parties are in agreement that the respondent was fully **informed of his *Miranda* rights** and that he invoked his *Miranda* right to counsel when he told Captain Leyden that he wished to consult with a lawyer. **(59)** It is also uncontested that the respondent was "in custody" while being transported to the police station.

(60) The issue, therefore, is whether the respondent was "interrogated" by the police officers in violation of the respondent's undisputed right under

Miranda to remain silent until he had consulted with a lawyer. **(61)** In resolving this issue, we first define the term "interrogation" under *Miranda* before turning to a consideration of the facts of this case.

A

(62) The starting point for defining "interrogation" in this context is, of course, the Court's *Miranda* opinion. **(63)** There the Court observed that "[b]y custodial interrogation, we mean *questioning* initiated by law enforcement officers after a person has been taken into custody or otherwise deprived of his freedom of action in any significant way." *Id.*, at 444 (emphasis added). **(64)** This passage and other references throughout the opinion to "questioning" might suggest that the *Miranda* rules were to apply only to those police interrogation practices that involve express questioning of a defendant while in custody.

(65) We do not, however, construe the *Miranda* opinion so narrowly. **(66)** The concern of the Court in *Miranda* was that the "interrogation environment" created by the interplay of interrogation and custody would "subjugate the individual to the will of his examiner" and thereby undermine the privilege against compulsory self-incrimination. *Id.*, at 457–458. **(67)** The police practices that evoked this concern included several that did not involve express questioning. **(68)** For example, one of the practices discussed in *Miranda* was the use of **line-ups** in which a coached witness would pick the defendant as the perpetrator. **(69)** This was designed to establish that the defendant was in fact guilty as a predicate for further interrogation. *Id.*, at 453. . . . **(70)** The Court in *Miranda* also included in its survey of interrogation practices the use of psychological ploys, such as to "posi[t]" "the guilt of the subject," to "minimize the moral seriousness of the offense," and "to cast blame on the victim or on society." *Id.*, at 450. **(71)** It is clear that these techniques of persuasion, no less than express questioning, were thought, in a custodial setting, to amount to interrogation.

(72) This is not to say, however, that all statements obtained by the police after a person has been taken into custody are to be considered the product of interrogation. **(73)** As the Court in *Miranda* noted:

> Confessions remain a proper element in law enforcement. **(74)** Any statement given freely and voluntarily without any compelling influences is, of course, admissible in evidence. **(75)** *The fundamental import of the privilege while an individual is in custody is not whether he is allowed to talk to the police without the benefit of warnings and counsel, but whether he can be interrogated. . . .* **(76)** Volunteered statements of any kind are not barred by the Fifth Amendment and their admissibility is not affected by our holding today. *Id.*, at 478 (emphasis added).

(77) It is clear therefore that the special procedural safeguards outlined in *Miranda* are required not where a suspect is simply taken into custody, but rather where a suspect in custody is subjected to interrogation. **(78)** "Interrogation," as conceptualized in the *Miranda* opinion, must reflect a measure of compulsion above and beyond that inherent in custody itself.

(79) We conclude that the *Miranda* safeguards come into play whenever a person in custody is subjected to either express questioning or its functional equivalent. **(80)** That is to say, the term "interrogation" under *Miranda* refers not only to express questioning, but also to any words or actions on the part of the police (other than those normally attendant to arrest and custody) that the police should know are reasonably likely to elicit an incriminating response from the suspect. **(81)** The latter portion of this definition focuses primarily upon the perceptions of the suspect, rather than the intent of the police. **(82)** This focus reflects the fact that the *Miranda* safeguards were designed to vest a suspect in custody with an added measure of protection against coercive police practices, without regard to objective proof of the underlying intent of the police. **(83)** A practice that the police should know is reasonably likely to evoke an incriminating response from a suspect thus amounts to interrogation. **(84)** But, since the police surely cannot be held accountable for the unforeseeable results of their words or actions, the definition of interrogation can extend only to words or actions on the part of police officers that they *should have known* were reasonably likely to elicit an incriminating response.

B

(85) Turning to the facts of the present case, we conclude that the respondent was not "interrogated" within the meaning of *Miranda*. **(86)** It is undisputed that the first prong of the definition of "interrogation" was not satisfied, for the conversation between Patrolmen Gleckman and McKenna included no express questioning of the respondent. **(87)** Rather, that conversation was, at least in form, nothing more than a dialogue between the two officers to which no response from the respondent was invited.

(88) Moreover, it cannot be fairly concluded that the respondent was subjected to the "functional equivalent" of questioning. **(89)** It cannot be said, in short, that Patrolmen Gleckman and McKenna should have known that their conversation was reasonably likely to elicit an incriminating response from the respondent. **(90)** There is nothing in the record to suggest that the officers were aware that the respondent was peculiarly susceptible to an appeal to his conscience concerning the safety of handicapped children. **(91)** Nor is there anything in the record to suggest that the police knew that the respondent was unusually disoriented or upset at the time of his arrest.

(92) The case thus boils down to whether, in the context of a brief conversation, the officers should have known that the respondent would suddenly be moved to make a self-incriminating response. **(93)** Given the fact that the entire conversation appears to have consisted of no more than a few off hand remarks, we cannot say that the officers should have known that it was reasonably likely that Innis would so respond. **(94)** This is not a case where the police carried on a lengthy harangue in the presence of the suspect. **(95)** Nor does the record support the respondent's contention that, under the circumstances, the officers' comments were particularly "evocative." **(96)** It is our view, therefore, that the respondent was not subjected by the police to words or actions that the police should have known were reasonably likely to elicit an incriminating response from him.

(97) The Rhode Island Supreme Court erred, in short, in equating "subtle compulsion" with interrogation. **(98)** That the officers' comments struck a responsive chord is readily apparent. **(99)** Thus, it may be said, as the Rhode Island Supreme Court did say, that the respondent was subjected to "subtle compulsion." **(100)** But that is not the end of the inquiry. **(101)** It must also be established that a suspect's incriminating response was the product of words or actions on the part of the police that they should have known were reasonably likely to elicit an incriminating response. **(102)** This was not established in the present case.

(103) For the reasons stated, the judgment of the Supreme Court of Rhode Island is vacated, and the case is remanded to that court for further proceedings not inconsistent with this opinion.

(104) *It is so ordered. . . .*

Mr. Justice MARSHALL, with whom Mr. Justice BRENNAN joins, dissenting.

(105) I am substantially in agreement with the Court's definition of "interrogation" within the meaning of *Miranda v. Arizona*, 384 U.S. 436 (1966). **(106)** In my view, the *Miranda* safeguards apply whenever police conduct is intended or likely to produce a response from a suspect in custody. **(107)** As I read the Court's opinion, its definition of "interrogation" for *Miranda* purposes is equivalent, for practical purposes, to my formulation, since it contemplates that "where a police practice is designed to elicit an incriminating response from the accused, it is unlikely that the practice will not also be one which the police should have known was reasonably likely to have that effect." *Ante*, [in omitted footnote]. **(108)** Thus, the Court requires an objective inquiry into the likely effect of police conduct on a typical individual, taking into account any special susceptibility of the suspect to certain kinds of pressure of which the police know or have reason to know.

(109) I am utterly at a loss, however, to understand how this objective standard as applied to the facts before us can rationally lead to the conclusion that there was no interrogation. **(110)** Innis was arrested at 4:30 a.m., handcuffed, searched, advised of his rights, and placed in the back seat of a patrol car. **(111)** Within a short time he had been twice more advised of his rights and driven away in a four-door sedan with three police officers. **(113)** Two officers sat in the front seat and one sat beside Innis in the back seat. **(114)** Since the car traveled no more than a mile before Innis agreed to point out the location of the murder weapon, Officer Gleckman must have begun almost immediately to talk about the search for the shotgun.

(115) The Court attempts to characterize Gleckman's statements as "no more than a few off hand remarks" which could not reasonably have been expected to elicit a response. *Ante*, at [sentence 92]. **(116)** If the statements had been addressed to respondent, it would be impossible to draw such a conclusion. **(117)** The simple message of the "talking back and forth" between Gleckman and McKenna was that they had to find the shotgun to avert a child's death.

(118) One can scarcely imagine a stronger appeal to the conscience of a suspect—*any* suspect—than the assertion that if the weapon is not found an innocent person will be hurt or killed. **(119)** And not just any innocent person, but an innocent child—a little girl—a helpless, handicapped little girl on her way to school. **(120)** The notion that such an appeal could not be expected to have any effect unless the suspect were known to have some special interest in handicapped children verges on the ludicrous. **(121)** As a matter of fact, the appeal to a suspect to confess for the sake of others, to "display some evidence of decency and honor," is a classic interrogation technique. See, *e. g.*, F. Inbau & J. Reid, Criminal Interrogation and Confessions 60–62 (2d ed. 1967).

(122) Gleckman's remarks would obviously have constituted interrogation if they had been explicitly directed to respondent, and the result should not be different because they were nominally addressed to McKenna. **(123)** This is not a case where police officers speaking among themselves are accidentally overheard by a suspect. **(124)** These officers were "talking back and forth" in close quarters with the handcuffed suspect, traveling past the very place where they believed the weapon was located. **(125)** They knew respondent would hear and attend to their conversation, and they are chargeable with knowledge of and responsibility for the pressures to speak which they created.

(126) I firmly believe that this case is simply an aberration, and that in future cases the Court will apply the standard adopted today in accordance with its plain meaning.

Mr. Justice STEVENS, dissenting.

(127) An original definition of an old term coupled with an original finding of fact on a cold record makes it possible for this Court to vacate the judgment of the Supreme Court of Rhode Island. **(128)** That court, on the basis of the facts in the record before it, concluded that members of the Providence, R.I., police force had interrogated respondent, who was clearly in custody at the time, in the absence of counsel after he had requested counsel. **(129)** In my opinion the state court's conclusion that there was interrogation rests on a proper interpretation of both the facts and the law; thus, its determination that the products of the interrogation were inadmissible at trial should be affirmed.

(130) The undisputed facts can be briefly summarized. **(131)** Based on information that respondent, armed with a sawed-off shotgun, had just robbed a cabdriver in the vicinity of Rhode Island College, a number of Providence police officers began a thorough search of the area in the early morning of January 17, 1975. **(132)** One of them arrested respondent without any difficulty at about 4:30 a.m. **(133)** Respondent did not then have the shotgun in his possession and presumably had abandoned it, or hidden it, shortly before he was arrested. **(134)** Within a few minutes, at least a dozen officers were on the scene. App. 37. **(135)** It is fair to infer that an immediate search for the missing weapon was a matter of primary importance.

(136) When a police captain arrived, he repeated the *Miranda* warnings that a patrolman and a sergeant had already given to respondent, and respondent said he wanted an attorney. **(137)** The captain then ordered two officers who were assigned to a "caged wagon" to transport respondent to the central station, and ordered a third officer to ride in the back seat with respondent. **(138)** While the wagon was en route to the station, one of the officers, Officer Gleckman, stated that there was a school for handicapped children in the vicinity and "God forbid" one of them should find the shotgun and hurt herself. **(139)** As a result of this statement, respondent told the officers that he was willing to show them where the gun was hidden. **(140)** The wagon returned to the scene and respondent helped the officers locate the gun.

(141) After a suppression hearing, the trial court assumed, without deciding, that Officer Gleckman's statement constituted interrogation. **(142)** The court nevertheless allowed the shotgun and testimony concerning respondent's connection to it into evidence on the ground that respondent had waived his *Miranda* rights when he consented to help police locate the gun. **(143)** On appeal from respondent's conviction for kidnaping, robbery and murder, the Rhode Island Supreme Court held that Officer Gleckman's statement constituted impermissible interrogation and rejected the trial court's waiver analysis. **(144)** It therefore reversed respondent's conviction and remanded for a new trial. **(145)** Today, the Court reverses the Rhode Island court's resolution of the interrogation issue, creating a new definition of that term and holding, as a matter of law, that the statement at issue in this case did not constitute interrogation.

I

(146) As the Court recognizes, *Miranda v. Arizona*, 384 U.S. 436 makes it clear that, once respondent requested an attorney, he had an absolute right to have any type of interrogation cease until an attorney was present. **(147)** As it also recognizes, *Miranda* requires that the term "interrogation" be broadly construed to include "either express questioning or its functional equivalent." *Ante*, at [sentence 78]. **(148)** In my view any statement that would normally be understood by the average listener as calling for a response is the functional equivalent of a direct question, whether or not it is punctuated by a question mark. **(149)** The Court, however, takes a much narrower view. **(150)** It holds that police conduct is not the "functional equivalent" of direct questioning unless the police should have known that what they were saying or doing was likely to elicit an incriminating response from the suspect. **(151)** This holding represents a plain departure from the principles set forth in *Miranda.*

(152) In *Miranda* the Court required the now-familiar warnings to be given to suspects prior to custodial interrogation in order to dispel the atmosphere of coercion that necessarily accompanies such interrogations. **(153)** In order to perform that function effectively, the warnings must be viewed by both the police and the suspect as a correct and binding statement of their respective rights. **(154)** Thus, if, after being told that he has a right to have an attorney present during interrogation, a suspect chooses to cut off questioning until counsel can be obtained, his choice must be "scrupulously honored" by the police. See *Michigan v. Mosley*, 423 U.S. 96, 104, *id.*, at 110 (WHITE, J., concurring in result). **(155)** At the least this must mean that the police are prohibited from making deliberate attempts to elicit statements from the suspect. **(156)** Yet the Court is unwilling to characterize all such attempts as "interrogation," noting only that "where a police practice is designed to elicit an incriminating response from the accused, it is unlikely that the practice will not also be one which the police should have known was reasonably likely to have that effect." *Ante*, [in omitted foonote].

(157) From the suspect's, point of view, the effectiveness of the warnings depends on whether it appears that the police are scrupulously honoring his rights. **(158)** Apparent attempts to elicit information from a suspect after he has invoked his right to cut off questioning necessarily demean that right and tend to reinstate the imbalance between police and suspect that the *Miranda* warnings are designed to correct. **(159)** Thus, if the rationale for requiring those warnings in the first place is to be respected, any police conduct or statements that would appear to a reasonable person in the suspect's position to call for a response must be considered "interrogation."

(160) In short, in order to give full protection to a suspect's right to be free from any interrogation at all, the definition of "interrogation" must include any police statement or conduct that has the same purpose or effect as a direct question. **(161)** Statements that appear to call for a response from the suspect, as well as those that are designed to do so, should be considered interrogation. **(162)** By prohibiting only those relatively few statements or actions that a police officer should know are likely to elicit an incriminating response, the Court today accords a suspect considerably less protection. **(163)** Indeed, since I suppose most suspects are unlikely to incriminate themselves even when questioned directly, this new definition will almost certainly exclude every statement that is not punctuated with a question mark from the concept of "interrogation."

(164) The difference between the approach required by a faithful adherence to *Miranda* and the stinted test applied by the Court today can be illustrated by comparing three different ways in which Officer Gleckman could have communicated his fears about the possible dangers posed by the shotgun to handicapped children. **(165)** He could have:

(1) directly asked Innis:

> Will you please tell me where the shotgun is so we can protect handicapped school children from danger?

(2) announced to the other officers in the wagon:

> If the man sitting in the back seat with me should decide to tell us where the gun is, we can protect handicapped children from danger.

or (3) stated to the other officers:

> It would be too bad if a little handicapped girl would pick up the gun that this man left in the area and maybe kill herself.

(166) In my opinion, all three of these statements should be considered interrogation because all three appear to be designed to elicit a response from anyone who in fact knew where the gun was located. **(167)** Under the Court's test, on the other hand, the form of the statements would be critical. **(168)** The third statement would not be interrogation because in the Court's view there was no reason for Officer Gleckman to believe that Innis was susceptible to this type of an implied appeal, . . . ; therefore, the statement would not be reasonably likely to elicit an incriminating response. **(169)** Assuming that this is true, . . . then it seems to me that the first two statements, which would be just as unlikely to elicit such a response, should also not be considered interrogation. **(170)** But, because the first statement is clearly an express question, it *would* be considered interrogation under the Court's test. **(171)** The second statement, although just as clearly a deliberate appeal to Innis to reveal the location of the gun, would presumably not be interrogation because (a) it was not in form a direct question and (b) it does not fit within the "reasonably likely to elicit an incriminating response" category that applies to indirect interrogation.

(172) As this example illustrates, the Court's test creates an incentive for police to ignore a suspect's invocation of his rights in order to make continued attempts to extract information from him. **(173)** If a suspect does not appear to be susceptible to a particular type of psychological pressure, the police are apparently free to exert that pressure on him despite his request for counsel, so long as they are careful not to punctuate their statements with question marks. **(174)** And if, contrary to all reasonable expectations, the suspect makes an incriminating statement, that statement can be used against him at trial. **(175)**

The Court thus turns *Miranda's* unequivocal rule against any interrogation at all into a trap in which unwary suspects may be caught by police deception.

II

(176) Even if the Court's new definition of the term "interrogation" provided a proper standard for deciding this case, I find it remarkable that the Court should undertake the initial task of applying its new standard to the facts of the present case. **(177)** As noted above, the trial judge did not decide whether Officer Gleckman had interrogated respondent. **(178)** Assuming, *arguendo*, that he had, the judge concluded that respondent had waived his request for counsel by offering to help find the gun. **(178)** The Rhode Island Supreme Court disagreed on the waiver questions, and expressly concluded that interrogation had occurred. **(180)** Even if the Rhode Island court might have reached a different conclusion under the Court's new definition, I do not believe we should exclude it from participating in a review of the actions taken by the Providence police. **(181)** Indeed, given the creation of a new standard of decision at this stage of the litigation, the proper procedure would be to remand to the trial court for findings on the basis of evidence directed at the new standard.

(182) In any event, I think the Court is clearly wrong in holding, as a matter of law, that Officer Gleckman should not have realized that his statement was likely to elicit an incriminating response. **(183)** The Court implicitly assumes that, at least in the absence of a lengthy harangue, a criminal suspect will not be likely to respond to indirect appeals to his humanitarian impulses. **(184)** It then goes on to state that the officers in this case had no reason to believe that respondent would be unusually susceptible to such appeals . . . . **(185)** Finally, although the significance of the officer's intentions is not clear under its objective test, the Court states in a footnote that the record "in no way suggests" that Officer Gleckman's remarks were designed to elicit a response. . . .

(186) The Court's assumption that criminal suspects are not susceptible to appeals to conscience is directly contrary to the teachings of police interrogation manuals, which recommend appealing to a suspect's sense of morality as a standard and often successful interrogation technique. **(187)** Surely the practical experience embodied in such manuals should not be ignored in a case such as this in which the record is devoid of any evidence—one way or the other—as to the susceptibility of suspects in general or of Innis in particular.

(188) Moreover, there is evidence in the record to support the view that Officer Gleckman's statement was intended to elicit a response from Innis. **(189)** Officer Gleckman, who was not regularly assigned to the caged wagon, was directed by a police captain to ride with respondent to the police station. **(190)** Although there is a dispute in the testimony, it appears that Gleckman may well have been riding in the back seat with Innis. **(191)** The record does not explain why, notwithstanding the fact that respondent was handcuffed, unarmed, and had offered no resistance when arrested by an officer acting alone, the captain ordered Officer Gleckman to ride with respondent. **(192)** It is not inconceivable that two professionally trained police officers concluded that a few well-chosen remarks might induce respondent to disclose the whereabouts of the shotgun. **(193)** This conclusion becomes even more plausible in light of the emotionally charged words chosen by Officer Gleckman ("God forbid" that a "little girl" should find the gun and hurt herself).

III

(194) Under my view of the correct standard, the judgment of the Rhode Island Supreme Court should be affirmed because the statements made within Innis' hearing were as likely to elicit a response as a direct question. **(195)** However, even if I were to agree with the Court's much narrower standard, I would disagree with its disposition of this particular case because the Rhode Island courts should be given an opportunity to apply the new standard to the facts of this case.

TASK 6.H.1. Case Brief

Write a case brief of *Rhode Island v. Innis* using the template on page 392. Also include a summary of the dissenting opinions in your brief.

TASK 6.H.2. Criminal Procedure Vocabulary Definitions (List 5)

Fill in each definition on the next page with the appropriate term from the list below. Consult a law dictionary or an English-to-English dictionary to confirm that you have matched each term with the correct definition. If multiple forms of a term are provided, you may not need to use all of the forms in the blanks.

evidentiary hearing *(noun)*
grand jury *(noun)*
indictment *(noun)*
inform [someone] of her/his rights *(verb)*
kidnapping *(noun)*
line-up *(noun)*
murder *(noun)*
photo array *(noun)*
robbery *(noun)*
sustain [the admissibility of evidence or an objection made at trial] *(verb)*

1. ____________________ is the unlawful seizing and taking away of a person against her will.

2. ____________________ is the unlawful killing of another human being. The exact definition varies from one state to the next, and many states prescribe different degrees depending on whether the killing was premeditated or planned.

3. ____________________ is the unlawful taking of property from another person by using verbal threats or physical force.

4. An individual is ____________________ of her *Miranda* rights when the police administer *Miranda* warnings.

5. A/an ____________________ is a type of eyewitness identification procedure used by law enforcement to identify a potential suspect. In this procedure, a witness is shown a collection of photographs to determine if she can recognize someone involved in the crime. Another popular type of eyewitness identification procedure is the ____________________, in which the witness is shown a collection of people, standing or sitting in a row (usually behind a one-way mirror).

6. A/an ____________________ is a criminal charge against the defendant. This charge is returned by a/an ____________________, which is composed of randomly selected individuals. (Note: these juries are not like regular trial juries. They do not find guilt, but rather determine if there is enough evidence to charge the defendant and go to trial. See Appendix D: Steps in the Criminal Justice Process.)

7. To ____________________ means to agree with or rule in favor of a party in court.

8. During a/an ____________________ a judge decides whether there is enough evidence to proceed to trial. This "preliminary hearing" often takes place after a prosecutor files a complaint against the defendant. (See Appendix D: Steps in the Criminal Justice Process.)

TASK 6.H.3. Questions for Discussion

Answer the questions on the next page to assist you during a class discussion of the case. Indicate the sentence(s) in which you found the answer to each question.

1. What's the definition of "interrogation" according to:

    a. Majority (Stewart)
    b. Dissent (Marshall)
    c. Dissent (Stevens)

2. How do the three judges apply the definition of interrogation to the facts of this case, and what is the outcome for each?

3. Which judge's definition and/or analysis do you find most convincing? Why?

4. Which of the following scenarios is MOST likely to be deemed by the Court as interrogation? Why?

    a. Police officers introduce themselves and give the suspect their business card. They tell the suspect that they are in charge of the investigation and that the suspect's full cooperation would be appreciated.
    b. A police officer calls another officer in the suspect's presence. The police officers discuss which street they should take to transport the suspect to a maximum security detention facility.
    c. A police officer gives the suspect a document containing the charges against him. Next to the charge of murder is written: "Punishable by death." The officer remarks to another officer in the room, "I bet he wants to talk now."
    d. Police officers arrive at the scene of a shooting. They find the victim, a 15-year-old boy, and the boy's mother. With the officers standing right next to her, the mother asks the boy, "What have you done?"

I. Criminal Procedure Case #6

The following case presents a somewhat unusual fact pattern. As you read, decide whether you believe the defendant in this case was interrogated while in custody. What does the Court say?

ILLINOIS v. PERKINS

Supreme Court of the United States, 1990.
496 U.S. 292, 110 S.Ct. 2394, 110 L.Ed.2d 243, 58 USLW 4737.

Justice KENNEDY delivered the opinion of the Court.

(1) An **undercover** government agent was placed in the cell of respondent Perkins, who was **incarcerated** on charges unrelated to the subject of the agent's investigation. **(2)** Respondent made statements that implicated him in the crime that the agent sought to solve. **(3)** Respondent claims that the statements should be inadmissible because he had not been given *Miranda* warnings by the agent. **(4)** We hold that the statements are admissible. **(5)** *Miranda* warnings are not required when the suspect is unaware that he is speaking to a law enforcement officer and gives a voluntary statement.

I

(6) In November 1984, Richard Stephenson was murdered in a suburb of East St. Louis, Illinois. **(7)** The murder remained unsolved until March 1986, when one Donald Charlton told police that he had learned about a homicide from a fellow **inmate** at the Graham Correctional Facility, where Charlton had been **serving a sentence** for burglary. **(8)** The fellow inmate was Lloyd Perkins, who is the respondent here. **(9)** Charlton told police that, while at Graham, he had befriended respondent, who told him in detail about a murder that respondent had committed in East St. Louis. **(10)** On hearing Charlton's account, the police recognized details of the Stephenson murder that were not well known, and so they treated Charlton's story as a credible one.

(11) By the time the police heard Charlton's account, respondent had been released from Graham, but police traced him to a jail in Montgomery County, Illinois, where he was being held pending trial on a charge of aggravated battery, unrelated to the Stephenson murder. **(12)** The police wanted to investigate further respondent's connection to the Stephenson murder, but feared that the use of an **eavesdropping** device would prove impracticable and unsafe. **(13)** They decided instead to place an undercover agent in the cellblock with respondent and Charlton. **(14)** The plan was for Charlton and undercover agent John Parisi to pose as escapees from a work release program who had been arrested in the course of a burglary. **(15)** Parisi and Charlton were instructed to engage respondent in casual conversation and report anything he said about the Stephenson murder.

(16) Parisi, using the alias "Vito Bianco," and Charlton, both clothed in jail garb, were placed in the cellblock with respondent at the Montgomery County jail. **(17)** The cellblock consisted of 12 separate cells that opened onto a common room. **(18)** Respondent greeted Charlton who, after a brief conversation with respondent, introduced Parisi by his alias. **(19)** Parisi told respondent that he "wasn't going to do any more time" and suggested that the three of them escape. **(20)** Respondent replied that the Montgomery County jail was "rinky-dink" and that they could "break out." **(21)** The trio met in respondent's cell later that evening, after the other inmates were asleep, to refine their plan. **(22)** Respondent said that his girlfriend could smuggle in a pistol. **(23)** Charlton said: "Hey, I'm not a murderer, I'm a burglar. **(24)** That's your guys' profession." **(25)** After telling Charlton that he would be responsible for any murder that occurred, Parisi asked respondent if he had ever "done" anybody. **(26)** Respondent said that he had and proceeded to describe at length the events of the Stephenson murder. **(27)** Parisi and respondent then engaged in some casual conversation before respondent went to sleep. **(28)** Parisi did not give respondent *Miranda* warnings before the conversations.

(29) Respondent was charged with the Stephenson murder. **(30)** Before trial, he moved to suppress the statements made to Parisi in the jail. **(31)** The trial court granted the motion to suppress, and the State appealed. **(32)** The Appellate Court of Illinois affirmed, 176 Ill.App.3d 443 (1988), holding that *Miranda v. Arizona,* 384 U.S. 436 (1966), prohibits all undercover contacts with incarcerated suspects that are reasonably likely to elicit an incriminating response.

(33) We granted certiorari, 493 U.S. 808 (1989), to decide whether an undercover law enforcement officer must give *Miranda* warnings to an incarcerated suspect before asking him questions that may elicit an incriminating response. **(34)** We now reverse.

II

(35) In *Miranda v. Arizona, supra,* the Court held that the Fifth Amendment privilege against self-incrimination prohibits admitting statements given by a suspect during "custodial interrogation" without a prior warning. **(36)** Custodial interrogation means "questioning initiated by law enforcement officers after a person has been taken into custody. . . ." *Id.* 384 U.S., at 444. **(37)** The warning mandated by *Miranda* was meant to preserve the privilege during "incommunicado interrogation of individuals in a police-dominated atmosphere." *Id.,* at 445. **(38)** That atmosphere is said to generate "inherently compelling pressures which work to undermine the individual's will to resist and to compel him to speak where he would not otherwise do so freely." *Id.,* at 467. **(39)** "Fidelity to the doctrine announced in *Miranda* requires that it be enforced strictly, but only in those types of situations in which the concerns that powered the decision are implicated." *Berkemer v. McCarty,* 468 U.S. 420, 437 (1984).

(40) Conversations between suspects and undercover agents do not implicate the concerns underlying *Miranda.* **(41)** The essential ingredients of a "police-dominated atmosphere" and compulsion are not present when an incarcerated person speaks freely to someone whom he believes to be a fellow inmate. **(42)** Coercion is determined from the perspective of the suspect. *Rhode Island v. Innis,* 446 U.S. 291, 301 (1980); *Berkemer v. McCarty, supra,* 468 U.S., at 442. **(43)** When a suspect considers himself in the company of cellmates and not officers, the coercive atmosphere is lacking. *Miranda,* 384 U.S., at 449 ("[T]he 'principal psychological factor contributing to a successful interrogation is *privacy*—being alone with the person under interrogation'"); *id.,* at 445. **(44)** There is no empirical basis for the assumption that a suspect speaking to those whom he assumes are not officers will feel compelled to speak by the fear of reprisal for remaining silent or in the hope of more lenient treatment should he confess.

(45) It is the premise of *Miranda* that the danger of coercion results from the interaction of custody and official interrogation. **(46)** We reject the argument that *Miranda* warnings are required whenever a suspect is in custody in a technical sense and converses with someone who happens to be a government agent. **(47)** Questioning by captors, who appear to control the suspect's fate, may create mutually reinforcing pressures that the Court has assumed will weaken the suspect's will, but where a suspect does not know that he is conversing with a government agent, these pressures do not exist. **(48)** The state court here mistakenly assumed that because the suspect was in custody, no undercover questioning could take place. **(49)** When the suspect has no reason to think that the listeners have official power over him, it should not be assumed that his words are motivated by the reaction he expects from his listeners. **(50)** "[W]hen the agent carries neither badge nor gun and wears not 'police blue,' but the same prison gray" as the suspect, there is no "*interplay* between police interrogation and police custody." Kamisar, *Brewer v. Williams, Massiah* and *Miranda:* What is "Interrogation"? When Does it Matter?, 67 Geo.L.J. 1, 67, 63 (1978).

(51) *Miranda* forbids coercion, not mere strategic deception by taking advantage of a suspect's misplaced trust in one he supposes to be a fellow prisoner. **(52)** As we recognized in *Miranda:* "[C]onfessions remain a proper element in law enforcement. **(53)** Any statement given freely and voluntarily without any compelling influences is, of course, admissible in evidence." 384 U.S., at 478. **(54)** Ploys to mislead a suspect or lull him into a false sense of security that do not rise to the level of compulsion or coercion to speak are not within *Miranda*'s concerns. . . .

(55) *Miranda* was not meant to protect suspects from boasting about their criminal activities in front of persons whom they believe to be their cellmates. **(56)** This case is illustrative. **(57)** Respondent had no reason to feel that undercover agent Parisi had any legal authority to force him to answer questions or that Parisi could affect respondent's future treatment. **(58)** Respondent viewed the cellmate-agent as an equal and showed no hint of being intimidated by the atmosphere of the jail. **(59)** In recounting the details of the Stephenson murder, respondent was motivated solely by the desire to impress his fellow inmates. **(60)** He spoke at his own peril.

(61) The tactic employed here to elicit a voluntary confession from a suspect does not violate the Self–Incrimination Clause. **(62)** We held in *Hoffa v. United States,* 385 U.S. 293 (1966), that placing an undercover agent near a suspect in order to gather incriminating information was permissible under the Fifth Amendment. **(63)** In *Hoffa,* while petitioner Hoffa was on trial, he met often with one Partin, who, unbeknownst to Hoffa, was cooperating with law enforcement officials. **(64)** Partin reported to officials that Hoffa had divulged his attempts to bribe jury members. **(65)** We approved using Hoffa's statements at his subsequent trial for jury tampering, on the rationale that "no claim ha[d] been or could [have been] made that [Hoffa's] incriminating statements were the product of any sort of coercion, legal or factual." *Id.,* at 304. **(66)** In addition, we found that the fact that Partin had fooled Hoffa into thinking that Partin was a sympathetic colleague did not affect the voluntariness of the statements. *Ibid.* Cf. *Oregon v. Mathiason, supra,* 429 U.S., at 495–496 (officer's falsely telling suspect that suspect's fingerprints had been found at crime scene did not render interview "custodial" under *Miranda*); *Frazier v. Cupp,* 394 U.S. 731, 739 (1969); *Procunier v. Atchley,* 400 U.S. 446, 453–454 (1971). **(67)** The only difference between this case and *Hoffa* is that the suspect here was incarcerated, but detention, whether or not for the crime in question, does not warrant a presumption that the use of an undercover agent to speak with an incarcerated suspect makes any confession thus obtained involuntary.

(68) Our decision in *Mathis v. United States,* 391 U.S. 1 (1968), is distinguishable. **(69)** In *Mathis,* an inmate in a state prison was interviewed by an Internal Revenue Service agent about possible tax violations. **(70)** No *Miranda* warning was given before questioning. **(71)** The Court held that the suspect's incriminating statements were not admissible at his subsequent trial on tax fraud charges. **(72)** The suspect in *Mathis* was aware that the agent was a Government official, investigating the possibility of noncompliance with the tax laws. **(73)** The case before us now is different. **(74)** Where the suspect does not know that he is speaking to a government agent there is no reason to assume the possibility that the suspect might feel coerced. **(75)** (The bare fact of custody may not in every instance require a warning even when the suspect is aware that he is speaking to an official, but we do not have occasion to explore that issue here.)

(76) This Court's Sixth Amendment decisions in *Massiah v. United States,* 377 U.S. 201 (1964), *United States v. Henry,* 447 U.S. 264 (1980), and *Maine v. Moulton,* 474 U.S. 159 (1985), also do not avail respondent. **(77)** We held in those cases that the government may not use an undercover agent to circumvent the Sixth Amendment right to counsel once a suspect has been charged with the crime. **(78)** After charges have been filed, the Sixth Amendment prevents the government from interfering with the accused's right to counsel. *Moulton, supra,* at 176. **(79)** In the instant case no charges had been filed on the subject of the interrogation, and our Sixth Amendment precedents are not applicable.

(80) Respondent can seek no help from his argument that a **bright-line rule** for the application of *Miranda* is desirable. **(81)** Law enforcement officers will have little difficulty putting into practice our holding that undercover agents need not give *Miranda* warnings to incarcerated suspects. **(82)** The use of undercover agents is a recognized law enforcement technique, often employed in the prison context to detect violence against correctional officials or inmates, as well as for the purposes served here. **(83)** The interests protected by *Miranda* are not implicated in these cases, and the warnings are not required to safeguard the constitutional rights of inmates who make voluntary statements to undercover agents.

(84) We hold that an undercover law enforcement officer posing as a fellow inmate need not give *Miranda* warnings to an incarcerated suspect before asking questions that may elicit an incriminating response. **(85)** The statements at issue in this case were voluntary, and there is no federal obstacle to their admissibility at trial. **(86)** We now reverse and remand for proceedings not inconsistent with our opinion.

(87) *It is so ordered. . . .*

Justice MARSHALL, dissenting.

(88) This Court clearly and simply stated its holding in *Miranda v. Arizona,* 384 U.S. 436 (1966): "[T]he prosecution may not use statements, whether exculpatory or inculpatory, stemming from custodial interrogation of the defendant unless it demonstrates the use of procedural safeguards effective to secure the privilege against self-incrimination." *Id.,* at 444. **(89)** The conditions that require the police to apprise a defendant of his constitutional rights—custodial interrogation conducted by an agent of the police—were present in this case. **(90)** Because Lloyd Perkins received no *Miranda* warnings before he was subjected to custodial interrogation, his confession was not admissible.

(91) The Court reaches the contrary conclusion by fashioning an exception to the *Miranda* rule that applies whenever "an undercover law enforcement officer posing as a fellow inmate . . . ask[s] questions that may elicit an incriminating response" from an incarcerated suspect. *Ante,* at [sentence 83]. **(92)** This exception is inconsistent with the rationale supporting *Miranda* and allows police officers intentionally to take advantage of suspects unaware of their constitutional rights. **(93)** I therefore dissent.

(94) The Court does not dispute that the police officer here conducted a custodial interrogation of a criminal suspect. **(95)** Perkins was incarcerated in county jail during the questioning at issue here; under these circumstances, he was in custody as that term is defined in *Miranda.* 384 U.S., at 444; *Mathis v. United States,* 391 U.S. 1, 4–5 (1968) (holding that defendant incarcerated on charges different from the crime about which he is questioned was in custody for purposes of *Miranda*). **(96)** The United States argues that Perkins was not in custody for purpose of *Miranda* because he was familiar with the custodial environment as a result of being in jail for two days and previously spending time in prison. Brief for United States as *Amicus Curiae* 11. **(97)** Perkins' familiarity with confinement, however, does not transform his incarceration into some sort of noncustodial arrangement. . . .

(98) While Perkins was confined, an undercover police officer, with the help of a police informant, questioned him about a serious crime. **(98)** Although the Court does not dispute that Perkins was interrogated, it downplays the nature of the 35–minute questioning by disingenuously referring to it as a "conversatio[n]." *Ante,* at [sentences 15, 18, 27, 28, 40]. **(100)** The officer's narration of the "conversation" at Perkins' suppression hearing however, reveals that it clearly was an interrogation.

> **(101)** "[Agent:] You ever do anyone?
> **(102)** "[Perkins:] Yeah, once in East St. Louis, in a rich white neighborhood.
> **(103)** "Informant: I didn't know they had any rich white neighborhoods in East St. Louis.
> **(104)** "Perkins: It wasn't in East St. Louis, it was by a race track in Fairview Heights. . . .
> **(105)** "[Agent]: You did a guy in Fairview Heights?
> **(106)** "Perkins: Yeah in a rich white section where most of the houses look the same.
> **(107)** "[Informant]: If all the houses look the same, how did you know you had the right house?
> **(108)** "Perkins: Me and two guys cased the house for about a week. **(109)** I knew exactly which house, the second house on the left from the corner.
> **(110)** "[Agent]: How long ago did this happen?
> **(111)** "Perkins: Approximately about two years ago. **(112)** I got paid $5,000 for that job.
> **(113)** "[Agent]: How did it go down?
> **(114)** "Perkins: I walked up [to] this guy['s] house with a sawed-off under my trench coat.
> **(115)** "[Agent]: What type gun[?]
> **(116)** "Perkins: A .12 gauge Remmington *[sic]* Automatic Model 1100 sawed-off." App. 49–50.

(117) The police officer continued the inquiry, asking a series of questions designed to elicit specific information about the victim, the crime scene, the weapon, Perkins' motive, and his actions during and after the shooting. *Id.,* at 50–52. **(118)** This interaction was not a "conversation"; Perkins, the officer, and the informant were not equal participants in a free-ranging discussion, with each man offering his views on different topics. **(119)** Rather, it was an interrogation: Perkins was subjected to express questioning likely to evoke an incriminating response. *Rhode Island v. Innis,* 446 U.S. 291, 300–301 (1980).

(120) Because Perkins was interrogated by police while he was in custody, *Miranda* required that the officer inform him of his rights. **(121)** In rejecting that conclusion, the Court finds that "conversations" between undercover agents and suspects are devoid of the coercion inherent in station house interrogations conducted by law enforcement officials who openly represent the State. . . . **(122)** *Miranda* was not, however, concerned solely with police *coercion.* **(123)** It dealt with *any* police tactics that may operate to compel a suspect in custody to make incriminating statements without full awareness of his constitutional rights. See *Miranda, supra* 384 U.S., at 468 (referring to "inherent pressures of the interrogation atmosphere"); *Estelle v. Smith,* 451 U.S. 454, 467 (1981) ("The purpose of [the *Miranda*] admonitions is to combat what the Court saw as 'inherently compelling pressures' at work on the person and to provide him with an awareness of the Fifth Amendment privilege and the consequences of forgoing it") (quoting *Miranda,* 384 U.S., at 467). **(124)** Thus, when a law enforcement agent structures a custodial interrogation so that a suspect feels compelled to reveal incriminating information, he must inform the suspect of his constitutional rights and give him an opportunity to decide whether or not to talk.

(125) The compulsion proscribed by *Miranda* includes deception by the police. See *Miranda, supra,* 384 U.S., at 453 (indicting police tactics "to induce a confession out of trickery," such as using fictitious witnesses or false accusations); *Berkemer v. McCarty,* 468 U.S. 420, 433 (1984) ("The purposes of the safeguards prescribed by *Miranda* are to ensure that the police do not coerce *or* trick captive suspects into confessing") (emphasis deleted and added). Cf. *Moran v. Burbine,* 475 U.S. 412, 421 (1986) ("[T]he relinquishment of the right [protected by the *Miranda* warnings] must have been voluntary in the sense that it was the product of a free and deliberate choice rather than intimidation, coercion, *or* deception") (emphasis added). **(126)** Although the Court did not find trickery by itself sufficient to constitute compulsion in *Hoffa v. United States,* 385 U.S. 293 (1966), the defendant in that case was not in custody. **(127)** Perkins, however, was interrogated while incarcerated. **(128)** As the Court has acknowledged in the Sixth Amendment context: "[T]he mere fact of custody imposes pressures on the accused; confinement may bring into play subtle influences that will make him particularly susceptible to the ploys of undercover Government agents." *United States v. Henry,* 447 U.S. 264, 274 (1980). See also *Massiah v. United States,* 377 U.S. 201, 206 (1964) (holding, in the context of the Sixth Amendment, that defendant's constitutional privilege against self-incrimination was "more seriously imposed upon . . . because he did not even know that he was under interrogation by a government agent") (citation and internal quotation marks omitted).

(129) Custody works to the State's advantage in obtaining incriminating information. **(130)** The psychological pressures inherent in confinement increase the suspect's anxiety, making him likely to seek relief by talking with others. Dix, Undercover Investigations and Police Rulemaking, 53 Texas L.Rev. 203, 230 (1975). See also Gibbs, The First Cut is the Deepest: Psychological Breakdown and Survival in the Detention Setting, in The Pains of Imprisonment 97, 107 (R. Johnson & H. Toch eds. 1982); Hagel–Seymour, Environmental Sanctuaries for Susceptible Prisoners, in The Pains of Imprisonment, *supra,* at 267, 279; Chicago Tribune, Apr. 15, 1990, p. D3 (prosecutors have found that prisoners often talk freely with fellow inmates). **(131)** The inmate is thus more susceptible to efforts by undercover agents to elicit information from him. **(132)** Similarly, where the suspect is incarcerated, the constant threat of physical danger peculiar to the prison environment may make him demonstrate his toughness to other inmates by recounting or inventing past violent acts. **(133)** "Because the suspect's ability to select people with whom he can confide is completely within their control, the police have a unique opportunity to exploit the suspect's vulnerability. **(134)** In short, the police can insure that if the pressures of confinement lead the suspect to confide in anyone, it will be a police agent." (Footnote omitted.) White, Police Trickery in Inducing Confessions, 127 U.Pa.L.Rev. 581, 605 (1979). **(135)** In this case, the police deceptively took advantage of Perkins' psychological vulnerability by including him in a sham escape plot, a situation in which he would feel compelled to demonstrate his willingness to shoot a prison guard by revealing his past involvement in a murder. See App. 49 (agent stressed that a killing might be necessary in the escape and then asked Perkins if he had ever murdered someone).

(136) Thus, the pressures unique to custody allow the police to use deceptive interrogation tactics to compel a suspect to make an incriminating statement. **(137)** The compulsion is not eliminated by the suspect's ignorance of his interrogator's true identity. **(138)** The Court therefore need not inquire past the bare facts of custody and interrogation to determine whether *Miranda* warnings are required.

(139) The Court's adoption of an exception to the *Miranda* doctrine is incompatible with the principle, consistently applied by this Court, that the doctrine should remain simple and clear. . . . **(140)** We explained the benefits of a bright-line rule in *Fare v. Michael C.,* 442 U.S. 707 (1979): "*Miranda*'s holding has the virtue of informing police and prosecutors with specificity as to what they may do in conducting custodial interrogation, and of informing courts under what circumstances statements obtained during such interrogation are not admissible." *Id.,* at 718.

(141) The Court's holding today complicates a previously clear and straightforward doctrine. **(142)** The Court opines that "[l]aw enforcement officers will have little difficulty putting into practice our holding that undercover agents need not give *Miranda* warnings to incarcerated suspects." *Ante,* at [sentence 80]. **(143)** Perhaps this prediction is true with respect to fact patterns virtually identical to the one before the Court today. **(144)** But the outer boundaries of the exception created by the Court are by no means clear. **(145)** Would *Miranda* be violated, for instance, if an undercover police officer beat a confession out of a suspect, but the suspect thought the officer was another prisoner who wanted the information for his own purposes?

(146) Even if *Miranda,* as interpreted by the Court, would not permit such obviously compelled confessions, the ramifications of today's opinion are still disturbing. **(147)** The exception carved out of the *Miranda* doctrine today may well result in a proliferation of departmental policies to encourage police officers to conduct interrogations of confined suspects through undercover agents, thereby circumventing the need to administer *Miranda* warnings. **(148)** Indeed, if *Miranda* now requires a police officer to issue warnings only in those situations in which the suspect might feel compelled "to speak by the fear of reprisal for remaining silent or in the hope of more lenient treatment should he confess," *ante,* at [sentence 43], presumably it allows custodial interrogation by an undercover officer posing as a member of the clergy or a suspect's defense attorney. **(149)** Although such abhorrent tricks would play on a suspect's need to confide in a trusted adviser, neither would cause the suspect to "think that the listeners have official power over him," *ante,* at [sentence 48]. **(150)** The Court's adoption of the "undercover agent" exception to the *Miranda* rule thus is necessarily also the adoption of a substantial loophole in our jurisprudence protecting suspects' Fifth Amendment rights.

(151) I dissent.

TASK 6.I.1. Case Brief

Write a case brief of *Illinois v. Perkins* using the template on page 392. Also include a summary of the dissenting opinion in your brief.

TASK 6.I.2. Criminal Procedure Vocabulary Definitions (List 6)

Fill in each definition with the appropriate term from the list below. Consult a law dictionary or an English-to-English dictionary to confirm that you have matched each term with the correct definition. If multiple forms of a term are provided, you may not need to use all of the forms in the blanks.

bright-line rule *(noun)*
eavesdrop *(verb)*
incarcerated *(adjective)*
inmate *(noun)*
serve a sentence *(verb)*
undercover *(adjective)*

1. A/an ____________________ individual is imprisoned (i.e., confined to prison).

2. When someone goes ____________________, she uses a fake identity in order to obtain information.

3. ____________________ is the act of secretly listening in on a private conversation.

4. Individuals who are kept in a prison or mental institution are referred to as ____________________. In the prison context, they ____________________ of a specified period of time. This sentence is determined by a trial judge.

5. A/an ____________________ is a rule that resolves a legal issue in a predictable way. The benefit of such rules is that they are easy for courts to administer and they create more certain results.

TASK 6.I.3. Questions for Discussion

Answer the following questions to assist you during a class discussion of the case. Indicate the sentence(s) in which you found the answer to each question.

1. What is the Court's holding?

2. Was the questioning of Perkins a "custodial interrogation"? Did the Court address this point?

3. Justice Kennedy (majority) and Justice Marshall (dissent) interpret the *Miranda* rule in slightly different ways.

a. According to Justice Kennedy, what are the concerns underlying *Miranda*?

b. According to Justice Marshall, what are the concerns underlying *Miranda*?

c. How are these different interpretations applied to the facts of *Perkins*?

d. Which interpretation do you find more convincing?

4. Is there an argument to be made that Perkins was compelled to make an incriminating statement?

J. Criminal Procedure Essay Question #3

Answer the following hypothetical using the previous cases in this chapter to inform your answer. Use a piece of paper or a blank document on your computer to outline your response before you begin writing.

Suggested response time: **35 minutes**.

QUESTION

Two police officers, Ted and Vicki, were dispatched to a mall after Rachel, an employee at one of the stores, reported that a man snatched her purse and ran off. The officers searched the mall looking for a suspect. After 15 minutes, they found Steve, who matched the description that Rachel had provided.

Steve was standing in line at a coffee shop when Ted and Vicki approached him. They asked Steve how long he had been at the mall, to which he replied, "About an hour, but that's none of your business." Ted and Vicki then each grabbed Steve by one arm. Ted said, "Okay buddy. You're coming with us." They led him to the store where Rachel was waiting. While Ted was still holding Steve by one arm, about five feet from Rachel, Vicki approached Rachel and within earshot of Steve, asked her if Steve was the person who had taken her purse. She responded, "Yes, I'm positive that was him." Hearing Rachel's statement, Steve explained, "Fine, I took her purse. But only because she owes me money." Ted subsequently arrested Steve and read him his *Miranda* rights.

Steve has been charged with assault and robbery. He has filed a motion to suppress the statements made at the mall on the ground that they were obtained in violation of his Fifth Amendment rights. You are the trial judge presiding over the case. How would you rule on the motion?

K. Criminal Procedure Case #7

Assume that a suspect is advised of her *Miranda* rights and is subsequently taken into custody and questioned. Per the *Miranda* decision, at this point, she can either invoke her rights, or she may waive her rights and make a statement. The following case provides some answers as to what constitutes an effective waiver.

NORTH CAROLINA v. BUTLER

Supreme Court of the United States, 1979.
441 U.S. 369, 99 S.Ct. 1755, 60 L.Ed.2d 286.

Mr. Justice STEWART delivered the opinion of the Court.

(1) In evident conflict with the present view of every other court that has considered the issue, the North Carolina Supreme Court has held that *Miranda v. Arizona,* 384 U.S. 436, requires that no statement of a person under custodial interrogation may be admitted in evidence against him unless, at the time the statement was made, he explicitly waived the right to the presence of a lawyer. **(2)** We granted certiorari to consider whether this per se rule reflects a proper understanding of the *Miranda* decision. 439 U.S. 1046.

(3) The respondent was convicted in a North Carolina trial court of kidnaping, armed robbery, and felonious assault. **(4)** The evidence at his trial showed that he and a man named Elmer Lee had robbed a gas station in Goldsboro, N. C., in December 1976, and had shot the station attendant as he was attempting to escape. **(5)** The attendant was paralyzed, but survived to testify against the respondent.

(6) The prosecution also produced evidence of incriminating statements made by the respondent shortly after his arrest by Federal Bureau of Investigation agents in the Bronx, N. Y., on the basis of a North Carolina fugitive warrant. **(7)** Outside the presence of the jury, FBI Agent Martinez testified that at the time of the arrest he fully advised the respondent of the rights delineated in the *Miranda* case. **(8)** According to the uncontroverted testimony of Martinez, the agents then took the respondent to the FBI office in nearby New Rochelle, N. Y. **(9)** There, after the agents determined that the respondent had an 11th grade education and was literate, he was given the Bureau's "Advice of Rights" form which he read. **(10)** When asked if he understood his rights, he replied that he did. **(11)** The respondent refused to sign the waiver at the bottom of the form. **(12)** He was told that he need neither speak nor sign the form, but that the agents would like him to talk to them. **(13)** The respondent replied: "I will talk to you but

I am not signing any form." **(14)** He then made inculpatory statements. **(15)** Agent Martinez testified that the respondent said nothing when advised of his right to the assistance of a lawyer. **(16)** At no time did the respondent request counsel or attempt to terminate the agents' questioning.

(17) At the conclusion of this testimony the respondent moved to suppress the evidence of his incriminating statements on the ground that he had not waived his right to the assistance of counsel at the time the statements were made. **(18)** The court denied the motion, finding that

> the statement made by the defendant, William Thomas Butler, to Agent David C. Martinez, was made freely and voluntarily to said agent after having been advised of his rights as required by the Miranda ruling, including his right to an attorney being present at the time of the inquiry and that the defendant, Butler, understood his rights; [and] that he effectively waived his rights, including the right to have an attorney present during the questioning by his indication that he was willing to answer questions, having read the rights form together with the Waiver of Rights . . . . App. A–22 to A–23.

(19) The respondent's statements were then admitted into evidence, and the jury ultimately found the respondent guilty of each offense charged.

(20) On appeal, the North Carolina Supreme Court reversed the convictions and ordered a new trial. **(21)** It found that the statements had been admitted in violation of the requirements of the *Miranda* decision, noting that the respondent had refused to waive in writing his right to have counsel present and that there had not been a *specific* oral waiver. **(22)** As it had in at least two earlier cases, the court read the *Miranda* opinion as

> provid[ing] in plain language that waiver of the right to counsel during interrogation will not be recognized unless such waiver is 'specifically made' after the *Miranda* warnings have been given. 295 N.C. 250, 255 (1978).
>
> See *State v. Blackmon,* 280 N.C. 42, 49–50 (1971); *State v. Thacker,* 281 N.C. 447, 453–454 (1972).

(23) We conclude that the North Carolina Supreme Court erred in its reading of the *Miranda* opinion. **(24)** There, this Court said:

> If the interrogation continues without the presence of an attorney and a statement is taken, a heavy burden rests on the government to demonstrate that the defendant knowingly and

> intelligently waived his privilege against self-incrimination and his right to retained or appointed counsel. 384 U.S., at 475.

(25) The Court's opinion went on to say:

> An express statement that the individual is willing to make a statement and does not want an attorney followed closely by a statement could constitute a waiver. **(26)** But a valid waiver will not be presumed simply from the silence of the accused after warnings are given or simply from the fact that a confession was in fact eventually obtained. *Ibid.*

(27) Thus, the Court held that an express statement can constitute a waiver, and that silence alone after such warnings cannot do so. **(28)** But the Court did not hold that such an express statement is indispensable to a finding of waiver.

(29) An express written or oral statement of waiver of the right to remain silent or of the right to counsel is usually strong proof of the validity of that waiver, but is not inevitably either necessary or sufficient to establish waiver. **(30)** The question is not one of form, but rather whether the defendant in fact knowingly and voluntarily waived the rights delineated in the *Miranda* case. **(31)** As was unequivocally said in *Miranda,* mere silence is not enough. **(32)** That does not mean that the defendant's silence, coupled with an understanding of his rights and a course of conduct indicating waiver, may never support a conclusion that a defendant has waived his rights. **(33)** The courts must presume that a defendant did not waive his rights; the prosecution's burden is great; but in at least some cases waiver can be clearly inferred from the actions and words of the person interrogated.

(34) The Court's opinion in *Miranda* explained the reasons for the prophylactic rules it created:

> We have concluded that without proper safeguards the process of in-custody interrogation of persons suspected or accused of crime contains inherently compelling pressures which work to undermine the individual's will to resist and to compel him to speak where he would not otherwise do so freely. **(35)** In order to combat these pressures and to permit a full opportunity to exercise the privilege against self-incrimination, the accused must be adequately and effectively apprised of his rights and the exercise of those rights must be fully honored. *Id.*, at 467.

(36) The *per se* rule that the North Carolina Supreme Court has found in *Miranda* does not speak to these concerns. **(37)** There is no doubt that this respondent was adequately and effectively apprised of his rights. **(38)** The only question is whether he waived the exercise of one of those rights, the right to the presence of a lawyer. **(39)** Neither the state court nor the respondent has offered any reason why there must be a negative answer to that question in the absence of an *express* waiver. **(40)** This is not the first criminal case to question whether a defendant waived his constitutional rights. **(41)** It is an issue with which courts must repeatedly deal. **(42)** Even when a right so fundamental as that to counsel at trial is involved, the question of waiver must be determined on "the particular facts and circumstances surrounding that case, including the background, experience, and conduct of the accused." *Johnson v. Zerbst,* 304 U.S. 458, 464. . . .

(43) We see no reason to discard that standard and replace it with an inflexible *per se* rule in a case such as this. **(44)** As stated at the outset of this opinion, it appears that every court that has considered this question has now reached the same conclusion. **(45)** Ten of the eleven United States Courts of Appeals and the courts of at least 17 States have held that an explicit statement of waiver is not invariably necessary to support a finding that the defendant waived the right to remain silent or the right to counsel guaranteed by the *Miranda* case. **(46)** By creating an inflexible rule that no implicit waiver can ever suffice, the North Carolina Supreme Court has gone beyond the requirements of federal organic law. **(47)** It follows that its judgment cannot stand, since a state court can neither add to nor subtract from the mandates of the United States Constitution. *Oregon v. Hass,* 420 U.S. 714.

(48) Accordingly, the judgment is vacated, and the case is remanded to the North Carolina Supreme Court for further proceedings not inconsistent with this opinion.

(49) *It is so ordered. . . .*

Mr. Justice BRENNAN, with whom Mr. Justice MARSHALL and Mr. Justice STEVENS joins, dissenting.

(50) *Miranda v. Arizona,* 384 U.S. 436 (1966), held that "[n]o effective waiver of the right to counsel during interrogation can be recognized unless *specifically* made after the warnings we here delineate have been given." (Emphasis added.) **(51)** Support for this holding was found in *Carnley v. Cochran,* 369 U.S. 506, 516 (1962), which held that in the absence of an allegation of an "*affirmative* waiver . . . there is no disputed fact question requiring a hearing." (Emphasis added.)

(52) There is no allegation of an affirmative waiver in this case. **(53)** As the Court concedes, the respondent here refused to sign the waiver form, and "said nothing when advised of his right to the assistance of a lawyer." *Ante,* at [sentence 15]. **(54)** Thus, there was no "disputed fact question requiring a hearing," and the trial court erred in holding one. **(55)** In the absence of an "affirmative waiver" in the form of an express written or oral statement, the

Supreme Court of North Carolina correctly granted a new trial. **(56)** I would, therefore, affirm its decision.

(57) The rule announced by the Court today allows a finding of waiver based upon "infer[ence] from the actions and words of the person interrogated." *Ante,* at [sentence 34]. **(58)** The Court thus shrouds in half-light the question of waiver, allowing courts to construct inferences from ambiguous words and gestures. **(59)** But the very premise of *Miranda* requires that ambiguity be interpreted against the interrogator. **(60)** That premise is the recognition of the "compulsion inherent in custodial" interrogation, 384 U.S., at 458, and of its purpose "to subjugate the individual to the will of [his] examiner," *id.*, at 457. **(61)** Under such conditions, only the most explicit waivers of rights can be considered knowingly and freely given.

(62) The **instant case** presents a clear example of the need for an express waiver requirement. **(63)** As the Court acknowledges, there is a disagreement over whether respondent was orally advised of his rights at the time he made his statement. **(64)** The fact that Butler received a written copy of his rights is deemed by the Court to be sufficient basis to resolve the disagreement. **(65)** But, unfortunately, there is also a dispute over whether Butler could read. See Tr. of Oral Arg. 22, 23. **(66)** And, obviously, if Butler did not have his rights read to him, and could not read them himself, there could be no basis upon which to conclude that he knowingly waived them. **(67)** Indeed, even if Butler could read there is no reason to believe that his oral statements, which followed a refusal to sign a written waiver form, were intended to signify **relinquishment** of his rights.

(68) Faced with "actions and words" of uncertain meaning, some judges may find waivers where none occurred. **(69)** Others may fail to find them where they did. **(70)** In the former case, the defendant's rights will have been violated; in the latter, society's interest in effective law enforcement will have been frustrated. **(71)** A simple prophylactic rule requiring the police to obtain an express waiver of the right to counsel before proceeding with interrogation eliminates these difficulties. **(72)** And since the Court agrees that *Miranda* requires the police to obtain some kind of waiver—whether express or implied—the requirement of an express waiver would impose no burden on the police not imposed by the Court's interpretation. **(73)** It would merely make that burden explicit. **(74)** Had Agent Martinez simply elicited a clear answer from Willie Butler to the question, "Do you waive your right to a lawyer?" this journey through three courts would not have been necessary.

TASK 6.K.1. Case Brief

Write a case brief of *North Carolina v. Butler* using the template on page 392. Also include a summary of the dissenting opinions in your brief.

TASK 6.K.2. Criminal Procedure Vocabulary Definitions (List 7)

Fill in each definition with the appropriate term from the list below. Consult a law dictionary or an English-to-English dictionary to confirm that you have matched each term with the correct definition. If multiple forms of a term are provided, you may not need to use all of the forms in the blanks.

relinquishment *(noun)*; relinquish *(verb)*
"the instant case" *(noun)*

1. To ____________________ means to voluntary give up, renounce, or surrender.

2. When courts speak of ____________________, they are referring to the case currently under review. Courts also use the term "the present case."

TASK 6.K.3. Questions for Discussion

Answer the following questions to assist you during a class discussion of the case. Indicate the sentence(s) in which you found the answer to each question.

1. What is the Court's holding?

2. Waiver is determined based on the "particular facts and circumstances" of a case. What kinds of circumstances do—and *should*—police officers and courts take into account?

3. Do you agree with Justice Brennan's dissenting opinion and suggestion? Why or why not?

4. Hypotheticals:[4]

   a. Suzanne is in custody and is read her *Miranda* rights. She makes no response. Officer Tom then starts to question Suzanne and Suzanne responds, incriminating herself.

      Can Suzanne's statements be admitted against her at trial?

   b. Assume instead that Suzanne states she understands her rights but then refuses to sign a waiver form. Officer Tom then says to her: "You don't have to sign the form, but we would like you to answer some questions for us." Officer Tom then interrogates Suzanne about the crime in question and Suzanne makes several incriminating responses.

      Can Suzanne's statements be admitted against her at trial?

   c. Assume instead that Suzanne states she will answer questions about the crime but will not give or sign a written statement because, in her words, "I know that could be used against me." She then proceeds to make several incriminating statements during the questioning.

      Can Suzanne's statements be admitted against her at trial?

   d. Ursula, handcuffed in the back seat of a police vehicle, was driven to the police station by Detective Jones. Ursula appeared to be very disoriented, fatigued, and obviously under the disorienting influence of narcotics. After arriving at the police station, Detective Jones advised Ursula of her rights. Ursula nodded affirmatively when asked whether she understood them. The detective then said to Ursula: "The sooner you come clean with us, the quicker we can get you help." The detective proceeded to question Ursula about the crime in question, reminding her several times in a forceful manner that it would be easier on her if she confessed. Ursula finally agreed to answer questions and eventually admitted committing the crime.

      Can Ursula's statements be admitted against her at trial?

---

[4] Hypotheticals adapted from ROBERT M. BLOOM AND MARK S. BRODIN, EXAMPLES & EXPLANATIONS: CRIMINAL PROCEDURE: THE CONSTITUTION AND THE POLICE 292 (7th ed. 2013).

5. Create your own question. For inspiration, review the list of common question types in Part II, Chapter 3.

L. Criminal Procedure Case #8

The final case focuses on an exception to the *Miranda* rule. As you read, determine what this exception is and in what situations it might apply.

NEW YORK v. QUARLES

Supreme Court of the United States, 1984.
467 U.S. 649, 104 S.Ct. 2626, 81 L.Ed.2d 550.

Justice REHNQUIST delivered the opinion of the Court.

(1) Respondent Benjamin Quarles was charged in the New York trial court with criminal possession of a weapon. **(2)** The trial court suppressed the gun in question, and a statement made by respondent, because the statement was obtained by police before they read respondent his "Miranda rights." **(3)** That ruling was affirmed on appeal through the New York Court of Appeals. **(4)** We granted certiorari, 461 U.S. 942 (1983), and we now reverse. **(5)** We conclude that under the circumstances involved in this case, overriding considerations of public safety justify the officer's failure to provide *Miranda* warnings before he asked questions devoted to locating the abandoned weapon.

(6) On September 11, 1980, at approximately 12:30 a.m., Officer Frank Kraft and Officer Sal Scarring were on road patrol in Queens, N.Y., when a young woman approached their car. **(7)** She told them that she had just been raped by a black male, approximately six feet tall, who was wearing a black jacket with the name "Big Ben" printed in yellow letters on the back. **(8)** She told the officers that the man had just entered an A & P supermarket located nearby and that the man was carrying a gun.

(9) The officers drove the woman to the supermarket, and Officer Kraft entered the store while Officer Scarring radioed for assistance. **(10)** Officer Kraft quickly spotted respondent, who matched the description given by the woman, approaching a checkout counter. **(11)** Apparently upon seeing the officer, respondent turned and ran toward the rear of the store, and Officer Kraft pursued him with a drawn gun. **(12)** When respondent turned the corner at the end of an aisle, Officer Kraft lost sight of him for several seconds, and upon regaining sight of respondent, ordered him to stop and put his hands over his head.

(13) Although more than three other officers had arrived on the scene by that time, Officer Kraft was the first to reach respondent. **(14)** He frisked him and discovered that he was wearing a shoulder holster which was then empty. **(15)** After handcuffing him, Officer Kraft asked him where the gun was. **(16)** Respondent nodded in the direction of some empty cartons and responded, "the gun is over there." **(17)** Officer Kraft thereafter retrieved a loaded .38–caliber revolver from one of the cartons, formally placed respondent under arrest, and read him his *Miranda* rights from a printed card. **(18)** Respondent indicated that he would be willing to answer questions without an attorney present. **(19)** Officer Kraft then asked respondent if he owned the gun and where he had purchased it. **(20)** Respondent answered that he did own it and that he had purchased it in Miami, Fla.

(21) In the subsequent prosecution of respondent for criminal possession of a weapon, the judge excluded the statement, "the gun is over there," and the gun because the officer had not given respondent the warnings required by our decision in *Miranda v. Arizona*, 384 U.S. 436 (1966), before asking him where the gun was located. **(22)** The judge excluded the other statements about respondent's ownership of the gun and the place of purchase, as evidence tainted by the prior *Miranda* violation. **(23)** The Appellate Division of the Supreme Court of New York affirmed without opinion. 85 A.D.2d 936 (1981).

(24) The Court of Appeals granted leave to appeal and affirmed by a 4–3 vote. 58 N.Y.2d 664 (1982). **(25)** It concluded that respondent was in "custody" within the meaning of *Miranda* during all questioning and rejected the State's argument that the exigencies of the situation justified Officer Kraft's failure to read respondent his *Miranda* rights until after he had located the gun. **(26)** The court declined to recognize an **exigency** exception to the usual requirements of *Miranda* because it found no indication from Officer Kraft's testimony at the suppression hearing that his subjective motivation in asking the question was to protect his own safety or the safety of the public. 58 N.Y.2d, at 666. **(27)** For the reasons which follow, we believe that this case presents a situation where concern for public safety must be paramount to adherence to the literal language of the prophylactic rules enunciated in *Miranda*.

(28) The Fifth Amendment guarantees that "[n]o person . . . shall be compelled in any criminal case to be a witness against himself." **(29)** In *Miranda* this Court for the first time extended the Fifth Amendment privilege against compulsory self-incrimination to individuals subjected to custodial interrogation by the police. 384 U.S., at 460–461, 467. **(30)** The Fifth Amendment itself does not prohibit all incriminating admissions; "[a]bsent some officially coerced self-accusation, the Fifth Amendment privilege is not violated by even the most damning admissions." United States v. Washington, 431 U.S. 181, 187 (1977) (emphasis added). **(31)** The *Miranda* Court, however, presumed that interrogation in certain custodial circumstances is inherently coercive and held that statements made under those circumstances are inadmissible unless the suspect is specifically informed of his *Miranda* rights and freely decides to forgo those rights. **(32)** The prophylactic *Miranda* warnings therefore are "not themselves rights protected by the Constitution but [are] instead measures to insure that the right against compulsory self-incrimination [is] protected." Michigan v. Tucker, 417 U.S. 433, 444 (1974); see Edwards v. Arizona, 451 U.S. 477, 492 (1981) (POWELL, J., concurring). Requiring *Miranda* warnings before custodial interrogation provides "practical reinforcement" for the Fifth Amendment right. Michigan v. Tucker, supra, 417 U.S., at 444.

(33) In this case we have before us no claim that respondent's statements were actually compelled by police conduct which overcame his will to resist. See Beckwith v. United States, 425 U.S. 341, 347–348 (1976); Davis v. North Carolina, 384 U.S. 737, 738 (1966). **(34)** Thus the only issue before us is whether Officer Kraft was justified in failing to make available to respondent the procedural safeguards associated with the privilege against compulsory self-incrimination since *Miranda*.

(35) The New York Court of Appeals was undoubtedly correct in deciding that the facts of this case come within the ambit of the *Miranda* decision as we have subsequently interpreted it. **(36)** We agree that respondent was in police custody because we have noted that "the ultimate inquiry is simply whether there is a 'formal arrest or restraint on freedom of movement' of the degree associated with a formal arrest," California v. Beheler, 463 U.S. 1121, 1125 (1983) (per curiam), quoting Oregon v. Mathiason, 429 U.S. 492, 495 (1977) (per curiam). **(37)** Here Quarles was surrounded by at least four police officers and was handcuffed when the questioning at issue took place. **(38)** As the New York Court of Appeals observed, there was nothing to suggest that any of the officers were any longer concerned for their own physical safety. 58 N.Y.2d, at 666. **(39)** The New York Court of Appeals' majority declined to express an opinion as to whether there might be an exception to the *Miranda* rule if the police had been acting to protect the public, because the lower courts in New York had made no factual determination that the police had acted with that motive. *Ibid.*

(40) We hold that on these facts there is a "public safety" exception to the requirement that *Miranda* warnings be given before a suspect's answers may be admitted into evidence, and that the availability of that exception does not depend upon the motivation of the individual officers involved. **(41)** In a kaleidoscopic situation such as the one confronting these officers, where spontaneity rather than adherence to a police manual is necessarily the order of the day, the application of the exception which we recognize today should not be made to depend on post hoc findings at a suppression hearing concerning the subjective motivation of the arresting officer. **(42)** Undoubtedly most police officers, if placed in Officer Kraft's position, would act out of a host of different, instinctive, and largely unverifiable motives—their own safety, the safety of others, and perhaps as well the desire to obtain incriminating evidence from the suspect.

(43) Whatever the motivation of individual officers in such a situation, we do not believe that the doctrinal underpinnings of *Miranda* require that it be applied in all its rigor to a situation in which police officers ask questions reasonably prompted by a concern for the public safety. **(44)** The *Miranda* decision was based in large part on this Court's view that the warnings which it required police to give to suspects in custody would reduce the likelihood that the suspects would fall victim to constitutionally impermissible practices of police interrogation in the presumptively coercive environment of the station house. 384 U.S., at 455–458. **(45)** The dissenters warned that the requirement of *Miranda* warnings would have the effect of decreasing the number of suspects who respond to police questioning. Id., at 504, 516–517 (Harlan, J., joined by Stewart and WHITE, JJ., dissenting). **(46)** The *Miranda* majority, however, apparently felt that whatever the cost to society in terms of fewer convictions of guilty suspects, that cost would simply have to be borne in the interest of enlarged protection for the Fifth Amendment privilege.

(47) The police in this case, in the very act of apprehending a suspect, were confronted with the immediate necessity of ascertaining the whereabouts of a gun which they had every reason to believe the suspect had just removed from his empty holster and discarded in the supermarket. **(48)** So long as the gun was concealed somewhere in the supermarket, with its actual whereabouts unknown, it obviously posed more than one danger to the public safety: an **accomplice** might make use of it, a customer or employee might later come upon it.

(49) In such a situation, if the police are required to recite the familiar *Miranda* warnings before asking the whereabouts of the gun, suspects in Quarles' position might well be deterred from responding. **(50)** Procedural safeguards which deter a suspect from responding were deemed acceptable in *Miranda* in order to protect the Fifth Amendment privilege; when the primary social cost of those added protections is the possibility of fewer convictions, the *Miranda* majority was willing to bear that cost. **(51)** Here, had *Miranda* warnings deterred Quarles from responding to Officer Kraft's question about the whereabouts of the gun, the cost would have been something more than merely the failure to obtain evidence useful in convicting Quarles. **(52)** Officer Kraft needed an answer to his question not simply to make his case against Quarles but to insure that further danger to the public did not result from the concealment of the gun in a public area.

(53) We conclude that the need for answers to questions in a situation posing a threat to the public safety outweighs the need for the prophylactic rule protecting the Fifth Amendment's privilege against self-incrimination. **(54)** We decline to place officers such as Officer Kraft in the untenable position of having to consider, often in a matter of seconds, whether it best serves society for them to ask the necessary questions without the *Miranda* warnings and render whatever **probative** evidence they uncover inadmissible, or for them to give the warnings in order to preserve the admissibility of evidence they might uncover but possibly damage or destroy their ability to obtain that evidence and neutralize the volatile situation confronting them.

(55) In recognizing a narrow exception to the *Miranda* rule in this case, we acknowledge that to some degree we lessen the desirable clarity of that rule. **(56)** At least in part in order to preserve its clarity, we have over the years refused to sanction attempts to expand our *Miranda* holding. . . . **(57)** As we have in other contexts, we recognize here the importance of a workable rule "to guide police officers, who have only limited time and expertise to reflect on and balance the social and individual interests involved in the specific circumstances they confront." Dunaway v. New York, 442 U.S. 200, 213–214 (1979). **(58)** But as we have pointed out, we believe that the exception which we recognize today lessens the necessity of that on-the-scene balancing process. **(59)** The exception will not be difficult for police officers to apply because in each case it will be circumscribed by the exigency which justifies it. **(60)** We think police officers can and will distinguish almost instinctively between questions necessary to secure their own safety or the safety of the public and questions designed solely to elicit testimonial evidence from a suspect.

(61) The facts of this case clearly demonstrate that distinction and an officer's ability to recognize it. **(62)** Officer Kraft asked only the question necessary to locate the missing gun before advising respondent of his rights. **(63)** It was only after securing the loaded revolver and giving the warnings that he continued with investigatory questions about the ownership and place of purchase of the gun. **(64)** The exception which we recognize today, far from complicating the thought processes and the on-the-scene judgments of police officers, will simply free them to follow their legitimate instincts when confronting situations presenting a danger to the public safety.

(65) We hold that the Court of Appeals in this case erred in excluding the statement, "the gun is over there," and the gun because of the officer's failure to read respondent his *Miranda* rights before attempting to locate the weapon. **(66)** Accordingly we hold that it also erred in excluding the subsequent statements as illegal fruits of a *Miranda* violation. **(67)** We therefore reverse and remand for further proceedings not inconsistent with this opinion.

(68) It is so ordered. . . .

TASK 6.L.1. Case Brief

Write a case brief of *New York v. Quarles* using the template on page 392.

TASK 6.L.2. Criminal Procedure Vocabulary Definitions (List 8)

Fill in each definition with the appropriate term from the list below. Consult a law dictionary or an English-to-English dictionary to confirm that you have matched each term with the correct definition. If multiple forms of a term are provided, you may not need to use all of the forms in the blanks.

accomplice *(noun)*
exigency *(noun)*
probative *(adjective)*

1. In order to be admissible, evidence must be ____________________; in other words, it must tend to prove some disputed point.

2. A/an ____________________ is an individual who helps another person commit a crime.

3. ____________________ refers to an urgent need or emergency. The adjective form is "exigent."

TASK 6.L.3. Questions for Discussion

Answer the following questions to assist you during a class discussion of the case. Indicate the sentence(s) in which you found the answer to each question.

1. Based on the cases you have read in this chapter, why *shouldn't* Quarles's statement about the gun be admitted against him at trial?

2. Why does the Court ultimately allow Quarles's statement about the gun to be admitted against him?

3. What are the potential problems with the rule enunciated by the Court? What are the benefits?

4. Hypothetical: Stevens summoned police to her home, advising them that a shooting had occurred. Upon arrival, the police found two wounded persons lying in the living room. The officers put Stevens in handcuffs and asked where the shooter was, but Stevens was evasive. After the police explained that the ambulance crew would not treat the victims until the scene was safe, Stevens admitted that she had shot the persons, believing

them to be burglars. In response to a later question, Stevens told the officers that she had left the gun in the bedroom, where they retrieved it.

May these responses and the gun be used against Stevens at trial?[5]

5. Create your own question. For inspiration, review the list of common question types in Part II, Chapter 3.

M. Criminal Procedure Essay Question #4

Answer the following hypothetical using the previous cases in this chapter to inform your answer. Use a piece of paper or a blank document on your computer to outline your response before you begin writing.

Suggested response time: **40 minutes.**

QUESTION

Tom, aged eighteen, has had a hard life. His parents abused drugs throughout Tom's childhood and died from a heroin overdose when he was eight years old. After being placed in foster care, Tom was physically abused by his foster parents for several years. When he was fourteen, Tom ran away from his foster home and dropped out of high school in the middle of his freshman year.

Over the next few years, Tom had a few part time jobs until he turned to full-time drug dealing (heroin). Lucky for Tom, despite dealing drugs for a couple of years, he flew under the radar for most of his first eighteen years of life and was never arrested or had much interaction with law enforcement. However, Tom's luck ran out four weeks ago when a reliable police informant identified him as a narcotics dealer.

For the past six months, Detectives Williams and Young have been investigating the narcotics ring which Tom is part of. One day they took the investigation to Tom's neighborhood and happened to spot Tom standing in a dark alley with a young woman. Tom had the woman pinned up against a wall and, despite her objections, injected something into her arm using a hypodermic needle. The detectives ran into the alley, drew their guns, and pointed them at Tom. Officer Williams yelled at Tom to put his hands up and drop the needle. Tom complied. Officer Young then asked Tom whether he had any other drugs or needles on him. Tom replied, "Yeah, I got more needles." Officer Williams instructed Tom to throw all the remaining needles to the ground. Tom emptied

[5] Hypothetical adapted from ROBERT M. BLOOM AND MARK S. BRODIN, EXAMPLES & EXPLANATIONS: CRIMINAL PROCEDURE: THE CONSTITUTION AND THE POLICE 317 (7th ed. 2013).

his pockets of needles and several bags of heroin also fell out. The detectives frisked Tom, cuffed him, led him to a police car, and placed him in the backseat.

While in the car, Officer Williams administered *Miranda* warnings and asked Tom if he understood his rights. He smiled at the officer and said, "I look stupid, but I know a lot of things." The officer did not ask any further questions and started driving toward the police station. On the seat next to Tom was a newspaper with a headline reading: "Promising singer escaped physically abusive relationship only to be raped three months later; last week, she took her own life." Tom, feeling a sudden pang of remorse, said, "I need to come clean. I raped that singer girl in the headline."

Tom has been charged with rape, assault, and possession of a class A substance (heroin) with intent to distribute. You are Tom's defense attorney. It is now before the trial and you must decide whether to file a motion to suppress any of Tom's statements that may be used against him. What's your decision?

N. Criminal Procedure Vocabulary Exercises (Lists 1-8)

EXERCISE 6.N.1. Fill in the Blanks

Fill in the blanks with the most appropriate form of the words and phrases in the list below. You may have to change word form to create a grammatically correct sentence. Some questions may have more than one correct answer.

administer	inmate
apprise	invoke
burglary	larceny
concede	line up
deny	motion to suppress
evidentiary hearing	photo array
exigency	probative
extort	relinquish
grant	sustain
incarcerate	take the stand
indict	undercover

1. The grand jury ____________________ the police officer on charges of voluntary manslaughter, finding that there was enough evidence to proceed to trial.

2. Monica had difficulty picking out the defendant in the ____________________ shown to her by the detectives. All of the pictures looked so similar. In addition, she didn't get a good look at her assailant's face because it was so dark when he assaulted her in the park.

3. After ____________________ for 12 years for a crime he did not commit, James was finally released from prison.

4. Kacey ____________________ her rights when she told the police officers that she did not want to speak to an attorney and was ready to confess to her crimes.

5. In ____________________ situations, police officers can circumvent the *Miranda* requirement. For example, if a police officer believes that there is an immediate risk to the public safety, she does not have to ____________________ *Miranda* warnings prior to interrogating a suspect.

6. Joseph ____________________ the statements he made at the police station. The trial judge ____________________ the motion and the statements were thus admissible.

7. Police officers ____________________ a confession from the suspect by employing deceptive tactics. Specifically, the officers told the defendant that his fingerprints were found at the scene of the murder so he "might as well confess."

8. Shortly after ____________________ my client's apartment, the defendant left the country. There is ample evidence to suggest that the defendant unlawfully broke into the apartment in order to steal my client's collection of rare guns and sell it on the black market overseas.

EXERCISE 6.N.2. Multiple Choice

Circle ALL of the words that may be used to complete each sentence.

1. After she arrested the suspect, the police officer ____________________ *Miranda* warnings.

    a. gave
    b. warned
    c. advised
    d. administered

2. *Miranda* warnings are designed to safeguard against ________________ interrogations.

    a. indigent
    b. coercive
    c. inculpatory
    d. incarcerated

3. The defendant ________________ for less than a month.

    a. was charged
    b. was convicted
    c. was prosecuted
    d. was incarcerated

4. When the ________________ appealed the state supreme court decision, she never imagined that the Supreme Court of the United States would grant certiorari.

    a. indigent
    b. petitioner
    c. respondent
    d. *Amicus Curiae*

EXERCISE 6.N.3. Error Correction

The following sentences are from students' exam answers. The highlighted portion of each sentence below contains one or more errors with respect to grammar and/or word use. Fix ONLY the highlighted portion of each sentence.

1. I grant the motion to suppress Marius's statement because the officer did not apply Miranda rights.

    Your correction:

2. Before questioning Marius, the police officers did not advise Marius of *Miranda* rights.

    Your correction:

3. The officer interrogated him without administering *Miranda* rights.

   Your correction:

4. When Casey was interrogating Aaron, he did not informed Aaron of his *Miranda* warnings.

   Your correction:

5. If individuals are not provided for their *Miranda* rights when they are under "custodial interrogation," any statement they make cannot be used as evidence against them.

   Your correction:

O. Additional Essay Questions

Answer the following hypotheticals using the eight cases in this chapter to inform your answers. Use a piece of paper or a blank document on your computer to outline your response before you begin writing.

Suggested response time for Question 1: **35 minutes.**

QUESTION 1

On September 5, 2018, Police Officer Andrea went to Bolton Middle School (BMS) to investigate an alleged sexual assault. She had received information from the school resource officer,[6] Cory, that Dan, 14 years old, might have been involved in the assault. Andrea went to BMS to interview Dan.

Dan was requested over the school intercom[7] to go to Principal Ellis's office. When Dan arrived, he was escorted into the Principal's office by Cory. Cory and Principal Ellis both left the office and closed the door behind them, while Andrea and Dan remained in the room. The room had windows that provided a view of

[6] A school resource officer is a law enforcement officer responsible for keeping children safe in schools.

[7] An intercom is a communication device that allows people to communicate between different rooms in a building.

the school parking lot. Andrea sat behind Principal Ellis's desk and Dan sat across from her with a view of the parking lot. Andrea was wearing plain clothes and her gun was hidden from view under her blazer. She showed her police badge to Dan and told him that she was a police officer who wanted to ask questions about an alleged sexual assault. When she asked Dan if they could talk, he said, "I guess. But I'm not talking if I'm under arrest."

Andrea explained to Dan that he was not under arrest, but that it would be important to answer her questions so that she could "get to the bottom"[8] of what happened. She then removed her badge and gun from under her blazer and placed them on the desk in between her and Dan. After ten minutes of talking about Dan's relationships with girls at BMS, Andrea asked if he had ever sexually assaulted anyone at school. Dan stated that he never had any intention of assaulting anyone, but admitted that his group of friends made a game out of going up to girls in the hallways and kissing them without their consent. When Andrea pressed Dan for more details, he became agitated and asked if he could talk to a school counselor instead. Andrea terminated the interview and permitted Dan to meet with his counselor.

One week after the interview, a petition was filed in juvenile court alleging that Dan had sexually assaulted a female classmate at BMS. Dan's attorney moved to suppress the statements made during the meeting between him and Andrea, arguing that the interview constituted "custodial interrogation" and that Dan should have been advised of his *Miranda* rights.

The trial judge denied the motion to suppress. The Court of Appeals reversed. You work in the District Attorney's (DA's) office as an assistant district attorney. Your supervisor has asked you to write an informal memo analyzing whether the DA's office should appeal the Court of Appeals' decision.[9]

Suggested response time for Question 2: **35 minutes**.

QUESTION 2

Victor was dating Wells' sister, Yolanda. On the evening of September 9, 2017, while barbecuing in the front yard of Victor's townhouse, the two men got into a dispute about a large sum of money that Victor allegedly owed Wells. The dispute quickly escalated into a physical altercation. In the course of the fight, Victor sustained injuries to his face and leg after Wells punched and kicked him. Victor stabbed Wells in the throat using a kitchen knife.

---

[8] To "get to the bottom of something" means to find out the (usually hidden) cause or explanation behind a bad situation.

[9] Hypothetical adapted from State ex rel. Juvenile Dept. of Multnomah County v. Loredo, 125 Or.App. 390 (1993).

Witnessing the fight, Yolanda called the police on her cell phone. Four police officers and an ambulance arrived at the scene shortly thereafter.

The officers found Wells lying in a pool of blood, seemingly unconscious. Victor, still holding the knife used to stab Wells, was arguing with Yolanda. Upon seeing the officers, Victor dropped the knife and held up his hands, saying, "Thank God you're here. I was scared for my life." Zach, one of the officers approached Victor, told him to put his hands behind his back, and handcuffed him. Victor was cooperative. Zach placed Victor in his police car and told him, "We'll go down to the hospital to get your face and leg checked out. We'll talk more there." In the meantime, the ambulance rushed Wells off to the hospital.

Victor arrived at the hospital in handcuffs, accompanied by Zach and his colleague, Xander. At the hospital, Victor was treated by Nurse Ames while Zach and Xander stayed with him in the examination room. Nurse Ames asked Victor several questions. She first asked how he had hurt his face and leg, to which Victor replied, "That animal, Wells, punched and kicked me." She then asked if Victor had stabbed Wells. Victor responded, "Yes." Nurse Ames informed Victor that Wells was in surgery and not doing well. Victor stated, "He deserves it. He almost killed me. If I'd had a gun, I would've shot him."

Upon hearing this, Xander informed Victor of his *Miranda* rights. Victor, a first-year law student, stated, "Dude, I'm practically a lawyer. I know my rights. Just don't record this conversation; I want it to stay between us." Zach then asked Victor, "So tell me. Why did you stab Wells?" Victor responded, "It's what I already said. Wells is so aggressive he would've killed me. I had to defend myself." Victor opened his mouth to say more, but suddenly stopped himself, telling Zach that he wouldn't be answering any more questions. Xander then advised Victor that it would be in his best interest to cooperate because Yolanda may be implicated in the crime if he doesn't tell the whole truth. Hearing this, Victor exclaimed, "Leave her out of it! She did nothing wrong. I'm the one who stabbed Wells. To tell you the truth, I've always wanted to kill that guy." Wells died from his stab wounds a couple of hours later.

Victor has been charged with first degree murder. He has filed a motion to suppress all of the statements he made on the night of the altercation with Wells. You are the trial judge. How would you rule on the motion to suppress?[10]

Suggested response time for Question 3: **35 minutes**.

QUESTION 3

Greg and Hailey are a married couple who hired a former employee, Jason, to murder their business partner, Kevin, in order to gain ownership over their interior decorating business. Jason is a parolee who had served two years in

[10] Hypothetical adapted from State v. Ybarra, 111 N.M. 234 (1990).

prison for defrauding[11] investors. Greg and Hailey instructed Jason to break into to Kevin's house, where he was supposed to murder Kevin and his wife, Leigh Anne.

The same day that Jason was contacted by Greg and Hailey, he got in touch with his attorney and explained that he did not want to follow through with the plan. Jason's attorney took him to the District Attorney's office, where Jason was equipped with an electronic listening device and instructed to record any incriminating conversations with Greg and Hailey. During one of these conversations, Greg mentioned that the murder should ideally take place at 11 p.m. on November 10, 2018. This conversation was monitored by Detective Marion and other detectives at the local police department.

On the afternoon of November 10, 2018, Detective Marion and her colleagues, Detectives Nora and Olivia, went to Greg and Hailey's apartment complex to arrest the couple. The three officers approached Greg and Hailey in the pool area of the apartment complex, which was fenced off from the street. Greg and Hailey were sitting by the pool on two lawn chairs. There were no other guests present. The officers were not in uniform, but showed their badges as they approached Greg and Hailey. Backup officers were just down the street, and Greg and Hailey could see flashing police lights from the pool.

Marion told Greg and Hailey that Kevin and his wife Leigh Anne had been murdered and that someone had been spotted running away from their home. Although these statements were not true, the detective made them to see how Greg and Hailey would react and whether they would come up with a story. In response to the news, Greg said, "Wow, that's too bad. Kevin was not only a colleague, but also a good friend."

Next, Marion asked Greg if he knew Jason. Visibly upset, Greg yelled, "It was all her idea!" and pointed to his wife Hailey. He added, "I never wanted to hurt anyone, but Hailey is obsessed with the idea of having the business to herself." At this point, Marion placed both Greg and Hailey under arrest and administered *Miranda* warnings.

Greg and Hailey were charged with conspiracy[12] to commit a felony.[13] Greg sought to suppress the statements he made by the pool on the ground that they were obtained in violation of his Fifth Amendment rights. The trial court found that Greg was not "in custody" at the time he made the statements and denied the motion. The Court of Appeals and State Supreme Court affirmed. The Supreme Court of the United States granted certiorari to review the case.

---

[11] To defraud means to cause injury or loss to a person by trickery or deceit.

[12] Conspiracy refers to an agreement between two or more people to commit an unlawful act, with the intent to achieve the agreement's objective.

[13] A felony is a serious crime that is usually punishable by imprisonment for more than one year.

You are a law clerk to Justice Sotomayor. She has asked you to write the first draft of her opinion.[14]

Suggested response time for Question 4: **35 minutes**.

QUESTION 4

While State Trooper[15] Norris was parked on the shoulder of a highway monitoring traffic, he heard the screeching of brakes and then felt a crash in the rear of his police vehicle. Looking in his rearview mirror, he saw that a red Honda had collided into his car.

Norris exited his vehicle and began walking toward the Honda when he heard a gunshot coming from the car. He noticed a hole in the windshield and saw two men, Oliver and Peter, struggling in the two front seats. A 12-year-old girl, Reese, was sitting in the back seat of the car. As Norris approached the Honda, Reese exited the car from the rear and stood next to the car frozen, shaking and crying. The rear door of the car remained open.

Norris trained his gun on Oliver and Peter, who, as it turns out, were fighting over a gun. Norris yelled at the men to drop the weapon, but they continued their battle. Norris radioed for assistance. He kept his weapon trained on Oliver and Peter while waiting for backup.

About one minute later, two other police officers, Stewart and Taney, drove by. They saw Norris as they passed and stopped their vehicle to come to his aid. Noticing the three police officers surrounding the car, Oliver and Peter abruptly stopped their struggle. Oliver had gained control of the gun and held it in his lap. Norris, Stewart, and Taney all trained their weapons on Oliver. Stewart yelled at Oliver to place the gun on the dashboard[16] of the car and to exit the vehicle. Oliver complied. Peter also got out of the car. While Norris still had his weapon trained on the two men, Stewart and Taney pushed Oliver and Peter, respectively, to the ground. They patted Oliver and Peter down for weapons. Reese was still standing by the rear door of the Honda, which was open, crying uncontrollably.

As Stewart was patting down Oliver, he noticed, through the open rear door of the Honda, an aluminum suitcase sitting in the back seat. He poked Oliver with his finger and asked, "Whose suitcase is that?" Oliver responded, "It's mine." Norris walked over to the rear seat and seized the suitcase. He opened it and examined the contents, which revealed a scale and a white powder that was later identified as cocaine.

---

[14] Hypothetical adapted from State v. Kennedy, 116 Ariz. 566 (1977).

[15] A state trooper is a law enforcement officer who is a member of a state police force.

[16] The dashboard is an interior panel underneath the windshield (front window) of a car in front of the steering wheel.

Oliver was charged with possession of a controlled substance with intent to distribute. He filed a motion to suppress the statement made at the scene of the collision on the ground that it was obtained in violation of his Fifth Amendment rights. The trial judge denied the motion. Oliver was eventually found guilty and sentenced to five years in prison and fined $5,000.

Oliver has appealed his case, arguing that his statement was improperly admitted into evidence. You are the appellate judge reviewing the case. Write your legal opinion.[17]

Further Reading

The following hornbooks provide more in-depth coverage of criminal procedure law. Titles marked with an asterisk (*) contain practice exercises in the form of hypotheticals.

*ROBERT M. BLOOM AND MARK S. BRODIN, EXAMPLES & EXPLANATIONS: CRIMINAL PROCEDURE: THE CONSTITUTION AND THE POLICE (8th ed. 2015).

*NEIL P. COHEN, MICHAEL J. BENZA, AND WAYNE A. LOGAN, QUESTIONS & ANSWERS: CRIMINAL PROCEDURE—POLICE INVESTIGATION (3d ed. 2016).

JEROLD ISRAEL AND WAYNE LAFAVE, CRIMINAL PROCEDURE: CONSTITUTIONAL LIMITATIONS IN A NUTSHELL (8th ed. 2014).

*JOHN KIP CORNWELL, THE GLANNON GUIDE TO CRIMINAL PROCEDURE (3d ed. 2012).

[17] Hypothetical adapted from People v. Roundtree, 135 Ill. App. 3d 1075 (1985).

Conclusion
Tips for International Students Studying Law in the United States

Academic culture tends to differ from one country or region to the next. In some countries, students are expected to use a level of formality with their instructors that would seem out of place or awkward elsewhere. Professors in some countries encourage students to work collaboratively in groups, while professors in other countries might view this as an act of cheating. Even within a single country, there might exist numerous academic "sub" cultures. For example, what is acceptable behavior in an undergraduate science class may not be appropriate in a graduate business class.

This chapter describes, in rather broad brushstrokes,[1] the culture of law school in the United States. It contains practical tips for navigating your law classes and relationships with professors and classmates. You may find this chapter informative if you have not yet studied at an institution of higher education in the United States. On the other hand, you might find that the suggestions contained in this chapter reflect what you already know, having attended university in your own country or having taken classes in the United States.

---

[1] If something is described in "broad brushstrokes," the description focuses on main ideas as opposed to details. This idiomatic expression originates from the art of painting. Brushstrokes refer to the paint left on a surface with a paint brush. Broad (or large) strokes painted with a thick, flat paint brush do not capture fine detail the same way as small strokes painted with a pointed paint brush. However, broad brushstrokes provide a picture of the general shape of things.

EXERCISE 1. U.S. Law School Culture Quiz

Read the following statements about law school in the U.S. and write "T" if you believe the statement is true, or "F" if you believe the statement is false. If you are not sure, write a question mark ("?").

1. _____ If you missed a class, you should ask your classmates what you missed before going to your professor.

2. _____ If you know you will be absent from class, it is best not to tell your professor and hope that she does not notice.

3. _____ If you tell your professor first, it is okay to miss class to pick up family members from the airport.

4. _____ Being two to three minutes late for class is acceptable so long as you are not disruptive when you enter the classroom.

5. _____ It is better to be a little late to class because you were eating lunch, rather than eat lunch during class.

6. _____ You have an assignment due on the course website by 11 p.m., but you know you will not be able to finish it on time. It is okay to turn it in at 3 a.m., as long as the professor receives it before class the next day.

7. _____ If you know that you cannot finish an assignment on time, it is okay to ask your professor for an extension.

8. _____ It is appropriate to call your professors by their first name.

9. _____ It is acceptable to disagree with your professor as long as you use a respectful tone.

10. _____ If you have a question for your professor about something you covered in class, it is better to ask her after class rather than during class.

11. _____ If you need to see your professor outside of class, you should stop by her office between 9 a.m. and 5 p.m.

12. _____ Forming a study group with three or four classmates is a good way to review materials and prepare for exams.

13. _____ It is an act of cheating to check your take-home exam answers with a classmate before submitting your exams.

14. _____ Weekends are primarily for relaxing, meeting up with friends, and traveling—not for studying or doing work.

Answers to each of the questions are contained in Sections A through F below.

A. Attending Classes

Every law school has an attendance policy. At most schools, this policy requires regular, punctual attendance and participation in classes. Failure to attend classes, participate in classes, or meet other class requirements could subject students to a lower grade, a failing grade, or a withdrawal from the course. Check your law school's student handbook for its attendance policy and make sure to follow it.

Also check the attendance policy of each course you are taking. These policies can be more stringent than the school's general attendance policy. Individual course policies are usually listed on a course syllabus.

While you should aim to attend every law class, understandably, emergencies happen. Sometimes you will have to miss class or arrive late. But exactly what counts as a legitimate excuse for missing or being late to class, and the most appropriate way to communicate with your professor that you need to miss or arrive late to class, differs from culture to culture. In one educational culture, it might be acceptable to simply not show up. In another culture, this might be frowned upon.

This section addresses U.S. educational norms about absence and lateness, focusing specifically on the law school context.

1. Absences

Statement 1
If you missed a class, you should ask your classmates what you missed before going to your professor.

This is **TRUE**.

Your professors would prefer that you attend every class. They spend a great deal of time preparing their lessons and feel that you will benefit from attending and participating in the class. They really want you to be there.

But your professors are also human. They understand that things come up and occasionally—though rarely—you might have to miss a class due to an emergency, illness, or other personal reason. Their understanding of your situation does not mean, however, that they want to be burdened with explaining what they covered in a class that *you* did not attend. Since you were absent, the responsibility is on you to figure out what you missed. You could look at your syllabus, your course website, and ask a reliable classmate about what the class covered. If the professor handed out any documents, you could ask the same classmate if you can make a copy of the document(s). Further, make sure to turn in any assignments that were assigned during the class. Only if you have a question that your classmate cannot answer, or a question for which you cannot find an answer in your course materials, should you go to your professor. This should usually be your last resort.

Statement 2
If you know you will be absent from class, it is best not to tell your professor and hope that she does not notice.

This is generally **FALSE**.

If possible, tell your professor that you plan to be absent *in advance of* the class session you will miss. This is especially important for small seminar classes of 20 or fewer students, in which your absence will be quite obvious.

As for larger lecture classes, if you know that you cannot make it to class, it is a good idea to tell your professor in advance that you will be absent. Students do sometimes decide to take a gamble—that is, not tell the professor and hope for the best. In a large lecture of more than 50 students, a professor might not notice that you are not there. It is also possible, however, that the professor will call on you exactly on the day that you have skipped class. This is an uncomfortable situation that the professor will almost certainly remember, and you can definitely expect to be called on again in the next class.

The following email is an example of an appropriate message to send to a professor.

From: Student Name student@school.edu>

Date: Fri, Nov 3, 2017 at 12:25 PM

Subject: Absence in today's lecture

To: Professor Name <professsor@school.edu>

Dear Professor [Last name],

Unfortunately, I am unable to attend class today. I have been feeling under the weather and my condition has not improved.

I will be certain to get notes from today's lecture from my classmates. If there is anything I can do to make up for my absence today, please let me know. Thank you for your time and understanding.

Best regards,

[Your full name]

This sample email provides just enough information, and not too much. If you must miss a class because you are sick, err on the side of giving less detail about your illness rather than more. Your professors usually do not want know every little detail about what ails you.

You should always try to send an email to your professor before missing a class. If you do not know in advance that you will be absent from class—maybe due to an emergency that arose on the morning of class—write to your professor as soon as you can. Again, this is particularly important for small seminar classes.

Statement 3

If you tell your professor first, it is okay to miss class to pick up family members from the airport.

This is **FALSE**.

This statement raises the question of what counts as a legitimate excuse for missing class. Generally speaking, illnesses, injuries, and other emergencies are valid excuses that any professor would accept. Examples of emergency situations usually include: your own hospitalization, a death or illness in the family (or of a close friend or significant other), or experiencing a crime. Students with families may also have emergencies related to securing childcare. If you have a child and her school is closed or a caregiver has an emergency and cannot take care of your child when you are due to be in class, your professor will probably understand if you need to miss one session.

Some students may want to miss class for a job interview as well. Professors take different approaches to this. Some professors see no problem with a student missing class for an interview, while others do not consider this a valid excuse. Whenever possible, schedule interviews when you are not supposed to be in class.

Situations that are not considered a legitimate excuse to miss class include: feeling tired (not sick), missing a train or getting stuck in traffic, leaving early for vacation, and picking up family members from the airport. These situations do not constitute valid excuses because they are all entirely avoidable. You can get more rest at night. You can leave your home earlier to account for traffic and delays. You can book tickets after classes get out. And regarding picking up family members from the airport, you have a few options. You could find tickets with an arrival time that does not conflict with your academic schedule; tell your family to wait for you at the airport; or arrange transportation for your family to arrive at a hotel or your home.

2. Latenesses

Statement 4

Being two to three minutes late for class is acceptable so long as you are not disruptive when you enter the classroom.

This is **FALSE**.

Entering a classroom after the class has begun is always disruptive to some degree, even if you crouch down and quietly tiptoe to the nearest seat. It is nearly impossible to enter a class that has already begun without drawing some attention to yourself.

In addition, being late to class, even just two to three minutes, may be considered disrespectful. In the United States, punctuality is highly prized. Being punctual to class, meetings, and appointments is viewed as a sign of respect for others' time. If you arrive on time, your class (or meeting or appointment) will end on time, thereby allowing your professor (or colleague or administrator) to tend to other business. Arriving late may send the inadvertent message that you do not value other people's time.

Note also that professors who teach small classes of fewer than 15 students may not begin class until most students are present. They do this in part because they do not want anyone to miss important information. They also do this because they do not want to repeat information unnecessarily. Needless to say, waiting for students to show up can be frustrating for the professor and the other students in the class who managed to arrive on time.

Statement 5

It is better to be a little late to class because you were eating lunch, rather than eat lunch during class.

This is generally **FALSE**.

Though it depends on the professor, eating during class is usually accepted. Professors understand that students are busy and have very short breaks between classes. For example, your schedule might have one day with three two-hour classes back to back with only 10 or 15-minute breaks in between. No one expects you to go without food for seven hours. Plan in advance and buy or bring lunch to class with you, especially if you know that you will not have enough time to get lunch between classes. Make sure, however, that if you eat during class, your food is neither smelly (e.g., a tuna sandwich) nor crunchy (e.g., tortilla chips). These can be disruptive.

As mentioned, punctuality is highly valued in the United States. Aim to be on time to every class.

B. Submitting Assignments

In most of your law classes you will have only a handful of assignments, or perhaps none at all, with the exception of a final exam. In courses that do require submission of assignments, law professors tend to be strict about submitting them on time.

Statement 6
You have an assignment due on the course website by 11 p.m., but you know you will not be able to finish it on time. It is okay to turn it in at 3 a.m. as long as the professor receives it before class the next day.

This is **FALSE**.

Though your professor may not read your assignment until later in the day (or later in the week or month), you are still obligated to submit your assignments on time. There are two reasons for this.

First, as mentioned, in the United States we place a premium on punctuality. Students are expected to come to class on time and submit their assignments by the due date. Punctuality is just as important in the academic setting as it is in a professional context (as well as in social situations). Second, accepting a late submission would raise issues of fairness. If one student has an extra three hours to complete an assignment that the other students do not, this hardly seems fair to those other students in the class. For this reason alone, some professors will not accept late assignments.

If your professor uses an internet-based learning management system (e.g., Blackboard, Canvas, TWEN, etc.), most likely she can see if you submitted a late assignment. On one site, for example, each assignment comes with a time stamp showing the exact time that the assignment was submitted. Any submission received later than the due date is marked in red. Other professors set up their course sites so that no late assignments can be submitted at all. In this case, if you were to miss a deadline, you would find yourself in the uncomfortable position of having to write to your professor to ask if you could still submit the assignment via email.

The bottom line: do everything in your power to submit all of your assignments on time. If an assignment is due at midnight, do not wait until 11:59 p.m. to upload it. Course websites can crash or your computer can give you trouble. Leave enough time to comfortably submit your assignment.

Statement 7
If you know that you cannot finish an assignment on time, it is okay to ask your professor for an extension.

This is generally **FALSE**.

Unlike some other educational institutions in the United States, the word "extension" is rarely used in the law school context. If you have an assignment due on Friday by midnight, that is when the professor expects to receive it. All law students have multiple competing demands on their time: classes, job search, externship, journal, and so on. You are not the only one with multiple obligations, so your professor probably will not make an exception for you.

This strictness about deadlines is part of the professionalization of law. It is unlikely that a managing partner at a law firm or a judge reviewing your case will give you an extension because *you* did not manage your time well. One aim of law school is to prepare you for this reality.

The exception to asking for an extension is, of course, an emergency. If you experience any of the emergencies listed above (see again the response to Statement 3), your professor will likely be sympathetic to your situation and grant an extension. If you have to miss a final exam, you should speak not only with your professor, but also make arrangements with your law school's office of student services or registrar to take the exam at an earlier or later date.

And if you truly must ask for an extension, do not ask for it an hour or two before the deadline—or worse, after the deadline has passed. Try to manage your time so that you always know in advance if you will have trouble meeting a deadline, and plan accordingly.

C. Relationships with Professors

International students often report that professors in the United States are more approachable than their counterparts in other countries. Although this may well be true, there are some "rules" for interacting with law professors both in and outside of the classroom.

Statement 8
It is appropriate to call your professors by their first name.

This is generally **FALSE**.

Law school is referred to as a "professional school" because every student attends law school to learn the profession of law. The professional nature of the law school permeates many different facets of the institution: the way professors and students dress,[2] speak, and conduct themselves.

Law students are often treated by the faculty not so much as students, but professional colleagues. Accordingly, many professors call students by their last name (e.g., Ms. Vazquez or Mr. White) and expect to be called by their last name, preceded by a title, as well. The preferred title is "professor" (e.g., Professor Vazquez), though professors with a Ph.D. might prefer "doctor" instead (e.g., Doctor White).

Regardless of how your professor calls you—that is, by your first or last name—you should *always* use a title ("professor" or "doctor") and the professor's last name. The only exception to this is if the professor gives you permission to call her by her first name. Do not assume that because a professor has a youthful appearance, you are automatically on a first name basis.

Statement 9

It is acceptable to disagree with your professor as long as you use a respectful tone.

This is **TRUE**.

In U.S. educational contexts, debate is not only acceptable, but often encouraged. Disagreeing with a professor is a sign that you are thinking critically about the subject matter instead of unquestioningly accepting everything that you read or hear. In the United States, debate and disagreement are viewed as indispensable for learning and progress.

When disagreeing with a professor (or classmate), you should, however, use a respectful tone. What qualifies as respectful is subjective and culturally determined. Generally speaking, a respectful tone in the United States means using an appropriate volume (i.e., not too loud) and appropriate language (i.e., no obscene or offensive language).

Statement 10

If you have a question for your professor about something you covered in class, it is better to ask her after class rather than during class.

This **DEPENDS**.

---

[2] Many law professors wear a suit to teach, though some opt for business casual attire. Although you do not need to dress up in a suit for your classes, do dress appropriately (e.g., jeans are fine, but sweatpants may not be). Opportunities for networking and meeting future employers may arise when you least expect them. You want to try to appear professional when they do.

Whether you should ask a question in class or after class depends on your question. Usually, questions about the previous night's reading material are best asked in class. If you have a question, chances are good that some of your classmates have the same question as well. If your question is long or focuses on a very specific detail that may be off topic, then it is probably best to ask after class when you and your professor can speak one-on-one.

Something to avoid is waiting to ask all of your questions until after class. Professors are often bombarded by questions immediately after class has finished, with a long line of students forming waiting to talk to them. This may cause them not only to feel rushed, but also to be late to an appointment or lunch.

A rule of thumb: if you have a question that you think will require a response of more than one minute or so, either go to your professor's office hours (this is usually posted on the professor's office door and/or contained in the course syllabus)[3] or write your professor an email to request an appointment to meet.

Statement 11
If you need to see your professor outside of class, you should stop by her office between 9 a.m. and 5 p.m.

This is **FALSE**.

Professors are not always in their office. Some teach class and then return home because they are more productive there. Professors do not necessarily work on a 9 to 5 schedule. As mentioned, your best bet is to visit your professor when you know she has office hours or to write to your professor to set up an appointment to meet face-to-face.

D. Relationships with Classmates

Law school can sometimes create a competitive atmosphere. This is because the "curve" used at a majority of U.S. law schools places students in direct competition with one another for grades. The curve refers to a "bell curve" representing a distribution of exam grades that looks like this:

[3] "Office hours" refers to a block of time during which a professor is available to meet with students to answer questions. Many, though not all, professors hold office hours. Some professors prefer students to write them an email requesting an appointment. You might see on the course syllabus the sentence: "Office hours by appointment."

Figure 1. Bell Curve

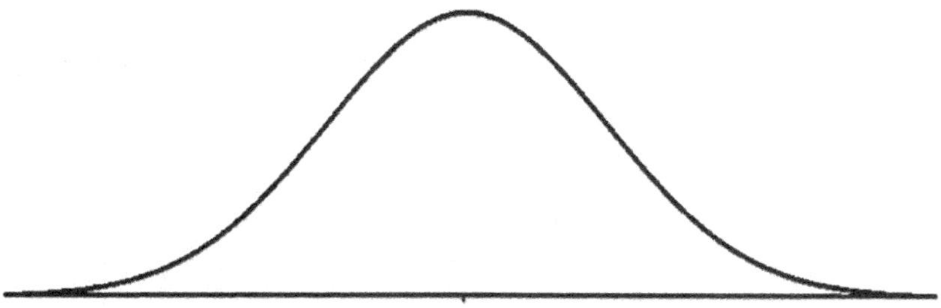

When students are "graded on a curve," the number of As, Bs, and Cs is determined in advance. For example, if students are graded on a "B curve," the majority of students must receive a B (e.g., the 50 percent that are in the middle, fat part of the curve). The rest of the students fall on either skinny end of the curve—for example, 25 percent receive As, A-s, and B+s, while another 25 percent receive B-s, C+s, Cs (or below). The curve means that when professors grade exams, they are permitted to give out only a certain number of each grade. Thus, your performance on a curved exam is relative to how others perform on the same exam. To get an A, for example, you have to write a better test answer than almost everyone else taking the exam.

Nearly every law school uses a curve to calculate grades. See your law school's student handbook to determine what the particular curve is for your school and degree program (most grades are curved to a B or B+).

In general, the curve promotes healthy competition among students, and it usually does not get in the way of forming lasting friendships with your classmates. The next two statements address how you can work together with those classmates and friends to prepare for exams—and, in turn, increase the likelihood that you find yourself at the top of the curve.

Statement 12
Forming a study group with three or four classmates is a good way to review materials and prepare for exams.

This is **TRUE**.

In your prior education you might have viewed studying as a solitary activity: you read, you reviewed, and you did practice exercises in the comfort of your own home or a quiet library. In law school, you could certainly continue studying in this way.

However, it is advantageous to supplement self-study with group study as well. Study groups, as they are known by law students, are a mainstay of American law school culture. Scott Turow, a Harvard Law graduate and author of

One L: The Turbulent True Story of a First Year at Harvard Law School sums up the function of study groups as follows:

> Study groups are another of the basics of [law school] . . . . A small number of students, usually between four and eight, meet regularly to discuss common difficulties which have arisen with course work. There is no set regime for study-group operation. Some groups merely hash over random questions; others use their time together to work out formal exercises; some spend the year developing long course outlines which are exchanged among group members before exams. Most of the faculty encourage the formation of study groups. They afford each student an opportunity for extensive talk about legal problems, something rarely possible in class.[4]

As suggested by Turow, a study group allows you to do what you cannot do in class or alone: talk through complex legal problems with classmates in a low-stakes environment. Study groups also provide an opportunity to learn from your classmates. As the saying goes, two heads are better than one—and three or four heads even more so. Consider forming a study group with classmates and friends taking the same courses as you.

Statement 13
It is an act of cheating to check your take-home exam answers with a classmate before submitting your exams.

This is **TRUE**.

A take-home exam is no less an exam than an in-class exam. While taking a take-home exam, try to isolate yourself from your classmates and do not talk to anybody about the contents of the exam while you are still taking it. Doing so would constitute cheating. If a friend in the same course asks you to take a lunch break during the take-home period, just say "no." You want to avoid putting yourself in situations where you might end up chatting about the exam. For the duration of the exam, pretend that the only thing that exists is you and the test. (Of course, do take bathroom, food, drink, and sleep breaks as necessary.)

---

[4] SCOTT TUROW, ONE L: THE TURBULENT TRUE STORY OF A FIRST YEAR AT HARVARD LAW SCHOOL 51 (2010).

E. Managing Your Workload

Statement 14
Weekends are primarily for relaxing, meeting up with friends, and traveling—not for studying or doing work.

This is **FALSE**.

Although it is important to strike a healthy balance between school work and your personal life, your course work should be a main priority during your time in law school. You will probably find yourself at the bottom of the curve if you "coast" during the semester and attempt to "cram" a semester's worth of information two days before the exam. It is practically impossible to learn hundreds of pages of dense case law and other legal materials in a matter of days and be adequately prepared for the exam (see again Part II, Chapter 4 on exam preparation).

Being a law student will require some adjustments to your social calendar. Though this does not mean saying goodbye to your family and friends forever, it might mean occasionally forgoing a social event so that you can do school work. Some students treat law school like a job: they attend classes and do their reading and other work from 9 a.m. to 5 p.m. (and also work a bit on the weekend). Others follow a less structured schedule and work in the evenings and mostly on the weekends. No matter how you plan your time, you will almost certainly need to do some studying or review on the weekends.

While school work should be a priority, do take care of yourself and find time to do the things you enjoy. This will allow you to better focus on your work when that is what you need to do.

The information provided in this book has been geared to prepare you for cultural differences you might encounter at a law school in the United States. Though this book does not completely list every difference you may encounter, after working with international students for many years, the authors chose topics they felt were the most challenging for international students and most important for their success. By following the suggestions in this book about writing documents; reading, discussing, and analyzing cases; taking exams; and navigating class and school environments, we know that you will be able to do well in your law school classes. When you know what is expected of you, you will be able to enjoy the process of learning law at a law school in the United States.

Resources and Further Reading

For a list of resources for law students studying in the United States, peruse the American Bar Association's "Resources for Law Students and Law Schools" webpage: https://www.americanbar.org/groups/lawyer_assistance/articles_and_info/law_student_resources.html. This site has links to useful articles, podcasts, and videos on topics ranging from bar admission to mental health.

For practical information about the LL.M. degree for both prospective and current international students, see also GEORGE E. EDWARDS, LL.M. ROADMAP: AN INTERNATIONAL STUDENT'S GUIDE TO U.S. LAW SCHOOL PROGRAMS (2011).

Appendix A. List of Torts Vocabulary Terms

List 1

allege *(verb)*
arguendo (adverb) (pronounced AR-GYOO-**EN**-DOH)
bring suit *(verb)*
common carrier *(noun)*
innkeeper *(noun)*
owe [someone] a duty of care *(verb)*
record *(noun)*
Restatement *(noun)*
social host *(noun)*
superior knowledge *(noun)*

List 2

amended *(adjective)*; amend *(verb)*
complaint *(noun)*
deceased *(adjective*; *noun)*
err *(verb)*
"exercise reasonable care" *(verb)*
foreseeable *(adjective)*
grant vs. deny *(verb)*
intoxicated *(adjective)*
reasonably *(adverb)*; reasonable *(adjective)*
"the case at bar" *(noun)*

List 3

claim *(noun*; *verb)*
deterrent *(adjective*; *noun)*
inebriated *(adjective)*
prima facie case *(adjective)* ("prima facie" is pronounced **PREE**-MUH **FAY**-SHUH)
vacate *(verb)*

List 4

assault *(verb*; *noun)*
bring an action *(verb)*
causation in fact *(noun)*; also referred to as "but-for cause"
cross-examination *(noun)*
directed verdict *(noun)*
discretion *(noun)*
present evidence *(verb)*
proximate cause *(noun)*
risk of harm *(noun)*

set aside the verdict *(verb)*
sustain an injury/injuries *(verb)*
testimony *(noun)*; testify *(verb)*
witness *(noun)*
verdict *(noun)*

List 5
abuse of discretion *(noun)*
burden of proof *(noun)*; have the burden of proving [something] *(verb)*
comparative negligence *(noun)*
contributory negligence *(noun)*
jury instructions *(noun)*; instruct the jury *(verb)*
medical malpractice *(noun)*
recovery *(noun)*; recover [damages] *(verb)*
return a verdict in favor of [someone] *(verb)*

List 6
damages *(noun)*; award damages *(verb)*
legally cognizable *(adjective)*
render *(verb)*
wrongful death *(noun)*

List 7
adequate vs. inadequate *(adjective)*
defective *(adjective)*
misuse *(noun)*

List 8
actual damages *(noun)*
incur [injuries or damages] *(verb)*
malicious *(adjective)*
petition for a writ of certiorari (*noun*; *verb*)
punitive damages *(noun)*
reckless *(adjective)*
wanton *(adjective)*
willful *(adjective)*

List 9
cost of custodial care *(noun)*
culpability *(noun)*; culpable *(adjective)*
derivative claim *(noun)*
loss of enjoyment of life *(noun)*
lost earnings *(noun)*
medical expenses *(noun)*

nonpecuniary damages *(noun)*
pain and suffering *(noun)*
pecuniary damages *(noun)*

Appendix B. List of Criminal Procedure Vocabulary Terms

List 1

admissibility *(noun)*; admissible *(adjective)*; "admissible in evidence"
apprise [someone] of her/his rights *(verb)*
cease *(verb)*
circumstantial evidence *(noun)*
coercion *(noun)*; coerce *(verb)*
compulsion *(noun)*; compel *(verb)*
exercise/invoke a privilege *(verb)*
exculpatory vs. inculpatory *(adjective)*
extort vs. obtain a confession *(verb)*
inadmissible *(adjective)*
incommunicado *(adjective)*
indigent *(adjective)*
probable cause *(noun)*
prosecute *(verb)*; prosecutor *(noun)*; prosecution *(noun)*
waive *(verb)*; waiver *(noun)*

List 2

advise [someone] of her rights *(verb)*
charge [someone] with a crime *(verb)*
convict [someone] of a crime *(verb)*
dispositive *(adjective)*
homicide *(noun)*
issue *Miranda* warnings *(verb)*
motion to suppress *(noun)*
per curiam (adjective)
petitioner *(noun)*
respondent *(noun)*

List 3

administer [*Miranda* warnings] *(verb)*
bench trial *(noun)*
concede *(verb)*
district attorney *(noun)*
first-degree burglary *(noun)*; burglarize *(verb)*
parolee *(noun)*; be on parole *(verb)*
read [a case] broadly *(verb)*
take the stand *(verb)*

List 4
age of majority *(noun)*
Amicus Curiae; *Amici Curiae (noun)* (pronounced UH-**MEE**-KUS **KYOO**-REE-EYE; UH-**MEE**-KEE **KYOO**-REE-EYE)
count of [name of offense] *(noun)*
delinquent *(adjective*; *noun)*
fact-intensive *(adjective)*
juvenile *(adjective; noun)*; juvenile detention *(noun)*
larceny *(noun)*
public defender *(noun)*

List 5
evidentiary hearing *(noun)*
grand jury *(noun)*
indictment *(noun)*
inform [someone] of her/his rights *(verb)*
kidnapping *(noun)*
line-up *(noun)*
murder *(noun)*
photo array *(noun)*
robbery *(noun)*
sustain [the admissibility of evidence or an objection made at trial] *(verb)*

List 6
bright-line rule *(noun)*
eavesdrop *(verb)*
incarcerated *(adjective)*
inmate *(noun)*
serve a sentence *(verb)*
undercover *(adjective)*

List 7
relinquishment *(noun)*; relinquish *(verb)*
"the instant case" *(noun)*

List 8
accomplice *(noun)*
exigency *(noun)*
probative *(adjective)*

Appendix C. Steps in the Civil Litigation Process

A. Pleadings

The term "**pleadings**" refers to the documents that parties submit to the court to initiate a civil action: complaint and answer.

1. Complaint

A lawsuit begins when the injured party (**plaintiff**) files a complaint with a trial court. A **complaint** is a legal document containing the plaintiff's reasons for bringing suit against the **defendant**. In the complaint the plaintiff alleges specific facts that give rise to a **cause of action**—that is, a basis for her right to money compensation or some other form of relief. The plaintiff must serve the defendant with the complaint and a **summons**, which calls on the defendant to file an answer.

2. Answer

An **answer** is a legal document in which the defendant either admits or denies each factual allegation made in the plaintiff's complaint. In the answer the defendant may raise **affirmative defenses**, which are defenses that the defendant must prove at trial (the plaintiff otherwise bears the burden of proving her claim). With an answer, a defendant may also choose to assert **counterclaims** against the plaintiff—in other words the defendant's *own* asserted causes of action against the plaintiff (i.e. a complaint against the plaintiff).

B. Discovery

Discovery is the fact-gathering phase of a lawsuit. During discovery, both parties request information and documents from the other side about their arguments and the evidence they plan to use to support them. There are three common methods of discovery: interrogatories, request for production of documents, and depositions. An **interrogatory** is a document containing a list of questions that the other party must answer, under oath, in writing. The answers to interrogatories help the parties gain more information about the case. **Requests for production of documents** are a series of written requests from one party to the other for documents related to the facts at issue in the case. A **deposition** refers to a hearing in which witnesses are questioned under oath regarding their knowledge of the facts surrounding the case. Depositions are a good way to ascertain how witnesses are going to testify at trial and therefore allow the parties to better prepare for court.

C. Pre-trial motions

A **motion** is a request made by one party for the court to rule on a certain legal issue. The court either **grants** (allows) or **denies** (rejects) a motion. Parties often file two kinds of motions before trial: a motion to dismiss the plaintiff's complaint and a motion for summary judgment.

When a defendant files a **motion to dismiss** the plaintiff's complaint, she asserts that the plaintiff has failed to state a cause of action for which the court can grant relief. Defendants often file motions to dismiss a complaint before filing an answer, with the hope that the court will dismiss the case before the parties have to proceed to discovery, which is often costly and time consuming. A motion to dismiss challenges the legal sufficiency of the plaintiff's complaint, but only based on the facts alleged in the complaint. For example, a court would likely grant a motion to dismiss the complaint in the following scenario: the plaintiff alleges that the defendant told her she got a horrible haircut, which hurt the plaintiff's feelings. Even if the facts alleged were true, the court would probably grant the defendant's motion to dismiss this complaint because the law does not recognize the defendant's actions as a tort.

A **motion for summary judgment** is an assertion that there are no genuine issues of material fact and the moving party is therefore entitled to judgment as a matter of law. Unlike a motion to dismiss, a party filing a motion for summary judgment can rely on facts and information outside of the plaintiff's complaint, including information gleaned through the discovery process. Recall the following illustration of a motion for summary judgment from Part II, Chapter 2: imagine a plaintiff's case against a defendant doctor in which the plaintiff alleges that the doctor performed her hand surgery on the wrong hand (e.g., the left instead of the right hand). If there is no dispute between the parties as to whether this fact occurred, the only question that remains is whether the defendant was negligent as a matter of law in performing the surgery on the plaintiff's left hand. Under these circumstances, if the plaintiff moved for summary judgment, she would probably be granted the motion. This is because there is no question as to whether the doctor performed the surgery on the left hand; the only issue that remains to be resolved is whether this act was negligent. Either party can file a motion for summary judgment.

(Note that parties can also file motions during and after trial.)

D. Trial

In an adversarial system of law, each party is represented by a lawyer who advocates on her behalf. The parties cannot speak freely in court to make their case; rather, they and other witnesses are questioned by their own lawyers (**direct examination**) and opposing counsel (**cross examination**). It is through such questioning that the "story" of the dispute emerges. The **testimony** of witnesses (again, elicited through an attorney's questions) and other **exhibits** (e.g., objects, photographs, records, reports, etc.) collectively make up the evidence used at trial. Attorneys for either side present their evidence to one of the most important players at trial: the jury.

1. The Role of the Jury

The jury is a group of people selected at random from the general population. Juries are responsible for hearing testimony and viewing the exhibits presented at trial by both sides to the dispute (plaintiff and defendant) and ultimately deciding who they believe and hence who should win the case. Juries are referred to as **triers of fact** or **factfinders** because their task is to "find" the facts—that is, determine which facts they believe are true based on the evidence they hear and review. At the close of a case, the jury goes to a **deliberation** room where it decides which side should win and, if it finds for the plaintiff, how much money to award the plaintiff. This decision is called the jury's **verdict**.

2. The Role of the Judge

In U.S. trial courts, judges play a rather passive role. They act as "referees," ensuring that all of the rules of evidence are followed, making decisions on motions, and instructing the jury on what law to apply to the facts of the case. The primary difference between the jury and the judge is that the jury decides **questions of fact** (i.e., what actually happened?) while the judge resolves **questions of law** (i.e., what law should apply?).

An example of a question of fact might be: based on all of the evidence presented at trial, did the defendant actually see the puddle of water on the supermarket floor that caused the plaintiff to slip and fall? And a corresponding question of law for the judge would be: what law applies when a plaintiff alleges that the defendant was careless in cleaning up a puddle of water on the supermarket floor? Judges do not make factual determinations at trial unless the parties **waive** (give up) their right to a jury trial. These are called **bench trials**.

E. Appeal

The party who loses at trial can **appeal** the judge's decision by arguing that the judge made one or more legal errors. It is important to note that the losing party cannot appeal a decision simply because she is unhappy with the final result. She has to allege specific **legal errors** made by the trial judge in resolving questions of law. Legal errors argued on appeal tend to fall into three categories:

(1) errors related to the admissibility of evidence (e.g., did the trial judge **err** in admitting the evidence?); (2) errors related to the grant or denial of motions (e.g., did the trial judge err in denying the motion?); and (3) errors related to jury instructions (e.g., did the trial judge err in instructing the jury in a particular way?).

If an appeal has been made by the losing party, an **appellate court** reviews the trial judge's decision and renders an opinion as to whether the judge made a legal error. The job of an appellate court is to review the *legal* decisions made by trial judges, not to "find" facts. Appellate courts accept the factual conclusions made by the jury, which the jury based on all of the evidence it heard and reviewed at trial. There is usually no new evidence presented on appeal.

If an appellate court agrees with the trial judge's legal decisions, it **affirms** the decision. If it disagrees with the trial court, the appellate court **reverses** the decision. When an appellate court reverses a decision, it often also **remands** (sends back) the case to the trial court for further proceedings—often a new trial.

Many U.S. states have a three-tier court system: a trial court, an intermediate appellate court, and a supreme court. A party's appeal to an intermediate appellate court is usually an **appeal as a matter of right**. This means that the intermediate appellate court must review the case. However, appeals to a state's highest court are often **discretionary**, though this may depend on the issue at stake. If an appeal is discretionary, the court is not obligated to review the case. In these situations, the losing party must petition for a **writ of certiorari** or a **leave to appeal**, which is a formal request for the court to hear the case.

Appendix D. Steps in the Criminal Justice Process

A. Investigation

This involves examining the crime scene and collecting evidence, canvassing the neighborhood for witnesses, interviewing witnesses and suspects, searching for physical evidence of the crime, and making arrests.

B. Charging

Once the prosecutor has examined all available information gathered during the investigation phase, she decides whether to make a formal accusation (a **charge**). Charges can be filed in different ways, depending on the jurisdiction and offense involved. Prosecutors initiate most criminal cases by filing a complaint or by seeking an indictment.

A **complaint** is a written document that contains the name of the defendant, the criminal charges against her, and a brief description of the alleged facts giving rise to the criminal charges. A judge holds a **preliminary hearing** to determine whether there is enough evidence to support the charges.

A prosecutor may instead present the case to a **grand jury**. In a secret proceeding, the grand jury, composed of randomly selected individuals, listens to evidence to determine whether charges should be brought. This charge is called an **indictment**.

C. Arraignment

Once the defendant has been charged, she is brought before a judge for arraignment. During the **arraignment** the judge informs the defendant of the charges against her. The judge also decides whether to hold the defendant in prison or release her (usually the defendant has to **post bail**, that is, pay money to be released). At the arraignment the defendant also pleads guilty or not guilty to the charges.

D. Discovery

During discovery, both sides (prosecution and defense) prepare for the trial. They read reports on the case, gather evidence about the crime, and decide which witnesses they should call to testify in court.

E. Plea Bargaining (Optional)

In some cases, the prosecution may offer the defendant a plea deal. A **plea deal** is an agreement between the prosecution and defendant that avoids a trial and may reduce jail time in return for the defendant admitting to having committed the crime. Though the judge is in charge of sentencing the defendant, the government may recommend reduced jail time.

F. Pre-trial Motions (Optional)

This is the phase where the prosecution and defense file and respond to motions. (**Motions** are requests for the court to decide on an issue). Common motions include motions to dismiss or a motion to suppress evidence.

G. Trial

During the trial, both sides (prosecution and defense) present evidence and question various witnesses to make their case. The judge oversees the trial and determines what evidence may be shown to the jury. The jury decides whether to **convict** the defendant or **acquit** the defendant of charges. Occasionally, defendants waive their right to a jury trial and the judge acts as the factfinder. These are called "bench trials."

H. Post-trial Motions (Optional)

If the defendant is convicted, she can file various motions, including a motion for a new trial.

I. Sentencing

After the defendant has been convicted, she is **sentenced** by the judge. The judge uses sentencing guidelines, with maximum and minimum sentences for different crimes, to make her determination. The death penalty can be imposed for certain serious offenses, though some states have abolished it.

J. Appeal (Optional)

If the defendant believes she was wrongly convicted or the sentence was unjust, the defendant can appeal to a higher court. Appeals often center on the legal/procedural decisions of the trial judge; for example, a defendant may argue that a motion to suppress was incorrectly denied.

Index

A

Absences from law school classes, 489–492
Academic legal analysis, 183–185
  criminal procedure, 377–485. *See also* Criminal procedure
  discussing cases, 227–231. *See also* Discussing cases
  elements of opinions, 199–217. *See also* Elements of opinions
  foundations of U.S. law, 187–197. *See also* Foundations of U.S. law
  reading cases, 199–226. *See also* Reading cases
  torts, 285–376. *See also* Torts
  writing about cases, 233–283. *See also* Writing about cases
Academic legal discourse, 7–8
  brainstorming, 60
  culture, role of, 10–23
  defined, 9–10
  discussion questions, 24–25
  drafting, 61
  editing, 156–159. *See also* Editing
  evidence to support ideas, 14–15
  footnotes, 23
  importance of, 9
  law review article as example, 23–60
  legal terms, definitions of, 25
  organizing ideas, 60
  outlining, 60
  paragraphs, 63–97. *See also* Paragraphs
  process of writing, 60–61
  professor, role of, 10–11
  proofreading, 159–177. *See also* Proofreading
  reader, writing with focus on, 12–13, 19–20, 94
  "reader responsible" cultures, 12
  revising and rewriting, 61
  sentences, 99–118. *See also* Sentences
  steps of thinking, 20–23
  transitions, 119–154. *See also* Transitions
  "writer responsible" cultures, 12–13, 115
  writing vs. discourse, 10
Acquittal, 512
Admissibility of statements from police interrogation. *See* Police interrogation of witnesses and suspects
Affirmance, 190, 217, 510
Affirmative defenses, 507
Analogy, reasoning by, 215
Analysis in IRAC framework, 264–268
  applying rule to hypothetical, 265–266
  counterarguments, 267
  framing points as arguments, 266–267
  policy justifications, 267–268
  rebuttals, 267
Answers, 507
Appeals
  affirmance, 190, 217, 510
  civil litigation process, 509–510
  criminal procedure, 512
  defined, 189
  legal errors, 509–510

as matter of right, 510
remand, 217, 510
reversal, 190, 217, 510
Appellate courts and judges, 189–190, 510
Arraignment, 511
Articles, definite and indefinite, 162–164, 167
Assignments in law school, submitting, 493–494
Assumption of risk, 333–337
discussion questions, 336–337
exercises, 336–337
sample case, 333–336
Attending law school classes, 489–493
Attribution, 79

B

Backward-looking transitions, 149–150
Bail, 511
Bankruptcy Courts, 192
Bench trials, 196
Beyond a reasonable doubt, 194
The Bluebook, 206–207
Boldface, 253
Brainstorming, 60
Breach of duty, 298–307
discussion questions, 306–307
exercises, 305–306
sample case, 299–304
Briefs, 233–247
benefits of, 240–247
class participation, helping with, 241
defined, 233
effective case briefing, 235–240
exam preparation, helping with, 241
facts stated in, 237–238
holdings stated in, 239
issues stated in, 238–239
language development, promoting, 242–247
obiter dictum, awareness of, 237
order of ideas, 244
paraphrasing in, 242–247
reasoning stated in, 240
"rule of the case," 236–237
rules or procedures stated in, 238–239
sample brief, 234–235
synonyms, use of, 242–243
text structure, 245
transitions, 244
word form, 243
Bullet points in course outlines, 252

C

Case method, 189
Cases
briefs, 233–247. *See also* Briefs
defined, 187
descriptions in, 71
discussion of, 227–231
disposition of, 216–217
dissenting opinions, 299
elements of opinions, 199–217. *See also* Elements of opinions
headings, 204–207
holdings, 212–214
issues, 210–212
procedural histories, 209
reading cases, 199–226. *See also* Reading cases
reasoning, 214–216
writing about, 233–283. *See also* Writing about cases
Cases of first impression, 188

Causation, 309–323
discussion questions, 321–323
exercises, 319–321
sample case, 310–318
Cause of action, 200
Certiorari, 193
Charging step in criminal procedure, 511
Checklists
course outlines, 254–255
editing, 157–159
proofreading, 160–167, 175–177
Choice of law essay questions, 278–280
Circumstantial evidence, 387
Citation
of case, 206–207
of sources, 79
Civil litigation, 507–510
affirmance, 190, 217, 510
affirmative defenses, 507
answers, 507
appeals, 509–510
certiorari, 193
complaints, 507
counterclaims, 507
discovery, 507–508
diversity of citizenship jurisdiction, 191–192
federal question jurisdiction, 191
judge, role of, 509
jury, role of, 509
legal errors, 509–510
pleadings, 507
preponderance of the evidence, 194
pre-trial motions, 508
remand, 217, 510
reversal, 190, 217, 510
summons, 507
trials, 508–509
Clauses, dependent and independent, 161–162, 167
Clinics and experiential classes, 258
Cohesion of paragraphs, 86–92
exercises, 89–92
Commenting on holdings of cases, 228–229
Common law, 187–189
Comparative negligence, 324–333
contributory negligence vs., 331
discussion questions, 330–331
exercises, 328–329
sample case, 324–328
Comparing cases, 230
Complaints
civil litigation, 507
criminal procedure, 511
motions to dismiss, 200
Complex sentences, 110–112
Compound-complex sentences, 112
Compound sentences, 109–110
Concluding sentences, 65
Conclusions
ending academic legal discourse with, 16, 18–19, 59–60
in IRAC framework, 268–269
Conclusory answers in exams, need to avoid, 275–276
Confessions. *See* Police interrogation of witnesses and suspects
Conflict facts, 208
Connecting words, 129–131
Contextualizing cases, 221
Contributory negligence, 324–333
comparative negligence vs., 331

discussion questions, 330–331
exercises, 328–329
sample case, 324–328
Conviction, 512
Counterarguments in IRAC framework, 267
Counterclaims, 507
Course outlines, 248–257
boldface, 253
bullet points, 252
checklists, 254–255
commercial outlines as supplement rather than replacement for, 256–257
effective outlining, 251–257
flowcharts, 255
format of, 248–251
highlighting, 253
long outlines, 256
major topics and subtopics, identification of, 251
organizing by topic rather than case name, 252
organizing for visual appeal, 252–255
past exams used to validate course outlines, 257
sample outlines, 248–250
short outlines, 256
tables, 253
time considerations, 256
underlining, 253
Court of Federal Claims, 192
Court of International Trade, 192
Courts of Appeals, 192–193
Court system, U.S., 189–193
Bankruptcy Courts, 192
certiorari, 193
civil litigation process, 507–510. *See also* Civil litigation
Court of Federal Claims, 192
Court of International Trade, 192
Courts of Appeals, 192–193
criminal procedure, 511–512. *See also* Criminal procedure
District Courts, 191–192
diversity of citizenship jurisdiction, 191–192
en banc, 191
federal courts, 191–193
federal question jurisdiction, 191
hierarchy of courts, 189–191
specialized courts, 192
state courts, 193
Supreme Court, 193
Criminal procedure, 183–184, 377–485, 511–512
acquittal, 512
appeals, 512
arraignment, 511
beyond a reasonable doubt, 194
certiorari, 193
charging, 511
conviction, 512
custodial interrogation, 395–433, 452–462. *See also* Custodial interrogation
discovery, 511
essay questions, 403–404, 436–437, 462, 476–477, 480–485
exceptions to *Miranda* rights, 470–476
Fifth Amendment, 377
interrogation. *See* Custodial interrogation
investigation, 511
Miranda rights, 378–395. *See also Miranda* rights

plea bargaining, 512
police interrogation. *See* Police interrogation
post-trial motions, 512
preliminary hearings, 511
pre-trial motions, 512
privilege against self-incrimination, 377, 378, 384–385
probable cause, 390
sentencing, 512
trials, 512
voluntary statements to police, 452–462. *See also* Voluntary statements to police
waiver of *Miranda* rights. *See* Waiver of *Miranda* rights
Critiquing claims of parties, 228
Cross examination, 509
Cultural norms of students and professors, 10–13
Custodial interrogation, 395–433. *See also Miranda* rights; Police interrogation of witnesses and suspects
defined, 378
determining custodial status, 452–462
determining questioning to constitute interrogation, 437–449
discussion questions, 402–403, 410–411, 432–433, 461–462
exercises, 401–402, 409–410, 430–432, 460–461
juvenile subjected to questioning, 412–430
sample cases, 396–401, 404–409, 412–430, 452–460

D

Damages, 352–366
defined, 200
discussion questions, 358–359, 366
exercises, 357–358, 364–366
loss of enjoyment of life, 359–366. *See also* Loss of enjoyment of life
nonpecuniary damages, 359–366. *See also* Nonpecuniary damages
punitive damages, 352–359. *See also* Punitive damages
recovery of, 200
sample cases, 353–357, 359–364
seeking/requesting damages, 200
Defendants, 285
Defenses
affirmative defenses, 507
assumption of risk, 333–337
comparative negligence, 324–331
contributory negligence, 324–331
volenti non fit injuria, 333–337
Definite articles, 162–164
Definitions, 73
Deliberation, 195
Dependent clauses
markers, 113
proofreading for grammar, 161–162
Depositions, 507–508
Descriptions, 70–71
Dicta, 237
Direct answers in exams, 269–270
Direct examination, 509
Discovery
civil litigation, 507–508

criminal procedure, 511
depositions, 507–508
interrogatories, 507
requests for production of documents, 507
Discussing cases, 183, 227–231
applying holding or reasoning to hypothetical, 229–230
commenting on holdings, 228–229
comparing to other cases, 230
critiquing claims of parties, 228
evaluating reasoning, 229
speculating about implications, 231
Dismissal of complaint, 200
Disposition of cases, 217–218
affirmance, 190, 217, 510
remand, 217, 510
reversal, 190, 217, 510
Dissenting opinions, 299
District Courts, 191–192
Diversity of citizenship jurisdiction, 191–192
Drafting, 61
Dress in law schools, 495*n*2
Duty to exercise care (negligence cases), 286–293
discussion questions, 292–293
exercises, 290–292
sample case, 287–290
in special relationships, 293–298

E

Economic policy arguments, 216
Editing, 8, 156–159
checklists, 157–159
exercises, 159
principles of, 156–157
in process of writing, 61
during timed exams, 177–178
Elements of opinions, 199–217
affirmance, 217
case headings, 204–207. *See also* Headings of cases
citation, 206–207
conflict facts, 208
discussion questions, 203
disposition, 216–217. *See also* Disposition of cases
facts, 207–209
holdings, 212–214. *See also* Holdings
issues, 210–212. *See also* Issues
legal facts (procedural history) vs. conflict facts, 208
name of case, 204–205
name of court, 205–206
name of judge, 207
naming conventions, 205
procedural histories, 209
procedural holdings, 213
procedural issues, 210–212
reasoning, 214–216. *See also* Reasoning in cases
remand, 217
reversal, 217
sample case, 200–203
substantive holdings, 213
substantive issues, 210–212
typeface, 204
Enacted laws, 188
En banc, 191
Evaluative reading strategies, 222–223
Evidence to support ideas, 14–15
Examples, use of, 70
Exams, 258–283
avoiding conclusory answers, 275–276

avoiding inventing facts, 276–277
briefs helping to prepare for, 241
choice of law essay questions, 278–280
direct answers, 269–270
editing during, 177–178
fact patterns in, 259–260
hedging, 269
instructions in, 274
IRAC framework, 263–269
"issue spotter" essay exams, 258–278. *See also* "Issue spotter" essay exams
mistakes to avoid, 270–278
multiple choice questions, 282
multiple issues, identification of, 270
organizing answer with headings, 273
outlining answer, 271–273
past exams used to validate course outlines, 257
policy essay questions, 280–281
proofreading during, 177–178
"red herrings," 270
rule application in, 274–275
short answer questions, 281
significance of facts, avoiding requiring reader to infer, 277–278
time management, 270–271
Exceptions to *Miranda* rights, 470–476
discussion questions, 475–476
exercises, 474–475
sample case, 470–474
Exhibits, 189, 509
Explanations of reasons and justifications, 71–72

F
Fact finders, 509
Fact patterns in exams, 259–260
Facts
briefs, stated in, 237–238
facts of the case, 207–209
legal facts (procedural history) vs. conflict facts, 208
legally relevant facts, 237–238
Fairness and justice policy arguments, 216
Federal courts, 191–193
Federal question jurisdiction, 191
Fifth Amendment, 377
First impression cases, 188
Flowcharts in course outlines, 255
Footnotes, 23
Formatting, 174–177
checklist, 175–177
consistency, importance of, 177
Forward-looking transitions, 150–151
Foundations of U.S. law, 183, 187–197
appeals, 189
appellate judges, 189–190
bench trials, 196
beyond a reasonable doubt, 194
case method, 189
cases of first impression, 188
civil litigation. *See* Civil litigation
common law, 187–189
court system, 189–193. *See also* Court system, U.S.
criminal procedure. *See* Criminal procedure
deliberation, 195

exhibits, 189
fact finders, 194
guilt, 194
jury system, 194–197
liability, 194
motions, 189
precedent, 187–188
preponderance of the evidence, 194
stare decisis, 188
testimony, 189
trial judges, 189
triers of fact, 194
voir dire, 196

G

Grammar, 159–167
articles, 162–164, 167
clauses, 161–162, 167
exercises, 166–167
nouns, 162–164, 167
parallel structure, 165, 167
passive voice, 164–165, 167
pronouns, 161, 167
subject-verb agreement, 160–161, 167
verbs, 160, 167
Grand juries, 511
Guilt, 194

H

Headings of cases, 204–207
citation, 206–207
name of case, 204–205
name of court, 205–206
naming conventions, 205
typeface, 204
Headings of sections, 142–147
caveat regarding, 146
defined, 142
exercises, 147
format of, 145–146
in law review articles, 143–144
as sentences, 146
subsections, 142
topic sentences and, 144–145
Hedging in exams, 269
Hierarchy of courts, 189–191
Highlighting
course outlines, 253
reading cases, 218–220
Holdings, 212–214
applying to hypothetical, 229–230
briefs, stated in, 239
caveat regarding, 213
commenting on, 228–229
procedural holdings, 213
signposting, 213
substantive holdings, 213
Hypotheticals
applying holding or reasoning to, 229–230
IRAC framework, applying rule to hypothetical, 265–266

I

Inadmissibility of statements. *See* *Miranda* rights; Police interrogation of witnesses and suspects
Indefinite articles, 162–164
Independent clauses
markers, 113
proofreading for grammar, 161–162
Instructions in exams, 261, 274
Intentional torts, 285
Interrogation. *See* Custodial interrogation; Police

interrogation of witnesses and suspects
Interrogatories, 507
Introductions
in academic legal discourse, 16–18, 26–29
in law review articles, 147–148
section introductions, 147–149
Investigation, criminal, 511
IRAC framework, 263–269
analysis, 264–268
conclusion, 268–269
issue, 263
rule, 263–264
Issues, 210–212
briefs, stated in, 238–239
caveat regarding, 210
in IRAC framework, 263
"issue spotter" essay exams, 258–278. *See also* "Issue spotter" essay exams
procedural issues, 210–212
signposting, 210
substantive issues, 210–212
"Issue spotter" essay exams, 184*n*2, 258–278
avoiding conclusory answers, 275–276
avoiding inventing facts, 276–277
direct answers, 269–270
fact patterns in, 259–260
hedging, 269
instructions in, 261, 274
IRAC framework, 263–269. *See also* IRAC framework
mistakes to avoid, 270–278
multiple issues, 270
organizing answer with headings, 273
outlining answers, 271–273
questions in, 260
"red herrings," 270
rule application in, 274–275
sample answers, 261–263
significance of facts, avoiding requiring reader to infer, 277–278
take-home exams, 259
time management, 270–271
torts essay questions, 259–261

J

Judges
appellate judges, 189–190, 510
bench trials, 196
name of deciding judge, 207
role of judge in jury system, 195–196, 509
trial judges, 189
Judicial administration policy arguments, 216
Judicial opinions. *See* Cases
Jurisdiction
diversity of citizenship jurisdiction, 191–192
federal question jurisdiction, 191
Jury system, 194–197
beyond a reasonable doubt, 194
deliberation, 195
fact finders, 194
guilt, 194
liability, 194
preponderance of the evidence, 194
questions of fact vs. questions of law, 195
role of judge and jury, 195–196, 509
service on jury, 196
size of jury, 196

triers of fact, 194
voir dire, 196
Juvenile subjected to police questioning, 412–430

L

Language development promoted by brief writing, 242–247
Lateness in law school
attending classes, 492–493
submitting assignments, 493–494
Law review articles
cohesion of paragraphs in, 86–88
definitions in, 73
examples in, 23–60, 70
headings of sections in, 143–144
introductions of sections in, 147–148
length of paragraphs in, 92–94
references to authority in, 75
statistics in, 74
substantive transitions in, 126–128, 130–131, 136–140, 150–151
topic sentences in, 63–64
transition words in, 135–136
unity of paragraphs in, 81–83
Law schools, 487–499
absences, 489–492
assignments, submitting, 493–494
attending classes, 489–493
classmates, relationships with, 496–498
class participation, 241
clinics and experiential classes, 258
course outlines, 248–257. *See also* Course outlines
culture quiz, 488–489
dress in, 495*n*2
exams, 258–283. *See also* Exams
lateness, 492–494
professors, relationships with, 494–496
seminar classes, 258
study groups, 497–498
workload management, 498–499
Legal analysis. *See* Academic legal analysis
Legal discourse. *See* Academic legal discourse
Legal errors, 196, 509–510
Legal facts (procedural history) vs. conflict facts, 208
Legally relevant facts, 237–238
Length of paragraphs, 92–96
exercises, 94–96
in law review articles, 92–94
LexisNexis, 206
Liability, 194, 285
Linear reading strategies, 217–220
highlighting, 218–220
marginal notes, 219–220
skimming, 218
underlining, 218–219
Long course outlines, 256
Loss of enjoyment of life, 359–366
discussion questions, 366
exercises, 364–366
sample case, 359–364

M

Main ideas

finding and identifying support for, 76–79. *See also* Support of main ideas
starting academic legal discourse with, 12–13
Making predictions about cases, 221–222
Marginal notes in cases, 219–220
Miranda rights, 378–395
case, 378–392, 405–409
discussion questions, 394–395
exceptions to, 470–476
exercises, 392–394
juvenile subjected to police questioning, 412–430
waiver of, 380, 463–469
Mistakes to avoid in exams, 270–278
Motions
civil litigation, 508
criminal procedure, 512
defined, 189
denying, 507
to dismiss complaint, 200
granting, 507
post-trial motions, 512
pre-trial motions, 508, 512
for summary judgment, 224, 508
Multiple choice questions, 282
Multiple issues in exams, 270

N

Negligence
assumption of risk, 333–337
breach of duty, 298–307. *See also* Breach of duty
causation, 309–323. *See also* Causation
comparative negligence, 324–331. *See also* Comparative negligence
contributory negligence, 324–331. *See also* Contributory negligence
damages, 352–366. *See also* Damages
defenses, 324–331, 333–337
defined, 285
duty to exercise care, 286–293. *See also* Duty to exercise care
elements of, 285
essay questions, 309, 323, 337–338, 366–367, 369–376
products liability, 338–352. *See also* Products liability
special relationships requiring duty of care, 293–298
volenti non fit injuria, 333–337
New York court system, 193
Nominalizations
defined, 100
problems with, 100–102
Nonpecuniary damages, 359–366
discussion questions, 366
exercises, 364–366
sample case, 359–364
Nouns, countable and non-countable, 162–164, 167

O

Obiter dictum, awareness of, 237
Opinions, 187. *See also* Cases
Oral examinations, 10
Organizing ideas, 60, 244
Outlining
answers in exams, 271–273

course outlines, 248–257. *See also* Course outlines
in writing process, 60

P

Paragraphs, 7, 63–97
attribution, 79
citation, 79
cohesion of, 86–92
concluding sentences, 65
editing checklist, 158
exercises, 65–69, 83–85, 89–92, 94–96
length of, 92–96
paraphrasing vs. quoting, 79–80
research, 79
support, 69–80
topic sentences, 63–69
transitions between, 134–142. *See also* Transitions
transitions within, 120–134. *See also* Transitions
unity of, 81–85
Parallel structure, use of, 165, 167
Paraphrasing
in briefs, 242–247
combination of techniques, 245–246
defined, 242
order of ideas, change in, 244
quoting vs., 79–80
synonyms, using, 242–243
text structure, change in, 245
transitions, change in, 244
word form, change in, 243
Passive voice, 102–103, 164–165, 167
Petition for writ of certiorari, 193
Plagiarism, 242*n*6. *See also* Paraphrasing
Plaintiffs, 285
Plea bargaining, 512
Pleadings, 507
Police interrogation of witnesses and suspects, 377
custodial interrogation, 395–433. *See also* Custodial interrogation
essay questions, 403–404, 436–437, 462, 476–477, 480–485
Miranda rights. *See Miranda* rights
privilege against self-incrimination, 377, 378, 384–385
voluntary statements to police, 452–462. *See also* Voluntary statements to police
waiver of *Miranda* rights, 380, 463–469
Policy essay questions, 280–281
Policy rationales, 215–216
Post-trial motions, 512
Precedent, 187–188
Preliminary hearings, 511
Preponderance of the evidence, 194
Pre-trial motions
civil litigation, 508
criminal procedure, 512
Privilege against self-incrimination, 377, 378, 384–385
Probable cause, 390
Problematizing reading strategies, 220–222
asking questions while reading, 221
connecting to real world purpose, 222
contextualizing, 221

making predictions, 221–222
Procedural histories of cases, 209
Procedural history of case, 208
Procedural holdings, 213
Process of writing, 60–61
brainstorming, 60
drafting, 61
editing, 61. *See also* Editing
organizing ideas, 60, 244
outlining, 60
proofreading, 61. *See also* Proofreading
revising and rewriting, 61
Products liability, 338–352
design defects, 338
discussion questions, 346, 351
exercises, 344–345, 350–351
manufacturing defects, 338
sample cases, 338–344, 347–350
warning, duty to provide, 338–344, 347–350
Professors
cultural norms for, 10–11
relationships with, 494–496
Pronouns, used as subjects and objects, 161, 167
Proofreading, 8, 155–156, 159–177
checklists, 160–167, 175–177
consistency, importance of, 177
exercises, 166–174
for formatting, 174–177. *See also* Formatting
for grammar, 159–167. *See also* Grammar
in process of writing, 61
for punctuation, 167–173
for spelling, 173–174
during timed exams, 177–178
Punctuality, 492, 493
Punctuation, 167–173
exercises, 168–173
Punitive damages, 352–359
discussion questions, 358–359
exercises, 357–358
sample case, 353–357

Q

Questions in exams, 260
Questions of fact vs. questions of law, 195
Quoting vs. paraphrasing, 79–80

R

Reader, importance to keep in mind while writing, 12–13, 19–20, 94
"Reader responsible" cultures, 11, 12
Reading cases, 183, 199–226
asking questions while reading, 221
connecting to real world purpose, 222
contextualizing, 221
discussion questions, 226
elements of opinions, 199–217. *See also* Elements of opinions
evaluative reading strategies, 222–223
highlighting, 218–220
linear reading strategies, 217–220
marginal notes, 219–220
predictions, making while reading, 221–222
problematizing reading strategies, 220–222
sample case, 223–226
skimming, 218
strategies, 217–226
underlining, 218–219

Reasonable doubt, 194
Reasoning in cases, 214–216
    by analogy, 215
    applying to hypothetical, 229–230
    briefs, stated in, 240
    economic policy arguments, 216
    evaluating, 229
    fairness and justice policy arguments, 216
    judicial administration policy arguments, 216
    policy rationales, 215–216
    rule application in, 215
    separation of powers policy arguments, 216
    social policy arguments, 216
Rebuttals in IRAC framework, 267
"Red herrings" in exams, 270
References to authority, 74–76
Remand, 217, 510
Requests for production of documents, 507
Research
    attribution and citation of, 79
    seminar classes requiring, 258
    statistics and, 73–74
Reversal, 190, 217, 510
Revising and rewriting
    in process of writing, 61
    sentences, 104
Rule application
    in exams, 274–275
    reasoning in cases, 215
Rule in IRAC framework, 263–264
"Rule of the case," 236–237

S

Sample answers in exams, 261–263
Sections, transitions between, 142–153
    backward-looking transitions, 149–150
    exercises, 147–149, 151–153
    forward-looking transitions, 150–151
    headings, 142–147. *See also* Headings of sections
    introductions, 147–149
    substantive transitions, 149–153
Self-incrimination, 377, 378, 384–385
Seminar classes, 258
Sentence fragments, 160
Sentences, 8, 99–118
    clear meaning, 108–114
    complex sentences, 110–112
    compound-complex sentences, 112
    compound sentences, 109–110
    concluding sentences, 65
    confusion, need to avoid, 105–108
    dependent clause markers, 113
    ease of understanding, 99–104
    editing checklist, 158
    enhancing rhythm and flow of writing, 115–117
    exercises, 104, 107–108, 114, 116–117
    independent clause markers, 113
    nominalizations, problems with, 100–102
    paragraph length and number of sentences, 92
    passive voice, problems with, 102–103
    revision of, 104

sentence structure, 108–114. *See also* Sentence structure
simple sentences, 109
topic sentences, 63–69. *See also* Topic sentences
varying length and type, 115–117
word forms in, 105–108
word order in, 99–104
Sentence structure, 108–114
in brief writing, 245
complex sentences, 110–112
compound-complex sentences, 112
compound sentences, 109–110
dependent clause markers, 113
error correction, 114
exercises, 114
independent clause markers, 113
simple sentences, 109
Sentencing, criminal, 512
Separation of powers policy arguments, 216
Short answer questions, 281
Short course outlines, 256
Simple sentences, 109
Skimming cases, 218
Social policy arguments, 216
Socratic Method, 184*n*1
Special relationships requiring duty of care, 293–298
discussion questions, 297–298
exercises, 296–297
sample case, 293–296
Speculating about implications of cases, 231
Spelling, 173–174
Stare decisis and precedent, 187–188
State courts, 193
Statistics, 73–74
Steps of thinking, 20–23
Strict liability, 285
Student papers
explanations in, 71–72
paraphrasing vs. quoting in, 79–80
topic sentences in, 65
Study groups in law schools, 497–498
Studying tips
absences, 489–492
attending classes, 489–493
classmates, relationships with, 496–498
culture quiz, 488–489
lateness, 492–494
professors, relationships with, 494–496
study groups, 497–498
submitting assignments, 493–494
workload management, 498–499
Subject-verb agreement, 160–161, 167
Submitting assignments in law school, 493–494
Substantive holdings, 213
Substantive transitions
connecting words, 129–131
examples, 126–127
exercises, 132–134, 151–153
key words, 140
in law review articles, 126–128, 130–131, 136–140, 150–151
structure of, 127–132
topic, reminding reader of, 140–141

topic sentences, incorporating into, 141–142
transitions between paragraphs, 136–142
transitions within paragraph, 121–125
Summary judgment, 224, 508
Summons, 507
Support of main ideas, 70–76
definitions, 73
descriptions, 70–71
examples, 70
exercises, 76–79
explanations of reasons and justifications, 71–72
references to authority, 74–76
statistics, 73–74
Supreme Court, U.S., 193
Supreme courts, state, 193
Synonyms, use in briefs, 242–243

T
Tables in course outlines, 253
Take-home exams, 259
Tenses of verbs, 160
Testimony, 189, 509
Time management in exams, 270–271
Topic sentences, 14, 63–69
exercises, 65–69, 83–85
headings of sections and, 144–145
in law review articles, 63–64
matching, 65–67
substantive transitions, use of, 141–142
writing, 67–69
Torts, 183–184, 285–376
assumption of risk, 333–337
breach of duty, 298–307. *See also* Breach of duty
causation, 309–323. *See also* Causation
common law, 285
comparative negligence, 324–331. *See also* Comparative negligence
contributory negligence, 324–331. *See also* Contributory negligence
damages, 352–366. *See also* Damages
defendants, 285
duty to exercise care, 286–293. *See also* Duty to exercise care
essay questions, 259–261, 309, 323, 337–338, 366–367, 369–376
intentional torts, 285
liability, 285
negligence. *See* Negligence
plaintiffs, 285
products liability, 338–352. *See also* Products liability
special relationships, duty imposed in, 293–298
strict liability, 285
volenti non fit injuria, 333–337
Transitions, 8, 119–154
backward-looking transitions, 149–150
in briefs, 244
connecting words, 129–131
defined, 119
editing checklist, 158
exercises, 124–125, 132–134, 142, 147–149, 151–153
forward-looking transitions, 150–151
matching, 132–134
within paragraph, 120–134
between paragraphs, 134–142
between sections, 142–153. *See also* Sections, transitions between

substantive transitions, 125–134, 136–142, 149–153
topic sentences, incorporating into, 141–142
transition words, 121–125, 134–136
Transition words
commonly used, 121–122
exercises, 124–125
in law review articles, 135–136
transitions between paragraphs, 134–136
transitions within paragraph, 121–125
Trial judges, 189
Trials
civil litigation process, 508–509
criminal procedure, 512
cross examination, 509
direct examination, 509
exhibits, 509
testimony, 509
Triers of fact, 194, 509

U
Underlining
in course outlines, 253
while reading cases, 218–219
Unity of paragraphs, 81–85
exercises, 83–85

V
Verbs, 160, 167
Voir dire, 196
Volenti non fit injuria, 333–337
discussion questions, 336–337
exercises, 336–337
sample case, 333–336
Voluntary statements to police, 452–462
discussion questions, 461–462
exercises, 460–461
sample case, 452–460

W
Waiver of *Miranda* rights, 380, 463–469
discussion questions, 468–469
exercises, 468
sample case, 463–467
Westlaw, 206
Witnesses, testimony of, 194–195
Word forms in sentences, 105–108
exercises, 107–108
identification of forms, 107–108
Word order in sentences, 99–104
briefs, changing in, 244
exercises, 104
nominalizations, problems with, 100–102
passive voice, problems with, 102–103
Workload management in law school, 498–499
"Writer responsible" cultures, 11, 12–13, 115
Writing about cases, 183, 233–283
briefs, 233–247. *See also* Briefs
course outlines, 248–257. *See also* Course outlines
exams, 258–283. *See also* Exams
Writ of certiorari, 193